IRS Best Practice in HR Handbook

Editor:
Neil Rankin

T0330600

Members of the LexisNexis Group worldwide

United Kingdom	LexisNexis IRS, 2 Addiscombe Road, Croydon, Surrey CR9 5AF
Argentina	LexisNexis Argentina, BUENOS AIRES
Australia	LexisNexis Butterworths, CHATSWOOD, New South Wales
Austria	LexisNexis Verlag ARD Orac GmbH & Co KG, VIENNA
Canada	LexisNexis Butterworths, MARKHAM, Ontario
Chile	LexisNexis Chile Ltda, SANTIAGO DE CHILE
Czech Republic	Nakaladatelstvi Orac sro, PRAGUE
France	Editions du Juris-Classeur SA, PARIS
Hong Kong	LexisNexis Butterworths, HONG KONG
Hungary	HVG Orac, BUDAPEST
India	LexisNexis Butterworths, NEW DELHI
Ireland	Butterworths (Ireland) Ltd, DUBLIN
Italy	Giuffré Editore, MILAN
Malaysia	Malayan Law Journal Sdn Bhd, KUALA LUMPUR
New Zealand	LexisNexis Butterworths, WELLINGTON
Poland	Wydawnictwo Prawnicze LexisNexis, WARSAW
Singapore	LexisNexis Butterworths, SINGAPORE
South Africa	Butterworths SA, DURBAN
Switzerland	Stämpfli Verlag AG, BERNE
USA	LexisNexis, DAYTON, Ohio

© Eclipse Group Ltd 2003.

A CIP Catalogue record for this book is available from the British Library.

ISBN 0 7545 2182 6

Cover design, production and typesetting by Brett Gamston
Printed and bound by Hobbs the Printers, Hampshire

Transferred to Digital Printing 2009

Visit LexisNexis IRS at www.lexisnexis.co.uk

Contents

Introduction

Welcome to this first edition of the *IRS Best Practice in HR Handbook*.

This handbook presents a one-stop guide to the effective management of people. Uniquely, we believe, it is based on the hard-won experience of those at the "sharp end" of modern best practice: personnel and HR managers, and their colleagues who specialise in recruitment, pay, equality, health, pensions or legal issues.

Thanks to them, IRS's researchers have been able to obtain detailed feedback about the key themes, problem areas and success factors associated with a wide range of personnel issues. More details of our research programme can be found in chapter 14.

The *IRS Best Practice in HR Handbook* tackles these issues thematically, devoting a chapter to each of the main aspects of the management of people. In every case, the chapters contain checklists, case studies and other examples of named practice, supplemented by findings about the state of play at present and of emerging trends and challenges.

This is not another of the many lawyer's guides available today. Instead, it concentrates on best practice, while using legal checklists and, where necessary, more detailed coverage of recent legislation to remind practitioners of the legislative dimension to their work.

We have tried to make it as easy as possible for you to find your way around this information-packed publication. There is a thorough index at the end of the book. A contents list appears on the preceding pages. And each chapter begins with a more detailed list of its own contents. There are, of course, also cross-references within the text to related chapters and sections.

Neil Rankin

1. Filling your vacancies

See also: 2. Cost-effective selection; 3. Using electronic media effectively; 4. Checking candidates' backgrounds; and 9. Equal opportunities and diversity.

This chapter covers:
- Overview;
- Cost-effective recruitment methods: for managers; IT specialists; sales staff; skilled workers; semi- and unskilled workers; new graduates; school-leavers and young people; and for all types of recruit;
- Developing recruitment and selection criteria: the development, use and updating of job descriptions and person specifications;
- Using competencies;
- Managing recruitment administration;
- Recruitment advertising;
- Recruitment advertising agencies;
- Jobcentres;
- Employment agencies;
- Headhunters;
- Recruitment fairs;
- Referral payments;
- Using schools, colleges and universities;
- Foreign workers; and
- Tackling skills shortages and other hard-to-fill vacancies.

Checklists in this chapter:
1. Acas on job descriptions
2. Guidelines for best practice in the use of job analysis techniques
3. Avoiding discrimination in person specifications and job descriptions
4. Competencies: the key issues
5. The key issues in effective recruitment advertising
6. Using recruitment advertising agencies: points to watch
7. Jobcentres: the points to watch
8. Using employment agencies: the key issues
9. Using headhunters
10. Recruitment fairs: the key issues
11. Referral schemes: the key issues
12. Alternatives to conventional recruitment advertising
13. Legal checklist

Case studies in this chapter:

A. Eden Brown

B. Examples of referral schemes

C. The Remainders Group

D. King's College Hospital NHS Trust

E. Centrica

Overview

Recruitment and selection provide the gateways to employment. If practice at this stage is faulty, then all subsequent personnel and HR processes, from induction and training, to appraisal and equal opportunities, will fail to deliver the high levels of performance that organisations demand.

Yet employers can rarely afford to "throw money at the problem" to ensure they recruit absolutely the best people. The costs involved are often so considerable, and the scale of recruitment often so large, that a balancing act is required between costs and effectiveness.

This first chapter in the handbook focuses on the initial stage of finding new members of staff, where employers set out to identify potential recruits through advertising, referrals, employment agencies and other such methods. Chapter 2 covers the selection stage, and examines the second phase of the hiring process, where potential candidates are assessed against the vacancy's requirements.

This chapter looks at the various recruitment techniques available to employers, presenting the actual experience of hundreds of personnel, HR and recruitment managers in finding the most cost-effective hiring solutions.

It begins with an analysis of the most cost-effective recruitment methods for seven major groups of staff, followed by an overview of methods as they operate for recruits as a whole. (Chapter 2 provides the same information in respect of the methods used to select staff.)

Then we focus on the ways in which employers identify their recruitment and selection criteria – through job descriptions, person specifications and competency frameworks – and examine practice in managing the administration of recruitment.

We then consider each of the main recruitment methods, one by one, before turning to the issue of skills shortages and feedback from employers that highlights the best ways of responding to such recruitment difficulties.

Cost-effective recruitment methods

All employers are faced with the same challenge when a vacancy occurs: how are competent, capable people to be found to fill the job? Sometimes, there may be internal staff who might be interested in the job; a member of staff might know of someone who could be suitable for the role; or potential recruits might have approached the employer with enquiries about possible job opportunities.

These fairly passive sources of recruits involve little or no cost. Conversely, many proactive recruitment channels – placing advertising, contacting employment agencies, and so on – can involve costs often running into thousands of pounds.

Which option is best? This depends, according to the experience of personnel, HR and recruitment professionals, on the type of job, the locality, the severity of skills shortages, and several other factors. But, all in all, their experience reveals a surprisingly large degree of consensus about the methods that present the best balance between cost and effectiveness.

This section provides their feedback according to seven major types of vacancy, followed by an overview for vacancies as a whole. Chapter 2 provides a parallel analysis in respect of the selection methods that are then applied to the pool of candidates these recruitment exercises have produced.

A. The cost-effective recruitment of managers

The most cost-effective methods of recruiting managers, according to the experience of personnel, HR and recruitment specialists, are, in descending order:
- advertising in national newspapers;
- using commercial employment agencies;
- advertising in specialist journals and/or the trade press; and, to a lesser extent
- advertising in local newspapers.

National newspapers: More than a third of the specialists we contacted (34.8%) identified national newspaper advertising as the method that has proved most effective for them.

Even when analysed by type of employer, national newspaper advertising appears in first, second or third position in all cases. It receives its strongest accolade among specialists working for public sector employers, where more than half (56.4%) identified it as their most successful method – whereas private sector firms gave relatively greater prominence to employment agencies.

Some of this difference in emphasis is no doubt due to the public sector's preference for open recruitment. Advertising is considered more transparent than recommendations from agency staff. Indeed, private sector recruiters are around four times more likely than the public sector to use an agency at all in their recruitment of managers (eight in 10 versus one in five, respectively).

Employment agencies: Almost as many of the specialists (just under three in 10 overall; 28.7%) told us that, in their experience, commercial employment agencies provide their single most cost-effective means of recruiting high-quality managers.

As we saw above, agencies are preferred by private sector employers. Almost half of manufacturers (46.7%) and four in 10 service sector firms (39.1%) told us that employment agencies are their most cost-effective recruitment method for managers. In contrast, only a minuscule 2.6% of specialists working in the public sector did so.

Specialist titles: The trade press and specialist journals represent overall the third most highly rated means of recruiting managers, with just under a fifth of the employers we contacted (19.1%) choosing them as their best source of quality applicants. Public sector employers are more likely to choose this method than those in the private sector. Again, the public sector's emphasis on publicly advertising its managerial vacancies accounts for some of this result. The high take up of advertising in the trade press and specialist journals by the public sector (90.2%) is witness to this policy.

Local papers: Beyond the big three recruitment methods, recruiters are more divided as to the best means of obtaining good-quality managerial applicants. Across all types of employer, the use of local newspaper advertising ranks fourth from top, although fewer than a 10th of recruiters (9.6%) chose it.

This medium is slightly more popular among services firms in the private sector (where 17.4% chose it) than the overall result, but, in contrast, it was not identified by a single recruiter in the manufacturing and production sector.

No other recruitment method was rated as being the most cost-effective option by more than 6.0% of the specialists we contacted.

B. The cost-effective recruitment of IT specialists

The most cost-effective methods of recruiting IT specialists, according to personnel, HR and recruitment managers, are, in descending order:
● using commercial employment agencies;
● advertising in specialist journals and/or the trade press;
● advertising in local newspapers; and, in equal measure;
● advertising via the internet.

Employment agencies: One in three personnel, HR and recruitment managers have found that employment agencies represent the most cost-effective means of recruiting IT specialists for their organisations.

Again, the public sector's aversion to using agencies means that hardly any such employers identified agencies as their best bet (only 2.9%). In contrast, more than half (55.2%) of the specialists working in the service sector and almost as many (46.1%) in the manufacturing and production sector chose agencies as their most cost-effective recruitment option.

Specialist titles: Overall, just over one in four (27.6%) of our contacts consider that advertising in specialist IT publications offers the most cost-effective way of recruiting IT specialists.

Considerably greater proportions of the public sector and manufacturing/production employers have found that this recruitment medium provides the most cost-effective method available to them (41.5 and 38.4%, respectively, against only 7.8% of employers in the service sector).

Local papers: One in seven (14.8%) of our contacts chose advertising in local newspapers as their most cost-effective option in preference to the above recruitment methods.

Personnel, HR and recruitment managers in both the public sector and the service sector are particularly pleased with this method (with 20.5% and 18.4%, respectively, citing it as their most cost-effective option). In contrast, not one of our contacts in the manufacturing and production sector chose it.

Electronic recruitment: Computers are, of course, the "tool of the trade" of IT specialists, and recruiters often turn to electronic recruitment when seeking to fill vacancies for such staff.

In all, two-thirds (66.3%) of employers now practise electronic recruitment for their IT vacancies, but it has yet to win over many personnel, HR and recruitment managers in terms of producing the best candidates in the most cost-effective way.

Overall, only one in seven (14.8%) of our contacts said that electronic recruitment represents their most cost-effective way of recruiting IT specialists.

The proportion rises to one in five in the public sector (20.5%) and one in six (15.7%) in the service sector. In contrast, only one in 13 (7.6%) of our contacts in manufacturing/production chose it – despite the fact that electronic recruitment is as widely used in that sector as the other two sectors.

No other recruitment method was rated as being the most cost-effective option by more than 7.0% of the specialists we contacted.

C. The cost-effective recruitment of sales staff

The experiences of personnel, HR and recruitment specialists concerning the most cost-effective methods of recruiting sales staff polarise along industrial lines – between those working in the service sector and those in the manufacturing and production sector. (Sales roles are uncommon in the public sector.)

In the service sector, the most cost-effective methods of recruiting sales staff, are, in descending order:
● advertising in local newspapers (where two-thirds, 62.2%, told us that this method represents their most cost-effective option); and
● using commercial employment agencies (where one in four, 24.3%, did so).

No other recruitment method was rated as being the most cost-effective option by more than 9.0% of the specialists we contacted who work in the service sector.

In the manufacturing and production sector, the most cost-effective methods of recruiting sales staff, are, in descending order:
● using commercial employment agencies (where more than four in 10, 42.9%, told us that this method represents their most cost-effective option);
● advertising in specialist journals and/or the trade press (where one in five, 19.0%, did so);
● advertising in national newspapers (where one in seven, 14.3%, did so);
● word of mouth; and, in equal measure;
● advertising via the internet (where one in 10, 9.5%, did so in both cases).

No other recruitment method was rated as being the most cost-effective option by more than 5.0% of the specialists we contacted who work in the manufacturing and production sector.

D. The cost-effective recruitment of skilled workers

The most cost-effective methods of recruiting skilled workers, according to the experience of personnel, HR and recruitment specialists, are, in descending order:
● advertising in local newspapers; and to a lesser extent
● advertising in specialist journals and/or the trade press; and
● using commercial employment agencies.

In addition, some of our contacts working in the manufacturing and production sector have found the following to be their most cost-effective method:
● word of mouth.

Local newspapers: Local newspaper advertising is rated by the greatest proportion of our contacts as being the most cost-effective means of generating a good-quality set of potential recruits for their vacancies for skilled workers (according to more than half, 58.6%, of employers). Many potential applicants will be drawn from the local labour market, where local newspapers have a wide circulation – potentially, to every household through the doorstep delivery of free titles.

Almost four times as many recruiters chose local newspaper advertising as their single most cost-effective recruitment medium for skilled workers as opted for any other technique. Public sector recruiters are much more likely to rate this as their most cost-effective method (seven in 10, 71.0%, did so), with around half of our contacts in the private sector doing so (53.6% of those in the manufacturing and production sector, and 50.0% of those in the service sector).

Specialist titles: Second, but highlighted by a considerably smaller proportion of employers, lies the use of specialist publications, such as the trade press, professional journals and specialist titles. Overall, one in six of our contacts (16.1%) reported that, in their experience, such media offer the most cost-effective recruitment method.

However, public sector recruiters are relatively more impressed by this method of recruitment than are their counterparts in the manufacturing and production sector (22.6% versus 7.1%; with the service sector falling in between, with 17.9% choosing it).

7

Employment agencies: In third place, in terms of the proportion of employers choosing it as their most cost–effective recruitment method, lie commercial employment agencies. Overall, just over one in 10 recruiters (11.5%) highlighted their use as being most cost-effective.

Specifically, though, while equal proportions of manufacturers and services firms in the private sector chose agencies for their effectiveness (one in six, 17.9%, in both cases), not one public sector employer did so.

The public sector's aversion to the use of agencies may be the result of its preference for open advertising as part of its commitment to ensuring equality of opportunity. And, of course, it might also be a reflection of any difficulties experienced by public sector employers in agencies' ability to meet their requirements.

Word of mouth: Among our contacts working for employers in the manufacturing and production sector, one in 10 (10.7%) have found from experience that word of mouth provides the most cost-effective means of finding recruits for skilled-worker vacancies.

However, this method was not considered as being their most cost-effective option by any of our contacts in other parts of the economy. No other recruitment method was rated as being the most cost-effective option by more than 4.0% overall of the specialists we contacted.

E. The cost-effective recruitment of semi- and unskilled workers

The most cost-effective methods of recruiting semi- and unskilled workers, according to personnel, HR and recruitment specialists, focus on a single medium:
● advertising in local newspapers.

However, just a few employers have found, from experience, that one of the following is more cost-effective:
● using jobcentres; commercial employment agencies; or word of mouth.

Local newspapers: By far the largest proportion of the personnel, HR and recruitment specialists we contacted told us they have found local newspaper advertising represents their most cost-effective means of recruiting semi- and unskilled workers (three-quarters, 73.2%, did so). Local newspapers are particularly effective options for public sector employers (eight in 10, 81.1%, chose them, against three-quarters, 72.7%, of service sector employers and only six in 10, 63.0%, manufacturers).

Jobcentres: The state-run network of jobcentres provides a free service to employers and jobseekers. Its emphasis on finding work for unemployed people, and the privatisation of its professional and executive division many years ago, tends to concentrate its focus on lower-level jobs. This emphasis is reflected in the widespread use of jobcentres made by the employers we contacted in order to fill their semi- and unskilled vacancies.

However, fewer than one in 10 (9.3%) of our contacts have found from experience that jobcentres are the most effective means of recruiting semi- and unskilled workers, with little difference in effectiveness being reported across the various sectors of the economy.

Employment agencies: One in 12 employers (8.2%) find that employment agencies provide the most cost-effective means of finding potential recruits to semi- and unskilled posts. Again, there is little difference in this experience between employers in the different economic sectors.

Word of mouth: Almost one in five (18.5%) of our contacts working in the manufacturing and production sector have found that word of mouth provides the most cost-effective means of recruiting semi-and unskilled workers.

In contrast, few services firms in the private sector (just 6.1%) have found that this is the case, and none at all in the public sector. However, the public sector is generally averse to using informal recruitment methods, such as word of mouth.

No other recruitment method was rated as being the most cost-effective option by more than 3.0% of the specialists we contacted.

F. The cost-effective recruitment of new graduates

The recruitment of new graduates to management-entry and similar types of programmes represents a specialist activity that is mainly confined to large employers and those operating in certain sectors, particularly consultancy, accountancy and financial services.

There are at least 20 different methods of recruiting new graduates to traditional, mainstream graduate-type roles that are practised by employers. However, just four techniques stand out, in terms of their being the most cost-effective methods in the experience of personnel, HR and graduate-recruitment specialists. These are, in descending order:

9

- campus visits, including the "milk round";
- former work-placement students; and to an equal extent, advertising via the internet where the employer's own website is used; and
- university careers services.

In addition, our contacts working in the manufacturing and production sector highlighted two further methods:

- students they have sponsored at university; and
- advertising in specialist journals and/or the trade press.

Campus visits: Four of the six most highly rated recruitment methods involve some form of reaching out to universities and their students: visits to campuses; contact with students who have undertaken work placements with the employer; the use of university careers services; and the sponsorship of students while at university.

Proportionately more of our contacts chose campus visits as being their most cost-effective means of recruiting new graduates than identified any other recruitment method (15.5% did so).

Work-placement students: The recruitment of new graduates is different in many ways to the normal process of filling organisations' vacancies. In particular, there are few other examples where employers are able to "preview" potential candidates months, perhaps years, in advance of hiring them.

For graduate recruiters, previewing undergraduates through work placements – with or without formal sponsorship arrangements – provides an important recruitment channel. As we saw above, former placement students represent a cost-effective means of recruiting a pool of potential new members of staff (14.1% of our contacts told us so).

As well as providing an opportunity for the potential employer and employee to get to know each other, work placements help undergraduates develop work-related skills and behaviours that employers value. For vocational courses, placements play a central role in students' learning.

Offering a placement requires time, effort and resources on the employer's part and should not be undertaken lightly. The National Centre of Work Experience (www.work-experience.org) has developed a set of guidelines to help employers, and they can advertise placement opportunities on the website of the centre's parent body, the Central Services Unit (www. prospects.ac.uk).

According to a survey of 90 graduate recruiters conducted by the Association of Graduate Recruiters and the Financial Times[1], work experience is highly valued by employers. Specifically, structured placements undertaken as part of a degree course are most valued, followed by any other type of work experience with an employer. However, gap years taken prior to attending university rank only seventh in order of the value placed on different types of work or life experiences. Gap years taken after graduation are even less valued, lying in ninth place. Surprisingly, participation in voluntary work comes even lower, at 10th place, in terms of the value placed on it.

Advertising via the internet: A further one in seven (14.1%) of our contacts told us that, in their experience, advertising graduate vacancies on their own organisation's internet site provides the most cost-effective recruitment method available to them.

There is a general shift away from using job boards – commercial internet sites dedicated to recruitment advertising – and other external sites in favour of using employers' own websites, and this is reflected in our contacts' feedback. Only 2.8% of them told us that external internet sites represent the most cost-effective method of recruiting new graduates.

In general, there are several potential disadvantages connected with using organisations' own websites to carry recruitment advertising. Unless a jobseeker is actively searching for a new position – by using a search engine or deliberately targeting a few organisations' sites to visit – then this form of internet recruitment can be a very hit-and-miss affair. In particular, it can often fail to attract the attention of individuals who are not actively searching for a new job.

The specialised nature of graduate recruitment, though, redresses some of this imbalance – particularly, where employers are well-known among undergraduates as desirable places to work (having a strong "employer brand"). In such cases, jobseekers will indeed meet recruiters more than halfway and actively seek out the corporate websites of such employers (the large consulting firms, City financial institutions, major retailers, some airlines, multinational corporations, and so on).

Organisations with the "clout" to attract undergraduates to their own websites also tend to have the financial and technical resources to exploit e-recruitment to a great extent. They will offer detailed, but engaging, insights into the nature of the company and the jobs available to graduates. There may be video sequences of actual employees talking about their work, and self-completion questionnaires that help visitors decide whether or not they would like working there.

University careers services: University careers services have had mixed "reviews", with some commentators arguing that they could provide more help than they do at present to employers in filling their vacancies and deliver more consistent levels of service. The recruiters we contacted, however, already make considerable use of these careers services, and rate them highly. In all, one in nine (11.3%) have found that university careers services provide their most cost-effective means of graduate recruitment.

To add some background to these bald facts, we also asked recruiters to tell us the extent to which they agreed that "university careers services are of help to employers in recruiting new graduates". More than three times as many agreed or strongly agreed with this point of view, as disagreed with it. Only one in five of those we contacted had no decided views either way.

In addition to the above recruitment techniques, our contacts working in the manufacturing and production sector highlighted two further methods: using sponsored students as a recruitment pool (where one in six, 15.2%, told us it was their most cost-effective method), and advertising in specialist journals and/or the trade press (where one in eight, 12.1%, did so).

No other recruitment method was rated as being the most cost-effective option by more than 10.0% of the specialists we contacted.

The best times to recruit new graduates: Despite the huge changes underway in higher education and the pressures besetting employers' recruitment activities, much graduate recruitment – undergraduate recruitment, strictly speaking for the most part – still follows a regular rhythm. The "milk round" of organised campus visits, the publication deadlines of careers directories and, of course, the dates of the long summer vacation all provide landmarks in the graduate recruitment year.

In most cases, employers tell us they find that their most productive recruitment activity is concentrated into a relatively short timespan. One-third (35.7%) of those we contacted have found that a single month in the year offers prime recruitment opportunities. The remainder nominate two, three or four months in all, but rarely more than this.

Many recruiters have found from experience that timing is both crucial and situation-specific. It is crucial in that tardy recruiters will lose the best undergraduates to other employers, while premature recruitment may find that many students are not yet ready to commit themselves to their choice of employment after university.

Unfortunately, too, finding the optimal recruitment timing depends on the activities of competitor employers, the nature of the university course, and many other internal and external factors. Across all the employers we contacted, while almost all of them were able to identify the best month or months in which to hire their future graduate recruits, there is little helpful agreement as to the specifics. Roughly equal proportions chose each of the four months, December to March, and almost as many nominated May or June. However, they reached their greatest consensus in respect of November as the prime hiring month, followed by October.

Getting the timing right is a matter of importance for employer and undergraduate alike. According to research undertaken for Pearn Kandola's *Graduate recruitment manual*[2], most private sector organisations recruit just once a year to their graduate-entry schemes, particularly so among financial services companies. In the public sector, though, roughly equal proportions run one scheme a year as run several.

G. The cost-effective recruitment of school-leavers

The most cost-effective methods of recruiting school-leavers and other young people, according to the experience of personnel, HR and recruitment specialists, are, in descending order:
● advertising in newspapers; and to a lesser extent
● recommendations from current members of staff; and
● contact and/or links with schools and colleges.

Press advertising: Half (49.0%) of the specialists we contacted told us that newspaper advertising represents the most cost-effective means of recruiting young people. In most cases, employers use local or regional titles in preference to more expensive (and less well-targeted) national newspapers.

Word of mouth: A further one in seven (14.0%) of our contacts have found that obtaining personal recommendations from current members of their workforces provides the most cost-effective recruitment method. This form of word-of-mouth recruitment is favoured by up to half of our contacts working in the service sector, but, in contrast, does not find favour with a single employer in the public sector, where this form of recruitment is frowned upon.

Links with education: Another one in seven (14.0%) of those we contacted prefer another recruitment method to find young people: making

13

contact, or developing longer-term links, with schools and colleges. However, different economic sectors have different experiences of this approach. While as many as three in 10 (30.0%) manufacturers have found that educational links provide the most cost-effective method, only one in 14 (7.0%) of our contacts in either the service sector or public sector have found this to be the case.

No other recruitment method was rated as being the most cost-effective option by more than 9% of the specialists we contacted.

H. Cost-effective recruitment: an overview

Above (in sections A to G), we analysed feedback we obtained from employers about the cost-effectiveness of various recruitment methods in respect of particular types of vacancy. Here, though, we draw on findings from the Chartered Institute of Personnel and Development's research[3] to provide an overview across all types of vacancies.

The most cost-effective recruitment methods, when generalised across all types of vacancy are, in descending order:
● advertising in local newspapers (24.8% of employers chose this method); and, to a lesser extent
● using commercial employment agencies (14.7%);
● advertising in specialist journals and/or the trade press (11.9%);
● advertising in national newspapers (8.8%);
● using jobcentres (8.6%);
● word of mouth (also 8.6%);
● electronic recruitment (5.8%); and
● speculative applications (5.6%).

No other recruitment method was rated as being the most cost-effective option by more than 4.0% of employers.

Interestingly, the Institute's research report contrasts the ratings given to particular recruitment methods' cost-effectiveness with their actual prevalence. It should be borne in mind that employers often make use of two or more recruitment methods for a particular vacancy, so it does not necessarily follow that the best methods are also the most widely used.

In fact, the extent of use of most recruitment methods reflects their actual importance to employers in delivering high-quality candidates at a reasonable cost. For example, jobcentres are the fifth most effective method, according to employers, and are the sixth most widely used technique.

But the institute does find a few contradictions. In particular, national news-paper advertising is reported as having greater importance for recruiters than its more limited use would suggest (it ranks fourth in terms of its value to employers, but only eighth in terms of its actual use). Conversely, electronic recruitment is much less important to employers than its current usage would suggest – it is the second most widely used method, but ranks only eighth in terms of its importance.

Developing recruitment and selection criteria

There is more pressure than ever before on organisations to make the most cost-effective selection choices. And the growing body of discrimination legislation means that employers with practices that fall short of objectivity and fairness could well face costly tribunal complaints.

Objectivity and fairness in recruitment take as their starting point the compilation of accurate job descriptions and person specifications, based on valid job analysis techniques (see checklists 1, 2 and 3). These techniques involve time, effort and expense, certainly, but can repay this investment through their contribution to much improved recruitment decisions. And, job descriptions and person specifications can contribute in other ways, particularly in providing the starting point for formal performance-management reviews, where an individual's actual performance is measured against the requirements of their job as spelled out in these documents. Job descriptions are also important starting points when undertaking job evaluation exercises, although comparison between different jobs depends on the descriptions having followed a common format and structure.

Current practice in using and updating job descriptions and person specifications is analysed below, and is based on feedback obtained by IRS from 250 personnel, HR and recruitment specialists. Some organisations use competency frameworks as alternatives to job descriptions and person specifications; *see the next section in this chapter for information on competencies.*

Job descriptions

State of play: Job descriptions are in widespread use, with more than eight in 10 (82.8%) employers using them (excluding the smallest workplaces).

They are most widespread in the public sector, where almost all (97.4%) such employers make use of them. In the private sector, in contrast, only seven in 10 (69.4%) services firms and two-thirds (66.0%) of employers in the manufacturing and production sector have introduced job descriptions.

In addition, the public sector is more likely to have developed job descriptions for all its jobs and roles (96.2% have done so), compared with only two-thirds (66.6%) of the service sector and only four in 10 (40.9%) employers in the manufacturing and production sector.

Usage is most patchy and selective in the manufacturing and production sector, where more than one in five employers (22.7%) have developed them for no more than a minority of jobs and roles.

In terms of workforce size, the prevalence of job descriptions increases in tandem with employee numbers, with three-quarters (74.2%) of employers with fewer than 250 staff having them compared with nine in 10 (88.8%) of the largest organisations with 10,000-plus staff.

Employers that have made a deliberate decision to reject the use of job descriptions most often do so because they fear they would create barriers and restrictions in organisations that value flexibility and informality.

Content of job descriptions

Feedback from the 250 personnel and HR specialists we contacted shows that job descriptions share many common features (checklist 1 contains Acas's advice on their content). In descending order of prevalence, they usually contain the following:
- job title (100% of employers' job descriptions contain this information);
- summary of the main purpose of the job (97.1%);
- principal job duties with brief descriptions of them (96.7%);
- a statement relating to other duties (81.2%);
- details of those reporting to job-holder (76.5%);
- date of the most recent update of the job description (55.4%);
- location (53.5%);
- grade of job (51.6%); and
- statement relating to changing duties (43.6%).

There are few differences in the content of job description between employers, in terms of their workforce size or economic sector. However, public sector job descriptions tend to be slightly more detailed in general and, in particular, are more likely to contain: details of the job-holder's direct reports (82.4% do so); the date that the job description was most recently revised (66.2%); and the inclusion of a statement relating to changes in duties (58.1%).

1. Acas on job descriptions

Acas gives the following advice about the content of a typical job description:

"This should detail the purpose, tasks and responsibilities of the job. A good job description should include:

● main purpose of the job – try to describe this in one sentence;

● main tasks of the job – use active verbs, like 'writing', 'repairing', 'machining', 'calculating', instead of vaguer terms like 'dealing with', 'in charge of'; and

● scope of the job – expanding on the main tasks and the importance of the job. Job importance can be indicated by giving information such as the number of people to be supervised, the degree of precision required and the value of any materials and equipment used.

A good job description is useful for all jobs. It can help with induction and training. It provides the basis for drawing up a person specification – a profile of the skills and aptitudes considered essential and desirable in the job-holder. It enables prospective applicants to assess themselves for the job and provides a benchmark for judging achievements."

Reproduced with permission from "Recruitment and induction", Acas, 2003, www.acas.org.uk.

Application of job descriptions

Once they have been drafted, job descriptions tend to be widely used by employers. The public sector is not only a relatively high user of job descriptions, but also makes greater use of them once they have been developed.

As well as their use in recruitment, job descriptions are also used in selection, performance management and in the analysis of training needs.

At least half of all employers that have developed job descriptions use them for these purposes:
● when developing selection criteria (used for this purpose by 83.4% of employers with job descriptions);
● as a guide when writing recruitment advertisements (82.0%);
● sending them to candidates as a means of providing some information about the vacancy (75.4% overall, ranging from 94.5% of public sector employers down to just 46.8% of manufacturers);

● as a reference point in formal performance-management reviews (69.8% overall, rising to 76.7% in the public sector); and
● to help in identifying training needs (55.6%).

Significant proportions of users also employ job descriptions for other purposes. At least four in 10 users employ them in the following ways:
● to provide them to employment agencies that are retained to supply recruits and temporary staff (46.2%); and
● as constituent parts of the contract of employment (39.6%, ranging from 53.4% of public sector employers to 38.4% of the service sector and just 15.6% of manufacturers).

Analysing jobs

Direct observation: Direct observation of existing job-holders at work can often provide insights into a job that cannot be gleaned in any other way, and is particularly useful for roles where most of the tasks being performed are visible and fairly narrow in scope, such as manual jobs.

However, there are several drawbacks to this technique. Employers must devote time and money to providing training for the observers in observational skills. And observation is not well-suited to tasks that are not visible or that vary considerably from day to day (where time-consuming follow-up observations would be required). The main problem, though, concerns the act of observing the individual, because this knowledge may alter their behaviour and lead them to perform the job in ways that do not reflect its true nature.

Interviewing job-holders: Observation is often improved by interviewing the job-holder to gain further information about some issues and explore others that are not capable of being observed. Interviewing is also a technique in its own right, where individuals performing the job and, often, their line manager, are asked to describe its duties. This technique is most effective where trained interviewers are used, and where interviewees are asked to prove concrete examples to illustrate the information they give about the job's duties.

Holding separate interviews with two or more individuals allows the interviewer to confirm and cross-reference the information to test its accuracy and fill in any gaps. In some cases, the interviews are not held one after the other, but with a group of interviewees who discuss the issues and are expertly led to draw out the main factors associated with performing the job. Group interviews may also be known as focus groups, particularly where the interviewer facilitates the discussion with well-timed questions, and allows the participants to exchange views and opinions with each other. Focus groups are frequently used in the analysis of jobs for the purpose of developing competency frameworks.

The main drawback with interviews lies in the interaction between interviewee and interviewer. Interviewees may feel threatened by what they perceive as an examination of their own performance, rather than the components of the job, and be hostile or uncooperative. They may wish to make a good impression, consciously or not, by downplaying the mundane parts of their work and exaggerating the importance of areas of responsibility. Interviewers with suitable training and experience can do much to overcome these problems, and the use of group interviews can also reduce them.

Documentary evidence: Organisations often have sources of documentary evidence that can be useful when analysing jobs, such as internally-developed training materials designed for individuals performing the job being analysed, and records from formal performance-management systems where individuals and their managers have discussed the person's main tasks and the skills involved.

As well as internal training materials, the lengthy descriptions of tasks contained in National Vocational Qualifications and Scottish Vocational Qualifications have been developed from fieldwork among a range of employers and could provide useful information, particularly for lower-level jobs. And individuals being assessed for the purposes of obtaining an NVQ or SVQ must usually compile a "portfolio of evidence" about their duties and the way in which they perform them, which job analysts could find useful for their purposes.

Beyond existing documentation, job-holders can be asked to keep logs or diaries for a period, recording the main duties they undertake and, perhaps, the way in which they performed them.

Job-analysis questionnaires: Job-analysis questionnaires are survey-based tools that gather information from individuals performing the job being analysed, and/or their line managers, about the major aspects of their duties. Employers can either design their own survey forms or use one of the products available in the marketplace.

Examples of off-the-shelf products include McCormick's Position Analysis Questionnaire (PAQ), the Job Component Inventory (JCI) and the SHL Work Profiling System (WPS). Licence fees, the purchase of materials and other costs are usually involved in using commercial products, and some publishers will require users to undergo accredited training before they are able to use their surveys.

Critical incident technique: A trained interviewer works with job-holders to gather information on incidents that were critical to achieving job objectives and were either handled extremely well or extremely badly. These incidents are then explored more deeply to determine what the interviewee actually did, and what skills are needed to cope effectively with the incident. The strengths of this technique include its focus on real-life events performed by the job-holder, and its ability to reduce interviewees' desire to exaggerate particular aspects of their role.

The main drawbacks of this technique are the need to use suitably trained and experienced personnel, and the time and resources required.

Repertory grid interviews: Around since the 1950s, the repertory grid technique can be used in various ways to develop job descriptions and person specifications. Essentially, though, a trained interviewer conducts an interview with someone who is very familiar with the job being analysed. The interviewee is asked to consider three factors at a time, and compare and contrast them, with the aim of drawing out the essential points of difference. Questioning about each group of three factors continues until all points of similarity and dissimilarity are exhausted, and then further groups of three factors are introduced, until all possible factors have been discussed with the interviewee.

The technique can be used to focus on tasks, in which case three tasks are chosen at a time (often, at random) by the interviewer, and the interviewee is asked to compare and contrast the skills and abilities required to perform them. Or, it can focus on people, where a line manager is asked to consider three individuals who work for them, and compare and contrast the ways in which they approach and perform their duties.

The main drawbacks of the repertory grid technique are that it can be extremely time-consuming, and that it demands high levels of skills on the part of the interviewer in both conducting the interviews and then analysing the information obtained from them.

Further information on job analysis can be found in checklist 2, which contains an extract from a free SHL publication, *Guidelines for best practice in the use of job analysis techniques* (available from www.shlgroup.com/uk).

2. Guidelines for best practice in the use of job analysis techniques

Job analysis provides a useful means of developing job descriptions and person specifications. The following advice about using job analysis techniques comes from psychometric test publisher and consultancy SHL:

The role of the job analyst
The role of the job analyst is easily taken for granted, and this can lead to problems. Effective analysts should:
● be properly trained in job analysis techniques;
● have a working knowledge of the organisation and the job in question;
● have good interpersonal skills; and
● be comfortable working as a group facilitator.

[. . .]

Communication
Communication is paramount to a successful job analysis project, and it is up to the analyst to make sure all participants are properly informed. Without proper communication, participants may be suspicious of the process and may not provide important information.

Communication with the participants should take place prior to a job analysis session and again at the start of the session. The briefing of participants should be comprehensive, open and honest, stressing that their cooperation is voluntary, but that their assistance and insights are essential to success.

Once the session begins, it is also important to:
● develop a rapport with the individual;
● avoid being judgmental;
● ask probing questions to clarify issues; and
● avoid turning it into a counselling session.

Identifying participants
Which people should participate in a job analysis exercise? They should be the ones most familiar with the job and how it is currently performed, and as such are often known as subject-matter experts (SMEs). Usually, job incumbents and line managers or supervisors are the most expert source of job information. However, anyone with detailed knowledge of the job may participate in the job analysis sessions.

It is good practice to take a sample of people who are representative of the target population in terms of age, gender, ethnic origin and background. Different perspectives on the job can produce a more rounded picture. The participants should feel comfortable with the process or activities that will be used, and be both able and willing to participate.

Briefing the participants
All subjects for job analysis studies should be fully briefed, either by letter or in person, before they go through a job analysis procedure. This briefing should explain such issues as:
● what job analysis is;
● why the job is being analysed;
● why the person has been chosen for the study;
● what the person will be expected to do;
● what the outcome of the study will be; and
● what preparation the person will need to do.

Interview protocol and question style
Interviewing subject matter experts for a job analysis relies upon the same basic principles as other types of interviews. Establishing rapport and being an active listener are important skills on the part of the job analyst. Again, it is good practice to inform the participant about what will be taking place, including information such as the purpose of the interview, the degree of confidentiality and the amount of time available. Make it clear that it is a two-way process, and that the candidate's views are very much welcomed.
● Use plenty of open questions during interviews.
● Don't be nervous about asking naïve questions, especially regarding technical vocabulary or company jargon.
● Be sure to ask for clarification.

Reproduced with permission from "Guidelines for best practice in the use of job analysis techniques", SHL, 2001, www.shlgroup.com/uk.

Updating job descriptions

Job descriptions can quickly fall out of date given the pace of change in today's organisations. Step-changes in corporate structures, staffing levels and other significant operational areas can act as trigger points for the review of job descriptions and other formal documents. But the type of incremental modifications that often takes place in employees' jobs is less perceptible and may pass unnoticed. This means it is all the more important for job descriptions and person specifications to be reviewed on each occasion that recruitment is undertaken.

In all, nine in 10 (89.9%) of the personnel and HR specialists we contacted told us that their organisations aim to keep job descriptions up to date. Most commonly, job descriptions are updated each time a job becomes vacant (two-thirds, 66.2%, of employers follow this approach), while far fewer (just over one-third, 37.8%) update them as part of the operation of their performance-management system. Employers in the manufacturing and production sector are relatively less likely to update their job descriptions through either of these (or any other) means.

Updating methods: Most employers (66.0%) that revise job descriptions involve the relevant posts' line managers and post-holders in the review process.

Some of our contacts told us that their updating process involves formal research methods. One in six (15.5%) employers use one or more job-analysis techniques including job analysis questionnaires, direct observation, repertory grid interviews and critical incident techniques. A further one in seven (13.3%) employers conduct straightforward interviews with post-holders.

Problems with job descriptions

Fundamentally, the usefulness of job descriptions depends on the accuracy and objectivity of the job analysis upon which they are based. Each of the main methods of drawing up job descriptions has its own drawbacks, as we saw above. Beyond these practical limitations, there are also two philosophical objections to the use of job descriptions.

First, they are intended to ensure that the parties to the employment relationship – the employee and employer – are equally clear about the role the individual is expected to perform. Some see this as a drawback. Formalising a job's duties in this way creates a certain rigidity, which may involve the employer negotiating with the employee each time a change in the job is required. This can result in a slow response to changes in the workplace and, sometimes, lead to a breakdown of the relationship between employer and employee.

However, the inclusion of a statement relating to the need for other duties to be undertaken from time to time can – to a certain extent – overcome this problem for temporary changes in job content. Job descriptions can also contain some reference to the possibility that duties will change over time – supplemented by inclusion of a phrase to the effect that the job-holder will be expected to cooperate where such changes are reasonable. What constitutes "reasonable" in such a scenario is another question.

Second, job descriptions have been criticised because they shift the emphasis towards the job and its tasks, and away from the person performing it. There is a school of thought that suggests that this encourages people to think in terms of being employed in a job and not for an organisation. This can result in employees focusing on their own particular job duties rather than on the needs of the organisation as a whole. And it can create a culture where individual performance and effort is seen as being of lesser importance than conformity to a collective, fairly mediocre standard applying to all job-holders.

Set against these criticisms is the consideration that recruitment and selection are unlikely to succeed where recruiters are not clear about what they are looking for among the candidates. Without a set of criteria obtained from an objective analysis of the vacancy, they will be forced to fall back on their subjective impressions of what counts. And once the recruit is in post, line managers will find it difficult to manage their performance without having a clear set of standards, derived from job analysis, against which to assess them.

Perhaps one answer to these conflicting views involves creating job descriptions and person specifications that are correct at the time they are produced – for the purposes of recruitment, for example – and then treating them as flexible, fluid statements that both employee and employer need to revisit and update on a regular basis once the individual has been appointed.

Person specifications

While the focus of a job description rests on the job itself, person specifications concentrate on the individual who performs the job in question. Person specifications aim to describe the characteristics of the individual who would be most suited to the demands of the role set out in the job description.

Often, though, employers find it difficult to resist the temptation to "gold-plate" their person specifications by pitching their requirements as high as possible. Where person specifications are not related accurately and precisely to the demands of the job, organisations expose themselves to two dangers.

First, recruitment will be flawed. Over-ambitious person specifications will lead to over-qualified candidates being recruited, with the risk that someone will be employed on the basis of false hopes and aspirations, which will not make for a good – or long-lasting – working relationship.

Second, employers will run the risk of complaints of unfair discrimination, should their recruitment criteria be too removed from the real demands of the job and this could have the effect of putting certain groups at an unfair disadvantage.

To minimise these dangers, the process of writing job descriptions and person specifications should be an integral part of implementing a policy of equal opportunities.

Use of person specifications

Person specifications are slightly less widely used than job descriptions, with 10 percentage points fewer employers having developed them (72.8% versus 82.8%).

Size and, therefore, the resources available to the organisation has little bearing on employers' use of person specifications, with around seven in 10 doing so, except among the very largest organisations with 10,000+ employees where their use is almost universal.

By sector, though, differences are marked. More than nine in 10 (91.2%) public sector employers have developed person specifications, while only six in 10 organisations in the private sector have done so (63.6% in manufacturing and production, and 64.2% in the service sector).

Person specifications are mainly used by employers for recruitment purposes. At least half of all employers that have developed person specifications use them for these purposes:
● when shortlisting applicants (used for this purpose by 89.0% of employers with person specifications);
● as a guide when writing recruitment advertisements (85.7%);
● in helping to develop interview questions (82.4%);
● as part of the process of screening, or preselecting, the initial group of applicants (59.8%); and
● sending them to candidates as a means of providing some information about the vacancy (53.8%).

With the exception of the penultimate use, in screening or preselection, public sector organisations make greater use of person specifications for the uses listed above than do employers in the private sector.

Areas covered in person specifications

According to Acas[4], factors to consider when drawing up the specification include:
● "skills, knowledge, aptitudes directly related to the job;
● the length and type of experience necessary;
● the competencies necessary;

● education and training, but only so far as is necessary for satisfactory job performance; unless the person is being recruited on the basis of future potential (eg graduate trainees), when a higher level of education may be specified; and

● any criteria relating to personal qualities or circumstances which must be essential and directly related to the job, and must be applied equally to all groups irrespective of age, sex, race, nationality, creed, disability, membership or non-membership of a trade union. To do otherwise is potentially discriminatory."

Feedback we obtained from 250 personnel and HR specialists shows that Acas's advice is broadly followed by many employers:

● skills and experience are found in more than nine in 10 employers' person specifications (98.8% and 95.0%, respectively);

● qualifications are included, as relevant, by a similar proportion (92.2%);

● however, education is included by as many as three-quarters of employers (75.2%), despite Acas's concerns;

● personal attributes are addressed by almost three-quarters (72.5%);

● while any special aptitudes required of job-holders are detailed by six in 10 employers (59.8%); and

● interests and motivation are included in four in 10 employers' person specifications (39.5%).

Person specifications, job descriptions and discrimination

Care needs to be taken when developing person specifications, in particular to ensure that the criteria included in them do not discriminate unfairly on the grounds of gender, ethnicity or disability.

The adoption of the EU's equal treatment Directive will mean that areas such as sexual orientation, religious belief, political views and age are, or will soon be included in discrimination legislation. And it is expected that existing disability discrimination law will be broadened to encompass indirect discrimination.

This means that HR practitioners need to ensure that any criterion that is potentially discriminatory against a protected group is objectively justifiable. It must, therefore, be genuinely necessary in the performance on the role, and must not be a device to benefit members of one group of the population. Employers should also audit job descriptions and person specifications to ensure that all reasonable adjustments are indicated that could be implemented to ensure the appointment or continued employment of individuals with disabilities.

3. Avoiding discrimination in person specifications and job descriptions

● Use objective methods of developing job descriptions and person specifications and, where cost-effective, use two or more methods in tandem;

● Ensure that job descriptions and person specifications do not contain directly discriminatory factors (for example, marital status, gender and, from 2006, age);

● Exclude factors from job descriptions and person specifications that are not essential to the job;

● Avoid "cloning" the characteristics of the current job-holder when compiling the job description and person specification (for example, are the current job-holder's age, length of service, years of experience, particular formal qualifications, etc, all necessary to the performance of the job?);

● Pay particular attention to mobility clauses (relating to the person's place of work) and other requirements that could restrict access to the job by certain groups (mobility requirements that are not essential are likely to constitute unlawful sex discrimination in that fewer women than men could fulfil them; age and length of service requirements might constitute indirect sex

discrimination against women, as well as age being direct discrimination once the forthcoming legislation is enacted by the end of 2006);

● Ensure job titles and other wording do not imply that the job is restricted to, or more suitable for, one gender or race (as well as avoiding "foreman" or "waitress", for example, the use of "he" in a job description or person specification could imply that the employer intends to discriminate unfairly; use alternatives, such as "they", "he or she" or "the job-holder");

● Examine every aspect of job descriptions and person specifications to ensure that reasonable adjustments have been made to accommodate individuals with disabilities, or indicate in these documents the areas where alterations could be made to do so (there is a danger that a too literal analysis of the current job could prevent individuals with disabilities from performing it; it is important to ensure that equally acceptable alternatives are explored – for example, where the telephone is used at present as a key means of communication, but where email or text-messaging could provide a suitable alternative; where some travel is involved, the job-holder may have a driving licence and use a car, but the use of public transport might provide a suitable alternative);

● Check that person specifications do not include, or encourage, assumptions about the groups that would provide the best fit with their requirements (stereotyping could take place, where some factors might be assumed to be most likely found in a younger person (flexibility; drive), or a man (physical strength; assertiveness), for example);

● Ensure that person specifications are not unnecessarily restrictive (for example, where a certain level of experience is required, this could include relevant skills and experience gained outside the workplace. Where formal qualifications are required, equivalent awards from outside the UK should be accepted provided this does not conflict with statutory requirements covering regulated professions; in other cases, refusal to accept an overseas qualification might constitute unfair race discrimination;

● Pay particular attention to person specifications that are based on a structure derived from a five- or seven-point plan – these usually include a heading of physical fitness that is often unnecessary in modern jobs and could discriminate unfairly against women and people with disabilities; such plans also frequently contain a heading of "disposition" that could encourage indirect discrimination based on assumptions and stereotypes;

● Audit existing job descriptions and person specifications for direct and indirect discrimination, and any omissions of reasonable adjustments to accommodate individuals with disabilities; and

● Ensure that job descriptions and person specifications are up to date, so that their requirements continue to reflect the actual, essential demands of the job.

Using competencies

Competencies are widely used in recruitment and selection processes, and represent one of the main areas of innovation and development in these processes. The large-scale survey of personnel, HR and recruitment specialists conducted by the CIPD[5] found that one in four (25.8%) of the 747 people contacted said that their organisation uses competencies to recruit or select candidates. A long-term project by IRS to track the use of competencies has found that they are used by more than 700 employers, having a combined workforce of more than four million. Although they were initially introduced by larger organisations, their use is spreading to medium-sized employers with workforces of a couple of hundred or more employees.

Competencies are sets of definitions of skills that any or all people-management practices can take as their starting point. For example, in recruitment, a job advertisement can use the competencies relevant to the vacancy as a means of describing it in the advert; application forms can be worded to obtain information from candidates about their skills and expertise as they relate to the competencies that recruiters are seeking. Information on the use of competencies in selection can be found in chapter 2. Here we provide an introduction to the ways in which employers identify competencies and use competencies in general.

The different types of competencies

Employers have two ways in which to define the jobs and skills they require:
● broader, softer skills and behaviours that apply to more than one particular type of job (for example, where customer care is important, this can be apply to many jobs and many specific tasks and actions within a job – other common examples are a concern for quality, an awareness of business or commercial realities, a willingness to cooperate with others in teams, and an ability to make decisions); and
● job-specific skills that usually apply to just one type of job (for example, to most staff involved in marketing, sales, IT support, or logistics).

To find lists of competencies that may be of use to them, employers have three choices:
● to develop the competencies themselves (with or without the input of an external consultant);
● to use ready-made sets of competencies offered by some consultancies (usually, the consultants will work with the employer to tailor them to its particular requirements); or
● to use NVQs (or Scottish Vocational Qualifications, (SVQs), which closely follow the NVQ approach and coverage of jobs). Even here, many employers do not introduce NVQs without modification; often, they find that the documentation needs simplifying or rewording in clearer English, or that some skills need more or less emphasis than given in the particular NVQ in order to reflect the range of skills that the employer itself requires.

Advantages and disadvantages of NVQs

Pros:

● **Ready-made:** NVQs (taken hereafter to include SVQs) are ready to use, and will have been carefully developed from large-scale research among employers, are regularly updated, and now cover a wide range of jobs and tasks. There is, therefore, a reasonable chance that there will be NVQs to suit an employer's requirements.

● **Recognition:** NVQs are, as their name implies, nationally-recognised awards. Provided the rules governing them are followed, employees have the opportunity to gain a national qualification that gives official recognition to their status as being a competent person without having to sit an examination. NVQs are primarily awarded on the basis of on-the-job assessment, meaning that employees who are already proficient need not undertake any further training nor sit an exam. The availability of a formal certificate can provide a powerful motivator to some employees to improve their performance and, where necessary, participate in training.

Cons:

● **Relevance:** Many employers find that NVQs lack sufficient relevance to their own activities and business priorities; even where they are potentially suitable, considerable revision and editing may be required to tailor them to an organisation's own needs.

● **Customer focus:** Few employers find NVQs easy to use; there are widespread criticisms of the large amount of documentation accompanying each NVQ, and of the difficulty in understanding the language and phraseology used in the materials.

● **Assessments:** Where employers use NVQs as a means of providing formal qualifications, they find that the procedure of obtaining an award is liable to antagonise and bewilder those involved. The assessment process usually involves assembling large amounts of evidence that shows the individual can satisfy the various aspects ("elements") of competence that make up each major part ("unit") of an NVQ. This can degenerate into a tick-box mentality that detracts from any training linked to the NVQ and from the intended motivational benefit of gaining a formal qualification.

● **Credibility:** NVQs have largely failed to gain the same reputation enjoyed by traditional vocational qualifications, such as BTEC and City & Guilds. This can reduce the intended motivational impact of encouraging employees to gain an NVQ.

Advantages and disadvantages of competencies

Non-NVQ types of competencies also have their good and bad points.

Pros:

● **Relevance:** Most employers develop competencies through a process of internal research, involving managers and employees in identifying the most important aspects of their jobs and in producing definitions and examples phrased in ways that are understood readily by them and that reflect the employer's own culture. This makes it likely that the competencies will be directly relevant to business needs, cultural values and managers' and employees' priorities.

● **Flexibility:** Unlike NVQs, competencies can take many formats, cover technical or behavioural skills (or both), and be revised internally as needs arise. Behavioural competencies are transferable (they are not related to particular tasks or jobs), so have some inbuilt flexibility to accommodate organisational changes and individuals' moves to different jobs.

Cons:

● **Resource-intensive:** The process of developing competencies involves considerable amounts of the time of both the project leaders and those they consult internally, and often requires the use of expensive external consultants.

● **Expertise:** Developing competencies requires an understanding of the competency approach, the methods of identifying and defining competencies, and the ways in which competencies can be applied.

● **High stakes:** Without this expertise, tight project management and a good involvement and communications strategy, competencies could turn out to be an expensive, high-profile failure that undermines the credibility of personnel and HR specialists.

● **Inflexibility:** Competency frameworks must be kept up to date or they will become irrelevant and discredited. Although it is possible to review them fairly easily, the initial time, effort and expense in producing the first version tends to deter employers from revisiting them.

● **Cloning:** Competencies that are identified through studying current job-holders may, in some circumstances, perpetuate the existing make-up of the people doing these jobs. This can happen where the jobs are dominated by particular groups (for example, many managerial roles are disproportionately filled by white males) and where the competencies emphasise the particular behaviours, skills and experience that these job-holders happen to possess. However, well-designed competencies that are audited for unfair discrimination, and have some forward-looking elements built in, will not lead to such cloning. Moreover, this is not a problem unique to competencies; it can also be found in job descriptions, person specifications, conventional

31

(non-competency-based) recruitment and selection, the attitudes of line managers when undertaking performance assessments, and so on.

● **Not forward-looking:** Linked to the cloning issue, competencies that are defined on the basis of current jobs and job-holders run the risk of reinforcing the status quo – they would not be forward-looking and take account of the future direction and aims of the organisation. However, well-designed competencies incorporate an aspect of future-proofing by involving senior managers who have strategic, policy-making roles and by taking account of their feedback on the future direction of the organisation and what this means in terms of the skills and behaviours that it will expect of its staff.

Identifying and defining competencies

Most organisations develop their competency frameworks through an internal research programme, often aided by advisers from an external consultancy. Our 10-year research programme into employers' use of competencies shows that there is now a model of identifying and designing competency frameworks that most employers broadly follow.

The project to introduce competencies is usually led by personnel, HR or training specialists, who, together with a small project team of line managers and an external consultant, conduct research among employees and managers within their organisation. The composition of the team and those who are consulted for the competency research affects not only the effectiveness of the competencies they devise, but also the degree of "buy-in" from the eventual end-users. For example, if line managers are not present in the project team, and have little or no input into the competency research, then our contacts have found that they are unlikely to accept the final result.

In fact, two-thirds of employers deliberately involve line managers at the design stage – either in a project group or as active participants in the research efforts used to develop the competencies. Employees, numerically if not politically, are more important end-users, and many – albeit slightly fewer – organisations also involve them in the process of designing competency frameworks.

Research among employees, managers and directors focuses on drawing on their insights about their organisation and its activities to compile definitions of performance, and the names to be used for each major aspect of performance. The latter will become the competencies themselves, while the definitions will provide the descriptions, explanations and examples of behaviour that inform users' understanding of what each competency means in practice.

The specific techniques used to gain this feedback vary from employer to employer. In most cases, though, one-to-one interviews are among the methods used. These are time-consuming, and may be restricted to the most important stakeholders and most influential individuals in the organisation. At senior level, interviewees are often asked about the future direction of the organisation as well as current requirements. This is one way that competencies can minimise built-in obsolescence, where they simply record performance as it mattered in the past.

Particularly where external advice is available, these interviews will use one or more special techniques, such as repertory grids, the critical incident technique or behavioural event interviews. These sophisticated types of interview require trained, experienced researchers. Their technical details vary (and go beyond the scope of this handbook, although a summary can be found earlier in this chapter in the section on Analysing jobs) but, to generalise, they enable the interviewers to obtain detailed descriptions of important competencies from the interviewees, who are chosen on the basis of their direct knowledge of the jobs being analysed. The interview transcripts also provide information that describes the competencies in action, and provide vivid examples of ways that performance could be observed by others.

Group meetings are one of the most common ways that employers develop their competency frameworks. These may take the form of a simple round-table discussion led by a member of the competency project team, which aims to get participants' views on important competencies and the ways in which these should be defined.

Alternatively, the project team may organise more formal, structured focus groups. Here, a small meeting led by a facilitator discusses issues and develops ideas based on a creative interaction of the participants. These can be particularly helpful in assisting participants to crystalise and articulate their views on what may be difficult or unfamiliar issues. For example, the competency project may wish to identify the characteristics of people who are seen as successful in a role or activity. A facilitated focus-group discussion can help individuals identify the type of person who would qualify as being defined as "successful", and provide a framework to help them think through the technical or behavioural skills that they believe contribute to this success.

At some point in the design stage, the project team will usually look outwards and conduct a form of benchmarking against one or more comparators. Almost all of our contacts tell us that their organisations incorporate some form of such external monitoring in the process of designing their own competency frameworks. At a minimum, this involves an examination of other employers' frameworks. More commonly, though, one or more of the design team will visit other organisations, discuss their experiences and be given an insight into the structure and content of their competencies.

Once the draft framework has been produced, employers have two choices: to attempt a full implementation or to use a pilot exercise in one department, group or grade of staff. A pilot programme has several advantages. It presents a further opportunity to involve employees and managers in the system at a formative stage (and, thus, increase their commitment to the end product). And, of course, it can provide a trial ground to identify areas for improvement at a stage where mistakes and problems will be restricted in scope. Just over four in 10 employers (44%) with competency frameworks incorporate a pilot stage in their development process – although private sector service firms are noticeably less likely to have a pilot stage than other organisations – while 54% of public sector bodies, and 52% of manufacturing and production firms, introduce competencies by using pilot programmes, only 30% of private sector services firms do so.

Comparatively few organisations, though, use pilots or other evaluation methods for the purpose of checking that their competencies comply with the law – particularly in terms of their impact on equal opportunities on grounds of gender, ethnicity or disability. While competencies are no more, or less, likely to encourage unlawful practices, recent and impending changes to discrimination legislation are bringing more and more aspects of personnel management into the legal arena, and personnel and HR specialists will need to be alert to these potential dangers.

Preparing the introduction of competencies

Each year, the various groups of personnel and HR specialists whom IRS contacts about their organisations' use of competencies identify the same issues that can make or break the effective use of competencies. They consistently highlight the importance of ensuring the motivation and the understanding of line managers and employees; in other words, of the end-users who will be working with the competencies on a day-to-day basis.

Employers have found that the involvement of managers and employees is essential and, as we noted above, a significant number ensure that as many end-users as possible are involved from the very first when their organisation's framework is being designed.

However, there are additional ways of building the commitment of employees and managers; it is a slow and painstaking process that usually requires a multi-stranded approach. Employers often adopt several methods, although few do so across the board – either in terms of the whole workforce or the whole range of methods available. Most commonly (among 78% of users), employers hold group briefings to explain the competency approach and the new framework. Also prevalent is the provision of training to managers about the use of competencies; usually, this will be mainly concerned with the practicalities of assessing their staff's competence.

Just over half of employers with competency frameworks provide training for employees, as distinct from their managers, but only one-third produce a special leaflet or brochure to explain the new framework. A similar proportion provides publicity via an existing channel of communication: the staff newsletter. Several organisations are also making use of their intranets to publicise competencies.

The methods that work best at gaining commitment are not necessarily those most commonly employed, however. We asked our contacts to nominate just one of the commitment and communication methods they have used as being the most effective in gaining support for the competency approach. This feedback shows that, while involving staff at the design stage is less commonly used than two of the other methods, it emerges as decisively the best way of achieving commitment (nominated by 42% of employers).

Group briefings follow in terms of effectiveness, although considerably fewer employers said so (only 28%). And at some distance after that is the provision of training to employees (13% of employers) and managers (10%). No employer considers that publicity – whether it is in the staff newsletter or a special publication – represents their most effective commitment tactic.

4. Competencies: the key issues

The experience of employers that have introduced competencies highlights several key issues that can make or break their effective use. This checklist draws on two sources: our long-term study of employers' use of competencies, and research conducted by Professor Adrian Furnham for the Careers Research Forum[6].

● Effective competency frameworks address three factors: accuracy, acceptability and accessibility.

● **Accuracy:** an accurate framework expresses the actual capabilities required for effective performance; it omits no essential ones, and excludes peripheral or superfluous ones. The descriptions of the competencies should be sufficiently specific and clear that they can be used in practice; however, they should not be so specific that subsequent revision and updating is impeded.

● **Acceptability:** to be effective, a framework should be accepted as accurate and helpful by the people who will use it. Acceptance is usually based on: how far the framework accords with their experiences, the apparent legitimacy of the design methodology and the degree to which the framework is in harmony with other priorities affecting the user.

● **A balance must be struck regarding the size and clarity of the framework:** large and detailed models are often difficult to use but, at the other extreme, a small model may contain descriptions that are too vague and broad to be of value.

● The accessibility of a framework can be improved over time.

Key issues and pitfalls:
● Employers should describe their frameworks as consisting of "competencies" only if this term is relevant to them and line managers.

● Many employers find that more than nine competencies is too many. The methods that work best when assessing individuals' competencies for performance-management purposes are those that are short, simple and comprehensible, rather than comprehensive.

● When designing the framework, it is unwise to rely entirely on consultants. A small, bright, dedicated and multifunctional working party for early research works well. The introduction of competencies tends to be more successful where the team has done extensive pilot work across the organisation.

● Many organisations attribute their problems with competencies to the long time taken to generate the framework. The critical issue lies in timing and managing expectations about when the framework will be finished and how it will help line managers and the organisation. Communicating clearly about purpose and progress right from the beginning can solve many of the problems.

● Allowing specialists to have a small number of three to four competencies to add to a short but manageable list of six to eight general competencies works well. Employers that resist introducing specific competencies often have the use of the whole framework threatened.

● The issues of finding a champion and gaining senior-level support are crucial.

● There are three phases to the successful implementation of all frameworks: phase one: planning/creating; phase two: implementing/launching; and phase three: maintaining. The vital phase of maintaining the system and ensuring it is used must not suffer from neglect, as it often does.

● The development of an expensively printed and complex manual containing details of the competency framework often discourages subsequent updating. In addition, framework design is often based on current, rather than future, organisational needs. There needs to be a balance between continuity and change. Competency frameworks need revisiting every two to three years to ensure they are still relevant. Resistance to updating is a common source of failure.

● There are three types of training that need to be provided to support all competency frameworks: (1) helping individuals agree their own objectives and competency-based success criteria; (2) training line managers to give staff feedback on their performance on a continuous basis; and (3) training assessors where competencies are given performance ratings.

● Competencies are often insufficiently linked to business plans. There needs to be greater integration, and frameworks need to be more flexible and updated more frequently.

● Competencies have undoubtedly brought about four clear benefits: (i) competencies have provided a common, shared, rich and descriptive language to describe people and performance; (ii) competencies have helped to realise the idea that performance needs to be measured in order to be managed, and that measurement can improve feedback; (iii) the competency approach leads to improved consistency across the whole organisation in the way in which people are managed; and (iv) competencies help focus on the need for development, and also identify ways of going about it.

● Keys to success: the characteristics of the successful introduction and use of competency frameworks are:

(a) frameworks should be not over-complex;

(b) they must be relevant to managers, employees and business objectives;

(c) they have to be fully supported in terms of staff and money, and championed consistently from the top;

(d) competency frameworks should be flexible to facilitate regular updating;

(e) the application of the competency system must be psychologically rewarding;

(f) the system needs to be initially linked to developmental opportunities for senior managers;

(g) the aims, deadlines and benefits of the competency project need to be spelt out clearly, regularly and simply; and

(h) the system must allow departments to add specific or technical competencies.

Effective uses of competencies

Feedback from personnel and HR specialists shows that employers use their competency frameworks in several different ways; often, the same employer uses competencies in two or more applications, such as recruitment and training. Their experience shows that the following (shown in descending order of effectiveness) are the most effective uses of competencies:

● to underpin training and development (helping to identify training needs and shape the content of training provision);

● in performance management (using behavioural competencies to broaden performance management to include the way in which a job is performed; using technical competencies to provide clearer definitions of what the job involves);

● recruitment and selection;

● helping to design jobs;

● to facilitate cultural change;

● in grading and job evaluation;

● in encouraging and supporting teamworking;

● succession planning; and

● as a factor when determining pay increases or bonuses★.

★ *The fact that competency-related reward comes last in this list is partly – but not entirely – a reflection that only three in 10 (29%) organisations that have adopted competencies use this approach.*

Managing recruitment administration

In some ways, recruitment and selection represent a public-relations exercise. The potential audience of a single recruitment advertisement could run into thousands of people. For the moment, they may be potential recruits, but for the remainder of their lives they have a different relationship with the organisation – as potential customers, clients or business partners.

Yet the two activities of marketing/PR and recruitment are often viewed entirely differently by the organisations concerned. Contrast the care that many employers give to the design and printing of corporate stationery and brochures with the low-key appearance and layout of recruitment adverts and application forms and the laid-back approach they take to candidate administration.

The areas of recruitment administration that personnel, HR and recruitment specialists tell us they are focusing on to improve their ability to fill their vacancies include:

● using e-recruitment to extend their advertising to individuals who might not see their conventional paper-based advertisements; e-recruitment has the added advantages of speed and, often, lower cost;

● introducing or updating software to make their recruitment administration more efficient and faster;

● offering additional, easier and faster ways to obtain details about a vacancy and submit an application – primarily, via email and the telephone; and

● keeping in closer touch with applicants so that they do not become disheartened and apply elsewhere.

More information about the ways in which employers are enhancing their "candidate-relationship management" can be found in chapter 2 in the section on Improving the cost-effectiveness of selection.

Application methods

We contacted 250 personnel, HR and recruitment specialists to find out current practice in offering candidates various ways to apply for a job. The recruitment difficulties that many of our contacts have experienced in the past three to four years have encouraged them to diversify, and become more candidate-friendly. Now, more than half of even smaller-sized organisations offer at least three different application methods for at least some of their vacancies:

● in writing (nine in 10 employers);

● via email (more than eight in 10); and

● using the telephone – mainly for initial enquiries and to request an application pack (seven in 10 employers, ranging from half of employers with fewer than 250 staff and seven in 10 employers with 250 to 999 staff, to three-quarters of larger employers).

In addition, some employers also use the following:

● recruitment advertising via the internet, with an in-built application process – such as an online application form or a hyperlink to an email message (more than four in 10, rising to half of larger employers); and

● a dedicated recruitment telephone line with a message-recording service for after-hours callers (four in 10 employers, ranging from one in five of those with fewer than 250 staff and four in 10 of those with 250 to 999 staff, to more than six in 10 employers with more than 10,000 staff).

Acknowledging applications

The acknowledgement of applications is greatly valued by candidates. Most individuals do not fire off multiple applications in a casual fashion, with little interest in the outcome. Instead, they generally invest time and emotional energy in the process, and have a psychological stake in their bid for a new job.

Where their applications are sent off, but are met with a deafening silence, how are candidates to know whether or not it has arrived safely? The post is not as reliable as it once was, and applications sent by email can easily disappear into the ether along with many other electronic messages.

Even an initial confirmation is not enough, unless the whole recruitment and selection process can be wrapped up in a couple of weeks. In these cases, a single letter or email to could acknowledge the application and notify candidates of the progress or outcome of their application.

Notifying candidates of the outcome of their application fulfils a basic need. Candidates have no means of guessing the result, given that employers' recruitment timescales vary so widely. Does a silence of two or three weeks mean that they have been rejected, or should they continue to be psychologically geared up for an interview?

Conversely, employers – even if they appreciate the need to keep candidates informed – are not always willing or able to provide this feedback. It can take considerable amounts of staff time to acknowledge applications or notify candidates of the outcome, as well as the expense of postage and stationery (although the cheaper, speedier and less formal medium of email is growing in popularity).

The main consideration appears to be the volume of applications. So, although the largest employers usually have the greatest resources at their disposal, they also tend to experience the greatest number of job enquiries. The feedback we obtained from personnel, HR and recruitment specialists shows that there is a rapid falling off in the practice of contacting applicants linked to the size of the workforce.

The majority (67.6%) of the smallest employers – defined as those with fewer than 250 staff – makes it their practice to acknowledge all applications.

This is not the case in respect of larger employers. Among employers with 250 to 999 staff, for example, fewer than half (47.0%) do so. This falls to just over one in three (36.1%) organisations with 1,000 to 9,999 staff, and to only one in five (22.2%) among the very largest organisations with 10,000+ staff.

In terms of economic sectors, there is a marked difference in practice between the public sector (where only one in six, 16.4%, acknowledge all applications) and employers in the private sector (where around six in 10 do so).

Time taken to acknowledge

Typically, there is a gap of four working days between the closing date for applications having passed and employers sending out acknowledgements to applicants. There is a little significant variation in timescales; only one in 12 employers that acknowledge job applications take longer than 10 days to do so.

Smaller employers are, on average, one day faster than larger organisations in this respect (taking 4.4 days and 5.4 days, respectively). However, although few public sector organisations acknowledge all applications, those that do so are one day faster than their private sector counterparts (4.6 days against 5.6 days).

Supplying information to candidates

Some employers make it their practice to provide background information to potential job applicants, beyond the scant details they are able to include in the limited space offered by a recruitment advertisement. The public sector has always been adept at sending out detailed application packs, containing information about the post, the recruitment process and, sometimes, details on the organisation itself.

But employers of all types are coming to realise that recruitment and selection is a two-way process; jobseekers make the decision whether or not to apply based on the information they have available about the vacancy and the employer. This provides two benefits. Well-crafted information-giving encourages potentially suitable individuals to apply, while discouraging those who are unlikely to meet the job's requirements or be happy with the organisation's culture. Not only does this provide a better-quality group of applicants, saving time and money on fruitless shortlisting and sending out rejection letters, but it avoids having to explicitly reject many individuals. No matter how carefully phrased, a rejection is likely to deter the individual from contacting the organisation – now or in the future – about other vacancies to which they could be much better suited. See chapter 2 for more information about self-selection.

In the case where employers send out further information to potential applications, below are the details that are most commonly provided, shown in descending order of prevalence:

● details of how to apply for the job (and, often, the recruitment timescale and its stages): provided by eight in 10 employers that supply further information to candidates;

● job description for the vacancy: eight in 10 employers;

● background information about the employer: six in 10 employers;

● person specification for the vacancy: almost six in 10 employers;

● details of a contact point or person for queries or further information: just over half of employers; and

● the organisation's equal opportunities policy: one in five employers (ranging from one in 10 or fewer private sector firms to more than one in three public sector organisations).

Recruitment advertising

Print media – national newspapers, the local press, trade magazines, specialist journals and the like – are heavily used to publicise job opportunities.

A survey conducted for the Chartered Institute of Personnel and Development[7] shows that almost nine in 10 (87.3%) employers make use, at some point and for at least some jobs, of the local press to advertise their vacancies (as a yardstick, employment agencies are only used by 63.7% of employers). In addition, two-thirds (66.4%) of employers place recruitment advertisements in specialist journals or the trade press. And just over half (53.4%) advertise for staff in national newspapers.

Many employers are reluctant to "put all their eggs in one basket", and often explore other ways of finding good-quality staff alongside their use of advertising. So, is the huge and expensive use of the press merely a recruiter's habit?

Research among employers in central London[8] shows that there is some logic to the use of advertising. Based on a massive project involving interviews with 1,188 employers, this study found that press advertisements represented the single largest source of successful applicants; that is, those who were actually hired from among all those who came forward. Specifically, the press was responsible for generating a quarter (26%) of successful applicants, followed by employment agencies (25%). Informal methods remain strong, though, and 22% of appointments were made via word-of-mouth sources. This same study also found that employers of all sizes share much the same experience of the effectiveness of press advertising.

One of the best reasons for employers' loyalty to recruitment advertising is that the British are inveterate newspaper readers and there is a strong national press – unlike the situation in the USA, for example.

According to figures from the National Readership Surveys quoted in BRAD[9] (a monthly directory of advertising rates and other such data), more than half of all adults (54.3%) read a national morning newspaper, and even more (57.6%) read a national Sunday paper. Local free papers are read by more than half of all adults (54.9%), while more than a quarter (29.7%) read a priced local paper.

Circulation figures are an unreliable guide to their total readerships. Most national newspapers, for example, are bought by one person but read by two or more. Moreover, someone who moves from a casual to an active interest in finding a new job will often buy a copy of a particular newspaper or magazine simply because it has a reputation as having the best selection of vacancies in the occupation or industry concerned.

Advertising can be a comparatively inexpensive form of recruitment. Even a four-figure sum for an advertisement in a national daily paper can, if it finds a good recruit, be cheaper than the use of an employment agency or headhunter. For some organisations, though, the balance tips firmly towards advertising because of what it is: a public, open invitation to apply for a vacancy. This can help to create a level playing field between different groups in the labour market, and is an issue to which we return below when considering equal opportunities and advertising. Advertising can also help organisations raise their profile and "build an employer brand".

In fact, any encouragement to use open forms of recruitment can pose a dilemma for recruiters. For some vacancies, conventional advertisements are unlikely to yield the best results. The rarified field of executive recruitment represents a prime example. In the private sector, certainly, few of those most suited to fill a top-level position will be scanning the situations-vacant columns. Informal approaches from headhunters are often most likely to whet such a person's appetite for the position. Sometimes, though, advertising is still employed, but adopts an informal approach – the employer's name is not disclosed and only basic details of its activities are provided. In these instances, readers are invited to approach the search consultant retained by the employer for further information about the vacancy.

Conversely, press advertising may be less successful for certain posts not because the medium is too formal and public, but because it is being challenged by modern technology. For many IT posts and graduate-entry schemes, the internet is becoming the recruitment medium of choice for both jobseeker and employer *(see chapter 3 Using electronic media effectively)*.

Even where recruitment advertising seems the best method of filling a vacancy, there is evidence that the way in which it is conducted can affect success rates, too. Psychologist Karel De Witte has drawn attention to five separate studies which show that recruits who had been found via press advertisements had higher rates of labour turnover than recruits who had been obtained from personal recommendations or unsolicited applications[10].

He believes the explanation lies in the amount of accurate information that candidates were given. Those who had been found by informal methods (recommendations and unsolicited applications) were likely to have obtained a more realistic appreciation of the demands of the job and the culture of the organisation.

Advertisements were less successful in finding applicants who were likely to remain in post, because people recruited through job advertisements "have much too high expectations about their job; those expectations are not countered by the recruiters, in order not to lose candidates".

Evaluating advertising's effectiveness

Karel De Witte's work and the findings he used are now dated. Fortunately, many recruiters now have access to their own data on the effectiveness of their advertising. According to the 102 employers that we contacted for in-depth information on their experience of using recruitment advertising, three-quarters (74%) monitor the effectiveness of recruitment advertising.

The downside, though, is that one in four employers do not compile such information, and this can only leave personnel, HR and recruitment managers exposed should questions be asked about their contribution to the business. With employers spending around £1 billion a year on recruitment advertising[11], a sizeable slice of this is being spent on trust.

The public sector is a major player in recruitment advertising, and our research shows that it is particularly vigilant in monitoring the effectiveness of this investment. More than eight in 10 (82%) of the public bodies we contacted conduct such evaluations. Services firms in the private sector are slightly less likely to evaluate their recruitment advertising, with just over three-quarters (77%) doing so. Manufacturers are least inclined to do so, with only six in 10 (59%) users of job advertising monitoring its effectiveness.

In specific terms, our analysis of personnel, HR and recruitment managers' practices shows that they monitor the effectiveness of their recruitment advertising in the following ways (shown in descending order of prevalence):
● the number of applications generated by a particular advertisement: almost all employers (93%) that conduct some form of evaluation adopt this practice; and
● the number of applicants from each publication or media source used in the recruitment campaign (78% do so).

Both these measures are based on the overall pool of applicants generated by an advertisement. Some employers go further and use quality-based indicators:
● two-thirds (66%) identify the publication or type of media that was responsible for producing the successful candidate(s);
● almost as many (61%) focus on the shortlist, and monitor each publication or type of media according to the number of individuals it generated, based on their presence in the shortlist for the vacancy;
● interestingly, though, recruitment advertising is least likely to be monitored in terms of its financial results. Only half (51%) of the employers that monitor advertising attempt to attach a unit cost per applicant, based on the total cost of the recruitment advertising for a vacancy, divided by the number of applicants generated by the advertisement; and
● proportionately, even fewer (41%) calculate how much a successful appointment has cost the organisation in terms of the amount it has spent on recruitment advertising.

First steps

Recruitment advertising is often undertaken in conjunction with an advertising agency (see the section later in this chapter on using recruitment advertising agencies).

Two fundamental decisions need to be taken, though, regardless of whether or not an agency is to be used:

1. **Does the vacancy need to be filled?** If someone is being replaced, this is an opportunity to consider whether parts or all of the work could be

reassigned to other employees, outsourced, automated or otherwise modified. Even newly created roles need to be analysed: how difficult and/or expensive will it be to find someone for the role as envisaged? Are there alternatives, such as outsourcing?

2. **What specifically is required?** A person specification is essential, setting out the skills, experience and qualities that the role demands as its basic requirements. The pace of change in most workplaces means that existing specifications are unlikely to be reliable and will have to be revised.

Competencies are increasingly being used in recruitment, either to replace person specifications or to amplify them. Competencies often offer a greater rigour and precision to the task of defining a recruiter's requirements. (For more information, see the section on Using competencies earlier in this chapter.)

Some basic information about the key activities of the role – a simplified form of job description – is also useful. These functional details will help to clarify recruiters' thinking and can be provided to applicants as a means of giving them an insight into the realities of the job. It might also be drawn upon in the advertisement, if relevant.

Armed with this information, recruiters who use an expert adviser can then provide a detailed, accurate and up-to-date brief on the vacancy. For those who go it alone, though, there is another preliminary step to take:

3. **Where to advertise?** Recruitment advertising is an exercise in free-market economics. The recruiter must find the best places to advertise where good-quality candidates are likely to see the vacancy, while taking account of the costs involved. Television has probably the greatest reach of any medium, yet its costs (and highly ephemeral nature) preclude it from almost all recruitment advertising. Although the use of the internet is growing rapidly, traditional print media continue to represent the mainstay of their recruitment advertising for most employers and most vacancies.

Choosing media

At the risk of over-simplification, recruitment advertising in the press can follow one of three routes.

First, for vacancies that are sufficiently highly paid to justify the expense of a home move and domestic upheaval, there are national broadsheet newspapers to choose from. This source provides access to a level of the labour market that cuts across geographical boundaries. Each paper tends to specialise in certain types of vacancy and, in the case of some newspapers, to vary its focus from day to day. So, for example, the Monday editions of a certain broadsheet might be devoted to public sector appointments, while its Tuesday issues might concentrate on vacancies for academic and related staff.

Advertising in national broadsheets is expensive, but, as the alternatives are either even more costly (the use of a headhunter or mainstream employment agency, for example) or are less effective, this can still be the most cost-effective option.

Second, at the other end of the spectrum, vacancies that are not highly paid, and not sufficiently specialised to have their own identifiable groupings (nursing, architects, engineers, etc), are probably most suited to advertising in local newspapers. The conurbations, such as Birmingham, Coventry and London, may have daily evening or morning papers, but in most areas these will be weekly in frequency (or even less often in the remotest areas).

Third, midway between these two poles lie the occupations whose incumbents identify themselves as having a common interest or profession and, importantly, also have one or more specialist trade or professional titles serving them. Specialist publications are often national in coverage, but their lower circulation means that they cannot usually charge the same high advertising rates as newspapers that circulate nationally or regionally.

However, circulation figures, or actual sales, can often be unsatisfactory guides as to the choice of a particular title in one of these three categories. The Guardian newspaper, for example, has relatively low circulation and sales figures, yet it overshadows competitors in having established a dominance for some types of vacancy. Many of those in a particular occupation will also know about this specialisation, and buy a copy (or borrow someone else's) on a few occasions[12].

The difficulty for recruiters where there is a poor match between the composition of a newspaper's regular readership and vacancy being advertised lies in the nature of most people's job search. For every active jobseeker who has already broken the psychological links with their current employer and made the decision to leave, there must be many more people who are merely vaguely interested in new opportunities. There is no automatic link between someone being an active jobseeker and them being the best possible candidate for a job. Therefore, publications whose readership corresponds closely to the relevant job market are very useful sources of candidates, given that the vacancy pages will be seen by many people who are merely browsing but might still be tempted by a suitable job opportunity.

Specialist titles are generally read for more than the collection of vacancies they advertise. So, with some exceptions, there is likely to be a closer fit between the overall market (the occupation) the recruiter wishes to target and the publication they read as a matter of routine. The same is true for local newspapers; readers will buy the title covering their locality and scan it for local news, house prices, small ads, etc. The same publication will also offer advertisements for jobs that are situated within one or more local travel-to-work areas.

Timescales are important, too. Advertisements should carry a closing date for applications, and this must take into account both the lead time required by the publication – the delay between the deadline for placing the ad in time for the next issue and its actual appearance – and how often the publication appears. A specialist journal, for example, might only appear once a month, and this could have a major impact on the timescale of the application process and, of course, on the speed with which the vacancy can be filled.

To compound the problem of working with publication frequencies, Margaret Dale, in her guide to recruitment and selection[13], adds that recruiters should take account of readers' habits. She says that the urgency with which they read a publication mirrors its frequency. Daily newspapers are usually read within one to two days, while a monthly, for example, may be put aside and not read for a couple of weeks.

Personal knowledge may be all that is required to identify the publications most relevant to a particular vacancy. Alternatively, or additionally, those working in the same part of the organisation as the post being filled will usually have a shrewd idea of the best sources of job advertisements. Newspapers and magazines displayed in libraries, the media directories they may have in their reference collections, and searching the internet can be additional sources of inspiration when selecting appropriate media.

One of the key sources for those involved in several recruitment exercises each year is BRAD (www.brad.co.uk), formerly known as British Rate and Data. This media directory is intended for buyers of all types of advertising in media that cover the UK and the Republic of Ireland. It has more than 13,000 entries, some of which are updated in each monthly issue. This is a costly publication (the online service costs £970 a year), but some large public reference libraries may hold copies and there is a pay-per-view facility on the BRAD website where advertising details on individual publications may be purchased for £10 per title once the site's search facility has narrowed down the possible choices.

Baiting the hook

There is rarely safety in numbers in terms of the response to a recruitment advertisement. An ideal ad for a single vacancy should generate a few, good-quality applications, thereby minimising the costs involved in responding to the applications, sifting them to produce a shortlist, sending out rejection letters and organising the remainder of the selection process.

Given that the best candidates could be happy in their current position, and might be merely scanning the jobs pages – to keep abreast of developments in competitors, salary movements, and so on – then the advertiser needs to find a means of grabbing the reader's attention.

Unfortunately, there is no one accepted best way of baiting the hook of a recruitment advertisement. One school of thought argues that informative adverts, with prominent job titles, some good background information on the vacancy and its requirements, will succeed in attracting readers.

Others, though, believe that unusual or striking advertisements are required. These might use colour to stand out (assuming most of the others are in monochrome) and an eye-catching statement or graphic, but will have had to sacrifice much of the information-rich content to make space for large headings and illustrations. This trade-off between elements of an advertisement is a simple matter of economics. Few organisations have the luxury of bottomless advertising budgets to increase the size of an advert as required.

Fashion, too, plays a part, although go-it-alone recruiters will be less exposed to such trends unless they slavishly follow what others are doing. There seem to be noticeable trends in the look and "feel" of recruitment advertising, just as there are in product adverts. For example, the use of amusing or exciting situations that is such a strong feature of car-makers' publicity can also be found these days in some advertisements for jobs.

The best of these cameos, though, have a serious purpose: to enable the reader or viewer to imagine themselves in the situation and get an insight into how they would feel if they were in one of the principal character's shoes. These are forms of "realistic job previews", an approach that aims to impart the essence of a vacancy to potential candidates and help them to decide whether or not the job would suit them. This self-selection can occur in other ways. The most traditional approach would be to pack an advertisement full of details about the job, its requirements and the organisation – and hope that the reader could untangle this mass of data and measure themselves against what is being implied.

Other, latter-day approaches include expressing the vacancy in terms of a few competency statements. If the language is vivid and the competencies genuinely based on essential key criteria, then this can be an effective form of self-selection.

Finally, self-selection can involve posing a series of questions that the candidate sees, or hears, and that aim to evoke some sort of reaction. Good reactions should encourage the person to apply for the job, while negative ones aim to dissuade. The internet can offer a greater edge here over traditional print-based advertising, because there is much more space to carry such questions and the responses can be interactive, giving the candidate immediate feedback.

According to a 1994 study by Dr Jonathan Hill of the Gallup Organization's selection research division[14], there is a definite science in composing the questions to be used in a recruitment advertisement. Among the evidence he cites are two studies that investigated the quality of responses to job advertisements with and without questions addressed to potential jobseekers. In both studies, the use of questions improved the effectiveness of the advertising. Significantly, though, the questions had been derived from a careful analysis of the characteristics of employees performing the job, and had not been made up in an unsystematic or intuitive way.

(For more information on improving recruitment and selection by encouraging candidates to undertake some self-selection, see chapter 2.)

Jargon and clichés

Competency statements, like other aspects of an effective recruitment advertisement, must be grounded in the real demands of the job in question. Too often, though, they appear in a degraded, unfocused form, with phrases such as "good team player", "high levels of motivation" and "self-starter".

Research conducted for the former Focus Central London Training and Enterprise Council found that vagueness, clichés and jargon are often an indication that the recruiter does not know what the job involves and has attempted to cast their net wide by using imprecise terms. Lack of insight into the necessary technical skills may be mirrored in the area of soft skills:

"If this is the situation for occupationally-specific skills, then the situation for the occupationally non-specific is even worse [. . .] Employers do not have the language to describe many of the softer key skills and, so, fall back on generalisms and euphemisms which convey a general meaning but which stand no chance of being measured in practice."[15]

According to Edward Moss of Edward Moss Communications in Leeds, clichés and jargon go beyond being space-wasters in recruitment advertisements: they can actually damage the reputation of the employer and deter potentially good applicants. "Must be a self-starter" often translates, he says, into "we haven't actually got a clue what we want you to do". And "good prospects" means that "you're bound to want to leave in a couple of years to go to a proper and better-paid job"[16].

At best, some potential applicants can "pick their way through" vague, cliché-ridden advertising copy, says Stuart Caldwell of recruitment advertisement agency TMP Worldwide, and make a reasonably sensible decision whether or not to apply for the vacancy. Others will not be so fortunate, and will either apply for jobs that turn out to be unsuitable, or fail to put themselves forward for ones in which they could perform very effectively. Either way, the advert will work against the interests of the employer[17].

The use of jargon – in the sense of technical language prevalent in an industry or occupation – is a contentious issue, even where it is precise in its meaning. On the positive side, such jargon may be a means of concisely and accurately portraying the demands of a job. However, on the downside, unless the recruiter is certain that the jargon is both accurate and entirely essential to a key demand of the job, its use will unfairly discriminate against some applicants. This could prevent the best applicants from being hired and may also be contrary to equal opportunities legislation.

Employer branding

The theory of "employer branding" is derived from mainstream advertising-industry practice, and involves building an identifiable brand for an organisation as an employer, in a similar way that some organisations build brands based on goods or services they provide. The aim is the same in both cases: to impress the reader (or viewer) so that they remember the brand, and to associate the brand in the person's mind with certain favourable connotations.

Brand-building is a difficult, expensive and long-term activity, so it is a serious step to consider. In most instances, though, the decision will have been taken at corporate level, and personnel, HR and recruitment managers will simply be expected to support an existing product- or service-related strategy. This may make itself felt through stipulations that the brand's slogan should appear on all recruitment advertisements ("the world's favourite . . ."), or that a logo be carried. The typeface and style used for the name of the organisation may also have been laid down.

Recruiters naturally aim to build on their strengths when seeking to attract applicants. The nature of the job, the location or salary may be their strongest point. In some cases, though, an established brand will represent one of the best ways of "stopping readers in their tracks". An organisation with a strong brand that has a favourable connotation in the labour market will attract jobseekers because working there "will enhance their future career prospects, self-esteem or social status," says Stephen Taylor[18].

Apart from a conveniently-available brand, recruiters have other cards they can play.

Effective content

A recruitment advertisement is no more than an invitation to apply for a vacancy. To be effective, it needs to reach its audience by ensuring that the correct media are chosen. The advertisement itself must be arresting so that readers who are merely browsing will have their attention grabbed for long enough for them to make an initial decision whether or not they would be suited to the job.

Much of the controversy surrounding the style and content of advertisements stems from the different schools of thought about the techniques that should be used to engage the reader's attention and, thereafter, to help them compare themselves against the job and its requirements.

There are some points, though, from research into the elements of job ads that contribute to successful recruiting. A major study for Focus Central London Training and Enterprise Council[19] analysed more than 9,000 recruitment advertisements published in a single month in 1999. The researchers investigated the amount of detail provided in the ads, based on counting the number of skills mentioned in each one. They then asked the employers concerned how many applications had been generated by the advertisement and whether they had been successful in finding someone who met all the selection criteria.

Overall, they found that: "Employers who 'invested' more money in the advertisement by specifying a greater number of skills tend to receive more applications for the job, and are more likely to have obtained all the skills, qualifications and experience that they require."

According to Wickland Westcott, a selection, assessment and development consultancy: "Research shows that potential candidates are drawn first to the job title, then to the salary indicator and, finally, to the location. If these three criteria broadly meet their expectations, then the rest of the copy will be scanned to see what scope the job offers. At this point, any entry requirements are probably noted and a mental tally done of matching experience."[20]

The Executive Search and Selection division of the PricewaterhouseCoopers consultancy asked almost 1,400 senior managers and directors what they considered to be the vital elements in recruitment advertisements that might attract them to apply[21]. They confirmed Wickland Westcott's assertion that the job title is often the most important factor for jobseekers, closely followed by salary. "These factors are much more important than the size and position of the advertisement, or whether the ad is in colour or includes pictures or graphics," the survey's report says.

Karel De Witte is frequently cited as a source of hard information on how jobseekers approach recruitment advertisements, in terms of such factors as their reading behaviour and the elements of an advert that attract their attention. However, although his work involved a cross-section of jobseekers, and was not confined to top managers and directors as the above two sources were, De Witte's research was conducted some years ago and carried out in Belgium[22]. So, his findings should be treated as food for thought, rather than hard-and-fast statements of fact.

He found that most jobseekers are casual browsers of the jobs pages. A recruitment advertisement that attracts their attention does not have to be situated on a particular page or place on a page (such as the centre top, or the middle), but will draw them in if it is well laid out, with a clear structure, and has a factor that they recognise quickly and easily. This may be the job title, organisation name, company logo or similar element.

Once they have paused in skimming the advertisements, they will make a decision whether or not to read more of the advert based on the job title and name of the employer.

Then, having decided to read on, De Witte found that jobseekers expect to be able to find detailed information about the job and its requirements, details of the pay and benefits package, and background information about the organisation itself.

There are, of course, many issues that a recruitment advertisement could cover. The Chartered Institute of Personnel and Development recommends that advertisements should be "clear" and "state briefly":

- "the requirements of the job;
- the necessary and the desirable criteria for job applicants;
- the activities and working practices of the organisation;
- the job location;
- the reward package;
- job tenure (eg contract length); and
- the application procedure."[23]

Including or excluding salary details

A close reading of the various findings and best-practice recommendations above shows that they highlight the inclusion of details about salary and benefits in recruitment advertisements. But a quick scan of jobs pages shows that many employers take the opposite view and do not reveal facts about their reward packages.

Descriptive statements may be a poor substitute for such facts. For example, Edward Moss's cynic's view of the phraseology of job ads, mentioned earlier, says that a vague phrase such as "attractive salary" is in danger of being understood to mean: "As it's so low, it's attractive to us".

Few jobseekers begin their jobsearch because they want higher pay, with the notable exception of low-paying sectors such as hospitality and retailing — most are prompted by dissatisfaction with the way they are managed or denied development. However, few will be attracted to a new position if the salary is lower than their present one. Denying potential applicants this key piece of information is likely to handicap recruiters by discouraging some potentially suitable people from applying.

However, recruiters seldom enjoy complete autonomy. Stephen Taylor makes the point that many organisations, particularly those with performance-related pay, keep salary levels confidential within the organisation and are, therefore, unlikely to allow disclosure outside it. A compromise of quoting a salary range may be possible, though.

Alternatively, the absence of a salary tag may be no more than a reflection that a recruiter has accurately targeted the market for a vacancy. One of the judges for the 2001 RAD awards for recruitment advertising, Maxine Packer, the graduate recruitment manager for Logica, is quoted by *Personnel Today* as saying that: "IT adverts don't tend to quote salaries, and it seems much more common to sell the job rather than the pay package. You don't see that so much in the sales category, where it is much more in-your-face, with single job adverts quoting salaries and benefits."[24] As with the choice of media, the point here lies in personnel, HR and recruitment managers ensuring that their recruitment advertising takes account of their target audience's habits, interests and expectations.

Speeding up recruitment advertising

How to apply: Providing the main details of the application procedure is such an important part of the recruitment process that its occasional omission from an advertisement is hard to explain. As well as contact details, potential applicants need to know how the employer intends to handle their application; in other words, how does the applicant begin to engage with the selection process?

Some employers use telephone-screening interviews as an initial step, some expect candidates to compose a letter of application, some will accept standard CVs, while some organisations rely on application forms. The dividing lines between these different approaches are not always clear to applicants.

For example, the same employer may use forms for manual and clerical workers, but accept CVs for managerial vacancies. And the public and private sectors take notably different approaches to the acceptance of CVs which, with the increasing cross-over of employees and jobseekers between the sectors, they need to reveal to all concerned.

Contact telephone details: The practice of giving a contact telephone number in job advertisements has increased in recent years. Making a phone call to obtain an application form or background information is much faster than the postal system. It also gives an employer the opportunity to make some informal contact with potential applicants. Provided that the experience gives a friendly and efficient impression, this can help in the process of developing the "psychological contract" with the new employee, which raises their commitment and lessens the likelihood of an early resignation.

For more senior jobs, particularly, the contact details may include an offer to telephone someone who can discuss the job with applicants – often, the line manager responsible for the role being filled or, perhaps, the incumbent if they are still in post.

Many employers have been improving the ways in which potential applicants can contact them in response to worsening recruitment difficulties.

The aim here is to make the recruitment process as easy and fast as possible, consonant with effective practice, both to encourage individuals who might not be actively seeking a new job and to gain an edge over rival employers who are also recruiting – see chapter 2 for more information.

Email and internet details: Many of the employers that we contacted now offer potential candidates the option of using email to lodge their application or request further information. Overall, two-thirds (65%) do so, ranging from just over half of employers in the public sector to more than seven in 10 in the private sector.

The inclusion of a website address adds a further, and potentially much larger, dimension to a recruitment advertisement. Corporate websites almost invariably contain information that could be useful to a potential applicant, giving background details on the organisation, its activities, sites, main departments and corporate values.

An increasing number of corporate sites also carry details of the organisations' vacancies. Following up such links gives a potential applicant access to all the opportunities available. If the vacancy they saw advertised in the press is not suitable, then one of these online vacancies may be.

And, the most sophisticated users of online recruitment will have corporate sites that can handle enquiries, provide further information (such as profiles of typical jobholders) and enable jobseekers to submit their applications electronically.

At present, fewer employers include details of a website in their press advertising than give their email addresses – probably, for the most part, for the obvious reason that their organisations have not yet set up a corporate website.

Of the employers we contacted, just over half give their website details, with little variation between public and private sectors in this practice.

On the face of it, it might seem unnecessary or odd to include an employer's email and internet details in a recruitment advertisement destined to appear in a traditional paper-based publication. However, many publishers have now launched online editions of their newspapers and magazines, and the same job advert could well appear in both formats for little or no extra cost to the employer. So, even if a reader would not necessarily welcome the provision of email and web details, an online user certainly would. The address will usually operate as a hyperlink giving a user single-click access to the employer's website or to an email enquiry form.

Equal opportunities in recruitment advertising

It is essential to ensure that the use of recruitment advertising does not lead to unfair discrimination. The prime goal of attracting the best candidates for the vacancy should be reason enough to ensure that the advertisement does not deter, or disadvantage, anyone unfairly. Moreover, employers and the media that carry their advertisements face legal action if they contravene equal opportunities legislation. The adverse publicity that even successfully defended cases attract can be unwelcome, as will be the financial cost of lawyers' fees and any fines or compensation awards where rulings go against the employer.

Lost business can be a further consequence of discriminatory recruitment advertising, as the Chartered Institute of Personnel and Development (CIPD) points out in its recruitment guide[25]. It says that: "Poor recruitment practices may leave applicants with an unfavourable opinion of the organisation, which may significantly affect their future relationship as customers or clients."

Poor practices "also give out the wrong messages to successful applicants, who may commence employment with negative impressions of the organisation," the CIPD adds.

Good advice is available from the Equal Opportunities Commission on avoiding discrimination on the grounds of sex or marital status, in its *Sex equality and advertising guide*[26]. The guide points out that preventing discrimination in recruitment advertising has become more difficult. Blatant sexism is "long gone", but there is now a greater danger that advertisements may reflect stereotypes and assumptions about what a man or woman can do that are less immediately obvious to those inside the organisation.

Similarly, the focus is shifting from specific, and obvious, discrimination through the job titles – "girl Friday", "handyman" – to the overall impact of a recruitment advertisement, in terms of whether or not it is considered to have broken the law. Nevertheless, the guide gives advice on such specific details as choosing neutral job titles, and on selecting images that give equal prominence to both sexes (or, where this is not possible, to providing a prominent statement that redresses the balance).

There is a parallel set of guidance from the Commission for Racial Equality covering discrimination on ethnic grounds, including colour, nationality, race and ethnicity[27].

Its guide *Job advertisements and the Race Relations Act* defines racial discrimination and shows how recruitment advertisements may contravene the law through either direct or indirect means. The various exemptions under the Race Relations Act 1976 are also explained. Further guidance is given in the Commission for Racial Equality's Race Relations Code of Practice for the Elimination of Racial Discrimination and the Promotion of Equality of Opportunity in Employment (available from the Commission for Racial Equality, tel: 0870 240 3697, www.cre.gov.uk).

Age

Age restrictions will not constitute direct unfair discrimination until legislation is enacted by late 2006. However, it is possible that they may already constitute indirect discrimination where fewer women than men (or vice versa) are able to satisfy the requirement. For example, where an advertisement specifies that the vacancy is suitable for people in their 20s, this could place greater limits on the ability of women to apply, than men, because relatively more of them might be temporarily away from the paid labour force while caring for young children[28].

Once age discrimination legislation is enacted by the end of 2006, personnel, HR and recruitment specialists will have to be particularly alert to the wording, images and overall impact of their recruitment advertisements. As well as easily-detected age limits, less noticeable practices are currently widespread.

The use of "maturity", for example, usually has one meaning for an employer (emotional stability, sense of proportion, etc) and potentially another for outsiders (stipulating that older people are required and not younger, immature ones). The current, unofficial Code of Practice on Age Diversity in Employment gives a further example: "'Only people with GCSE English need apply' seems reasonable, until you consider that many older people left school before GCSEs were introduced. So, 'GSCEs' rules them out as candidates, even though they may have the necessary communication skills."[29]

Broadening recruitment

The choice of media used for recruitment advertising can play a role in improving equality of opportunity. Many employers with an equal opportunities policy are now reviewing their media choices in order to broaden their recruitment pool. Alongside mainstream media, such as national broadsheet newspapers, organisations are experimenting with the use of specialist media that have a particular audience in the community, such as ethnic minority groups, women, gays or lesbians. There are printed newspapers and magazines serving these and other groups and a growing number of internet sites, some of which have launched web pages dedicated to recruitment advertising.

In addition, employers' advertisements can encourage applications by individuals from under-represented groups. A statement to the effect that "[name of employer] positively welcomes applications from all sections of the community" is so general as to avoid any consideration of unlawful reverse discrimination, although its generalised nature will similarly lessen any impact.

There are instances where the law permits an advertisement to give special encouragement to individuals from one sex or a particular ethnic group to apply, provided that it is under-represented in the type of job being filled. (There is also an exemption in the sex and race discrimination Acts where the sex or ethnicity of the worker is a "genuine occupational qualification", which allows discrimination in recruitment.)

More specifically, a statement welcoming applications from people with disabilities is not barred under the Disability Discrimination Act 1995. It is often likely that the Act's requirement that employers should make "reasonable adjustments" to facilitate the employment of people with disabilities will include making the information about the vacancy available in different formats, such as large print, tape, on disc or via email[30]. But an advert could turn this into a positive advantage in terms of encouraging applications from individuals with disabilities, and explicitly state that the employer can provide the vacancy details in such ways.

Monitoring for equality: Some employers, particularly those in the public sector, have adopted equal opportunities, or diversity, policies, of which the organisation's recruitment practices are often seen as playing a fundamental role. Recruitment advertising is favoured, as we noted above, because it is more open and accessible than most other ways of finding applicants. In such circumstances, monitoring the effectiveness of advertising can go beyond keeping tabs on the quantity and/or quality of applicants it generates. Additional measures include monitoring the make-up of the group of applicants according to their gender, race, whether or not they are people with disabilities, age, religion (in Northern Ireland), and so on.

5. The key issues in effective recruitment advertising

In the experience of personnel, HR and recruitment managers, these are the key issues in effective recruitment advertising:

● **Good management:** It is important to conduct recruitment and recruitment advertising within an effective framework. A contact working for a financial services company highlighted the importance of "having a resourcing plan; a clear understanding of your needs and the marketplace; and an excellent working partnership with external suppliers".

● **Appropriate media:** Many employers we contacted emphasised the importance of identifying the most appropriate media for the vacancy being filled.

● **Equality:** Identifying the most appropriate media may not be straightforward, where the source does not attract a good cross-section of the community. A contact of ours in a city council advised the use of "other forms of media which are less 'traditional' than paper-media advertising, especially raising the organisation's actual profile in the community".

The content, images and overall message of an advertisement should be carefully considered to ensure that it does not unfairly discriminate against protected groups. Where particular groups are under-represented, advertisements are permitted to give positive encouragement to individuals from these groups to apply.

● **Timing:** The timetable of the recruitment and selection process needs careful planning to make sure that the advertisement will appear at a suitable time and gives a suitable period for applications to be sent in. This involves consideration of the frequency of the publication concerned and when readers are likely to see the advert. In some instances, a vacancy may need to be filled before the advertising process can be completed.

● **Eye-catching:** Advertisements must attract the attention of casual readers as well as those who are already intent on moving to a new employer.

● **Sell the job:** Depending on the organisation's needs, it may be necessary to be upbeat in tone and avoid precise criteria.

● Conversely, depending on the type of vacancy and other factors, it may be more appropriate if the advertisement is highly informative and detailed. A bookseller told us that: "When placing ads, [we need] to be precise as possible in what type of person we are looking for and what qualifications are required."

● **Branding:** Advertising can be more effective where an employer already has an established brand (a reputation); where appropriate, recruitment advertising can be used to build a brand; or, in other cases, it may have to adhere to an established corporate branding policy. A personnel contact of ours in a garden centre told us that: "We are known locally, so our reputation helps us." A contact in a financial services company highlighted the value of adopting a single approach to advertising: "[It is] important to establish a consistent branding/message across the organisation."

● **Salary details:** Their inclusion is controversial, but evidence shows it can improve the effectiveness of recruitment advertising.

● And do not forget to include contact details and other key selection information, such as the closing date and the way in which candidates should lodge their applications.

Recruitment advertising agencies

Recruitment advertising suffers from over-familiarity. More or less every employer will use advertising to fill some vacancies, and readers of most newspapers and trade journals encounter pages of such advertisements in every issue. Yet producing a cost-effective advertisement is no easy matter. Finding the appropriate media, devising the wording and design of the advertisement, and dealing with often complex advertising rates require expertise, experience and a degree of flair. It is not surprising that many employers turn to specialists for advice.

Out of a group of just over 100 employers contacted by IRS that make use of recruitment advertising, we found that four out of five (79%) use recruitment advertising agencies. It is their experience that forms the core of this section.

Use of recruitment advertising agencies

Users of recruitment advertising agencies tend to be larger employers, often because the volume of their recruitment makes it easier to justify using such services. The public sector is more likely to retain agencies than either private sector services or manufacturers (87%, 70% and 68%, respectively).

Public sector bodies are also large employers, in the main. So, their size may be more relevant than the nature of their ownership. But the public sector often has a different approach to recruitment. It tends to be more formal and structured, and emphasises the open advertising of vacancies. Where an employer has a policy of advertising most or all of its vacancies, there may be economies of scale in placing this work with an advertising agency.

To support this explanation, our research shows that the public sector prefers to place all its recruitment advertising with an agency, with private sector services and manufacturers being more inclined to be selective and use agencies for some of their vacancies only.

The services that employers expect their agencies to perform are shown below in descending order of use:
● **providing media advice:** Identifying appropriate media for the vacancy in question and, where applicable, the most suitable timing for the advertisement's publication (for example, some national newspapers specialise in certain types of vacancy on certain days of the week);
● **advising on presentation:** Providing advice on the presentation of the advertisement – its appearance, style, graphics and so on;

● **negotiating discounts:** Obtaining reductions in the advertising charges levied by publishers, and passing these savings on, in some form, to the client employer. In fact, the ability of agencies to obtain such discounts represents a major attraction for employers. Most employers lack the knowledge and bargaining power to gain media discounts, and this means that an agency's fees become more competitive compared with the costs involved were the employer to place the advertising itself. In some cases, employers may find that they spend no more on an agency's fees than if they had paid for the advertisement themselves, and also receive for the same price a broader range of services than merely publishing the advertisement;

● **advising on the text:** These three services of placing advertising, advising on presentation and negotiating discounts are used by three-quarters or more of the employers that retain a recruitment advertising agency. Far fewer – just over half the users – expect or wish their agencies to give advice on the text of the advertisement that the employer has written;

● **writing the text:** Fewer still, just over four in 10, want their agency itself to write the text of their recruitment advertisements; and

● **handling responses:** Only one in eight users want their agencies to handle responses to their vacancy advertisements. (Within this group, firms in the private sector are much more likely to use such response handling than their counterparts in the public sector.)

Choosing an agency

There are only a few factors that influence employers' choice of a particular recruitment advertising agency, according to the feedback we have obtained from personnel, HR and recruitment managers:

● **track record:** An agency's proven effectiveness and/or personal experience of its services is paramount (being cited by 88% of agency users), far surpassing all other possible reasons;

● **reputation:** Allied to this, but at some distance behind, almost half of users take account of an agency's general reputation for its performance and effectiveness; and

● **proposal:** This is followed closely by the agency's specific performance when tendering/presenting for the contract that the employer then awarded to them.

The following additional factors are not particularly significant:

● **personal recommendation:** One in six employers take account of a personal recommendation as a factor when choosing an agency;

● **equal opportunities:** A similar proportion has regard to an agency's commitment to equality of opportunity;

● **cost:** Even fewer, one in eight, employers choose an agency partly, or wholly, on their tender having been the lowest of those invited to bid for the contract; and

● **kitemarks:** Very few employers, just one in 25, take account of kitemarks, awards and other factors that might have a bearing on an agency's reputation or concern for quality. Only 3% of users said that an agency having ISO 9000 approval (the international quality-conformance standard) would influence their choice of which agency to use. And only 4% take account of the accolade represented by the agency having gained an industry award for its advertising. This is not particularly surprising as, unlike some industries, there are a number of award schemes with no single one seizing the public imagination.

Effective relationships with advertising agencies

The previous section considered the services that employers expect their recruitment advertising agencies to provide. Conversely, though, agencies can only deliver an efficient service if their client employers engage in a two-way process. One of our contacts who works for an engineering firm pointed out that "communication is essential. If you don't provide them [agencies] with enough relevant information, you can't moan when they don't help you."

Employers may be using a set of criteria to choose an agency, but much of this information will also be vital for the agency to know – for example, expectations about the services required and the priority that should be given to factors such as cost versus flexibility or timeliness.

Much of this background material will have been included in the initial brief, or invitation to tender. But it is important to ensure that it is up to date – and revised regularly once the contract has been awarded – and that the agency has, in fact, understood what is required. This lack of understanding seems to be a common problem.

For example, some employers suspect that agencies' enthusiasm for winning new contracts can overshadow their attention to the detail of what the employer requires. One contact in a university personnel department told us that the problems with their agency stem from "not providing 'the goods' following tender". A contact working for a London borough put it this way: "do not always deliver what they have promised".

Another a private sector employer told us of "lack of understanding/grasp of our organisational structure means lots of rework. Also, limited value added when developing ads for technical and scientific positions, usually because they don't understand the role."

So, as well as briefing the agency on organisational issues, the agency should be given some background about the nature of the typical vacancies for which it will be expected to provide advertising and other services. Job descriptions, person specifications and, if time and resources permit, a briefing by telephone or in person, should be provided by the employer.

Contracts and formalities aside, the employers we contacted broadly favour one of two approaches towards their relationship with their agency (or agencies).

Some believe that employers should "be firm with agencies or they will take you for a ride", as one of the employers we contacted (a retailing supplier) put it. In a similar vein, a national campaigning organisation talks of the importance of "regular meetings, not accepting poor work, always pointing out mistakes, making sure it's your agenda". More overtly, a contact in an engineering company says that their approach is to "let the advertising agency know we have an alternative company ready and waiting . . . [there are] plenty of agencies on our books".

Conversely, other employers believe in "making sure you work in partnership, have service-level agreements, regular meetings, report back on progress" (said a major engineering company). Another contact emphasised the need for a "good relationship with key personnel, built up over a period of time; mutual trust" (an adult education organisation).

The emphasis on partnership and taking a longer-term view of the relationship between the employer and agency has led one of our contacts, a transport company, to argue that "you need to treat the agency staff as if they were your own staff; do not underestimate the amount of time required to manage the agencies".

Somewhere between these potentially opposing views about handling the agencies lie employers whose contacts of ours talked of mutual rights and obligations. The employer should provide clear, adequate information, set out its expectations and provide honest, but constructive, feedback. The agency should then deliver what has been agreed. While frank and constructive exchanges should be cultivated, ultimately, an employer should walk away from an agency that seems irredeemably incapable of fulfilling its side of the contract.

Many employers we contacted raised other issues concerned with their relationships with agencies. The importance of working well at an individual level was raised by several contacts. "Build a good working relationship with one person at the agency," said a contact in a fire and rescue service. Certainly, employers that emphasise an approach based more on a longer-term partnership will find it difficult to do so if there is no continuity in the agency staff with whom they work.

The deterioration of an agency's performance, mentioned by our retailing contact above, was also picked up by other employers as a problem they have experienced, and one that they advise others to guard against.

An NHS trust found that the agency was gradually increasing the size of the typeface used and, to accommodate this, had been increasing the overall size of the advertisement – with the result that costs were also rising. Fortunately, the agency ceased this habit after the trust drew it to its attention.

More generally, several employers considered that their agency had become complacent as time went on – "loss of enthusiasm/service over time", in the words of an insurance company we contacted.

Some agencies seem incapable of paying attention to detail – even in areas as fundamental to their business as the wording and accuracy of the advertisements they produce. A charity complained to us of "typing errors, wrong copy dates and inappropriate copy". Other contacts of ours told us of errors in the text, poor wording, "poor proof-reading" (mentioned by several contacts including a further education college, an NHS trust and a mobile telephone company). Given that many employers will turn to agencies because they hope to gain access to staff who are expert in writing advertising copy, laying it out to best advantage and proof-reading it, these experiences are worrying indeed.

In all, four in 10 (39%) employers we contacted that use agencies report having experienced problems with them. This rises to half (48%) of the employers that use agencies to advertise just some of their vacancies (only just over a quarter (28%) of the employers that use agencies for all of their vacancy advertising report experiencing problems). These differences in experience could be interpreted as a vote in favour of establishing close relationships with agencies; employers that use agencies on a more ad-hoc basis are likely to find it harder to do so.

Evaluating performance

Many problems with agencies will be all too apparent to the client employer. But the overall performance of an agency is more difficult to track without some formal mechanisms being in place. For example, response rates to advertisements require systems to gather this information. Assessing the data is difficult, though, as there are seldom situations where like-for-like comparisons can be made. In this respect, employers that only place some of their advertising with an agency, and retain the rest, have an advantage.

They could, for example, compare the response rates for comparable vacancies from a department or location, where in-house staff conduct the advertising, with rates where an agency is used. Or employers that use agencies could compare response rates for comparable vacancies with other employers that do not, in a form of benchmarking.

Costs, too, are another quantifiable area where evaluations can be made against alternative approaches to advertising: the use of in-house staff, other agencies or, indeed, compared with other methods of recruitment.

Overall, six in 10 (61%) employers we contacted evaluate the performance of their recruitment advertising agencies. Employers that use agencies for just some of their vacancies are slightly more likely to conduct evaluations than those that use agencies for all their vacancies (67% compared with 59%).

This may be an indication that the selective use of agencies lends itself more easily to evaluation, or that this group of employers is more sceptical about using agencies and is more vigilant as to their performance. On a sectoral basis, manufacturers are much less likely to evaluate performance than either private services firms or the public sector (47% against 67% and 66%, respectively).

Key issues to watch

Many of the employers we contacted for this research went out of their way to share their experience of using recruitment advertising agencies, and of the pitfalls they have encountered. Together with the other information we have gleaned, we have distilled this into checklist 6.

The reader will see that the issues covered by the checklist range from such pre-contract matters as the services the successful agency will be expected to provide and the factors that will form the selection criteria when choosing between agencies, to ways of working with an agency, the possible problem areas with its performance, and ways of evaluating the agency's contribution.

6. Using recruitment advertising agencies: points to watch

The key issues connected with using recruitment advertising agencies, according to employers' own experience:

● **Services:** Agencies offer an increasing range of services, including response handling and sifting/screening applications. Decide which services will be required, and set them out in detail in the tender document or background papers. Decide whether the contract will cover all vacancies or just some, and the criteria for identifying eligible vacancies, if the latter approach is chosen.

● **Choice:** Identify the factors that will determine the choice of agency, and their relative importance. Some of this information will be useful to the agencies bidding for the contract because it clarifies the employer's expectations.

● **Relationship:** Decide the desired form of relationship with the successful agency. Will it emphasise compliance and control, or a long-term partnership?

Many employers recommend giving time and attention to establishing and maintaining good communication with the agency, including regular meetings, providing frank but constructive feedback, and openness. Productive, informed relationships are easiest to develop where one or a few agency personnel provide continuity of service to the employer.

Employers stress the importance of providing full information and briefings about the employer's culture, business activities and types of vacancies. When vacancies occur, employers emphasise the importance of providing job descriptions and person specifications, and ensuring that these are up to date, informative and focus on key issues. Briefing the agency on the minimum selection criteria that the employer will use is also recommended.

● **Agency performance:** Employers have found that the following problems can occur, and advise others to be alert to them:

❑ customer focus: giving insufficient attention to the customer by failing to ensure continuity of staff handling the account, and not giving time and attention to understand the employer's requirements; being unreceptive to feedback on their performance;

❑ timeliness: delays in responding to the employer; not producing copy on time; missing publication deadlines;

❑ quality of copy: factual errors; typographical mistakes; poor reflection of the vacancy's requirements; poor layout and design;

❏ costs: advertisements being larger and, therefore, more costly than agreed; failure to negotiate suitable media discounts, or to reflect the discounts in overall contract price;

❏ creativity versus practicality: failure to get the balance right – being too creative at the expense of practicality, or, conversely, lacking ideas and flair;

❏ media knowledge: being unable to identify the most suitable media, particularly for specialist or hard-to-fill vacancies;

❏ failing to continue to be as enthusiastic and committed as when the contract was first awarded; and

❏ administration: inaccurate, or tardy administration; in particular, failing to provide accurate invoices.

● **Evaluation:** Establish in advance the ways in which the agency's performance will be assessed, and communicate this to the agency because it further clarifies the employer's expectations. Formal performance monitoring may require benchmarking data against which the agency can be compared. Will equal opportunities monitoring be used? If so, decide the extent to which the agency will be involved in monitoring and, more generally, in advising on choice of media to reach under-represented groups.

Jobcentres

What if you had access to a national chain of employment agencies with more than 1,500 branches, covering every town and city in Britain? And what if this agency chain offered to advertise your vacancies and list your jobs on its internet site – all for free?

Such an agency already exists, of course, in the shape of the state's jobcentre network, run by a government agency, Jobcentre Plus, which in turn is part of the Department for Work and Pensions. The network handles around one in three of all vacancies in the economy, has well over a third of a million jobs on its internet recruitment site at any one time, and is widely used by employers.

But the fact that there are hundreds of commercial employment agencies, with employers prepared to pay what may be substantial levels of fees to use their services, indicates that jobcentres rarely provide the complete answer to a recruiter's needs.

The potential benefits

Jobcentres grew out of the old employment exchanges, and provide details of vacancies – particularly for the benefit of unemployed people – and a growing range of related services. Their parent body has taken over responsibility for government training programmes for unemployed people that used to be run by Training and Enterprise Councils until their abolition in 2000.

The government also uses jobcentres as a conduit for administering work-related state benefits, such as the Jobseeker's Allowance. The government is now gradually integrating these functions into a working-age agency called Jobcentre Plus.

The jobcentre network has benefited from the government's drive to use the internet to help modernise public services, and has received more than £500 million to introduce new computer systems that link all jobcentre sites. One major outcome of this project is its online recruitment site *(see below)*, which offers public access to the whole jobcentre network's current vacancies. In addition, visitors to jobcentres will be able to access the vacancies via touch-screen terminals, called Jobpoints. Some 9,000 of these have been introduced and will eventually cover the whole jobcentre network.

Most people who lose their jobs find work within a few months, so the job-centres' access to a large pool of current vacancies is an important part of the state's help for the unemployed. Employers are central to this. After all, if they did not let jobcentres know of their vacancies, then the supply of jobs for unemployed people would dry up. Unlike some other European countries, employers are entirely free to use competing, commercial employment agencies if they do not like the state's network.

So, efforts are being made to encourage employers to use jobcentres by offering a good service and providing it for free. Government ministers and officials responsible for the system acknowledge that employers are equally important customers of jobcentres, alongside unemployed people. A set of special service commitments has been drawn up called the Jobcentre Plus employers' charter (this was being revised as this handbook went to press).

The charter provides a set of minimum service standards that employers can expect when dealing with any of the jobcentre offices. It includes:
● checking the vacancy details carefully and offering a copy of them to the employer;
● providing a named contact who will handle the vacancy;
● being contacted by the vacancy manager within two working days to dis-

cuss the vacancy; the manager will provide information about the local labour market, relevant employment legislation and Jobcentre Plus services that assist with the employment of people with disabilities;
● enabling employers to specify their preferred method of receiving applications from jobcentre users; and
● publishing the employer's vacancy immediately after receiving details via the telephone, or within two hours when details are received by post, fax or email.

Being the local access point to state support for unemployed people and others of working age, jobcentres can offer employers subsidised or free services that might help them fill their vacancies. For example, jobcentres are access points for the New Deal, which offers training grants and subsidies to employers taking on eligible unemployed people (for more information, see chapter 5 Induction, training and development). There is also the Work Trial scheme, where employers can try out an unemployed person in a job for up to 15 working days.

People with disabilities are covered by a range of services under the government's Access to Work programme that could be of benefit to employers, and which can be accessed via jobcentres. Services include advice about recruiting and employing individuals with disabilities (and keeping them in work if existing employees become disabled), and the provision of grants and resources to make any necessary adaptations and adjustments.

Internet recruitment site

Jobcentre Plus's central database holds details of around 250,000 vacancies at any one time. These vacancies can now be accessed "24 hours a day, seven days a week" by jobseekers and employers alike via the agency's website. The agency plans to provide an internet route for employers to manage their own vacancies online (scheduled for introduction in summer 2003), and has already piloted such a scheme. This will be a significant development for employers. As well as the instant and highly accessible nature of the service, it will enable employers to take control of the recruitment process. Not only will an employer be able to notify new vacancies online, it will have the facility to input any changes to existing ones.

It is envisaged that one click on the vacancy button on the www.jobcentreplus.gov.uk website will activate an automated dialogue that records and validates the employer's vacancy. The employer will then receive an email to confirm that details of the vacancy have been recorded. In order to preserve overall quality control of the process, employers will first be required to register using the "Employer Direct" telephone number (tel: 0845 601 2001).

Employers are asked to comply with their statutory responsibilities, such as equal opportunities and minimum wage legislation, as a condition of their registration. There are strict rules governing the online recruitment process, and the website for jobseekers gives advice on what action to take if they believe that the rules are being infringed.

Anyone actively looking for work who has access to a computer can search online for suitable vacancies, although, at the moment, applications must still be made through a jobcentre. This may change, though. It is also planned that employers will be able to search candidates' CVs online. Jobseekers will be able to input details of their career history, skills and type of work they are looking for into a CV bank. Employers can then conduct their own search for suitable job candidates. Other plans include the intention to alert jobseekers by email to specific vacancies if it is felt that they have the suitable skills and experience for the job. This means that jobcentres will actively promote employers' vacancies, but in a targeted fashion.

Employer Direct

Employer Direct is the centralised new service for employers provided by Jobcentre Plus. Before the creation of the new agency (jobcentres were formally part of the Employment Service), around 700 of the 1,000 jobcentres dotted around the country were responsible for dealing with local employer vacancies. Now, a call to the single low-cost national telephone number (0845 601 2001; open 8am to 8pm Monday to Friday and 10am to 4pm Saturday) enables employers to notify their vacancies, and kickstarts the recruitment advertising process.

Within minutes of contacting Employer Direct, the vacancy is entered into the jobcentre network's internet recruitment site (www.jobcentreplus.gov.uk), so the details are instantly accessible across the country and beyond.

In many jobcentres, the job details are no longer printed on racks of cards but are accessed by a network of more than 9,000 "jobpoints". These are described as "easy-to-use, touch-screen kiosks" where jobseekers can obtain information about vacancies using criteria such as location, employment category and salary. As a person looking for work can call up job details for any part of the UK, this new facility means that potentially an employer is casting a much wider recruitment net.

The rationale for introducing Employer Direct is the fast-changing and increasingly competitive labour market. The Department for Work and Pensions, which is responsible for Jobcentre Plus, believes that a single contact point for employers to place their vacancies will produce a more responsive and faster service, vital to meeting employers' recruitment needs today.

The technological developments, such as the ability to notify and manage vacancies online, are considered vital in view of the rise in electronic business. Another development involves the incorporation of third-party vacancies in its online recruitment site, such as those from newspapers' classified sections and commercial employment agencies. By adopting this approach, the government is emulating the practice of public employment services in countries such as Australia and the USA.

The infrastructure to support Employer Direct involved establishing a network of 11 regional customer service centres. These are spread across the UK and include Portsmouth, Liverpool, Telford, Peterlee in Durham and Bromley in Kent.

As well as recording vacancy details from employers, the call centres' customer service representatives monitor subsequent recruitment activity. A named call centre contact will make a follow-up call to an employer about two weeks after it notified a vacant post to check progress on recruitment. If the employer is not satisfied with the level of interest shown in the vacancy, the call centre employee will contact the employer's local jobcentre for help in filling the post.

When an employer telephones the single national number for Employment Direct (calls are distributed around the customer service centres according to the availability of an operator), an adviser takes down the vacancy details using a computer-assisted process. The basic information the adviser requests includes:
● job title;
● place of work;
● duties to be performed;
● experience/qualifications required;
● personal qualities needed;
● preferred method of application; and
● contact details.

This standard procedure ensures that adequate and consistent information is obtained from employers.

Although the customer service centres have now replaced local jobcentres as the initial point of contact with employers, jobcentre staff still have an important role to play in facilitating the recruitment process. Local vacancy service managers have retained responsibility for the middle part of the process by fielding jobseekers' enquiries about vacancies, sifting through applications to assess their suitability for particular vacancies and arranging interviews on behalf of employers.

Jobcentre managers also review all new vacancies in their local area on a daily basis in an attempt to match job requirements to potential candidates. They will also be contacted by one of the call centres if a local employer is having trouble in filling a vacant post.

A spokesperson for one of the Brighton jobcentres points to the advantages of the new centralised system, such as more choice for both employers and job-seekers and greater efficiency. One possible disadvantage of the new system is the reduced contact time that jobcentres now have with local employers.

For example, a recruiting organisation ringing the national number should get connected to the geographically nearest service centre, but the call will be redirected to another part of the country if the lines are busy. This means that the call centre employee taking details of the vacancy will not necessarily have knowledge of local employment issues.

Jobcentres still work hard to reinforce their regional links with employers, however, with a variety of different activities. Employers are encouraged to interview prospective recruits at their nearest jobcentre, and regional offices stage regular job fairs as well as organising visits to local companies.

The drawbacks

The prime drawback for employers of using jobcentres stems from their divided loyalty. Unlike commercial agencies, where employers represent their sole client group, jobcentres must serve the needs of government in reducing unemployment. They, therefore, have two groups of clients: unemployed people as well as employers.

Conflicts of interest can arise. For example, the personnel, HR and recruitment managers we contacted who have experience of using jobcentres told us that rigorous job-matching can be sacrificed sometimes for the goal of getting someone back into work. The jobcentres' policing role, in ensuring that claimants are actually looking for work, represents a further potential troublespot. Some employers find that individuals merely "go through the motions" of applying for a job, simply to satisfy jobcentre staff that they are serious about gaining employment in order to satisfy the conditions for continuation of state benefits.

But the main difficulty associated with jobcentres' dual focus relates to the fact that unemployed people do not represent a cross-section of the labour force – particularly, at times when the economy is performing well and redundancies are relatively scarce.

Official statistics from the *Labour Force Survey* show that unemployed people, especially those out of work for an extended period, tend to be less well-educated, have fewer qualifications, and are lower skilled. So, employers find that there are fewer potentially suitable candidates for vacancies that demand higher levels of education, qualifications or skills – typically, managerial, professional, technical and some skilled manual jobs.

Jobcentres used to take account of this fact through a service dedicated to the needs of these higher-level workers, the Professional and Executive Register (PER). However, PER was privatised in the 1980s, with the result that jobcentres' focus on lower-level jobs was heightened still further.

At present, many employers – particularly, those in the private sector – do not notify their higher-level vacancies to jobcentres because they are unlikely to provide many suitable jobseekers. And, as a result, many managers, professionals and technicians who are considering swapping jobs – but who are not out of work – do not consider using the jobcentre network because there are few suitable vacancies.

This represents a vicious circle that the relatively recent launch of the nationwide jobcentre internet site could perhaps help to break in the future. The online service will enable easier use by employers (with online notification of vacancies once this becomes available). In-work jobseekers may be tempted to use the site as part of a wider trawl of internet job boards, particularly if the jobcentre network achieves its aim of enriching its site with vacancies held by employment agencies

Suitable vacancies

Few employers notify jobcentres of their whole range of vacancies, managerial as well as clerical, skilled as well as unskilled. Of the employers we contacted that use jobcentres, three times as many pick and choose which vacancies to pass on to jobcentres as adopt the practice of providing details of every single vacancy regardless of its level or function.

There are differences, though, largely due to the reasons why employers use jobcentres in the first place. In the private sector, employers tend to be hard-nosed, and look for results. They notify their vacancies in the hope that they will be filled. So, more than six times as many private sector services firms are selective about notifying their vacancies, as pass on details of all of them. In the manufacturing and production sector, none of the firms we contacted adopts a blanket approach: they all pick and choose among their vacancies before deciding which to pass on to jobcentres.

The big exception comes from the public sector, where many more organisations have a policy that, regardless of results or suitability, they will notify their jobcentre of every single vacancy (or, at least, those that are not restricted to internal candidates). In fact, in the public sector, as many employers pass on all vacancies as adopt a selective approach.

Going into this in more detail, employers that pick and choose the vacancies that they notify to jobcentres tell us that their choice is based on level. Clerical, administrative and secretarial jobs are most likely to be notified to jobcentres, followed by unskilled and semi-skilled manual jobs, such as drivers and routine operatives. At some distance behind are vacancies for craft and skilled manufacturing jobs, including food preparation, welding, electrical trades, construction, machining and textiles.

Least likely of all to be notified to jobcentres are vacancies for managers, professionals and associate professionals (the latter includes nurses, paramedics, technicians and para-legals).

Deciding to use jobcentres

Employers' reasons for using jobcentres present a mix of business sense and altruism, or social responsibility. Feedback we obtained from personnel, HR and recruitment managers shows that the main reasons why employers use the jobcentre network are as follows (shown in descending order of importance):

● **Cost:** The only reason given by the majority (51%) of employers relates to the fact that the use of the jobcentre network to advertise vacancies and obtain recruits costs the employer nothing apart from its own staff time;

● **Social responsibility:** One-third (32%) of employers use jobcentres because they believe it is the right thing to do. For example, a contact in a pharmaceutical company told us that there were no substantive reasons for using jobcentres, "just to 'do our bit' in the community". A city council said "[we have] a commitment to working in partnership with them on increasing employment opportunities for the community". In fact, more than half of all public sector employers we contacted have a policy that all their vacancies (or, in some cases, just their externally-filled vacancies) will be notified to jobcentres. This contrasts with a quarter of private sector services firms and just one in 20 manufacturers;

● **Proven effectiveness:** Both cost considerations and having a corporate policy of working with jobcentres speak little for the positive contribution of jobcentres to employers' recruitment. However, three in 10 employers (31%) using jobcentres report that their proven effectiveness is a motivation for their use;

● **Equal opportunities:** For a substantial minority of employers (one in five; 21%), jobcentres' commitment to equality of opportunity constitutes a good reason for using them. Jobcentres, as an arm of government, are in a politically sensitive area, and employers have a reasonable assurance that they will conform to the requirements of the law. Their operations are transparent in that vacancies are posted up in jobcentres and, now, on the internet, and it is possible to identify those that appear at odds with discrimination legislation or the minimum wage. Over the years, there have been several instances of campaigning bodies and politicians drawing attention to alleged breaches of the law by the vacancies handled by jobcentres, or contravention of good practice. Officials can be expected to be alert to such dangers. In addition, jobcentres' wide distribution provides a community focus for employers' recruitment and, coupled with the fact that the vacancies are all publicly advertised, this provides an attractive service to employers committed to equality of opportunity and to organisations adopting diversity initiatives;

● **Reputation:** Few employers become clients of jobcentres because of their reputation (just 4% do so) or through personal recommendation (1%), although personal experience of their effectiveness plays a much greater role in employers' decisions to use them as we saw above. This means that encouraging employers to obtain direct experience of using jobcentres, and ensuring they are satisfied with the result, represents a fruitful opportunity for government policy makers. In contrast, they face an uphill battle if they rely on advertising or gimmicks to encourage employers by raising the profile and reputation of jobcentres; and

● **Other factors:** As well as the reasons reported above for using jobcentres, our contacts mentioned several other factors that motivate them. The most common, cited by 6%, is that jobcentres are a means of gaining access to the local labour market. Although each office is linked electronically, and is covered by the new national website of jobcentre vacancies, some employers consider that their local jobcentre remains a focus for the community. It is the place that unemployed people usually attend when signing on for benefits and renewing their claims, and jobcentres often occupy a high-street site that keeps them in the public consciousness. A major utilities company told us that it uses the jobcentre because it "keeps within the local/travel-to-work area and, therefore, [gives us a] higher chance of success". A chemicals company told us that jobcentres are "successful in filling local vacancies in the towns away from the bigger cities". More generally, a university said that using the local jobcentre means its vacancies "have access to the local community".

7. Jobcentres: the points to watch

In the experience of personnel, HR and recruitment managers, these are the main issues to consider when using jobcentres in recruitment:

● **Type of vacancy:** Many employers find that jobcentres are better suited to filling some types of vacancies than others. These tend to be below managerial, professional and technical levels.

● **Equal opportunities:** Jobcentres can play a valuable role in improving equality of opportunity in recruitment. They have policies about unfair discrimination, and provide access to the local community to job opportunities, all of which are advertised and freely available.

● **Candidates may not match the specification:** Jobcentre staff need to be fully briefed to ensure that a reasonable matching of candidates to the vacancy criteria is undertaken. Employers advise checking that these requirements are understood and are put into practice. It is also important to give feedback to the jobcentre when problems occur.

● **Candidates may not be serious jobseekers:** One aspect of jobcentre staff's role involves supervising people claiming work-related state benefits. It may be unavoidable that some candidates put forward are only applying, or even being shortlisted for interview, to retain their entitlement to unemployment-related state benefits.

● **There may be communication difficulties:** Try to build a good working relationship with the jobcentre staff.

● **Service levels are variable:** The speed and quality of service may vary from one member of jobcentre staff to another and, particularly, between different jobcentres. Giving feedback and building longer-term relationships may help to raise service levels.

● **Coverage:** Jobcentres may offer an effective means of gaining access to the local labour market.

Problems experienced

Most employers (64%) that use jobcentres told us they had not experienced any problems in the service they receive. Interestingly, the relatively higher usage of jobcentres by the public sector has not resulted in them experiencing more problems. In fact, only a quarter (23%) told us that difficulties had occurred. This is much the same as the proportion of employers in the manufacturing sector that reported problems to us (26% of jobcentre users) – and considerably fewer than their counterparts in private sector services firms (where 57% have encountered problems).

Incidentally, it does not seem that organisations with a blanket policy of notifying all their vacancies to jobcentres have laid themselves open to greater problems and hassles. Relatively fewer of these employers reported problems in their use of jobcentres than those where they were selective about which vacancies to pass on. In theory, there is a greater chance of unsuitable candidates being put forward where each and every vacancy is notified to the jobcentre. In these cases, jobcentres are more likely to be given the types of managerial, professional and technical vacancies that other employers keep back, and which are less suited to the typical jobcentre patron.

It is important to put the problems that employers using jobcentres experience in some context. In each case – employers as a whole; and analysed by sector: private sector services firms, manufacturers, and the public sector – considerably greater proportions of employers using commercial employment agencies told us they had experienced problems than did those that use jobcentres.

Employment agencies

The UK is unusual in having a large and influential job-placement service under private ownership. In several other European countries, for example, private agencies were banned for many years and, until the forthcoming EC Directive is implemented, often continue to be strictly controlled as to the services they can offer.

Here, the state-owned network of jobcentres is often seen as competing effectively at the lower end of the labour market *(see the previous section in this chapter)*, while commercial agencies have established a very strong position for other types of worker.

As well as supplying recruits, commercial agencies are often the first port of call for employers wishing to make use of temporary workers of all types.

In fact, more employers use agencies as a source of temporary workers than do so to fill permanent positions. And agencies' share of the total market for temporary workers seems to have been increasing steadily, according to a study reported in the *Human Resource Management Journal*[31].

Figures showing the size and income of agencies bear witness to the sector's importance in the UK. At any one time, it has been calculated that 700,000 people are working as temps, according to the Department of Trade and Industry[32]. And research commissioned by the same department estimates that employers pay some £18 billion a year to agencies[33].

Forthcoming legal changes

Two legal developments unprecedented in their potential impact on the use of agencies are about to shake up this marketplace. First, the government has published its final proposals for changes to the legal regulation of agencies (described in detail below in the section on the law). The new Regulations, whose implementation date has not yet been announced, will limit agencies' ability to levy transfer fees on employers that recruit their temporary workers, and require them to improve their selection and screening of temps and potential recruits.

Second, and even more significantly, an EC Directive on agency workers – still at the draft stage as this edition of the handbook went to press – could have a major impact on employers' use of temporary agency workers when it is implemented in the UK. Agency temps will have to be given equal pay, holidays, hours of work and other conditions to permanent members of staff doing similar work in the employer using the temps. It is also possible that, instead of controlling transfer fees (also known as "temp-to-perm fees") as the domestic legislation will do, the Directive may complete ban them. The result of the Directive may be higher agency fees, a reduction in employers' use of temps and the closure of many agency businesses. For more information on the draft Directive, see the section below on The law on agencies.

The marketplace

One of the most notable features of the current employment agency marketplace in the UK is its highly fragmented and localised nature. Even four years ago, prior to a period of sustained growth, there were some 11,950 agency offices in the UK, according to the Department of Trade and Industry's research cited above.

Most agencies do not specialise in either supplying temporary workers or helping to recruit permanent employees. According to the department's research, only one-third (37%) specialise in either of these ways. Out of this 37%, 23% concentrate on permanent recruitment, while surprisingly few – just 14% – deal solely with the supply of temporary workers. However, many agencies develop specialisms in other ways, mainly by focusing on a particular locality, industry, occupation, or a combination of these factors.

Employers therefore face a bewildering choice. The sheer number of agencies makes the selection of a supplier a difficult, time-consuming matter. Nor is the agency industry well-organised at present, so that employers could draw up a shortlist of potential suppliers by contacting a single representative body. Even the best-known umbrella organisation, the Recruitment and Employment Confederation, is estimated by the government to cover no more than 50% of all agencies.

Moreover, recruiters' own knowledge of agencies is often challenged by the ever-changing nature of the industry. According to the government research, one in six agencies (17%) are new entrants, although this rises to four in 10 (41%) in respect of agencies serving the hotels and restaurants trade.

Agencies' services

The appeal for employers of agencies' temping services lies in their potential to provide stop-gap staff at short notice. They provide cover for absences, offer skills where only a temporary need exists, or where vacancies are unfilled because of recruitment problems, and usually avoid the legal complications of direct recruitment by the employer. Such staff are generally either employees of the agency or are self-employed.

Permanent recruitment through agencies offers several advantages, depending on the vacancy being filled. In some occupations, agencies are jobseekers' preferred route into new permanent jobs, and employers' gain best access to these segments of the labour market through the use of an agency.

In other cases, agencies act as a back-stop where vacancies prove difficult to fill through employers' own efforts. They may have jobseekers on their books, or uncover other potential candidates through advertising, referrals or the use of online recruitment.

More generally, agencies can help employers improve their recruitment by shortening the lead times involved. Where they can supply potential recruits from their books, employers may be able to avoid time-consuming and costly recruitment advertising to provide a field of candidates.

Costs

Agencies' charges tend to involve complex cost structures. Even the seemingly straightforward process of supplying temporary workers can involve various permutations of charges and penalty clauses. The hourly/daily/weekly rate, for example, may be based on the typical short-term demands of employers, but, where a longer-term need is identified, it may be possible to negotiate a reduction in charges. Generally, though, recruitment expert Stephen Taylor says that "hourly rates for agency workers are invariably double those paid to regular employees."[34]

In the **NHS**, acute staffing shortages mean that 10% of shifts are staffed by nurses from agencies and in-house staffing "banks", according to the Audit Commission. Agency nurses are typically paid 20% more than the NHS's directly employed bank nurses, the commission says, and agencies also levy an average commission charge of 20.5%.

However, the commission also found that there are huge variations in agency charges, and concluded that "there is scope for [NHS] trusts to achieve savings by negotiating with agencies". It found that while one in three trusts paid 25% or more in commission, one in six paid less than 10%[35].

Interim management commands particularly high rates. This is a specialised form of temporary work involving executives who provide managerial expertise to companies. According to the Russam GMS "snapshot survey"[36], the average daily rate at the end of March 2003 was £461, rising to £512 among IT interim managers.

Frequently, an agency's contract for the supply of temporary workers will also impose a charge should the employer then recruit the person as a permanent member of staff. These transfer, or "temp-to-perm", fees have received considerable publicity over the past couple of years, following the government's lengthy preparation of new Regulations covering employment agencies.

The government's "regulatory impact assessment" of the impact of its forthcoming new Regulations[37] commissioned research from BMG into current agency practice. It finds that while the majority of agencies impose temp-to-perm fees, one in five do not. This minority may have its own reasons for not doing so, but the assessment adds that many instances are the result of employers actively negotiating preferential terms. Usually, though, this is dependent on the employer having first hired the temporary worker involved for a "reasonable length of time", it says.

The BMG research shows that agencies imposing such charges generally adopt one of two approaches:
● a straight commission based on salary; this is used by 58% of agencies and averages 15% of pay; or
● a combination of commission and flat fee; this is used by the remaining 42% of agencies.

The arrangements for charges in respect of agencies' role in permanent recruitment are even more variable and complex than in their provision of temps. Depending on the level/status of the vacancy, and the type of service required, an agency may charge a straight commission, based on a proportion of the vacancy's annual salary, an overall fee (perhaps paid in stages), or some other arrangement.

A ready-reckoner published in *Personnel Today*[38] magazine quoted agencies' typical overall charges for supplying recruits for three common types of vacancy: a secretary/administrator (10% of annual salary), a sales manager (13%) and a marketing director (13%). In each case, the bill included an initial visit to the employer, handling responses to a recruitment advertisement or recruitment website, initial telephone interviews and drawing up a shortlist.

Agencies' costs represent significant amounts of money that organisations will have to pay. However, it seems that many employers know what to expect in terms of their scale of charges. A survey of 155 employers using agencies for temporary workers, reported in *Human Resource Management Journal*[39], found that ensuring the "cost of the contract is low" was a major priority for only 2.6% of them. Nevertheless, employers are canny enough to take cost into consideration when choosing between agencies (see below).

Agencies' ability to levy temp-to-perm fees will be restricted under the forthcoming updated version of the Conduct of Employment Agencies and Employment Business Regulations and, eventually, may even be banned completely under the proposed EC Directive.

The Regulations will impose a "quarantine period" of eight weeks, being the break in continuity between the end of a temporary worker's contract with an employer and the date when it is able to recruit them without being obliged to pay a temp-to-perm fee.

Alternatively, the employer will be able to notify the agency that it intends to recruit a temporary worker supplied by it, and extend the length of time that it uses the temp – a so-called "notice period". The new Regulations leave the length of the notice period to negotiation between the agency and employer, but, after it has been served, the employer will be able to recruit the temp without any requirement to pay a transfer fee to the agency. Agency terms that appear to contradict either or both of these provisions will be unenforceable under the new Regulations.

The Regulations will have a particular impact on two groups of employers that are currently able to enjoy a VAT concession. Reed Executive, the employment agency that fought the case creating the Inland Revenue concession, estimates that the new Regulations will add 10% to 14% to the cost incurred by banks and charities in using agency temporary workers.

Finally, agencies will incur additional costs, which may be passed on to employers, through a requirement in the new Regulations that they improve their pre-employment checks on workers (see below). In theory, this change could be cost-neutral, in that employers would always have conducted reference and other checks; now, it is the agencies that are required to do so. However, it assumes that employers will be content to rely on agencies to perform this task.

Employers may still prefer to conduct their own pre-employment screening, particularly where the work involves sensitive tasks – such as confidential information or handling money – or where the work takes the person into contact with vulnerable groups, such as children or adults in care.

Choosing an agency

We asked 100 personnel, HR and recruitment specialists who have experience of using employment agencies for their feedback on the key issues associated with their effective use, and on the potential pitfalls awaiting the unwary.

In terms of making a choice of an agency, their feedback shows that employers rely on what they know when they choose an agency. Above all else, the proven effectiveness of an agency is of paramount importance (being a factor cited by 91% of the employers we contacted). And where they are not personally familiar with an agency, half of all employers (50%) will take account of its reputation when deciding which of the many agencies to use.

Both of these factors assume that the agency has a track record, which a potential client-employer then uses as a guide to its present and future standards of service. However, the high turnover of staff in many agencies, particularly during the hiring boom of recent years, means that the quality of service provided in the past cannot always be a reliable guide to present and future conditions. And the sixth of agencies that are newcomers to the industry each year will not even have a service record on which to base this judgment.

Third, in terms of the criteria used by employers to select an agency, involves employers actively matching their requirements against those that an agency can offer. Half (50%) of employers take account of an agency's specialist expertise in their own industry, in the local labour market, in the occupation(s) that the employer is interested in, or a combination of these factors.

Cost represents a major discriminating factor, and four in 10 (41%) employers take it into consideration.

An agency's commitment to ensuring equality of opportunity, however, seems to be of minor importance to employers, and fewer than one in four (22%) of them take it into account when choosing an agency. This is likely to change. Certainly, the Race Relations (Amendment) Act 2000 places an onus on public sector employers to take a more active stance in ensuring all their personnel practices support equality of opportunity on the basis of ethnicity. And what improves equality on race grounds is also often likely to help reduce discrimination on the grounds of gender, disability and age, too.

External quality "kitemarks" currently carry little weight either. An agency's membership of a professional association, such as the Recruitment and Employment Confederation (which has a code of conduct, but which has relatively few agencies in its membership that offer permanent recruitment), or an agency's possession of the international quality standard, ISO 9000, are important to fewer than one in six employers (13% and 9%, respectively).

Practice in using agencies

Employers often use agencies to supply temporary workers for certain types of job – particularly, clerical, secretarial, nursing, care and computing staff – but use agencies for different occupations when they wish to recruit permanent workers.

In particular, while nine in 10 (89%) employers use agencies to supply clerical and secretarial staff to fill temporary gaps in their workforces, this proportion almost halves (to 46% of employers) in respect of using agencies to supply the same types of staff for permanent vacancies.

There is a similar pattern – where agencies are used much more heavily for temporary workers than permanent recruits – in respect of personal and protective services (covering such jobs as hairdressers and support staff in caring roles), operatives and assembly workers, and, to a lesser extent, craft and skilled manufacturing jobs.

Conversely, proportionately far fewer employers tell us that they use agencies to supply managers on a temporary basis as use them to find permanent recruits (31% versus 65%), although this is partly explained by the lower demand by organisations for interim managers.

Differences exist between different types of employer, too. In particular, employers in the public sector generally follow their private sector counterparts' use of temporary workers, but change their approach in respect of filling permanent vacancies.

For example, 97% of the public sector employers we contacted use agencies for clerical and secretarial staff to provide temporary cover, and 85% of private sector firms do so. But only 12% of the public sector fills its permanent positions for clerical and secretarial staff through agencies, against 65% of the private sector. Such differences are almost certainly due to the public sector's emphasis on public, open recruitment, usually through advertising, causing it to avoid agencies because they obtain candidates from many informal sources, often via self-referral.

Recruiting agency temps

In theory, the use of temporary workers supplied by an agency provides an ideal probationary period to judge their performance and consider offering them a permanent position, should one arise.

However, apart from any equal opportunities considerations, two obstacles stand in the way of this approach. First, as we saw in the section immediately above, many employers have more work opportunities for temporary agency staff – particularly in some occupations, such as clerical and secretarial work – than have permanent vacancies they need to fill. So, opportunities are often relatively uncommon.

And second, agencies are concerned that employers will "cream off" their best temps, and use agencies as an unpaid recruitment service. As a result, most agencies – around eight in 10, as we saw above in the section on costs – insert clauses in their contracts with employers that impose a financial penalty known as a transfer, or temp-to-perm, fee.

Nevertheless, it seems that many employers are not deterred. Among the 100 employers represented by the personnel, HR and recruitment managers who gave us feedback for this research, we find that nine in 10 (90%) offer at least some of their permanent vacancies to temps supplied by an agency. Surprisingly, the public sector is not adverse to using this route – eight in 10 (79%) do so – despite its far lower incidence of using agencies in a direct way to help with its recruitment of permanent staff. This percentage compares with 92% of manufacturers and 97% of private sector services firms.

While our research shows that many clients of agencies practise temp-to-perm recruitment, its present scale – in terms of the actual number of temps being hired – seems modest. The government's regulatory impact assessment, cited above, quotes statistics from the Recruitment and Employment Confederation to show that eight in 10 temps (80%) continue in this capacity from year to year, and are not being recruited as permanent workers by client employers.

Problems with agencies

Problems with agencies are a common occurrence, according to the employers we contacted. More than one-half (57%) of employers with experience of using agencies have encountered difficulties, although the public sector is markedly more content (only 31% of users have experienced problems) than either manufacturers (62% of employers in this sector have encountered problems) or, in particular, private sector services firms (where 74% have experienced problems).

Employment agencies seem to cause more difficulties for their client employers than either recruitment advertising agencies or the much-maligned network of state jobcentres. While 57% of users have complaints about employment agencies, this falls to 37% in the case of jobcentres, and falls still further to 34% in the case of recruitment advertising agencies (based on matched samples of employers).

But difficulties provide valuable learning points for others, and checklist 8 draws on this feedback, together with more general observations given to us by the employers we contacted.

Above all, once an employer has identified the criteria that it will use to choose an agency, and the type of relationship it wishes to foster, our contacts stress the importance of providing full information and background briefings to the staff of the chosen agency. However, they add that this must be a two-way process. Frequently, agency staff appear unable or unwilling to absorb this information and use it when selecting temps or potential recruits to put forward to the employer.

Many employers complain, too, that agency staff fail to brief jobseekers adequately about the organisation or the job. (Although, as with direct recruitment, lack of preparedness may be due to the jobseeker's lack of interest or motivation.)

Candidate suitability is obviously a key issue, and is the most frequent cause of complaint we received from the employers we contacted. Some agencies send individuals whom the employer considers to be wholly unsuited to the work involved; others consider that the person meets some of their requirements, but does not provide a complete match. Alternatively, agencies may adhere to the brief, but consequently fail to send any or sufficient candidates for interview.

Some employers complain that agency staff hope that quantity will compensate for quality, in terms of the balance between the number of candidates they put forward and their potential suitability.

While the ability of an agency to provide staff to specification represents the fundamental reason for using it, employers sometimes seem to expect the impossible. Where skills are in short supply, even the best agency will struggle to meet employers' demands. In fact, some employers mentioned that they welcomed some honesty. If an agency cannot provide an exact match, they would prefer that they were told of this and given the chance to consider the individuals on that basis.

Another key potential advantage of using agencies, as opposed to finding candidates through recruitment advertising, lies in their responsiveness. Agencies should have access to a pool of jobseekers that they can draw on as soon as an employer contacts them. However, some employers told us of untoward delays and, more generally, of agencies failing to meet agreed deadlines for the supply of temps or job interviewees.

Cost, too, represents an issue of concern to current and potential clients of agencies. Cost-effectiveness should be established, and monitored. But some employers also experience higher than expected bills, sometimes due to overcharging, and a few told us of disputes about the level of temp-to-perm fees incurred when they recruited an agency's own temporary worker.

Finally, it is important to evaluate suppliers' performance. While conformance to contract is important, some form of benchmarking can provide a wider perspective – such as cost per recruit compared with instances where in-house resources are used. The increasing practice of monitoring recruitment to ensure equality of opportunity also raises practical issues, in ensuring that agency activities, such as shortlisting, are covered by the procedure. However, potentially, it also provides a further source of data to evaluate agency performance.

8. Using employment agencies: the key issues

The key issues connected with using employment agencies, based on feedback from personnel, HR and recruitment managers' own experiences.

● **Choice:** Identify the factors that will determine the choice of agency, and their relative performance. Identify where and how an agency will offer a more cost-effective service than using internal resources.

● **Relationship:** Decide the desired form of relationship with the successful agency; where will it lie on the scale of shorter-term compliance and control, at one end, or a longer-term partnership, at the other end?

Many employers recommend giving time and attention to establishing and maintaining effective communication with the agency, including holding regular meetings, providing frank but constructive feedback, and adopting an attitude of openness to the agency's input and the disclosure of information. Productive, informed relationships are easiest to develop where there is a single point of contact with the agency, and there is some continuity of service.

Employers stress the importance of providing full information and briefings about the employer's culture, business activities and types of work required of recruits and temporary workers. For permanent recruitment, employers emphasise the importance of providing job descriptions, person specifications and key selection criteria.

● **Agency performance:** Employers have found that the following problems can occur, and advise others to be alert to them:

❑ customer focus: agencies giving insufficient attention to the customer by failing to ensure continuity of staff handling the account, and not giving time and attention to understand the employer's requirements; being unreceptive to feedback on their performance; giving more priority to agency sales targets than meeting customer needs;

❑ candidate suitability: sending temps or potential recruits who do not meet the specification; insufficient candidates; substituting quantity for quality in terms of potential recruits sent for interview;

❑ understanding: failing to understand the employer's requirements; failing to impart these details and background information on the employer to job-seekers;

❑ timeliness: delays in supplying staff; not meeting agreed deadlines; not being flexible and responsive where urgent staffing needs arise;

❑ costs: inaccurate billing; over-charging; disputes over temp-to-perm fees; and

❑ poaching: recruiting the client employer's own staff as agency temps or on behalf of other employers.

● **Evaluation:** Establish in advance the ways in which the agency's performance will be assessed, and communicate this to the agency because it further clarifies the employer's expectations. Formal performance monitoring may require benchmarking data against which the agency can be compared. Will equal opportunities monitoring be used? If so, decide the extent to which the agency will be involved in monitoring.

The law on agencies

Permanent recruits supplied by an agency naturally enjoy the same legal status and protection as other employees, and the actions of employers and the agencies acting as on their behalf are covered. The role of agencies as "gatekeepers" in the recruitment process of both temporary and permanent workers causes particular concern in terms of its significance for equal opportunities, and there have been several investigations conducted into agencies by the relevant statutory bodies in Great Britain. The Commission for Racial Equality, for example, pays special attention to agencies in its employment Code of Practice[40]. *For more information on equal opportunities, see the section Equal opportunities and agencies below.*

Employers using temporary workers from an agency, as well as the agencies themselves, are required under existing legislation to ensure workers' health and safety and not to discriminate unfairly against them. The national minimum wage and the 1998 Working Time Regulations also apply to such workers.

Temporary workers' employment status has been unclear and, with it, the respective rights and responsibilities of employer and employee (or, indeed, of self-employed persons). One of the main purposes of the forthcoming Conduct of Employment Agencies and Employment Business Regulations is to clarify the legal position of employer.

These Regulations will replace outdated 1976 legislation, but have been repeatedly delayed and have been through several versions from 1999 onwards. Once an implementation date is announced – probably in late 2003/early 2004 – some sections of the Regulations will be phased in over a three-months period, including their provisions relating to transfer fees.

The Regulations identify two types of agency: an "employment business", which supplies temporary workers to employers, and an "agency", which supplies recruits to employers who then become the employer's own employees. Businesses and agencies will have to make clear to both individuals and employers the basis under which they are operating.

Both employment businesses and agencies will have to gain individuals' agreement to the terms of the arrangement between them, including the type of agency services it is providing. Businesses must clarify the temp's contractual status: either as an employee of the employment business or being self-employed, and provide a copy of the agreement (or a written statement of particulars). Agencies will continue to be barred from charging jobseekers for assistance in finding employment, with the exception of professional sportspeople, models, actors, composers and related professions.

Importantly, employment businesses will have to pay temporary workers for periods when they work for an employer, regardless of whether or not the agency has itself been paid by the employer, or whether the temp can produce a timesheet or other document that the employer should have provided or signed.

Better vetting

The forthcoming Regulations try to ensure that employers, as well as the workers, will be clear as to the basis of their use of an employment business or agency. The details to be agreed and spelled out in a single document supplied before any services are provided include:
● the status of the firm, showing whether it is acting as an employment business or agency;
● the process to be followed if any of the workers proves unsatisfactory to the employer;
● the fee involved, how it will be calculated, and the terms relating to refunds or rebates; and
● in respect of agencies, whether the agency has the authority to act on the worker's behalf and enter into agreements on their behalf.

Any variations in the above terms will have to be mutually agreed, and a revised document will have to be supplied to the employer. Importantly, the Regulations will tighten up the requirements concerning pre-employment checking that employment businesses and agencies must observe. In a "belt-and-braces" approach, the Regulations spell out the steps that they will have to take in respect of both establishing employers' requirements and individuals' abilities and bona fides.

Employment businesses and agencies must first obtain "sufficient information" from the employer in order to "select a suitable workseeker", and this must include:

● the name of the employer and the nature of its activities;
● the date on which the temp or recruit is required, and the likely duration of the work;
● the position ("including the type of work a workseeker in that position would be required to do"), its location, hours of work, and known health and safety risks;
● "the experience, training, qualifications and any authorisation" that the employer considers necessary, and/or are required by law or a professional body; and
● in respect of an agency, the minimum pay and benefits that the employer "would offer to a person in the position", the frequency that the pay and benefits are paid, and the notice period involved.

As well as the above points, businesses and agencies should confirm the identity of the individual seeking work as a temp or permanent employee, and that the person meets the employer's criteria – the necessary experience, training and other factors set out above. Finally, they will have to confirm that the individual is willing to work in the position concerned.

All of this information will then have to be supplied to the employer in respect of the individuals that are proposed as temps or recruits. Additionally, for temps, the business must let the employer know whether the temps are its own employees or are self-employed. Employers must be given the relevant information at the time the individual is offered to the employer, or within three working days in writing (or electronically), if it was originally given verbally.

The above provisions relate to information that the employer and individual will have to supply, but the Regulations additionally require employment businesses and agencies to undertake some investigations themselves.

They must identify any requirements imposed by law or a relevant professional body relating to the job that either the individual or employer must satisfy to do the work – and take all reasonable steps to pass on this information.

And, as well as conducting the above checks and investigations before someone is offered to an employer, agencies and businesses will be required to pass on to the employer any information that they later obtain that indicates the individual might, after all, be unsuitable. For permanent recruits, agencies will have this duty for a period of three months after first introducing the person to the prospective employer.

Sensitive posts

All of these provisions about employment businesses' and agencies' matching of individuals to employers, and of basic pre-employment checks, are heightened in the forthcoming Regulations where the work is of a sensitive nature. This is defined as work where professional qualifications are required by law, or where the work involves people aged under 18 or vulnerable adults.

In these cases, not only must employment businesses and agencies satisfy the matching and pre-employment screening duties mentioned above, but they must also – before an individual is supplied to the employer – obtain copies of any qualifications and two references, and pass copies to the employer. Additionally, for work with the under-18s and vulnerable adults, "all other reasonably practicable steps [must be taken] to confirm that the workseeker is not unsuitable for the position concerned". These steps are likely to include using the Criminal Records Bureau to obtain a "standard" or "enhanced" criminal record check on the individual *(see chapter 4 Checking candidates' backgrounds for more information)*.

Finally in connection with the new Regulations, they will also limit agencies' ability to levy temp-to-perm fees, as we described above in the section on costs.

In the pipeline, though, are further legal changes that will have considerable implications for agencies' and employers' costs in the form of an EC Directive on agency workers.

EC Directive on agency workers

The EC intends to introduce a Directive on the working conditions of agency workers, although the final draft had not been agreed by the time this edition of the handbook went to press. Despite lobbying by the British government, the CBI and other employers' organisations, it is likely that the Directive will have a major impact on the operation of the market for agency temps in this country. Once it has been agreed by the EC, the UK and other member states will have between two and three years to implement it, although there may be a phasing-in period for some of the Directive's provisions.

Some of the specifics of the Directive will be left to the UK to determine, so its precise provisions will not be clear until the government issues its proposals. However, the Directive is likely to insist that its provisions about equal treatment between temps and a client employer's own staff must apply to all agency temps, including those working part-time, and cover public sector, private sector and not-for-profit employers' use of temps.

Apart from any objectively justifiable differences in treatment that the government may permit, agencies will be required to ensure that their temps "receive at least as favourable treatment in terms of basic working and employment conditions" as a "comparable worker" in the organisation where the temps are currently working. In particular, this includes pay, hours of work, paid holidays, and lunch and other breaks. A "comparable worker" is defined as someone in the organisation who is in an "identical or similar post", taking account of the skills, qualifications and length of service required.

Agencies will have to identify the nature of comparable terms and conditions, such as salaries, and identify comparable workers, and may have to obtain these details from the employer wishing to use the agency to supply temps. Where pay rates, in particular, are higher among the employer's own workforce, it is highly likely that agencies will pass on the cost of raising temps' pay in the form of higher fees paid by the organisation using the temps.

In addition, employers where agency temps are working will be required to give them equal access as their own employees to their "social services". This is likely to include employers' "social facilities", such as canteens and restaurants, childcare facilities and transport laid on for workers. There is an exception to this requirement where there are "objective reasons against this".

Employers where temps are working will be required to notify the temps of any vacancies that arise among their permanent workforce. It is possible that clauses in agencies' contracts preventing employers from recruiting temps could become null and void, with the result that transfer (temp-to-perm) fees will be abolished, although the current debate about the content of the draft Directive raises the possibility that transfer fees may be restricted rather than abolished completely.

The possible exceptions that member states may choose to allow are:
● periods of work lasting less than six weeks with the same organisation – this is the main focus of the controversy and disagreement about the draft Directive; the UK government wishes to increase this qualifying period so that short temping assignments are not covered, while some other member states want the Directive's provisions to apply from the first day that a temp begins working with an employer;
● participants on government training programmes;
● temporary workers who have been given a permanent contract by their agency that ensures they are paid between assignments; and
● differences in treatment between temps and the employees of the organisation that is using the temps, provided these are "justified by objective reasons".

Equal opportunities and agencies

Employment agencies represent an important source of permanent and temporary labour for British employers, and this gives agencies a significant influence over the degree to which the labour market is free from, or prone to, unfair discrimination.

Agencies are covered by the anti-discrimination legislation in their own right. But where their clients put pressure on them to discriminate unfairly, both they and their client employers could be liable for prosecution. In addition, both self-employed temps and those employed by agencies are protected against unfair discrimination carried out by client employers, even though they are not members of the employer's own staff.

As well as ensuring that agencies do not discriminate unfairly – for example, by failing to recommend jobseekers or temps to an employer purely because of their gender, ethnicity or disability – employers should take account of two further considerations.

First, many agencies are small in scale, and are often based in particular geographical areas. Where they do not take steps to broaden their access to potential recruits and temps, there is a danger that the individuals they recommend to employers will be unrepresentative of society as a whole. The Commission for Racial Equality's Code of Practice on employment, for example, says that there might be a prospect of the agency and/or employer committing unfair indirect discrimination where the employer confines itself "unjustifiably" to those agencies that "because of their particular source of applicants, provide only or mainly applicants of a particular racial group". (However, the Code also says that this consideration might equally apply to certain jobcentres, careers offices and schools that employers use as sources of recruits.)

Second, agencies do not always gain access to potential recruits and temps through open advertising – in fact, most individuals on their books are likely to come via self-referrals or recommendations from individuals' colleagues, families or friends. The lack of openness in this initial stage of recruitment causes concerns to some employers, particularly those in the public sector, and it often makes far less use of commercial employment agencies than private sector firms for this reason.

Case study A. Eden Brown

In contrast to concerns about employment agencies' potential to have an adverse impact on equality, at least one employment agency has won an award for its activities to overcoming barriers to work. Eden Brown gained the government's Age Diversity in Recruitment Award of Excellence in 2000 for its initiatives to improve the employment prospects of older people among its own staff. Its managing director says that the agency aims to "attract, develop and retain the best and most diverse talent in a sector that is traditionally perceived as 'young'"[41].

It has reviewed all its personnel management procedures, to ensure that direct and indirect discrimination is not being practised. In the area of recruitment, the review has led to the development of a new set of standards for its advertising that ensure it does not include any mention, or indirect reference to, age-related conditions. A human resource manager is now involved in every selection interview to ensure that corporate policies are being observed and are explained to potential recruits.

Regular monitoring of its workforce composition has been introduced, and this confirms that the company's initiatives have helped to broaden the age profile of its employees.

Headhunters

Search-and-selection consultants, otherwise known as "headhunters", can help with hard-to-fill, high-level or commercially-sensitive vacancies.

Headhunters approach and secure potential recruits for a key vacancy through a series of complex and discreet negotiations. Most headhunting firms maintain databases of individuals with an established track record in the occupations or industries that the firm covers, and can also act as intermediaries by approaching someone that their client has identified.

Often, headhunters act as "poachers", approaching the best members of staff employed by the competitors of their client employer. This is an activity that the client would find difficult, or distasteful, to carry out themselves (although a few very large companies have set up in-house headhunting units), but which a skilled intermediary could perform while the client remains at a distance. Given that poachers can turn gamekeepers – a headhunter could as easily poach one of their client's staff on behalf of another employer – many of the reputable firms have a code of conduct that prevents them approaching individuals who work for a current or former client. This can cause problems where the headhunter acts for many clients, particularly in the same industry, because this ring-fencing can cut off a client from what might be many of the most important sources of recruits.

More directly, headhunters often advertise openly for candidates when acting on behalf of an employer, although they usually conceal their client's identity (using such phrases as "a major force in fast-moving consumer goods"; or "a well-established West Midlands pharmaceuticals manufacturer"). Potential applicants are directed to contact the headhunter rather than the client, and the consultancy then usually undertakes initial shortlisting on the basis of a telephone conversation and submission of a CV. This may then lead to an initial interview and, perhaps, the use of one or more psychometric tests. The shortlist of candidates may then be presented to the client for its consideration and final selection.

9. Using headhunters

Feedback from personnel, HR and recruitment specialists with experience of using headhunters' services highlights several important issues:

● **Skills 1:** Headhunters should be able to demonstrate an excellent knowledge of the market they operate in, good communication skills, integrity, competence, loyalty and accuracy.

● **Skills 2:** In addition, because consultants also need to have regular, two-way communication with the client employer, they should possess good customer-care skills and considerable levels of project management expertise.

● **Choice:** The confidentiality surrounding the use of headhunters means that it may not always be possible to obtain details of a consultancy's previous clients and approach them for recommendations. However, anonymised data on completion rates and the level of repeat business should be available. Colleagues, friends and personnel, HR and recruitment contacts in comparable organisations may be a good source of recommendations. For many potential clients, the reputation and track record of an individual consultant are equally, or more, important than those of the consultancy as a whole.

● **Size:** Headhunter consultancies range in size from multinationals to very small operations. Large firms may have better networks and databases of contacts, access to larger numbers of experienced staff and the ability to offer a wider range of services. Where they advertise a vacancy on behalf of a client, their own reputation might encourage responses from suitable individuals. However, smaller firms may have developed specialist expertise in particular industries or occupations. A code of conduct that prevents headhunters approaching employees of former or current clients may favour smaller consultancies, because it will mean they are likely to be able to approach a larger number of individuals than some of the major headhunting firms.

● **Relationship:** It is important that the client employer carefully defines the service, and expected outcomes, that the headhunter is expected to deliver; brief the headhunter fully on the vacancy and the organisation; and ensure that the relationship between the headhunter and the employer is actively managed. A relationship between one consultant and one member of the employer's staff tends to work best, where there is two-way communication and feedback, and where the relationship develops over time so that both sides gain an in-depth knowledge of each other.

● **All eventualities:** The contract with the consultancy should also cover issues that might cause conflict if they arise later, such as the position regarding candidates who are put forward by the headhunter and then leave, or are dismissed, shortly after appointment.

● **Confidentiality:** To be effective, headhunters will obtain sensitive information about the client employer; therefore, a guarantee of complete confidentiality should be obtained at the outset of the project.

● **Suitability:** Headhunters' services are expensive – their fees are usually based on a sizeable percentage of the vacancy's annual salary, plus administration expenses – it is therefore important to identify in advance the added value that the consultancy will bring to the employer's ability to find the best candidates. Our contacts report that it is often best to use headhunters where the target group for the vacancy is well-defined.

Recruitment fairs

Many people associate recruitment fairs with the graduate "milk round", where organisations bidding for the best new graduates set up stands on campus. However, their use is much more diverse than this particular application. Special recruitment events range from a small-scale open day organised by a single employer to a grandiose, three-day exhibition attracting thousands of visitors. Some careers fairs have a broad focus, while others are sector-specific and geared to attracting potential recruits to jobs in the media, for example.

In most cases, the stands that employers mount at recruitment fairs are staffed by their own employees. They should have been sufficiently briefed in advance to be in a position to advise about current and future vacancies in the organisation, and project a strong image of the company as an attractive employer. Some employers take a proactive stance, and distribute application packs and application forms at the event. They may use their staff to screen enquirers for their suitability as potential recruits. In this case, their representatives on the stand should have already received adequate training in selection techniques and in issues concerned with equal opportunities.

According to research undertaken for the Chartered Institute of Personnel and Development (CIPD)[42], three in 10 (30%) employers are involved in some kind of promotional event or fair to help their recruitment activities. These include open days or evenings where "prospective applicants are invited to attend and gain some insight into the organisation and available vacancies", and attendance at externally arranged careers events held at schools and university campuses.

Although most recruitment fairs are concerned with the recruitment of young people, particularly graduates, some also cater for jobhunters looking to return to employment or wanting a career change. Another possible approach involves fairs that target particular sections of the workforce, such as minority groups. For example, several large UK employers, including the police service and the Inland Revenue, have organised recruitment stalls at Gay Pride events.

Many local fairs, particularly those organised by a single employer, are often responses to localised skills or labour shortages, and often involve employers in sectors with high levels of labour turnover, such as retailing or hospitality. One-off fairs are usually linked to a business start-up, such as the opening of a new supermarket or hotel, where many vacancies need to be filled as quickly as possible.

Blue-chip companies tend to be the major participants in the large, commercially run recruitment fairs. In some cases, these organisations cannot afford not to have a presence at such events. For instance, attendance by the major high-street banks at an event organised for the financial services sector is a must, given the need to push the brand as well as attract top talent. The CIPD compares the competition between leading employers for the best individuals with the rivalry that exists between Premier League football teams[43].

Another reason why larger firms can be expected to participate in the Olympia-type fairs is that they can justify the financial outlay because of the numbers of graduates they recruit. Their graduate intake has the potential to pay dividends in terms of future contribution as middle and senior managers to the organisation's goals.

Large-scale employment exhibitions are a big money-spinner and represent an industry in their own right. The opportunities available range from direct participation in one of the many commercial fairs, where recruitment agencies and event organisers stage, typically, two- or three-day events with stands for hire by individual organisations, to engaging an external company to manage the project on the employer's behalf.

There is a plethora of commercial event organisers vying for business. And it is sound business sense to undertake careful research before entering into a contract to rent display space or take advantage of other services on offer. For example, it is usually an easy task to research the success of the organiser's previous employment exhibitions, such as where and how well the event was advertised, and the number of visitors. Some employers participating in a recent event – particularly, those having a similar size, business activity or location to the enquirer's own organisation – could be approached for their feedback on its success and whether or not they consider participation to provide a cost-effective means of filling their vacancies.

A company's involvement in a recruitment event can be almost entirely handed over – at a price – to an agency that will oversee the advertising and liaise with universities or other bodies, as well as being present on the day to undertake interviews and follow up shortlisting and other recruitment matters. A note of caution here: most event organisers are exactly what the name suggests and are not necessarily recruitment specialists.

The benefit of outsourcing on this scale is that, depending on the track record and reputation of the event organiser, the employer is taking advantage of a well-oiled machine. The company will offer established processes and advertising channels, and will take the strain if the organisation of the fair cannot be managed effectively in-house. But employers can pay heavily for the privilege.

The cost of hiring a stand for two days at a modestly sized regional recruitment fair (45 companies exhibiting) in Bristol, for example, ranges from £600 for a basic stand to £5,500 for "branding the event", which includes stall hire, promotional literature, advertising and sponsorship of the fair.

Sector-specific fairs: Industry-specific recruitment fairs are available for most employment sectors; for example, the Engineering Recruitment Show, supported by the Institution of Electrical Engineers, which features around 30 employers looking to recruit to engineering jobs.

The Recruitment and Employment Confederation (REC), the professional body for the recruitment industry, believes that participation in sector-specific recruitment fairs can be very successful. A spokesperson told us that: "We advise our member organisations that they are likely to gain the most out of careers events that cater for a particular industry, for example, an event organised to meet recruitment shortages in the IT sector. The really huge fairs, with thousands of employer stalls, can be overwhelming for both jobseekers and companies."

Small-scale fairs: A small event organised by an individual company can be more focused in meeting that company's recruitment needs than being just one participant in a large-scale fair involving dozens of employers. Local fairs can attract jobseekers living or working in the area, and give them the opportunity to meet employees and gain a realistic impression of the organisation.

Aylesford Newsprint, which employs around 400 staff at its paper-manufacturing plant in Kent, organises an open evening for recruitment to its Modern Apprenticeship scheme. Around 120 people attended the company's 2001 event, providing an opportunity for potential recruits to meet both employers and apprentices already established on the scheme.

Brewers Fayre, the pub restaurant chain, organised a one-off roadshow in autumn 2001 in the North West to tempt chefs to work in the South East, where the company has experienced recruitment difficulties. The manager of the company's Village Inn in Swanwick, Southampton, was one of those active in the recruitment campaign and told us: "Our search for new chefs took us to the North West where we received a positive response from applicants interested in changing careers and moving south."

Two open-house sessions were held at a Liverpool hotel in November 2001, which resulted in 39 on-the-spot interviews. Of these, 16 candidates were driven directly to one of the chain's restaurants in the South East to receive on-the-job training. The recruitment drive was a success and resulted in eight new recruits.

Fairs for new graduates: Most of the large UK higher education establishments hold their own graduate recruitment fairs, managed by the institution's careers service. Most of these fairs run from May to January, with the majority of events taking place in the autumn.

For example, the University of Edinburgh's 2002/03 programme comprised three events to "bring employers face-to-face with students and recent graduates" on campus:

● a Careers Opportunities Fair for final- and penultimate-year students from a number of Scottish higher education institutions;
● a Graduate Fair in June "designed to help exhibiting organisations fill remaining vacancies"; and
● an Internship and Vacation Opportunities Fair for non-final-year students and those seeking seasonal work.

The first port of call for employers looking to recruit significant numbers of graduates should be the careers services of higher education institutions that offer courses in relevant disciplines. The careers staff employed there will have specialist knowledge of graduate recruitment. Even if the employer does not plan to make use of their organised careers events and interview programme, they are still likely to have valuable advice to help conduct a successful recruitment campaign.

10. Recruitment fairs: the key issues

● **When to use them:** Participation in recruitment fairs can be expensive, so make sure the cost is justified.

● **The same golden recruitment rule applies:** Consider what type of event will attract the most suitable pool of potential candidates for the organisation's recruitment needs. It may be that a smaller-scale open day will be more effective than having a stand at one of the more grandiose commercial events.

● **If you're going to do it, do it well:** Even a small affair requires careful planning and a big commitment of resources to make a good impression.

● **Stand out from the crowd:** Use the event to build the organisation's profile by presenting a positive and realistic impression of the organisation. The

exhibition stand should be attractive and imaginative to draw visitors in, and should carry plenty of corporate literature to distribute once their interest is engaged.

● **Stand and deliver:** Make sure the representatives on the stand have the skills required to do credit to the employer; a careful balance needs to be struck between being too upbeat (and giving a false impression of the reality of the job and the organisation) and being too laid back (and failing to engage visitors' interest). The representatives will also require training in recruitment and equal opportunities issues where visitors are given advice about their suitability for the vacancies on offer.

● **Follow up:** A recruitment fair is not a one-off event but should be an integral part of an organisation's recruitment process. The CVs or application forms gathered on the day should be considered and responded to promptly.

Referral payments

Informal recruitment practices have always played a major role in the operation of the British labour market. In all, six in 10 (61.7%) employers use word of mouth and other informal networks as part of their recruitment methods, according to the Chartered Institute of Personnel and Development's survey of almost 750 personnel, HR and recruitment specialists[44].

This means that informal recruitment is more widespread than either recruitment advertising or the use of corporate websites to publicise job vacancies, and is only marginally less popular than the use of jobcentres.

Much informal recruitment involves networking, where jobseekers approach people they know and enquire about work opportunities, or contacts of theirs pass on details to them about specific vacancies. The jobseeker may have a friend, family member or neighbour who works for an employer where a vacancy arises, and their contact knows enough about the jobseeker's circumstances and background to think that they might be interested in the position.

These fairly casual types of referral do not offer a strong likelihood that the vacancy and the jobseeker will be well matched. But where the employee knows a good deal more about the jobseeker – and where the employee has given the jobseeker a good understanding of the vacancy and the organisation's culture – then the chances of a good match are much greater.

Indeed, there is some evidence that insightful personal referrals represent a better source of recruits than the considerably more costly option of recruitment advertising (as found, for example, by Karel De Witte; see the section above on recruitment advertising).

Some employers have taken personal referrals a stage further by offering financial inducements – known as referral payments or bounty payments – where staff refer a jobseeker who is successfully recruited by the organisation. The financial payment and higher profile attached to such schemes can considerably increase the prospects of employee referrals uncovering potentially valuable recruits. Staff will be more aware that their employer positively welcomes referrals, and the payment encourages them to recommend individuals most likely to meet the vacancy's requirements.

Alongside these advantages, there are two main downsides, though, to bounty payment schemes:

1. Equal opportunities: There is a viewpoint that referral schemes can encourage "cloning", on the theory that employees are most likely to refer jobseekers who are like themselves (eg middle-aged white males being more likely to mention a vacancy to another middle-aged white male than to a teenage women of Pakistani ethnic origin, for example). However, most individuals have a reasonably wide circle of acquaintances, as well as their immediate family and friends. The same white middle-aged male may, for example, hear that the daughter of their newsagent is looking for a new job and mention it next time they call in to the shop.

Certainly, referral schemes are the opposite of formal, open recruitment and restrict the ability of individuals to gain the job to those who hear about it on the grapevine. But employers rarely rely on one method of recruitment to fill their vacancies, and most of the personnel, HR and recruitment specialists we contact tell us that informal recruitment provides what may be a useful adjunct to more formalised procedures, such as advertising.

2. Administration: While some employers avoid the time-consuming and expensive process of acknowledging applications and notifying unsuccessful candidates, it is more difficult to avoid doing so where referrals from current employees are involved. They will often see themselves as the applicants' sponsors, and it is likely to damage employee relations where those making referrals consider that the jobseekers have been treated discourteously.

Employers' use of referral schemes seems to ebb and flow with the tide of skills shortages, and grew in extent in the late 1990s in the face of increasing recruitment difficulties.

11. Referral schemes: the key issues

● **Payment:** Most schemes offer a direct financial payment – although a few donate the bounty in cash or kind to a charity. The level of payment needs to be sufficiently attractive to encourage employees' involvement, without being too generous. Employees' expectations are likely to be shaped by the typical wage levels in the organisation. It may be worth offering two or three tiers of payment, depending on the difficulty with which particular vacancies can be filled. A few employers provide rising levels of payment to encourage employees to make more than one referral. However, some employers have found that schemes with different types, and levels, of payment lose their appeal because employees find them difficult to understand.

● **Terms and conditions:** Most employers make it clear that the bounty payment will only be made in respect of candidates that are actually appointed;

some require a minimum period of service (often, three to six months). There have been experiences, particularly in low-paid jobs, where employees collude with friends to obtain the bounty, at which point the friend resigns and the employee refers another friend to the employer.

● **Ineligible staff:** Some employers bar certain members of staff from their referral schemes, usually personnel/HR specialists and senior managers and, less frequently, line managers. These employers take the view that recruitment is part of these members of staff's normal duties and they should not be eligible for additional reward for performing it. In some employers, though, the bar on line managers only applies to vacancies for staff who report directly to them.

● **Internal publicity:** The most successful schemes seem to be those where employers make strenuous effects to publicise them on a continuous basis.

● **Administration:** To maintain employees' interest in the scheme, employers find that it is necessary to acknowledge all referrals made by members of staff. Standard letters and forms are less motivating than personalised communications, such as personalised emails or a telephone call. Candidate administration is also important, given that the jobseekers' opinions of their treatment will be passed back to the employees who made the referral. Rejections will have to be handled particularly sensitively.

● **Maintenance:** All forms of bonus scheme require regular review and renewal to keep them fresh and continue to act as an effective incentive. Payments should be uprated periodically, and the terms and conditions should be reviewed. Some employers have experimented with coupling the bonus payment with the chance to enter a prize draw for a significant prize, as a means of renewing interest in their scheme.

Case study B. Examples of referral schemes

The **Bank of Scotland** reviewed its referral scheme in 2002, according to *Personnel Today*[45], as part of a drive to recruit 1,500 additional staff. The bonus was doubled to £1,000, rising to a maximum of £5,000 for employees making multiple successful referrals. The bank estimated that up to one in five of its 220 new business development specialists and up to half of vacancies for junior support roles were recruited via employee referrals.

News agency **Reuters** has told us that a review of its recruitment and retention strategy has led it to give greater emphasis to its referral scheme. Now, between 10% and 20% of vacancies are filled via referrals, a considerable increase on the previous situation.

Financial services company **Alliance & Leicester** has developed introduction cards that employees are encouraged to give to people they know who are

Using schools, colleges and universities

Educational establishments provide a fruitful source of recruits for many employers, particularly where organisations are seeking young people or new graduates.

Young people

Among employers that have vacancies for school-leavers and other young people, six in 10 (59%) of those we contacted told us that they use their local schools, sixth-form colleges and further education colleges as sources of recruits. When asked to choose their single most cost-effective method of recruiting young people, the employers we contacted highlighted local newspaper advertising (chosen by the largest proportion), employee referrals and schools and colleges (both with the second-highest proportions).

Simply informing educational establishments that the employer has a vacancy for a young person is seldom sufficient. Indeed, several employers have told us that the official education league tables mean that schools have an incentive to encourage pupils to stay on in education, rather than moving into employment at age 16 or 18.

Instead, employers often maintain a wide range of links with educational establishments. Partly, this helps foster a relationship with the institutions and also gives them access to potential recruits – for example, when they offer work experience or go into schools and give careers talks. But, more broadly, some employers become involved in order to exert a positive influence on the quality and subject content of courses. And some employers see their educational work as part of being publicly spirited, becoming involved in local schools and other community activities out of a sense of social responsibility.

In descending order of prevalence, these are the main ways in which employers that recruit young people become involved with schools and colleges:

● offering work experience to students (practised by 92.0% of employers with some form of educational involvement);

- staff giving talks in schools or colleges (56.0%);
- hosting workplace visits by groups of students (55.0%);
- attending careers days (51.0%);
- offering students the opportunity to practise their interview techniques (30.0%);
- encouraging staff to become school governors (27.0%);
- taking part in a formal partnership with local schools (25.0%);
- donating equipment (19.0%); and
- donating money (16.0%).

For more information, see section G. The cost-effective recruitment of school-leavers earlier in this chapter.

New graduates

Employers' involvement with universities is a central, well-established aspect of their recruitment of new graduates. Attendance on campus for careers fairs represents the most effective recruitment method at their disposal, according to the employers we contacted that recruit new graduates. And the use of university careers services represents the fourth most effective method.

In descending order of prevalence, these are the main ways in which employers that recruit new graduates become involved with universities:
- using university careers services, including proactively contacting them and providing them with information about their organisations (86.8%);
- making campus visits (59.2%); and
- offering work placements (51.3%).

For more information, see section F. The cost-effective recruitment of new graduates earlier in this chapter.

Foreign workers

The free movement of citizens within the EU, and the wider European Economic Area, gives employers access to a much broader labour market of potential recruits. Jobcentres offer a free service where suitable vacancies can be advertised on the international EURES network and, of course, the internet is a truly worldwide means of publicising employers' vacancies. However, employers are usually restricted in their ability to recruit workers from outside the EU and EEA through work permits, immigration controls and other Regulations.

See chapter 4 for information on the recruitment of foreign workers.

Tackling skills shortages and other hard-to-fill vacancies

Skills shortages and labour difficulties are a recruiter's nightmare. In some sectors and occupations, problems are endemic; while in others, the ease with which employers fill their vacancies ebbs and flows with the health of the economy.

In some cases, high levels of unemployment exist alongside ever-present labour difficulties[47]. For example, some inner London boroughs have among the highest rates of joblessness of any part of the UK, yet the high concentration of hospitality employers in these locations must often turn to overseas workers to fill their vacancies.

It is worth recalling that employers are exposed to skills shortages and other recruitment difficulties when new jobs are created through business expansion or reorganisation, or when existing staff leave their posts. In both situations, much can be done to avoid encountering recruitment problems purely by reducing an organisation's exposure to the external labour market.

Newly-created jobs can be filled internally through promotion, retraining or upskilling. This may create a knock-on effect where vacancies occur elsewhere, but these may involve less-skilled, and easier to fill, jobs. As a bonus, promotion and developmental job moves can be powerful motivators and help employers increase their retention of staff.

Vacancies that occur through what is misleadingly called "natural wastage" can also be managed, by developing focused, cost-effective initiatives to tackle the reasons that encourage staff to leave. Given that recruitment and retention are merely the opposite ends of the same spectrum, what benefits one area often helps the other.

Where recruitment and selection practices are improved, this will often lead to more suitable candidates being appointed – candidates who are more closely matched to the vacancy's requirements and who are more attuned to the culture of the organisation. Such staff are likely to be more happy in their work and, therefore, less likely to leave prematurely.

And, where retention is managed and labour turnover is reduced, then fewer recruits will be required. *Employers' cost-effective retention practices are analysed in chapter 7 Retaining the best staff.*

This section in chapter 1 on skills shortages examines employers' responses from five different angles:

1. an overview of the prevalence of skills shortages and employers' responses to them;

2. improving the recruitment and selection process itself;

3. making greater, or more sophisticated, efforts to recruit staff;

4. offering financial incentives; and

5. providing other benefits and conditions.

1. An overview of the current situation

The extent of recruitment problems: Recently, we contacted more than 430 personnel and HR specialists and asked them about their experience of skills shortages and other recruitment difficulties, and then asked them to tell us of the ways in which they were attempting to resolve these problems.

These specialists told us that skills shortages and other recruitment difficulties remain widespread. When we analysed a matched sample of people that we had also contacted a year previously, we found that the proportion of employers with recruitment-related problems had hardly diminished – seven in 10 (69.3%) were currently experiencing problems against three-quarters (75.0%) a year previously.

The public sector remains worst affected by difficulties in filling vacancies (with 78.6% experiencing difficulties), although there have been some improvements recently – primarily, we believe, because of increased funding that has boosted morale and enabled greater recruitment efforts to be made.

Difficulties are also widespread among services firms in the private sector (72.4%), and there has been little recent improvement in the extent of their problems.

However, skills shortages and other recruitment difficulties are least prevalent among companies in the manufacturing and production sector, although this is only a relative statement because more than half (57.9%) are affected. The continued job losses in this sector have played a part in reducing the extent of recruitment problems, and there has been a 17-percentage-point reduction in the proportion of employers affected.

Typical responses: Despite the continuing prevalence of recruitment difficulties, most of the personnel and HR specialists we contacted told us that their organisations are using just a couple of methods to overcome them.

Just over half of employers experiencing recruitment difficulties have readvertised the affected vacancies and/or increased the starting salaries they were offering. And almost half have turned to agencies or headhunters as a source of recruits, where their own efforts have failed.

Ironically, the three most commonly employed measures mentioned above are also among the mostly costly options that employers could explore.

In addition, almost one-half of organisations have tried to broaden their search by advertising on the internet. Increasingly, feedback from personnel, HR and recruitment specialists shows that employers are turning to their corporate websites, where the costs are minimal and, in most cases, hidden, instead of paying to advertise on a commercial job board.

All in all, these are the main responses to skills shortages and other recruitment difficulties that employers tell us they are taking (shown in descending order of prevalence):
- readvertising (53.0%);
- improving starting salaries (52.0%);
- instructing employment agencies/headhunters (47.3%);
- advertising on the internet (47.3%);
- offering flexible hours of work (31.7%);
- being flexible about selection criteria (29.9%);
- speeding up the recruitment process (28.8%);
- introducing/increasing relocation expenses (10.0%); and
- offering a starting bonus (golden hello) (7.5%).

Only one in six (16.1%) employers use methods that are not listed above.

2. Improving recruitment and selection

Over the years, we have contacted thousands of personnel, HR and recruitment specialists; their feedback shows that there is a considerable amount of activity being undertaken to improve recruitment and selection practices in the UK – much of which is being driven by skills shortages.

The nature of these improvements is analysed in detail in chapter 2 in the section "Improving the cost-effectiveness of selection". Here, we highlight the initiatives being adopted by employers that have a particular relevance for tackling skills shortages.

Certainly, salary is a major factor in attracting recruits, but the recruitment and selection procedures used by employers can themselves contribute to the difficulties employers experience in filling some posts. Here are the main ways in which employers are addressing these practices:

● **Ease of applying for a job:** Unnecessary barriers to submitting an application will deter would-be candidates and send them in the direction of more agile competitors. Email and recruitment advertising via the internet are being increasingly used to make the application process as fast and painless as possible.

● **Speed of response:** Once having applied, candidates will become frustrated if there is a lengthy silence from the employer. They may look elsewhere and apply for another vacancy and, where they have several applications pending, a competitor with a faster process will gain the advantage. Again, email is being increasingly used to acknowledge applications; more generally, employers are giving greater priority to acknowledging all applications and to doing so within a shorter space of time. Some employers are investing in software that speeds up their administration of recruitment and selection, or are upgrading their existing systems.

● **Faster recruitment:** Many employers, too, are aiming to reduce the overall time they take from the vacancy occurring to their final selection decision. Some employers tell us that their adoption of recruitment advertising on the internet enables them to reduce the timescale of the recruitment process, because adverts can be published within hours, rather than waiting for the next issue of a weekly or even monthly paper-based publication to appear. Some employers, too, are making greater efforts to reduce unnecessary delays in sifting applications, calling individuals for interview and conducting reference checks. This may require encouraging line managers to give greater priority to their recruitment and selection responsibilities, or of finding ways to work round resource constraints that slow down the process.

● **User-friendly:** There are, too, several different ways in which employers can make themselves more encouraging to would-be applicants. A named contact, with their telephone number, can be given as a source of information and advice to enquirers. The contact, and others involved in recruitment, can be given training in relevant interpersonal skills to ensure that they have a friendly, customer-focused attitude. Reception staff who meet and greet applicants can be properly briefed and trained to provide a professional, yet welcoming atmosphere. Those administering selection tests and those conducting selection interviews can be briefed and trained to strike a good balance between professional detachment and an encouraging, fairly informal and low-key manner. And application forms and other recruitment-related documentation can be reviewed to make them as attractive, engaging and understandable as possible.

Case study C. The Remainders Group

The Remainders Group employs around 1,400 staff in its four retail discount bookshops: The Works, Book Depot, Banana Bookshop and Booksale. The company has put in place a number of integrated initiatives that aim to benefit both recruitment and retention.

Its HR manager told us that: "We found that the majority of people were leaving within the first six months of employment. It was therefore essential that we looked at our recruitment approach in the first instance. The company has made a big investment in training for line managers in areas such as recruitment, disability, disciplinary and objective-setting, which has had a big impact on both recruitment and initial retention rates."

As a result of the training, managers are now more confident in areas such as questioning candidates, making selection decisions and managing performance.

Case study D. King's College Hospital NHS Trust

Based in an inner-city district of London, the trust faces acute difficulties in recruiting and retaining staff. It has introduced a range of initiatives, and has found that improvements to its recruitment practices have also benefited its ability to retain employees.

The trust continually aims to narrow the gap between the expectations of would-be recruits and the reality of the role. "New employees will be disappointed, and possibly leave, if the job does not match up to their expectations," its staff resourcing manager told us. "We therefore make sure that candidates are given realistic information about the job, and we encourage people to visit the hospital so that they can view their prospective working environment."

3. Recruitment efforts

The failure of a recruitment campaign is often employers' first indication that they may be facing a skills shortage or other recruitment difficulty. At this stage, they are already a considerable way down the track and may not have the time to devise an alternative strategy. As a result, many employers simply readvertise the same vacancy, often in the same publication.

But, with some prior warning and forethought, there are many other recruitment methods through which personnel, HR and recruitment specialists can attempt to find suitable candidates; see checklist 12 below.

12. Alternatives to conventional recruitment advertising

Based on the experiences and feedback of personnel, HR and recruitment managers, these are the main alternatives to conventional recruitment advertising used by employers, particularly when confronted by skills and labour shortages – many of these options are covered in more detail in this chapter:

● advertising in different types of printed media, such as women's magazines;

● asking recent recruits and established employees about their perception of working for the organisation and its most attractive aspects, and emphasising the positive aspects in revamped recruitment advertising messages;

● retaining external specialists to advise on recruitment advertising;

● advertising on buses and at bus stops;

● using the internet to advertise vacancies;

● providing recruitment displays and leaflets in local supermarkets;

● leaflet distribution to local households;

● taking part in a recruitment fair;

● holding a well-publicised jobs open day (or evening) on site or at a local venue, such as a hotel;

● radio advertising;

● approaching army placement centres responsible for the re-employment of former services personnel;

● targeting unemployed people as potential recruits, particularly where job-centres and other local organisations are involved in providing work-preparation courses (such as the New Deal);

● targeting former members of staff or, more generally, suitably qualified individuals who have taken a career break;

● launching or revamping "refer-a-friend" schemes;

● forging links with local schools and colleges, and with universities that offer courses in relevant subjects – provided that young people and/or new graduates are specifically sought as recruits by the organisation – such as by offering work placements, giving careers talks, offering sponsorships to undergraduates, encouraging staff to become school governors, donating equipment and supplies, and offering an input into curriculum development;

● keeping a file of unsolicited applications and/or unsuccessful, but potentially suitable, applications for later use as vacancies arise;

● targeting refugees, asylum seekers and overseas workers as sources of recruits;

● taking a long-term view by "building the employer brand" – adopting a sustained publicity programme to promote the employer as a desirable place to work;

● using an employment agency or headhunter, or changing current providers of these services; and

● reviewing recruitment criteria and changing the organisation of work internally, so that external recruitment is less dependent on finding scarce high-level skills and experience.

Case study E. Centrica

Utility and services company Centrica has been tackling some of its recruitment difficulties by targeting unemployed people. It has been running one-week work-preparation courses in conjunction with the jobcentre network. Participants are drawn from the jobcentres' client groups of unemployed people, such as long-term unemployed people, individuals with disabilities and single parents. The courses have had high success rates, with many participants being recruited to hard-to-fill call-centre jobs. The company has found that the initiative also helps its diversity efforts to broaden its workforce, so that the staff reflect the variety of backgrounds and needs of its customers[48].

4. Financial incentives

Many employers' first reaction to their recruitment difficulties is to assume that they are being outbid by competitors that can afford higher salaries and better benefits. Certainly, few jobseekers who voluntarily leave their current jobs will opt for a lower-paying alternative, all other factors being equal. And vacancies with starting salaries that are way below the going rate are unlikely to find many of the most able candidates clamouring to fill them.

The key, according to most of the personnel, HR and recruitment specialists we contact, lies in ensuring that starting salaries and all other salary levels in the organisation are in line with market rates – wherever financially feasible. Salary surveys, feedback from recruits and job applicants, details shown in job adverts, surveys conducted by IRS, data passed on through networks of contacts, pay clubs and a host of other sources are used by our contacts to ensure their pay levels remain competitive.

Location payments

The main drawback for many employers in relying on matching the market rate when recruiting staff lies in the fact that disposable income varies significantly across the UK. Most sources of market pay data focus on gross pay or earnings, and rarely reflect the additional costs affecting a particular town, city or region. Housing costs are, of course, the major variable, but lower-paid workers would also be particularly influenced by significant variations in transport costs.

Historically, London's high living costs have been addressed through location payments – usually, non-pensionable supplements that can be uprated, frozen, or (very rarely) reduced or abolished as local prices change.

In retailing, many employers have created two, three or more parallel sets of salary scales: a main, national one, and others that incorporate pensionable location elements. Where several local salary scales exist, each has a different location element, reflecting local prices and, particularly, the degree of difficulty that the employer's local stores experience in filling their vacancies.

Large factories and other manufacturers often addressed the cost of transport to their works by providing works buses. Employees travelled free or paid subsidised fares. But the decline of manufacturing has led to the disappearance of many such schemes, although many employers offer free parking for employees' cars and some have experimented with subsidies to encourage car-sharing or the use of bicycles, or have cooperated with local authorities to improve public transport links to their offices and sites.

The decline of public transport, its expense, inflexibility and lack of service for many workers with unsocial hours, has encouraged the use of private cars for travel to work. The advent of congestion charges will, potentially, have a considerable financial impact on many employees – particularly where, as in London, the charges only affect some districts and not others. Low-paid workers are often concentrated in jobs with unsocial hours and will be disproportionately affected by daily commuting penalties. Where two employers offer similar jobs, with similar salaries, but one is inside the £5 a day zone and the other is not, then one of them faces a considerable handicap in its ability to recruit and retain employees.

Several employers in London have been investigating offering payments to compensate workers for the congestion charge. **The London Ambulance Service** has introduced a payment for staff who work shifts, affecting some 400 people, worth £550 a year per person[49].

In the **NHS**, the unaffordable cost of housing in London is being addressed by providing more than 2,800 homes for rent at up to 40% below market rates, together with the development of staff hotels close to major hospitals in the capital. **Hammersmith Hospital NHS Trust** has been building housing for its staff and has been considering the use of special portable flat-pack homes[50].

Alongside the public sector, private transport operators often experience considerable recruitment difficulties in areas of high costs. The London bus operations of **Go-Ahead** have been offering subsidised accommodation in a bid to reduce shortages of bus drivers. Recruits can live in one of the 50 houses that the company has bought, and pay rent at half the market value for six months. Each house accommodates between three and six people. As well as helping to reduce its recruitment difficulties, the company told *Personnel Today* magazine that the initiative has contributed to a reduction in labour turnover from 45% to less than 25%[51].

Relocation

Job markets operate at several different levels. Some types of job are usually filled by local residents; others can attract people willing to undertake a longer commute on a daily basis. And some, generally at managerial, professional and technical level, can tap into a national pool of workers who may be willing to relocate their homes and families.

In the cases where vacancies are likely to attract candidates who may need to move home, some employers offer a relocation package as a recruitment incentive. The precise combination of benefits varies, but they are usually one-off payments, although a few employers offer longer-term help with mortgage interest costs through subsidised loans.

We contacted 50 personnel and HR specialists whose organisations offer relocation assistance to new recruits. These are the most common benefits they offer, shown in descending order of prevalence (the costs being either met either wholly or partially by the employer):

- estate agents' and solicitors' fees;
- stamp duty;
- the legal fees involved in obtaining a mortgage;
- temporary accommodation costs;
- removal expenses;
- storage costs;
- weekend return visits to the recruit's home while living in temporary accommodation;
- paid time off for the home move;
- househunting costs;
- paid time off for househunting;
- financial assistance when moving to a higher-cost area;
- help with selling the current home, such as guaranteeing the sale price; and
- offering a subsidised bridging loan.

Market premia

Direct intervention to ratchet up starting salaries is often avoided, wherever possible, because of the distorting effect it can have on the employer's salary structure as a whole. Instead, many organisations prefer to offer unconsolidated supplements – "market premia" – to provide an added financial incentive where particular vacancies prove difficult to fill.

Market premia often considerable flexibility; they can target a few types of vacancy or even a particular sought-after individual; they can increase over time as difficulties grow, or exclude new vacancies that arise once skills shortages have reduced.

However, as pay specialist e-reward points out: "Market supplements are essentially divisive and can create dissatisfaction amongst those who do not receive them. Every attempt should be made to avoid paying them, other than in exceptional circumstances."[52] There are, too, potential difficulties with equal pay legislation, unless an employer can show that any difference in treatment between a man and a woman doing the same job, or work of equal value, is not related to their gender and is objectively justifiable.

Recruitment incentives

Market premia offer medium- to long-term payments to recruits where skills shortages exist, but some employers adopt an alternative (sometimes, complementary) strategy of providing a one-off cash sum to new recruits: a recruitment incentive, otherwise known as a "golden hello".

These financial inducements have been fairly common in some industries for many years, normally for prestige, hard-to-fill, top jobs, such as executive positions. However, the practice took on a new lease of life in the late 1990s when economic conditions led to widespread skills shortages.

Apart from executive vacancies, financial incentives have been offered by some employers in their recruitment of new graduates. Blue-chip companies aiming for the cream of each year's new graduates have often found it difficult to fill their vacancies with recruits of the high calibre they require, despite the ever-increasing number of university places. Some of the incentives are depicted in terms of providing a young person with the means of starting a career. The money is intended to buy a business suit, help with travel and home-finding costs, and so on. In other employers, the financial incentive has been paid in instalments to help the new graduate pay off the debts they have incurred while studying.

Golden hellos are very much the exception, though, and the majority of employers recruiting new graduates do not offer them. Among the graduate recruitment specialists we contacted, only 8% of their organisations have such a scheme.

In fact, the public sector represents the main area of growth in golden hellos, with incentives being targeted towards areas of acute skills shortages, such as doctors and teachers.

Sponsorship schemes

In addition to starting bonuses for new graduates, there is a long tradition of providing financial support to potential graduate recruits while they are at university. Our annual research programme into employers' graduate recruitment practices consistently finds that around three in 10 organisations that recruit graduates offer a sponsorship programme. However, manufacturing remains the heartland of sponsorship, with half (48.6%) of such firms that recruit new graduates sponsoring one or more students, against just one in seven (13.5%) services companies.

These programmes provide a cash sum, a bursary, while the individual is studying, and pay them a salary for the periods when they spend time working with the sponsoring employer. Our latest research finds that a typical bursary is worth £1,000 a year. And sponsored students are paid a midpoint monthly wage of £958, rising to £1,442 among manufacturers, when working with their sponsor.

Organisations tend to review their programmes regularly, and practice is focusing on restricting the bursaries to the final year of study, rather than paying them throughout the university course. In addition, there are often eligibility restrictions linked to particular skills that the employer needs. Most commonly, sponsorship schemes are open to students on courses in various engineering and electronics disciplines. The numbers of students taking many of these courses are in long-term decline, and employers' – primarily manufacturers' – skills shortages are compounded by the trend for many of those graduating from such courses to go into other occupations.

Employers tell us that sponsorships increase the likelihood of finding suitable recruits for hard-to-fill vacancies. The close and lengthy association between sponsored student and employer often leads to a successful result; typically, employers obtain a 70% success rate in converting sponsored students to new recruits. Not only does the sponsorship give the employer the time and opportunity to get to know a great deal about the abilities and motivation of the individual, but the student is more likely to make a sound choice of employer based on an informed knowledge of the reality of the job and organisation.

Manufacturers that we contacted told us that the use of sponsorship programmes represents one of their three most effective ways of recruiting new graduates.

Reasons for offering an incentive

The personnel and HR specialists we contacted about their recruitment incentives tell us that they offer them because they:
● provide a high-profile means of attracting the best candidates;
● represent a response to the bonuses offered by competitors; and
● enable them to respond to marketplace pressures while leaving their grading structure unaltered.

Terms and conditions

There appears to be a mixture of terms and conditions attached to the operation of incentive payments to new recruits. Some organisations have strict rules about the repayment of the money if the person leaves before a stated period, while others stipulate exactly what the money should be spent on.

118

When we contacted employers about their practices in 2001, financial services company **HSBC** stipulated that graduates leaving before the end of the executive trainee programme had to refund one-twelfth of their payment for every month not worked. And at **Exxonmobil**, employees had to refund the £750 they received when accepting a job offer if they did not actually start work with the company; otherwise there were no other terms and conditions attached to the sum. Graduates at **Boots** had to repay their bonus of £1,000 if they left within their first two years of employment.

Payment levels

Golden hellos are often worth several thousand pounds, often in the £1,000 to £3,000 range for new graduates, although some of the largest management consultancies and accountancy firms have offered as much as £10,000. However, the higher payments tend to be carefully targeted at areas or times of acute skills shortages, and are often withdrawn or reduced at short notice.

The government offers golden hellos of £4,000 and repays the student loans of new teachers where they spend at least half their time teaching subjects in state schools where skills shortages are most acute. Currently, these subjects include English, maths, modern languages, IT and science. Bursaries of £6,000 are also available to eligible postgraduate students on teacher training courses.

Golden hellos were introduced for further education lecturers in 2002, offering payments of up to £4,000 for recent recruits to subjects where skills shortages exist, including construction, engineering, design and technology, and IT.

In the NHS, the golden hello scheme introduced in 2001 for doctors, consultants and GPs has been extended to returning staff, and payments have been increased to a maximum of £12,000 in areas of particular skills shortages.

5. Other recruitment incentives

One of the most exciting developments in tackling recruitment difficulties involves three measures that have great appeal for many potential recruits, that can enhance employees' performance, and yet often involve little direct cost to the employer. Two of these measures relate to so-called "work–life balance" factors, while the third taps into many employees' desire for self-improvement.

All three options are showing initial signs of proving effective in reducing recruitment problems, but, equally significantly, are also helping organisations to improve their ability to retain employees and reduce absence rates. The same initiatives thus have the potential to offer a coherent approach to the management of employees' performance.

Flexible working

Many adults lead increasingly complicated lives, balancing caring commitments with work, and trying to find time for social activities in what is often an overlong working week. Employers that have experimented with offering recruits (and existing employees) some control over their working hours through different working patterns are finding that it represents an effective recruitment incentive. The main options being offered, usually in place of standard, full-time jobs with a fixed 9–5 pattern, include part-time work, flexible hours of attendance, term-time work and extended periods of (usually unpaid) leave.

Where flexible hours of attendance are on offer, employers' options include compressed working weeks, where longer hours are worked on some days, allowing an early finish on the fifth day or even compressing normal hours into four days a week. Or employees may be offered flexitime, where there are required core hours of attendance (10–3, for example), but where the employee can manage their time either side of this period provided their hours add up to the expected working week, fortnight or month. Taking this flexibility a stage further, some employers have set up annualised hours schemes, where employees' required hours of attendance are calculated on a yearly basis, giving them (and, often, the employer) the option of longer hours at some times in the year – for example, during school terms – and shorter hours at others.

Where shift systems are in operation, employers may offer flexibility around the shift hours, or allow employees to swap shifts to accommodate caring and social commitments.

Adding impetus to the move to offer flexible working, a new statutory right to request flexible working came into force in April 2003. This is restricted to parents of minors, but six in 10 of the personnel, HR and equality specialists we contacted about this right told us that they expect their employers to extend it to their workforce as a whole.

More information on flexible working, including the statutory right, can be found in chapter 9 Equal opportunities and diversity (including two case studies, H and I) and chapter 12 Attendance and absence (including two further case studies, C and D).

Childcare

Quality childcare provision is scarce and expensive in the UK. The Equal Opportunities Commission says that a nursery place costs an average of £128 a week. In most other European countries, childcare places are heavily subsidised, with parents paying around 30% of the cost. In the UK, parents pay around 75% of the fees[53].

This means that parents in low-paid or part-time jobs are effectively working to pay for the cost of having their child looked after while they are out earning money.

The commission estimates that around one in 10 employers already provide help with childcare, mainly through subsidises that assist with parents' childcare costs. A few employers offer direct assistance, through workplace crèches or cooperative schemes where two or more organisations organise and run a nursery for the benefit of their combined workforces.

We contacted more than 50 personnel and HR specialists working for employers that already offer childcare assistance to gain their feedback on current practice. They told us that the two main reasons for offering childcare assistance are that it improves their organisations' ability to recruit and retain employees.

Most commonly, these are the main features of employers' childcare schemes:
● providing an advisory and referral service about childcare options and provision;
● offering assistance to employees with a child of nursery-school age;
● providing financial assistance towards childcare costs;
● setting up an on-site nursery (a few employers do so in partnership with another employer or organisation, while even fewer provide a nursery away from the workplace);
● there are usually only limited places available in employers' nurseries, with competition between staff for them;
● therefore, many employers with nurseries set up waiting lists; most often, a simple queuing system is used, although some employers take account of the employee's length of service, their need for assistance or whether they are single parents or have a child with disabilities;
● where subsidies are provided, most employers restrict them to employees meeting certain criteria, these vary, but include the number of hours worked, whether they are the primary carer, their financial resources or having worked a minimum period of service;

● subsidies are usually restricted to children below a certain age, often five years old; and

● only a few employers cater for school-age children through schemes that cover out-of-school hours and holiday times.

Among the employers we contacted, childcare places were subsidised by the employer paying capital costs and maintenance, with the employee's contribution representing the direct cost of the day-to-day operation of the nursery. However, instead of a flat-rate hourly or daily fee, many employers with nurseries operate a scale of charges that depends on such factors as the child's age and the employee's salary.

Contributions towards employees' external childcare costs vary significantly from employer to employer, with weekly payments worth anything between £10 and £55.

Training

Providing tailored training and development opportunities represents one of the most effective ways of retaining valued employees (see chapter 7 Retaining the best staff). But some employers are integrating training in their recruitment strategies as a means of reducing their skills shortages. The training provides both a means of giving recruits the skills required in the post, but also can act as an incentive, encouraging candidates to apply to an employer that provides this benefit.

The government-subsidised Foundation Modern Apprenticeships and Advanced Modern Apprenticeships can provide employers with trained young people (only those aged under 25 are currently eligible in most cases), where they have gained their skills and experience through a combination of on-the-job working and training, and college-based tuition.

These apprenticeships can attract able young people who do not want to continue in full-time education; the ability to "earn while learning" is being used as a unique selling point. *See chapter 5 Induction, training and development for more information on the apprenticeships and the New Deal programmes.*

Some employers set up their own training programmes, where recruits take part in an intensive course that gives them the skills required to fill jobs where the employer experiences recurrent recruitment difficulties when trying to find fully-trained candidates. Some such schemes involve partnerships with the jobcentre network or other state agencies, where unemployed people are offered pre-recruitment training. Those successfully completing the course and meeting the employer's recruitment criteria are then offered jobs. Several such initiatives have taken place in recent years where a large-scale recruitment exercise is being launched; for example, where a large supermarket is being built and unemployed people from the local community are given training to help them gain some of the new jobs.

Finally, research for the government into organisations' recruitment difficulties makes this observation: "Employers who are engaged in the continuous development and training of their staff appeared, from the case studies, to experience fewer recruitment problems. This was a consequence of having trained people coming through the occupational hierarchy to fill skilled jobs as they arose and lower labour turnover (itself associated with training and development)."[54]

13. Legal checklist

● Recruitment practices should not discriminate unfairly, although there are very limited exceptions where the employer can show an objective reason for so doing – Sex Discrimination Act 1975; Race Relations Act 1976; Disability Discrimination Act 1995; Part-Time Workers (Prevention of Less-Favourable Treatment) Regulations 2000; Fixed-Term Employees (Prevention of Less-Favourable Treatment) Regulations 2002; Trade Union and Labour Relations (Consolidation) Act 1992; and Codes of Practice associated with these Acts

● Recruitment practices in the public sector must support equality of opportunity on the grounds of ethnicity – Race Relations (Amendment) Act 2000.

● All aspects of recruitment can potentially discriminate unlawfully against one or more groups (see the relevant sections in this chapter), and should be reviewed for direct and indirect bias; monitoring of recruitment procedures, stage by stage, can provide additional information about areas of potential concern.

● Legislation covering employment agencies will be modified and increased once the forthcoming Conduct of Employment Agencies and Employment Business Regulations are approved; in addition, a draft EC Directive on agency workers will have considerable consequence for employers' use of agency temps once the Directive is eventually implemented. (See the section on Employment agencies in this chapter for more details of both measures).

2. Cost-effective selection

See also: 1. Filling your vacancies; 3. Using electronic media effectively; 4. Checking candidates' backgrounds; and 9. Equal opportunities and diversity.

This chapter covers:
- Overview;
- Improving the cost-effectiveness of selection;
- Cost-effective selection methods: for managers; IT specialists; sales staff; skilled workers; semi- and unskilled workers; new graduates; school-leavers and young people; and for all types of recruit;
- The validity of different selection methods;
- The main selection methods: application forms and CVs; interviewing; testing; assessment centres; competency based selection; biodata; and graphology;
- The role of self-selection; and
- Record-keeping.

Checklists in this chapter:
1. Improving the cost-effectiveness of recruitment and selection
2. Application forms: improving their effectiveness
3. Interview techniques
4. Developing an interviewer guide
5. Improving equal opportunities in interviewing
6. Choosing an off-the-shelf test
7. Test use and equal opportunities
8. Assessment centres: the key issues
9. Legal checklist

Case studies in this chapter:
A. Peugeot
B. Amery-Parkes and Cornwall County Fire Brigade
C. London Borough of Harrow
D. Danzas
E. Staffordshire Police
F. Scottish Equitable
G. Capital One Bank
H. Halcrow Group
I. Pret a Manger

Overview

The fact that this chapter on selection is one of the longest in this handbook bears testimony to the complexity surrounding this important aspect of personnel management. Here, we analyse best practice from three different angles.

First, we highlight the ways in which employers are improving the cost-effectiveness of their practices. They are doing so in many different ways, often implementing initiatives that are mutually reinforcing. Changes that make their practices more candidate-friendly make it easier to compete in the labour market, but they also introduce the risk that the overall number of unsuitable applications will soar. So, many organisations are coupling such moves with ones that aim to improve their ability to screen applicants out at the earliest possible stage in the process. The joined-up thinking at work here means that this section of chapter 2 addresses improvements in both recruitment and selection practices.

Second, we examine the most cost-effective methods of selecting applicants, again based on the actual experience of large numbers of personnel, HR and recruitment professionals.

And third, we discuss each of the main selection methods in turn in the final sections of this chapter.

Even with this extensive treatment, some issues have had to be dealt with elsewhere. In particular, the use of references, the recruitment of ex-offenders and overseas workers, the use of the Criminal Records Bureau and other methods of checking candidates' backgrounds are covered in chapter 4. And chapter 3 covers the role of electronic media in recruitment and selection.

Improving the cost-effectiveness of selection

Greater efforts are being made to improve the cost-effectiveness of recruitment and selection, according to the feedback that IRS has obtained from personnel, HR and recruitment professionals in recent years. The scale of this activity is impressive. Practitioners are addressing both the recruitment and selection aspects of the process of hiring new staff. And while some of the 350+ people we contacted are doing so under duress – in the face of tighter cost controls or budget cuts – others are taking the initiative even where cost is not the issue.

The moves seem part of the increasing professionalism and stronger holistic approach of the personnel, HR and recruitment professions to ensure that their organisations receive the best value for money and the best possible choice of candidates.

Some of their activities tackle headline problems, such as controlling the cost of agency fees, others, though, are more subtle. For example, ensuring that candidates are kept informed, treated courteously and are subject to the shortest possible delays before their applications are considered makes the organisation less likely to lose good applicants to other employers. Acting in this way may involve additional costs, but can actually save money in the long run by avoiding failed recruitment exercises that prompt a second round of costly advertising, and by making it easier to recruit individuals with greater performance potential.

A sharper competitive edge

A quarter of organisations find that they lose good candidates to competitors because their own recruitment and selection processes take too long to complete. A key priority for these and many other employers is to shorten this timespan, and they are doing so in several different ways.

E-recruitment: In particular, almost six in 10 (56.8%) employers are turning to electronic recruitment – the use of the internet and emails – to reduce the time taken to advertise vacancies and receive completed applications. Sometimes, the best candidates are those who are not actively looking for another job. They may be browsing the internet for another purpose and come upon a recruitment advertisement that an employer has placed on its own website or on a dedicated job board. Where they can then express an interest in the job by the simple means of clicking on a link and, indeed, being able to submit their CV or a completed application form online, then recruiters are taking full advantage of the speed and immediacy of the web. *(See chapter 3 Using electronic media effectively for more information on using the internet and emails in recruitment and selection.)*

Technology: Recruiters are using technology in additional ways to improve their relationships with candidates. More than a third (37.7%) of employers have introduced or improved the technology they use in recruitment. For example, they have upgraded their internet and email access to broadband, or introduced or improved their use of recruitment-related software that enables them to produce standard letters and track candidates' progress.

The resources at an employer's disposal, and the number of applications received each year, make the use of technology a more cost-effective option for larger employers. So, while just over a fifth (22.7%) of smaller firms with fewer than 250 employees have introduced or improved recruitment-related technology, half (50.0%) of the largest organisations (with 10,000+ employees) have done so.

Streamlining: Almost one in three (31.7%) organisations have been rethinking their management of recruitment and selection. In most cases, they have taken steps to involve line managers more extensively in the process, although some employers – mainly large ones – have gone in the opposite direction and appointed a recruitment specialist to have overall responsibility for ensuring the efficiency of their hiring practices.

Employers that involve line managers more fully in recruitment and selection usually combine this with a realignment of the role played by their personnel or HR manager(s) towards acting more in an advisory or strategic capacity. But, for their part, many personnel and HR managers have told us that this new approach does not always work. Tensions develop between line managers and their advisers, or line managers find that they lack the time, knowledge, skills or interest involved in assuming a greater role in recruitment and selection. In such cases, personnel and HR specialists find that they have to give greater support and advice to ensure line managers perform their recruitment and selection duties in a professional manner.

Interestingly, the size of an employer's workforce does not seem to affect the decision to give line managers greater responsibility for recruitment, although there are differences across the economy. The practice is most widespread among firms in the manufacturing and production sector (44.4% having done so), and is least common in the public sector (28.2%) and among private sector services firms (30.7%).

Screening: Employers' widespread use of e-recruitment to improve the cost-effectiveness of recruitment has a potential flaw in that it can encourage applications from larger numbers of unsuitable candidates. This inflicts higher costs on organisations, given that each application must be read by one or more selectors. There are, too, the costs of acknowledging the receipt of their applications and notifying candidates of the outcome.

To address the potential increase in the quantity of applications, three in 10 (29.3%) organisations are taking steps to improve their initial screening procedures. They are aiming to either prevent some candidates from applying or ensuring that unsuitable applications are sifted out at the earliest opportunity.

There are various ways in which this issue is being tackled, with some employers adopting two or more of them. For example, the content and layout of recruitment advertisements is being improved to ensure that potential candidates have a clearer idea of the vacancy's requirements. Advertisements are expensive and have space constrictions, so many employers are coupling this move with the provision of additional background information on the job, the organisation and its culture, which they either post to enquirers or make available on the internet.

Many employers in the public sector have a long tradition of compiling application packs that they post to candidates. But some of them, and a growing number of private sector employers, are now loading this information on their internet sites. Individuals who are browsing the web have immediate access to these details, without the delay and hassle of contacting the employer and waiting for materials to arrive through the mail. Employers' costs are reduced, where the information is loaded free of charge onto corporate sites, and they do not incur heavy postage costs for the copies that individuals print out or download themselves.

Some organisations, too, are focusing on the use of self-selection materials that take this provision of background information a stage further. The information is worded and laid out in such a way that applicants are encouraged to relate their own skills, abilities and career interests to the context of the vacancy and the employer. Self-selection may involve no more than a carefully worded series of short questions, or it can take the form of a self-completion questionnaire *(for more information, see the section on self-selection towards the end of this chapter)*.

These tactics focus on managing candidates before the point that their application reaches the employer. But many employers are also addressing the issue of screening at the point of entry by introducing or improving their use of application forms to make shortlisting easier and more accurate. Where forms enable selectors to make quick assessments of each candidate's skills and abilities in a consistently objective and rigorous way, then the organisation will save time and resources, and potentially improve the quality of the resultant shortlist of candidates. And, as we will see in the section below on selection tests, some employers are administering psychometric tests earlier in the selection process as a means of enriching the information they can use for shortlisting purposes.

In terms of cost-effectiveness, measures to improve screening and self-selection tend to be justified where employers have relatively large numbers of vacancies and job applicants. While half (50.0%) of the largest organisations (with 10,000+ employees) have taken such steps, only around one in three or fewer of firms with workforces of fewer than 10,000 people have done so.

Multiple, speedier application routes: Most personnel, HR and recruitment managers tell us that their organisations are taking an increasingly flexible approach about the ways in which candidates can contact them and submit applications.

By supplementing the traditional method of written correspondence with the use of email, the telephone and, to a lesser extent, dedicated recruitment answering machines for out-of-hours enquiries, employers aim to speed up the recruitment process, and make it easier for candidates to apply.

In all, almost nine in 10 employers (88.7%) now accept communications from applicants via email, ranging from handling initial enquiries to accepting completed application forms or CVs. The use of email is as common in larger as in smaller organisations, and in the public as in the private sectors of the economy.

Two-thirds (68.5%) of employers also encourage enquiries by telephone. But, in this case, larger organisations' access to the necessary resources to handle what might be hundreds of enquiries a week or month is reflected in differences in practice. Only half of smaller firms (52.9% of those with fewer than 250 staff) are able or willing to promote the use of the telephone in their recruitment, while three-quarters (75.0%) of employers with 10,000-plus staff do so. Similarly, almost nine in 10 (87.3%) public sector bodies – which tend to have larger-than-average workforces – give potential applicants a telephone number to call, while only around six in 10 private sector organisations do so (57.5% of services firms and 61.3% of the manufacturing and production sector).

Taking this a stage further, most employers' telephone lines are only staffed during office hours, but candidates often find it easiest to submit job applications in the evenings or weekends. So, four in 10 (42.7%) employers have installed dedicated recruitment answering machines where callers can leave out-of-hours messages.

As well as requiring a separate line and the necessary equipment, employers must have staff available who can deal with what is likely to be an onerous workload from large numbers of messages. And they must be able to respond to these callers on the next working day, otherwise the potential advantages of using this method will turn into negative publicity. As a result of these logistical factors, three times as many large employers as small ones provide recruitment answering machines (20.5% of firms with fewer than 250 staff, doubling to 42.4% of those with 250 to 999 staff, and rising to 62.5% of the largest organisations with 10,000+ staff).

Keeping in closer touch: There is a danger that candidates will become discouraged or disenchanted if employers do not contact them about their application, with the result that the best candidates may be lost to competitors. The ways in which employers are improving their relationships with candidates includes: acknowledging the receipt of their applications, giving them a likely timescale for the recruitment and selection process, contacting them when delays occur and, finally, letting them know about the outcome of their application. The use of email systems enables automated responses (perhaps with attachments, such as details of the recruitment timescale), while personnel-management software packages also increase the ease and efficiency of generating letters to candidates.

Although larger employers have relatively greater resources at their disposal, they still tend to resist devoting the staff time, resources and postage costs required to acknowledge candidates' applications. Two-thirds (67.6%) of smaller firms (fewer than 250 staff) routinely acknowledge all applications, while only just over one-fifth (22.2%) of the largest organisations (10,000+ staff) do so. By sector, the practice is very rare in the public sector (where only one in six, 16.4%, do so), rising to six in 10 or more in the private sector (59.8% of services and 65.9% of manufacturers).

Typically, the 250 personnel, HR and recruitment managers we contacted told us that it takes four days for an application to be acknowledged by their organisations, although it takes longer for larger employers and those in the public sector to do so. Many of those we contacted consider that they could do better, as delays can lead to candidates losing interest in the vacancy or forming an unfavourable impression of the organisation's efficiency.

Just over half (55.9%) have recently taken action to reduce this time lag, although larger employers and the public sector have been relatively more active (100% and 84.5%, respectively) – but they had a more pressing need to do so, as we have just seen.

Cost controls

External suppliers are a source of considerable expertise when employers recruit and select candidates, but this comes at a price. Most personnel, HR and recruitment managers have been reviewing their use of employment agencies, headhunters and recruitment advertising agencies to ensure they get the best value for money possible.

As well as negotiating better deals with their existing agencies, employers have been particularly active in the past two to three years in examining alternative options. While many have "shopped around" to see what other suppliers have to offer, others have investigated replacing external sources with in-house provision.

In many cases, the managers we contacted have told us that their re-examination of external suppliers has been driven by a desire to improve the cost-effectiveness of recruitment and selection, rather than being linked to a need to reduce expenditure. In fact, some employers – mainly but not exclusively in the expanding public sector – have simultaneously been given larger recruitment budgets while engaging in cost-cutting on the supplier front.

The particular reasons for the use of a supplier vary according to each employer's requirements and circumstances, and the responses to their cost-effectiveness audits naturally differ. So, while it may be logical to expect that employers will tend to reduce their use of external suppliers as a means of saving costs, some organisations have gone in the opposite direction – because that is the right solution for them.

In all, of the organisations we contacted that have audited their use of employment agencies, more than four in 10 (46.4%) have reduced their usage, but a further three in 10 (30.4%) have increased it. The balance swings the other way among smaller employers with fewer than 250 staff, where one in three (33.3%) have reduced but half (50.0%) have increased their use of agencies, finding them a cost-effective means of sourcing new recruits. Typically, smaller firms are relatively larger users of agencies, and often prefer them to the use of expensive recruitment advertising as a means of gaining access to potential candidates.

Headhunters provide a specialised, in-depth service where senior or specialist vacancies need to be filled. As well as using conventional recruitment advertising, they have access to databases of potential candidates, use networking to approach individuals on a confidential basis, and also undertake the initial screening or shortlisting process. These services are difficult to replace, unless, like much of the public sector, there is resistance to using informal recruitment. Instead, mainstream public advertising is preferred.

There has, therefore, been less change in terms of the use of headhunters – although, the economic downturn has inevitably affected the volume of vacancies they handle. Most often, employers' audits of headhunters' cost-effectiveness has led to no change in their use, while roughly similar proportions of other employers have decided to either increase or decrease the use they make of headhunters' services. In a few very large employers, in-house search and selection services have been set up as replacements for outside providers.

Finally, in terms of external recruitment-related providers, agencies supplying advertising expertise have come under close scrutiny. Recruitment advertising agencies offer a range of services, from designing the advertisement and suggesting its wording and style, to identifying suitable media and negotiating the advertising costs with publishers. Some "total-service" agencies also offer response-handling, where the agency handles and acknowledges their applications.

In all, recruiters' review of their use of advertising agencies has been neutral (35.5% of employers) or negative (with 42.1% reducing their use). Few – just 13.2% – have made the decision to increase their use of these providers.

Recruitment advertising agencies have done particularly badly from employers' cost-effectiveness audits because it is relatively easy to replace their services from internal sources. Personnel, HR and recruitment specialists may take over the task of writing the advertisements and dealing direct with publishers. However, on the down side, employers are unlikely to be able to emulate agencies' ability to negotiate discounts from publishers. But many employers have been reducing their use of conventional print advertising – either because of the economic downturn's impact on their recruitment volumes or because of greater use of corporate websites as a means of advertising their vacancies.

1. Improving the cost-effectiveness of recruitment and selection

Based on an analysis of the feedback we have obtained from hundreds of personnel, HR and recruitment managers, below are the main ways in which they are taking action to improve the cost-effectiveness of their recruitment and selection practices.

1. Improving employers' ability to compete for recruits:

● **Electronic recruitment:** Introducing or increasing the use the internet to advertise vacancies more widely, coupled with the use of email to speed up the receipt of applications, and make it easier for quality candidates to lodge their applications;

● **Technology:** Introducing or increasing the use of technology to speed up the acknowledgement of applications and, thereby, to improve contact with candidates;

● **Line managers:** Giving line managers a greater role in recruitment and selection in order to streamline the process and ensure they "buy in" to appointment decisions;

● **Quality:** Measures to make it easier for candidates to apply for jobs can create problems of quality; many employers are also improving their screening practices to deter unsuitable candidates before they apply or to enable them to reject applications more easily and reliably;

● **Multiple routes:** Alongside the internet and email, employers are increasingly encouraging candidates to contact them by telephone, with some introducing dedicated recruitment answering machines for out-of-hours callers; and

● **Keeping in closer touch:** Many employers now acknowledge receipt of all applications, and many are also reducing the delay in sending out these acknowledgements.

2. Auditing external providers

● Employment agencies, headhunters and recruitment advertising agencies are being audited for their cost-effectiveness.

Cost-effective selection methods

Cost-effectiveness in selection depends on many factors, not least the balance between spending more on higher-cost recruitment methods or selection techniques and the actual improvement in the number and quality of candidates. Well-designed and run assessment centres provide some of the best ways of selecting candidates, but they are also among the most costly of all to develop and use. Few employers would contemplate running a two-day centre to recruit a receptionist, while they might do so for middle-manager appointments.

Despite the wide range of organisation-specific considerations, there is broad agreement among personnel, HR and recruitment specialists about the particular selection methods that their experience shows provide the best balance between expenditure and results. Naturally, the methods of choice vary according to the vacancy being filled. (The most cost-effective recruitment methods – the techniques used to find applicants – are covered in chapter 1.)

A. The cost-effective selection of managers

The most cost-effective methods of selecting managers are, in descending order:

● face-to-face interviews;

● assessment centres; and to a lesser extent

● application forms, CVs, and competency based selection.

Interviewing: Despite the fact that employers usually deploy their most expensive and time-consuming methods when filling managerial vacancies, face-to-face interviews stand head and shoulders above any other selection tool in terms of their reported cost-effectiveness. Almost half of all the personnel, HR and recruitment managers we contacted (48.3%) chose it in preference to any other method – a considerably higher proportion than chose the next most highly rated approach (assessment centres).

The dominance of interviewing in the selection process has puzzled many occupational psychologists. It is notorious for the low results it achieves in identifying potentially suitable recruits. Interviewing is also wide open to many extraneous influences: the mood of the interviewers; the impact of candidates' clothing, body language, ethnicity, gender, and so on. Yet employers consistently report that it represents the key to their selection decision.

However, it is often forgotten that interviewing is perhaps the only selection method that every organisation uses. Assessment centres, for example, are highly thought of, yet remain a minority pursuit because they require access to considerable technical expertise to design and conduct them, and are costly in terms of staff time and other resources. So, even if a relatively greater proportion of employers considers assessment centres to be the best selection method, their low usage inevitably reduces their score. (It is also worth remembering that almost all assessment centres include one or more interviews as part of their battery of selection methods.)

Assessment centres: At some distance behind interviewing, a proportion of employers has nominated assessment centres as their preferred method (four in 10 did so; 39.2% – against 48.3% in respect of interviewing). Provided they have been carefully designed and conducted, assessment centres have repeatedly been found to provide the best means of identifying suitable managerial recruits. Generally, too, they also command respect and credibility among the applicants who participate in them. Assessment centres, being expensive and resource-intensive, tend to be most common among larger organisations. Among those with workforces of 10,000-plus, almost half of the employers concerned chose them as their best selection method, against only three in 10 that did so in respect of interviews.

Competencies: This technique has now entered mainstream personnel practice. It provides an approach to specifying the skills that employers require, both in terms of specific job-related skills and knowledge and in respect of the broader way in which jobs are performed. In most cases, competency frameworks contain definitions of each constituent competency and more detailed assessment information. The latter provides a good starting point for recruitment and selection exercises.

Competencies are the fourth most highly rated method of selecting managers. However, this relatively low score ignores the fact that they provide the foundation for most assessment centres, helping to design the centres, the centre's exercises and the scoring techniques used. Among the employers we contacted, a large majority of assessment-centre users (87.5%) base their centres on competenceis and, as we saw, assessment centres are the second most credible selection method after interviews.

Application forms and CVs: These are the main direct-application methods used by employers for managerial appointments and, in such cases, almost always provide the means by which first- or second-stage shortlists are compiled. In other words, these two methods provide an important gateway to later, more in-depth parts of the selection process.

Overall, application forms and CVs lie in third and fifth place in terms of their status as being the most effective selection methods, according to the employers we contacted. In the public sector, CVs are rarely accepted – even for managerial vacancies – and the importance of forms rises correspondingly. As an illustration, three-quarters of the public sector employers we contacted (72.5%) will only accept application forms, against 5.8% of private sector services firms and 6.2% of manufacturers.

No other selection method was rated as being the most cost-effective option by 1.0% or more employers.

B. The cost-effective selection of IT specialists

The most cost-effective methods of selecting IT specialists are, in descending order:
- face-to-face interviews;
- tests of specific skills and abilities; and to a much lesser extent,
- application forms and assessment centres.

Interviewing: Almost four in 10 (38.8%) of all those we contacted have found that interviewing remains the most cost-effective means of selecting good quality IT staff. Interviews are felt to be the most cost-effective selection method by recruiters in all sizes of organisations.

Tests of specific skills and abilities: While interviewing is seen as the most cost-effective means of selecting IT specialists, many personnel, HR and recruitment specialists find that the insights given by suitable psychometric tests provide valuable information on which to base selection decisions. Technical skills lie at the heart of IT professions, and tests of specific skills, or more general aptitude for computing work, provide an important way of ensuring organisations are making informed selection decisions. Using such tests is also likely to be attractive to potential candidates.

Overall, three in 10 (30.0%) personnel, HR and recruitment specialists consider that tests are more cost-effective tools than interviewing when selecting IT staff, rising to more than one in three (36.5%) private sector services firms.

Application forms and assessment centres: No other method comes close to interviewing and testing as being highly rated by those we contacted, although a few chose either application forms or assessment centres as the most cost-effective means of selecting applicants for IT vacancies.

No other selection method was rated as being the most cost-effective option by 6.0% or more employers.

C. The cost-effective selection of sales staff

The most cost-effective methods of selecting sales staff are:
- face-to-face interviews; and to a much lesser extent
- assessment centres.

Interviewing: More than half (54.1%) of the employers consider that face-to-face interviewing provides the single most cost-effective means of identifying sales staff with potentially high performance. In many instances, interviews can provide a good means of assessing skills that are often crucial to sales roles: the ability to communicate, be persuasive, show self-confidence and, generally, deploy good interpersonal skills. While there are some suitable tests of sales ability and sales potential, fewer than 5% of the personnel, HR and recruitment managers we contacted believe that testing offers the single best means of selecting sales staff.

Assessment centres: While few employers will use assessment centres for routine sales vacancies, they may feature in recruitment to more specialised roles, such as higher-level sales management, or selling involving key accounts or big-ticket products. In all, almost one in five (18.0%) employers told us that assessment centres provide the single most cost-effective selection option at their disposal for sales staff.

No other selection method was rated as being the most cost-effective option by 5.0% or more employers.

D. The cost-effective selection of skilled workers

There are some 3.7 million skilled trades people in the UK, in such industries as construction and building trades, metalworking, engineering and electrical work, agriculture, textiles and printing. According to the employers we contacted, the most cost-effective methods of selecting individuals to such roles are:
- face-to-face interviews; with a few employers preferring
- tests of specific skills and abilities; or
- application forms; or
- assessment centres.

Interviewing: Face-to-face interviewing is considered to be the most cost-effective means of selecting skilled trades people by far the largest single group of employers we contacted. In all, some 44.4% chose it in preference to any other method – almost four times as many as chose the next most highly rated technique: selection testing.

Tests: The work performed by skilled trades people is often more suited to the use of skills tests than many other roles. However, only one in eight employers (12.2%) consider that tests of specific skills and abilities provide the best means of selecting such workers, although this does represent the second-highest proportion, after interviewing.

Application forms: For skilled trades people, application forms attracted the third largest proportion of employers as being their single best selection method, although this represents only a minority of those we contacted (11.1%). Among public sector organisations, however, application forms attracted the second largest proportion of employers (23.3%).

Assessment centres: While few employers use assessment centres when recruiting skilled trades people in general, they may feature in the recruitment to more specialised or demanding roles. In all, one in 10 employers

(10.0%) told us that assessment centres provide the single best selection option at their disposal for some of their vacancies for skilled trades people.

No other selection method was rated as being the most cost-effective option by 7.0% or more employers.

E. The cost-effective selection of semi- and unskilled workers

The most cost-effective methods of selecting individuals for semi- and unskilled vacancies are:
● face-to-face interviews; with a small proportion of employers, mainly in the public sector, preferring
● application forms.

Interviewing: The use of interviewing comes into its own at the lowest levels of the labour market, where employers find it difficult to justify the time and expense of using more demanding methods of selecting candidates. A simple application procedure and an interview are often the limit of the process.

At least twice as many of the employers we contacted singled out interviewing for its effectiveness in selection as opted for another method and, in all, half (48.5%) of them chose it.

Application forms: One in six (17.8%) managers prefer application forms as their most cost-effective method, rising to almost a quarter (23.5%) among public sector employers.

Tests: A further one in 10 (9.9%) cited the use of tests of general ability/aptitude as being their best means of finding potentially effective recruits. Two other types of testing attracted smaller proportions of employers: tests that involve performing a sample or mock-up of the work involved (6.9%), and tests of specific skills and abilities (4.9%).

No other selection method was rated as being the most cost-effective option by more than 4.0% of employers.

F. The cost-effective selection of new graduates

The recruitment of new graduates to management-entry and similar types of programmes represents a specialist activity that is mainly confined to large organisations and firms operating in financial services, consultancy and accountancy.

The most cost-effective methods of selecting new graduates for traditional, mainstream graduate-type roles are:
- assessment centres; and
- face-to-face interviews.

Assessment centres: These are the selection method of choice when employers hire new graduates. Most new graduates have no "track record" on which to base a selection decision, and the ability of assessment centres to provide insights into candidates' performance in work-relevant tasks helps to overcome this problem. In many cases, however – particularly for graduates with non-vocational degrees – employers are more interested in their potential than their immediate work-related skills. Assessment centres score here, too, as they give insights into many transferable competencies – such as interpersonal skills, self-confidence and leadership – that indicate the suitability or otherwise of candidates.

Employers rate assessment centres very highly indeed. They are considered the single best method of making cost-effective selection decisions in respect of new graduates by more than half of all the employers we contacted (58.1%). However, assessment centres are relatively less frequently used by smaller employers because of the time, expense and necessary expertise required. So, while more than eight in 10 (84.2%) of the largest organisations (with 10,000+ staff) told us that assessment centres are most cost-effective, fewer than one in three (31.8%) of the smaller employers (with fewer than 1,000 staff) did so.

Interviewing: More than twice as many employers chose assessment centres as opted for a rival selection method, in terms of its cost-effectiveness. At some distance, just over one in four (28.4%) preferred face-to-face interviews. These can be seen as an alternative. Where assessment centres are relatively little used, employers consider that interviews offer the best means of selecting graduates. So, among smaller employers, more than four in 10 (45.4%) chose interviews, while only one in 20 (5.3%) larger organisations – where assessment centres are almost universally used – chose interviewing as their best method.

No other selection method was rated as being the most cost-effective option by 5.0% or more employers.

G. The cost-effective selection of school-leavers

The most cost-effective methods of selecting school-leavers and other young people are:

● interviews; and
● trial periods of employment.

Interviewing: In terms of the most cost-effective method of selecting young people, one technique stands out: the interview. More than two-thirds (69.0%) of employers told us that the interview works best for them when selecting good-quality young people.

Trial periods: These are a relatively little used option in the recruitment and selection of young people, but receive a disproportionately high vote of confidence (15% of employers consider them their most cost-effective method).

This indicates more organisations could consider using trial periods than presently do so – particularly, given that their rating is even higher in some parts of the economy than the overall results suggest. In smaller firms, especially, trial periods are seen as highly effective, following closely after interviews in terms of being the single most effective selection technique (48% and 32%, respectively). Manufacturers also value trial periods, with over a fifth (22%) choosing them as their most effective technique. Conversely, few employers in the public sector choose them (only 3%, against 90% for the selection interview). This is partly a reflection of their relatively low use in that sector – possibly, due to policy reasons – with less than half as many employers using them as among employers as a whole (16% versus 38%).

No other selection method was rated as being the most cost-effective option by more than 7.0% of employers.

H. Cost-effective selection: an overview

Above (sections A to G), we analysed feedback we obtained from employers about the cost-effectiveness of selection methods in respect of particular types of vacancy. Here, though, we draw on findings from the Chartered Institute of Personnel and Development's research[1] to provide an overview across all types of vacancies.

The most cost-effective selection methods, when generalised across all types of vacancy are, in descending order:
● interviews (32.5% of employers chose this method);
● application forms (18.8%);
● CVs or letters of application (18.4%);
● tests of specific skills (7.1%);
● competency based selection (5.0%);
● assessment centres (4.5%).

No other selection method was rated as being the most cost-effective option by more than 4.0% of employers.

Interestingly, the Institute's research report contrasts the ratings given to particular selection methods with their actual prevalence, and highlights those that employers could investigate introducing.

Generally, the confidence invested by personnel, HR and recruitment managers in particular selection techniques closely corresponds to their actual usage. Of the five most commonly used methods, four also appear among the top five that are considered to be most cost-effective.

The mismatch between relatively high cost-effectiveness and relatively low usage centres on just two selection techniques: competency based selection (ranked fifth in terms of importance, but only 10th in actual usage) and, to a lesser extent, assessment centres. These are ranked sixth in importance, but only ninth in current usage.

Validity

The accuracy of different selection methods in identifying candidates who could become high-performing members of staff provides crucial information when undertaking a cost-effectiveness assessment. However, selection is only as good as the information on which it is based – the analysis of the skills, abilities and other requirements of the vacancy being filled – and the way in which the selection techniques are put into use and the evidence is weighed up by selectors.

Selection methods are usually rated on a 0 (lowest) to 1 (highest) scale in terms of their effectiveness, but there is considerable debate about the actual scores that should be given to each method and, as a result, whether one method is relatively more effective than another. However, with these caveats in mind, here is a typical set of ratings[2] (the different techniques are explained in the sections that follow later in this chapter):

Testing: ability and aptitude tests: 0.5 to 0.55

Assessment centres: 0.4 to 0.6

Interviews: structured: 0.32 to 0.5

Biodata: 0.3 to 0.4

Testing: personality questionnaires: 0.2 to 0.4

Application forms: 0.2

Interviews: unstructured: 0.15 to 0.2

References: 0.15

The main selection methods

Application forms and CVs

Application forms, CVs and letters of application are the prime ways in which employers gather the information they need to shortlist the candidates who will then be asked to undertake further selection methods, such as testing and interviewing. As gatekeepers, helping to determine whether or not an applicant is rejected at the first hurdle, it is vital that application forms and CVs are used effectively. However, while the pros and cons of interviewing are endlessly debated, and the issue of psychometric testing remains as controversial as ever, little attention is paid to the mundane end of the hiring process.

Forms and CVs are often treated as natural alternatives. Many employers, particularly in the private sector, use application forms for certain types of vacancy. But for other vacancies, particularly higher-level ones, application will be expected via CV. However, in the public sector, many employers have tried to avoid accepting CVs and routinely write back to applicants enclosing a form to be completed. In recent years, though, difficulties in recruiting staff have encouraged some public sector bodies to take a more relaxed view and accept CVs for certain posts, particularly at professional and managerial level.

In fact, information on current practices obtained by IRS from recruitment, personnel and HR specialists shows that few other areas of personnel management demonstrate such a marked public–private sector divide as attitudes towards the acceptability of forms and CVs.

In organisations under public ownership, almost three out of four employers (72.5%) will refuse to accept job applications that do not use the official application form. In contrast, more than eight in 10 employers in the private sector have no such policy. They will accept CVs, particularly for more senior vacancies, as well as other forms of application, such as formal letters.

Attitudes towards the use of application forms and CVs also reflect the resources of the organisation, as well as the nature of its ownership. Smaller employers favour more informal recruitment and selection methods, and often rely on CVs – in some cases, to the exclusion of application forms, although more commonly involving the acceptance of both CVs and forms. Generally, the larger the organisation, the more likely it is to require jobseekers to use its approved application form and to reject CVs or other approaches.

It is worth bearing in mind, however, that the nature of the UK economy means that private sector employers tend to be over-represented among small and medium-sized organisations, while the public sector dominates the group of large and very large organisations. So, research findings of practice in larger employers as a whole are usually heavily influenced by public sector activities.

Ironically, though, at the same time as the public sector is becoming more likely to accept CVs in respect of some types of vacancy, the private sector is moving in the opposite direction. This is being driven by the adoption of electronic forms of recruitment. Employers that have gone a stage further beyond simply posting their job advertisements on the internet, and have introduced interactive application methods, are finding that it is more efficient to use online application forms as their method of choice.

This trend is in its early phase, however. Six in 10 employers (60.0%) involved in electronic recruitment accept CVs emailed to them, while only one in three (33.1%) accept completed application forms online.

Application forms

Application forms are widely acknowledged as representing an integral part of the selection process. Research undertaken by the Chartered Institute of Personnel and Development (CIPD) has found that application forms come second only to interviews as the most popular selection tool, with 80% of respondents using them in recruitment[3].

Application forms also seem to justify their continued inclusion in employers' selection processes. According to the CIPD's research, the personnel and HR specialists it contacted found, in their experience, that forms play an important part in the final selection decision, again coming only second to interviews in that respect.

Forms generally constitute the first stage of selecting people for new positions. The basic information they provide – such as personal details, educational background and work experience – is typically used as the basis for identifying those who will go forward to the next part of the selection process. In many cases, most applicants are rejected purely on the basis of the information they provided on the application form.

This, alone, makes an application form as important as any other part of the selection process. But, in addition, the information on the form is often used as a point of reference in respect of those who are shortlisted, particularly by interviewers.

One additional purpose of application forms that is frequently overlooked is their role as a PR tool. Forms are distributed widely by employers. Not only are they seen and used by all job applicants in respect of vacancies where forms are mandatory, but they also reach many other individuals who may have considered applying and then changed their mind. Well-designed, visually appealing forms that are relatively easy to complete will help to support an organisation's image of being a good place to work. Fuzzy photocopies of forms containing densely packed lists of poorly arranged questions will convey the contrary message, regardless of the reality.

As we note in the section below on equal opportunities, many employers develop a single form that they use for a wide range of vacancies, with the result that the questions on the form have to cover a wide range of eventualities. This can make it harder for selectors to conduct shortlisting and exasperate applicants when they are asked to provide information that has little relevance to the job in which they are interested. Research commissioned by the Society of Personnel Officers in Local Government into public sector recruitment found that long application forms put candidates off completing them[4].

One solution to the problem of the rigidity of application forms is to tailor the form to specific vacancies. Forms designed with a core set of questions, supplemented by focused questions for each vacancy or group of vacancies, can help ensure a balance between consistency and flexibility. Given that the most effective application forms are those that pay close attention to the job description and person specification *(see chapter 1)* for the post in question, their validity as a selection method could be greatly enhanced by being designed to be more specific to each post.

Word-processing software available on PCs makes this an easy task. The basic form, with blanks for job-specific questions, could be set up as a template and copied to all those who have the responsibility for recruitment, together with a simple set of guidelines on the template's use. Corporate logos could be scanned in and pasted into the document as a picture insert. Alternatively, the covering page of the form and its standard set of questions could be professionally designed and printed in large quantities. Additional pages of questions tailored to the needs of particular vacancies could then be produced on a PC and simply attached to the covering sheet as required.

Case study A. Peugeot

Coventry-based car manufacturer Peugeot is one company that has changed the design and content of its forms to improve the reliability of its shortlisting process, and cut down the number of people taken forward in the selection process. The application form for one group of workers now includes questions relating to individuals' experience of shiftworking, for example, and the equal opportunities section has also been expanded.

The old application form, which had remained unchanged for a number of years, did not provide Peugeot with enough information to screen out inappropriate candidates. A company spokesperson told us that the new forms have proved successful, helping the company to identify applicants who do not meet its requirements but who may have been invited for production-line tests and interview under the previous system.

Forms and equal opportunities

The growth in interest in diversity policies has focused attention on recruitment and selection. These processes represent the gateway to employment and can make or break any diversity initiative. Diversity extends the principles of equal opportunities beyond protected groups, such as ethnic minorities, to the community as a whole. The usual aim of diversity initiatives is to broaden the workforce, not only for reasons of social equity but in the belief that it provides the means of ensuring the organisation has the widest base of skills, talents and experience at its disposal.

Application forms are widely considered, particularly in the public sector, to be an important way of increasing the objectivity of selection decisions, and it is possible that their use is increasing as result of the interest in diversity. Certainly, the new legal obligations on public sector bodies to foster equality of opportunity mean that they will be encouraged to use application forms to the exclusion of other methods. Forms also provide a convenient vehicle for the gathering of data about the profile of applicants (their ethnicity, gender, age, disability, and so on) that employers require to validate their procedures to ensure they do not discriminate unfairly.

One employer in our research told us that its diversity initiatives include providing "advice to applicants on how to complete their application form, [as well as] removing all personal information from application forms before they are seen by the shortlisting panel". Another mentioned that forms provide a useful method of emphasising an organisation's commitment to equal opportunities or diversity. In this case, the organisation is now including "diversity statements in advertising material and [on] job application forms".

However, such organisations have to compete in the same labour market as many other employers. Many jobseekers' experience of recruitment practices, particularly in the private sector, does not prepare them for the use of application forms, and this can put organisations that insist on their use at a competitive disadvantage. One public sector authority, for example, told us that "we have to . . . try to make it as easy as possible to allow applicants to apply, eg the internet and CVs accepted at the preliminary stage".

Why are application forms considered to be fairer than the use of CVs? Certainly, there are advantages and disadvantages associated with each method of application. The main benefit of the application form is that it sets a level playing field: all applicants are required to answer the same questions in the same way, which should aid objectivity. The advantage, in this instance, lies in helping selectors be as objective and systematic as possible.

An application form also offers advantages to the person completing it, in that, like any form, it offers a ready made structure that removes much of the uncertainty from the process of providing information. In contrast, astute applicants submitting a CV will aim to tailor their standard document to the needs of the employer. This involves attempting to understand its selection criteria, draw out the individual's relevant skills and experience, and structure it in such a way that their best points stand out. A well-researched and structured application form does this work for the jobseeker.

But application forms are rarely well-researched, designed and laid out. Many employers, indeed, have one standard form that has to suit all possible types of vacancy. It encourages them to develop a "catch-all" form that asks a range of questions in the hope that some of them will be relevant to the vacancy being filled at the particular time. This means that many questions will ask generic questions about previous experience, formal qualifications, training courses and so on, in order to provide a mass of detail from which selectors will be able to extract the specific details that relate to a particular job.

It is common practice for distinctions to be made on application forms between "current" and "previous" employment. This could deter, or work to the a disadvantage of, a candidate who has taken a break to look after a child or older relative or who is unemployed. Nationally, unemployment is relatively more common among some ethnic minority groups than others, and much less so among whites. Similarly, the practice could discourage a person from applying if they have concerns about the length of time they have been in their current position. This could particularly affect older people, who often have longer periods of job tenure.

The Equal Opportunities Commission's Guidelines for equal opportunities employers[5] advises that "some questions on application forms could be unlawful" for one or two reasons. First, a question may constitute "less favourable treatment" of one gender, even where the form is completed by applicants of both sexes. Second, the way in which the information supplied on the form is used may constitute unlawful discrimination.

The Commission adds that some questions could send out the message that the organisation intends to practise unfair discrimination, even where no such intention exists. This could deter some applicants, lead to an atmosphere of mistrust and (although it does not say this explicitly) encourage tribunal applications from unsuccessful candidates. Answers to such questions could also make it more difficult for selectors to do their job objectively and fairly.

"Examples of such questions deal with family, ages of children, married/single/divorced status, intentions about engagement and/or about having children, intimate personal questions and so on," it says. Where medical information is sought, it adds that questions should be carefully worded to be neutral rather than being directed at one sex.

Application forms could also work against equality of opportunity on the grounds of ethnicity. For example, forms that use a level of English that is more demanding than that required in the job being filled could discriminate against some individuals from ethnic minority groups or, more generally, against applicants with lower levels of literacy. Similar considerations apply where forms instruct candidates to complete them in their own handwriting. This could discriminate against the same groups and also against some candidates with disabilities. As well as being good practice to take account of such considerations, they are reflected in the Commission for Racial Equality's Employment Code of Practice which is admissible in relevant tribunal cases.

Information that should have no bearing on the selection decision is also often collected via application forms, such as marital status (including titles such as Mrs and Miss), age or date of birth and nationality. Not only could selectors be subconsciously influenced by such details, their inclusion could also encourage applicants to believe that the organisation has not treated them fairly. Acas – and several other bodies – recommends[6] that this information, and medical details, should be collected via a tear-off section or separate sheet.

Indeed, the collection of medical information presents broader issues to consider. While employers are reluctant to recruit someone who is liable to take frequent or extended periods of absence, the inclusion of questions about medical details can deter applicants with disabilities from applying – particularly, where questions about disabilities and health appear after each other on the application form.

Medical questions are generally permissible under the Disability Discrimination Act 1995. But employers do have an alternative where they follow up job references. As chapter 4 shows, employers frequently ask current and former employers about applicants' absence records, and the general practice of following up references at a late stage, usually not until the preferred candidate for the post has been identified, means that this information would only need to be obtained in respect of a few individuals.

Designing an application form so as to gather information on the skills and attributes of the candidate that are relevant to the job is one way of addressing the above issues.

The result of the use of generic application forms is that applicants will often be required to complete questions that have little or no obvious relevance to the job they are interested in – the form will lack "face validity". For example, applicants for a senior managerial job could well be asked to list the subjects and grades of all their GCSEs or O-levels, despite most of them having taken these examinations perhaps 15 or 20 years previously, and being convinced that the information will be disregarded by selectors.

Application forms should provide the means of focusing on important work-related abilities. But where they are used in a mechanistic way, there is a danger that they create an additional hurdle that can work against equality of opportunity and effective selection. Candidates with previous experience of applying via forms – or who are simply good at form-filling – can gain an advantage over other applicants who may be equally or better qualified for the job. This problem arises because many employers' application forms follow the same pattern, in terms of the information required and the order in which it is requested on the form, so that individuals with previous application experience get to "know the ropes". And within particular organisations, the tendency to use a standard catch-all form for all vacancies can favour candidates who are willing and able to answer all the questions, no matter how tangentially related to the job, over other applicants who may be less proficient in form-filling.

The debate about the relative merits of CVs and forms continues, particularly in terms of their impact on equality of opportunity. Some public sector organisations, where forms have traditionally been used as a means of promoting equality, are becoming more convinced that forms are the better means of lodging an application. Others, in contrast, have growing doubts about this view. Brighton and Hove City Council, for example, has been reviewing its reliance on forms, and told us that there is a view that permitting CV applications in some cases would open up the recruitment process to members of the community who may find it difficult to complete the standard form.

Data protection

There is now another compelling reason for not using a standard application form across all vacancies. The Employment Practices Data Protection Code has significant implications for the use of application forms. The Code, which provides guidance on the interpretation of the Data Protection Act 1998, covers areas such as privacy, transparency, necessity and currency. The Code is likely to be implemented later in 2003 or in the first half of 2004.

In terms of necessity, information should be collected only when it is needed for selection. This casts doubt on the use of standard forms as, by their very design, they invariably request information that is not specifically relevant to a particular vacancy. Under the Code, personnel and HR professionals should ensure that the information requested on a job application form is not "excessive, irrelevant or inadequate".

The Code specifies that if sensitive information is collected, such as that relating to racial or ethnic origin, political opinions or sexual life, at least one "sensitive-data condition" must be satisfied. The specific circumstances in which such data can be obtained are spelled out and include reasons such as: a legal obligation in connection with employment; where the individual in question has given explicit consent; or as part of equal opportunities monitoring.

The Code sets out these further benchmarks with reference to job applications:

● "state, on any application form, to whom the information is being provided and how it will be used, if this is not self-evident;

● only seek personal data that are relevant to the recruitment decision to be made;

● only request information about an applicant's criminal convictions if that information can be justified in terms of the role offered. If this information is justified, make it clear that spent convictions do not have to be declared, unless the job being filled is covered by the Exceptions Order to the Rehabilitation of Offenders Act 1974;

● explain any checks that might be undertaken to verify the information provided in the application form including the nature of additional sources from which information may be gathered; and

● provide a secure method for sending applications."

2. Application forms: improving their effectiveness

● Wherever possible, tailor the form to the particular needs of the vacancy.

● The questions should relate to the purposes for which the form is intended, such as shortlisting, obtaining formal permission to conduct reference-checks and ensuring applicants provide a formal declaration of the accuracy of the information.

● Shortlisting usually involves concentrating on ensuring candidates meet essential minimum criteria; the form should be designed to elicit this, and – in order to reduce its length and complexity – only this, information.

● Information that is only required of the successful candidate need not be collected from all applicants, such as national insurance details, date of birth, marital status and being legally able to work in the UK.

● Forms should contain details of the return address and closing date; where a standard form is used, details of the vacancy for which the application is being made are also required.

● Information for monitoring purposes, that is used to check that the selection process is not unfairly discriminating against particular groups, should be gathered on a separate form. Details that should be irrelevant to the selection decision – such as date of birth or age, marital status, nationality and disability – should not be requested on the application form; they could subconsciously influence selectors and could undermine candidates' confidence in the objectivity of the selection process.

● However, it may be useful to include a question on the application form itself giving individuals with disabilities the opportunity to request reasonable adjustments to the selection procedure, under the terms of the Disability Discrimination Act 1995.

● Employers should ensure that the use of application forms does not disadvantage particular groups; for example, that the standard of literacy used in the questions or is required to answer them is not more demanding than the job itself demands; applicants with disabilities should be able to submit their application in ways that reflect reasonable adjustments to accommodate their disability, such as submitting an alternative version using a PC or typewriter, or one recorded on tape.

● The number of questions and the length of application forms should be commensurate with the demands of the vacancy being filled, and aim to be as short as possible.

● The space allotted to each answer should reflect its importance in affecting the selection decision and the amount of information that candidates are likely to wish to provide.

● Selection criteria should be interpreted carefully to avoid unfair discrimination and rejecting potentially valuable candidates. For example, formal qualifications are often used as a proxy for required minimum levels of knowledge, and using the form to obtain evidence of such knowledge could be more useful that asking about paper certificates. Some types of skill – particularly transferable ones such as decision-making, organisation, assertiveness and the ability to work with others – can be developed and demonstrated in several contexts, not just at work, and forms could be designed to collect this information.

● Application forms are more effective in gathering some types of information about candidates than other selection methods, and forms should build on these strengths. For example, forms are better than interviews in gathering factual details of a job-relevant nature, and covering formal aspects such as obtaining signed declarations and consents.

● Each version of an application form should be piloted to ensure its questions, layout, design and structure are candidate-friendly, and that selectors find it easy to use in shortlisting candidates according to job-relevant criteria.

● The process of supplying application forms, through the post, using email or via the internet, affords a good point of contact with candidates that should be used to provide them with background information about the job and organisation, a monitoring form and the key selection criteria being used.

● Application forms should ask candidates to be honest and instruct candidates to sign their name to attest to this; the form should state that the information they supply will be verified and that significant inaccuracies could result in disqualification or dismissal.

Interviewing

Interviews are the most widely used – and often the most widely condemned – of all selection tools, an irony that has long been recognised.

The criticisms are well documented and often based on convincing research evidence, the most frequent focusing on the unreliability and poor predictive quality of traditional interviews compared with more sophisticated selection methods such as some forms of psychological testing. At worst, some critics argue that hiring decisions based on interviewing can be no better than tossing a coin. Almost as damning are the accounts in the popular press of some interviewers' eccentric approach to interviewing job candidates, asking bizarre questions or indulging in "stress interviewing" that owes more to interrogation techniques than the skilful, yet polite investigation of candidates' abilities.

The fact remains that interviewing is a universal practice. Even if employers were to wish to discontinue it, the resistance of candidates would prevent them. This reflects the dual purpose of the process. Interviews are selection techniques in their own right, but they also provide a crucial means of establishing a relationship between the prospective employer and the individual that no other commonly used selection method seems able to replicate.

Would-be recruits wish to view the environment in which they would be working, meet prospective managers and, perhaps, colleagues, and get a taste of the culture and atmosphere of the organisation. Another key feature that would be difficult to replace involves the opportunity for both parties to undertake some negotiation concerning issues such as salary levels and possible start dates.

An interview should be an interactive, two-way process: not only is the candidate's potential suitability for the post under consideration, but the organisation is open to scrutiny as a prospective employer. Although the selector is generally in a more powerful position, the final decision in the process rests with the favoured candidate in deciding whether or not to accept an offer of appointment. The PR opportunity for projecting a favourable but realistic impression of the organisation should therefore not be mishandled.

The multi-purpose nature of interviewing – selection technique, a meeting to help social or psychological bonding, the chance for applicants to learn more about the employer, a negotiation session to thrash out contractual issues – provides a major explanation for the high esteem in which employers hold it. When those with experience of recruitment and selection are asked for their feedback on the most important aspects of the process, interviewing consistently comes top of the poll (with the single exception of assessment centres in the minority of employers that use them; *see the section earlier in this chapter*).

The key point to bear in mind when conducting interviews is that their success in selecting the most suitable candidates can vary markedly depending on the approach that is adopted. There is a wide range of techniques that can enhance the effectiveness of interviews. Their predominance as a selection practice makes it even more vital that employing organisations consider incorporating the most effective forms of interviewing in their practices. As well as the information and analysis in this handbook, the reader may be interested in *Guidelines for best practice in selection interviewing* issued by SHL, the psychometric-test publisher formerly known as Saville & Holdsworth (free from www.shlgroup.com).

3. Interview techniques

Setting aside distinct interview approaches such as structured interviewing *(see checklist 4)*, there are several important guidelines to bear in mind when steering the interview process. (*See checklist 5* for equal opportunities issues in interviewing.)

● **Training:** All interviews should have received adequate training in interviewing skills and issues related to ensuring equality of opportunity.

● **Planning and preparation:** Interviews should be based on carefully analysed job criteria and accompanied by an interviewer guide *(see checklist 4)*. Interviews should draw on information already available on the candidate, such as obtained from the application form or CV. It is often preferable to use teams of two or three interviewers, but there should be prior discussion about each person's role, the questions they will ask, and so on. The time allocation, time for pre- and post-interview reviews, arrangements for conducting candidates to and from reception, refreshments, interview expenses, and a quiet, undisturbed room should all be organised in advance.

● **Information exchange:** Candidates will expect to obtain information from interviewers as well as giving it to them; however, much information can be provided by other means, saving valuable interview time.

● **Closed questions:** Unless designed to clarify a small and simple point, closed questions that require only a "yes" or "no" response should not be asked. An example of such a question could be: "Do you work well as part of a team?" If this type of questioning is used too frequently, it would result in a stilted dialogue that could prevent any useful exchange of information. Some closed questions are also easy for interviewees to guess the required answer ("Are you punctual?"; "Do you like challenges?").

● **Leading questions:** These questions are also capable of suggesting the required answer. A typical introduction to this type of question is: "Do you agree that...", thereby giving a strong indication of the expected answer. The interviewee is faced with either passively agreeing with what is effectively a statement rather than a question, or contradicting the interviewer. Interviewers should therefore take care to draft neutral questions that do not contain an opinion, implied or otherwise.

● **Multiple questions:** Interviewers should also refrain from asking multiple questions that address more than one issue at a time. Apart from the confusion this creates for the candidate, it is usually the last question that will be answered. An example of this type of question would be: "What did you learn from the experience, has it changed your approach to dealing with customers, and how have you applied the lessons in your current role?"

● **Hypothetical questions:** Situational or hypothetical questions have limited uses. They may be able to provide insights into ways in which interviewees would approach an unfamiliar part of the job, but they are vulnerable to candidates who exaggerate or falsify their answers.

● **Providing explanations:** Asking candidates to provide explanations for their successes or failures[7] does not necessarily provide reliable information; some types of answer have been found to influence interviewers more favourably than others of equal validity, and individuals are not necessarily able to understand their own motives and emotions. The practice is also open exaggeration or falsification by the interviewee.

● **"Stress" questions:** These are sometimes used as part of a deliberate interviewing strategy. This type of question is combative and designed to put the candidate under pressure to gauge reactions to stressful or difficult situations.

There are several reasons why such an aggressive interviewing approach should be avoided. It places the interviewee in an uncomfortable and unfair position, and the reactions shown are likely to be artificial and unreliable as a measure of behaviour. It can provoke a reaction by the candidate against the employer, which they could pass on to their friends and family. This might rebound against the organisation in deterring future applications and in losing customers.

More immediately, stress questioning can provoke a strong reaction on the part of the interviewee, and interviewers must be able to handle the emotions they evoke and ensure that the situation does not get out of hand. This demands considerable levels of skill that are best developed through the provision of suitable training.

● **Open-ended questioning**: The most effective questions are open-ended ones that encourage candidates to respond fully. These questions usually start with words such as "what", "when" and "why". To avoid long, rambling answers, variations can be made to the open format that narrows the scope of the reply; for example: "Tell me about a situation where you have had to make a difficult decision at work recently".

● **Probing**: Another useful technique linked to the open-ended approach is the follow-up or probing question, which may be used to obtain supplementary information from the interviewee. The format for this type of questioning may be open or closed. For example, an open-ended question would be: "Can you elaborate on what advice you gave to the client?" while a closed, probing question could be: "How many employees reported to you at that time?" Probing questions can be effective, and it is hard to imagine an interview taking place without the need to clarify some of the interviewee's responses in more depth. Indeed, candidates will often expect interviewers to pose follow-up questions, and some types of structured interview formats that preclude the use of probing may seem unnatural and intimidating. The only drawback to follow-up questions lies in when they are used too frequently, which can create an interrogatory atmosphere for the candidate.

● **Opening questions**: Effective interviewing should begin on a positive note, with a few simple questions geared towards putting the candidate at ease. This will set the tone for the interview. Questions and issues of greater complexity should be raised in the middle part of the interview, with the final part reserved for clarifying any issues that were raised during the interview.

● **Active listening**: This is a vital skill for an interview situation, and enables the interviewer to concentrate on what is being said and act as a positive presence for the candidate. Body language assumes a significant role here and it is possible to create a relaxed environment, where the candidate feels confident, just by nodding or smiling encouragingly at appropriate moments (be aware, though, that there are cultural and ethnic differences in body language).

Feedback and summarising are other techniques that can be employed to good effect, to reflect on or clarify the interviewee's responses.

● **"Pet" questions:** Many interviewers, particularly line managers untrained in selection techniques, develop one or more favourite questions that they believe offer the key to choosing able candidates. These questions are unlikely to have been validated for their actual effectiveness, and are often thrown in with little or no regard to the order, structure or job-relevance of the interview schedule. The answers are likely to be used subjectively, and such questions can disconcert candidates because of their lack of relevance or disruption to the proper flow of the interview.

● **No-noes:** Rudeness, abruptness, lack of attention to the candidate (such as using the telephone), making personal remarks and poor timekeeping by interviewers (unless unavoidable and accompanied by an explanation) will discourage applicants from giving their best performance at interview; more generally, they will give a poor impression of the prospective employer and encourage applicants to go elsewhere.

Structured interviewing

The one consistent and clear message that emerges from much of the research into selection interviewing is that structured interviews offer far superior results in predicting future job performance than their unstructured counterparts.

Structured interviews, as their name implies, provide interviewers with a framework that they follow when interviewing each candidate. The questions are derived from an analysis of the selection criteria for the vacancy (which, in turn, are usually based on accurate and up-to-date job descriptions and person specifications; *see chapter 1 for information on these tools*). The questions are worded carefully to elicit evidence from the candidate about the degree to which they satisfy the key selection criteria, and the order in which they are asked is carefully considered to present a logical, understandable sequence that helps the candidate engage fully with the interview.

How far should the structure dictate the format of the interview? Here, attitudes and practice vary considerably.

No deviation: Some employers, particularly those in the public sector, consider that much of the benefits of using the technique will be lost if the structure is adapted in any way. This means that each question is asked in exactly the same way, using the same wording. And follow-up questions – where replies are ambiguous or incomplete, for example – are either asked of all candidates or none at all.

The advantage of this approach is that much greater consistency is produced, in that each interviewee is treated as equally as possible.

The two main disadvantages are, first, that the interview can appear stilted and unnatural. Some interviewers may actually read out the questions almost as a dictation exercise, without any pretence at spontaneity. Candidates can be unnerved by this atmosphere, particularly where they do not obtain any feedback to their answers. Questioning can become a polite, low key form of interrogation. Second, refusing to sanction the flexible use of follow-up questions means that some candidates could be asked unnecessary, and apparently nonsensical, questions, while other might give unsatisfactory answers that the prescribed probing question might not address. Given that the aim of interviewing should be to obtain as much evidence as possible of candidates' potential suitability, failure to clarify or amplify answers could be a disservice to both parties.

More flexibility: In other organisations, though, the interview structure is used with varying degrees of flexibility. Some interviewers may, for example, ask the questions in a way that comes more naturally to them, in terms of their vocabulary and method of expression. And follow-up questioning may not be pre-determined, but used when and where necessary according to the answer that a particular candidate has just given.

The advantages and disadvantages of adopting a more flexible approach to structured interviewing are mirror images of those mentioned immediately above. A limited amount of flexibility can give a more lively, natural and informal feel to the interview, helping to put the candidate at their ease and, thus, giving them the best chance of presenting themselves to their best advantage. However, the consistency that structured interviewing offers over less formal methods can be undermined where interviewers deviate from the "script". And the greater objectivity of the technique can be reduced where this deviation has been prompted by interviewers' conscious or unconscious reactions to particular interviewees.

Case study B. Introducing structured interviewing

Birmingham-based firm of solicitors **Amery-Parkes** has been updating its interviewing procedures. It has introduced a system for recording each stage of the interview process, which includes the interview panel's structured interview and assessment, with pre-prepared questions based on a competency framework. Interview records are retained for at least six months, mainly for feedback purposes. Training for interviewers has also been reviewed.

Cornwall County Fire Brigade has also adopted a structured approach to conducting its "point-of-entry" selection interviewing. Although a national framework for the fire service ensures consistency by setting out the specific areas that interview questions should cover – such as health and safety, interest in the fire service, and equality and fairness – the exact content and wording can be determined locally. The questions must, however, be designed so that candidates have the opportunity to demonstrate certain competencies that are set out on the interview sheet next to the appropriate question.

All questions asked at the interview are prepared beforehand by the panel members, and only the panel member who set a particular question may put it to the candidate and ask any supplementary questions. All panel members will have a copy of the question and a suggested model answer so that they are competent to assess candidates' answers. These are scored from one to six on a rating scale, which includes an explanation for each score. The process is designed to be as objective and fair as possible. Each panel member scores independently and, at the end of the interview, the ratings are averaged to determine which candidates were successful. Candidates are provided with feedback on their assessment where possible as part of a "debrief".

Assessment guides: Many structured interviews use an interviewer assessment guide, that provides both a prepared script of questions and a scale for measuring candidates' responses; *see checklist 4 for more information.*

Many employers are adopting structured interviewing, according to feedback obtained by IRS from personnel, HR and recruitment managers. This is particularly true among those with larger workforces. Just under half (47%) of organisations with workforces of 250 to 999 use the technique, rising to three-quarters (74%) of those employing more than 10,000 people.

The incidence of structured interviews is at its lowest in larger manufacturing and production companies (where around one-third use it), and highest among public sector employers (where as many as nine in 10 use it). Local councils, for example, have a strong tradition of developing highly structured interview formats, the use of a panel of interviewers (with two, and often three or more, interviewers) and standard questioning that includes set questions on equal opportunities issues.

The CIPD points to the very poor predictive ability of unstructured interviews in its recruitment guidelines and recommends[8] that, to have any value, interviews should:

● always be conducted or supervised by suitably trained individuals;

● be structured to follow a previously agreed set of questions mirroring the person specification or job profile of the vacancy; and

● allow candidates the opportunity to ask questions.

4. Developing an interviewer guide

An interviewer guide is one of the key characteristics that distinguishes a structured interview. Its goals are simple: to ensure that the interview questions are arranged in the most logical order, and that all candidates are asked the same questions in the same sequence. The guide should contain both the questions and a rating scale to mark each candidate's answer to each question, complete with benchmark answers if a behavioural format is adopted. As well as acting as a blueprint for the way in which the interview should progress through each of its stages, the guide paves the way for consistent measurement of candidates' suitability for the post.

Although the development of such a guide requires time and effort, there are several benefits to be gained. Once a guide has been developed, its skeleton can be applied to different jobs, although the specific questions and typical answers will need to be altered. The interviewer guide can also be used in its entirety for future hiring rounds for the same position, providing the job profile does not change. This will save preparation time in the future, particularly if the job category is one with several people in post. An important advantage of having a structured interview plan is that it reduces the risk of discrimination claims, as there will be evidence to show that all candidates were dealt with in a consistent manner and judged on objective criteria.

● **Preliminary guidance:** This should provide advice on basic points, such as the need to treat all candidates the same throughout the interview and ask the same questions. It is worth reminding interviewers to avoid any questions that could be construed as discriminatory, such as those dealing with age, domestic responsibilities or marital status. The guidance should highlight the need for the interviewer to take notes and to ensure that information on the candidate, such as CV and/or application form, is close to hand.

● **Organise the questions:** As well as the need to ask job-related questions based on a person specification and/or the competencies required for the role, the questions should flow in a logical manner. Organise the material by grouping together questions that address similar topics and start the interview with simple questions, moving on to the more complex issues as the interview progresses.

● Develop a measurement section: Each question should be accompanied by the performance expectation based on the benchmark answer, together with examples of "good", "average" and "poor" responses. The competency requirements to achieve each task should also be included in order that the interviewer has a clear understanding of why each question is being asked.

● **Starting the interview:** The interview should begin with the aim of making the candidate feel at ease. Explain the interview process; for example, if it is a panel interview, outline who will be asking the questions, their names and positions in the organisation. If more than one interview is planned, advise the interviewee of the schedule for the different interviews and who they will be meeting.

● **Closing the interview:** Candidates should have the opportunity to have their own questions answered. Describe the next steps in the schedule and when the interviewee can expect to have feedback on the results of the interview.

Interviewing and equal opportunities

The main risk associated with interviews, and the reason for much of the criticism levelled against them, is the vulnerability of the interviewer to making subjective decisions. In its most blatant form, this could leave the recruiting organisation open to claims of discrimination. Both the Commission for Racial Equality[9] and the Equal Opportunities Commission[10] recommend that all interviewers are given training in the anti-discrimination statutes.

There are some obvious areas to avoid in questioning a candidate, such as queries concerning marital status or the number of children they have. Even if the same question were asked of all candidates, regardless of gender, such a question could still be construed as discriminatory against women.

There are other, more subtle errors that can creep into the selection process. The danger is slipping into making prejudiced assumptions based on the interviewer's own personal system of beliefs. This can result in unfair stereo-typing, where the interviewer's own opinions are projected onto the candidate without any objective reference to job-related criteria. It can be difficult to eliminate all traces of subjectivity from the interviewing process, but it is possible to create an environment that greatly reduces the risks.

5. Improving equal opportunities in interviewing

● Interviewer training can improve their awareness of their own assumptions and biases, help develop the skills involved in conducting more objective, non-discriminatory interviewing, and enhance awareness of the relevant legislation.

● More objective methods of interviewing – notably, structured interviewing based on thorough job analysis – can be introduced.

● Some candidates with disabilities may require reasonable adjustments to be made to the interview location, timing or its procedure. An interviewee may require a companion, for example to provide signing for a candidate with hearing difficulties or to provide support where a candidate has learning difficulties.

● Irrelevant personal details, such as age and ethnicity, can be removed from the information given to interviewers and others involved in selection.

● Decisions about a particular candidate's suitability should be based on objective information. Where particular issues are involved – such as flexibility, ability to travel long distances and/or stay overnight, ability to work shifts (or, for people with disabilities, discussions about more general issues concerning their ability to perform the job) – these should be discussed objectively with the candidate. Assumptions about suitability based on gender, sexual orientation, marital status, caring responsibilities, partner's occupation and circumstances, ethnicity, nationality, religion, disability, trade union membership and (forthcoming) age may amount to unlawful discrimination.

● Evidence of suitability for the vacancy should avoid being related to specific ways in which the suitability might have been acquired; for example, questions concerning leisure or sporting interests might put women at an unfair disadvantage (domestic responsibilities on top of work commitments could reduce women's opportunities to pursue such interests); similarly, mechanistic judgments based on years of service tend to favour men given that women may have broken periods of service due to childcare responsibilities.

● Interviewing could involve pairs of interviewers. Bias and subjectivity can be reduced where more than one assessment of each interviewee is available, particularly where the interview panel involves a mix of genders, ethnicities, ages and experiences of disabilities. In addition, claims of harassment or discrimination against a particular interviewer will be more difficult to substantiate where one or more witnesses are present.

● The regular use of monitoring, where applicants are tracked through each stage of the selection procedure according to their gender, ethnicity, disability and age, can highlight areas where discrimination may be occurring and further investigation is warranted.

Case study C. The London Borough of Harrow

The London Borough of Harrow has put in place a number of measures to ensure that interviews are not only bias-free but promote diversity. All interviews follow a structured format and are carried out by no less than two interviewers. Moreover, for senior appointments, the panel must include an ethnic minority member of staff, and this practice is recommended for interviews at all levels. As a representative from the Employee Relations Unit told us: "We try to ensure that interview panels are balanced in terms of ethnicity and also gender. This not only helps combat discrimination but also promotes the council's image as an equal opportunities employer." The council regularly reviews its recruitment and selection processes to ensure that they continue to be effective.

Number of interviewers

One important and unavoidable decision for recruiting organisations is to decide on the number of interviewers. There are various pros and cons to all the possible formats. One-to-one interviews are the simplest to arrange and have the advantage of creating an informal and unthreatening atmosphere for candidates. This format is perhaps most suitable for an initial screening exercise. Feedback from personnel, HR and recruitment managers obtained by IRS shows that, overall, one-third (32%) conduct face-to-face interviewers with a single interviewer present. The incidence of the one-to-one approach is greatest among private sector services firms, with six in 10 (59%) such companies favouring a single interviewer compared with just 3% of public sector organisations.

The downside to this approach is that a lone interviewer will find it onerous to listen effectively to what the candidate is saying, take notes and consider what points to explore in more detail, all at the same time. This type of interview is also more open to allegations of bias or malpractice, as there is no opportunity to check perceptions or assumptions with another interviewer, nor call on them as a witness to help refute such claims.

These drawbacks can be alleviated to some extent by the use of two interviewers or a panel interview. There is almost no limit to the number of interviewers that can be present in a panel interview, but it should be remembered that facing more than two or three people across a room could be an intimidating experience and is unlikely to encourage a relaxed and informative dialogue. A possible solution is to conduct sequential interviews, where the candidate is interviewed by several people consecutively, but sees no more than one or two interviewers at a time. This approach would enable interviewers to exchange opinions on the candidate's suitability for the post, but would avoid the artificial and potentially unproductive environment created by a panel interview.

The key point to remember with both panel and sequential interviewing is to agree beforehand what areas each interviewer will cover. Otherwise, some issues will be covered twice, others missed entirely, and panel members could talk across each other, with the result that candidates will be confused and form an unfavourable impression of the organisation.

Case study D. Danzas

Danzas, a transport and logistics company, favours one-to-one interviews over panel interviews. It considers that panel interviews, where three or more people ask questions, can be intimidating and adversarial, and prove difficult to manage. It limits the number of interviewers to a maximum of two and, if necessary, its managers conduct interviews with candidates consecutively. Overall, the company views other selection tools, such as technical capability and interpersonal skills testing, as more reliable although it has found that interviews can serve as a useful vehicle to judge more subjective elements of the appointment such as cultural fit.

The number of stages involved in the interview process represents a further important consideration affecting an organisation's selection practices. Not only do some organisations conduct sequential interviewing, where each candidate may be interviewed separately by two or more interviewers, but considerably greater numbers of employers call back some candidates for a second-stage interview after the initial interview has been used to compile a reduced shortlist. The remaining candidates are then interviewed afresh by the same panel or different members of staff. In some cases, the final stage may be more of a formality undertaken with the favoured candidate to discuss contractual details. Broadly, the more senior the job, the more likely it is for there to be more than one interview stage.

Calling candidates back to attend successive interview stages is a time-consuming and costly arrangement, and one that inevitably slows down the process of reaching a final decision. This can mean that employers must leave vacancies unfilled for longer periods, incur higher reimbursement costs for interviewees' travel expenses, and must allocate greater amounts of staff time to interviewing. Slower-footed employers also face the possibility that the best candidates could receive job offers from competitors.

Conversely, the process of ensuring that candidate and prospective employer are closely matched in their requirements may require more than one interview. The psychological aspect of interviewing where candidate and employer come to know each other and form a bond can also take longer to achieve than the duration of an initial interview. Both these considerations tend to be most relevant to more senior positions.

Situational interviewing

Situational interviewing aims to obtain insights into candidates' transferable skills, by extrapolating their answers to hypothetical ("What if .. ?") questions to important parts of the job being filled. The concept assumes that candidates' immediate reactions – their typical attitudes and behaviours – to such questions will reveal those they are most likely to bring to bear on a situation they encounter in the job.

Situational interviewing can involve asking candidates to adopt a problem-solving approach ("What would you do if . . . ?"). As with all types of situational interviewing, the interviewee is not required to relate the answer to their direct experience.

The advantage of situational questioning is that, in one sense, it creates a level playing field, particularly if the interview is structured so that all candidates are presented with the same predetermined questions and situations. All candidates have a fair chance of crafting an appropriate answer, even if they have never encountered an identical or similar scenario.

This also raises the main concern with situational formats. Although this approach does not preclude candidates drawing on previous examples where they have displayed relevant competencies or abilities, a fast-thinking candidate can provide the "right" answer while offering no guarantee that they would react the same way were the situation to recur once they were appointed.

The validity of situational interviewing as a selection technique should therefore be considered carefully. Validity is a key criterion for evaluating the effectiveness of any selection method and refers to the accuracy of the conclusions that can be drawn from any particular technique. Asking scenario-type questions that are not based on a candidate's real experience may heighten the lack of precision with which it is possible to predict future job performance from statements made at interview.

Behavioural questioning

Behavioural questioning – also termed the Patterned Behavioural Description Interview – is probably the least common technique adopted by organisations but, if done properly, can yield reliable results. Behavioural interviewing focuses exclusively on actual events or "critical incidents" in the candidate's past to enable the interviewer to hear evidence of how the candidate has previously demonstrated the behaviours and abilities considered essential to the post. The reasoning behind this approach is that individuals are likely to have faced many situations that are similar in terms of the competency requirements needed to deal with them effectively, even though they may have taken place in different contexts.

As the aim is to draw out past incidents of when the interviewee has shown those abilities or behaviours that are relevant to the current job, behavioural questioning is usually used in competency-based interviews. An example may be a job in which time management is considered a core competency. A behavioural question might involve asking for an illustration of how the candidate has prioritised tasks of equal importance and conflicting deadlines. Although it may be easier for the candidate to draw parallels with past job-related situations, this does not have to be the case and it should be acceptable for an individual to recount non-work experiences, providing the examples display evidence of the competency requirement.

When questioned, interviewees will often supply quite a broad description of a past incident. If this is the case, supplementary questions will need to be asked by the interviewer to probe for more detail about how the candidate behaved.

Case study E. Staffordshire Police

Staffordshire Police uses a wide range of selection techniques to assist in the recruitment, selection and promotion of staff. Despite the broad range of options available, interviewing remains the most popular selection method for the organisation. Interviews are essentially used to obtain evidence of transferable skills, as practical skills, knowledge and aptitude would be assessed through other methods.

There are several ways in which candidates are supported in advance of the interview. They are provided with information about the vacancy, such as the scope of the job, as well as the role profile and person specification. In addition, they are informed of the nature of the selection process, including test procedures where appropriate, and advised to use the internet to find out more about the organisation. Internal candidates applying for promotion are also advised who is on the panel, and provided with coaching and guidance from process experts.

The number of interviewers is dependent on the level of the appointment, but it would always be a panel interview. The organisation favours this approach because it allows someone to ask the questions, another person to listen and act as a "safety net", and a third interviewer to take notes. At least one interviewer will be an independent HR representative. The interview is intended to be a two-way process, and includes the opportunity for the candidate to view the environment they will be working in and for Staffordshire Police to "sell the role" and promote itself as an employer.

A structured approach is adopted for interviewing. This focuses on core questions relating directly to the competency area. The questions are scripted beforehand, linked closely to the person specification and job description, and are consistently used for each of the candidates. The candidates are also asked supplementary questions designed to probe specific areas of the candidate's response. Care is taken to ensure that these are in line with the behavioural indicators of the competency area.

The focus of the interview is on the candidate providing examples of what they have done in order to provide evidence of behaviour or performance, in line with the premise "the best indicator of an individual's future performance is evidence of their past performance". The follow-up questions, that must still relate to the vacancy's profile and competency areas, are used to draw out more detail on the action taken by the candidate in a particular event, and the results achieved. The organisation is careful to avoid closed questions, leading questions, multiple questions, self-assessment questions and personally intrusive questions.

Staffordshire Police also believes that there is no place for hypothetical questions, as there is a risk that, if appointed, the person in post may not do what they said they would do. It told us that: "The golden rule is that a hypothetical question will give a hypothetical answer and may elicit only a textbook answer, opinion or pure speculation."

The aim for interviewers in assessing candidates is to "observe, record, classify and evaluate". Contemporaneous notes are taken that form an accurate record of the interview: the objective here is to support the objectiveness and fairness of selection decisions. Individual interviews are rated in respect of each competency. The rating scale used when assessing performance is based on seven categories:

7. Demonstrates exceptionally strong level at all times (higher than 98% of other candidates);

6. Markedly exceeds requirements of the post;

5. Sometimes exceeds requirements of the post;

4. A sound and acceptable performance: the standard expected to meet the requirements of the post;

3. Generally acceptable but occasional shortcomings in performance;

2. Some areas for development: training needs identified; and

1. An extremely low score (lower than 98% of other candidates): significant training needs identified.

Interviewers are required to undergo a four-day comprehensive training programme covering effective interviewing skills. The programme includes the legal perspective, such as equal opportunities awareness and learning from observing model interviews. Evaluation of interviews, such as "dip sampling" (for example, reviewing interview notes) and benchmarking against other forces, is considered essential to preserving their robustness as a selection tool. External auditing of the process is also carried out.

Behavioural interviewing can provide a powerful means of matching candidates to softer types of selection criteria because it ensures that interviewees are questioned in such a way that they provide hard evidence that they have already displayed the desired behaviour in the past. From the opposite perspective, there is also a stronger foundation to justify why someone was not appointed to a position, as the selector is able to cite the lack of evidence of specific behaviours and attributes from the candidate.

The main pitfall associated with the behavioural interviewing technique is asking for information about behaviours that are not strictly relevant to the role. This can be overcome by careful preparation beforehand, and adopting a tightly structured interview format where interview questions are based on the person specification and the competencies, or transferable soft skills, required for the role.

The proper method for developing behavioural questions involves using the critical incident technique, the repertory grid or behavioural event interviewing to record events that are pivotal to the success of the job. It is not possible to provide details of these specialised techniques within the confines of this handbook, but, broadly, they each involve a form of questioning by a trained interviewer. The interviewees are chosen for their detailed knowledge of the job being analysed – usually, jobholders and their supervisors – and the questioning is pursued until the most important aspects of the job, and of the most successful jobholders, can be identified.

The resulting behavioural statements are then used to develop benchmark answers and a scale is used to score the interviewees' responses. As well as the benchmark answer, examples of good, average and poor responses can be incorporated into the interviewer guide. This helps to create a framework for standardised assessment that contributes greatly to the effectiveness of the selection interview.

Behavioural questioning presents a more time-consuming and challenging approach to interviewing, but it is the painstaking preparation and job-related content of the questions that helps guarantee its success.

Telephone-based interviewing

Not surprisingly given the rise of telecommunications and call centre businesses, telephone interviewing is becoming more popular as a selection tool, particularly as a means of initially screening potential candidates. Telephone interviews were undertaken by one in six (17%) respondents to the CIPD's recruitment survey[11].

Our own research among personnel, HR and recruitment specialists shows that telephone interviewing is much more commonly used in the private sector than it is among public sector organisations.

There are various ways of conducting telephone interviews, from highly informal discussions to the use of automated telephone systems that take candidates through a carefully structured menu of options. Purposes vary, too.

Selectors may merely telephone applicants to clarify specific points on their application form, or telephone interviews may be used as the initial gateway establishing that the candidate meets certain basic criteria qualifying them to proceed further. For example, a vacancy may be restricted to candidates with a particular qualification or level of education, and a quick telephone call can establish this and then arrange for the caller to be sent an application pack. Those who do not satisfy the requirements are politely rejected, with the result that selectors have far fewer inappropriate applications to read and reject when undertaking shortlisting.

Or the gateway may be based on some form of psychometric test, where candidates' answers are used to create a profile of their likely suitability for the role, and inform the decision whether or not to let them progress to the next stage of the application process.

The best-known example of this approach involves do-it-yourself retailer **B&Q**. It has set up a recruitment response centre that uses an automated telephone screening interview system as a preliminary screening process. Job hopefuls are presented with a series of statements designed to assess whether or not they would be suited to the company in key areas such as attitude to work and customer service. The company wanted to create a system that helped it to manage a large volume of job applications in a cost-effective and efficient manner and to achieve consistency at this early selection stage. The only information subsequently passed on to recruiting managers is job-related and does not include personal details; this provides a valuable means of reducing the likelihood that subjective issues could influence selectors.

Telephone conversations can also be effective ways of assessing an individual's spoken communication skills and, in relevant circumstances, their powers of persuasion or argumentation – skills that may be relevant, for example, in connection with the recruitment of sales executives, marketing staff or public relations professionals. Finally, the telephone may be used as an alternative means of conducting a normal face-to-face job interview, such as for the purposes of a first-stage interview where candidates live a long distance away from the workplace.

The same basic rules apply here as for other forms of interviewing. The interview should be highly structured, follow a prepared script and ask standard questions of each candidate. The interviewer should take notes throughout and ensure the candidate has the opportunity to ask questions. A particular consideration is the lack of visual cues between candidate and interviewer (until video phones come into widespread use), that provide indications when the other person should speak. Their absence can lead to long silences punctuated by both parties talking at once. In addition, interviewers have far less control over the conditions under which the interview is being conducted – at worst, the interviewee may be using a mobile telephone in a noisy, public place. Booking an appointment for the interview and providing sets of instructions on such matters help to overcome such problems.

Although generally much shorter in length than the face-to-face variety, telephone interviews can be a very effective selection practice, particularly if there is a large pool of candidates.

Case study F. Scottish Equitable

Financial services company Scottish Equitable has offices in Scotland, England and Northern Ireland, employing some 3,000 people in all. Its diverse recruitment activities range across all business functions, from mail loggers to customer servicing, IT, legal, sales and senior management. The company has a very positive attitude to telephone screening as a cost-effective recruitment tool.

Entry-level telephone screening is outsourced through an agency in Edinburgh, and comprises a basic check of work history, mobility and career aspirations. Included in the script are some competency-based questions.

Telephone screening for all other professional-level positions is conducted in-house, with interviews lasting up to an hour. There is some attention to work experience, but the main focus is on critical competencies and requirements for the job, both technical and behavioural. Data collected is restricted to "need-to-know" details – name, address, salary and where the candidate would be willing to work. Psychometric testing is done at a later phase, and not via telephone.

According to Scottish Equitable, the advantages of using telephone screening are that it:

● enables a much better candidate match, reducing the need for in-house interviews;

● constitutes an equitable process;

● minimises interview stress;

● produces a saving of interview time and costs with a reduction in interview numbers;

● offers a means of recruitment at a significantly lower cost than using an employment agency;

● facilitates the vetting of candidates from non-traditional sources (that is, other than agency referral, where pre-vetting has already been done); and

● achieves a recruitment success ratio of 4 in 10 as opposed to 1 in 10 without telephone screening.

Not all areas of Scottish Equitable's business use telephone screening to the same degree. An example: customer services uses it primarily at entry level, and outsources some assessment functions. However, at Aegon UK, the parent company, phone screening is a prerequisite of all recruitment.

According to Scottish Equitable, there are no disadvantages when telephone interviewing is used as a pre-screening tool. It does not use phone screening at the secondary level of recruitment. While the company agrees that lack of familiarity with phone screening can mean some people – both applicants and interviewers – are initially uncomfortable with the process, it has found that the response is very positive once the benefits become clear.

Access to interview notes

It is well-known that individuals now have a legal right to gain access to the notes that are made about them at interview, under the Employment Practices Data Protection Code which supplements the Data Protection Act 1998.

However, the Code (which is expected to be implemented in late 2003/early 2004) does not oblige employers to make interview notes, nor that the notes should be comprehensive, nor that the notes should be preserved. The Code's "benchmarks" – the issues that reflect statutory requirements – merely say, in connection with job interviews: "Ensure that personal data that are recorded and retained following interview can be justified *as relevant to, and necessary for,* the recruitment process itself, or for defending the process against challenge" (our emphasis). In other words, individuals will normally have a right of access to notes about them that happen to have been made, provided that the employer has decided to retain them (given that the Code advises only notes that are "relevant to, and necessary for" the purposes of selecting the applicant need be retained).

Testing

The use of testing in selection enjoyed a huge boom in the final decades of the last century, but has reached a plateau. The take-up of personality questionnaires, in particular, has slowed – some surveys even indicate that their use has gone into a slight reverse.

Not all types of psychometric testing are as controversial or limited in scope as personality questionnaires, and interest has been focusing on finding and using work-related tests that provide a sample or emulation of the typical duties involved in the job being filled.

Work-sample tests are perhaps the oldest forms of testing: asking a candidate to "Show me that you can do this job", by observing them performing it in action. Much modern work is complex and less easy to undertake in a dry run, however. Even typing tests – updated into the use of keyboards and using common PC programmes such as Word and Excel – can capture only some aspects of many administrative roles these days.

Where it is possible to find instruments that are relevant to the job, and administer and assess them professionally, then work-sample tests provide some of the most powerful ways to select candidates for a job.

Tests directly related to the work involved in a vacancy represent the most commonly used type of testing, according to research among almost 750 personnel and HR managers by the Chartered Institute of Personnel and Development (CIPD)[12]. Just over half (53.9%) of employers use tests of specific skills.

And more than one in three (36.9%) organisations assess candidates' literacy and/or numeracy. A similar proportion (31.9%) employs instruments that assess candidates' abilities in broader way. Finally, just over one in three (34.8%) organisations use personality questionnaires.

Why test?

Employers use various methods in their selection procedures in order to get to know more about the candidates, and then employ the knowledge gleaned from these sources to match the candidates against the requirements of the post being filled. Psychometric tests represent some of these potential sources, and are particularly valuable where other selection methods cannot provide the same breadth or depth of information on candidates.

For example, other selection methods may use the candidates themselves as the source of information that selectors need – through application forms or at interview, for example. But some forms of work-sample testing aim to demonstrate whether or not the claimed skills exist in practice by getting the candidate to carry out tasks that put these skills into practice. Other tests, such as those that investigate a candidate's potential aptitude for certain types of work (such as their aptitude for computer-related roles, or having an aptitude for sales roles) may uncover information of which candidates were themselves unaware.

Personality questionnaires, which are not tests as such, should be approached differently, in that they provide information that has no right or wrong interpretation, but afford insights into candidates' innate personality traits that might make them more or less suitable for the vacancy.

While they demand high levels of expertise in their choice and use, psychometric tests are not "magic bullets" that solve employers' recruitment problems, although personnel, HR and recruitment specialists may come across some managers who believe otherwise.

Case study G. Capital One Bank

Nottingham-based credit card business Capital One Bank has used cognitive/numerical testing and work-style assessment in the selection of employees for many years, alongside the use of competency based interviewing. It told us it has found that, correctly used, testing is one of the most effective and job-related ways of selecting individuals. Although the company makes use of off-the-shelf tests, it also designs its own. It was involved in a large-scale exercise to assess the validity of a new battery of tests, as well as the use of personality assessment. This validation study involved 1,300 existing employees – much larger than is the norm with such studies – to see how accurately the measures under consideration predicted actual job performance.

Types of test

Work-related tests: These instruments aim to test individuals in specific skills and abilities. Tests that involve performing a sample of an important aspect of the vacancy being filled, can, if properly developed and assessed (and checked that they do not unfairly discriminate), have some of the highest levels of predictive validity *(see below)* of not only any type of test, but also of any selection method.

Ability and aptitude tests: These instruments provide information about candidates' abilities and aptitudes for either a range of related roles, such as computer programming or sales representatives, or broader underlying characteristics, such as reasoning, numerical or spatial abilities.

Personality questionnaires: These controversial instruments are not pass-or-fail tests and, strictly speaking, do not "test" candidates at all, but provide insights into the degree of emphasis of their different personality traits. According to the British Psychological Society, these instruments "assess disposition. Dispositions describe our preferred or typical ways of acting or thinking [...] they attempt to measure how much or how little we possess of a specific trait or set of traits (eg gregariousness, empathy, decisiveness)".[13]

Employers usually aim to use the insights provided by personality questionnaires as points of comparison with the behaviours and attitudes they believe the vacancy requires. Higher-level jobs often give greater emphasis to behaviours and attitudes than purely technical ability. Certainly, employers in the UK tend to use personality questionnaires far more for managerial recruitment (and graduate development programmes leading to managerial positions) than for other types of job.

There is a body of opinion that some types of behaviour or attitudes that employers have found to be directly relevant to performance in a role are less amenable to training and development than others. In particular, fundamental personality traits may alter little once an individual reaches adulthood. For this reason, some researchers and academics argue that it is better to recruit on the basis of personality than to try to alter some traits through the training and development of existing employees. So, where a thorough job analysis has identified that some underlying behaviours or attitudes are important aspects of the role, then the use of personality questionnaires may constitute valuable aspects of the selection process.

However, it is equally true that strong criticisms are made of the concept of using these instruments. The very basis of the theories underlying them is disputed, as is their predictive validity *(see below)*. Critics argue that some personality instruments are poorly designed, and that better ones may still be misinterpreted and misused. In addition, personality questionnaires often give candidates greater scope to distort their answers, deliberately or unconsciously, than other forms of testing, and this raises its own problems in using the questionnaires' results.

Case study H. Halcrow Group

Engineering consultancy Halcrow first introduced personality questionnaires when selecting senior managers for newly created positions following a corporate reorganisation. Existing employees, such as project managers and operations directors, had to apply for these new positions, and testing was considered the best way of reaching an objective assessment of each individual.

Following advice from an external recruitment consultancy that has its own occupational psychology unit, Halcrow identified a particular personality questionnaire as being the most relevant test to achieve its objective of getting people into the right roles. Previously, the company says, individuals had "drifted" into senior management positions from a technical background, whereas testing has been successful in ensuring the right people are now in the right positions. A weighted scoring sheet was used in the selection process, with the testing results accounting for around 20% of the overall individual marks.

Staff undertaking the profiling, which was conducted and assessed online, each received a report and had the opportunity to discuss the results with the psychologist making the assessment. A few employees disputed the results, but Halcrow is very pleased with the outcome and personality profiling is now used for selection to all senior roles.

Choosing tests

Tests, like other selection methods, must relate to the demands of the vacancy being filled. Just as the questions asked at interview should aim to provide insights into the candidate's abilities as they relate to important aspects of the job, so, too, should the use of testing. This requires a thorough analysis of the vacancy, in terms of the most important skills and abilities that are required for high performance in the job.

Some skills and abilities may be capable of being tested in a relatively simple way, such as keyboard skills, the ability to operate common computer programmes or having good telephone skills. Even here, though, the knowledge and experience of skilled jobholders should be used to ensure that the test focuses on important aspects of these skills and abilities, and assesses them in a realistic, objective way. Particular care should be taken to ensure that such tests do not put external applicants at a disadvantage because the content of the test involves knowledge or information specific to the organisation.

Some large employers develop more sophisticated types of test to suit their particular needs, but this requires considerable resources, large numbers of staff doing work similar to that being tested and sufficient numbers of vacancies to justify the endeavour.

Other employers will have to buy tests on the open market from one of the many test publishers – see checklist 6 for factors to consider when making a choice of test.

6. Choosing an off-the-shelf test

There are high stakes involved in using testing. Inappropriate or misapplied tests, or misused test results, can lay users open to claims of unfair discrimination where compensation awards are unlimited. Poor practice can also alienate potential recruits and hinder, rather than help, the search for the best candidates.

● **Training:** The choice of suitable tests requires prior knowledge of the underlying concepts of psychometric testing; therefore, those involved in choosing tests should be suitably trained (including training in equal opportunities issues) in advance.

● **Job-relevance 1:** The demands of the vacancy should be analysed carefully, and only tests that provide useful information on important aspects of the job should be used.

● **Job-relevance 2:** Reputable publishers should provide clear information about the purpose of each of their tests, the types of skills, abilities and, often, typical occupations, for which the test is suited. Test results are often compared with the typical profile of others in the community, based on data in the test's user guide. These "norm groups" should be relevant to the vacancy being filled; otherwise, interpreting the results will be difficult and, perhaps, misleading.

● **Appropriateness:** In addition, publishers should indicate the level in terms of educational standard or level of responsibility (managerial, supervisory, etc) for which the test is intended. Tests may use levels of communication or intellectual demand that may be too high for the vacancy; this could amount to unlawful discrimination, as well as being unsuited to finding the best candidates.

● **Culture:** Some tests have been developed outside the UK, and may not be suitable for use here. Test publishers should be expected to provide information on the location of the research used as the basis for developing and validating their tests. Some US tests, for example, have subsequently been adapted and validated by research among British individuals. In addition, test publishers should have undertaken research to investigate their tests' potential unfair discrimination on the grounds of gender, ethnicity, nationality and age.

● **Development groups:** Tests should be developed and validated by administering them to large groups of individuals; reputable publishers should provide details of the size and make-up of these groups *(see Culture above)* and, the results of this research.

● **Reliability:** There are several ways in which tests can be powerful, or valid. They should be "reliable", in that, when applied to the same individuals under the same conditions, they yield the same results. Reputable publishers should provide evidence that they have validated their tests for reliability. A test's reliability is often rated from 0 upwards; 0.7 to 0.9 is often considered to be an acceptable range here.

● **Validity 1:** Tests are "valid" when they measure what they are intended to measure. Crucially, for selection purposes, a test's "predictive validity" relates to its ability to measure candidates' potential to be good performers in the job for which they are being assessed. Researching a test's predictive validity is difficult, as it often involves following up the same candidates once appointed, and being able to reach judgments on their effective performance according to objective criteria. Large numbers of individuals would have to be involved to provide solid evidence of a test's predictive validity. It is therefore uncommon for test publishers to be able to give much information about this crucial factor. Where it exists, a rating system from 0 upwards is often used; 0.2 to 0.45 is often considered to be an acceptable figure.

● **Validity 2:** However, personnel and HR managers can, themselves, monitor their use of tests and follow up candidates who are appointed by checking subsequent performance ratings from formal performance reviews, and by checking labour turnover data, dismissals during the probationary period and by talking to line managers of the individuals.

● **Other indicators:** The British Psychological Society is publishing a series of test reviews; summaries are available free of charge from its website, while the full reports can be purchased as printed copies or for a relatively modest fee via its website (details from the British Psychological Society, tel: 0116 252 9530, www.psychtesting.org.uk). In addition, reputable test publishers should require all potential users to be trained to acceptable levels of competence, based on the standards developed by the British Psychological Society. They may also require additional training in using a particular test. Where a test is claimed to be quick to complete, easy to use and analyse, and effective in predicting performance, particular caution should be exercised. Its publisher should be asked to provide evidence to support these claims. The experience of undertaking a test oneself, or the recommendation of a colleague, is an unreliable guide, particularly in the case of personality questionnaires.

Using tests

Tests should never be used as the sole means of rejecting or selecting candidates. Even the best-designed, most relevant test can only provide an insight into some of the skills and abilities required.

Most often, personnel and HR managers tell us that they use tests once they have undertaken their shortlisting process – in other words, where they have used the information on the application form or CV to reduce the number of applicants to a manageable number.

Some employers then invite the shortlisted candidates to attend and undertake one or more tests; the results, together with the application form/CV, are then used to reduce the shortlist to those who will be called for interview.

But, in most cases, candidates who have already been chosen for interview are tested, either just before their interview or just afterwards. Tested beforehand, the results are available for interviewers to use to inform their questioning of candidates. Where the test or tests are taken after interview, the results may be used as part of the decision about which candidates will be called back at a later date for a second-stage interview.

There has been some growth in using testing at earlier phases of selection. B&Q is the best-known example of the organisations that have introduced testing as a pre-recruitment screening device (its test is telephone-based; *see the section above on telephone-based interviewing for more details*). Some employers that use assessment centres have brought forward their use of some tests, in order to ensure those who participate in this costly, time-consuming technique are suited to the vacancy.

Administering tests

Test administration and analysis requires training, careful preparation and execution.

It is good practice to advise candidates in advance that they will be tested, and the length of time required. Tests take time to complete and candidates may have not allowed sufficient time where they have other appointments, have taken a limited amount of time off work or having caring responsibilities. Time pressures can heighten their anxiety when undertaking a test and put them at a disadvantage. This could well affect their test results.

For fairness and reliability, candidates should take the test in the same controlled environment, even where they do so individually rather than at the same time. Increasingly, test publishers are producing online versions of their tests, but most of them are intended to be taken under supervision. Tests that candidates can undertake remotely – for example, while sitting at home using their personal computer – are controversial, in that the employer has no control over the environment and, in particular, cannot guarantee that the test-taker is the candidate themselves and not a friend or relative.

Again, good practice requires that candidates should be able to practise the test before the test proper begins. This involves asking them to complete a few sample questions, thereby helping them to become familiar with the test's approach and what is expected of them. It can also encourage them to relax and feel comfortable. Where candidates potentially come from differing backgrounds and experiences, the use of practice questions provides an important way of reducing unfair discrimination.

Test administrators and analysts should all receive training. Most reputable test publishers will require users to have obtained the level of competence laid down by the British Psychological Society for their particular type of test (details from the BPS, tel: 0116 252 9530, www.psychtesting.org.uk), and may also require users to undergo specific training in the particular test itself.

It is also good practice to provide feedback to candidates on their test results. This should only be undertaken by someone who has been trained in analysing the test(s) involved and, preferably, has also received training in counselling skills.

Undertaking a test can evoke unwelcome memories of sitting examinations at school or university, and can ask a great deal of a candidate. In addition, the process of taking a test can seem intrusive – particularly so, where personality questionnaires are used – and demands levels of commitment that the effort and attention involved in giving feedback helps to recognise. There is, too, the understandable human desire to discover "How did I do?".

There are different levels of feedback, from simply providing a copy of the same results that the selectors received, to a fairly low-key one-to-one debriefing, and to a more extensive counselling-type session on the implications of the results.

Current practice among employers is divided on the provision of feedback. Just under half (48%) of employers always offer it, while a slightly smaller proportion (43%) does so if candidates request the information. However, they are more likely to do so without being asked where more intrusive or demanding types of testing are involved – particularly, personality questionnaires.

Test results must not be disclosed to unauthorised personnel, and should be kept securely. *(For more information, see the section on record-keeping later in this chapter.)*

Testing and equal opportunities

Testing is a high-profile activity and has attracted considerable attention here and in the USA in terms of its potential to discriminate unfairly – particularly, against ethnic minorities.

Guidelines *(see below for sources)* and Codes of Practice under the various anti-discrimination Acts recommend that employers should ensure that all aspects of test use do not discriminate unfairly – see checklist 7.

7. Test use and equal opportunities

● Everyone involved in choosing and administering tests should have received suitable training, as should all those who will analyse and interpret test results;

179

● Ensure that the vacancy has been carefully analysed and that tests are chosen that are relevant to the most important skills and abilities involved;

● Tests should also be chosen on their basis of being appropriate to the type and level of vacancy, and that have been robustly developed and validated, particularly in terms of lacking unfair bias *(see also checklist 6 Choosing an off-the-shelf test)*;

● Advise candidates in advance that they are to be tested, and how long this will take;

● At an appropriate stage in the application process, give candidates the opportunity to state that they have a disability that requires reasonable adjustments to be made to the process, and discuss with them the nature of the adjustments involved;

● Where tests or test conditions must be adapted to accommodate individuals with disabilities, consider involving the test publisher for their advice where an externally developed test is being used. There are particular considerations about the choice of tests and their administration in respect of applicants with disabilities, and further guidance should be sought, such as from the sources shown later in this chapter;

● Ensure that candidates receive a friendly welcome at reception and by test administration staff;

● Test administration staff should aim to develop a low-key atmosphere that puts candidates at their ease, paying attention to developing a rapport with candidates;

● Instructions given to candidates should not disadvantage individuals unfairly, such as those whose first language is not English or who have hearing difficulties; staff should ensure that candidates understand what is required, and encourage general questions about the testing process;

● Sample test questions should be provided for candidates to complete before the test proper is undertaken;

● Test results should never be used as the sole basis for rejecting or selecting candidates; particular care should be taken where a benchmark score from a test is used to assist in making selection decisions to ensure that this does not unfairly discriminate against particular groups;

● The use of particular tests should be reviewed periodically;

● Test use should form part of equal opportunities monitoring practices.

The Code of Practice on Sex Discrimination: Equal Opportunity Policies, Procedures and Practices in Employment from the Equal Opportunities Commission[14] states that the use of selection tests should be specifically related to job or career requirements, and should measure an individual's actual or inherent ability to do, or train for, the job or career. It recommends that tests should be reviewed regularly to ensure that they remain relevant, and that they do not lead to unjustifiable bias.

The Code of Practice for the Elimination of Racial Discrimination and the Promotion of Equality of Opportunity in Employment from the Commission for Racial Equality[15] recommends that selection criteria and the use of tests are examined to ensure they relate to the requirements of the vacancy, and are not unlawfully discriminatory. In particular, "Selection tests which contain irrelevant questions or exercises on matters which may be unfamiliar to racial-minority applicants should not be used (for example, general-knowledge questions on matters more likely to be familiar to indigenous applicants)." In addition, the Code says that staff involved in recruitment and selection should be given training in this role and in factors that could lead to unfair discrimination, such as stereotyping.

In terms of individuals with disabilities, the way in which tests are taken can be a particular source of unfair discrimination. Individuals with sight impairments or difficulties with manual dexterity present readily understandable reasons for ensuring that tests are chosen, or adapted, to ensure they do not face unfair disadvantages.

But tests can lead to unfair discrimination in other ways. For example, individuals with hearing impairments who communicate through signing rather than spoken English may be screened out by tests involving spelling and grammar. Individuals with visual disabilities may be screened out by tests requiring abstract reasoning. And personality questionnaires may screen out individuals who are protected by the Disability Discrimination Act 1995 because of a psychological illness where they score poorly on a measure of "emotional stability".

The Code of Practice on the Elimination of Discrimination in the Field of Employment against Disabled Persons or Persons who have had a Disability[16] highlights the role of tests in potentially discriminating unfairly. It says that the Disability Discrimination Act 1995 does not prevent employers from using selection tests, but that: "Routine testing of all candidates may still discriminate against particular individuals or substantially disadvantage them. If so, the employer would need to revise the tests – or the way the results of such tests are assessed – to take account of specific disabled candidates, except where the nature and form of the test were necessary to assess a matter relevant to the job. It may, for instance, be a reasonable adjustment to accept a lower 'pass rate' for a person whose disability inhibits performance in such a test. The extent to which this is required would depend on how closely the test is related to the job in question and what adjustments the employer might have to make if the applicant were given the job."

"For example, an employer sets a numeracy test for prospective employees. A person with a learning disability takes the test and does not achieve the level the employer normally stipulates. If the job in fact entails very little numerical work and the candidate is otherwise well-suited for the job, it is likely to be a reasonable adjustment for the employer to waive the requirement."

"For example, an employer sets candidates a short oral test. An applicant is disabled by a bad stammer, but only under stress. It may be a reasonable adjustment to allow her more time to complete the test, or to give the test in written form instead, though not if oral communication is relevant to the job and assessing this was the purpose of the test."

The Act's requirement that employers make "reasonable adjustments" applies both to the work (and surroundings) and to the use of testing. So, as well as considering whether a test is appropriate or can be adapted, employers might also have to consider whether the skills and abilities that the test is designed to measure could be adjusted.

Test publisher ASE has produced guidance on testing individuals with disabilities[17]. It gives an example of this double implication of making reasonable adjustments: "A person with dyslexia should be given an opportunity to take a written test orally, if the dyslexia seriously impairs the individual's ability to read. If the ability to read is a job-related function that the test is designed to measure, the employer may be acting reasonably in requiring that person to take the written test."

"However, even if this is the situation, a reasonable adjustment should be considered. The person might be accommodated with a reader, unless the ability to read unaided is an essential function of the job."

Despite taking precautions, employers will not know whether or not their use of tests is unfairly discriminating against particular groups unless they monitor the results of their recruitment and selection practices *(see chapter 9 Equal opportunities and diversity)*.

Further information on the equal opportunities issues concerned with the use of testing is available from several sources, including those shown in the next section.

Further information on using testing

Psychometric testing is a complex subject and some further sources of information are shown below.

Equal opportunities issues:

● *International guidelines for test use*, International Test Commission, free of charge from www.intestcom.org;

● *Guidelines for testing people with disabilities*, SHL, free of charge from www.shlgroup.com;

● *Equal opportunities guidelines for best test practice in the use of personnel selection tests*, SHL, free of charge from www.shlgroup.com;

● *Guidelines for test users: testing people with disabilities*, ASE, free of charge from www.ase-solutions.co.uk.

General issues:

● The British Psychological Society has set up a website dedicated to providing information on test use (www.psychtesting.org.uk). This contains much free information, including: *Psychological testing: a user's guide*; *Psychological testing: a test-taker's guide*; information on internet-based testing; the Code of Good Practice for Psychological Testing; and free summaries of its reviews of tests. Full test reviews are available to purchase either from the website or in printed format from the BPS (tel: 0116 252 9530). However, the BPS does not provide recommendations about the choice of particular tests.

● The International Test Commission has set up a website providing some information, and has developed *International guidelines for test use*, which are available free of charge from its site (www.intestcom.org);

● *Best practice in the management of psychometric tests: guidelines for developing policy*, free of charge from www.shlgroup.com;

● The British Psychological Society has also published a book, *Understanding psychological testing*, by Charles Jackson (1996, price £13.95; it can be ordered from bookshops or from: www.bpsblackwell.co.uk); and

● The Chartered Institute of Personnel and Development has produced a brief guide "Psychological testing", in its *Quick Facts* series, which is available free to CIPD members at www.cipd.co.uk.

Assessment centres

Assessment centres bring together a powerful mix of different selection methods, and assess groups of candidates over an extended period – typically, between half and two days at a time. Since their creation by the military in the Second World War, they have been adopted by many employers and, according to a survey of employers conducted by the Chartered Institute of Personnel and Development (CIPD)[18], just over a quarter (27.4%) of organisations now use them.

But their power depends on careful and skilled preparation, and an investment of considerable amounts of time, effort and money. This inevitably means that employers have to ration their use, and mainly reserve them for the recruitment of new graduates, managers and some professional staff. It also means that many employers lack the resources to introduce assessment centres. The same CIPD survey found that proportionately four times more organisations with the largest workforces (2,000+ employees) use them as do the smallest firms (those with fewer than 100 employees). Specifically, just over half (51.5%) of the largest, an eighth (13.1%) of the smallest and a quarter (25.3%) of medium-sized organisations use assessment centres (medium-sized firms are defined in the survey as having between 250 and 499 staff).

Among those employers using them, most consider the time, effort and expense to have been well-spent. According to the experience of the recruitment, personnel and HR managers we have contacted, assessment centres are considered to represent their most effective means of selecting staff. For new graduates, in particular, assessment centres are rated as being significantly better than any other selection method.

Assessment centres have gained a reputation as the Rolls-Royce of selection methods. Like the luxury cars, they are expensive to design, run and maintain, but can be highly efficient in what they do. This can make them a solid investment. Less happily, some employers are primarily attracted by their prestige and kudos, and may be more concerned with their outward show than spending the time and effort required to use them properly. They may turn, instead, to low-cost imitations that lack the reliability of the original.

There is no single definition of an "assessment centre", but there is general agreement that it involves all of the following elements:

● a group of candidates who are brought together at the same time and place;

● that the same series of selection methods is undertaken by each candidate;

● these methods involve a combination of collective and individual selection techniques;

● the selection methods are designed to reveal how candidates would actually perform in the organisation should they be appointed;

● the selection methods are designed around the actual demands of the vacancy;

● the performance of the candidates is evaluated by at least two assessors; and

● the event is sustained over a relatively long period, generally lasting at least half a day and often taking two days.

The key point, though, is that the use of assessment centres increases the fairness of the treatment given to the candidate and fairness of the final appointment decision, because candidates are assessed in more than one situation, against pre-determined, objective criteria, and by more than one assessor.

Occupational psychologist Steve Whiddett gave a convincing explanation of the logic behind assessment centres in his presentation to the Chartered Institute of Personnel and Development (CIPD) Recruitment Forum conference in 1996: "The research shows that no single selection tool is going to cover a whole job. A mix of tools are needed to look at a range of behaviours. The reliability of less controlled tools can be increased by using more than one assessor. Cost-effectiveness can be increased by simultaneously assessing several applicants. What we now have is a multiple assessment process – usually referred to as an 'assessment centre'."

Designing and running an assessment centre is a serious undertaking, requiring considerable investment in time, resources and – in all but the largest organisations with their in-house experts – requiring the input of a suitably experienced and qualified external adviser. The assessors, all or most of whom are usually managers from the host organisation, have to be trained and then must find the time to run the centre.

The organisation is asking a great deal of the candidates themselves, as well as of its own managers, and should be prepared to offer successful and unsuccessful candidates alike some in-depth feedback on their performance. Knowing that feedback will be offered can also benefit the organisation. If assessors know that their judgments will be passed on to the candidate, this can help maintain the discipline of ensuring that assessments are as objective as possible.

Attempts to short-circuit any of these steps not only undermine the effectiveness of the centre – in effect, the investment will be wasted because poor appointment decisions will be the result – but can also inflict psychological damage on participants. An assessment centre is an intense experience for candidates, requiring a great deal of commitment and energy. If it is mishandled, the reputation of the organisation will be undermined. Conversely, a well-conducted centre can help promote the image of the employer. In fact, many organisations judge their investment in assessment centres in terms of both their ability to select the best candidates, and their role as a marketing tool for the "employer brand" – the image of the employer among employees and potential employees as being a good place to work.

Guidelines

At present, there are no official best-practice recommendations or code of conduct governing the general use of assessment centres in the UK, although a useful set of guidelines has been developed by test publisher SHL (*Guidelines for best practice in the use of assessment and development centres*, free from www.shlgroup.com).

Back in 1989, the USA's Task Force on Assessment Center Guidelines produced a series of standards for that country (these are reproduced in Charles Woodruffe's *Development and assessment centres*[19] – a standard text, now in its third edition). But, in the UK, the British Psychological Society's working party is still formulating its proposals and it is not known when these will be available. Our own analysis of the key issues involved in designing and conducting effective assessment centres is shown below in checklist 8.

8. Assessment centres: the key issues

● Establish the purpose of the assessment centre: Is it to recruit staff? If so, how will internal applicants be involved? Is it to identify individuals with promotion potential? Is it to help individuals understand and develop their skills (a "development centre")? If more than one purpose is intended, how will these aims be reconciled? Ensure that senior management support the use of the assessment centre.

● Identify whether or not the organisation has internal expertise to design and conduct an assessment centre; if not, identify suitable external advisers and conduct a tendering process.

● Determine the basis of assessment: If there is a vacancy to be filled, how will be key demands of the job be identified and used to design the assessment centre's selection methods? If recruitment is to a more generic role, how will the skills and abilities required be identified and used to design the centre?

● Decide whether competencies should be used as the basis of designing and assessing the different parts of the centre, or whether more directly work-related aspects of the job should be used. (Competencies, in this context, are transferable, underlying skills, often "softer" or behavioural in nature.)

● Design the centre so that it closely, and honestly, reflects the culture of the organisation and the demands of the vacancy (skills, behaviours, actual tasks and context). The exercises should be purpose-built to reflect the job demands, and not bought off-the-shelf.

● Psychometric tests are commonly used in assessment centres; only those that are appropriate to the types of vacancy being filled should be used; the choice and administration of tests should take account of the factors shown in checklists 6 and 7 in this chapter.

● The elements of the assessment centre (exercises, interviews, tests) should be integrated, so that they use the same business context or scenario, involve a mix of individual and group work and different types of exercises, and flow from one element to the next.

● The duration and location of the centre should be suited to the aims of the centre, and the optimum number of candidates should be determined. Methods of selecting candidates should be identified. For external selection, some form of pre-selection is often required to limit numbers.

● Well-designed and conducted assessment centres are less likely to involve unfair discrimination than other selection techniques, but equal opportunities issues should be given careful consideration (for more details see the text in this chapter).

● Assessors should be selected who have the aptitude for the role; most of them should be line/senior managers from within the organisation. They should be given extensive training in observing candidates, recording behaviours, and scoring them against the competencies/work aspects used to design the centre. At least two assessors should observe the same candidate(s) in each exercise.

● Assessors should be given checklists of performance to assess candidates against; where competencies are used, there should be examples of positive and negative behaviours. A form to record their observations and give scores for each exercise should be developed for assessors' use.

● The method of calculating a score for each candidate's performance in each exercise, and in the assessment centre as a whole, should be developed. The purpose and importance of the post-centre assessors' discussion ("wash up") should be determined: Will it produce final scores by consensus? Will it discuss anomalies or difficult cases? Or will it merely review the overall scores that have been calculated mathematically?

● Where aspects of the centre require more than observation by the centre personnel – such as role plays, interviews and test administration – suitable people should be identified to provide this input, and be trained and fully briefed (test administrators and scorers should be trained to the standards required by the British Psychological Society and the relevant test publishers).

● Candidates should be briefed on the essential details of the assessment centre, including the competencies/work demands used as its basis, and how performance will be observed and assessed, and be given practise materials for any psychometric tests that will be used.

● The content, format and style of the feedback to candidates should be determined, and one or more individuals with the aptitude for this sensitive role should be identified and given training.

● The centre should be piloted, using internal staff or other volunteers.

● The outcomes of the assessment centre should be evaluated: Did the assessors reach broadly the same conclusions in terms of the same exercises and the same candidates? How effective did the successful candidates prove to be in the job? Did participants find any aspects of the centre objectionable or unsatisfactory? Monitoring data on job applicants at each stage of the recruitment and selection process should be gathered, and checked to ensure that unfair discrimination is not taking place.

Extending and evolving usage

Assessment centres have been in use since the Second World War, and have been used by one of the UK's largest recruiters – the Civil Service – since 1945. However, only in the past two decades has their use taken off.

According to Paul Iles, writing in 1991, only one in 14 (7%) British employers used assessment centres in 1973, rising to one in five (19%) by 1984[20]. More recently, the best evidence of their use comes from the annual recruitment survey conducted for the CIPD. This shows that usage rose from three in 10 (29.1%) employers with 50 or more staff in 1998 to one in three (33.9%) in 2000[21]. However, the resources required to conduct assessment centres mean that they are mainly found in larger organisations and, even then, are usually reserved for the recruitment of managers, professionals and new graduates.

Not only have assessment centres been taken up by increasing numbers of employers, but the organisations using them have been putting them to a wider range of purposes. From their wartime use in officer selection, and the well-documented example in the USA of AT&T's use to assess staff's managerial potential, assessment centres have expanded to include the assessment of development needs of existing staff, and in the selection of team leaders, of skilled manual workers and other non-managerial grades. The Trades Union Congress, for example, has used them to recruit trainee organisers who have spearheaded its campaign to increase union membership.

But assessment centres have changed in other ways. Partly, this has come about because some employers have become less willing to take the claims of assessment centres' powers of prediction at face value, and have been investigating and modifying their practices.

Following a series of research studies that found comparatively high rates of success ("predictive validity") in centres' ability to identify the best candidates in terms of their subsequent job performance, the pendulum has swung back somewhat. Several experts in the field have argued that such studies have unintentionally "cherry-picked" the best assessment centres – those that have been well-designed, conducted and evaluated – and have created an artificially high expectation that all assessment centres will be equally effective. For example, occupational psychologist Clive Fletcher has said that: "There is a real danger that some so-called assessment centres are less effective, and possibly less fair, than simpler assessment methods."[22]

The work relevance of centres

In one notable trend, employers are adapting their assessment centres to build in greater work relevance; they know that close linkages between the centre's design and the requirements of the job help to improve its ability to identify the most suitable applicants. The Society of British Aerospace Companies, for example, introduced an assessment centre process developed for it by Jonathan Lee Recruitment that aimed to improve the recruitment of engineers. The centres were held partly in aerospace factories and were based on the competencies required to perform the job being filled.

A study of assessment centres by Sharpe Research for the Cabinet Office[23], as part of a recent project to improve the Civil Service Fast Stream, found that centres "took place on or near the employer's own premises; it seemed to be important to all recruiters that candidates visited their offices at some point to get a feel for the organisation and its people, its atmosphere and culture". At fast-food retailer Pret a Manger, each external assessment centre begins at 6.30am in one of the company's shops, where candidates "shadow" a manager or team leader for four hours.

Similarly, many employers have taken steps to ensure that the exercises and interviews in their centres more closely reflect real life in their organisations. They are checking that the centres capture the reality of the skills required: both their nature and the context (if interpersonal skills are required, whether they are required in teams or in one-to-one settings, for example). And simulations are being used more extensively and realistically. At the **Halifax**, a major financial services company, a report in *The Times* says that the company's external advisers helped it modify its assessment centre into a single simulation: a seven-hour business scenario. The newspaper quoted its group succession planning manager as saying that: "We find this simulation-based approach so successful that we're adopting it for middle-manager assessment and graduate selection."[24]

Some organisations have rejected competencies – overarching definitions of the way that work is approached and performed – as the basis of their centres' design, in favour of task-based definitions, which they use to create the activities and to provide assessors with observation and assessment guides. This switch is controversial, and some experts argue that the task-based approach is not well-suited to many of the more complex and demanding types of vacancy for which assessment centres are typically used.

The design of assessment centres is coming under scrutiny in broader ways, too. Centres that consist of a series of self-contained exercises lose some of their ability to provide a realistic insight into the job and of candidates' potential performance in it, and can be disruptive for participants. Consequently, efforts are being made to ensure that each exercise flows into the next and, where simulations or scenarios are used, that each exercise uses the same context – the same business challenge, or the same people and events.

There has been a debate about the particular attributes of a candidate that should be assessed: should a centre take account of personality, given that it is much less changeable than an individual's personal competencies or technical skills? Some experts, such as Margaret Dale and Paul Iles, believe not. They say that: "We feel that assessment centres were never designed, nor should be used, to measure stable personality traits, but situation-specific skills. The multiple exercises used in centres are not simply there to provide multiple opportunities for the measurement of the same stable trait."[25]

Rapid organisational change, and the likelihood of this continuing in the future, has heightened some organisations' attention to the importance of sustaining their core values. Given that jobs, roles and the tasks involved are likely to change significantly, it becomes more important to consider the core values underlying the organisation's activities, and to take account of them in the assessment centre. Both employer and candidate stand to gain if their values are shown to coincide.

Some employers are now administering some or all of the psychometric tests they used to include in their centres at a previous stage of the selection process. This makes the best use of the time available in the centre, and still allows the test results to form part of the information used in making assessments.

At soft-drinks manufacturer **Britvic**, its graduate recruitment programme administers tests in two phases. Numerical and verbal reasoning tests are administered in its phase-one centre. Then, candidates who go forward to stage two complete a personality questionnaire prior to the second centre.

Attention to candidates

In recent years, recruiters have found that the best candidates are increasingly sought-after by other would-be employers, and this has had implications for their use of assessment centres. Those that are seen to make unreasonable demands of candidates are likely to become notorious and, where there is competition for staff, applicants will go elsewhere.

The Civil Service investigation into its fast-stream programme, mentioned above, showed that many employers that use assessment centres have been trying to reduce the length of their recruitment process, so that sought-after applicants do not lose interest and take up a job offer from a competitor. The government report recommended that, while there are constraints on greatly reducing the period involved in the civil service process, efforts should at least be made to keep in contact with candidates on the progress of their application.

The way in which applicants are shortlisted to be called to a centre also provides opportunities to improve both the centre's effectiveness and the candidate-friendly nature of the recruitment system. Centres are expensive to run, and it is rarely possible or desirable to invite all applicants to attend. As a result, some employers have improved their selection techniques to ensure that this sifting is as objective and effective as possible. Some employers have enhanced their application forms, for example, by including more questions directly linked to the selection criteria that are used as the basis for designing their assessment centres. They have found that such forms not only help selectors to draw up a shortlist of centre participants, but also provide insights into their own strengths and interests that assist candidates to self-select. The information gathered by the application form can also be used as part of the centre process in respect of candidates who go forward to this stage of selection.

The shortlisting process is also being used by some employers to ensure that the chosen candidates are suited to the assessment centre method. This minimises the risk of a strongly negative reaction by participants which they would then communicate to others.

Applicant selection takes on an added dimension where a centre involves both external and internal applicants. The two groups may not be compatible. Internal candidates have an inside knowledge of the organisation, often of the specifics of the vacancies involved, as well as the corporate culture. They may know how to perform so as to make a favourable impression on the assessors, many of whom will be managers drawn from within the organisation, and could already be known to participants.

Conversely, the organisation will know much more about internal applicants than external ones, and this may not be to their advantage. As well as supervisors' knowledge, there could be appraisal ratings, absence records and other insights that are not as readily available in respect of non-company personnel. There is no guarantee that these advantages and disadvantages will cancel themselves out, though, and create a level playing field across the group of candidates as a whole. This has led some employers, including Pret a Manger, to make special provision for internal applicants – in its case, through a parallel centre separate from the one used for external applicants.

Equal opportunities in assessment centres

Assessment centres bring together a battery of selection methods and the considerations that apply individually to them – interviewing, testing, and so on – in ensuring equality of opportunity also apply to their use in combination.

More generally, though, those who will act as assessors should receive adequate training in this role to ensure they base their judgments on objective, job-relevant factors, and are aware of – and minimise – personal biases and assumptions based on gender, ethnicity and disability.

The typical use of centres for higher-level vacancies means that there may be few women or ethnic minority candidates who are selected to attend an assessment centre. SHL's guidelines, mentioned above, note that: "This issue [of there being only one women or participant from an ethnic minority] is particularly pertinent in interactive exercises, such as a group discussion. The assessors may need to take this into account when evaluating the participant, but, on the other hand, this could be a realistic situation. It is good practice to ensure that one of the assessors represents the minority group."

As with any selection process, the operation and outcomes of assessment centres should be monitored to provide information on their effectiveness and to detect any unfair discrimination.

Case study I. Pret a Manger

Fast-food retailer Pret a Manger aims to fill around 60% of its managerial vacancies from internal candidates. In recognition that internal and external candidates applying for a management position may not be on an equal footing, there are two distinct assessment centre processes for each group.

The company aims to run one internal and one external assessment centre each month. The first stage of the process is the same for all candidates and consists of an application form, psychometric testing and an initial screening interview. The results of all three are taken into account before candidates undergo the assessment centre process.

The psychometric testing involves numerical and verbal reasoning, and a personality questionnaire. The personality section of the questionnaire was developed with the input of around 60 Pret a Manger managers to ensure that it measures "real Pret behaviours". A software package produces a report based on the test answers that suggests specific questions to follow up with the candidate.

The assessment day for external candidates begins at 6.30 am at one of the company's shops. Each would-be manager shadows a Pret manager or team leader for four hours, learning the tools of the trade such as making coffee and dealing with customers. Pret a Manger considers that the morning session provides an excellent way of getting across the reality of the job and the ethos of the organisation, which could not be achieved as effectively in an artificial setting. It also gives candidates an opportunity to assess whether the company's environment is one in which they would feel comfortable working.

The general manager responsible for the store then completes a feedback sheet on the candidate's performance against set competencies. This means that, by the time the assessment tests start, there is already a substantial amount of information to inform the selection process. Candidates will have been supplied with details of what to expect at the assessment centre well in advance of the day itself.

Up to eight candidates attend the centre in any one session. The ratio of assessors to candidates is high: three assessors to four or five candidates, rising to four assessors if there are six, seven or eight candidates. All assessors are company personnel, ranging from store managers to HR people who are trained to recognise the behaviours outlined in Pret's competencies. The company is keen to involve its own managers in recruitment. It gives them a sense of ownership of the process, and they are seen as the best people to judge whether or not candidates match up to the organisation's expectations.

Following an initial icebreaker, the first test is a group exercise involving a "leaderless project". The group is presented with an issue or problem that needs solving by consensus, and each candidate is measured against three key competencies: leadership, communication and tenacity/resilience. Half-an-hour's preparation time is allowed beforehand. The second exercise follows a communal lunch and is a one-to-one interview. Situational and behavioural questions based on Pret's competency framework follow up the results of the psychometric test and feedback form.

The final test is a presentation, made in the presence of candidates and assessors. Candidates are expected to talk on a subject that is downloaded from the internet that day. If possible, the topic is related to the food industry, and past presentations have ranged from "the history of English tea parties" to "the coffee bean". The brief is to make the presentation interactive, visual (a flipchart is provided) and interesting. Audience participation is welcomed, as is a sense of humour.

Following the assessment day, assessors have a "wash up" where they compare notes on the suitability of candidates. A summary sheet is completed which also outlines participants' development needs, regardless of whether or not they were offered a job. This is then handed to candidates before they leave. As the company has a rolling management recruitment programme, it will take on all the candidates attending the session who are considered suitable.

Pret a Manger found that existing employees attending the assessment centre were noticeably more nervous than their external counterparts. The company has therefore developed an alternative assessment day that mirrors the assessment centre process but, instead, takes place on the job. Candidates undertake the same exercises as external candidates but in a work environment – such as a presentation to the shop team and an exercise that tests leadership – and are measured against the same competencies. In one sense, the management recruitment process is even more rigorous for internal candidates, as their applications must first have been endorsed by at least three managers.

A scaled-down version of the assessment centre has been developed for candidates applying to work as team members in a new store. Around 16 candidates attend a four-hour session, where they take part in games designed to assess competencies such as teamwork, communication and listening skills. The process is considered to provide an additional benefit, in that it begins to build the team spirit considered so vital to the company's culture.

Other techniques

Competency-based selection

Competencies are widely used in recruitment and selection, and represent one of the main areas of innovation and development in these processes. The large-scale survey of personnel, HR and recruitment specialists conducted by the CIPD[26] found that one in four (25.8%) of the 747 people contacted said that their organisation uses competencies to recruit or select candidates.

Competencies do not represent a specific selection method, unlike interviews or tests, but provide a means of establishing the criteria that interviews, tests and other selection practices can use to define a vacancy's requirements and assess candidates against them.

The use of competencies is widespread in the UK, particularly among large organisations, although their use is spreading to medium-sized employers with workforces of a couple of hundred or more employees. A long-term project by IRS to track the use of competencies has found that they are used by more than 700 employers, having a combined workforce of more than four million. The methods of identifying competencies are outlined in chapter 1.

Competencies began to be introduced in the UK in the 1970s and 1980s as a means of establishing the selection criteria to be used in assessment centres, and most centres continue to use them for this purpose. This has shaped the focus of competencies in selection. Assessment centres are most commonly used in the recruitment of new graduates, managers and some professional staff, where employers are most interested in assessing candidates' transferable skills, such as leadership, decision-making, customer focus and interpersonal skills. The terms "competency" and "competencies" are often now used to relate to these softer types of skills, although competencies are also widely (and increasingly) used to define technical, job-related skills and knowledge.

Competencies are no more than definitions of skills that particular jobs, or even the whole workforce, require. It is the precision with which the skills can be defined, and the detail with which the definitions are spelled out, that makes the use of competencies in selection so potentially powerful. However, the process of producing these definitions demands considerable time (several months), expertise and, often, the use of external consultants to see it through.

Competencies rarely succeed without a considerable amount of initial and ongoing involvement from employees and line managers – this process of involvement is the single most important key to success, according to the series of research studies among users that IRS has carried out over the course of a decade.

And their implementation and use is seldom successful without a sustained communication and training exercise, so that the end-users understand and accept the concept of competencies. In other words, the introduction and use of competencies should not be taken lightly.

A well-designed competency framework enables each job's requirements to be readily identified, and provides a definition of each competency, together with several examples of how assessors (including line managers for performance-management purposes) could identify that an individual possesses the competency in question. To make matters easier, most frameworks divide each competency into performance levels, and give examples of performance for each level involved. Some employers' frameworks supplement this information with a set of examples of how not to perform the competency, known as "negative indicators". For use in recruitment and selection, the competency framework needs to be as detailed as possible, giving selectors as much information as possible about the evidence they should be seeking from candidates.

Recruitment advertisements are often phrased to highlight key competencies, although many employers' use has degenerated to jargon ("team player"; "will to win"), instead of using them in a rigorous way derived from an analysis of the vacancy's specific requirements. At the selection stage, most aspects of the process can be designed to incorporate an assessment of competencies.

Application forms, for example, are increasingly being adapted so that selectors can use evidence of competencies as part of the shortlisting process. Commonly found questions can elicit information about technical, job-related competencies, while transferable, softer, types of competencies require a tailored approach. One fairly uncommon method involves listing the core competencies that are crucial to the vacancy, giving a description of each one so that candidates understand their meaning, and asking them to provide examples of ways in which they have demonstrated the competency in question.

However, this approach's unfamiliarity may deter potentially good candidates from applying, and confuse others so that they fail to complete the form satisfactorily. It can also demand levels of communication skills and analytical ability that might make it unsuitable for some roles, bearing in mind the recommendations of the Code of Practice for the Elimination of Racial Discrimination and the Promotion of Equality of Opportunity in Employment.

A simpler approach, more commonly found, takes a less overt route to obtaining competency-related evidence. Here, specific questions about more familiar competencies – such as teamworking, communication skills and problem-solving – are asked on the application form, to which candidates provide fairly structured answers.

Self-selection techniques that are based on competencies are used by many employers. The recruitment advertisement, or other material that candidates are likely to see, highlights the essential aspects of the vacancy and is worded in such a way that encourages potential applicants to relate their own interests and skills to what is required. This technique has been found by some employers to reduce the quantity of unsuitable applications, while encouraging potentially suitable candidates to apply.

Popular newspapers and magazines often contain self-completion question-naires, and some employers take advantage of the attraction and popularity of this approach to create surveys related to job requirements. The quiz poses a series of questions, often linked to core competencies, and candidates fill in their answers.

At their most developed and sophisticated, the tests give model answers to highlight the degree that candidates would suit the job and vice versa, or they might provide a scoring guide and the overall result would indicate their compatibility. Some employers' recruitment pages on the internet contain interactive versions of such quizzes, so there is less effort required on the test-taker's part. Indeed, a few employers have incorporated these tests as a formal part of the application process, and the result acts as a gateway to gaining access to an online application form, or to a message regretting that the candidate is unsuitable for this particular vacancy.

Interviews can also incorporate competency-based questions; this works particularly well when structured interviews based on interviewer guides are used (*see the section on interviewing and checklist 4 earlier in this chapter*). The precision of well-defined competencies, directly related to essential aspects of the vacancy, enables the development of questions that gain evidence of interviewees' competence. Importantly, provided the evidence criteria are satisfied, the evidence can come from any part of the candidate's experience, without being confined to work settings. This can be a means of ensuring that selection does not preclude candidates from unconventional backgrounds, and is a useful means of implementing equal opportunities and diversity policies.

Interviewers will find they have a ready made means of scoring candidates' answers where the interview questions have been based on competencies that are defined according to various levels of performance, each of which is accompanied by examples of acceptable evidence.

Biodata

Biodata has never gained more than a foothold in the UK, and only around 1% of employers now use it. It involves a rigorous programme of research to identify the key attributes shared by the most successful performers in a particular job, based on isolating those that standard performers and poor performers do not also possess in common. As its name indicates, biodata (short for biographical data) looks for aspects of individuals' backgrounds.

On the basis that these can act as predictors of successful performance in others, selectors then design application forms or special questionnaires that elicit information about this biodata and use it as part of the shortlisting process. The best analogy to the use of biodata is the use of actuarial data by life-assurance companies, where research has found that certain factors in individuals' backgrounds are linked to greater or lesser risks in terms of longevity.

Developing biodata requires large numbers of individuals performing the same, or similar, jobs, and access to the expertise required to undertake the research and subsequent validation to identify relevant criteria. Also, or perhaps more importantly as a drawback, the technique often lacks "face validity" – there is usually no obvious link between aspects of biodata and their relevance to recruitment and selection – and candidates can react strongly against its use.

In addition, traditional forms of biodata relate to aspects of individuals' backgrounds over which they may have little or no control, and this is likely to make it increasingly offensive to many people. The likelihood of its use constituting unlawful discrimination should be thoroughly investigated before introducing biodata. ("Use of biodata, like other tests, needs careful control to avoid any possibility of discrimination or invasion of privacy," advises Acas[27].)

Graphology

Graphology is another controversial technique that also remains on the margins of employer practice in the UK. While it has its adherents, graphology or handwriting analysis, is used by fewer than 1% of British employers, although it is much more common in France and some other Francophone countries.

According to research evidence cited by recruitment expert Stephen Taylor, graphology has the same power of identifying potentially good candidates as astrology – zero, or no better than chance[28]. A review of research by the British Psychological Society into the use of graphology has found that few studies exist and, of these, most are unfavourable[29].

The role of self-selection

Only in exceptional cases are candidates in a completely subordinate, take-it-or-leave-it, position. They usually have a choice, and the decision to work for the employer is one that they will have played a part in making alongside the recruiters themselves.

The contribution of candidates to recruitment and selection begins from the initial point where individuals come to hear of the vacancy, where they go through an internal decision-making process as to whether or not to send in an application. After that, each stage of the selection process is likely to see candidates re-evaluating their decision. A long delay, or complete absence of communication, after lodging their application may discourage them, and send them into the arms of another employer. A complex application form, a seemingly irrelevant selection test or an interview that betrays a lack of courtesy or consideration could all be decision points where the candidate withdraws. This is all before the point where the successful candidate sits down and talks terms with the recruiters about starting dates, salary and other terms and conditions.

Self-selection is receiving increasing attention by astute employers because they recognise its importance in adding strength to the "psychological contract" between each employee and the employer. First impressions can have a strong influence on the recruit's attitudes to their new job and their employer, their motivation, performance levels and, ultimately, the likelihood of them leaving prematurely to join a competitor.

But, perhaps more urgently, employers tell us they are concentrating on self-selection because they find it difficult to fill their vacancies with high-performing recruits. For many jobs, employers are competing against each other for a limited supply of jobseekers. They need to do what they can to encourage potentially suitable applicants to come forward, and self-selection can help in this regard. Equally importantly, it can dissuade potentially unsuitable individuals from sending in an application. This reduces employers' costs – there will be fewer applications to shortlist, and fewer rejection letters to produce and send out. And it also means that the candidate has "rejected" themselves, rather than suffering the embarrassment of being rejected by someone else. This maintains goodwill, and a "self-rejected" candidate who was unsuited to one vacancy may be ideal for another and may be more inclined to re-apply to the employer as a result.

However, not all employers give the same amount of attention or importance to full and frank disclosures about the nature of the jobs they are trying to fill. In extreme cases, where competitors are portraying their organisations and jobs in unrealistically attractive ways, recruiters might place themselves at a disadvantage if they were to be too open and honest. This might reduce the number of applicants, but could still help the employer to ensure that the people they recruit are doing so in full knowledge of the demands of the job and the facts of organisational life. Recruits that do not experience clashes between their expectations and the reality of their new job are likely to "show greater commitment to the organisation, greater job satisfaction, better performance and longer tenure"[30].

The importance of self-selection means that it has already cropped up several times in this chapter. At the outset, when we focused on ways in which personnel, HR and recruitment managers are improving the cost-effectiveness of their recruitment and selection, we noted that they are including self-selection in their range of initiatives.

They are improving the information available to potential candidates about the vacancy, the organisation and its culture. Job advertisements are being reworded and redesigned to this end, and application packs are being introduced or improved. The potential of the internet is being exploited as a cheap, fast and readily updated medium to provide background information. Some employers, particularly for higher-level jobs, are inviting potential candidates to telephone a named individual who can discuss the vacancy with them and, astutely carried out, help the individual relate their own abilities to those required.

The public sector, in particular, has been adept at compiling packs of information that are sent out routinely to candidates, including corporate information, a job description, terms and conditions and, perhaps, the person specification. Some employers are experimenting with providing information on the selection criteria they will use – where organisations are using competency based selection, the criteria are likely to be sufficiently detailed (definitions, explanations and examples of performance) for external candidates to understand and relate to it.

Some organisations are taking this a stage further. The background information is worded and laid out in such a way that applicants are encouraged to relate their own skills, abilities and career interests to the context of the vacancy and the employer. Self-selection may involve no more than a carefully worded series of short questions, or it can take the format of a self-completion questionnaire.

The questions are unlikely to be effective unless they go beyond platitudes ("Are you a team player?"), and take the most important aspects of the job and convert them into hard-hitting questions. Competencies – carefully constructed definitions of the key aspects of a job – provide a ready source of such questions and answers, where employers have already researched and developed competency frameworks. Several organisations are using competencies for this purpose.

At their most developed and sophisticated, self-selection tests have been created that give model answers to highlight the degree that candidates would suit the job and vice versa, or use a scoring guide for each answer, where the overall result would indicate the individual's potential compatibility. Some employers' recruitment pages on the internet contain interactive versions of such quizzes, making it easier and more interesting for potential candidates to undertake them. Indeed, a few employers have incorporated these tests as a formal part of the application process, and the result acts as a gateway to gaining access to an online application form, or to a message regretting that the candidate is unsuitable for this particular vacancy.

Beyond these initial stages, some stages of the selection process itself can encourage self-selection. The use of tests that replicate important aspects of the vacancy, such as work-sample tests or tests of aptitude in certain skills or roles, can provide clear insights for candidates into their potential suitability for the job. Assessment centres usually emphasise work-related scenarios in the exercises they use, and again these can foster self-selection. The extended nature of most assessment centres, and the frequent use of senior managers as assessors, also give candidates insights into the organisation's culture and values. And interviews that are precede or are followed by a tour of the workplace, and introductions to line managers and colleagues, can fulfil much the same purpose of helping candidates discover whether they would be happy in that particular work environment.

Record-keeping

Maintaining accurate and confidential records of selection procedures makes sound business sense. Each recruitment episode involves employers getting a pool of candidates together, and then assessing their skills, experience and other abilities. This involves considerable time, effort and expense, and many employers do not want to lose sight of individuals who may have been among the top two or three candidates, or who could well be suitable for other vacancies that arise in the future.

At telecoms company **Vodafone**, for example, applicants' details are now being stored in a "talent bank", which provides an immediate source of potential recruits as and when vacancies arise, helping the company reduce the time taken to fill posts.

These increasingly common practices will be covered by the provisions of the Employment Practices Data Protection Code when it comes into force later in 2003 or early 2004. The Code says that employers should: "Advise unsuccessful applicants that there is an intention to keep their names on file for future vacancies (if appropriate), and give them the opportunity to have their details removed from the file". This could easily be carried out by inserting a statement and tick box on application forms, or, where they are not used, by including a suitable statement in recruitment advertisements or in the rejection letters sent to applicants.

More generally, the Code provides guidelines and recommendations about the safe storage of selection-related records, and the length of time that details should be kept.

Apart from developing talent banks of unsuccessful candidates, selection records can be useful to employers in respect of the applicants who are appointed. The process of selecting the candidate often provides the most focused and extended assessment of their current and potential abilities that the employer will ever undertake. But few organisations seem to make conscious use of these insights once the individual is in post. This information could greatly help to inform the nature of the induction, initial training and longer-term development that the appointee receives, and assist when decisions are made about their future promotion.

Records, too, provide employers with documentary evidence where individuals make complaints to an employment tribunal, for example, under the anti-discrimination Acts. And requiring those involved in selection, particularly line managers, to maintain accurate, objective records of their actions and decisions helps impress on them that recruitment and selection should be taken seriously and handled professionally – if for no other reason than their actions could be investigated at a later stage.

More generally, accurate records enable the workings of the procedures to be monitored to ensure no unfair discrimination is taking place against individuals or groups.

Whatever records are kept – handwritten notes, completed forms or electronically stored files – there are legal implications for their security, confidentiality and period of storage. The Data Protection Act 1998 requires secure, confidential storage, the rights of access by employees to their records (having given due notice in the prescribed way), and that records "shall not be kept for longer than is necessary for that purpose or those purposes". Guidance on storing records is given in the Employment Practices Data Protection Code.

For more information on the implications of data protection for applicants' rights of access to interviewers' notes, and for the use of application forms, see "data protection" in the sections earlier in this chapter on Interviewing and Application forms, respectively.

While neither the Data Protection Act 1998 nor the Employment Practices Data Protection Code set limits on record-keeping, they expect that the period concerned should reflect a real business need and take account of other legal requirements. For example, records may be relevant to potential claims on the grounds of unfair dismissal or unlawful discrimination; in such cases, individuals usually have three months to lodge a complaint.

The Chartered Institute of Personnel and Development recommends that application forms and interview notes should be retained for one year[31].

9. Legal checklist

● Protected groups should not suffer unfair discrimination in recruitment and selection procedures – Sex Discrimination Act 1975; Race Relations Act 1976; Disability Discrimination Act 1995; Part-Time Workers (Prevention of Less-Favourable Treatment) Regulations 2000; Fixed-Term Employees (Prevention of Less-Favourable Treatment) Regulations 2002; Trade Union and Labour Relations (Consolidation) Act 1992; and Codes of Practice associated with these Acts.

● Recruitment and selection practices in the public sector must support equality of opportunity on the grounds of ethnicity – Race Relations (Amendment) Act 2000; guidance from the Commission for Racial Equality recommends that public sector employers should conduct regular reviews of their personnel policies and monitor their use to ensure there is no unfair discrimination on the grounds of ethnicity.

● Reasonable adjustments to accommodate applicants with disabilities should be made to both the selection criteria of the vacancy and the procedures involved in recruitment and selection – Disability Discrimination Act 1995.

● Further information on equal opportunities can be found in the sections covering particular selection methods in this chapter.

● Individuals have a general right of access to manual and electronic recruitment and selection records about them, including interview notes – Data Protection Act 1998 and its Employment Practices Data Protection Code. See also the section in this chapter on interviewing.

● The security, confidentiality and retention periods of employee records must follow the data protection principles – Data Protection Act 1998 and its Employment Practices Data Protection Code. See also the section in this chapter on Record-keeping.

3. Using electronic media effectively

See also: 1. Filling your vacancies; 2. Cost-effective selection; 11. Managing performance 2.

This chapter covers:
- ● Overview: an introduction to using electronic media effectively;
- ● Email and internet policies;
- ● Personnel's use of electronic media;
- ● Electronic recruitment and selection;
- ● Electronic induction materials; and
- ● Electronic-based training.

Checklists in this chapter:
1. Email and internet policies: the key issues
2. Effective e-learning: the key issues
3. Legal checklist

Case studies in this chapter:
A. KPMG
B. Woolworths
C. HFC Bank

Overview

Personnel and HR specialists have rarely been at the forefront of employers' use of electronic media. According to research for the Department of Trade and Industry (DTI), the introduction of email, internet access and corporate websites has been driven by the personal interests of directors, closely followed by the influence of IT staff or IT consultants[1]. As a result, the legal and human resources implications of electronic media have often been overlooked.

But electronic usage has reached such a peak that the need to draw up a policy is now pressing. The same DTI research shows that almost 90% of employers now have access to email, with almost four in 10 of their employees sending and receiving external emails on a daily basis. Even the majority of the smallest employers, with fewer than 10 staff, have email access (58%), and this steadily increases in tandem with workforce size (79% of employers with 10 to 49 staff; 92% of employers with 50 to 249 staff; and 96% of employers with 250 or more staff).

Just over 90% of employers have at least one computer with access to the internet, and almost four in 10 of their employees use the internet at least once a month. As with email, the majority of employers of all workforce sizes have access (ranging from 63% of employers with fewer than 10 staff, to 98% of those with 250 or more staff). In addition, 80% of employers have now set up their own corporate website on the internet (this ranges from 40% of employers with fewer than 10 staff, to 93% of employers with 250 or more staff).

Widespread usage of electronic media increases the risk of damage to employers' equipment through computer viruses and to their reputation through failures to protect confidential data from hackers. Staff who make excessive use of emails and the internet for personal reasons will waste valuable time, and run up costly telephone bills where employers have dial-up access (increasingly, though, organisations are switching to permanent connections). And, often more seriously, staff who send inflammatory emails – with rude, bullying, provocative or racist content, for example – will cause considerable damage to relationships both inside and outside the organisation.

There is, too, the increasing possibility that unregulated email and internet use will lead to costly legal action. In the landmark case of Western Provident Association v Norwich Union, an internal email message that circulated within Norwich Union was found to be defamatory of its rival Western Provident. The case cost the defendant £450,000 in damages and legal costs. Even had the court not stepped in and ordered Norwich Union to preserve the offending emails, it is usually possible to retrieve messages from computer systems even when they have ostensibly been deleted by senders and recipients. Emails are deceptive, appearing to be the most ephemeral of media, but actually having the permanence (and legal status) of written or typed correspondence *(see legal checklist at the end of this chapter for more information)*.

At much the same time as the Norwich Union case, the government enacted legislation that now makes it difficult for employers to monitor email and internet use – the Human Rights Act 1998. However, this piece of legislation is but one of many with implications for email and internet use – such as the Data Protection Act 1998 and the Protection from Harassment Act 1997, as well as the anti-discrimination laws – that makes the development of effective policies essential.

More creatively, though, electronic media present fresh opportunities for personnel and HR specialists. Intranets (internet-type networks within organisations) and email systems enable the rapid dissemination of policies, information updates and other personnel material at far less cost than traditional printed paper-based publications.

And in one specific aspect of personnel and HR work – recruitment and selection – electronic media have been adopted enthusiastically to improve the cost-effectiveness of these practices.

Email and internet policies

Email and the internet are not going to go away. Instead of denying access or restricting their use to a select few, many employers would be better advised to create policies and systems that ensure email and the internet are used as productively as possible to improve organisational effectiveness.

As we saw above, research for the DTI shows that four in 10 employees now use emails on a daily basis. Much of this involves internal messages, but emails provide an ideal medium for external communication in appropriate circumstances. Customers and other external parties increasingly expect to be able to contact organisations by email, and it is far cheaper than using the telephone when conducting overseas business.

As for the internet, it offers a wealth of information that is often more costly or difficult to obtain from other sources. Given that most employers have set up a corporate website – often, though, of a limited nature, the next logical step for them is to develop it into an active interface with customers and the general public. While the collapse of the dotcom boom has brought some sanity to the exaggerated predictions for the profits to be made from electronic commerce, nevertheless, many organisations continue to use the web to buy and sell products and services.

And employers, through their personnel and HR specialists, are making increasing use of emails and the internet to recruit and select staff *(see below)*, reinforcing the need to ensure that effective policies and procedures are in place.

Acas (the Advisory, Conciliation and Arbitration Service) is a source of advice on formulating policies on email and internet use[2].

1. Email and internet policies: the key issues

Personnel and HR specialists' experience of developing policies concerning the use of emails and the internet highlights the following as the main issues to consider:

● Knee-jerk reactions: Policies should aim to guide and channel employees' use of emails and the internet in a positive, pragmatic way, rather than over-reacting to perceived problems or attempting to prevent any and all access;

● Involvement: The best policies are often those that are developed with the involvement of line managers and staff; at least, this increases the likelihood of the policies being accepted and observed;

● Simple is best: Policies should avoid the temptation to be over-complex or use technical jargon;

● Clarity: Employers should set out their expectations of employees' conduct in a clear, concise way. Any limitations on the use of emails and the internet should be spelled out clearly. The likely consequences of infringements of the policy should also be made clear, including the means by which action will be taken (for example, through the normal disciplinary procedure);

● Communicate it: It is vital that the policy should be effectively communicated to all managers and employees. It should form part of the induction programme; copies of the policy should be given to each member of staff – employers recommend that each person should sign a form to confirm they have received and read it – and reference copies should be stored in convenient locations. It may be useful to include coverage of the policy in training programmes provided for managers. Where the organisation has an intranet (an internal communications system involving a network of computers, with the look and feel of the internet), the policy should be made available through it;

● Review it: The policy needs to be reviewed to ensure it is keeping pace with developments in the law and email/internet technology (routinely every two years, or as required when major legal/IT developments occur); and

● Police it: Regular reminders should be sent to staff about the policy, and conformance with it should be checked by line managers. Breaches of policies are widespread, according to employers, and should be addressed in the ways set down by the policy, rather than being ignored and, therefore, implicitly condoned.

State of play: Personnel and HR managers tell IRS that their organisations' policies on employees' use of emails and the internet most commonly cover the following issues:

- the downloading of material that may be infected with computer viruses;
- loading unapproved software on to employers' computer equipment;
- accessing inappropriate websites;
- using abusive or objectionable language in emails;
- circulating pornographic material;
- sending emails containing inappropriate comments about colleagues or competitors;
- using emails to commit sexual harassment;
- sending emails that are defamatory;
- making excessive use of emails or the internet during working hours;
- copying or downloading material or software in breach of copyright;
- sending or passing on chain letters via email;
- sending emails that have the effect of entering into unauthorised contracts;
- providing guidance on effective use of emails, particularly avoidance of excessive distribution of emails to reduce information overload; and
- covering a range of other factors, including gambling online, using chatrooms, and accessing internet sites that are dedicated to illegal drug use, pornography or terrorism.

Personal use

Employers' policies should clearly set out the limits on employees' use of emails and the internet for their personal use. There is no one best answer, although many organisations do not impose an outright ban on personal use, and the choice must depend on the employer's business, background, culture and other factors. In particular, existing attitudes and policies towards the personal use of telephone calls and, to a lesser extent, computer equipment, will greatly influence employees' (and line managers') attitudes towards emails and the internet. Where an employer has always prohibited, or strictly limited, personal use of the telephone, it will be much easier to gain acceptance for a similar restriction on emails, for example.

Acas recommends that: "Most policies will seek to establish a balance between business and personal use, whilst encouraging staff to develop effective computer skills. In most organisations, workers respond well to trust and follow agreed policy guidelines in a responsible manner. The organisation may choose not to be too restrictive so as to prevent damage to existing employment relations."[3]

Where personal use is allowed, some organisations restrict it to employees' own time. However, this will have the effect of causing a surge in use during lunch hours that may slow down the email system or other staff's work-related access to the internet. Other employers tell us that they permit personal use during work time, but require employees to behave "responsibly" or use emails and the internet "reasonably". In other cases, a few organisations require employees to reimburse the cost of connection charges; however, this is difficult to enforce, complicated and cumbersome to administer, and is increasingly irrelevant because of the move from dial-up connections to permanent access.

Automated controls

Policies frequently prohibit employees from accessing websites of a suspect nature, such as those concerned with pornography. Some organisations back this up by setting controls on their internet-browser software to bar access to designated websites – particularly, chatrooms – and those where certain words or phrases are detected – for example, "sex" or "drugs".

While these controls help to ensure employees observe the policy, they are not fool-proof and are no substitute for properly formulated guidelines. Many objectionable sites will escape them, while, conversely, the controls may bar access to content that is of legitimate interest (a personnel or HR specialist might be barred from sites providing information where the "sex" content relates to sex discrimination or sexual harassment, for example).

Many policies contain provisions that all or some external emails should contain a standard form of disclaimer or other warning. The aim is to ensure that the message is treated as confidential and not passed on to others, and that the employee does not inadvertently enter into a binding contract or create some other form of liability. (In most instances of employees' use of emails and the internet, employers are vicariously liable for the actions of their staff.)

To back up this requirement, many employers are introducing systems that automatically attach the standard disclaimer and warning to every email sent by members of their staff.

Monitoring

It is frequently difficult to police the personal use of emails and the internet through simple observation, when the employees concerned routinely use computers and these media as part of their normal work. Some organisations have, therefore, introduced a practice of monitoring electronically all email and/or internet traffic, or conducting spot-checks on it. The knowledge that a spot-check, even where these are rarely performed, might uncover their infringement of corporate policy can greatly improve employees' conformance with email and internet procedures.

However, the practice of monitoring is increasingly subject to legal intervention, particularly since the introduction of the Human Rights Act 1998. Article 8 of the Act confers a broad right to privacy in the workplace, qualified by certain exceptions. An employer's monitoring might qualify under one of these exemptions, particularly where employees have been made fully aware that the practice is used – in any event, notifying them is a requirement of the Telecommunications (Lawful Business Practice) (Interception of Communications) Regulations 2000.

The Human Rights Act 1998 is directly enforceable by employees of "public authorities"; in other types of employer, courts are required to take account of the Act when hearing relevant cases. For example, an employee might complain that the monitoring had infringed their right to privacy to such extent that it constitutes a fundamental breach of their contract, and lodge a complaint of constructive dismissal. In this case, an employee could draw on the Act's provisions in support of their complaint.

Acas suggests that employees' right to privacy under the Human Rights Act 1998 and the practice of monitoring could be reconciled by providing a non-monitored means of communication for employees' private use. This could take the form of a dedicated telephone line for staff use, or personal email addresses in an email system.

Instead of such special provision, it may be desirable to adopt a policy of gaining employees' express consent to such monitoring. This could have the effect of waiving employees' relevant rights under the Act and, thereby, enable the monitoring to continue.

In addition, monitoring is covered by principles contained in the Data Protection Act 1998. Detailed guidance on the implications of the Act for employers' monitoring of emails and telephone calls will be contained in the Employment Practices Data Protection Code of Practice. Publication of the relevant section of the Code has been delayed.

Also of potential relevance will be proposed improvements in the protection of employees' personal data from the European Commission, including monitoring practices. These provisions are at the consultation stage.

Personnel's uses of electronic media

A great deal of personnel and HR specialists' time is taken up by routine administration: keeping records, revising policies and procedures, providing basic information on terms and conditions, and so on. The advent of electronic media – particularly, email systems and intranets – has the potential to revolutionise this work, as well as raising the profile and contribution of personnel and HR specialists within the organisation. (Intranets are internal communication systems using a network of linked computers, with the look and feel of the internet.)

Employers inform us that the most common forms of electronic media used for personnel-management purposes are, in descending order:
● use of a general intranet;
● a special section of the intranet dedicated to personnel information;
● email (mainly to send out information on revised policies and procedures, and distribute staff newsletters); and
● specialist software (personnel-information systems; payroll software; etc).

The use of electronic media for personnel management provides several benefits, in employers' experience. In particular, employers report:
● improved communication with employees and line managers;
● greater coverage and accuracy of record-keeping;
● reduced administrative workload (particularly, where line managers and employees are able to obtain information unaided, and update their own records); and
● lower costs through the reduction in paper and printing charges where documents are available electronically.

The list below shows, in descending order, the most commonly found types of personnel information published on employers' intranets; in each case, the material is intended for open access by employees and line managers:
● policies;
● various rulebooks and codes of conduct;
● health and safety information;
● details of training courses;
● the staff handbook; and
● benefits information.

Electronic recruitment

Personnel and HR specialists have seized on the potential of the internet, emails and organisations' intranets to improve the cost-effectiveness of their recruitment and selection practices. According to the Chartered Institute of Personnel and Development (CIPD)[4], three-quarters (74.9%) of employers now engage in some form of electronic recruitment. Just over half of employers (51.7%) use their corporate websites to post vacancies on the internet, while fewer than one in three (28.9%) use commercial recruitment sites, otherwise known as "job boards".

Employers' experience of electronic recruitment is generally positive, without being exaggerated, according to the CIPD. Based on feedback from almost 550 employers, its survey found that users agree that the internet and emails represent "really useful recruitment tools", and that these media are "very cost-effective". And despite the well-publicised drawbacks of electronic recruitment – particularly, its poor targeting that leads to large numbers of unsuitable applicants – only one in 10 employers consider that it is "frustrating, costly and time-consuming".

Certainly, the market and infrastructure for electronic recruitment have matured. According to government statistics[5], the proportion of households having access to the internet more than trebled between 1999 and 2002 to 44% overall. Once other means of accessing the web are included (such as using employers' facilities), almost half (46%) of the adult population use the internet at least once a month. While usage is not consistent across different age groups, social classes, income bands and regions, the internet still compares favourably with the reach of most conventional forms of recruitment advertising.

In terms of infrastructure, there are hundreds, perhaps thousands, of commercial websites containing recruitment advertising; and most traditional paper-based publications that carry job ads now publish them simultaneously online. Even the jobcentre network has launched a nationwide online registry of job opportunities, representing the largest such source across the UK, having some 350,000 to 400,000 vacancies at any one time (www.jobcentreplus.gov.uk).

From the software point of view, there are now many packages available to employers to help them use their own websites for recruitment advertising, handle the applications and even conduct some selection screening or testing via the internet.

Several websites have published useful checklists about the use of online recruitment, such as that of the Internet Recruiters' Network and Association[6].

State of play: Most employers are using electronic media in a limited way in their recruitment and selection. Most commonly, personnel, HR and recruitment specialists inform us that their organisations advertise vacancies on their own website, and use email to handle enquiries concerning actual and potential vacancies. Slightly less commonly, they say that their employers use email to accept CVs sent in by applicants. Considerably fewer, though, send out and accept completed application forms via email.

The use of external websites to advertise vacancies, usually for a fee, is rare among medium-sized and smaller employers (undertaken by one in six or fewer of such firms, according to our feedback), but is practised by considerably greater proportions of larger organisations (reaching two-thirds of employers with 10,000-plus employees).

Very few medium-sized and smaller employers use their websites to publish background information about the vacancy and other relevant details for jobseekers, although this is more common among larger organisations. The use of the internet to administer selection tests is rare among employers, regardless of their workforce size.

Why use it?

Electronic recruitment and selection is being used by employers, personnel, HR and recruitment managers tell us, for the following reasons:

● **Cost control:** Increasingly, employers are advertising vacancies on the web because it is cheaper than conventional forms of advertising or the fees charged by employment agencies. Half of smaller employers we contacted have made changes to reduce their hiring costs, of which the introduction of online recruitment (or its increased use) is by far the most common action they have taken. To achieve these economies, employers are increasingly preferring to use their existing corporate websites, instead of paying companies to use their commercial websites.

● **Effectiveness 1:** Advertising on the web plays a similar role to advertising in the press in that individuals who are not actively looking for a new job can come across a vacancy by chance while they are browsing, and be encouraged to apply for it. Web advertising potentially appeals to a different group than conventional press readerships, has a much wider reach geographically, and has a longer exposure than conventional media where adverts tend to appear in a single issue of a publication.

● **Effectiveness 2:** But, recruitment advertising on the web offers a key advantage over paper-based media in that it can be tailored to jobseekers' requirements: once a jobseeker has found a site that may interest them, the site usually offers the ability for the individual to create their own profile of the jobs they are interested in (job type, salary, location, etc) and be shown only those vacancies that meet these criteria; some sites also send email alerts to individuals when vacancies matching their profile are loaded onto the site.

● **Agent of change:** Adopting electronic methods of recruitment and selection provides an opportunity, or lever, to improve the whole process – from the design of recruitment adverts and application forms, to the way in which candidates are kept informed of the progress of their application.

● **Speed:** Electronic recruitment is widely reported to us by employers as helping to speed up their recruitment process, thereby reducing costs and preventing sought-after candidates from being lost to competitors while their application is being processed.

Both the **BBC** and **Swansea Council**, for example, have found that their introduction of online recruitment has helped improve the quality of applicants seeking jobs with them. The BBC receives around half of all applications online, and believes that the quality is slightly higher than those using traditional methods. It attributes this to the fact that its website enables the corporation to provide more information about vacancies, such as their responsibilities and the skills required, than paper-based advertising permits[7]. In the first month of its use of online recruitment, Swansea Council received 10% of its applications online, and believes that the internet has widened its pool of potential recruits, as well as helping to improve the quality of applications[8].

The speed and broad reach of the internet is being used by several major retailers and hospitality employers to fill their vacancies for seasonal and temporary staff. At **New Look**, it believes the profiles of its customers (16 to 25 years) and typical Christmas-period recruits (20 to 25 years) closely match those of the age groups most likely to look for work over the internet. The **Tussaud's Group** has also begun hiring seasonal staff via the web, and both it and New Look expect this to become a growing trend. They find they are able to target their online advertising to the relevant groups, increase the speed of the recruitment process and enjoy longer exposure for their advertising than offered by daily newspapers[9].

215

Step by step

Electronic recruitment and selection offers many possibilities to personnel, HR and recruitment specialists, and need not require high levels of technical knowledge, huge expenditure or massive IT systems. In fact, most employers tell us that their use is modest.

Many employers, as we saw above, have already set up a basic website – usually, for corporate PR purposes, and which gives details of their services, the organisation's history and contacts for further information. It is usually a simple step to use this site to carry details of current vacancies.

Three issues immediately present themselves, however.

1. Most of the advantage of electronic recruitment advertising will be lost if jobseekers are not able to follow up the vacancy straight away. At the very least, applicants must be able to send an email to the employer making enquiries about the vacancy. Ideally, they should be able to undertake the whole application process via the same website, whether this involves completing an application form online or sending their CV and covering letter.

2. Organisations must be able to handle the enquiries and applications they receive by email. Employers report that they often fall down in this respect.

3. It is important to ensure that the website remains current. Frequently, employers fail to remove details of vacancies whose closing date has passed – or forget to provide details of the closing date.

More generally, though, personnel and HR specialists should give careful thought to the benefits they expect to gain from using their organisation's corporate website. Advertising on such sites is almost as limited as the traditional practice of posting details of jobs at the gates of the employer's factory or office block. Both practices are accessible to passers-by – in internet terms, largely those individuals who happen to be visiting an organisation's site.

Certainly, some search engines will index these electronic vacancies, but these services are notoriously hit-and-miss, and often overlook potentially relevant web pages. Alternatively, users often find that their search has thrown up many hundreds of hits that they cannot possibly follow up.

Job boards try to overcome this problem of relying on chance visits by "driving" traffic to their sites. They advertise on television and in paper-based publications, attend careers and other exhibitions, and form partnerships with special-interest sites that users might actively seek out. Once they have logged on to such a site, a special "click-through" display encourages them to visit the job board. In addition, job boards aim to draw people to their sites by making the visit as enticing as possible. Almost all of them carry information that jobseekers might want to read: guides to compiling CVs, interview tips and techniques, careers guides, and so on. However, this activity, and their profits, has to be paid for by the fees charged to employers when they advertise their vacancies.

Job boards come in all shapes and sizes. There are vast, often international, sites that carry a wide range of vacancies (although rarely for lower-level jobs); there are others focused on a single country (such as Scotland) or region (such as London). And there are those that concentrate on specific types of vacancy (new graduates or managers, for instance) or occupations (health, computing or engineering, for example).

It is worth remembering, though, that some job boards will advertise employers' vacancies without charge. Some sites carry free recruitment advertising; others are run by newspaper and magazine publishers and reproduce advertisements that employers originally paid to have published in their normal paper-based editions. This raises the point that even conventional advertisements should consider providing an email address or details of the employer's website, as these will prove particularly useful for those who see the online version of the vacancy details.

Setting up **consortia** of employers to launch recruitment websites is being piloted in the public sector as a means of increasing the benefits and reducing the costs involved. Their sites do not rely on individual employers' corporate websites, which many applicants may overlook, but use a dedicated site covering all the participating employers' vacancies. The scale of this activity, and the press attention it generates, can help to encourage visits to the site.

In Surrey, for example, **Surrey County Council**, 11 district councils in the county, a local NHS hospital and the ambulance service launched a joint recruitment site in early 2003. The site is expected to carry as many as 1,000 vacancies a year. Cost savings by just one of the participants, **Runnymede Borough Council**, are expected to reach £50,000 a year[10].

Similarly, 10 **NHS** trusts in south-west London are involved in a scheme to launch a website that will carry internal and external vacancies for its constituent employers[11].

It is relatively simple to include a link on a web page, such as page carrying a recruitment advertisement, to an email enquiry form. Potential applicants can use this to request an application pack, send in their CV or even return a completed application form.

Online application forms represent a refinement, or step up, in employers' use of electronic recruitment and, as we saw above, are less widely used. Employers inform IRS that such forms are most effective where they are designed specifically for online use, and offer a facility enabling applicants to save their forms and continue to complete them at a later date, before finally clicking a button to send them to the organisation.

Case Study A. KPMG

KPMG is a multi-site professional services firm and a major recruiter of new graduates. It originally attempted to rework its paper-based application form for online use, but discovered that this took three hours to complete and was difficult to use as a selection tool. It then redesigned its form, stripping it down to the essentials, and incorporating an online screening tool. The company told us that: "We had been seeking a whole plethora of information which we weren't using to make decisions – or, if we were, we shouldn't have been because it was subjective." The new form takes one hour to complete. The on-site information to candidates points out that: "You will quickly see that the KPMG application form is radically different from those you are normally asked to complete. The form has been designed to make it easier for you to apply and enable us to make an objective decision about how well you fit the profile of graduates we aim to recruit."

Few employers, though, take advantage of a relatively easy, yet potentially valuable, aspect of the internet: its ability to provide large amounts of information at low cost, and update it easily, quickly and cheaply. All applications involve a measure of self-selection, in that the applicant compares their interests, skills and experience with what the organisation and the particular vacancy have to offer. Occupational psychologists have found that encouraging self-selection helps to improve the quality of job applicants: those that decide to apply tend to be more suited to the job and are more motivated to work for the organisation. But this depends on employers being able to provide potential applicants with suitable background information *(for more information, see chapter 1 Filling your vacancies and chapter 2 Cost-effective selection)*. The internet enables employers to make this information readily available – it is there on the website without applicants having to request it and wait two to three days for a postal delivery – and it can be updated easily as the details change.

Some organisations, mainly large, well-resourced companies, have taken this a stage further, and provide video clips of real-life employees talking about their jobs. They may also offer interactive question-and-answer facilities that provide background information painlessly and, in a subtle yet effective way, encourage would-be applicants to think carefully about their suitability for the vacancy.

Linked to this, a few employers – again, mainly very large organisations with considerable resources – have introduced electronic forms of selection. In some organisations, where electronic application forms are used, the job-seeker must first complete an online screening questionnaire. Software is used to check the person's replies against pre-determined criteria, and only those who meet certain minimum standards are allowed access to the application form. The others receive a polite message that they do not meet the job's criteria, and may be advised to check for alternative vacancies or apply at a later date.

Abbey National, the financial services company, has adopted a middle way. It offers jobseekers an online self-assessment questionnaire that provides immediate feedback, but which is not used to screen out unsuitable applicants ("This questionnaire is not assessed; it has been designed for you to ensure that you will be happy in a role of this kind. It asks you what you would do in each situation, and then gives you immediate feedback on what we consider to be the correct answer within Abbey National").

Some organisations, additionally or alternatively, administer psychometric tests via the internet. Many commercial test publishers have produced electronic versions of their existing paper-format tests, while some employers have developed their own in-house online tests. Both types of test enable candidates to answer the questions online, and they and the recruiters receive immediate feedback as to their potential suitability for the vacancy in question. The process is much faster and cheaper to administer than conventional testing, but it has several serious drawbacks.

First and foremost, because the candidate is not present in person, it is possible for them to get help in answering the questions or, indeed, for another person to complete the test in its entirety. Some measures can be taken to reduce these risks, but they cannot be eliminated entirely. Second, the lack of human interaction means that the feedback given to test-takers will be a poor substitute for a detailed, sensitive one-to-one debriefing. Candidates may be given a contact number to call for further personal feedback from a trained assessor, but, again, this does not entirely overcome this inherent drawback.

Which jobs?

Employers in the private sector usually restrict their use of electronic recruitment and selection to certain types of vacancy – primarily, those for new graduates, computer specialists or managers of any description. (Practice in the public sector differs, in that many such organisations often publish all their vacancies on the web as a matter of routine.)

The use of the internet is, in fact, now the norm for graduate recruitment, and some organisations refuse to accept applications submitted by conventional, paper-based means. Our research among recruiters of new graduates shows that more than eight in 10 employers use the internet, rising to 100% among large organisations.

But probably the majority of employers now also uses online recruitment for computer specialists and managers. And a significant minority also uses the medium for vacancies for skilled workers and sales staff. Among these and other types of vacancy, usage is much more common among larger organisations. But the conscious use of online recruitment (as opposed to placing advertisements in the press that the publications then automatically publish online) remains much less common in respect of clerical staff and semi-skilled and unskilled manual workers.

For example, **B&Q**, the DIY retailer, is using the internet to appoint up to 1,000 managers linked to its store-expansion programme. It is building on the success of a recently established management-careers website, which already generates almost a quarter of all applications for managerial vacancies[12].

Effectiveness

When personnel, HR and recruitment specialists are forced to choose just one recruitment method as being most cost-effective, their experience rarely leads them to single out the use of the internet or emails.

However, filling vacancies for new graduates represents the prime exception. Here, the use of the employer's own website ranks joint second in terms of the proportion of personnel, HR and recruitment specialists telling us that it is their most cost-effective recruitment method.

In respect of managerial vacancies, though, electronic recruitment lies in fifth place, well behind such traditional methods as national-press advertising. Similar feedback from employers was given in respect of computer specialists (joint fourth); sales staff (sixth place); and skilled workers (joint fourth).

Case study B. Woolworths

The recruitment of managers and assistant managers for the 800 stores owned by Woolworths has been improved through its adoption of electronic media. The overall cost has fallen from £16,000 to £4,000 for a store manager, and from £10,000 to just under £4,000 for an assistant manager – mainly, because the new system has been linked to an improved selection process. Greater numbers of unsuitable candidates are sifted out at an earlier stage in the process. In addition, Woolworths has been able to shorten the time required to recruit managerial staff. Between the introduction of the new system in May 2001 and the end of 2002, the company handled more than 17,000 applications online, and more than nine out of 10 of its managerial applications are now lodged electronically.

Case study C. HFC Bank

HFC Bank, like Woolworths, used the introduction of electronic recruitment and selection to improve its whole hiring process. The bank also achieved cost savings, primarily by reducing its dependence on employment agencies and, thereby, cutting the fees it pays to them. It adopted a dual approach, advertising vacancies on its corporate website, but also paying for advertising on commercial job boards – the choice of job board varies according to the nature of the vacancy. The bank has introduced a single software-based system to handle its applications, regardless of whether the application originates from a press advert or online. In addition, it has introduced software that automatically sifts electronic applications (applications are made by submitting CVs, not application forms) based on the key skills required for the particular role. The software also ranks candidates according to the degree to which they match the vacancy criteria. Candidates who meet the criteria are fast-tracked to a job interview, and are contacted by email, giving them a unique reference code and a telephone number to call to book their appointment. The bank's introduction of electronic recruitment has achieved considerable savings in time, reducing the recruitment process by an average of just under a week per vacancy, and expects to save £500,000 a year.

E-learning

There is a considerable amount of hype concerning the use of electronic media to deliver training to employees. Generally, electronic methods have high initial costs that are only recouped where economies of scale are involved, such as those involving:
- large numbers of recruits whose induction can cover the same topics; or
- large numbers of learners requiring training in the same skills at broadly the same level.

The cost-effectiveness of using e-learning is at its greatest where a further factor is involved:

● groups of employees that are difficult (or expensive) to bring together for conventional, face-to-face training, such as shift workers, individuals who work in several distant workplaces, and those whose absence at the same time would handicap production or customer service (such as a group of retail assistants or check-out operators).

Recent feedback obtained by IRS from personnel, HR and training specialists shows that electronic forms of learning are not seen as particularly useful. Only one in five of those we contacted told us that e-learning is very effective. In contrast, seven in 10 rated team-based or group-based training as being very effective in facilitating learning.

At present, around one in three organisations use electronic methods when providing training to their employees, according to the CIPD[13]. While most research, including our own, finds that employers generally expect to increase its use, the current state of play is that only a small proportion of total training time is represented by electronic delivery methods. According to the CIPD, only one in 17 employers use e-learning media to a considerable extent.

Moreover, e-learning occupies an IT ghetto, at present. The CIPD research, which polled 500 employers, found that by far its most common use relates to the development of IT skills, followed by other technical training and, at some distance, management-related skills.

Electronic induction materials

So, at present, many forms of electronic-based induction and learning are only cost-effective for large organisations. However, developments in technology are opening up more possibilities to smaller employers, and publicly-funded e-learning opportunities are being improved, as well.

For example, employers tell IRS that a major aspect of the successful induction of new recruits lies in providing them with a resource pack of essential information *(see chapter 5 Induction, training and development)*. Most of the latest generation of personal computers contains a CD drive with the ability to "burn" CD-ROMs – in other words, to copy files from the PC onto a large-capacity CD. It is then an easy matter to organise the various induction materials that will already have been created on a computer, load them onto a CD, and provide each inductee with their own copy. Because each recruit's CD could be prepared just before they are appointed, it will automatically contain the latest version of the relevant files.

Some employers tell IRS that they are adopting this practice of using CD-ROMs for induction materials. Some go further, and post the disc to recruits before their first day at work – bearing in mind that more and more households have PCs with CD drives – helping recruits "get up to speed" as quickly as possible and reducing the unfamiliarity of their new surroundings.

Gail Nugent of e-learning specialist IQdos suggests that this electronic induction resource could include:
- a diagram of the corporate structure;
- a brief history of the organisation, its main activities and values;
- photographs (scanned in or taken with a digital camera) of key personnel, such as the management team;
- a location map of the office, a layout plan of the building highlighting key locations (such as fire exits) and addresses of other sites;
- the staff handbook; and
- the main employee policies, such as disciplinary and grievance procedures, personal use of email and internet facilities, harassment and bullying codes and absence procedures.

Thought should to be given to how electronic induction packs are to be used – particularly, where new recruits are expected to begin using them prior to joining the organisation. Instructions, question-and-answer lists and simplified versions of more detailed material will encourage use. Otherwise, there is a danger than inductees will be overwhelmed with information and the use of CD-ROMs will do more harm than good.

However, as Gail Nugent points out, employers can take electronic induction a stage further without incurring excessive costs and by using proprietary software to create simple interactive packages. New recruits could be asked to work through modules of information, and key in replies to an interactive quiz after each segment. The answers would show the recruit the extent to which they had assimilated the material and, if necessary, direct them to review some elements of the module to improve their knowledge. A repeat quiz would then be taken. Satisfactory completion of the material, as witnessed by the test, could then be filed by the employer as part of the individual's learning record. In regulated sectors, such as finance, this would also contribute towards evidence that the employee meets the competence requirements of regulatory bodies.

Increasing numbers of organisations are introducing intranets, where their various PCs are networked and a central computer acts as a server, providing an internal version of the internet. Intranets are ideally suited to the storage of quantities of information, and could contain a set of intranet pages dedicated to induction-type information. The provision of a central point for this information also makes it easier to update the contents and ensure that the latest version is the one that is being generally used in the organisation. Like the internet's click-through links, intranet connections enable users to move easily to related documents and files. And, again like the worldwide web, intranets can carry pictures, diagrams, maps and other visual material as well as text files.

Electronic-based training

For many years, employers have been able to hire or purchase off-the-shelf training packages that are run on computers – initially, via floppy discs, then CD-ROM and, now, via the internet and corporate intranets. These courses were (and continue to be) more or less cost-effective depending on the number of trainees, the relevance of the subject matter, employers' access to alternative resources (such as a trainer or college course) and, of course, the cost of the package itself. Many such offerings cover standard IT skills for users or specialists; some cover standard personal skills.

More recently, government-backed initiatives to improve the UK's competitiveness have improved the availability of electronic-based learning. learndirect, in particular, is developing a range of computer-based courses at low or no cost, as well as providing a free national helpline for enquiries about training opportunities (freephone: 0800 100 900; www.learndirect.co.uk; learndirect is the new name for the University for Industry). learndirect has a growing nationwide network of local learning centres, each with a suite of computers, internet access and access to a range of e-learning-based courses commissioned by learndirect.

Public libraries (some of which are also learndirect centres) are being equipped, through National Lottery funding, with computers and internet access for public use, and there have been experimental schemes where library staff have been trained to act as learning advisers to help adults use computer-based facilities to learn new skills.

These external developments, as well as improvements in the availability and price of hardware and software, mean that e-learning is gradually coming within the reach of employers. At present, though, even the largest employers are often taking a "tentative and exploratory" approach to e-learning, according to recent research among a cross-section of employers by the CIPD[14].

Some employers set up dedicated learning-resource centres of their own. These can range in scale from a single computer in a back office of a supermarket to large factories or head offices that have a whole suite of computers and other equipment, with libraries of books, journals and e-learning courses and several training specialists on hand to give advice and tuition.

However, these centres impose a fairly formal style of learning – trainees must request time off work, physically visit the site and, often, book in advance to ensure that the resources are free. Many employers, as the CIPD research found, reap the greatest benefits from e-learning where employees can adopt a more flexible approach – fitting in their learning at times when they are less busy, without having to leave their workplace or place bookings. Doing so, though, requires employees to have computer equipment of their own, or close at hand.

As the feedback gained by IRS from employers with experience of e-learning has shown, e-learning is seldom capable of being a direct substitute for conventional learning. The latter provides human support, the former does not. Most trainees need not only help with using the relevant hardware and software involved in e-learning, but also psychological support and encouragement. Learning as isolated individuals at a computer screen is a different experience to learning as part of a group. Indeed, some groups of employees – such as some manual workers – may lack even basic computer skills. They will need training in the technical skills associated with computer literacy, and help with confidence-building to encourage them to tackle such unfamiliar equipment.

Employers involved in the CIPD research found that off-the-shelf e-learning packages are most suited to their needs when they address standard IT skills – such as the Windows operating system, Word, Excel, HTML and Java. Indeed, the medium, as much as the message, is ideally suited to IT-related training. However, employers report greater difficulty in finding off-the-shelf materials that are relevant to employees' other skill needs. Learners can become demotivated where the training is obviously not fully relevant to their own needs, as well as wasting valuable time in learning skills that they will be unable to practise in their jobs. Moreover, the CIPD found that many e-learning courses are reported by employers as being of poor quality.

The alternative – producing bespoke e-learning materials – has both cost and resource implications. Some organisations are using authoring tools and developing (or customising) materials in-house; others are commissioning them from external consultants or publishers. Not only does this require time and expense, but the fact that the materials have been developed for a specific purpose also means that employers find they become out-of-date fairly rapidly.

2. Effective e-learning: the key issues

Effective e-learning depends on the following factors – over and above issues of cost-effectiveness in its use compared with traditional forms of training – shown in descending order of importance:

● ensuring that learners are motivated to learn: the content of the e-learning materials must be seen by learners as relevant and culturally-sensitive and, wherever possible, capable of adapting to individuals' different learning styles; in addition, individuals must be given the motivation to use e-learning as a training medium;

● providing suitable support to learners: a named person or contact point should be available so that learners can obtain answers to any questions they may have about the content of the material or its use;

● ensuring that learners are able to find time in their working day to use e-learning, that the timescale of the training takes account of their pattern of occasional or limited use, and that trainees' study time is "protected" from interruption, wherever possible.

Source: E-learning: the learning curve, Chartered Institute of Personnel and Development, 2003, www.cipd.co.uk.

3. Legal checklist

● Emails containing confidential information should not be disclosed to unauthorised individuals – Data Protection Act 1998; employees' implied duty under contract law.

● Employers are usually liable for defamatory remarks in employees' emails – Defamation Act 1996; precedent set by Western Provident Association v Norwich Union.

● Employers are usually liable for unlawful discriminatory remarks in employees' emails, and the distribution of internet content of a pornographic, racist or related content – Sex Discrimination Act 1975; Race Relations Act 1976; Disability Discrimination Act 1995; Protection from Harassment Act 1997.

● Employers are usually liable for bullying conducted via employees' emails – implied duty under contract law.

● The practice of monitoring of employees' personal emails should be made known to them, and follow legal frameworks – Data Protection Act 1998; Telecommunications (Lawful Business Practice) (Interception of Communications) Regulations 2000; Human Rights Act 1998; Regulation of Investigatory Powers Act 2000.

● Employers are usually liable for employees' unlawful or unauthorised copying of copyright material, including software – Copyright, Designs and Patents Act 1988.

● Safety of workstations – Health and Safety (Display Screen Equipment) Regulations 1992.

● Electronic recruitment and selection must observe the same equal opportunities principles as apply to traditional hiring processes, and not discriminate unfairly – Sex Discrimination Act 1975; Race Relations Act 1976; Disability Discrimination Act 1995; Trade Union and Labour Relations (Consolidation) Act 1992; and Codes of Practice associated with these Acts.

● Related to this, recruitment and selection processes that do not use non-electronic alternatives must ensure they take account of individuals covered by the Disability Discrimination Act 1995, particularly in respect of reasonable adjustments.

● Electronic recruitment and selection processes used by public sector employers must be checked by them for unfair discrimination on the grounds of ethnicity – Race Relations (Amendment) Act 2000.

● The use and storage of applicants' records must follow the data protection principles – Data Protection Act 1998 and its Employment Practices Data Protection Code.

● Online recruitment must observe the relevant provisions of the forthcoming Conduct of Employment Agencies and Employment Businesses Regulations 2002.

4. Checking candidates' backgrounds

See also: 1. Filling your vacancies; 2. Cost-effective selection; and 3. Using electronic media effectively.

This chapter covers:
- Overview: an introduction to conducting checks on candidates;
- Job references;
- Pre-employment screening;
- People with criminal records; and
- Foreign workers.

Checklists in this chapter:
1. References: the current state of play
2. The reasons why employers use references
3. Improving the effectiveness of references
4. Policies on reference-giving: the main factors
5. Improving pre-employment checking
6. Reducing unfair discrimination against ex-offenders
7. Legal checklist

Case studies in this chapter:
A. The National Portrait Gallery
B. Hanover Housing Association
C. Portsmouth Education Department
D. Reading Buses
E and F. Costain and Balfour Beatty
G. FedEx Express
H. The National Health Service

Overview

Undertaking pre-employment checks on new recruits constitutes a routine part of many employers' personnel practices. However, there are special considerations about four issues, and these provide the focus for this chapter.

The first two factors concern the use of particular practices: following up job references and undertaking pre-employment screening more generally. Reference-checking is an area of concern for many personnel, HR and recruitment specialists. Recent legal precedents have persuaded a growing proportion of employers to reduce the references they give to the equivalent of "name, rank and serial number". But, at the same time, an understandable concern to protect the public from dangerous or otherwise criminal individuals has heightened pressure on organisations to follow up references when undertaking recruitment. The same pressures are encouraging the use of more consistent and thorough pre-employment checks on potential recruits.

The second set of factors relates to two categories of applicant where special pre-employment checks may be necessary: individuals with criminal convictions, and applicants from outside the EU. In both cases, there have again been recent legal changes that have had an impact on effective personnel practice, and we examine the issues involved.

Job references

The death of references has been confidently expected for many years. Until recently, the practice of laboriously following up testimonials was seen as an anachronism – a throwback to the "characters" that decided the fate of servants in Victorian times. But, latterly, high-profile scandals involving the recruitment of dishonest, incompetent or homicidal employees have led to the passage of legislation designed to protect the public and, consequently, to greater pre-employment screening being undertaken by a wide range of employers.

The law

The law relating to references has developed piecemeal, from court decisions and from Acts of Parliament focusing on addressing abuses in particular occupations and industries. The lack of a single or prime source of legislation has probably heightened the impact of a number of legal cases in recent years, such as *Spring v Guardian Assurance*[1]. In general, there is no legal obligation for an employer to provide a reference in respect of a current or former employee, unless required to do so under a contract of employment, other agreement or in occupations and industries that are regulated, such as financial services.

However, a refusal to supply a reference to a current employee who has complained of discrimination might be interpreted as victimisation under one of the discrimination statutes. A House of Lords judgment (*Chief Constable of West Yorkshire Police v Khan*[2]) has relaxed this requirement to some extent. This legal precedent permits courts to consider the reasons for the refusal to supply a reference. In *Khan*, the House of Lords found that the reason related to the employer's current defence of a discrimination complaint, and not to a desire to victimise the individual.

In respect of former employees, refusal to provide a reference may constitute victimisation under the Sex Discrimination Act 1975, as confirmed in the case of *Coote v Granada Hospitality Ltd (No.2)*[3]. Until they are amended, this is not the case for groups covered by either the Race Relations Act 1976 or the Disability Discrimination Act 1995. These Acts currently only protect those in employment at the time of the act complained of: *Adekeye v Post Office (No 2)*[4] and *Jones v 3M Healthcare Ltd and others*[5], respectively.

This position is likely to change shortly. The government expects to amend the Disability Discrimination Act in October 2004, and is likely to have amended the Race Relations Act 1976 by summer 2003. (In both cases, the changes are part of a package of amendments required to implement the provisions of "Article 13" agreed by the European Union.)

Negligence

Where a reference is supplied, the employer and person writing it have a common-law duty of care to both the subject of the reference and its recipient. For example, the current employer and the personnel or HR manager supervising the reference would have a duty of care towards both an employee of theirs who has applied for a job with another employer, and towards the potential employer as well. The duty involves ensuring that the reference is accurate and fair – both in terms of what the reference says, and any significant details that are left out – and a claim for negligence might arise where the duty of care has not been met.

The landmark case of *Spring v Guardian Assurance*[6] involved a claim against Spring's former employer, Guardian Assurance, which reached the House of Lords. His reference was so damning that it was described as the "kiss of death", and he failed to gain the re-registration with the relevant financial-services regulatory body that would enable him to continue his career. While a claim of malicious falsehood (defamation) failed because of the "qualified-privilege" defence (*see below*), he succeeded in a claim of negligence. It was found that the employer had not checked its facts, and had made unsubstantiated allegations. The case established that the duty of care covers not only the person receiving a reference, but also the individual who is the subject of it.

In *Cox v Sun Alliance Life Ltd*[7], Mr Cox brought a court action for negligence against his former employer, on the grounds that inaccurate references –

one of which had been given over the *telephone* – had led to his subsequent difficulties in finding and keeping employment. The Court of Appeal upheld the original county-court judgment that his former employer had failed to take reasonable care to be either accurate or fair.

On the other hand, the temptation to omit any controversial or critical information from a reference may also lead to a breach of the law. References do not have to be comprehensive, but should not give a misleading impression when their recipients read them, whether this is due to the inclusion of inaccurate information or to the omission of important facts (*Bartholomew v London Borough of Hackney*[8]).

Barrister Daniel Barnett warns employers[9] to: "Treat any requests for references that come in within the next three months [after an employee's departure] with caution. It is common practice for employees' advisers [involved in claims for unfair dismissal] to try to obtain a reference from an employer in the hope that the employer will not refer to the reasons for dismissal within the reference. This will then be used against you at a tribunal hearing as evidence that your stated reason for dismissal was a fabrication." He suggests that employers could either refuse to supply a reference (unless they are required to do so, for example employers in financial services), or insert a standard phrase that: "It is this company's policy not to give any information on the capability or conduct of any employee. This should not be seen as an adverse reflection on [the individual]."

However, a refusal to supply a reference where the individual has lodged a claim of unfair discrimination could be seen as discriminatory in itself, as we saw above, unless all requests for references were treated alike. In other words, the employer would have to introduce a policy of refusing to supply any references. This would be a major blow to the use of references by employers in general.

Defamation – libel and slander – in respect of false information in references is more difficult to prove. The concept of "qualified privilege" enables referees to claim they believed the statements were true, while the individual faces the difficult task of proving that the referee acted with malice.

Mutual trust

As well as the common-law duty of care, references are also subject to the concept of the implied term of mutual trust and confidence. The law considers this term forms part of every contract of employment. In another well-known case, *TSB Bank plc v Harris*[10], the bank supplied a reference that revealed several complaints about Ms Harris of which she herself was unaware. The complaints might or might not have been factually correct, but the Employment Appeal Tribunal ruled that "simply to be accurate in what is said may not lead to a 'reasonable and fair' reference".

As well as potential negligence claims from new employers or former employees, employers supplying references to current employees that do not follow the above principles may be subject to a claim of constructive dismissal if the employee resigns as a result.

Unsatisfactory references

Employers typically obtain references at a late stage in their appointment process. However, job offers are legally binding contracts, and they cannot usually be withdrawn simply because a reference contains information that changes the recruiters' decision about the appointment – unless it reveals that the candidate has lied. To do so might leave the employer open to a claim for breach of contract – that is, for compensation for earnings lost during the applicable notice period. To avoid this, it is common practice to offer employment on a conditional basis – "subject to satisfactory references". In *Wishart v NACAB*[11], the Court of Appeal considered that "satisfactory" meant only that the employer must consider the reference in good faith.

Employment agencies and references

Employment agencies often act on behalf of employers in finding potential recruits and helping to shortlist them. The Conduct of Employment Agencies and Employment Businesses Regulations 1976 require agencies to undertake some basic pre-employment checks before they recommend an individual for employment. The precise details are due to change with a new set of similarly-titled Regulations which are expected, after several years' delay, to come into force by the end of 2003. In any event, personnel, HR and recruitment specialists must take a view about whether or not agencies' checks are adequate for their purposes and, if not, determine which of them need to be repeated.

Under the 1976 Regulations, agencies must obtain sufficient information from the individual to be able to ensure they meet the employer's requirements. In particular, where the vacancy is covered by any legal requirements, the agency has to make all reasonable enquiries to ensure that the individual can satisfy them.

The forthcoming Regulations state that an agency must not introduce a potential recruit (or supply a temp) "unless it has obtained confirmation of the identity of the work-seeker; that the work-seeker has the experience, training, qualifications and any authorisation which the hirer [ie the employer] considers are necessary, or which are required by law or any professional body, to work in the position which the hirer seeks to fill". Agencies are also required to pass on to the employer the details they obtained under this requirement, and to inform them of any information they obtain that indicates the potential recruit or temp may be unsuitable for the vacancy.

There are two additional requirements where agencies are supplying potential recruits or temps for certain types of post.

1. Where the work involves contact with children or vulnerable adults, or where the vacancy is covered by legal or professional requirements, agencies must undertake reference checks (they must have "obtained two references from persons not related to the work-seeker who have agreed that the reference they provide may be disclosed to the hirer"), and obtained copies of relevant qualifications which they should also pass on to the employer.

2. For posts involving contact with children or vulnerable adults, agencies must take "all other reasonably practicable steps to confirm that the work-seeker is not unsuitable for the position" – this is likely to involve obtaining disclosures from the Criminal Records Bureau.

At present, it is uncertain whether or not the requirements in the forthcoming employment agency Regulations that agencies should undertake pre-employment and reference checks will apply to commercial internet recruitment sites (often known as "job boards"). One of the industry's representative bodies, the Association of Online Recruiters, maintains that most of its members would be forced out of business if this were to be the case[12].

Data protection and references

References that employers receive about job applicants are covered by the Data Protection Act 1998. Although it is commonly believed the Act gives individuals the right to gain access to references about them, in fact, they are excluded from the access requirements (under Schedule 7 of the Act). The exceptions to this disclosure exemption are that the reference was not given in confidence, and that the reference cannot be disclosed without revealing the identity of another individual (including the referee), or that it has not been possible to gain the named individual's consent to disclosure.

In such cases, the Act says that it may be possible to disclose part of the reference, provided this does not reveal the referee's identity.

However, two publications from the Office of the Information Commissioner[13] have since considerably limited the Act's exemption for references, by applying it solely while a confidential reference is "in the hands of the organisation which gave it". Once the reference has been received by the intended recipient, these publications say that the exemption does not apply. There would, though, still be a breach of the referee's own rights if their identity were to be revealed without consent. One of these publications, the Employment Practices Data Protection Code, says that "the recipient is entitled to take steps to withhold information that reveals the identity of other individuals, such as the author of the reference".

The Code, which has aroused considerable controversy, is being issued in four instalments and will not take effect until all four parts have been published. The controversy has caused publication delays and the remaining instalments are not expected to be available until the final quarter of 2003. In addition, the Information Commissioner has announced that the first two parts of the Code will be revised and simplified in 2004 to follow the new style being adopted for parts three and four.

Part one of the Code recommends that:
- only details directly relevant to a particular vacancy, and that will be used as part of the selection process, should be obtained from job applicants;
- the role of references is to confirm the factual details that applicants supply;
- the reference procedure should be explained to applicants. This includes the nature of the information that will be requested;
- applicants must give their consent to this procedure; and
- employers should "give the applicant the opportunity to make representations should any of the checks produce discrepancies".

Some personnel and HR managers tell us that they already seek referees' permission to disclose the references they provide to the individuals concerned, although, in practice, this will only apply to the successful applicant once they have been recruited by the new employer. Where permission has not been sought, however, it is difficult to see how the Code's requirement to conceal the identity of the referee can be observed. In almost all cases, job applicants themselves provide the details of their referees, and will usually know the name or job title of the person in the organisations concerned who is charged with providing references to prospective employers. The simple deletion of the referee's name will not preserve their confidentiality.

The other provisions of the Code are notably at odds with current practice, according to the large-scale research that IRS has conducted among personnel and HR specialists. Most potential employers are interested in information from references that goes beyond the Code's restriction to the verification of factual details (see below). In particular, they are interested in applicants' absence records, their performance and referees' opinions of the person's suitability for the vacancy.

Nor do employers usually explain the reference procedure to applicants and the kind of information that will be requested from referees – apart from some employers' practice of telling applicants of the timescale for following up references. In fact, the timescale is such – references are usually followed up after the final interview – that employers will find it difficult to honour the Code's requirement that employers should "give the applicant the opportunity to make representations should any of the checks produce discrepancies". An exchange of correspondence would not be particularly suitable, leaving the options of telephoning the applicant or inviting them back for a further interview to discuss the reference.

Record keeping

There are legal implications for the security, confidentiality and period of storage of references and other information obtained about job applicants. The Data Protection Act 1998 requires secure, confidential storage, the rights of access by employees to their records (having given due notice in the prescribed way; *see above for the exemptions relating to references*), and that records "shall not be kept for longer than is necessary for that purpose or those purposes". Guidance on storing records is given in the Employment Practices Data Protection Code 2002.

While neither the Act nor the Code offer set limits on record-keeping, they expect that the period concerned should reflect a real business need and take account of other legal requirements. For example, records may be relevant to potential claims on the grounds of unlawful discrimination; in such cases, individuals usually have three months to lodge a complaint. These considerations highlight the need to ensure that records are filed safely and securely, and kept for as long as is relevant under the law and the organisation's requirements.

Regulated employment

Just as there is no general obligation on employers to provide references, there is no universal requirement to obtain references in respect of people applying to work with the organisation. However, some occupations and industries are covered by legislation designed to protect the public from unqualified or dangerous workers, where reference-checking is a legal requirement.

Employers in the financial services industry are now covered by the Financial Services and Markets Act 2000 and the supervision of the Financial Services Authority (FSA). The FSA has introduced a "training and competence" approach that aims to ensure workers in the industry obtain and maintain minimum levels of competence. Among its requirements, employers are expected to use reference-checking as part of their pre-employment screening processes to ensure that recruits have the necessary knowledge, skills, experience, training and relevant qualifications. Employers obtaining references are expected to explore all avenues where they are entitled to receive information on applicants. And employers asked to supply a reference are required to do so, and to provide all relevant information of which they are aware. The extent of the pre-employment screening may vary according to whether or not the applicant is already registered with the FSA, the nature of the job and the individual's own background. Credit-worthiness checks may be needed, usually via a specialist agency, although candidates' permission will first be required.

More generally, the latest Conduct of Employment Agencies and Employment Businesses Regulations, which are expected to be implemented by the end of 2003, will place a legal onus on employment agencies to undertake reference checks (they must have "obtained two references from persons not related to the work-seeker"). This requirement applies to both temporary workers and permanent recruits they supply to posts where qualifications are required by law or any professional body, or where the posts involve working with children or vulnerable adults.

These types of job are also likely to be covered by the new system of disclosures from the Criminal Records Bureau *(see the section below on the bureau)*, whereby employers are able to obtain details of applicants' criminal convictions and other criminal activity. However, even in such cases, employers are advised by the bureau to "engage in a full range of pre-employment checks"[14], such as obtaining suitable job references.

Using references in practice

Reference-checking is one of the most widely practised recruitment methods, coming fourth in prevalence after interviews, application forms and

CVs, according to the recruitment survey from the Chartered Institute of Personnel and Development (CIPD)[15]. Just under three-quarters of employers use references in their appointment decisions, although there is a sharp divide between private and public sector practices. While only some seven in 10 private sector firms – applying to roughly similar proportions of manufacturers and service sector firms – use them, this rises to almost nine in 10 public sector bodies.

1. References: the current state of play

● References are taken up by the majority of employers when deciding whether or not to appoint someone.

● Employers use reference-checking in respect of all their vacancies, typically, rather than being selective.

● In the private sector, following up references usually occurs once the appointment decision has been taken. The most common timing in the public sector occurs after the job interview, but before the final decision has been taken.

● Most employers prefer to obtain written (or emailed) references, and send out a standard questionnaire or form for referees to complete, together with some basic information about the vacancy.

● There is a growing contradiction between the information that employers are willing to provide in the references they give to others, and the details they want others to give to them. Almost all employers are willing to provide references about current/former employees, but most now have a policy controlling what is said. Typically, this restricts reference-giving to personnel and HR specialists, and limits the content to factual data.

In contrast, when most employers are in the position of requesting references, they are usually interested in as much informal, qualitative information and opinion from referees as possible.

● Very few employers in the UK supplement references with pre-employment screening or other checks on applicants.

● Despite the poor reputation of the use of references, most employers are broadly satisfied that they play a useful role in recruitment, and most have acted on them by deciding not to appoint a particular candidate.

● Employers' practice relating to employees' access to references is in a fluid state. A minority gives access to references provided by outsiders, while almost half give access to references they supply to others.

Few users of references confine reference-checking to particular vacancies or candidates, preferring a simple, uniform policy, according to the employers contacted by IRS. We find that more than eight in 10 users apply a policy of reference-checking across the board, leaving just a small minority that is selective.

Smaller employers are as likely to follow a universal approach as are larger organisations, and it is no more prevalent in the public sector than in services firms in the private sector. However, manufacturers that use references are comparatively less likely to have a policy of following up references for each and every vacancy or candidate, although the majority still does so.

The small proportion of employers that picks and chooses when to follow up references takes this decision according to one or more factors. Most commonly, the level of the vacancy acts as a trigger, with fewer basing their reference-checking according to the type of vacancy involved. A few employers make random checks, while others follow a variety of other approaches, such as obtaining references for permanent appointments, but not for fixed-term or temporary workers.

When references are taken up

References typically occupy the final stage in the lengthy process of filling a vacancy, according to the feedback IRS has obtained from personnel, HR and recruitment specialists. A decision is usually made on a favoured candidate, and he or she is offered appointment "subject to satisfactory references". In all, seven in 10 employers wait until this point before they follow up references.

Fewer than a quarter obtain references at the stage before this: when interviews have been completed, but before the choice of candidate has been made. Finally, one in 14 employers conduct their reference checks even earlier in the process, before interviews take place.

Smaller employers (those with fewer than 250 employees) are even more likely to leave reference-checking until the end of the selection process, with more than nine in 10 doing so. Conversely, the public sector places much greater weight on following up references earlier in the process. While, as we saw, seven in 10 of employers as a whole wait until the job offer has been made, only three in 10 public sector employers do so. Instead, half obtain references after the final interview, but *prior* to the selection decision. And one-fifth conduct their reference checks before any interviews are held – a proportion five times larger than found among private sector employers.

Decisions about the timing of reference checks will partly be influenced by the importance attached to the information obtained from referees. Where references are given a narrow role of merely confirming basic factual details, then it may be appropriate to delay their use until after a job offer has been made.

There may be delays in obtaining references, and candidates who have been offered a job – albeit conditionally – are less likely to become impatient and take up a job offer elsewhere than those who are still moving through the selection process and have no reason to think they are likely to be appointed. Moreover, a candidate who is fairly certain of being able to move to another employer will be far more relaxed about asking their present employer for a reference and, in so doing, informing them of their active search for a different job.

On the other hand, there are also good reasons why the earlier use of references should be considered. References are merely one source of information on the candidate and it does not necessarily follow that a referee's word should always be preferred to the details supplied by the candidate. There may be factors such as bias on the part of the referee, lack of direct or recent knowledge of the applicant, or simple errors of fact, that affect the status of the reference as a completely reliable source. This means that candidates should be given the opportunity to discuss conflicting information (a recommendation of the recent Data Protection Code, for example; *see the section on the law above*), and this may be best done in the formal setting of the interview. This, in turn, has implications for the timing of reference checks. Moreover, where recruiters give a greater role to references as an information source on candidates, they may want to feed them into an earlier stage of the selection process.

At the National Portrait Gallery in London *(see case study A)*, obtaining references earlier on in the recruitment process is seen as a means of improving the quality of the feedback that referees supply. The gallery's personnel manager told us that this can encourage the applicant and their current employer to discuss the vacancy and their potential suitability for it.

Nick Cowen and Rowena Cowen have suggested that employers could adopt a twin-track approach. Following up references is time-consuming and resource intensive, they point out; moreover, approaches to applicants' current employers can cause difficulties for the individuals involved. Instead, they propose that a reference from a *former* employer is obtained for each shortlisted candidate, prior to any job offer. Such references would serve to confirm past achievements and past appointments, excluding those from the person's current job. They would also help to minimise the need to withdraw job offers. Then, once an appointment decision has been made, a reference is obtained from the potential recruit's *current* employer to complete the checking process[16].

Case study A. The National Portrait Gallery

The National Portrait Gallery employs around 180 staff, ranging from curators to retail assistants, and from managers to support staff. The gallery checks references for all potential recruits and asks job candidates to supply details of three referees on its standard application form. Candidates are invited to tick a box as to whether references can be obtained prior to interview. In fact, in the majority of cases, the gallery is able to take up references before the interview process. It points out that the job circuit for galleries and museums is fairly small, and jobhunters are likely to have already approached their managers to gain support for a career move.

The process for requesting references is carried out in tandem with inviting candidates for interview. A structured form, together with a copy of the job description and person specification, is sent out to referees. Factual information, such as job tenure, reason for leaving and attendance record, is requested on the candidate, as well as the referee's opinion on the candidate's suitability for the vacancy. The gallery finds that employers are generally forthcoming when providing comments on suitability for the post, which it attributes in part to the more transparent process that is encouraged by seeking references up front. It believes that asking for references at an early stage may prompt applicants to discuss their application with their managers.

If the recruitment process reaches the stage where, following interview, no references have been received for the most suitable candidate, a conditional job offer can be made. The gallery makes every effort to obtain all three references, but, at the very least, aims to gain feedback on a person's employment history for the past five years. Referees are given the option to return references by post, fax or email in a bid to speed up the process.

Because of the potential for physical loss from the collection, and some staff having access to children, security checks on all staff are carried out using the services of government agencies. These checks include criminal convictions and childcare lists. It finds the service very effective, but lengthy; therefore, its offer letter clearly states that the job offer is conditional on acceptable checks having been made. The gallery uses the telephone to follow up or clarify any information that is provided in writing, but prefers to receive written references. While it believes that telephone interviews encourage frankness, the discipline of providing a written reference compensates by encouraging referees to think more carefully about the information they are providing.

Line managers have the authority to provide references on current or former employees, but they must be copied to the personnel department. The gallery's employee handbook provides guidance on reference writing and stipulates that the reference should contain factual information only.

All in all, the gallery considers that references are an important part of the selection jigsaw and are helpful in verifying factual details, but they cannot be considered in isolation. A reference can confirm the view of a candidate that is formed during the selection process.

At whatever point at which references are taken up, personnel, HR and recruitment specialists need to ensure that the process is administered properly. In particular, a record needs to be kept of the dates that references are requested, and follow-up action taken when they are not received within a pre-determined timescale. According to the CIPD, failure rates can be very high, with as many as two-thirds of reference requests being unanswered[17].

Written or verbal?

Personnel, HR and recruitment specialists tell us that their organisations overwhelmingly prefer formal references, making their requests in writing (or email) and receiving the reference in the same medium. There is little evidence of a switch to using the telephone or face-to-face interviews to obtain references, despite many employers' perceptions that written references are becoming less informative.

More than three-quarters of employers we contacted always obtain written references (by letter or email), and a further fifth do so on occasion. Hardly any employers invariably rely on verbal references.

For the vast majority of organisations using references in recruitment, the telephone is merely a fallback. When there is no response to a reference request, or when time is short, then a referee may be contacted by telephone. Often, though, the employers involved tell us that they would then ask for the details to be confirmed in writing.

This is the practice in the Hanover Housing Association, for example *(see case study B)*. It contacts referees where time is of the essence, but uses a similar set of questions to the one that appears on its written reference request to ensure it obtains information on the same issues – and referees are subsequently asked to confirm their feedback in writing.

When requesting written references, recruiters can simply ask the referee to compose a free-form letter, perhaps with some guidance as to what details should be included. Or they can supply a form for the referee to complete. In fact, more than eight in 10 employers that use written references also make use of a reference questionnaire or form that they send to the referees. And most of them invariably do so; with only a small minority doing so from time to time.

The public sector, surprisingly, given its greater formalisation of many recruitment practices, is not only a relatively lower user of forms and questionnaires (although a majority still does so), but also is less likely to use them on each and every occasion.

Providing background information

Conversely, public sector employers are assiduous information-givers when contacting referees. Each one of those we contacted supplies at least some background information about the vacancy when requesting references, while more than a third of services firms and manufacturers in the private sector supply nothing at all. Moreover, in terms of the extent of the background details supplied, public sector employers are almost always more likely to be forthcoming. For example, fewer than a half of private sector firms provide a job description relating to the vacancy, but almost all public sector organisations do so. And well under three in 10 private sector firms supply a person specification, while more than nine in 10 of the public sector does so.

Almost a quarter of public sector bodies go further, and give referees details of the main selection criteria for the vacancy in question – way ahead of private sector practice, where such details are supplied by fewer than one in 10 firms.

On the other hand, when a public sector employer contacts a referee, it either expects the person to know about the organisation or does not rate this as a priority area for information giving. Only one in 13 public sector employers supply information about the organisation itself, while private sector recruiters are almost twice as likely to do so.

Use of the information in references

Weighing up the information that referees supply is rarely an easy task, even where some form or structure is provided. In many cases, though, a reference is seen as a simple safety net against flagrant deceptions on the part of the candidate, rather than contributing in a fuller way to the appointment decision.

Potentially, though, a reference can provide information and feedback on a wide range of issues relating to the candidate. It can confirm, or disclose for the first time, the candidate's current salary, for example, and verify basic details such as the person's job title and employment dates.

Personnel, HR and recruitment managers tell us that they are interested in many different types of information when reading applicants' references *(listed in checklist 2)*. The three most popular topics are the applicant's absence record, the referee's opinion of the candidate's performance and their opinion of the person's suitability for the vacancy in question.

Many employers have now formulated a policy on what can and cannot be included in the references supplied to others *(see below)* – usually, to prevent the expression of opinions and the inclusion of other non-factual information. But, even such employers are ready to seek, and use, such qualitative feedback when they are in the position of obtaining references from others, according to our research. More than three-quarters of employers with a restrictive reference-giving policy are interested in referees' opinions of candidates' performance, and almost two-thirds are interested in referees' opinions about candidates' suitability for the vacancies being filled. Employers without policies limiting the content of references they supply are even less inhibited. More than nine in 10 are interested in opinions about performance, and more than three-quarters are interested in opinions concerning suitability for the vacancy.

2. The reasons why employers use references

References can provide many different insights into the candidate's abilities and performance. Feedback we obtained from personnel, HR and recruitment managers enables us to rank these factors on the basis of their popularity. The list is shown in descending order of popularity; the first eight factors are used by at least half of all recruiters.

- Absence record
- Opinion of candidate's performance
- Opinion of candidate's suitability for vacancy
- Work history
- Punctuality
- Disciplinary record
- Responsibilities of current job
- Motivation/commitment
- Gaps found in CV/application form
- Current salary
- Qualifications

- Criminal convictions
- Credit-worthiness
- Reason for leaving
- Membership of professional etc body
- Honesty/integrity
- Whether would re-employ

The box above shows the areas in references of most interest to recruiters as a whole, but there are some notable differences in approach according to the types of employer involved. For example, employers in the public sector are relatively more interested in gaining information from referees on candidates' absence records than employers in the private sector. This reflects the typically higher absence rates found in public services, and the government's emphasis on taking action to reduce them.

Particularly interesting, though, is the public sector's relatively greater interest in two qualitative areas: referees' opinions concerning candidates' performance and referees' opinions regarding candidates' suitability for the vacancy. Conversely, referees' information about applicants' current salaries represents a subject of interest to a considerably greater proportion of private sector services firms, than it does to either manufacturers or the public sector.

In terms of workforce size, smaller employers are more interested than larger ones in referees' information on applicants' current salary, and their views on the candidates' performance, their suitability for the vacancy and their motivation or commitment.

Effectiveness of references

Reference-checking will only confound its critics if it is shown to affect the final recruitment decision. The feedback obtained by IRS from personnel, HR and recruitment managers with experience of using references provides evidence that this is indeed the case.

First of all, the information obtained via references does affect employers' recruitment decisions.

In six out of 10 employers using references, they tell us that references have had a direct impact on some recruitment decisions, with these organisations rejecting at least one candidate in a typical 12-month period or failing to confirm a provisional offer of appointment. In a quarter of employers, references have led to the rejection of at least three candidates in a year, with one-twelfth rejecting five or more people. And, importantly, employers with sensitive posts – such as work with children and vulnerable adults, or in financial services – are proportionately more likely to reject applicants because of their use of references than employers as a whole. For example, only a quarter of this group fail to reject any candidates because of unsatisfactory references, against almost twice as many employers without such sensitive vacancies. Moreover, employers with sensitive posts are more likely to reject larger numbers of applicants because of their use of references than is the pattern in employers without posts of this type.

Second, the majority of personnel, HR and recruitment specialists with direct experience of using references has told us that they are useful, or very useful, to them. This holds true in all industries and size of organisation, with the exception of smaller employers with workforces of fewer than 200 employees, where most hold no strong views and only a minority actively consider references of being of use to them.

Case study B. Hanover Housing Association

Hanover Housing Association provides sheltered accommodation for elderly people, and employs around 600 employees, nearly half of whom are estate managers on sheltered housing schemes for the elderly. References are taken up for all job candidates, following final interview. If the housing association has reached a selection decision, a letter will be sent to the favourite candidate indicating an intention to offer them the job. Following the receipt of satisfactory references, the personnel department writes again, confirming the conditional offer of appointment and enclosing a copy of the contract.

The housing association always obtains written references on potential recruits by sending referees a structured form covering the following areas:

- position held and salary;
- honesty and capability;
- reliability;
- ability to get on with others;
- ability to work well under pressure;
- absence record, including significant periods of absence;
- details of any disciplinary action;
- whether or not the referee would re-employ the person;
- any reason why Hanover Housing Association should not employ the person; and
- additional information that the referee can provide if they wish.

If there is a need to appoint someone as quickly as possible, line managers initially assume responsibility for collecting references over the telephone. But, in such cases, a generic script ensures that it collects the same information as referees provide on the structured form used for written references. The recruitment team then follows this up by asking referees to complete the written form. The housing association has rejected several potentially suitable candidates because of unfavourable references. It always carefully follows up negative information, or any blanks in the data provided.

The housing association is happy in principle to supply references for current or former employees, and these contain the same type of information that it expects to receive from referees. However, in view of the growing body of case law on references, limitations are placed on the extent of information given out. Only personnel specialists have the authority to write references, and there are specific restrictions on what the references should contain. For example, when providing details of an employee's sickness-absence record, only the number of absent days will be indicated.

The association is using the Criminal Records Bureau as part of its pre-employment checking, and obtains "enhanced disclosures" concerning those individuals who will be working with vulnerable adults.

The psychology of references

The CIPD's guide to references[18] talks of the "reliability and validity problems" affecting them. First of all, the choice of referees could be influenced by job applicants' desire to make a good impression – left to them, they will not offer the names of referees who they suspect will give them a bad reference. But, recruiters can counteract this by avoiding so-called "character references", and stipulating that the choice of referees must conform to certain criteria. For vacancies that are unlikely to attract applicants straight from school or university with little work experience, recruiters can stipulate that the references must be supplied by the candidates' two most-recent employers.

Second, referees themselves can provide a distorted impression of the applicant, either intentionally or unconsciously. They may dislike the person, may be having an "off day" when they receive the reference request, may remember one negative incident that colours the whole reference, or may simply lack the expertise to present the facts without bias.

Conversely, the reference may be misleadingly positive. Many people dislike giving bad news, and may understate or conceal information that is unfavourable to the individual. Their recollection of the person may be influenced by a few strongly positive incidents that crowd out important, but unflattering, aspects of their performance. Referees may be concerned about legal liability where a reference contains critical details, and employers that give employees access to their references may encourage referees to avoid any negative statements, particularly where the two individuals are likely to come into contact in the future. Employers that are eager to help a under-performing member of staff find alternative employment will also have a motive for presenting the candidate in the best possible light.

Obtaining at least two references can reduce the impact of this subjectivity, as can the use of reference questionnaires sent to referees for their completion. These forms provide a structure for referees, encouraging balanced disclosure of information and, hopefully, a more considered and objective approach. Similarly, referees will be better informed if they are sent some basic information about the vacancy, such as the selection criteria and the job's requirements and duties.

However, there is scant scientific data on the validity of references. Reilly and Chao's major 1982 study that synthesised and weighted available research (a "meta-analysis") found that references had a low average score of 0.14[19]. However, another meta-analysis, by Hunter and Hunter[20], found some high scores among the average, indicating that references *could* be capable of helping to identify applicants who will turn out to be effective performers in their new job – but that references often fail to achieve this standard.

Improving the effectiveness of references

The potential to transform reference-checking from a paper-shuffling exercise into an important contributor to hiring decisions is supported by an investigation conducted by Paul Dobson. "In theory, they have a very sound basis," he says. "That is, the use of past samples of behaviour to predict future performance. The majority of referees will have had the opportunity to observe the applicant over a quite long period of time, in a natural setting, undertaking tasks of direct relevance to the target position."[21]

Paul Dobson's review led him to highlight the issues that could contribute to effective reference-checking. Like other researchers, before and after him, his conclusions also demonstrate the difficulty, levels of expertise and large amounts of time that are involved in raising references' validity. Checklist 3 brings together the main issues regarding the use of references, based on the feedback provided by the employers we contacted, and the work of Dobson and other researchers and writers.

3. Improving the effectiveness of references

Feedback obtained by IRS from personnel, HR and recruitment specialists, and other research, highlights the following issues as being important in the effective use of employment references:

● **Administration:** Identify the ways in which candidates will be informed of the mechanics of the reference-checking process. Ensure there is an effective system to administer reference checks and chase up late responses.

● **Timing:** Determine the point in recruitment at which references will be followed up. Left until a late stage, the number of candidates and the consequent workload will be reduced, the loss of good candidates caused by delays in obtaining references will be reduced, and the potential damage to candidates' careers with their current employer will be minimised. However, earlier use provides the opportunity for references to play a greater role in recruitment decisions, and for any queries or inconsistencies to be discussed at interview. It may be possible to follow up most references at an earlier stage, avoiding the current employer until later.

● **Choice of referee:** Referees should have first-hand, recent knowledge of the applicant where they are expected to provide information on the person's performance; other referees or contacts may be required where simple fact-checking is involved. If possible, it is useful to obtain more than one reference concerning the applicant's abilities and performance (a nominated referee could be asked to name other potential referees who also know the applicant well; however, this will require clearance with the applicant). A referee should be able to verify the information they give; they should not be used to confirm details of which they have no direct knowledge.

● **Structure:** Many researchers believe that referees are most likely to provide comprehensive and pertinent replies where they are given a structure. This can involve a questionnaire posted to referees, or structured interview schedule for verbal references. The questions should be based on the key requirements of the vacancy, derived from job analysis. Referees should be asked to provide details of observed performance (good or bad) in respect of each aspect.

● **Verbal or written:** Some researchers argue that an interview (face-to-face or by telephone) is preferable because referees may be more candid, and because it allows experienced interviewers to probe ambiguous or ostensibly biased replies, and obtain evidence for the information given. Conversely, some researchers argue that written interviews may be more considered and allow time for facts to be checked, and their formality can encourage honesty and objectivity. Basic, but effective enquiries should be carried out in both types of reference to confirm the identity of the referee.

● **Background details on the vacancy:** Providing basic information about the vacancy to referees may help them tailor their replies to the recruiter's requirements. Some researchers believe that providing fuller information, such as the key skills, experience and qualities sought, will further enhance the reference's relevance. Others argue that referees cannot be expected to "get inside the heads" of the recruiters, and fully understand such details.

● **Interpretation:** Referees are not necessarily more accurate or unbiased than job applicants. Where possible, at least two references concerning work performance should be obtained in order to permit checks for consistency and agreement. Those providing written references can be contacted for further information or clarification. Applicants should be given the opportunity to account for discrepancies or a referee's critical assessment.

● **Access:** The apparent contradiction between the Data Protection Act and the forthcoming Code of Practice regarding employees' access to their references has not yet been resolved. The Act exempts confidential references from access; the Code is much more limited – *see the section on the law above*. The law also requires references to be treated in confidence and kept securely.

Case study C. Portsmouth Education Department

In Portsmouth Education Department, teachers are recruited directly by schools in the city, while recruitment is undertaken centrally by the department for headteachers and support staff, such as advisers and educational psychologists. It follows the written reference-checking policy that applies across Portsmouth City Council. The policy runs to three pages and provides detailed guidance on areas such as providing references following disciplinary investigation or dismissal, and the disclosure of references. The policy is communicated to line managers and serves as an important guideline for all those involved in the recruitment process.

The department adopts a rigorous process when checking candidates' references: all references are checked, preferably prior to interview. It requests permission to take up references when job applicants are invited to attend for interview. If they decline at this point, they are asked again when attending for interview, and it is made very clear that the department will not make a job offer until references have been checked. However, it finds that most candidates are happy for their referees to be contacted in advance.

A significant number of prospective employees selected by the education department will be recruited to vacancies that involve working with children. Although it is considered vitally important that proper checks are carried out on such candidates, the department consistently applies the same approach to all job candidates, irrespective of the type of vacancy.

The department takes up three references for headteacher posts and two for all other vacancies. The policy dictates that at least one referee must be the candidate's most recent employer and, preferably, all references should bear testament to the person's ability to perform the job in question. Although the department has occasionally obtained a reference by telephone if necessary, it is not the preferred choice. If time is running short, it will contact a referee by telephone, but always request that any information supplied on a candidate is backed up subsequently through a written reference. A structured letter is sent to all referees, requesting information on the following areas:

- work history;
- responsibilities of current or most recent job;
- absence record;
- punctuality;
- disciplinary record;
- motivation and commitment;
- the referee's opinion of the candidate's performance; and
- views on the candidate's suitability for the vacancy.

Although line managers and personnel specialists have the authority to supply information on areas such as conduct and suitability for the vacancy, no specific details are disclosed to third parties. Managers are also aware that, where issues relating to performance or conduct are provided in a reference, the subject of that reference must be made aware of the disclosure.

The department believes that reference-checking plays an important role in its selection process, but only in the context of the overall process. The department has never rejected someone on the sole basis of a bad reference. If a negative testimonial is received, the candidate's unsuitability for the post is usually borne out by the whole selection process and there is no need to rely on the reference alone. In addition, the department has noticed that, in the light of increasing legal liability, referees are more guarded in the information they supply on current or former employees.

Providing references

As we saw above in our legal summary, employers have no general obligation to provide a reference for a current or former employee, although there are a few major exceptions to this freedom. Almost all employers, though, tell us that they will happily provide a reference for current and former employees.

The almost universal willingness to provide references does not mean that employers make no attempts to manage and control the process. In fact, the contrary is the case. As we shall see below, two-thirds of employers now have a policy that restricts the type of information that can be supplied in references, and almost all of them control who in their organisation has the authority to act as a referee.

Very few employers allow anyone in their organisation to respond to a reference request. Even then, some employers make use of a central gateway (usually in the form of the personnel or HR manager) through which all outbound references must pass. This provides an opportunity to keep central records of references and monitor their content.

Even line managers' freedom to act as a referee is circumscribed. They will be the most suitable person to provide an informed reference, having first-hand knowledge of the subject of the reference ("the only valid employment references are by individuals with first-hand detailed knowledge of a candidate's work"[22]). But in almost six in 10 organisations, they are not permitted to send out a reference. This restriction, in particular, provides evidence of the long-term trend away from providing detailed references. Instead of giving feedback on an individual's motivation, performance and attitudes – where personal knowledge of the subject is essential – employers are confining themselves to giving "name, rank and serial number". This basic factual information requires no more than access to the subject's personnel records, and personnel and HR managers are ideally placed to act as such new-style referees.

In the remaining organisations – the four in 10 giving line managers the authority to act as referees – several of the employers we contacted told us that the gatekeeping role of personnel and HR specialists still operates. One national charity, for example, said that "If a reference is provided by the line manager, HR has to see this and authorise it prior to sending". Others depicted their arrangement as a "partnership" between line managers and the personnel or HR manager – but with the same effect of ensuring the involvement of staff trained in the legal issues surrounding references and of good practice in supplying details that can be substantiated.

The central role of personnel and HR specialists is reflected in our research's finding that almost nine 10 employers permit them to act as referees. In fact, in just over half of employers as a whole, *only* personnel and HR specialists and no others can supply references. Conversely, in no instance of all those employers we contacted, does an organisation allow line managers to act as referees while preventing personnel and HR specialists from so doing.

There are differences in practice between the main sectors of the economy. The private sector is much more likely to exclude all but personnel and HR specialists from acting as referees – this is the case in two-thirds of private sector services firms and three-quarters of manufacturers. But the practice is rare in the public sector, with only one in seven such organisations having this policy.

Information restrictions

A series of well-publicised legal judgments – some of which were mentioned in the legal section above – have caused many employers to become cautious about the information that they supply to others in references.

Restrictions on the individuals who can act as referees may represent one means of reducing employers' potential legal liability. More directly, though, almost two-thirds of employers now have a policy that places limitations on the information that referees can include in the references they supply to others. One of our contacts, an office-supplies company, put it this way:"Just some concern over liability with references. Therefore, we provide minimal information for subsequent employers, ie dates of employment, position held, reason for leaving (eg resigned)."

The private sector is more wary than organisations in the public sector. Seven in 10 services firms and manufacturers in the private sector have imposed such restrictions, while just over four in 10 public sector employers have done so.

The role of personnel and HR specialists as gatekeepers of reference-giving plays a part in employers' policies regarding information disclosure. Organisations that allow their personnel and HR managers and no others to act as referees are less likely to have a policy restricting the content of references. This provides confirmation that employers use their personnel and HR specialists to monitor and control the content of references written by others in the organisation, as well as using them for record-keeping purposes.

4. Policies on reference-giving: the main factors

We have analysed feedback we obtained from personnel, HR and recruitment managers in organisations with a policy restricting the content of references to highlight the main features involved. Primarily, the policies aim to prevent referees expressing opinions and require them to keep to factual details. More specifically, the policies explicitly allow the following areas to be included in references given out to others. Shown in descending order or prevalence, they are:

● dates of employment;
● job title and/or position in organisation;
● reason for leaving;
● absence record;
● *performance record;*
● responsibilities of present job; and
● *current salary.*

However, almost as many employers told us that the topics italicised in the above list – performance and salary – could *not* be supplied as told us that they were permitted.

Employee access

We noted above *(in the "Data protection" section of this chapter)* that there is some uncertainty surrounding individuals' rights of access to confidential references concerning them. The Data Protection Act 1998 itself exempts them from access rights, while subsequent guidance from the Office of the Information Commissioner restricts the exemption to the brief period while a confidential reference remains in the hands of the organisation that is to supply it. In other words, once the reference has been received by the organisation that requested it, the exemption disappears and individuals have access rights – provided that the identity of the referee has been removed.

This confusion in what is required by law is reflected in employers' current practices, we have found. At present, just over a third of employers will, in principle, permit their employees to gain access to references about them that others – such as a former employer – have written about them. Manufacturers are most likely to grant such access (more than four in 10 do so), followed by the public sector (one-third do so) and private sector services firms (three in 10 do so). Analysed by workforce size, the smallest employers (those having fewer than 250 employees) are most likely to grant such access (half do so), while around a third of employers with larger workforces have adopted this policy.

In terms of references that employers themselves write about their current or past employees and supply to others, then relatively greater numbers of organisations permit access. In all, just under half do so. In this respect, the public sector is most likely to grant access (two-thirds do so), followed by manufacturers (just over four in 10 do so) and private sector services firms (four in 10 do so). There is little difference in such access policies between employers of different workforce sizes.

At present, therefore, more employers will give employees access to references they supply to others, than do so in respect of references they request from other organisations. However, just over three in 10 employers have introduced an even-handed policy, granting access to all types of reference (inward and outward bound).

The mechanics of granting employees access are naturally easier in respect of references that the organisation itself supplies. It can set out its policy and communicate it to all those entitled to act as referees, as well as informing the workforce of its access rights.

However, references that others outside the organisation supply to it present more difficulty. It would be a breach of faith, and of data protection rights, to disclose such references without the referees' knowledge and permission – unless the reference were to be anonymised. But, as noted above, the simple removal of the referee's name, and even their organisation, is unlikely to conceal their identity – given that the employee will usually have been the source of these details when applying for the job.

To get round this issue of referee confidentiality, some employers told us that the initial request for a reference also informs the referee that the information will be made available to the employee concerned. Either the reference is supplied on that basis (or the referee has the option of refusing to provide one), or he or she has the option of withholding their consent to access.

At Portsmouth City Council *(see case study C)*, its general policy on references states that "reference requests must ask for express consent from the writer to disclosure". It adds that "In the event that the question is not answered, this should be taken as withholding consent."

In terms of references supplied by the council to others, the policy sets out the logic for employee access: "Since a reference given by the city council for a current employee should contain no surprises for the employee concerned, it is good practice to share such references with the employee and explain the content, which should already have been discussed at appraisal."

Some organisations, though, adopt an ad-hoc approach to providing access to references written by others. An employer contacted for our research said that access was available: "If asked for, and only with consent of ex-employer", implying that an access request would initiate an approach to the referee for their permission. Several other contacts also pointed out that they require the referee's consent. One organisation, though, said that access requests are granted, "but details are removed".

Pre-employment screening

References are just one of the means at employers' disposal to check the bona fides of job applicants. For sensitive posts, such as working with children, there is a vetting system in place where employers can obtain disclosures from the Criminal Records Bureau. And, where relevant, employers can have applicants checked against lists of unsuitable people maintained by government departments. For some financial posts, particularly those regulated by the Financial Services Authority, employers may wish to conduct checks for county-court judgments, bankruptcies, disqualification from being a director and general credit-worthiness. Specialist agencies are often used to undertake such checks. Indeed, some such as Experian, maintain databases with credit ratings of individuals.

The standard of checking and vetting for sensitive posts has been driven up in recent years, partly because of self-regulation and government legislation intended to remedy weaknesses exposed by several high-profile instances where unqualified or dangerous individuals gained employment through falsified applications. But, more generally, employers may be more concerned about conducting reference and other checks because of perceptions that inaccurate or downright deceitful job applications are increasingly common.

According to the Risk Advisory Group[23], lies and inaccuracies rose by more than one-fifth in a sample of 877 of the CVs that it checked on behalf of client employers during a three-month period. In all, it says it found that just over half of these CVs "showed some form of discrepancy". However, as most such surveys show, it adds that "most of these discrepancies are harmless omissions or honest mistakes, and need not affect the hiring decision".

The difficulty seems to lie in candidates being confused about the acceptable boundary between effective self-presentation and deliberate distortion. The Risk Advisory Group believes that economic factors – the greater competition for jobs since the 11 September terrorist attacks and the downturn in the economy – are encouraging greater deception on the part of candidates. Other commentators blame social changes, arguing that impression management – "spin" – is a sign of the times.

There are now several agencies, such as the Risk Advisory Group, Experian, RWC and Equifax, that offer services linked to the verification of candidates' details, usually known as "pre-employment screening". These services range from obtaining standard references, to qualifications checking (Experian has an arrangement with British higher education institutions that it claims speeds up the process of confirming academic qualifications), credit checks and verifying home addresses. Bankruptcies, present and past directorships, media coverage of the person, membership of professional bodies, and confirming dates of birth are also on offer. Reputable agencies always require the candidate's prior permission for such checks and some share the results of their searches with the individual.

At present, though, employers rarely undertake pre-employment screening unless required to do so by law or where the post is particularly sensitive or crucial, such as the chief executive or head of finance. Despite contacting personnel, HR and recruitment managers in a wide range of employers, we could find very few examples of organisations that have undertaken or commissioned screening. In all, just one in seven organisations use some form of screening, but, in fact, this primarily concerns regulated vacancies where the Criminal Records Bureau is involved.

Guidance[24] from the Forum on the Employment of Ex-offenders in Care Settings, which has been endorsed by the Criminal Records Bureau and more than a score of other organisations, emphasises that the use of the Criminal Records Bureau is not a substitute for effective pre-employment screening and good management practices – even in respect of sensitive posts that are covered by standard or enhanced Bureau disclosures *(see below)*. "Good recruitment policies in general will often provide a better guide to applicants' suitability for posts," it says. "By carefully scrutinising applicants at earlier stages in the recruitment process, looking for inconsistencies and gaps in the information they provide, asking the right questions in interview concerning suitability for posts on offer, taking up references and, where necessary, questioning referees, you will be in a much better position to determine whether you have a suitable person for your vacancy." These considerations are particularly important given that delays and backlogs in the Criminal Records Bureau have led to the postponement of some disclosure arrangements.

One aspect of pre-employment screening is required of all employers, however. Employers must ensure that their recruits are eligible to work in the UK, according to the Asylum and Immigration Act 1996. To avoid possible liability under race discrimination law, all candidates must be treated equally *(see section later in this chapter for further information)*.

5. Improving pre-employment checking

Personnel, HR and recruitment specialists can play an important role in improving pre-employment checks, even where their employers have not introduced formal screening processes. For example, the ability of candidates to deceive employers or exaggerate their suitability for a vacancy can be reduced in all or any of the following ways:

● candidates can be warned at application stage that the details they supply will be checked and serious inaccuracies will be grounds for rejection or dismissal, should this come to light after appointment; research has found that this proves effective in encouraging more honest applications;

● where formal qualifications are required, the successful applicant can be asked to produce original copies of their certificates when they report for work;

● where professional membership or qualifications are required, checks can be made at source to verify that the successful applicant's details are as stated;

● simple checks should be incorporated in the reference-checking process to ensure that referees are whom they claim to be; to reduce the work involved, this again could be restricted to successful applicants only; reference practices themselves can be improved through the choice of referee, the use of structured reference forms, supplying referees with background information about the vacancy, comparing references from two or more sources to identify bias or collusion;

● interviews can be improved[25] to reduce candidates' "impression management" by training interviewers in effective interview techniques; focusing on verifiable details, such as achievements and work responsibilities; using follow-up questions to explore suspicious, incomplete, contradictory or evasive answers; ensuring that questions are directly relevant to the job or candidate; and warning interviewees that answers will be noted down and may be checked (however, this should be done in a fairly low key manner to ensure that interviewees are not intimidated and fail to give of their best); interviewees should also be given full opportunity and encouragement to display their skills, knowledge and experience;

● where psychometric tests are used in selection, it may be preferable to focus on tests that are capable of observation (such as work samples and assessment centres), rather than relying on candidates' descriptions; but, where this is not possible, using tests that contain some form of internal validation to uncover attempts to distort the results;

● in addition, where off-the-shelf tests are used, ensure that they contain alternative questions to avoid the "practice effect" where applicants who have encountered the same test elsewhere are able to perform much better than those with no such experience;

● ensuring that the recruitment and selection process as a whole uses methods that are as objective and verifiable as possible;

● making all appointments conditional on satisfactory references and other checks, and linked to the successful completion of a probationary period;

● following up pre-employment checks with effective day-to-day supervision of the individuals once they are appointed; where the appointment involves work with children or vulnerable adults, or large sums of money, ensure that there is a culture that encourages others to raise any concerns they may have about the individual's behaviour or performance; and

● applications can be scrutinised for inconsistencies and gaps in education or employment histories (however, applicants who are eligible for protection under the Rehabilitation of Offenders Act 1974 can conceal their convictions, and employers that discover them by chance are required to ignore them – see *next section*).

People with criminal records

The process of confirming the bona fides of job applicants – following up references, using the Criminal Records Bureau *(see next section)*, checking application details, and so on – could well uncover individuals who have criminal records. In some circumstances, employers are legally able to demand such information and take account of it in their hiring decisions under the Rehabilitation of Offenders Act 1974. In other situations, though, the law attempts to protect ex-offenders from unfair discrimination. And there is increasing pressure on employers not to do so. For example, the CIPD is campaigning on this issue, while, separately, the government is undertaking a consultation exercise about a possible extension of the Act's protection.

Many employers adopt a different, harsher, view towards applicants with criminal records than they do in respect of other groups covered by anti-discrimination legislation – "evidence shows that, of all things to put an employer off, a criminal record is the worst," says the CIPD[26]. However, the legal protection accorded to ex-offenders is much less extensive than that relating to individuals who suffer discrimination on the grounds of gender or ethnicity. And not only might ex-offenders face considerable discrimination as a group, but employers' attitudes are often affected subjectively by the nature of particular offences. Yet, as the CIPD points out: "No two offences are exactly alike."[27]

Not only is unwarranted discrimination against ex-offenders morally unjust, it is misguided for business reasons in that it restricts employers' access to the labour market. In contrast, some employers that have been particularly affected by skills shortages and other recruitment difficulties have encouraged applications from ex-offenders as a means of filling their vacancies. Personnel, HR and recruitment specialists provide a source of expertise to help employers formulate fair and effective policies relating to ex-offenders to ensure they comply with their legal and moral obligations, and also find the best recruits to fill their vacancies.

Case study D. Reading Buses

Reading Buses had been unable to fill all its vacancies for bus drivers for a two-year period, despite improving pay and conditions and readvertising posts. It turned to ex-offenders as a potential source of recruits, according to *People Management* magazine[28], gaining Prison Service approval to being able to contact local prisons with a view to recruiting inmates once they had completed their sentence. It sent information packs about jobs with the bus company to the young offenders' institution in Reading and two other prisons nearby. The company considered the nature of the job, which involved driving and contact with the public, and decided that three types of offence would automatically disbar applicants from employment: sexual offences, other crimes of violence and driving-related convictions. Each applicant is asked to be honest about the crime and sentence they received, and is screened by both the prison resettlement service and the bus company.

The CIPD recommends that employers should draw up a policy that takes an objective, measured approach to the recruitment and employment of ex-offenders. The CIPD has published several free guides to help personnel specialists develop a policy, including a guide to conducting risk assessments to identify the degree of risk involved in recruiting an ex-offender: *Employing people with conviction; Employing people with criminal records;* and *Employing people with criminal records: risk assessment* (all available from www.cipd.co.uk).

In addition, employers that are registered with the Criminal Records Bureau for the purposes of receiving standard and enhanced disclosures are required to develop a policy and make it available to all applicants – a sample policy is available free from the Criminal Records Bureau, www.disclosure.gov.uk. A shorter sample policy, particularly aimed at employers in health and social care, is available from the Forum on the Employment of

Ex-offenders in Care Settings (in *Recruiting safely*, free via link from www.disclosure.gov.uk).

These guides assume that employers know about a potential recruit's criminal past — but rehabilitated ex-offenders legally are able to conceal their convictions under certain circumstances *(see next two sections)*. The main points of an ex-offender's policy are shown in checklist 6.

6. Reducing unfair discrimination against ex-offenders

All the available research shows that ex-offenders are likely to face unfair discrimination in recruitment and employment unless personnel, HR and recruitment specialists provide advice and information to counteract it. For example, research by the Joseph Rowntree Foundation[29] found that even employers with equal opportunities policies are likely to discriminate against ex-offenders. Frequently, they are not covered by such policies, and line managers often distinguish between "deserving" and "undeserving" groups of people as a reason for not applying the policies' principles to ex-offenders. Often, employers are likely to reject applicants on the basis of the class of their offence without considering the nature of the job or the individual concerned. Some practices are likely to put employers in breach of the law. The foundation's research, guidance from the CIPD and feedback from employers highlights the following issues as being factors that can reduce unfair discrimination against ex-offenders:

● make line managers and others involved in recruitment aware of the statutory requirements of the Rehabilitation of Offenders Act 1974;

● include ex-offenders in the organisation's existing equal opportunities policy, if it has one;

● if not, devise a policy concerning the recruitment and employment of ex-offenders (employers that are registered users of standard and enhanced disclosures are required to develop a policy and make it available to all applicants – a sample policy is available free from the Criminal Records Bureau, www.disclosure.gov.uk);

● include the treatment of ex-offenders in the training given to recruiters;

● do not require existing employees to obtain and disclose basic disclosures;

● do not ask applicants about convictions that are unspent under the 1974 Act, unless the job is exempt;

● take account of risk factors when analysing a vacancy's requirements for recruitment purposes, and only request to see a basic disclosure where it might be directly relevant;

● to reduce the workload, consider restricting such requests to applicants who have been made a conditional job offer;

● encourage honesty from applicants by stating that appointments not exempt from the Act are made on merit alone and, for jobs with a risk factor, asking for information on criminal records to be supplied under separate cover to a named individual;

● do not automatically bar all or certain categories of ex-offenders from employment (unless subject to statutory or professional restrictions);

● where a vacancy has risk factors attached, identify which types of offence would be relevant and, even then, ensure that the candidate has the opportunity to discuss and answer the employer's concerns about their suitability;

● ensure that basic disclosures are kept securely and are safely destroyed after a set period;

● consider applying the principles from the Criminal Records Bureau's Code of Practice to basic disclosures; and

● after appointment, ensure there is effective day-to-day supervision; where the appointment involves work with children or vulnerable adults, or large sums of money, ensure that there is a culture that encourages others to raise any concerns they may have about the individual's behaviour or performance.

Rehabilitated offenders

It is worth bearing in mind that most offenders "grow out" of their criminal disposition at a relatively early age in their adult lives. The impact of discrimination against ex-offenders is likely to affect them for the rest of their lives even though they have returned to being honest citizens. The peak age of offending is 18, and the majority of offenders cease to offend after the age of 25.

The Rehabilitation of Offenders Act 1974 was, and is, intended to "strike a balance between giving reformed offenders the chance to reintegrate themselves into society and the need to protect society from those who might offend again," according to the Home Office. The legislation tries to achieve this balancing act by enabling some offences to be "spent" after a period of time – the rehabilitation period – which means that offenders are not required to tell employers about such convictions.

It ensures that serious offences, denoted by prison sentences (including suspended sentences) of 30 months or more, are never "spent". However, the Act's provisions about other offences are extremely complicated, with many different rehabilitation periods, and this can only have contributed to employers' unfamiliarity with the law. For most types of sentence, there are four different fixed rehabilitation periods, each of which is subdivided into (generally shorter) periods covering offenders who were under 18 years old when convicted, and those above that age. There are three further categories where the rehabilitation period varies.

Overall, the fixed rehabilitation periods range – for people aged 18 years and older – from five years for those on probation (or, for example, who were fined, given a community-service order, a compensation order or a curfew) after February 1995, to 10 years for those with prison sentences of more than six months but less than 30 months. Rehabilitation periods are extended where individuals reoffend; however, as noted above, sentences of more than 30 months are never spent.

Many jobs and professions are specifically excluded from the Act's rehabilitation provisions. In these cases, employers can ask job applicants for details of all their convictions, regardless of whether or not they are spent. These exemptions include:
● posts involving access to children, young people, the elderly, disabled people, alcohol and drug abusers, and the chronically sick;
● certain jobs concerned with national security;
● professions that are regulated by law, such as accountants, chemists, doctors, dentists and nurses
● healthcare work, generally; and
● work concerned with the law, such as barristers, solicitors and police officers.

In addition, jobs and professions involving work with children are covered by the Protection of Children Act 1999 and the Criminal Justice and Court Services Act 2000. These Acts prohibit certain individuals from working in such occupations, including those who are named in various government lists, and those convicted of certain offences against children, such as murder, rape and incest.

When a job is not exempt under the Rehabilitation of Offenders Act 1974, and the offence has been spent, individuals are legally entitled to lie about the conviction. For example, they do not have to answer truthfully to such a question on an application form or at interview. This non-disclosure is a statutory right and, therefore, employers may not refuse to employ someone simply because of the act of concealment. In addition, employers that obtain information about a spent conviction may not use it as the basis for a refusal to employ the person concerned where the vacancy is not exempt from the Act.

The current review of the Rehabilitation of Offenders Act 1974 is not only intended to update its exemptions, but also to address the Act's low profile by making it easier to understand. According to the CIPD[30], there is a general lack of awareness of the Act among both offenders and employers, which, together with evidence of widespread discrimination against ex-offenders looking for work, has meant that it has failed to live up to expectations. It is likely that some rehabilitation periods will be shortened, although this is not likely to apply to the maximum 10-year one applying to serious offences[31].

The Criminal Records Bureau

The vetting of job applicants for sensitive posts exempt from the Rehabilitation of Offenders Act 1974 has changed significantly with the setting up of the Criminal Records Bureau (tel: 0870 909 0811; www.crb.gov.uk and www.disclosure.gov.uk). The bureau has experienced many difficulties since its launch in March 2002 and, so far, has not met either the government's or employers' expectations of it. There have been delays in processing applications for disclosures of criminal records and, as a result, some occupations have been temporarily excluded from the bureau's coverage and the launch of the third of its services – "basic disclosures" available to any enquirer – has been repeatedly postponed.

While the delays in obtaining "standard" and "enhanced" disclosures have undoubtedly caused problems for the employers and individuals concerned, the furthest-reaching implications of the bureau's activities will be felt once basic disclosures are made available to employers.

At present, employers are unlikely to know about the criminal convictions of their employees or job applicants, unless their work is exempt from the Rehabilitation of Offenders Act 1974. Research for the Home Office indicates that this development is likely to affect considerable numbers of people, because the Act already covers the vast majority of ex-offenders. Only sentences of 30 months or more are never "spent". But only a small minority of offenders sentenced by the courts – 7% in 1997 – even receive a sentence of immediate custody, and most of these – 66% of adult prisoners – serve sentences of less than 12 months.

Disclosures

Part V of the Police Act 1997 laid the foundations for the establishment of the Criminal Records Bureau, which is intended to provide a "one-stop-shop service" for access to criminal record information, police records (from the Police National Computer and, in some cases, local police force records), and information on lists held by the Department of Health and the Department for Education and Skills.

The Criminal Records Bureau will eventually issue three levels of disclosure, of which the standard and enhanced levels are currently available:

● **basic disclosures:** these will be available for general purposes and will only show current, unspent convictions, based on information held by the Police National Computer. It is likely that the individual concerned will have to apply for the disclosure (this is under review; *see below*), and it will be issued to them and no other person. It will be at the individual's discretion whether or not they show the disclosure to a third party, such as an employer. The disclosure will not be job-specific and may be used more than once;

● **standard disclosures:** these are primarily intended for posts that involve working with children or vulnerable adults, although they may also be issued for people entering certain professions, such as law and accountancy. The standard disclosure contains details of all convictions held on the Police National Computer, including current and spent convictions, as well as details of any cautions, reprimands and final warnings. If a job involves working with children or vulnerable adults, the disclosure will indicate whether or not information is held on the Department of Health and the Department for Education and Skills lists of those who are banned from such work; and

● **enhanced disclosures:** these are intended for posts involving a far greater degree of contact with children or vulnerable adults. The type of work will include regularly caring for, supervising, training or being in sole charge of such people. Examples include teachers, and scout or guide leaders. Where local police records contain additional information that might be relevant to the post the applicant is being considered for, the chief officer of police may release information for inclusion in an enhanced disclosure. Exceptionally, additional information (typically, concerning current police investigations) may be sent under cover to the employer *(see below)* and should not be revealed to the applicant.

Applications for standard and enhanced disclosures must be countersigned by a person or body registered in advance with the Criminal Records

Bureau. Registered bodies are those that, due to the nature of their work, are likely to ask exempted questions. Such organisations might have a duty of care to children or adults in their charge or recruit people specified in the Rehabilitation of Offenders Act 1974 Exceptions Order. Individuals within the registered body who are able to countersign disclosure applications have their details held on a register by the bureau. Smaller employers and voluntary organisations can use an "umbrella body" to countersign applications. There are around 8,500 registered bodies, seven times more than the 1,200 organisations that were able to gain access to criminal records under the previous system.

At present, the government is reviewing the operation of the Criminal Records Bureau and is undertaking consultations about various proposed changes to procedures. In particular, it is proposing that:
● the number of registered bodies should be reduced, based on each organisation handling a pre-determined number of disclosure requests a year. Other organisations would be required to register via an umbrella body;
● that the fees charged by umbrella bodies should be controlled, in view of complaints from some employers that their charges are too high;
● registered bodies and umbrella bodies should be responsible for confirming the identity of the individuals about whom they seek disclosures, and for ensuring that the application forms are completed satisfactorily; there would be powers to withdraw registration from organisations that fail to meet these requirements;
● the level of disclosure (standard or enhanced) will be specified for each exempt occupation, in order to reduce the number of more time-consuming enhanced-disclosure requests;
● the inclusion of fingerprints in some disclosure applications is to be investigated, where "the sensitivity of the employment role to be undertaken makes this appropriate"; and
● the provision of basic disclosures will not be introduced until the system for standard and enhanced disclosures is working satisfactorily; there will be consultation about changing the proposed system so that requests would be routed via registered bodies (rather than the individual as planned).

Following the consultation period, several of the proposed changes will require amendments to existing legislation via the current Criminal Justice Bill.

Safeguards

Standard and enhanced disclosures contain extremely sensitive information, and are only available to employers entitled to ask exempted questions under the Exceptions Order to the Rehabilitation of Offenders Act 1974. The

Criminal Records Bureau has published a Code of Practice and employers' guidance for recipients of these higher-level disclosures to ensure that they are handled fairly and used properly[32]. The bureau is empowered to refuse to issue a disclosure if it believes that a registered person, or someone on whose behalf a registered person has acted, has failed to comply with its Code.

The Code covers all recipients, and obliges them not to discriminate unfairly against the subject of disclosure information. Registered persons are obliged to have a written policy on the recruitment of ex-offenders, and must give a copy to applicants for jobs where a disclosure will be requested. Any individual or body at whose request applications for disclosures are countersigned must also have a written policy.

The Code of Practice makes it clear that people who are or may be the subject of disclosure information should know in advance that it will be requested, and should be made aware of the use to which it will be put. Application forms must spell this out, while also stating that a criminal record will not necessarily be a bar to obtaining a position. Employers are also required to discuss any matters revealed in the disclosure with the person seeking the position before withdrawing an offer of employment.

Recipients of disclosure information are not allowed to pass it to persons who are not authorised to receive it – unauthorised disclosure is an offence under Section 124 of the Police Act 1997. Disclosures must be securely stored, and must not be retained any longer than is required for the particular purpose for which they were obtained. Generally, the period involved is no later than six months after the date on which recruitment or other relevant decisions have been taken.

A basic disclosure, in contrast to higher-level ones, will be sent solely to the individual who requests it (although the government is consulting about changing this procedure to one where registered bodies must lodge the request). Employers could ask their *current* employees, as well as jobseekers, to obtain a basic disclosure and show it to them (or, under the proposals, to agree to the employer lodging a disclosure request on their behalf). Employees can refuse, and retrospective checks can only be carried out if the employee's contract or conditions of employment state that a police check may be carried out.

Basic disclosures

Ironically, some of the safeguards in place concerning unfair discrimination towards ex-offenders and the safe-keeping of sensitive records will not apply to basic disclosures. Unlike standard and enhanced disclosures, these will not be restricted to particular posts or employers. In theory, job applicants (potential employees and volunteers) do not have to supply a basic disclosure to an employer, but, depending on the state of the labour market, the applicant may have little practical choice. There may be many applicants for a job, and the employer may state or imply that only those producing disclosures will be interviewed or offered employment.

Unless personnel, HR and recruitment managers ensure that their organisations' practices are fair and unprejudiced, the introduction of basic disclosures is likely to lead to widespread discrimination and poor practice. For example, rigorous research commissioned by the government's Department for Work and Pensions[33] found that:

● employers will attempt to use basic disclosures in respect of around half (45% to 56%) of all vacancies;

● the use of criminal record information (both the basic disclosure and other information) in recruitment is likely to be used in around two-thirds (68% to 71%) of vacancies, compared with 63% at present; and

● the proportion of vacancies for which criminal record information would be sought – and where strong disadvantage would ensue from a criminal record – could rise by between five and seven percentage points, depending on the offence.

The research was based on telephone interviews conducted with 1,000 employers in establishments with at least 10 employees, and covered the recruitment process, policy towards people with criminal records, knowledge of the Rehabilitation of Offenders Act, and the treatment of employees who are convicted. Further, qualitative research was carried out with 20 employers across a range of industry sectors. This investigated the relevance of the type of offence involved in influencing employers' decisions to recruit a person with a criminal record. It also looked at employers' views on what were considered to be acceptable periods of time before a conviction became spent, and the impact of experiences of offending at work on their views and approaches towards recruiting people with criminal records.

The increases in the use of criminal record information are likely to be proportionately greatest in the industries where usage is comparatively low at present, according to the research – in particular, financial services, wholesale and retailing, manufacturing, real estate and construction. The latter is likely to have a particularly strong impact on people with criminal records if, as is believed, many people with criminal records work in the construction sector.

The increasing use of criminal record information is also expected to vary by occupation, with the greatest expected increase involving occupations where a criminal record is currently least often sought: clerical and secretarial jobs, managers and administrators, and plant and machine operatives. For these occupations, the basic disclosure is predicted to lead to the use of criminal record information in between one quarter and one third more vacancies, suggesting that the basic disclosure will bring about a change in approach to criminal record information within these occupations. The rise in use of one of the lowest skilled occupations – plant and machine operatives – suggests a particularly high impact on people with criminal records.

For *existing* employees, the research found that employers expect to use the basic disclosure to check for a criminal record as follows:
● in as many as one in five workplaces (between 10% and 20%) in respect of particular types of job;
● in as many as one in seven workplaces (between 8% and 15%) in respect of particular employees; and
● in as many as one in seven workplaces (between 11% and 15%) for *all* employees working there.

The Criminal Records Bureau plans to encourage the basic disclosure to be used only when a conditional job offer has *already* been made, with recruiters asking applicants to obtain a disclosure at that stage. However, this runs counter to the implications from the research findings, which indicate that employers are less likely to discriminate unfairly if they discuss the findings of the basic disclosure with the ex-offender. With the increased use of criminal record information in recruitment, the possible lack of understanding of what specific offences denote and the probable greater accuracy of the information, it will be even more important that people with criminal records are given the opportunity to discuss their record with the employer.

Disclosures from the Criminal Records Bureau are covered by the Data Protection Act 1998 and its associated Employment Practices Data Protection Code 2002. The Code (which, as we noted above, is not yet in force) sets four "benchmarks" that employers are expected to observe. In particular, employers should only request any of the three levels of disclosure where "it is necessary for the protection or conduct of business". Requests that are "excessive" will breach the Code. Basic disclosures should not be obtained by "enforced subject access": putting pressure on individuals to obtain a basic disclosure about themselves and then passing this on to the employer (or, as most recently proposed, giving their consent to the employer obtaining the disclosure). And, even where disclosures have legitimately been obtained, employers should not retain this information "unless there is an over-riding reason for doing so. Usually, it will be sufficient to record that the check has been carried out and its result. In any event, do not retain the information for more than six months."

The Criminal Records Bureau's own Code of Practice, which covers standard and enhanced disclosures only, also contains provisions concerning the storage of disclosures. It says that disclosures and records of them should be kept only as long as they are required for the reason that the employer requested them. This, the Code adds, will usually be "not more than six months".

Foreign workers

The business case for employing overseas workers has been moving rapidly up the political agenda in recent years. Unable to ignore the acute skills shortages in some sectors of the economy, the British government has been increasingly open to discussing migration in economic terms.

The message that emerged in early 2002 from the White Paper on economic migration – *Secure borders, safe haven: integration with diversity in modern Britain*[34] – is that foreign workers strengthen the economy and help create job opportunities for all. As a Home Office minister has said: "The government is opening up ways for people to come and work here legally, in ways which can boost our economy, increasing the number of work permits issued and creating schemes for specific skill levels and industries."

The government has published several pieces of research to support its argument. One report on migration[35] by the Home Office points to the high calibre of people moving to the UK, many of whom have degree-level qualifications and are already well-established in their careers. The research cites four main benefits of attracting skilled foreign labour to work in the financial, IT, health and biotechnology sectors:
● providing a new source of scarce skills;
● diversity of knowledge and expertise;
● easing longer-term skill shortages; and
● positioning the UK as a genuine global marketplace for highly skilled people.

Another Home Office paper[36] showed that the inflow of migrant labour into the UK has had a positive effect on the pay of all workers. According to the research, an increase in immigration equivalent to 1% of the resident workforce leads to an increase of almost 2% in the wages of indigenous workers.

The chancellor's November 2002 pre-budget report continued the theme of immigration as a positive influence for UK business, and made a commitment to step up the number of work permits for overseas workers. Among the measures announced were an additional 5,000 work permits to be issued for the agricultural industry and a new small business unit within Work Permits (UK) to advise employers on methods of recruiting more easily from abroad. There has already been a dramatic increase in the number of work permits issued to skilled foreign workers: the estimated total of 175,000 for 2002 was more than three times higher than the 54,000 permits issued in 1997.

Immigration and work permits are now dealt with by the same government department – the Home Office – the work permit system previously having been administered by the former Department for Education and Employment. This affords the government greater opportunity to deal with labour migration in the round by proposing an "end-to end" process for dealing with asylum seekers and putting forward a cohesive framework for immigration, nationality and asylum.

The White Paper mentioned above has been followed by the Nationality, Immigration and Asylum Act 2002, which is being implemented in stages. The legislation puts into practice the government's twin-track approach of providing a controlled, business-friendly route for the migration of skilled workers while aiming to reduce illegal immigration. The government has made clear that its first priority is "to help those UK nationals without work find it" and maintains that illegal immigration will not be tolerated.

Patterns and trends

The growing trend to bring in more skilled workers from overseas has been widely welcomed by the business community, although a note of caution has been sounded by some employer bodies that migration should not form an alternative to training people in this country. The Confederation of British Industry, for example, has pointed to the immigration laws as an important way of bringing into the economy much-needed skills that are not being provided by the UK's own labour market. However, it wants more to be done throughout the European Union (EU) to improve skill levels.

Notwithstanding the concerns expressed by some sections of business for developing the UK's skills base in the long term, many private and public sector organisations have jumped at the chance to plug their staff shortages by recruiting overseas workers.

In 2001, foreign people made up around 10% of the UK's working-age population. There are currently around 2.5 million known foreign-born people in the UK jobs market. At least one-fifth of these are EU residents who have a right of access to the UK, but the overwhelming majority originates from further afield.

The appointment of overseas sportspeople to senior positions in the UK is no longer a cause of comment. There is a similar trend of importing top talent in British business, and not just within the private sector. But not all appointments of overseas workers are as high profile or as high level. The 2002 annual recruitment and retention survey[37] conducted for the CIPD found that one in six employers had introduced strategies for recruiting in foreign countries in the previous 12 months.

Broadly, there are three main categories of overseas workers:
● those who are not restricted as to their length of stay and/or their freedom to work in the UK, such as European Economic Area (EEA) nationals and overseas nationals with settled status (the EEA comprises the EU states and Iceland, Liechtenstein and Norway; from June 2002 Swiss nationals have had the same rights as EEA nationals);
● those who do not need a work permit and can take up employment for a fixed period of time, such as au pairs; and
● those who must hold a work permit to work in the UK.

Employers may wish to recruit foreign workers for a number of reasons, for example, to fill either temporary or "hard-to-fill" vacancies, where there is a shortage of UK workers with the required skills. An appointment could also involve the transfer of an EEA or non-EEA national from an overseas division of the UK organisation, for instance, to lead a specific project.

Case studies E and F. Costain and Balfour Beatty

Costain, a major international construction group based in Maidenhead, has recruited around 40 overseas staff from Europe, the Middle East and Asia to work on UK-based projects. It costs the company £80,000 to recruit eight overseas recruits, including advertising and interviewing, but not including relocation costs of around £12,000 per employee. Its HR director told us that the skills shortages in some areas, such as project management, make it cheaper to bring in overseas staff on UK market rates, providing the employee is retained for at least two years.

Balfour Beatty Rail Projects, part of the construction and rail group Balfour Beatty, has recruited engineers from countries as diverse as India, Australia and South Africa to help meet its recruitment needs. The company has also been instrumental in bringing the shortage of qualified engineers to the attention of Work Permits (UK), with the result that engineering is now included in the national shortage-occupation list which gives eligible foreign workers easier access to the British labour market.

The company has recruited around 100 engineers from abroad to work in the UK or in company's offices outside the UK. "Rail engineers from countries such as India and Australia are well-suited to work on UK railways, as often it was the UK in old colonial times that laid the first railways in these countries," the managing director of Balfour Beatty Rail Projects told IRS.

The company also ensures that new overseas recruits are well equipped to adapt to both the new working environment and a new country. "Candidates are interviewed in their home country and, once they arrive in the UK, HR makes sure that they have all the information they need," the company added. "As well as the basic issues, such as accommodation and work permits, cultural integration is also considered very important."

Work permits

The work permit scheme was established in 1991 to help plug skills gaps by allowing employers to fill certain vacancies with foreign workers. The scheme enables employers to recruit skilled workers from overseas who are not nationals of an EEA country or Switzerland, and are therefore not entitled to work in the UK. Work permits are issued for named workers in relation to specific posts, and it is the prospective UK employer's responsibility to make the application. Permits are usually granted for jobs that require qualification to degree-level and at least three years' experience using specialist skills, acquired through the type of job for which the permit is sought. A new work permit must be obtained each time an overseas worker changes employer, or changes the type of work they are doing for an employer.

The work permit system has undergone a major overhaul designed to make it faster and easier to recruit non-European residents to selected occupations where there are acute skills shortages, such as the engineering and medical professions. In 2000/01, more than 18,000 permits were granted under this fast-track system. The list of shortage occupations is updated regularly. For example, almost all IT-related occupations were removed from the list in September 2002 as skills shortages in that industry were thought to have eased considerably. This means that employers hoping to recruit most IT staff from overseas now have to prove that a recruitment search has failed to produce any suitable candidates from within the EU.

In addition, the maximum work permit period has been extended from four to five years. Speedier administrative procedures for the processing of both first-time permit applications and renewals have also been put in place. The aim is to decide 90% of all complete work permit applications within one day of receipt.

For business and commercial work permits, employers can apply up to six months in advance of when they want the overseas worker to start employment in the UK. Overseas employers are not eligible to apply for work permits unless the organisation has a presence in the UK. Recruitment or employment agencies are not eligible to apply for work permits either.

There are six main categories under which work-permit applications can be made:
● business and commercial – for non-EEA workers where the vacancy may otherwise be filled by a "resident worker";
● sportspeople and entertainers – allowing UK employers to recruit cultural artists and sportspeople and some technical support people from outside the EEA;
● training and work experience – enabling non-EEA people to undertake work-based training for a professional or specialist qualification, or a period of work experience;
● internships – allowing students from outside the EEA studying first or higher degree courses to undertake an internship with a UK employer;
● GATs – special arrangements made under the General Agreement on Trade in Services allowing employees of companies based outside the EU to work in the UK on a service contract awarded to their employer by a UK-based organisation; and
● the Highly Skilled Migrant Entry Programme (HSMP) – allows highly skilled individuals to migrate to the UK.

Business and commercial permits

There are two categories of application under which business and commercial work permits may be granted: "tier 1" and "tier 2" applications. Work permits are issued with a minimum of checks under the "tier 1" category, and include appointments from the shortage-occupation lists and at board level.

The guidance for tier 2 applications contains more stringent criteria for the employment of overseas workers. For example, the employer must show that there a genuine vacancy and demonstrate why the post cannot be filled with a "resident worker", that is, an individual who is a national of one of the EEA countries. Evidence must also be provided to show that a recruitment search has been conducted within the EEA. This includes the requirement to advertise in two national magazines or trade journals and, if appropriate, on the internet.

Another type of application that can be made under the business and commercial arrangements is a multiple-entry work permit. This allows workers who are based overseas to enter the country for short periods of time on a regular basis to work, rather than obtain a work permit each time they enter the country. Full details of the work permit scheme and information on the procedure for applying, which includes the option of making an application by email, can be found on the Work Permits (UK) website at www.workpermits.gov.uk.

Highly Skilled Migrant Entry Programme

The HSMP is a recent initiative designed "to allow individuals with exceptional personal skills and experience to come to the UK to seek and take work". In contrast to the stringent criteria for work permits generally, whereby permits are granted only to named employers in respect of specific vacancies, this scheme allows the migration of individuals who do not have a prior offer of employment. Overseas nationals who enter the UK under the HSMP can either apply for jobs on their arrival or become self-employed.

The programme is administered on a points system and, to be successful, individuals must score at least 75 points in areas such as qualifications, work experience, past earnings and achievement in the applicant's chosen field. The points system was revised in January 2003, and the emphasis was shifted away from achievement towards work experience. This is likely to enable more applications to succeed than in HSMP's first year, when the success rate was just over 50%.

In addition to the points requirement, individuals must demonstrate their ability to continue to work in their chosen field on moving to the UK, and be able to support themselves and their families without recourse to public funds. Nearly 1,000 individuals entered the country under the HSMP in its first two years, following its launch as a pilot scheme in January 2001. Its success in attracting "particularly talented individuals" to move to the UK has resulted in the scheme now being made permanent.

Low-skilled migration

While there has been a dramatic increase in the number of skilled migrants entering the UK, there are still very few routes whereby individuals at the unskilled end of the labour market can enter the UK to take up employment. The lack of a formal channel allowing unskilled workers into the country has paved the way for foreign nationals to either cross the border illegally or to try and use the asylum route to gain entry.

The pressure has been building, however, to introduce more formal migration channels to ease recruitment difficulties at the middle and lower end of the skills spectrum. Developing a legal route for potentially a much bigger labour pool undoubtedly presents more challenges and is a political minefield for the government. Its White Paper cited above identified "a clear need for short-term casual labour within the UK", and put forward some mechanisms for meeting the recruitment needs of specific sectors of the economy that are experiencing a shortage of low-skilled workers.

The Seasonal Agricultural Workers' Scheme (SAWS) is being reviewed, and there are plans to implement sector-based, short-term working schemes for the hospitality and food manufacturing industries. SAWS covers the short-term recruitment of overseas full-time students aged between 18- and 25-years-old (and those aged under 30 years old who return as SAWS supervisors) to work in agriculture.

The hospitality and food manufacturing schemes will build on the principles of SAWS to meet the demand for temporary labour within these specific sectors of the UK economy. The proposals are currently under consultation and are due to be implemented in 2003.

In a similar approach, the Working Holidaymakers Scheme, whereby around 40,000 Commonwealth people aged between 17 and 27 enter the UK annually on a holiday basis for up to two years, will also be extended to help fill recruitment gaps. A consultation paper suggests measures such as relaxing the restrictions on the type and amount of work that holidaymakers can do during their stay, and advertising "hard-to-fill" vacancies to young people in eligible countries.

The European Commission also has proposals for a common asylum and immigration policy for the EU. A draft directive[38], if implemented, will grant non-EU nationals the right of residence for them and their families in order to seek work.

Asylum seekers

In 2002, there were 71,365 applications for asylum from non-EU nationals, at least one-third of whom were granted leave to stay in the UK. Until recently, this group represented a potential source of untapped talent, because a person who had applied for asylum in the UK could ask the Home Office for permission to work if the application had been outstanding for at least six months. A significant proportion of asylum seekers is made up of skilled individuals, such as doctors and business people, who were in paid employment before they came to the UK. However, two developments have considerably restricted employers' access to asylum seekers.

There were always huge barriers for organisations wanting to recruit from this group. Many employers feared that they would fall foul of immigration law, or were put off by the red tape. But, the Nationality, Immigration and Asylum Act 2002 has removed the right to an in-country appeal for individuals from 10 countries in Central and Eastern Europe (such as the Czech Republic, Latvia and Poland) who enter this country to seek asylum. The number of people travelling to the UK from these countries is therefore expected to fall dramatically.

In a separate legislative development, the almost automatic right that asylum seekers previously had to work has also been withdrawn for new asylum seekers. As Michael Bradshaw, a solicitor with employment law specialist Charles Russell, explains: "From 23 July 2002, asylum seekers were no longer granted permission to work in this country where their application had been outstanding for six months, although this change in the law was not retrospective. Therefore, an asylum seeker who had already applied for the right to work before this date could still have been granted it. The main piece of advice we give to employers is that they must have a proper system of checks in place to ensure that job applicants are legally entitled to work here." He points out that employers can expect fewer and fewer asylum seekers to be able to work, a development that has hit the leisure industry particularly hard.

The combination of these two changes in asylum law has considerably reduced the opportunities for employers to consider asylum seekers as a means of easing skills shortages. Looking ahead, however, the 10 countries whose residents no longer have a right of appeal in this country are the same 10 countries that are due to become full EU members in May 2004. This means that, with their new status as EEA nationals, not only will the citizens of these countries no longer need to seek asylum in order to live in the UK, they will also be entitled to work here (from June 2002 Swiss nationals have had the same rights as EEA nationals).

Immigration and asylum law

In addition to requiring a work permit, overseas nationals are also likely to require a visa – or "entry clearance" as it is officially known – before they can enter the UK. These should be obtained from another government department, UK Visas (information on applying for a visa can be found at www.ukvisas.gov.uk). The spouse and children of people who hold work permits need entry clearance in all cases.

Under Section 8 of the Asylum and Immigration Act 1996, employers can be fined up to £5,000 per worker if they appoint people who do not have official permission to work in the UK. There is a statutory defence against prosecution under Section 8 available, which requires that the recruiting employer sees evidence that the individual is entitled to take up employment, and do so before the person starts work. The evidence must be one of the documents listed in the Act (the Home Office operates a documents helpline, tel: 020 8649 7878); the employer must see the original document, and not a copy; and the employer must keep the document or a copy of it, or make a record of it. There is an extensive list of specified documents, such as one issued by the Inland Revenue (for example, a P45 or P60), a British passport, or a certificate of registration or naturalisation as a British citizen.

Under the later Immigration and Asylum Act 1999, anyone giving advice on work permits and immigration status to people considering migrating to the UK must be registered as an immigration adviser with the Immigration Service. Employers have been exempt from this requirement, but the exemption was due to expire on 31 December 2002. The Immigration Services Commissioner (OISC) has indicated, however, that the exemption is likely to be extended. This means that employers will retain the right to give immigration advice to employees and potential employees without first having to seek registration.

Employers have to manage a delicate balancing act in their recruitment practices in order to avoid breaking contrasting sets of legislation in respect of foreign workers. While trying to avail themselves of the statutory defence against prosecution under Section 8 of the Asylum and Immigration Act 1996, recruiters can fall into the trap of making assumptions about a person's ethnic background that could lead to liability for conducting unlawful racial discrimination.

The Race Relations Act 1976 requires employers not to discriminate unfairly on the grounds of nationality, race or ethnicity. Direct discrimination is defined as treating a person less favourably on racial grounds – for instance, rejecting all job applicants who do not have a British passport. Indirect discrimination occurs when a condition or requirement is imposed that applies equally to everyone but is harder for people from particular racial groups to satisfy, and which cannot be justified. An example could be asking job candidates to undertake a language test when language skills are not a specific requirement of the job.

An employer could allow discriminatory attitudes and practices to creep into the recruitment process unwittingly, for example, by asking only candidates who appear to have a different ethnic or national origin about their immigration status.

Code of Practice

Following concerns that a number of recruiting organisations had, intentionally or otherwise, broken the Race Relations Act 1976, in May 2001 the Home Office introduced a Code of Practice[39] under the Immigration and Asylum Act 1999. The Code sets out the responsibilities of employers under the Race Relations Act 1976, and describes how they can use the statutory defence in a way that avoids unlawful race discrimination. Although the Code is not legally enforceable, failure to observe its contents is admissible as evidence in tribunal proceedings. It is worth remembering that there is no ceiling on awards granted by tribunals in discrimination cases.

The only obligations on the employer in relation to the authenticity of the documentation proving that the individual has permission to work in the UK is that it is an original and that it appears to relate to the job applicant in question. There is no onus on the employer to determine whether or not it is fraudulent. The Code advises that in order to claim the statutory defence, simple checks can be built into an organisation's normal recruitment procedures, but emphasises that these must be incorporated in a non-discriminatory manner.

This means that the recruitment process should not take into account assumptions about applicants' ability to work in the UK, particularly on the basis of their ethnicity. And the request to see documentation proving a right to work in the UK should be asked of all applicants who have reached that particular stage in the recruitment process. The Code says that the request can be asked at any stage – for example, those shortlisted for first interview; those called back to a second interview; or, most simply, the one applicant who has been selected for appointment – and depends on what is most convenient for the employer. However, the request should focus on the ability to work in the UK, and not the individual's immigration status ("such enquiries could mislead you into taking decisions which might constitute unlawful racial discrimination," the Code says).

It should be noted that the statutory defence in relation to section 8 of the Asylum and Immigration Act 1996 applies only to the checking of documents *before* employing someone. There is, therefore, no requirement to check the immigration status of *existing* employees and this practice should be avoided by employers. The Commission for Racial Equality has issued detailed guidance for recruiters[40].

Overseas recruitment

Personnel, HR and recruitment specialists who work for employers that wish to bring foreign workers to the UK on a regular basis need to be up to speed with the legal framework, and ensure that their organisations have in place robust policies and procedures for the workers' recruitment and selection. Internet recruitment could be a useful tool in reaching a wide international pool of candidates: it is quick, cheap and provides coverage around the clock. An online recruitment strategy needs to be carefully managed, however, as a job advert posted on the web could attract an unmanageable volume of responses *(see chapter 3 Using electronic media effectively for more information on online recruitment)*. Care should be taken to advertise vacancies on appropriate websites, and it may be worth investing in selection software that will carry out an initial screening exercise.

Case study G. FedEx Express

FedEx Express, a subsidiary of the global express transportation company FedEx Corp, needed a tool that could service its global reach and massive candidate response rate. It adopted Monster's "one-stop HR solution", Monster HR, which helped it handle, manage and screen candidates from one location.

The experience of FedEx Express explodes the myth that online recruitment only works at an executive level. As the HR manager of FedEx Express in the UK, Ireland and Scandinavia told us: "We anticipated success using Monster in our IT and executive professional fields. However, we were pleasantly surprised by the success in our frontline positions, such as couriers, warehouse agents and clerical jobs, and this success is replicated across all our European markets, especially in France, Italy, Spain and the UK."

In the likely event that an organisation wants to conduct face-to-face interviews with overseas candidates, a decision will need to be made as to whether these will be carried out in the UK or in the candidate's home country. Various factors will influence the best course of action, such as the level of appointment, the number of candidates (and countries), and whether the recruiting organisation has a presence in that country. The advantage of interviewing in the UK is that it may be possible to interview the candidates in one sitting while also providing the opportunity for potential recruits to visit both the organisation and country where they may be working.

Where particular countries are being targeted, some employers have found it helpful to retain local recruitment consultancies to advise on the best recruitment methods and conduct initial screening interviews with applicants. A manageable shortlist is produced that can be interviewed within a short period, either by sending interviewers out from the UK or paying for interviewees to travel here.

There are several practical issues that personnel and HR practitioners need to familiarise themselves with when recruiting overseas workers, not least of which is drawing up a suitable contract of employment. The CIPD suggests[41] the following checklist of items should be considered when drawing up the contract:
● the expected duration of the assignment;
● termination during an assignment and the period of notice at the end of an assignment;
● details of pay, including (for secondments) who pays and in what currency, and other financial benefits such as relocation costs and pension contributions;
● taxes and social security payments;
● applicable law during assignment, for example, foreign nationals employed in the UK have the same statutory employment rights as their British counterparts but may also be subject to the mandatory employment laws of their home country; and
● having a dual contract for employees who divide their working time between the UK and another country.

In terms of remuneration, in most cases the terms and conditions for overseas employees should be identical to that of their UK colleagues who are performing the same job. The exception is secondments, where the employee's salary would normally continue to be paid by the overseas employer. The tax implications of employing overseas nationals are complex, and professional advice should be obtained before any contract of employment is negotiated and drawn up.

Settling in

As well as complying with the "hard" legal and contractual issues associated with importing overseas labour, organisations also need to be aware of the softer issues that come into play when individuals leave their home country behind and move to the UK to work. Adjusting to a new job *and* a new country can throw up a host of challenges for the immigrant worker, such as employment for the spouse or partner and dealing with a different work culture. Some of the practical issues – for example, finding a new home, temporary accommodation and schooling for the children – could be dealt with under the employing organisation's relocation policy, if it has one, although this often applies only to existing employees. Alternatively, aspects of the provision that an employer has in place for relocation could be reflected in a new policy specially designed for overseas workers.

Employers that recruit from abroad also need to understand that different countries can have very different work cultures. This may manifest itself in migrant workers having diverse attitudes to organisational issues such as communication, management style, reward practices and teamworking. It is very important that a climate of tolerance and appreciation of different cultures is cultivated within the UK organisation, so that overseas staff do not feel alienated. Management training should include specific guidance on how to help integrate employees who are new to the country, and deal with particular issues that may arise.

The construction group **Costain** provides support for new overseas employees to help them orient themselves to the new country. "It is vital that the person and their family settle in and want to relocate," its HR director told us. "We have only had a 10% drop-out rate in 18 months." Overseas recruits are put through six months' training in their role, as well as in the company and UK culture to help them settle. Costain is also careful to ensure that overseas employees' spouses and partners are happy and, where possible, places families close to the homes of other staff.

Extra support may therefore be needed at the induction stage and beyond to help orient overseas recruits into their new environment. This could include special orientation sessions in addition to the organisation's usual induction programme that deal with the broader social and political issues of adjusting to a new country. An overseas worker will need to get to grips with the wider challenge of becoming part of UK society, and one way an employer can help is by assigning an existing employee as a "buddy" to act as an informal source of support. If the organisation employs a number of staff from a particular country, an "expat" network can really help the new employee feel at home.

Case study H. The NHS

The National Health Service has seen a considerable influx of overseas workers in recent years. One of the key elements of the "National Health Service Plan", launched in July 2000, was to increase the number of staff in the NHS and to find new ways of working to increase capacity. The target to employ 20,000 more nurses by 2004 has already been met, helped by the success of international recruitment campaigns run by the NHS. By early 2002, around 15,000 nursing staff from countries as far afield as Australia and the Philippines had arrived to work in the UK's health trusts. Other targets included in the NHS plan to increase the medical workforce are to employ 7,500 more consultants and 2,000 more general practitioners by 2004. The Department of Health believes that overseas doctors can make a key contribution to these targets.

The head of NHS employment at the Department of Health told IRS: "Training places are increasing, more qualified professionals are returning and the 'Improving Working Lives' initiative means that we are retaining existing staff. However, we still need committed, fully trained healthcare professionals, which is why the NHS is recruiting from abroad. It is important that these new recruits are supported while they make the transition into living and working in a new country. The NHS can provide the full package of support including language coaching and further education and training, which is one of the reasons why the health service is so successful at attracting medical staff from other countries."

Josie from the Philippines came to Epsom in January 2002. She says: "Nursing in the UK is different from nursing in the Philippines; the basic principles are always the same, but the family does not play a large role here. The people at the hospital are very supportive, and they've helped me adjust to the way they work. Also, my English improved very quickly through talking with patients and doctors every day. Since I've been here, I've learnt much in my profession and also in relating to other people, both professionally and as an individual. Coming here can be a big adjustment and hard work, but, if you'd like to change your life financially and professionally, it's really worth it."

Maria from Zaragoza, Spain began nursing in Epsom in February 2002. She says: "When I first started here, the most difficult thing was listening to English speakers, but now I understand patients and colleagues very well; my English has improved greatly. We have more direct involvement with patients here than in Spain, so it is important that you can communicate well. The NHS trust encourages you to train up to E Grade, which is good experience and advances your career. It was easy coming over here, because the trust helped me with most of the essentials I needed."

7. Legal checklist

● Protected groups must not be put at an unfair disadvantage as a result of checks on job applicants that have a bearing on their recruitment – Sex Discrimination Act 1975; Race Relations Act 1976; Disability Discrimination Act 1995; Trade Union and Labour Relations (Consolidation) Act 1992; and Codes of Practice associated with these Acts.

● Personnel practices in the public sector must be checked for unfair discrimination on the grounds of ethnicity – Race Relations (Amendment) Act 2000.

● There is no general obligation to supply a reference, unless required by a contract, other agreement or where occupations and industries are regulated.

● Refusal to supply a reference to an individual who has complained of discrimination might be interpreted as victimisation under the relevant anti-discrimination statute *(see this chapter for more details)*.

● Employers and referees supplying a reference have a common law duty of care towards the subject and the recipient, and have an implied term of mutual trust and confidence towards current employees.

● Employment agencies are required to undertake basic pre-employment checks on applicants and temps – Conduct of Employment Agencies and Employment Businesses Regulations 1976. The forthcoming revised version of the Regulations will strengthen these requirements.

● The use, storage and subject access of references are covered by the Data Protection Act 1998 and the Employment Practices Data Protection Code *(see this chapter for more details)*.

● Some regulated posts, particularly those involving contact with children, young people and vulnerable adults, require employers and employment agencies to undertake extensive pre-employment screening.

● Convictions involving sentences of less than 30 months are "spent" after certain periods of time, linked to the age of the offender and the conviction. Once spent, individuals can conceal their convictions from employers and prospective employers; however, certain jobs are exempt from these provisions – Rehabilitation of Offenders Act 1974 (the Act is under review).

● Individuals convicted of certain offences against children are banned from work with children – Protection of Children Act 1999; Criminal Justice and Court Services Act 2000.

● Employers' access to criminal records of employees and jobseekers has been significantly extended under the Police Act 1997. Registered employers are able to obtain standard and enhanced disclosures in respect of certain regulated posts from the Criminal Records Bureau; basic disclosures will be available at a future date. Registered employers must observe a Code of Practice.

● The government is consulting about changes to Criminal Records Bureau procedures, and may introduce legislation to enact some changes *(see text in this chapter for more details)*.

● Employers must not appoint new recruits without seeing original documentation that shows the individuals have the right to work in the UK – Asylum and Immigration Act 1996.

● The process of requesting and using this documentation should also comply with the Race Relations Act 1976; the Code of Practice issued under the Immigration and Asylum Act 1999 also applies.

5. Induction, training and development

See also: 3. Using electronic media effectively; 10. Managing performance 1; 11. Managing performance 2.

This chapter covers:
- Overview;
- Induction;
- Training and development: an overview;
- Training budgets, expenditure on training, and calculating training expenditure;
- Why train?;
- The key issues in managing training, including: establishing the case for training; gaining commitment to it; conducting training needs analyses; personal development plans; development centres; and Investors in People;
- Evaluating training;
- Some special legal issues;
- Government programmes and subsidies: Modern Apprenticeships; the New Deal; the Union Learning Fund; learndirect; and Individual Learning Accounts;
- Training delivery: the key options 1: on-the-job training, including coaching; mentoring; secondment; and action learning;
- Training delivery: the key options 2: off-the-job training, including training linked to qualifications; and NVQs;
- Management development; and
- Volunteering and e-learning.

Checklists in this chapter:
1. Effective induction: the key issues
2. Issues to address in induction
3. Induction: the current state of play
4. Calculating the costs of not providing training
5. Managing training: the key issues
6. Personal development plans: the key issues
7. Investors in People: employers' experience
8. Evaluating training: the most effective methods
9. Modern Apprenticeships: success factors

Overview

Induction, training and development provide vital foundations for an employer's management of employees' and managers' performance. Induction familiarises new members of staff with their job, colleagues, vital legal requirements such as health and safety, and less tangible but still essential issues such as corporate culture. Without effective induction, recruits are unlikely to start off in a confident, well-prepared manner and will soon lose their initial enthusiasm.

Much of what makes up good practice in terms of effective induction is no more than sound common sense coupled with effective management and pre-planning. Yet, it is rarely handled as well as it should, largely because new recruits' supervisors see it as an unwelcome chore in an already busy day, and because it is such an unglamorous part of organisational life. New recruits and those promoted internally think otherwise.

Training and development, in contrast, can gain an almost mythical status as a panacea for personality clashes and "problem" employees. Managers may be keen that "courses" are arranged to sort out the difficulties they face. Or, equally unhelpfully, may resist any training expenditure on the grounds that it represents no more than a costly means of providing their employees with a passport to better opportunities with the organisation's competitors.

The challenge for training, personnel and HR specialists is to ensure their organisations take a step back, and analyse their needs in a clear-sighted manner, so that induction and training are based on an analysis of business needs, and that they are evaluated to show they achieve their aims.

Induction

The first few months of a new recruit's employment are among the most crucial they will ever spend with the organisation. New employees usually start out with high hopes, considerable enthusiasm and a willingness to prove themselves. Yet, all too often, poorly-handled induction blights these aspirations, and the recruits fail to achieve their full potential or simply move to another employer.

In fact, most organisations could manage induction more effectively. At any given time, around one in every 20 of the UK's working population is in the first three months of a new job, according to Stephen Taylor, author and lecturer in HR issues. And, almost one in five new starters leave an organisation before the end of their first three months. Many of the 250+ employers we have contacted about their induction practices highlighted areas where their own programmes (and others') could benefit from improvements.

On the face of it, induction is not a high-status task for personnel, HR and training specialists to engage in. It is often a duty that line managers and supervisors try to avoid, or skimp, if they can. Yet, induction can be improved at little or no expense apart from modest amounts of staff time. And it is easy to attach costs and benefits to improvements in induction, so that the input of specialists can be demonstrated as adding value to their organisations.

In particular, it is relatively easy for most employers to gather statistics on labour turnover and break this down by length of service. The data is likely to reflect the national pattern of a high rate of turnover that plunges dramatically after two years' service. And it is also possible to calculate the costs of recruitment. Once induction has been reformed, improvements in turnover rates – all other things being equal – can be attributed to these reforms, and the benefits costed in terms of savings in recruitment costs.

Improving induction programmes is largely a matter of common sense. People are individuals, and "sheep-dip" induction is rarely suitable for their differing needs and interests. Humans are incapable of absorbing large amounts of data in short spaces of time, particularly when stressed by starting a new job in unfamiliar surroundings. And different methods of communication and training each have their advantages and disadvantages. Effective induction uses the best points of each one – reference packs (printed or electronic) for bulky information that needs to be consulted from time to time; face-to-face meetings with senior members of staff; and so on.

1. Effective induction: the key issues

IRS asked more than 250 personnel, HR and training specialists about aspects of their induction processes that are particularly effective in introducing new recruits and helping them to achieve optimal performance. We have analysed their feedback according to the three broad sectors of the economy; in each case, the issues are shown in descending order of importance to induction's effectiveness.

At the end of this checklist is a list of areas where current practice could be moved up to best practice, based on employers' own experience and recommendations.

See checklist 2 for the main subjects that could be covered by induction.

Private sector services firms:
● The involvement of key people from different parts of the organisation in giving new recruits an introduction to their activities and departments;

● The role of personnel, HR and training specialists in developing and managing induction programmes;

● The quality of information or welcome packs of reference information given to new recruits;

● A corporate induction day: bringing recent recruits together to meet each other and be given an overall briefing on issues of common interest about their new organisation; and

● The role of line managers: ensuring line managers play an important part in delivering induction and, where responsibility is shared with personnel, HR or training specialists, that they work together effectively.

Manufacturing and production industries:
● The involvement of key people from different parts of the organisation in giving new recruits an introduction to their activities and departments;

● The quality of information or welcome packs of reference information given to new recruits;

● The role of personnel, HR and training specialists in developing and managing induction programmes; and

● Health and safety: giving special attention in induction to the importance of health and safety at work.

Public sector:
● The involvement of key people from different parts of the organisation in giving new recruits an introduction to their activities and departments;

● The quality of information or welcome packs of reference information given to new recruits;

● The flexibility to tailor the programme to meet the needs of individuals and specific job functions;

● A corporate induction day: bringing recent recruits together to meet each other and be given an overall briefing on issues of common interest about their new organisation; and

● The role of personnel, HR and training specialists in developing and managing induction programmes.

Learning from mistakes
Many employers' induction programmes are unsatisfactory, they tell us. Here are the main ways in which their experience shows these shortcomings could be addressed:

● Ensure that the induction programme is delivered consistently and to the same high standard: Some line managers do not treat induction as a serious issue and may skimp on certain aspects of it, or give more attention to some recruits than others; in other employers, the programme is not sufficiently structured and this encourages inconsistency;

● Greater involvement of line managers: Linked to the above, line managers need to be heavily involved in the induction of employees who will report to them; at present, line managers are often reluctant participants. Organisations should clarify the aims and objectives of induction; communicate this; and agree the respective roles and responsibilities of line managers and personnel/HR/training specialists;

● More time should be devoted to induction: Often, too much information and familiarisation is crammed into a short space of time; employers recommend that the induction programme should be relaxed and phased in gradually – the "survival" and must-have details (such as health and safety) should be covered in days one and two, with other topics being prioritised and covered over a period of several weeks or months, interspersed with productive work on the recruit's part;

● Where possible, technology should be used to support induction, such as providing essential information as reference guides on an intranet or CD-ROM; and

● Evaluating the effectiveness of induction (see below).

Inducting different groups

The most effective approach to induction, according to personnel, HR and training managers, takes account of the special needs of particular new recruits. Generally, they tell us that they find the best way of approaching this issue is to identify areas where a common approach works well, and customise the rest.

For example, there are legal requirements that organisations have to fulfil, specifically with regard to health and safety, and all recruits can be given the same induction in such areas. However, employers may have to go further. The Management of Health and Safety at Work Regulations 1992 requires employers to make a suitable and sufficient assessment of the risks to the health and safety of employees and identify groups of workers who might be particularly at risk. If there are such groups, then induction will have to be tailored to them and the special risk factors they might face.

Managers: Recruits who will have managerial responsibilities will need induction in additional areas, such as people management and budgetary procedures. They will also require more detailed induction than non-managerial staff in order to build effective working relationships with senior managers, key individuals in other departments and divisions, and so on.

Supervisors, team leaders and managers who have been promoted internally may need more personal support during their induction phase. Instead of working alongside a group of colleagues, they may well have to make the difficult transition to assuming managerial control over them. They may require support to build and maintain their confidence, and access to someone who can discuss the new problems they face.

Young people: Conversely, some recruits will need extra attention in issues of an entry-level nature. Recent school, college or university leavers will need particular attention when joining a new organisation. Besides clearly outlining their position in the organisation, employers will need to introduce these individuals to the world of work and the work ethos, as graduates or school leavers may have a very limited experience of employment. Highlighting training and development opportunities is particularly important for new starters in this category.

Recruits who are unfamiliar with working environments may need additional induction in respect of health and safety procedures and policies within the organisation. And, when employing people under the age of 18, there are particular statutory requirements of employers. The Health and

Safety (Young Persons) Regulations 1997 require employers to assess risks to young people under the age of 18 before they start work and take into account their inexperience, lack of awareness of existing or potential risks and immaturity.

Returners: Individuals who are returning to work after a break of some years – such as those who have taken a break to care for a child or elderly relative or who have been unemployed for a long period – are likely to feel a certain level of apprehension about re-entering the workforce. Not least, information technology and business administration will have changed since they were last employed, and extra attention should be given to these areas. The socialisation process of introducing the recruits to their colleagues, supervisors and corporate culture needs to be given more attention and monitoring. Extra training and help should be offered to allow restarters the opportunity to settle into the organisation.

Special return-to-work courses have been developed by some employers, particularly the NHS for nurses and local education authorities for schoolteachers. These programmes cover changes in technology and offer a refresher course in the knowledge and skills required to do the job. For example, nurses will need to be updated on drug protocol, dosage, usage and type.

Disabilities: Special consideration needs to be given to recruits with disabilities. Employers are required to make "reasonable adjustments" to work, equipment and premises under the Disability Discrimination Act 1995. While each person's needs should be identified as soon as possible during the recruitment process, and not left until the individual reports for work, the induction process itself may need adaptation. For example, sight impairments may require alterations to induction documentation and tours of premises should take account of individuals with mobility difficulties. Advice on employing people with disabilities is available from Jobcentre Plus, the organisation running the state jobcentre network.

Ethnic minorities: The Advisory, Conciliation and Arbitration Service (Acas) recommends that recruits from ethnic minorities should be inducted in the same way as others, but "attention should be paid to any sensitivities"[1]. Employers may need to be aware and take account of any particular cultural or religious customs of new employees who are part of an ethnic or religious minority so that misunderstandings do not occur.

Employers in the public sector are now required, under the Race Relations (Amendment) Act 2000, to ensure their personnel practices support equality of opportunity on grounds of ethnicity. The Commission for Racial Equality's guidance recommends that public sector employers should conduct regular reviews of their personnel policies and monitor their use to ensure there is no unfair discrimination on the grounds of ethnicity.

Others: Induction should be sufficiently flexible to accommodate the needs of recruits who do not follow the standard 9 to 5 working week. Shift workers, in particular, could be excluded where induction is held at fixed times, but part-timers, job sharers and others could also miss all or part of their induction if their needs are not taken into account. It may be possible, for example, to modify the induction programme, temporarily agree a variation in recruits' hours of work, or use both approaches, to ensure that all new members of staff are able to participate in the full programme. The Part-time Workers (Prevention of Less Favourable Treatment) Regulations 2000 stipulate that part-timers should not be excluded from training purely on the basis of their part-time status.

2. Issues to address in induction

Guidance from Acas, reproduced with permission from *Recruitment and induction*, Acas, 2003, www.acas.gov.uk.

"It is good practice to let new starters have a copy of this list – this enables them to follow what is happening and will act as a reminder of anything missed or that needs particular attention. It should be the responsibility of both management and new starter to ensure that all relevant items are properly covered during the induction period."

	Carried out by	Date	Comments
Reception			
Received by			
Personnel documentation and checks completed – P45			
NI number			
Swipe/security card			
Introduction to the company			
Who's who			
History			

Products/services/markets

Future plans and developments

Terms and conditions of employment

Contract of employment issued

Hours, break, method of payment

Holidays

Clocking on/flexi-time/reporting
procedures

Probationary period

Period of notice

Sickness provisions

Pension provisions

Maternity/paternity/parental leave
provisions

**Equal opportunities and employee
development**

Equal opportunities policy

Training needs and objectives

Training provision

Further education/training policies

Performance appraisal

Promotion avenues

Policy/procedures to prevent bullying
and harassment

Employee–employer relations

Trade union membership

Other employee representation

Employee communications and consultation

Grievance and disciplinary procedure

Appeals procedure

Organisation's rules

Smoking policy

General behaviour/dress code

Telephone calls

Canteen/break facilities

Cloakroom/toilets/lockers

Health and safety

Risk assessment

Preventative and protective measures

Pregnant women and new mothers

Emergency procedures

Health surveillance (if appropriate)

Awareness of hazards – any particular to type of work

Safety rules

Emergency procedures

Clear gangways, exits

Location of exits

Dangerous substances or processes

Reporting of accidents

First aid

Personal hygiene

Introduction to safety representative

**Welfare and employee
benefits/facilities**

Sports facilities

Protective clothing – supply,
laundry, replacement

Medical services

Savings schemes (including share options)

Transport/parking arrangements

Company discounts

The job

Introduction to manager/supervisor

Requirements of new job

Standards expected

Co-workers

Supervision and work performance
appraisals

Source: Recruitment and induction, Acas, 2003, www.acas.org.uk.

Involvement of line managers

Just over half of all employers expect line managers and personnel/
HR/training specialists to contribute equally to the induction of new
employees. Specialists obviously can contribute their expertise in people
management and training, while the central importance of the relationship
between employees and their line managers requires managers' involvement
in inducting the staff who will work for them.

In other cases, organisations either place full responsibility for induction on their people and training managers or, conversely, leave it entirely to line managers to organise and deliver.

Unfortunately, line managers often fail to give induction the attention and priority it deserves, according to the employers contacted by IRS.

Essentially, it seems that practitioners believe that line managers either fail to apply induction procedures and policies in a consistent way, or do not take induction seriously enough. The irony is that line managers will benefit from their employees experiencing an effective induction process, rather than personnel, HR and training practitioners. It may be that line managers have failed to appreciate that induction is a business-critical activity, and treat it as a routine job they can leave to personnel, HR or training specialists to tackle.

For example, a small public sector employer we contacted told us that: "We really need to get line managers to take their responsibilities for induction more seriously." A large manufacturer told us that: "We will have to look at introducing measures to manage the performance of managers in the induction process."

At present, the tension between specialists and line managers is tangible, and there is a need to ensure that recruits do not pick this up – and, more positively, for organisations to take action. The aims and objectives of their induction programmes need to be reviewed and restated, so that all parties are clear about the aims and objectives of this process. Then, their respective roles and responsibilities should be agreed and set down. Where specialists and line managers are expected to take joint ownership, the best means of doing so productively need to be explored.

Involving other staff

Many employers routinely involve other staff in delivering induction programmes, over and above line managers and personnel, HR and training specialists. They tell us that involving health and safety officers, IT staff, senior managers, and so on, provides a dual benefit. These individuals are often best placed to provide specialist information and briefings to new recruits, but their involvement also ensures that they and the recruits are brought into contact in a reasonably informal manner.

Health and safety officers: Most commonly, health and safety staff are involved in induction (six in 10 employers do so), explaining health and safety policies and practices, evacuation procedures and so on.

IT specialists: Half of all employers involve IT staff in induction. Most organisations now operate IT systems, and IT staff are not only best placed to explain them, but need to be introduced to recruits in their role as sources of help and advice when problems are encountered later on. This is also the opportunity to introduce new employees to any email and internet policies the organisation may have developed, covering basic points of etiquette and rules and restrictions on personal usage (developing such policies is covered in chapter 3, Using electronic media effectively).

Colleagues: A basic aspect of induction normally involves taking recruits round their workplace and being introduced to individuals whom they will be working with as colleagues. But a quarter of employers now go further and involve recruits' colleagues in aspects of the formal induction process – generally, in an effort to ensure that effective working relationships are given the best possible start. The growth of team-based working structures makes this an even more important consideration.

A minority of employers has set up "buddy" systems as part of induction, where an experienced member of staff is asked to look after a new recruit. Their role is to provide a source of information and encouragement while the individual is settling in to their new job.

Practice varies considerably. A few employers have created formal buddy systems, where the buddy is responsible for delivering some aspects of the induction programme (such as showing the recruit round their workplace, introducing them to other employees, pointing out the location of fire exits, toilets, exits and so on), and might act as a mentor.

More often, though, the relationship is informal, and buddies are seen as enabling employees to raise concerns and ask for information that they may hesitate to take up with their line manager. For example, in even the best induction programme recruits will forget some facts or points of procedure, but may not wish to ask their line manager to repeat the information. Or they may be uncertain about how to act in a situation, but may be reluctant to appear in a poor light by asking their line manager for advice. Well chosen, a buddy can ensure that the recruit gets the information and advice needed to perform as effectively as possible and, where necessary, is encouraged by them to seek help from their manager or other member of staff.

Chief executive: A minority (one-fifth) of employers ensures that the chief executive or managing director meets new recruits as part of the induction programme. Slightly fewer (one in six employers) make an attempt to involve a representative from each department or section in induction, so that recruits gain a rounded introduction to their new organisation. Obviously, larger and more scattered organisations may find this much more difficult to achieve.

Trade union: And, finally, the minority of employers that recognises a trade union also often includes an introduction to the union in its induction programme. This may be limited to the distribution of literature about the trade union and an application form, or it may involve a trade union representative giving a presentation at one of the group induction sessions. Trade union involvement in induction may be a formal obligation under the terms of the employer's recognition agreement with the union(s).

3. Induction: the current state of play

Most employers make some attempt to familiarise new recruits with their workplace, their colleagues and the aims and workings of the organisation.

Tailoring induction: At present, only one-third of employers tailor their induction process to the particular needs of the recruits involved, with little variation in this proportion by industry or workforce size.

The third of organisations with customised provision generally follow one of three approaches:

● providing a core induction programme that is supplemented with extra provision for recruits in particular jobs or functions (this is particularly common among small and medium-sized organisations);

● adopting a twin-track, with one induction programme for non-managerial recruits and a separate one for managers; or

● creating entirely customised programmes for different types of job (this approach is particularly common among manufacturers, and reflects the highly specialised nature of many jobs in this sector; it is also popular among small and medium-sized organisations).

Methods in use: Personnel, HR and training managers say that these are the main methods used to provide induction, shown in descending order of prevalence:

● face-to-face meetings between recruits and their colleagues, line managers and other key members of staff – employers highlight the importance of scheduling these meetings, so that those involved do not forget about their commitment and prepare for them in advance;

● welcome packs of essential information: assembling a one-stop resource pack of key policies and procedures, lists of contacts, forms and so on that provides new recruits with a survival guide to working in the organisation (some organisations load the pack onto a CD-ROM or floppy disc and send it to the recruit to read before they start work);

● training sessions;

● making information available via the organisation's intranet (a system where an employers' computers are networked so that centrally-stored information can be searched and accessed in ways that have the look and feel of the internet); and

● group meetings of recent recruits, where they can meet each other, be introduced to senior members of staff and receive induction information of general relevance to new starters.

Evaluating induction

It makes sense to update the induction programme in line with any changes in policies and procedures. It can be damaging for the organisation and a negative experience for the new employee if they discover their induction has been based on policies and procedures that are out of date. Not only is it going to create a bad impression, but out-of-date information on statutory requirements could expose the organisation to prosecutions and bad publicity.

Organisations wishing to make a good impression with new employees should ensure that all aspects of the induction programme are in line with latest policies within the organisation. It may be difficult to coordinate, as different individuals may have responsibilities for different policies, but every effort should be made to ensure inductees are presented with the most up-to-date working practices.

"Formal and informal induction processes need to be based on what new employees need. You should ask recent recruits of six months' or a year's standing to help you design your programme," recommends Stephen Taylor, an expert in recruitment and retention issues[2].

Rather than presenting recent inductees with an intimidating blank sheet of paper, he suggests asking them to recall the aspects of their new job and employer that caused them the greatest stress in their first few weeks of starting work. In addition, what would they have wanted to know more about? What did they find confusing? And what unpleasant surprises could they have been warned to anticipate?

Organisations that conduct research among employees who leave voluntarily have a further source of information to review the effectiveness of their induction. Some employers interview staff before they leave ("exit interviews") or send them a survey form to complete ("separation questionnaires"). Feedback from those who left within six or 12 months of starting work should be given particular attention, Taylor says, to investigate whether or not any patterns emerge. Was there a main source of discontent? Is it possible that the conditions that led to their resignation could have been addressed through effective induction?

Those who have been at the receiving end of an induction programme are best placed to be focus of an evaluation as to its effectiveness. But, as well as asking them directly, participants' experience can be assessed in other ways. Labour turnover data has been mentioned above – if there are high rates of resignations (or dismissals due to unsatisfactory performance, timekeeping or attitude), then induction may need improving (although the soundness of the recruitment process itself should also be checked).

The organisation's performance-management system will also give insights into whether or not new recruits are establishing rapidly and satisfactorily. New recruits are often given more frequent formal performance reviews than established staff – six-monthly, instead of annually, for example. And line managers' day-to-day management of their staff should also uncover any areas of concern. So, as well as canvassing the recruits, line managers' views and insights are also valuable.

In addition, though, the content of induction needs to be reviewed on a regular basis. Organisational procedures and structures change rapidly, and there may be changes to legislative requirements, too.

In all, three-quarters of employers undertake a regular review of their induction practices. Most commonly, in descending order of prevalence, they do so in these ways:
● reviewing and updating induction in line with changing policies and procedures (both external and internal);
● after consultation with recruits who had taken part in the induction programme;
● continuous updating and improvements (however, this involves setting up systems to ensure that frequent changes to the programme are communicated effectively to all those involved and may be difficult for larger organisations);
● reviewing induction on an annual basis; and

● updating induction in line with improvements in relevant technology, particularly the introduction and improvement of intranets.

Case study A. Claridge's hotel

The luxury hotel Claridge's won the top "employer of the year" accolade at the 2002 National Business Awards. This would not have seemed possible just four years previously: customer satisfaction was running at only 50% and labour turnover was 73%.

While the hospitality sector is not known for its high retention rates, it was decided that a major cultural-change programme was needed to improve both customer and staff loyalty. As a result of a whole raft of cultural and HR initiatives that have been put in place, customer satisfaction has increased to 94% while employee satisfaction is now measured at 88.1%. Staff turnover has been slashed by almost two-thirds to 28%.

The first step in the change programme was to create a new vision and values for the hotel, with employees at the centre of the approach. As the hotel's HR director told IRS: "The philosophy is now 'one team, one hotel', and it was vital from the start that employees felt valued and respected in the new working environment."

The senior management team carried out an employee attitude survey in order to gauge employee opinion in key areas, and used the results to draw up an action plan to rectify areas of dissatisfaction. Some positive changes, such as redecorating the staff canteen, were carried out immediately. This showed employees that management was serious about improving Claridge's as an employer.

Recruitment and selection processes were also revised to support the new working environment. Behavioural interviewing techniques were introduced to ensure that would-be recruits have the appropriate attitudes and behaviours to fit the new culture.

As part of the induction programme, each new employee stays overnight as a guest of the hotel in order to appreciate the customer's perspective and the contribution that employees make to the guest's comfort.

Employee involvement and communication are integral to the new employment relationship at Claridge's. The previously mundane staff meetings have been transformed into a lively and open debate about organisational issues. A regular newsletter has been introduced, a monthly birthday celebration is held for all staff with birthdays falling in that month, and a champagne breakfast is organised every three months for the night shift to keep them up-to-date with developments. The hotel has also set up a number of project teams involving staff, such as the "communication and cooperation team", that is responsible for coming up with new ideas to boost internal communication. Management style is another area that needed changing, and leadership training was introduced to encourage teamwork and foster practical management skills, such as coaching and giving praise to staff. At least one off-site development event is now held annually for each of the different layers of management, to reinforce the new culture and management style.

One area considered key to turning around the employment relationship at Claridge's, at the same time boosting retention rates, is the raft of employee-recognition schemes that has been introduced. An "employee of the month" scheme enables staff to make nominations, and the winner receives £150 in vouchers and their photograph joins the portrait gallery of past winners outside the staff canteen. Following on from this scheme is the "employee of the year" contest. The 2003 winner received a two-week luxury cruise in the Caribbean.

The highlight of the hotel's employee-recognition strategy is "Going for Gold". The "gold" refers to a pot of gold envelopes that sits in the HR director's office, waiting for an employee to take a lucky dip and pull one out. This opportunity arises if the employee has been given a "going for gold" card, indicating that they have successfully demonstrated one of Claridge's core values. The gifts contained in the envelopes do not necessarily have high monetary value. But they have a high perceived value for employees, such as an extra day's annual leave, an extra hour for lunch, or a ride home in a limo. The top prize is an all-expenses-paid night in Claridge's penthouse suite that would normally cost a guest more than £3,800.

Training and development

Overview

In this chapter, we survey the main themes and approaches concerned with planning and delivering training and development, based on current and best practice. We begin out of sequence by focusing on training expenditure – simply, because this topic continues to represent an issue of keen interest to training, personnel and HR professionals.

Expenditure on training

Training specialists, together with their personnel and HR colleagues, are keenly interested in the amount that other organisations spend on training. Primarily, they wish to use this information as ammunition to argue the case for an increase in their own budget, or when resisting moves to make spending cuts.

Training budgets

Many organisations fail to quantify their spending on training in whole or part; in some cases, they do not even have a budget set aside for this purpose.

The authoritative government survey *Learning and training at work*[3] has found that between a fifth and a third of medium-sized employers do not have a training budget (36% of those with 25 to 99 employees and 18% of those with 100 to 199 employees). However, budgets are nearly universal among larger organisations (only 9% of those with 200 or more employees do not have them).

The survey only gives a broad breakdown by industry, and this indicates that the public sector is twice as likely to have budgets set aside for training pur-poses than does the production sector (made up of agriculture, mining, the utilities and construction) – 67% and 33%, respectively.

Our own research conducted in 2002 found that training budgets may be devolved to departmental or site level. Generally, employers often approach the budget in terms of spending a certain amount of money each year per employee, while fewer organisations base their budgeting on a percentage of payroll. Spending patterns vary significantly across employers, of which some variation is explained by their differing needs and contexts. For example, highly skilled technical work may require much greater investment per head than standardised, lower-level training which can enjoy considerable economies of scale and be delivered in a much shorter timescale.

Even where budgetary figures are produced, many organisations actually spend more than the amount in question without realising it, according to the CIPD. Its investigation of the mechanics of costing training expenditure shows that "using training budgets as a measure would mean seriously under-estimating the true costs of training"[4].

It has found that fewer than half of the budgets set by employers include any training-related capital expenditure, the salaries of in-house trainers and support staff or the salaries of trainees while they are being trained.

Training spending

Despite the keen interest in gaining benchmarking data about employers' training expenditure, there are few sources of this information, and even fewer that appear on a regular basis.

Partly, the lack of data is explained by the difficulty and expense involved in obtaining it. Survey researchers often come up against the same problem: employers are very keen to obtain this information, but are usually unable (or, sometimes, unwilling) to supply it. It seems that few organisations actually keep detailed records of where their training investment is spent. For example, a large-scale investigation sponsored by the Chartered Institute of Personnel and Development (CIPD) asked 7,000 members about their organisations' training expenditure, but received replies from only 129[5].

One of the best regular sources of training expenditure used to be the People Skills Scoreboard series, a research method introduced in the engineering sector that was later applied elsewhere. The scoreboards are based on postal questionnaires of employers in a particular broad industrial sector, and were organised – usually with government funding – by the relevant "national training organisation" for the sector. However, national training organisations are being gradually replaced by new "sector skills councils", and there is currently some uncertainty about whether or not many titles in the series will continue. There is likely, at least, to be a hiatus until the new skills councils become fully operational.

Below, we review some of the major sources. In most cases, the data cover the headline costs of off-the-job training, while ignoring or under-estimating on-the-job training and such costs as trainees' and in-house trainers' salaries.

Overview: The statistics on employers' training expenditure shown below indicate the difficulties of using the information for benchmarking purposes. There are huge differences in the findings of the various surveys, from under £100 a head a year up to as much as £5,000.

National surveys indicate a per-capita annual expenditure ranging from £361 (CIPD) and £400 (Capita) to £632 (a government survey from 2000, although this rises to £1,024 where on-the-job training is included).

In manufacturing and production industries, survey findings range from £269 to £900. In private sector services, the costs range from £167 to £5,000. And in the public sector, costs range from £87 to £159. However, most surveys generalise individual employers' training expenditure, and particular organisations can spend considerably more or less than the average or midpoint figures suggest.

Nationwide: In September 2001, the CIPD's survey of 129 employers mentioned above obtained statistics on their training expenditure. The figures, in comparison with others shown here, may be slightly exaggerated because of the large number of manufacturing companies in its research (a sector that tends to spend relatively greater amounts on training). The CIPD found an average cost of £361 per employee in 2000/01, but the low response to its survey meant that no analyses for particular industries could be provided.

A 2002 survey by Capita found that employers with fewer than 25 employees spent £400 per worker per year on training, while employers with more than 25 employees spent £350[6].

In 2000, that year's issue of the government's annual *Learning and training at work* survey obtained expenditure details from 711 English employers. Across the economy, it found that spending averaged £1,024 a head – a real-terms increase of a quarter since its previous research into costs carried out in 1993. Of the £1,024, £632 was spent on off-the-job training and £392 was devoted to on-the-job training. However, the average amounts gloss over several marked variations in practice.

For example, only two-fifths of employers used off-the-job forms of delivery, while considerably more – two-thirds – provided on-the-job training. This means that the typical employer spent less than £1,024 simply because it used cheaper, on-the-job forms of delivery.

In addition, larger employers are often able to gain economies of scale when organising training; in other words, the cost per head is often lower when large numbers of trainees are involved. So, the survey found that smaller employers spent twice as much per head, on average, as the largest ones: £1,627 for firms with 10 to 24 employees compared with only £873 for those with 500 or more employees.

The survey also provided figures for training expenditure based on each trainee. Only a proportion of employees receives training in any one year, so the amounts are naturally higher. In the 2000 survey, spending averaged £4,488 per trainee, ranging from £5,522 in the smallest firms to £2,798 in the largest (that is, 10 to 24 employees compared with 500 or more employees).

Sector by sector: In spring 2002, IRS published details of several organisations' annual training budgets[7]. Here are some examples, with their workforce numbers – and our own usually conservative estimates of spending per head of staff – shown in brackets.

● **Manufacturing:** a midpoint cost of £362 a year, including: **Claverham:** £100,000+ for formal training (316 employees; £316); **Control Techniques:** £60,000 for formal training plus ad-hoc spending of around £40,000 a year (1,500 employees; £67); **Nissan Motor Manufacturing (UK):** £10.2 million for formal training (5,000 employees; £2,040); **Vosper Thornycroft Shipbuilding Group:** about £500,000 (980 employees; £510); **Barry Callebaut (UK):** £90,000 on formal training (220 employees; £409); **Ryalux Carpets:** £100,000 on formal training (350 employees; £286);

● **Service sector:** a midpoint cost of £167 a year, including: **HOK International:** £90,000 (200 employees; £450); **Meta4 UK:** minimum of 3% of paybill for formal training (76 employees); **Natural Environment Research Council:** £270,000 (2,600 employees; £104); **Portal Software (Europe):** about £250,000 on formal training, based on about £1,000 per employee (220 employees; £1,000); **Safeway Stores:** £15 million on formal training with extra spending for teams and departments as justified (90,000 employees; £167); **Stagecoach Buses, East London:** £350,000 on formal training, and ad-hoc spending of about £100,000 (3,200 employees; £141);

● **Public sector:** a midpoint cost of £87 a year, including: **Derbyshire County Council:** £2.5 million on formal training (35,000 employees; £71); **Dudley Social Services:** £700,000 on formal training (2,000 employees; £350); **Essex County Council:** 1.5% of paybill on formal training, equating to about £2.5 million (28,720 employees; £87); **Kingston Hospital:** £600,000 on formal training (3,500 employees;

£171); **Pembrokeshire and Derwen NHS Trust:** £125,000 on formal training (3,000 employees; £42); **Wrightington, Wigan and Leigh NHS Trust:** £350,600 based on approximately £53 a head of staff, with additional spending on teams and departments according to need (6,500 employees; £53); and **York College:** £400,000 on formal training (700 employees; £571).

Local government: The 2002 edition of the annual People Skills Scoreboard for local government[8] polled 140 authorities, and found that they spent an average of £159 per employee per annum (0.9% of payroll), excluding the cost of trainees' salaries. However, amounts varied considerably. Spending averaged £107 per employee among Welsh unitary authorities (0.6% of payroll), rising to £243 in Northern Ireland and £301 in London boroughs (1.6% of payroll).

Engineering: The 2001/02 edition of the People Skills Scoreboard for the engineering industry[9] was the fourth in a hitherto annual series (it has now moved to an 18-month cycle), and surveyed 772 employers. On average, engineering employers spent £269 per employee per annum on off-the-job training (representing 0.22% of sales revenue and 1.34% of payroll).

Sub-sectors within the engineering industry spent widely varying amounts per head, as did individual employers (the survey gives training expenditure details for each named survey participant). The highest cash amount among those surveyed was £313 per head at R.B. Precision Engineering. Among sub-sectors, spending per head ranged from £130 in basic metals (0.54% of payroll), £170 in metal products (0.9% of payroll), £200 in both electrical equipment (1.2%) and "other transport" (1.1%), and £240 in mechanical equipment (1.1%), to £340 in automotive (0.9%), £370 in electronics (2.09%) and £576 in aerospace (2.18% of payroll).

Construction: The 2001 People Skills Scoreboard for the construction industry[10] found that the 93 participating companies spent an average of £287 a year on directly employed workers' off-the-job training, worth 1.5% of payroll and 0.2% of turnover. The highest absolute expenditure among those surveyed was found at Hearthstead Homes (£1,216 per person). In terms of on-the-job training, the average expenditure was £171 per person.

Chemicals: The 2000 People Skills Scoreboard for the chemicals industry[11] found that off-the-job training expenditure averaged £900, or 3.7% of payroll and 0.2% of sales. For on-the-job training, the amount was £2,300 (7.1% of payroll and 1.6% of sales) – although the on-the-job results were based on only a few respondents.

Broadcasting: Television broadcasters spent around £58 million on training in 2000, according to research by Skillset, including £30 million at the BBC, more than £8.3 million among ITV companies, £4.5 million at Channel 4 (900 employees; worth approximately £5,000 a head), £564,000 at S4C (200 employees; worth approximately £2,820 a head) and £6.6 million at BSkyB (1,300 employees; worth approximately £5,076 a head). In commercial radio, more than £1 million was spent by GWR (550 employees; worth approximately £1,818+ a head)[12].

Property services: The 2002 People Skills Scoreboard for property services[13] covered occupations including surveying, facilities management, estate agency, and the valuation of property, antiques and fine art. It found that the largest proportion of the 110 organisations surveyed spent 1% or less of their turnover on on-the-job training, with a similar percentage being devoted to off-the-job training.

Calculating training expenditure

Many training, personnel and HR managers could well find that producing accurate calculations of the true cost of training acts as a hostage to fortune, given the difficulties that many face in maintaining or increasing the training budgets they already receive.

As we noted above, few organisations take account of more than the most basic headline costs of training. Fewer than half of all employers with training budgets include the cost of trainees' salaries – in other words, the opportunity costs where the trainee could have been productively employed instead of being involved in training. Yet, the CIPD in its research mentioned above found that salary costs are often the single largest component of training expenditure. In fact, the compilation of accurate training accounts could well lead to the known headline cost rising by 50% or more.

However, should such detailed calculations be desired (perhaps, for internal use among training, personnel or HR staff) two fact sheets produced by the CIPD provide useful starting points: *Costing your training* by Frances and Roland Bee, and *Costs of training* by Mike Cannell (both are available free of charge from www.cipd.co.uk).

In a book by training consultant Tony Newby (*Cost-effective training: a manager's guide*, Kogan Page, 1992, www.kogan-page.co.uk), he makes the point that it can be equally as valuable to calculate the costs incurred by not providing training. Fundamentally, as he points out, the key issue is not how much training costs, but whether the costs are justified in terms of the returns gained by the organisation. A definition of good training, Newby says is that: "It is an investment (of organisational resources and individual effort) that yields identifiable improvements in job performance."

His book also contains a checklist to help calculate training expenditure, but it accompanies this with a checklist of the costs incurred when training is not provided (see checklist 4).

Where time and resources are limited, it may be more productive to focus on making a case for training through the latter type of calculations suggested by Newby and also investigating whether or not government financial support might be available to subsidise some of the organisation's training costs (*see the section below on government programmes*).

4. Calculating the costs of not providing training

Source: Cost-effective training, Tony Newby, Kogan Page, 1992.

"A checklist of examples of inadequate work performance which may respond to training."

Aspects of work performance	Does it happen here?	Best guess at £ cost	Best guess at £ gain by training
Customer complaints			
Equipment downtime			
Delivery delays			
Breakages			
Lost sales			
Accidents			
Quality failures			
Staff turnover			
Recruitment errors			
Ineffective training			
Uncontrolled overheads			

Bad debts

Stock-control problems

Excessive inventory held

Capacity underutilised

Contract deadlines missed

Loss of market share

Absenteeism

Shortage of promotable staff

Excessive overtime working

Add your own examples here

Note: In addition to Newby's suggestions, further, more specific examples could include:

● the cost of defending tribunal complaints;

● the number and nature of staff grievances (both could indicate a need for training in people-management skills);

● failure to gain, or delays in gaining, business-relevant quality awards (ISO 9000; EFQM; etc);

● the number and nature of formal disciplinary warnings and sanctions;

● the number of recruits whose employment is terminated during their probationary period;

● the use of specialist consultants or temporary staff to provide scarce skills;

● failed IT projects;

● failed acquisitions or mergers; and

● an inability to exploit the potential of the internet and/or electronic commerce because the skills to do so were not available.

Why train?

Training as a concept often polarises opinion within organisations. In some employers, the provision of training is taken as an article of faith, that it is a "good thing" in its own right.

In others, in contrast, training is seen as an inherent waste of time and money. Hire-and-fire managers may talk in terms of training being a convenient excuse to avoid confronting under-performance or incompetence by more direct means. Alternatively, they may believe that training merely improves the marketability of employees, who, once trained, are promptly poached by competitors who avoid the effort and expense of delivering the training themselves.

The aim, though, for most training, personnel and HR professionals is to demonstrate that training is an integral part of organisational strategy and its day-to-day operations. They cannot afford to rely on benign attitudes to training, given that a change of leadership, a worsening economic climate or other developments can occur at any time. And, in organisations where hard-nosed management prevails, training will always have to prove its worth.

● Checklist 4 above provides a starting point for professionals to begin to make the case for investment in training.
● Benchmarking the size of training budgets in comparable organisations in the same industry, locality, or both, may help to advance the argument that the proposed expenditure is reasonable and is one that competitors find capable of absorbing as part of their overheads.
● There may be government subsidies available, too, to reduce the costs involved (although these usually come with "strings attached").
● And, for each training programme or process, evaluation evidence needs to be obtained and used to demonstrate that the proposed objectives have been met and that tangible benefits have been achieved as a result.

The government's increasing concern about the competitiveness of the UK economy has given "training" an almost mystical quality as being good in its own right. At the same time, the search for more politically-acceptable terms for training has intensified: training is now often called "learning" or "personal development".

But, whatever the label, it is certainly true that all citizens should be encouraged as a matter of public policy to gain learning-to-learn skills and attitudes. But employers are usually more concerned with immediate costs and benefits, rather than lifelong self-development. Most training should lead to a direct, observable benefit to the organisation. It provides only one of several options to achieving that end, and it is not automatically the case that it will always be the most cost-effective.

For example, most occupational psychologists agree that training can only do so much. The further one moves away from technical skills towards softer skills and behaviours, the harder it gets for training to achieve a cost-effective result in the short- to medium-term.

Adrian Furnham, who is Professor of Psychology at University College London, and a well-known writer and researcher on occupational psychology issues, puts it this way: "Our personality, intelligence and many of the attitudes and beliefs that flow from them do not change. [. . .] Once one has become an adult, very little changes. Intelligence levels decline modestly, but change little over the working life. The same is true of abilities, be they with language, numbers, music or lateral thinking."

As for basic personality traits, he says that: "Most people like to think that personality can change, particularly the more negative features, such as anxiety, low self-esteem, impulsiveness or lack of emotional warmth. But data collected 50 years apart give the clear message: 'Still stable after all these years'. Extroverts become marginally less extroverted; the acutely shy seem a little less so, but the fundamentals remain the same."[14]

The implication is that the alternatives to training become more cost-effective, and attractive, where personality, intelligence and some deep-seated behaviours and attitudes are the issues. In addition, where the gap between current skills and those required is great, then training may not prove cost-effective.

In either of these scenarios, organisations can do one or more of the following, depending on the costs involved and whether or not each option represents a serious alternative (recruitment, for example, depends on there being suitable candidates available at a salary the employer can afford):
● recruit individuals with the attributes or higher-level skills they need;
● outsource the activities involved to an external company;
● use self-employed or agency staff;
● redesign the job or function, to spread the attributes/skills required over several members of staff (or deskill the work so that attributes/skills are required at a lower level); or, indeed
● accept that no-one is perfect, and find ways of using more of the attributes and skills that the individual already possesses, and either accepting their imperfections in other areas or find other individuals who can pro-

vide the complementary attributes and skills to create rounded performance.

The growth of team-based working is facilitating the latter approach, where
the skills, experience and knowledge that an organisation requires for a particular type of work can be provided on a collective basis by the team's
members as a whole, although particular individuals in the team may have
their own strengths and weaknesses.

Training is most likely to be cost-effective, and provide a realistic alternative
to these other options shown above, where it is based on a reasonably short-
term cause and effect.

Training can have an equal value where it develops trainees' self-confidence
– over and above specific work-related skills – with the result that they
become less anxious about the inevitable climate of change that now prevails in most organisations. Employees who are more confident in themselves and in their ability to learn new skills are more likely to accept change
and have more flexible attitudes.

Allied to this, some employers – particularly those employing manual and
semi-skilled workers – have introduced "employee development programmes". These offer free, or subsidised, courses in almost any subject,
sometimes in working hours but often during personal breaks and after
hours. The aim is to involve individuals in learning – any learning – and
make it an enjoyable experience (many courses involve leisure pursuits,
such as car maintenance, using a home PC or learning French or Spanish
for foreign holidays). Ultimately, the hope is that the experience will
encourage those concerned to accept work-related training and changes
to modernise their working practices. The first and best-known such
scheme is Ford's EDAP (employee development and assistance programme).

Finally, though, some training is only cost-effective because it helps to retain
staff who demand it as almost a perk. Professionals, in particular, are often
focused on ensuring that their career is developed and that whoever happens to be their current employer shares with them the burden of "continuing professional development" (CPD, sometimes translated as continuing
personal development). Such workers are often in short supply and there
may be no cost-effective alternative to providing them with training on a
fairly regular basis. However, the training ensures that these staff maintain
their professional skills and knowledge – some of which, in any case, the
employer may find directly useful. (In addition, expensive residential "con-

ferences", preferably in exotic locations, are favoured by some senior managers and directors as a perk of the job, and training managers may be expected to arrange, or simply pay for, their provision.)

The key issues in managing training

Training is a profession in its own right, although many employers do not appoint training managers but rely on personnel and HR specialists, line managers and external providers to manage their training provision for them.

Only the main themes of such a complex subject as the management of training and development can be covered in a general handbook. The themes are shown in checklist 5.

5. Managing training: the key issues

● Understand the organisation's corporate strategy, its main objectives and as much of the day-to-day activities as possible;

● Embed training in as many relevant processes as possible, particularly day-to-day performance management, formal performance reviews, return-to-work/absence practices, recruitment and induction, and business-planning activities;

● Gaining senior-management commitment to obtaining Investors in People accreditation is a means of embedding training, although the costs and benefits of gaining and maintaining accreditation should be evaluated;

● Involve line managers in identifying and planning training provision, because this will increase their commitment to it, encourage them to support the trainees and motivate them to help with the evaluation of the training's effectiveness;

● Be proactive: take training out into the organisation and identify areas where training could improve effectiveness; create a business case with costings (checklist 4) where training could provide a cost-effective benefit to the organisation;

● Ensure individuals' training needs are identified objectively and clearly; aim to create a consensus about the way in which training priorities will be set;

● Provide training to line managers in assessing training needs (probably via basic supervisory and line manager training programmes) and in trainer skills to those who will deliver on-the-job training and coaching;

● Compare the cost-effectiveness of remedying training needs through training against alternatives, such as recruitment and outsourcing;

● When planning training provision, take account of individuals' learning preferences, feedback on the most effective methods and possible economies of scale;

● Consider whether off-the-job training is the best option and, if so, whether it would be more cost-effective to organise and/or deliver it in-house, buy in external expertise or send trainees to open courses;

● Take account of organisational realities when planning training (spending constraints; the demands of professionals for continuing professional development, the interest of some senior managers in incentive-type conferences and so on); and

● Create a process for the evaluation of training, based on effective identification of training needs, prior assessment of abilities, effective training specification and delivery, and final evaluation; aim to provide an evaluation report that quantifies the benefits of training and supply this to trainees and line managers.

Winning support for training

The pressures on line managers and senior managers seem to be constantly increasing, and their packed work schedules mean that they will often be keen to offload people-management issues where their organisation has appointed personnel, HR or training specialists.

Unfortunately, although this ensures that the activities are managed professionally, and in compliance with the law, it also means that they come to be seen as peripheral to the mainstream life of the organisation. This, in turn, means such activities can be seen as adding little value – as costs rather than investments – that can be reduced without inflicting too much damage to the performance of the business.

Specialists, therefore, depend on winning line and senior managers' support for their work, both philosophically and in concrete cash terms.

In respect of training, most analyses of training needs depend on line managers' involvement – through their responsibility for performance management. And, once a need has been identified, the manager must be willing to release the member of staff to participate in the training. Provided managers have been won over, and understand how the training will benefit the individual and themselves (through improved performance, meeting targets, and so on), then their cooperation is more likely to forthcoming.

In the same way, the trainees need to be motivated to participate in the training. Their involvement in the discussion of their training needs in relation to the demands of their job, identifying the likely ways of resolving them (taking account of their learning styles or preferences) and in giving their feedback on the training provision, can help to improve their own "buy in". Many organisations also link longer-term training provision to the achievement of formal qualifications, and this official recognition of their improved skills can provide a powerful motivator for some individuals. In addition, some employers offer financial incentives to employees who complete certain training courses.

Some organisations have identified this issue of employee buy in as a key aspect of effective training, and are taking steps to give more ownership of training issues to the individuals concerned. However, to be a reality, this relies to a considerable extent on the presence of a supportive organisational culture, the commitment of individuals' managers and the availability of the necessary resources – such as training-resource guides, access to professional advice and support, and the necessary funding and paid time off from the employer.

Training and development expert Ian Cunningham recommends[15] that training, personnel and HR specialists should focus on helping line managers find solutions to their problems. Starting with training as the answer or, even, getting managers' help to fill vacant places on courses, sends out the unwelcome message that: "We have a solution; let's see if we can bend your problem to fit it."

Moreover, he advises being realistic and not "over-selling" the achievements that training can produce, and being astute enough to choose the right moment to approach a busy manager to discuss training issues– such as when they are not particularly stressed, or working to a tight deadline or facing another immediate challenge.

Analysing training needs

As case study B indicates, some employers approach the identification of training needs in a two-pronged approach. At the level of the organisation and major departments, they consider the implications of their business plans, new projects and pressing issues – such as an increase in customer complaints, or slump in performance – in terms of the skills they require, and then attempt to identify any skills that are in short supply.

This process is likely to be postponed or forgotten in the fast pace of organisational life, so many employers attempt to formalise it in some way.

At a local level of the individual employee and team, they compare the skills each job requires against those offered by the employees concerned. Again, this process is often formalised – perhaps more commonly than the one where organisational needs are discussed. Most commonly, employers tell us that they use their formal performance-management systems to ensure that training needs are assessed.

Many employers do so as part of the normal review system, where the (usually annual) formal meeting discusses past performance and achievements, and looks ahead to the coming year. A discussion of the skills, knowledge and experience required in the employee's job highlights potential training needs, informed by the assessment of their past performance and their aims for the next 12 months.

However, some employers uncouple the discussion of training needs from the performance review – particularly, where the review is linked to a decision about the employee's pay. Many employees would understandably be wary of discussing their areas of under-performance for the purposes of planning their training were this honesty to rebound on them in the form of a lower pay award or bonus. Putting a distance, in terms of timing, between the two types of review represents an attempt to reduce the impact of performance-related pay on training discussions.

Case study B. Emerson Process Management

Engineering company Emerson Process Management has a training policy covering its workforce of around 600 employees, which includes a process of training-needs analysis. Individuals' training needs are identified in a two-way approach, involving top-down and bottom-up assessments.

Line managers, assisted by HR specialists, are responsible for conducting the analyses. The top-down approach aims to identify the needs that are implied by departments' requirement to help achieve corporate objectives. Departmental managers conduct a review on a regular basis; the training procedure advises that this might be undertaken annually in tandem with budget-setting, or "some other stimuli, such as the introduction of new products or services, or perhaps the need to respond to customer concerns and complaints". The review interprets departmental responsibilities to help achieve corporate objectives in terms of individual tasks and skills.

They then use the performance-management system's assessment of each employee's skills to identify any skills gaps that should be addressed. "This gap analysis will allow the manager to identify systematically the overall training needs of their section or department. They must then plan how to meet that need," the procedure continues.

Bottom-up, individual training needs are identified through the formal performance-review meeting that each employee receives at least once a year. The discussions can range widely, including career aspirations as well as immediate training needs, and the company advises that "Not all training suggestions will become agreed training needs, as there must be [an] agreed business benefit."

Both the top-down and bottom-up approaches include preparation for the evaluation of training effectiveness that takes place after the training has been provided.

However, line managers and training, personnel and HR specialists have to walk a fine line between encouraging employees to take an interest in developing their skills and ensuring that the training can be justified in business terms, as well as being the best approach to resolving the skill need. There is also potential for tensions to occur between line managers, who may see training as the main response to under-performance, and training, personnel and HR specialists who might want to encourage the managers to adopt a more proactive role in developing competence on a day-to-day basis.

Case study C. Ministry of Defence

The Ministry of Defence has recently revised the performance-management system it uses for its civilian workforce of around 90,000 employees, giving more attention to discussing the way in which tasks are performed and to the preparation of development plans for each individual.

In the formal review meetings, line managers highlight at least three strengths, but they also identify three areas that would benefit from further development. In collaboration, the line manager and employee use these as the basis for a development plan. Plans may not necessarily reflect weaknesses, but could be formulated to strengthen existing skills or to develop them in response to planned changes in operational requirements.

Personal development plans

Increasingly, the discussions between individual employees and their line managers about their training needs is linked to the creation of a personal development plan (PDP). Not only are PDPs tailored to the particular needs of the employee concerned, but they are seen by the employee to be customised in this way. This knowledge often increases the motivation of the employee to take part in training and make best use of it.

It also provides a forum whereby both the individual and their line manager discuss training needs in such a way that they produce a formal document setting out their conclusions. The process thus involves line managers more closely in analysing their employees' training needs and encourages them to support the training they undertake – for example, by encouraging their staff to take up training opportunities, arranging for their work to be covered while they are training, and providing opportunities for the employee to put into practice the skills they have learned.

Two-thirds of larger organisations contacted by IRS now regularly provide their employees with PDPs, although the proportion is likely to be considerably lower among organisations with smaller workforces.

In some cases, PDPs are produced by another means: as a key output from a special extended assessment of individuals' training needs known as a "development centre". This approach is discussed in the next section.

Case study D. SecondSite

SecondSite Property Holdings handles the disposal of surplus property from the British Gas portfolio. It provides PDPs to its workforce of fewer than 100 employees. The plans are developed as part of the formal performance-review meetings between each employee and their line manager, and individuals are asked to send a copy to HR specialists so that they can be used to compile an overall training plan for the company based on key development requirements. HR specialists aim to correlate the training needs highlighted in the PDPs across the business to ensure best use is made of resources and to rationalise training provision. Reference is made to line managers to confirm that there is a real training need and establish the level of priority that should be given to it.

The introduction of PDPs provides a formal system of documenting each employee's training needs. The potential benefits of such systems depend, however, on careful preparation and the consideration of several important issues, as checklist 6 shows.

319

6. Personal development plans: the key issues

Increasing numbers of employers are introducing personal development plans (PDPs), but they will only prove effective in encouraging cost-effective training where some important issues are considered in advance. PDPs will not succeed where they are introduced without careful preparation and ongoing support.

● Who will be able to draw up a PDP – the whole workforce, or will they be reserved for non-manual staff, managers or other groups? (Increasingly, employers are covering their whole workforce; originally, many PDP schemes were restricted to managers and were outcomes from development centres);

● Will there be assistance to help those involved draw up PDPs? (Many employers provide a checklist or form to be completed during the meeting at which the PDP is drafted; some provide training to line managers and, perhaps, employees in developing PDPs);

● Who will be responsible for drawing up the PDP – the individual employee, their line manager, or both? (Many employers either expect this to involve a shared responsibility or put the employee in the driving seat);

● How much structure will the PDP have? (Practice varies; many employers provide forms to help compile PDPs that create a basic structure for the plan, and this may resemble the list of objectives and personal goals compiled during the formal performance review: each training need is listed, with ideas for ways in which it can be addressed, a likely timeframe for meeting the need, the person(s) who will help in addressing it, ways in which the training can be evaluated, and so on);

● What time frame will the PDP cover? (Often, one year);

● And, linked to this, how often will progress against the PDP be reviewed? (Often, annually with six-monthly progress reviews);

● What will the PDP cover – immediate training needs, longer-term training needs, training linked to broader career aspirations? (Practice varies, but often covers skill needs that can be addressed during the life of the plan – one year, for example – together with some broader areas for development);

● Who will ensure that the training needs incorporated in the PDP conform to organisational requirements – for example, where training is planned that extends beyond business-related skills to areas that fall outside corporate policy? (Line managers are usually expected to ensure that PDPs conform to corporate policy, or they may have to be copied to the training, personnel or HR manager for approval);

● Who will be responsible for implementing the PDP – the individual employee, their line manager, or both? (Employers take different approaches; in many cases, the line manager is expected to help the employee implement the plan by providing support, encouragement and resources; in others, it involves a shared responsibility; or, increasingly, employers place the onus on the employee as part of a wider move to transfer responsibility for training to the individuals involved);

● How much emphasis on formal training will the PDP have? (Increasingly, employers are using PDPs to encourage a solutions-based approach to training needs, where the full range of training opportunities is involved – they want their employees and managers to change their attitude that training always involves a course towards considering more creative, and often lower-cost, solutions – these may emphasise learning in the workplace);

● To what extent will the PDP describe potential solutions to training needs – will it be fully prescriptive, highlight some likely learning opportunities or leave this to be determined by the person(s) responsible for implementing the PDP? (Employers often create support systems to accompany the launch of PDPs, such as directories of training courses, useful books and videos, and ideas for learning activities in the workplace, together with the provision of advice and support from line managers, backed up by the input of training, personnel or HR professionals); and

● How will the cost-effectiveness of PDPs be evaluated? (Employers often struggle with implementing effective evaluation systems; PDP systems are often particularly difficult to evaluate.)

Development centres

Development centres provide another means of conducting training needs analyses and creating personal development plans (PDPs). Instead of a meeting or interview, discussed in the previous section, development centres bring to bear a whole battery of assessments in order to analyse individuals' strengths and weaknesses. As their name suggests, they are closely allied to the assessment centre technique (described in chapter 2 Cost-effective selection); the main difference between them is the purpose for which they are used: training or recruitment.

Development centres bring together several individuals for an extended period of assessments – often, for a day or two – and usually involve several work-related assessments, such as psychometric tests, work simulations and interviews. The aim is to cover all aspects of each participant's skills, although the centres often give more emphasis to transferable or "soft" skills.

In addition, the act of bringing together a group of participants who share some common attributes often, intentionally or not, improves networking and builds relationships.

Some employers' centres take this aspect of centres a step further and create groupings of participants who will help each other in carrying out their PDPs. Participants may meet each other on a regular basis after the centre and discuss the progress of their personal development, and facilitate learning opportunities for others in their group – for example, by arranging site visits, shadowing or secondments, or helping to facilitate work-related projects.

Being time-consuming, resource intensive and expensive to develop and run, development centres are usually reserved for key members of staff – senior managers or those on a high-flier programme, for example – and are most often found among larger organisations.

Employers often borrow the techniques involved without necessarily using the term "development centre" and may also blur the distinction between the purposes of assessment and development centres. For example, a development centre may also involve an element of judgment about participants' suitability for promotion. Charles Woodruffe, one of the UK's foremost experts on assessment and development centres, advises against confusing their purpose in this way. "Assessment and development do not go well together. [. . .] Rightly or wrongly, the assessees will be motivated to outwit the assessors if performance [in the centre] will affect their careers. That is not the frame of mind to confront development needs."[16]

Case study E. Johnston Press

Johnston Press has only a small head-office staff and a relatively flat organisational structure, and relies heavily on a dispersed team of managing directors and senior managers. It has set up a one-year development programme for its senior executives. Participants are nominated by their line managers, and are brought together in groups of six in learning sets. Each group is led by an external consultant who acts as a "learning-set adviser". At two-monthly intervals, each participant hosts one of the components of the programme at his or her site.

Initially, during an intensive two-day period, a development centre takes place that identifies each participant's strengths and weaknesses by making comparisons with the competency framework developed by company (the competencies identify the main transferable skills considered vital to achieve corporate goals, such as creativity and vision).

Personality questionnaires are completed and, to establish an initial standard of performance, 360-degree assessments take place to give feedback on perceived performance.

The information – such as "strong on leadership but weaker in analytical thinking" – is discussed between participants and their line managers (these are divisional managers or company managing directors). From this process, a learning contract is agreed and personal development plans are drawn up.

The one-year programme also includes three two-day modules that focus on: leadership and taking the initiative; communicating and influencing; and analytical thinking and creativity. During the modules, participants can "buy air time" for themselves, which provides an opportunity to talk about their needs and the challenges they face in their everyday roles. The company encourages its staff to raise particular issues in this way as part of its ethos that encourages employees to take responsibility for their own learning.

One of the modules takes the form of a business simulation run by the human resources director, which aims to develop a better understanding of the business. Mentoring skills are practised through behavioural observation of a fellow participant, followed by peer-to-peer feedback and coaching. At the end of the business-simulation module, participants give a presentation to the operations director, or chief executives, on a simulated business plan.

Each time that development centres are run, one of the managing directors is invited to attend as an observer. The company has found that this enhances knowledge about the competency framework, provides an opportunity to experience at first-hand the strength of the outputs and extends "buy-in" for the use of competencies.

The process of observation for managing directors is not a passive one. It involves working with an external consultant on their coaching skills and considering the language and methods involved in providing effective feedback. During development centres, observation is made of the six people who make up a particular learning set during the one-and-a-half-day period, entailing 12 observations, write ups and feedback sessions.

Participants in the programme may choose to discuss their weaknesses with their own managing director, but no markings are given for behaviours. Likewise, there is no pass or fail in assessments that are formed during the development centre. However, it is usual practice to highlight three competency strengths, but also identify another three that could benefit from additional work and development.

Investors in People

Investors in People (IiP) is an accreditation scheme that encourages effective, business-focused personnel management. Employers wishing to gain accreditation must commission an accredited external consultant to assess their personnel-related processes against the national IiP standard. Accreditation lasts for a maximum of three years before re-assessment is required.

IiP began life as a training-related set of requirements, specifying in some detail the way in which accredited employers were to conduct their personnel and training processes. The aim was to foster improvements in the quality and quantity of training undertaken by British employers as part of government policy to improve national competitiveness. A significant revision of the IiP scheme in 2000 has made it much less detailed, shifting the focus from the practices involved to their outcomes. Market research has found that the revised standard has greater appeal for employers, as being more relevant to their businesses and being written in a "less jargonistic" way[17].

The benefits of gaining IiP accreditation attract considerable controversy. Detractors argue that holding IiP accreditation adds little to organisations' reputation, particularly compared with such kitemarks as the international quality series ISO 9000. Critics also argue that it requires a costly, and still fairly bureaucratic, effort to gain accreditation, which gives few benefits to the organisations concerned in terms of enhanced productivity or profitability.

Supporters maintain that, with many thousands of employers holding accreditation, progressive organisations cannot afford to be left out. They point to the evidence of many employers' reported benefits, although these tend to focus on personnel and training issues, rather than bottom-line results. Even so, its supporters say that IiP offers an important lever for personnel, HR and training professionals to improve the management and development of employees, gain greater investment in these activities and raise their own status. The Chartered Institute of Personnel and Development is "fully supportive" of IiP[18].

State of play: Significant proportions of employers have gained IiP accreditation, according to government statistics[19], ranging from half of larger organisations (500-plus employees) and 45% of medium-sized ones (with 200 to 499 employees), to around a third of smaller enterprises (37% of those with 100 to 199 employees and 31% of those with 25 to 99 workers). In addition, around another 10% of employers in each category have announced they intend to gain accreditation. The body in charge of IiP, Investors in People UK, estimates that around one in four of all employees now work for an organisation with accreditation.

7. Investors in People: employers' experience

Feedback from personnel, HR and training managers obtained by IRS over several years shows that employers' experience of gaining Investors in People (IiP) accreditation is as follows:

● Planning: Careful planning of the work required for the organisation to meet the IiP standard usually pays dividends. Most employers find that the estimated time and costs involved were not exceeded;

● External advice: Most organisations sought outside assistance with their bid for IiP status, most commonly from official bodies managing IiP, although a significant minority paid for consultancy advice;

● Timescale: The time required from initially gaining internal agreement to aim for accreditation and achieving IiP status varies according to the organisation's own circumstances, but the typical time is around 15 months, based on a midpoint figure;

● Costs: The costs of gaining IiP status are even more influenced by employer specifics, but could be in the order of £7,000 to £9,000 (financial support may be available, however, particularly for very small organisations);

● Changes: Most commonly, the evaluation of training has had to be addressed by employers wishing to achieve accreditation, and this often poses the greatest challenge of any IiP-related changes;

● Two of the three main reasons why organisations set out to gain IiP status are training-related: ensuring that their investment in training is directly linked to business needs, and a desire for a general improvement in the quality of training. Additionally, gaining external recognition for existing good practice is often a powerful motivator;

● Most employers realise these ambitions, and these three factors are the main reported benefits experienced as a result of working for, and gaining, IiP accreditation (although by fewer organisations in each case than set out to enjoy them);

● The time taken for the actual assessment varies, although the average is five days; where organisations do not pass their assessment, the repeat process takes around the same length of time;

● Bottom line: Most organisations are not motivated to gain IiP accreditation as a means of improving their productivity or profitability, and few of those we have contacted have found that IiP has benefited them in these areas. However, ensuring that training expenditure becomes more cost-effective and business-related is a legitimate and valuable aim, and benefit, in its own right.

The standard: IiP consists of four "principles":
● **Commitment** (to training employees so they help achieve business objectives);
● **Planning** (ensuring that employees understand their organisation's objectives, and the part that their own job plays in achieving them);
● **Action** (putting commitment and planning together to ensure that business-related training is provided); and
● **Evaluation** (evaluating the impact of the expenditure on training and other employee-related practices on individual and corporate performance).

Each principle is subdivided into several indicators (there are 12 in all), each of which is accompanied by one or more examples of evidence that could show the indicator is being put into action. For example, one of the two indicators under the "action" principle is that "people learn and develop effectively". There are five examples of evidence shown for this indicator, including asking new members of staff to confirm that they have received an effective induction. The full standard is available to download free of charge from www.iip.co.uk.

As well as the main standard, Investors in People UK is developing a range of associated products, including a leadership and management standard, a recruitment and selection model, and a benchmarking tool called the Investors in People profile (also available from www.iip.co.uk).

Nationally, as we have noted, the scheme is run by Investors in People UK, but it is managed locally by local Learning and Skills Councils and, for small employers, the Business Link network, and these are the initial points of contact for organisations.

Evaluating training

The Investors in People standard places great emphasis on the evaluation of training, and acting on the findings, for good reason. Without proper actionable information on the results of providing training, there is no evidence that the money has been well spent, nor any information about areas in which training could be improved. Evaluation evidence is not only vital to organisational effectiveness, it provides invaluable information for training, personnel and HR managers to support their case that their employers should take training seriously and devote adequate resources to it.

However, many – perhaps, most – employers find the evaluation of training to be an almost impossible task, and efforts rarely extend beyond issuing "happy sheets" to trainees at the end of their courses.

The difficulties in conducting effective evaluations are undeniably formidable. The resources, particularly staff time, to undertake it may not be forthcoming, or simply not exist as workloads continue to increase. The practical problems in linking cause and effect are complex – there is often a great deal of organisational "noise" that gets in the way of attributing a particular result to the input of training. And, at the end of the day, the result may not be sufficiently clear cut to be convincing – or may be politically unpalatable. What if the evaluation shows there is no case for training?

8. Evaluating training: the most effective methods

Many employers struggle to conduct through evaluations of their training activities. However, based on their current practices, the following (in descending order of effectiveness) are the evaluation methods that they tell us are proving to be most effective:

● Post-course questionnaires;

● Interviews with trainees;

● Changes in trainees' formal performance-management assessments;

● Questionnaires completed by trainees' line managers;

● Observations of the trainees at work;

● Changes in metrics, such as output and productivity;

● Success rates in gaining formal qualifications;

● Test results;

● Assessment of progress in implementing trainees' personal development plans;

● Changes over time in the results of employee attitude surveys;

● Course log books; and

● Customer surveys.

Gaining trainees' views

"Happy sheets" are often decried as inadequate evaluation methods. They merely ask trainees for their impressions of the training; not only could this be subjective and influenced by many extraneous factors, but they give little insight into whether or not trainees have been able to apply what they have learned, and if they have benefited as a result. However, such questionnaires contribute most where groups of trainees are involved – collective feedback that shows a consistent trend could well highlight problem areas. And they are invaluable for motivational reasons – they show that the organisation takes the training seriously and wants the participants' feedback on it.

But this motivational function could be carried out equally effectively through debriefings conducted by trainees' line managers. This is particularly appropriate where the training was preceded by a meeting between these parties, such as a performance review that highlighted training needs. Debriefings thus represent part of the same process, and could involve an agreement on ways in which the individual could be given sufficient opportunity to put the training into practice and, perhaps, to look ahead to further training that might complement what has just occurred.

Debriefings, too, can be seen part of the function of day-to-day performance management by line managers. Training that is intended to help improve an individual's performance should be discussed between them, and this could help motivate the trainee to practise their new skills and, thus, reinforce their learning. Line managers' perceptions of any changes in employees' performance, following training, are also a vital part of conducting training evaluation. Involving them at this stage adds weight to their role and could increase their motivation to take a full part in evaluations, given that early involvement could help demonstrate the relevance of evaluation to their own responsibilities and targets.

Line managers' feedback

Line managers inescapably play an important role in any evaluation system. They observe first hand the performance of their employees, and should notice any changes in their performance and behaviour after training – particularly if the managers have been involved in identifying training needs and planning training to remedy them.

More formally, they will be responsible for conducting formal performance reviews where changes in performance should be discussed and analysed.

The records from the reviews provide what should be a more objective and considered point of reference to complement feedback obtained from managers closer in time to the training event.

Metrics

Formal performance-management reviews often aim to attach measurable targets to aspects of employees' performance, and these provide a means of assessing changes in performance following training. However, as we discuss in chapter 10 (*Managing performance 1*), it is increasingly difficult to quantify employees' work in meaningful ways, although some aspects of it may be capable of such measurement.

In addition, work-related tests have traditionally been used to evaluate training – the "test–retest" method. The test could simply comprise an accurate sample of the aspect of the individual's work that will be covered by the intended training. Or it could involve a questionnaire or other type of more formal test. The same test is then repeated at a suitable interval after the training, having given the trainee time to put their skills into practice, and the results are compared.

Employers tell us that broader metrics are also analysed for evidence of the impact of training, particularly changes over time in repeated employee attitude surveys (opinion polls of an organisation's staff about their job satisfaction, attitudes to proposed changes, and so on), and changes in labour turnover rates. These broader measures are, by their nature, more removed from the training and are open to the influence of a wider range of factors.

Control groups

Instead of focusing solely on trainees, the effectiveness of training can be investigated by comparing any differences over time between reasonably similar groups of employees, where one group receives training and the other does not. Changes analysed could include changes in on-the-job performance, job-related targets (sales, output, customer complaints, etc), attitudes and motivation, absence rates, resignation rates, and so on.

Evaluation models

There are many different models or techniques available that are intended to help employers conduct training evaluations, of which the best known is probably the one devised by Donald Kirkpatrick in 1959[20]. An analysis of his and several later models by the Institute for Employment Studies indicates that they share the same basic approach, which involves approaching evaluation from four different levels[21]:

- **reaction:** trainees' response to the training, including its content, the process used and the trainers (methods include post-course questionnaires and debriefings with line managers);
- **learning:** the extent to which trainees have assimilated the training (methods include test–retest);
- **behaviour:** the extent to which trainees apply the learning in their work (methods include observation by line managers, the use of metrics, control groups and formal performance reviews); and
- **results:** the impact of the training on corporate performance (methods include metrics such as sales, output and profits; and softer measures, such as changes found in successive employee attitude surveys).

However, a book by Tony Newby[22], which contains his own model, makes the valuable point that evaluation should not focus exclusively on the delivery of training. If, for example, the prior stage of the analysis of training needs is flawed, then no matter how good the training provision, it may still not be effective. In fact, he says, each aspect of planning, delivering and following up training should be related to the process of evaluation. Careful identification of training needs, for example, should produce a blueprint that can be used as the basis of assessing changes in the individual's skills after the training has been put into practice.

His book also highlights the importance of cultural or political factors in organisational life. For instance, he advises that: "People take time to absorb new ideas [such as the introduction of effective evaluation]. It is a sound principle to build on strengths and to concentrate on initial efforts at evaluation where people are most receptive and the pay-offs are likely to be greatest. 'Ownership' of evaluation projects is important. In the early stages, it is better that people work on the evaluation of training activities for which they personally have some responsibility."

In addition, in a further dose of political reality, he suggests that new programmes could be evaluated, because an evaluation has more chance of being accepted "in a spirit of enquiry", whereas targeting a well-established training programme could encourage those with a vested interest in it to become defensive.

Newby recommends that training, personnel and HR managers approach reforms to training evaluation (or its first-time introduction) in a measured way, based on setting priorities, easy wins, and gathering momentum and political support on the way:

- **Importance:** Target evaluation on training where its success or failure has the most serious consequences;
- **Timescale:** Will the results of the evaluation be available in time before the same type of training is repeated? If it is a one-off type of training, will the results be applicable to other training envisaged for the future?;
- **Costs:** Will the evaluation be cost-effective, in terms of the cost of conducting the evaluation compared with the cost of the training and, also, the potential losses were the training to fail?; and
- **Impact:** Is the evaluation likely to achieve any results, given the political/cultural climate in the organisation?

Additional methods

On a fairly subjective level, trainees could be asked to keep an on-the-job diary where they note down the ways in which they are applying their training to their daily tasks. This provides some insights into the impact of the training, and has the additional benefit of encouraging trainees to reflect on what they have learnt and, thus, reinforce the training.

More sophisticated methods of evaluating training are available that go beyond the confines of this handbook. For example, suitably trained staff can employ the critical incident technique or repertory grids, and administer and interpret psychometric tests.

Some special legal issues

As well as general legal considerations – such as anti-discrimination laws – that apply equally to training as other aspects of employment, there are some specific statutory developments with a bearing on the provision of training.

Rights to paid time off for training

From September 1999, certain young employees have had a statutory right to be given paid time off by their employers to undertake education and training under the Right to Time Off for Study or Training Regulations 1999.

The right relates to employees aged 16 and 17 (and 18-year-olds who change employers while engaged in relevant training under the rights) who have failed to gain a "level 2" qualification before entering employment. They have the right to request paid time off so that they can be qualified to level 2.

Being below level 2, under the national classification, means that the young person must have failed to obtain one A-level at grades A to E, five GCSEs at grades A★ to C, or a National Vocational Qualification at level 2, among other qualifications.

Notably, small firms are not exempt from the Regulations, and there is no minimum period of qualifying service, nor a minimum number of hours worked each week. The choice of course is left to the individual, and could include GCSEs as well as vocational (work-related) formal qualifications. However, the rights exclude youngsters who are in full-time education.

The onus lies on the employee to claim their right, and their course must be linked to a formal nationally-recognised qualification – although they could move towards level 2 in stages, so that the initial course does not necessarily have to offer a qualification at level 2. Employers must give "reasonable" amounts of paid time off for the purposes of following the course, but do not usually have to bear the costs of the training itself (which is usually met from public funds).

The use of "reasonable" means that where and when the time off is taken should take account of the employer's business needs, as well as the study programme that the young person wishes to follow. This means that some employers' own training courses could satisfy the Regulations, where they lead to a level-2 formal qualification. In such cases, the study could combine on-site and off-site training, and training delivered in modules or blocks, rather than regularly each week. However, as a yardstick, the government suggests that one day a week, on average, would be reasonable.

An estimated 100,000 to 120,000 young employees are covered by the Regulations, but research to date indicates that both the youngsters and their employers know little about these rights and are not yet making much use of them.

Union learning representatives

The Employment Act 2002 amends the Trade Union and Labour Relations (Consolidation) Act 1992 to create a new type of trade union representative: the "union learning representative". The amended 1992 Act sets out representatives' duties – which primarily involve promoting learning opportunities among trade union members. Representatives must be appointed under their union's rules (the union must already be recognised by the employer), and their details given in writing to the employer. They must receive suitable training for their role.

Once the statutory conditions have been met, learning representatives will have similar rights to trade union representatives to paid time off, facilities and protection against victimisation and dismissal. Members who consult their learning representative are entitled to unpaid time off for this purpose.

According to the amended 1992 Act, the right to paid time off for union learning representatives is intended for the following purposes:
● analysing members' training needs;
● providing information and advice about training-related issues (and not just those that relate directly to their work);
● arranging training for members;
● promoting the value of training among members;
● consulting the employer in respect of the above activities; and
● preparation time in relation to the above activities.

The activities are restricted to employees who are "qualifying members of the trade union"; that is, employees who are members of a trade union recognised by the employer and who make up the constituents of the union learning representative.

Union learning representatives, unlike normal union representatives, must have received appropriate training as a requirement of gaining their legal status (the trade union must write to the employer giving the learning representative's name and confirming that they have met the training requirement).

The paid time off – which covers training for their role as well as the representatives' duties – must be "reasonable", and Acas has amended its existing Code of Practice on Time Off for Trade Union Duties and Activities to include union learning representatives.

So far, the Labour Research Department estimates that there are around 4,500 union learning representatives, although this number could soar to as many as 22,000 by 2010[23]. Many of the current representatives have already been trained through programmes receiving public funding under the Union Learning Fund initiative (see below). According to a 2001 report from the Campaign for Learning and the Trades Union Congress, learning representatives were receiving five days' initial training on average, with one in three attending follow-up training[24].

Case study F. Manchester Airport

Manchester Airport has set up a network of "training champions" – employees who act as an important communication link between the company's training department and individual members of staff. The champions let training staff know of their constituents' suggestions for additional training provision, help in the evaluation of training and, if they wish, can be trained in training skills so they can help deliver courses. Champions meet on a regular basis to discuss training programmes that could be of benefit to employees working for the airport.

Compulsory consultation

The Trade Union and Labour Relations (Consolidation) Act 1992, as amended by the Employment Relations Act 1999, requires employers with more than 20 employees to grant recognition to a trade union under certain conditions (note that the recognition provisions are already under review by the government).

The new rights are summarised in chapter 8 Employee involvement and representation. But, of relevance here is the provision that an employer may be required to consult a recognised trade union about training issues. This will apply where a trade union has been given statutory recognition rights by the Central Arbitration Committee (CAC) (that is, in the absence of a voluntary agreement with an employer) and, additionally, where the union and employer have failed to agree on the content of the resultant recognition agreement.

Under such circumstances, the CAC will impose its own bargaining and consultation provisions. These include a stipulation that the employer will be legally required to consult and inform the trade union at least every six months on its training policy, training provision and planned training provision in respect of employees in the bargaining unit for which the union has been given statutory recognition.

To date, the new recognition rights have served to encourage employers to conclude voluntary agreements (there are advantages in doing so; see chapter 8), and there are few instances of compulsory recognition where the bargaining provisions have been imposed by the CAC. Potentially, though, the requirement for employers to sit down with a trade union and discuss training-related issues could have a considerable impact on the nature of industrial relations in the UK. It could mark a break with the traditional approach where employers have often not been involved in consulting or informing trade unions about training.

Government programmes and subsidies

The government has launched several long-term training programmes that provide financial help to employers as well as a host of short-term and experimental schemes on a national and regional basis.

Modern Apprenticeships

Modern Apprenticeships could be considered to be the government's flag-ship programme, in terms of the numbers of trainees and the amount of public subsidy. In essence, an employer that takes on a young apprentice under the programme receives financial assistance towards the cost of their training. There are many conditions attached, however, and the programme has many detractors.

Indeed, the programme has been almost constantly reviewed and reworked since its launch by a previous Conservative administration, which aimed to help reinvigorate the apprenticeship tradition and spread it from manufac-turing to the service and public sectors.

Most recently, Modern Apprenticeships have been merged with a lower-level scheme for young people called National Traineeships and changed into a two-tier programme of Foundation Modern Apprenticeships at level 2 in the national qualifications system, and Advanced Modern Apprenticeships at level 3. In addition, the technical subject matter of the courses has been boosted and separately assessed. Previously, trainees were awarded a National Vocational Qualification, but now can also gain a tech-nical certificate. Responsibility for the programmes has moved to the Learning and Skills Council and its regional councils.

There is also a government-sponsored enquiry underway intended to reduce the high rates of non-completion (around half of all trainees do not gain even a part-qualification) and increase the numbers of appren-tices and participating employers. There is now an official target that, by 2004, three in 10 (28%) of all young people will undertake a Modern Apprenticeship.

Around two-thirds to three-quarters of employers know about the original apprenticeship programme, with awareness increasing in tandem with workforce size, although slightly fewer know about the later foundation

335

scheme[25].

There is a growing range of apprenticeship programmes available – around 150 in all – from accountancy and business administration to plumbing, printing and engineering. Each course takes between one and three years to complete, depending on the occupation and whether the foundation or advanced programme is being followed. Information on Modern Apprenticeships is available from the Learning and Skills Council (tel: 08000 150 400; www.realworkrealpay.info) and its local offices, or from one of the Sector Skills Councils that cover a particular industry (www.ssda.org.uk).

Employers enter a formal agreement about their participation, which covers such factors as the particular programme, its level, the training involved and the stipulation that the apprentice must work towards a National Vocational Qualification, be assessed against the national "key skills" (literacy, numeracy and basic computer skills) and aim to gain a technical certificate. The employer and apprentice must also conclude a formal agreement, setting out their respective rights and responsibilities.

Generally, employers are required to take on the apprentice as an employee, pay them a salary, provide on-the-job training, and ensure they are given sufficient paid time off to pursue their off-the-job studies. However, Foundation Modern Apprenticeships could involve work placements for trainees, without a contract of employment; in such cases, the trainees receive a weekly allowance of at least £40.

The formal off-the-job training must be overseen by an accredited "learning provider", usually a college or a training company. Some large employers manage the programmes in-house. Modern apprenticeships are currently restricted to young people aged 16 to 24 years, but this is to be relaxed in the future.

Public subsidies cover part of the total cost incurred by employers in training a modern apprentice. In engineering, which involves some of the highest costs of any programme, the Engineering Employers' Federation estimates that subsidies cover around 30% of employers' expenditure on training 16- to 18-year-old apprentices (£14,560 of £50,000)[26].

9. Modern Apprenticeships: success factors

Based on our feedback from employers and other research, below are some factors that can contribute to successful Modern Apprenticeships (the complexity of the programme means that this cannot be a detailed checklist).

● **Suitability:** Although there are around 150 different apprenticeship programmes, many of which are offered at two different levels, employers should carefully check that a programme is available that matches their needs. And, where there is a possibility that trainees could move from foundation to advanced levels, that the programmes facilitate a smooth progression. Assessment against a National Vocational Qualification can present particular problems because it may involve tasks or skills that the apprentice's job does not offer. In such cases, employers should develop a scheme of exposing apprentices to a broader range of tasks and skills through job rotation, secondments or job enrichment.

● **Learning provider:** Employers often report that the relationship with their learning provider is unsatisfactory, in particular, that the training is of insufficient quality. Where a choice of provider is possible, careful selection is important, as is the maintenance of an ongoing relationship with the provider, discussing the trainee's progress, and ensuring that their on-the-job training and the provider's off-the-job training complement and reinforce each other.

● **Careful recruitment:** Apprenticeships require a long-term commitment from trainees, and considerable care should be taken when recruiting individuals to ensure they have the necessary motivation and aptitude. Employers have found that the concept of "earning while learning" is a considerable incentive to those young people who are not attracted to pursuing full-time academic education. However, realistic explanations of the job and apprenticeship programme are not always provided by employers. And some employers find that schools and colleges do not cooperate with their recruitment efforts. Providing work-experience opportunities to students, taking part in careers events and hosting open days for would-be apprentices and their parents have proved useful to some employers as ways of recruiting apprentices.

● **Full support:** Employers' participation in Modern Apprenticeships should be based on an identified business need for access to skills developed in the medium-term through this training programme, rather than being seen as a short-term means of gaining public subsidies. In particular, trainees require the support and encouragement of their line managers, and this is more likely if the organisation as a whole is committed to the programme. Generally, employers tend to gain most benefits from their participation when they contribute a relatively large proportion of the costs.

● **Bureaucracy:** Although the government is making efforts to reduce the red tape involved in participating in Modern Apprenticeships, some personnel and

HR managers we contacted advise employers to be prepared for the official bureaucracy, and that rule changes may be made that affect apprenticeships already under way as well as newly-agreed ones.

● **Key skills:** Participation in the key skills component of the apprenticeship is high-ly unpopular among trainees. In many cases, it is treated separately as a taught ele-ment that evokes unwelcome recollections of trainees' school days. Instead, learn-ing providers could be encouraged to integrate the key skills to some extent so that they are developed through work-based learning. The current review of Modern Apprenticeships is investigating the role and future of key skills.

● **NVQs:** Modern Apprenticeships involve trainees in working towards a National Vocational Qualification, and employers will need to ensure that trainees are given adequate support and encouragement to that end. The qualifications are accompanied by documentation that many find offputting and difficult to interpret, and the assessment process can appear bureaucratic and time-consuming.

The New Deal

One aspect of the government's New Deal programmes – which aim to help unemployed people find jobs – offers employers subsidies when they take on participants and then release them for training.

The New Deal initially focused on the large numbers of young people who were out of work in the mid-1990s. It was launched nationally in April 1998 against a background of considerable goodwill, and a great many employers signed up as supporters, offering places to New Deal trainees.

The New Deal has developed over time, and undergone considerable fine-tuning. The core programme now covers people aged 18 to 24 who have been registered as unemployed for six months or more. Most youngsters in this group are automatically referred to a New Deal adviser, and go through a "gateway" stage of assessment, initial training and help with job-search tactics.

They then have to take part in one of several options – one of which involves a six-month work placement with an employer. The New Deal trainee is paid by the government, and a subsidy is paid to the employer to help with the costs involved in releasing the trainee for training and providing a mentor. The subsidy is worth up to £60 a week.

For employers, the New Deal can offer some of the advantages afforded by the Modern Apprenticeship schemes: help with the training and recruitment of young workers, and access to a state subsidy. In addition, many employers aim to play a role in helping their local community, and the New Deal is a prime way of doing this. However, there are relatively few New Deal trainees in areas of tight labour markets – where employers would most need an additional source of recruits – and the official website warns organisations that there may be a delay in finding participants in such localities.

Many thousands of young people have taken part in the core New Deal programme, although the overall reduction in unemployment in recent years has helped to reduce the numbers involved. There has been considerable controversy over the cost-effectiveness of the programme and its success rate.

Generally, employers are more likely to be involved in Foundation or Advanced Modern Apprenticeships than they are with the New Deal for young people.

In addition, the New Deal has been extended to adults aged 25 years and over who have been out of work for 18 months or more (the employer subsidy is worth up to £75 a week for this group), as well as people with disabilities and single parents. These programmes tend to offer fewer services and options than the one devoted to young people, but all include a strand where participants can be placed with an employer.

There is also a voluntary programme for older jobseekers aged 50 years and over, where employers that recruit someone on the programme may receive a grant of up to £600 to help train the new recruit. Individuals are eligible for Working Tax Credits for up to a year; these are intended to ensure wages are as or more financially attractive than claiming out-of-work state benefits.

Further information on the New Deal is available from local jobcentres or www.newdeal.gov.uk.

The Union Learning Fund

Earlier in this chapter, we noted that the government has introduced rights for a new role of "union learning representative" and that much of the preparatory training of volunteers has been provided under its Union Learning Fund.

Employers can benefit from public funding under this initiative where they are involved in a training programme that promotes involvement in learning – "projects have to show they could get more people to take up courses to improve their skills, self-confidence and employability"[27]. From the start of the fund in 1998 to the 2003 spending round inclusive, the government will have provided more than £30 million in subsidies to more than 400 projects. As its name suggests, the funds are given to projects that are led by one or more trade unions, often in partnership with employers, and bids must be submitted by the union(s), not employers.

A government survey of employers that have taken part in Union Learning Fund projects found that the subsidies have mainly been used to help train their employees in basic literacy, numeracy and computer skills, as well as training union learning representatives and helping to set up workplace learning centres.

Employers told the researchers that their main reasons for participation were to have a more motivated and committed workforce, to encourage employees to be more receptive to taking part in training and to raise employees' skills.

All in all, they considered that the funding had helped to improve the self-confidence of employees, and fostered better communication between managers, their employees and trade unions. Having received initial funding, three-quarters of the employers were confident that the training activities would continue in the future[28].

Responsibility for the fund transferred to the Learning and Skills Council in April 2003.

learndirect

learndirect began life as the government's University for Industry, and offers free information on careers and the availability of training courses. Its database (which can be searched via its website) covers more than 600,000 courses offered by a wide range of public and commercial training providers. learndirect also commissions courses where gaps in provision are identified; some are free or subsidised. It is also supporting the creation of a nationwide network of local learning centres, each with a suite of computers, internet connections and access to a range of e-learning-based courses commissioned by learndirect.

Primarily, it is intended to be used by individual adults, rather than their employers, although learndirect has a consultancy devoted to providing training services to organisations. However, the vocational focus of learndirect means that many of the courses could be suitable in helping employees develop their skills, and use of the service could form part of the discussions concerning an employee's personal development plan. learndirect says that many users of its advice service are "seeking a change in their careers or courses to enhance their existing jobs".

learndirect's free national helpline is on 0800 100 900 (open 8am to 10pm daily); its internet site is at: www.learndirect.co.uk. In its first five years, the helpline handled five million calls.

Individual Learning Accounts

Individual Learning Accounts (ILAs) were intended to encourage individuals in the workforce who have few or no formal qualifications and experience of post-schooling learning to participate in training and become more employable.

The scheme, which was launched in September 2000, involved individuals registering with the national ILA Centre and being allocated an account number. They then simply quoted this number when contacting a training provider to undertake learning. At the same time as making contact with the provider, they also paid their own share of the cost of the training. The provider subsequently claimed the balance of the training-course fees from the ILA Centre.

However, a House of Commons investigation[29] found that many accounts missed their intended audience (40% were opened by professionals), and that subsidies had been improperly paid. By the time of their suspension in November 2001, more than 2.6 million accounts had been opened. In summer 2003, the government finally announced that ILAS would not be revived.

Training delivery: the key options

It is obviously important for training, personnel and HR managers to ensure that the training methods they use represent the most cost-effective and appropriate solutions to their organisations' needs. Overall, though, employees prefer face-to-face methods, particularly those where they have an immediate opportunity to put the learning into action.

Research by the CIPD among more than 750 individuals has found that these are the most popular methods[30]:

● on-the-job training (defined as "being shown how to do things, then practising them"): favoured by just over 50%, this is more than three times more popular than any other method;

● off-the-job training ("being taught in a meeting room or classroom situation"): 16%; and

● other forms of on-the-job training, such as informal tuition or coaching ("from colleagues and other people you work with"): also 16%. No other method gained 10% or more of the votes.

Our own research is based on the experience of training, personnel and HR specialists. It, too, finds that interactive methods are rated most highly (according to the effectiveness of the various methods), although this covers both off-the-job training based on group sessions and on-the-job training with one-to-one tuition.

Conversely, we have found that the least effective methods, according to specialists' experience, are passive training options. Lectures, presentations and training manuals are all rated poorly, as are e-learning methods – even those that include an element of interaction with the software programme.

On-the-job training

Employers are increasingly turning to on-the-job training as their delivery method of choice. There is a trend towards providing training to greater proportions of employers' workforces, but for shorter periods of time and by shifting delivery away from off-the-job courses towards work-based methods.

As we saw above, on-the-job training is popular among trainees and is considered to be an effective option by the specialists organising it. Surveys by the government and the CIPD, both cited above, confirm that on-the-job training is also the most widely provided method of learning.

As a method, on-the-job training suffers from over-familiarity. It is often dismissed as "sitting next to Nellie", although learning from others in a practical rather than theoretical sense, and then reinforcing the training by putting it into practice, is nothing to be ashamed of – particularly, where "Nellie" has been equipped with some basic trainer training. The main national training surveys mentioned above show that employers devote a large proportion of their investment in training to on-the-job learning, perhaps the largest share of it.

Guidance from the CIPD[31] on this method suggests that on-the-job training is most suited to developing job-specific skills, rather than broader skills and behaviours that are not tied to a particular job or role.

For: On the plus side, the CIPD points out that on-the-job training is eminently flexible, can easily be tailored to the training needs and learning styles of individuals, and be arranged at times that suit them and the person delivering the training.

The immediacy of the training means that trainers will find it easier to assess whether or not the trainees are understanding the training, and tailor their delivery accordingly.

Finally, the practical nature of this method means that the training can be reinforced by performing the skills required, and repeated as necessary until the individual is confident and practised.

Against: On the minus side, on-the-job training is deceptively informal, and may encourage trainers to skip the preparation that is essential to an effective learning experience.

Line managers and the trainees' colleagues must be consulted and involved, so that they provide support and encouragement.

And, as we noted above, the person providing the training – who is often not a specialist trainer – must be given some training in trainer skills for the training to be effective.

Finally, on-the-job training can be time-consuming, particularly where the trainer has to repeat the training with other trainees.

There is often an obvious choice as to the person who will deliver the training, as it is usually someone who is experienced in the skills or tasks being imparted. However, this can also encourage a casual approach by the organisation. Without some forethought, and discussion between the person chosen and a training, personnel or HR manager, there is a risk that more than just the good points of the trainer's performance will be imparted to the trainee. The trainer may not be following approved routines or processes in their job, or may have a jaundiced attitude to their duties or the organisation.

A review of the would-be trainer's formal performance assessments and/or a discussion with their line manager should reveal such shortcomings. It may then be necessary to discuss these concerns with the trainer, or, failing that or where the meeting does not resolve the problems, another person may have to be chosen to deliver the training.

Coaching straddles the line between on-the-job and off-the-job forms of training. The employee is coached and encouraged, usually by their line manager, to improve their performance, and this can be done while being supervised on the job or in meetings convened for the purpose, special coaching sessions and other off-the-job forums.

Coaching builds on the relationship that exists between the individual and their manager, and also enables employers to reinforce line managers' responsibility for managing their staff's performance. The face-to-face interaction involved in coaching is, as we saw, a firm favourite as being an effective learning medium.

According to research by the CIPD, formal coaching systems rarely cover the whole workforce, but are usually reserved for managers or, sometimes, for white-collar staff more generally[32]. A case study of coaching in the Royal Mail appears in chapter 10 of this handbook.

Mentoring is not necessarily linked to learning provision, as it usually involves creating a formal relationship between pairs of inexperienced and experienced members of staff, often based on the mentor being of greater seniority than the mentee but without any direct line relationship.

At its most limited, mentoring acts as an unofficial adjunct to an induction programme, with meetings between participants allowing the mentors to act as sounding boards and confidants. They will be able to share their greater knowledge of the culture and politics of the organisation and, perhaps, act as an ally or supporter in helping their mentee make the most of developmental opportunities. Their knowledge of the organisation also enables them to put the individual in touch with influential people and help with networking more generally. Most organisations with formal mentoring systems reserve them for managerial staff.

A broader role for a mentor occurs at more senior levels, where a consultant (usually one external to the company) acts almost as a careers counsellor, helping the participant explore their hopes and intentions for the future and whether their current career and employer are right for them. Their networking abilities mean that such mentors can also help their mentees move to another employer more suited to their needs. Alternatively, some employers are using this broader mentoring role to help retain key members of staff, by allowing them to discuss their ambitions and help satisfy them.[33]

Secondment takes on-the-job learning to a new stage, by physically relocating the trainee to a different role or workplace in order to broaden their skills, knowledge or experience. In some cases, organisations lend members of their staff to outside bodies, often to charities and schools.

Secondments can be difficult to arrange, and may arouse concerns among both the employees' line managers about loss of valuable personnel and among the participants, who may fear that their career progression could be hampered. But they can be an important means of exposing participants to new challenges, which, with adequate preparation and ongoing support and training, can be effective learning experiences.

As well as being potentially developmental, secondment presents a means of providing fresh interest to employees where promotion opportunities are becoming limited – particularly, given the trend towards flatter organisational structures or where there is little labour turnover.

Placements need not be long lasting, nor necessarily full time. For secondments to charities or schools, the individual could combine this work on a part-time basis with doing some of their normal duties. Or participants could be seconded to a special project or working group, either on a whole- or part-time basis.

However, part-time arrangements require careful management to avoid the participant shouldering additional work by juggling two potentially full-time roles, with the result that they may be too pressurised to learn much from the experience and could become less, nor more, motivated to stay with the organisation.

The type of secondment also has implications for the individuals and their hosts. Where employees are seconded to charities or schools, for example, the host will expect to gain access to levels of expertise that imply the individual should have already gained considerable experience and skills.

Short-term charitable work often falls under the umbrella of volunteering, which is discussed below.

Action learning takes on-the-job learning a stage further by formalising both the work involved and the way in which learning is structured. "Action learning" in its pure form involves bringing small groups of learners together in action learning "sets". Each participant develops one or more work-related projects – often, of a problem-solving nature – that they pursue from start to finish. During the course of the project, learners meet in their sets to discuss their projects, their aims for it, their progress and, importantly, the learning experiences that the project creates for them. Members of the group support each other, and discuss and question each others' ideas and experiences (and, thereby, highlight the key issues and reinforce the learning).

The time-intensive nature of action learning, and the often high-level projects involved, mean that this approach is usually reserved for managers or management trainees. Although the process of action learning, and the use of sets, appears self-managing, it actually requires effective preparation and facilitation by the learners' employer.

In particular, where problem-solving is the basis for the projects, there is considerable risk that the projects could rebound on the trainees. The projects may fail and the trainees lose credibility and, perhaps, self-confidence. But, equally or more importantly, projects that succeed could jeopardise the participants' futures by challenging the status quo and upsetting vested interests. Full prior consultation with senior managers and the trainees' own managers is required to investigate their awareness of the risks involved and the degree to which they are prepared to give public support for the projects and the trainees' actions.

Off-the-job training

The importance of developing a cost-effective approach to training, founded on identifying training needs linked to organisational objectives, becomes particularly important in the case of off-the-job training. Some line managers approach training from the opposite perspective, focusing on apparent solutions rather than first principles – "let's run a course".

Some line managers and members of senior management may have a misplaced confidence in their ability to deliver effective training courses to groups of employees. Where politically possible, each person required to talk to groups of trainees should themselves undertake some preparatory training in presentation skills and in learning theory and practice.

As well as using internal staff, off-the-job training often involves the use of external providers who may run a course for the organisation – either on or off site. Wherever possible, this course should be tailored to the needs of the organisation, rather than merely being the standard offering simply transplanted to another venue. Finally, there is a wide range of external, or open, courses where the organisation's trainees will sit alongside those from other employers. This can provide opportunities for networking, exposure to new ideas and solutions, and an opportunity for trainees to take time away from their workplace and gain a broader perspective on their organisation's own processes and activities.

Off-the-job training, particularly where trainees attend open courses, can be expensive and it is important to identify the full costs involved (travel time and costs, any overnight stays, trainees' salaries and lost output while away from work, and course fees), as well as the potential and actual benefits.

Where groups of trainees attend a course, there is an implicit assumption that they have similar training needs with broadly similar levels of prior skills and knowledge. Training-needs analyses are all the more important in such cases, to demonstrate that this assumption is well-founded. These assessments may show that such similarities do not exist, with the implication that a single, uniform course will not provide a suitable training method.

With any intended course, the aims and objectives should be established in advance, together with the methods that will be used to evaluate its effectiveness. Courses should have structured training programmes carefully developed and discussed with stakeholders.

Linked to qualifications

There is a huge range of work-related qualifications available in the UK, despite more than two decades of government reforms intended to simplify and improve the situation.

Many organisations use vocational qualifications as part of their training provision. Often, the qualifications are accompanied by detailed curricula and end-of-course assessments that can reassure employers that their trainees are being equipped with skills they need in their jobs. Importantly, too, some qualifications enjoy a status and reputation that act as a powerful motivator encouraging trainees to get the most from their course. In some regulated occupations, accredited formal qualifications are required as a means of ensuring that employees meet certain minimum standards of competence.

According to government statistics[34], at least six in 10 organisations encourage employees to gain formal qualifications, through such means as providing paid time off for study, paying course fees, and reimbursing the cost of books and materials. The proportion of six in 10 (60%) relates to employers with workforces of between 25 and 99 employees, but this increases rapidly among larger organisations: three-quarters (74%) of those with between 100 and 199 employees; eight in 10 (80%) of those with 200 to 499 employees; and almost nine in 10 (88%) among workforces of 500-plus.

However, the expense of such training means that it is usually confined to relatively few employees at any one time in all but the largest organisations. The Chartered Institute of Personnel and Development (CIPD) has found that professional qualifications are most likely to be supported by employers, followed by other types of vocational qualification, with postgraduate and undergraduate business-related courses being slightly less likely to win their backing[35].

In only a minority (40%) of the organisations surveyed by the CIPD were all types of employees eligible for financial support in order to gain a formal qualification. Generally, trainees' line managers are consulted about the decision whether or not to back their course and, significantly, the nature of this support. The full costs are not necessarily met by employers. Decisions tend to weigh up both the type of course involved and the status or type of job of the trainee. However, some sectors are more flexible than others, notably financial services, where formal qualifications are often a mainstream part of training activity.

Generally, around seven in 10 employers attach conditions to their financial support, most commonly by inserting a clawback clause requiring repayment of fees should the trainee leave the organisation within a certain period – most commonly, two years.

National Vocational Qualifications

National Vocational Qualifications (NVQs) and their Scottish counterparts Scottish Vocational Qualifications (SVQs) denote a particular kind of work-related qualification that has been developed, structured and assessed according to national guidelines. Some long-established awards have been reformatted as NVQs and hold dual status, but most NVQs have been specially developed as brand-new qualifications.

NVQs are modular, with each unit representing the basic building block that a trainee can use to build up their assessments gradually and gain a full award, should they not do so in one attempt.

Unlike traditional work-related qualifications, NVQs do not have a syllabus as such, nor end-of-course examinations – indeed, they are not dependent on trainees undertaking a course of study. The aim of NVQs is to set minimum standards of work competence; therefore, an individual who is already fully skilled can apply for assessment and, potentially, gain an NVQ without having to undergo further training or attend a course. Originally, NVQs did not describe the basic work-related knowledge that was required, but, increasingly, this is being incorporated into the qualifications.

In general, brand-new NVQs have failed to gain the status and recognition that some traditional vocational qualifications have enjoyed, although they now cover around 75% to 80% of all occupations in the UK. In particular, they have failed to make many inroads into professional-level qualifications (with the exception of qualifications in management), which has not helped to raise their profile.

The distinct nature of NVQs and the way in which their documentation is written and structured have aroused great controversy. Some employers find NVQs and SVQs to be relevant to their needs, and encourage their employees to gain these qualifications. Others, though, find it difficult to deal with the language in which they are written, find it difficult to meet the assessment requirements, and are not convinced that the amount of time and paperwork justifies the end result.

Certainly, the extensive involvement of employers in formal qualifications that we saw above is not fully reflected in their use of NVQs and SVQs. Overall, the same government survey found that only four in 10 employers in England offer NVQs, and participation is declining among organisations with 200 or more employees. Firms with fewer than 200 employees are, in contrast, becoming more involved in NVQs.

The statistics also show that NVQs have failed to penetrate many sections of the economy. In only parts of the public sector, urged on by government support for the qualifications, do more than half of all employers offer these awards. In financial and business services, in contrast, no more than one-fifth of firms have adopted them.

More detailed, but less recent official statistics[36] investigated individuals' involvement in NVQs and SVQs, as opposed to their employers. These show that NVQs appear to be in decline, while traditional types of vocational qualifications continue to increase year on year.

Statistics for 2000/01 show that 5% fewer NVQs and SVQs were awarded than in the previous year, while traditional qualifications grew by 10%. Overall, 428,000 NVQs and SVQs were awarded in 2000/01, compared with 553,000 traditional qualifications.

However, the position is likely to be even worse than this, as the official figures for traditional qualifications cover only those conferred by three of the largest awarding bodies, while the statistics for NVQs and SVQs are largely complete.

Most NVQs and SVQs are offered, and gained by, employees in lower-level, lower-skilled jobs (at levels 1 and 2 of the national qualifications framework; level 1 is a prevocational level, while level 2 is equivalent to one A-level at grades A to E or five GCSEs at grades A* to C). In 2000/01, 70% of all NVQs and SVQs were awarded at levels 1 and 2.

Case study G. Examples of using NVQs

The **Tyne and Wear Fire Brigade** uses National Vocational Qualifications (NVQ) courses for its uniformed staff; the NVQs were developed as part of a national drive to increase safety standards among firefighters. The Fire Fighting Operations suite of NVQs does not have a qualification at level 1 (pre-entry level), and Tyne and Wear does not use the level 2 award. Instead, its employees work towards gaining a level 3 qualification. This consists of 22 units, 12 of which are compulsory with a further two being chosen from the 12 optional ones. Each unit consists of between two and four elements.

Firefighters working towards the NVQ are assessed internally, and more than 300 employees have been trained for this role with a further 15 or so having been trained as internal verifiers who supervise the assessments. The assessors and verifiers have gained relevant NVQ units in these roles (the "D" units). All new entrants must be trained according to the NVQ's requirements, although existing staff are already qualified under the previous system and only participate in NVQs on a voluntary basis.

A spokesperson told us that their brigade was confident the move to using NVQs would provide a consistent training experience for fire crews across the UK and assist in reducing fatalities.

The **Walton Centre NHS Trust** is a Liverpool-based centre specialising in neuroscience. It is using NVQs in Care at levels 2 and 3 for its healthcare assistants. The trust has gained accreditation to assess its own employees' competence in order to award NVQs, and provides training based on the NVQs to raise healthcare assistants' skills and also to help them with career progression. In addition, it has produced a learning pack to accompany the NVQs that reinforces the theory behind the practical aspects of healthcare assistant work covered by the NVQ.

Several healthcare assistants have used the course as a stepping stone to undertake nurse training. The trust has found that offering NVQs and the ability to move to full nurse training is improving its ability to recruit and retain healthcare staff in what is always a difficult area of the labour market.

Gilesports, a chain of sports shops based in Merthyr Tydfil, has been using NVQ-related training as part of a retention strategy linked to store expansion. It has developed a course tailored to its own needs, according to *Personnel Today* magazine[37], that still enables trainees to gain a formal NVQ. It has found that the course appeals to staff because it is work-based, while still offering them a formal qualification, and is increasing their motivation to participate in the company's training provision.

Management development

Formal qualifications

We noted above that managerial qualifications were one of the few areas where NVQs had made inroads into professional occupations. Known most commonly as "MCI" (Management Charter Initiative) qualifications, these belong to a suite of awards at levels 3, 4 and 5 in mainstream supervision and management, together with specialist awards in such areas as quality management. The sudden closure of the MCI in 2000 has yet to sink into the public consciousness, mainly because its qualifications are being maintained at present while a fundamental review is underway.

Simultaneously, a government-backed investigation into the standards of management and leadership in British organisations led by the Council for Excellence in Management & Leadership recommended a series of reforms to management qualifications. The government endorsed most of its proposals, and changes are likely to be announced in due course.

Meanwhile, two well-established providers of management qualifications merged in late 2002, when the Institute for Supervision and Management (ISM) merged with NEBS Management. The new body, the Institute of Leadership & Management (ILM) (tel: 020 7294 2470; www.i-l-m.com), is a charity owned by the City & Guilds, and will continue the merged bodies' emphasis on providing formal qualifications and courses for team leaders, supervisors, first-line managers and middle managers. A range of new managerial qualifications was launched at the time of the merger.

Recently, too, another major provider of managerial training has gained its Royal charter, leading its name to change from the Institute of Management to the Chartered Management Institute (tel: 01536 204222; www.managers.org.uk). The long-established portfolio of courses provided by the Industrial Society has been sold to Capita, following the reorganisation of the Society into the Work Foundation. The courses are now provided by Capita Learning and Development (tel: 0870 400 1000; www.islearning.co.uk).

There are many other qualifications in management offered by business schools and other providers, such as MBAs, CMS and DMS (Master of Business Administration, Certificate in Management Studies and Diploma in Management Studies), although these qualifications are also available from some of the organisations mentioned above.

At present, though, many managers lack formal vocational qualifications, and develop their skills and experience over time, through progression and job rotation within their organisation and by planned career moves to new employers. Younger managers will be increasingly likely to possess a first degree, simply because of the growing participation in higher education by school leavers, although their courses often do not contain a business component.

Acas has produced a model syllabus for employees newly-promoted to supervisory level. Covering a five-day period, the course could be run in-house if expertise and time is available (*Supervision*, Acas, March 2003, free from www.acas.gov.uk).

Case study H. London Borough of Islington

The London Borough of Islington commissioned Middlesex University to develop a customised postgraduate management development programme for 90 middle managers drawn from across the borough's departments. The programme aims to improve standards of customer service to the borough's residents. It was designed to take account of previous training provision and the identification of development needs, and includes skills such as change management, development of self and others, project management, finance and accounting, and people and performance management.

One of the council's elected members responsible for customer service said that the programme would deliver higher standards of service to the public by increasing the confidence, competence and motivation of the managers and their own employees.

Issues in management development

"Management development" is the name given to the training of current and prospective managers, and embraces short programmes lasting two or three days as well as those that take a longer-term perspective. It frequently represents a high-cost area of an organisation's training expenditure, because the training is often personalised, one-to-one and intensive. But this recognises the crucial importance of having access to well-developed managerial skills to organisations' performance and survival.

Employers' management development practices were investigated in 1999 by occupational psychology consultancy Human Qualities (www.human-qualities.co.uk). Based on feedback from 60 employers, it found that the following were reported as being the most effective methods of developing managers (shown in descending order):
● internally-run training courses;
● work-based projects;
● the use of coaching;
● the use of competency frameworks (lists and definitions of the key skills that organisations require of their managers in order to achieve corporate objectives, usually derived from in-depth research and consultation); and
● 360-degree assessment.

Interestingly, several of the methods reported as being most effective were also those that had been introduced most recently: coaching, 360-degree assessment and managerial competencies. Development centres, too, were becoming more popular, as was a shift in perception that more of the responsibility for management development should be assumed by the participants and less by the sponsoring employer.

In the past, the development of supervisors and managers, particularly newly-promoted members of staff, concentrated on equipping them with the basic skills of management that their previous experience in technical roles had not emphasised. In particular, skills related to the management of people and budgets were usually covered by this initial training.

Latterly, though, organisations have changed and the skills they require of managers have evolved. Employees are likely to experience one or more reorganisations and change programmes during their time with any particular organisation. Their managers must be able to provide leadership, support and motivation during these periods of upheaval.

Innovations in services and products now have to be brought to implementation in shorter periods, and managers will play an important part in providing leadership, problem-solving and teamworking skills to ensure time to market is as short as possible. Relationships between managers and the managed are changing, too, in many organisations. There is often a trend towards greater group working, for particular projects, over the long term or using both approaches simultaneously. And managers often have to lead by example and by inspiring others, rather than being able to rely on direction and firm control.

And the pressures on costs and successive rationalisations have given greater attention to ensuring that each individual's performance is as effective and sustained as possible. So, managers' ability to manage their employees' performance on a day-to-day basis, to provide coaching and assess their staff's training needs, has risen up the corporate agenda.

According to research by the Institute for Employment Studies[38], these trends and changes have increased the importance of developing additional skills during management development – particularly, the following eight skills:

- having the ability to look ahead;
- coping with change and helping others to handle it;
- being self-reliant and resilient, and showing emotional awareness and maturity;
- being able to build relationships;
- working across boundaries, particularly during mergers and acquisitions;
- working in and managing teams;
- having high levels of business awareness, including knowledge of competitors; and
- possessing the ability to learn and undertake self-development.

Case study I. The Imperial War Museum

Around 60 of the Imperial War Museum's senior managers took part in its first leadership and management development programme. Based on competencies, the six-day course aimed to develop participants' skills in key areas, such as leadership, strategy, managing change and self-awareness. The head of personnel at the museum said that: "As a museum, we're facing many challenges, such as improving our collections, generating revenues and meeting our attendance targets. This programme is a positive and imaginative response to these challenges, as it will equip our managers with appropriate modern management skills."

The programme was split into two modules, each of three days, and was run five times with groups of 12 managers attending each course. Roffey Park, a management development organisation and management consultancy, won the contract to design the programme. It ran a series of focus groups, involving staff from all branches of the museum, to identify the competencies and skills that managers require in order to be successful in the organisation.

The skills and competencies provided the foundation for the training, and were also used to create a 360-degree feedback questionnaire. This was completed prior to the course in respect of each participant, and identified their strengths and areas requiring development. The first module of the programme included a session giving managers feedback on their questionnaire results.

In all, the programme's two modules addressed core competencies and skills covering: leadership; strategy; managing change; self-awareness; influencing others; personal power and control; organisational culture; "micro-politics"; teamworking; performance management; communications; and coaching. In addition, optional workshops addressed areas such as: handling conflict; negotiation skills; managing from a distance; delegation; motivation; stress management; and creative problem-solving. The results of the programme were assessed by measuring changes resulting from managers' improved competencies and skills, and their management style.

Management development appears to be rising in priority among employers, with the amount of training and the proportion of managers trained both increasing over time. While single courses continue to be used, they are often prompted by specific events, such as a business reorganisation or an intake of several new managers at the same time.

These courses are often be delivered in short concentrated bursts of training, but where general managerial skills are the focus (as opposed to new skills required by a reorganisation, for example), courses are increasingly being "unpacked" into longer-term and more diverse types of training. According to the same research by the Institute for Employment Studies, a classroom-based course of a few days is now often presented in the form of modules, involving a series of one- or two-day workshops held every few months that are interspersed with on-the-job learning, such as action learning, mentoring or coaching.

This type of provision is more flexible, in that the work-based aspects in particular can be tailored to each participant's own needs. Some participants might not need to undertake particular modules and, with small groups typically involved, each module can also be adapted to a considerable degree to the needs of those taking part. However, this implies that each manager's training needs have been analysed in an effective way prior to the course, and that there is a source of supervision and support to help them while the programme is under way.

Increasingly, as we noted above in the section on personal development plans (PDPs), PDPs are methods of choice in mapping out the development needs of each manager. Some organisations may help participants compile them as part of, or in parallel with, a performance-review system. Others, though, may organise development centres (see above) where a major outcome is the creation of a PDP for each participant.

As we saw immediately above, the skills covered by management development are being broadened to include those increasingly required by today's pressurised business environment. These are often broad, transferable skills – "soft" skills or behaviours, known in many organisations as "competencies". Our own long-term research concerning employers' use of competencies finds that their use is increasing, and is percolating down from the largest organisations to those of medium size (those with a few hundred employees or more). Many first-time users of competencies now tend to adopt them for their workforce as a whole, but some continue the original pattern of introducing them for managers (often, for management-development purposes) before extending their use more widely.

The use of 360-degree assessment is often found to be helpful in identifying development needs, particularly in terms of managers' soft skills. Such assessments are often part of the preparation for development centres, but many organisations use 360-degree assessment as a tool in its own right. The manager and a number of others complete a confidential questionnaire that asks them to rate the manager according to a series of predetermined skills – often, based on the framework of managers' personal competencies.

Some of those involved are automatically included: the manager's own manager and some or all of their own direct reports, but there is usually, too, an element of choice. The participant can nominate some of their colleagues to provide feedback. This upwards, downwards and sideways triangulation of perspectives on the manager's skills produces the 360-degree assessment.

Where there is a high degree of agreement between these different sources, the managers concerned often find the feedback from 360-degree assessments to represent convincing and powerful insights into their own methods of working, their strengths and weaknesses. Handled sensitively, the process can provide a spur to undertaking personal development, starting with a PDP that takes account of the feedback from the assessment process.

However, 360-degree assessments are resource intensive, and require specialist knowledge and skills to develop the questionnaires used, analyse them and present the findings to the participant. The large quantities of data generated by the questionnaires mean that software is usually required to analyse them.

Management development often requires special skills to organise and deliver it, and many employers involve external specialists in its provision, even where they tackle other types of training in-house. As well as independent consultants and small firms offering such services, there are major, multinational consultancies, as well as providers of training courses, business schools and management institutes. There are many different possibilities; an occupational psychologist with suitable experience may be retained to provide coaching or organise action-learning sets, for example. Or a provider may develop and deliver the series of training modules.

The increasing availability of forms of e-learning (see below) provides an additional option, alongside more traditional forms of distance learning and the use of external courses (particularly, those leading to a formal qualification).

The need to identify the most suitable providers and delivery methods, relate these to the needs of individual participants, and ensure that the development programme runs satisfactorily, demands considerable levels of expertise that training, personnel and HR specialists are often best placed to provide.

Case study J. The NEC Group

Each year, 5.5 million visitors use the five purpose-built exhibition, concert and conference venues managed by the NEC Group in locations in and around Birmingham. The group has been improving its personnel practices and has introduced a competency framework covering its permanent workforce. The framework forms a crucial part of performance management and, in particular, in providing a foundation for performance and development reviews.

Working on a consultancy basis, members of the HR team support line managers in their assessment of employees' competence, including the provision of training in conducting assessments. The training may take the form of individual coaching by HR staff, or participation in courses on performance management. The company has made appraisal-skills courses mandatory for all managers. Managers are being encouraged to set clear objectives and hold regular reviews about each employee's performance.

Performance reviews include a discussion of plans for developing new skills and personal competencies. Plans can include measures such as widening experience in other functions, multiskilling and specific project-based development.

Whenever possible, the NEC Group avoids a classroom approach and prefers to rely on coaching, mentoring and the use of performance feedback.

The company's focus on employee development has included much time and effort being put into the development of leadership skills and behaviours. As part of its leadership programme, managers receive 360-degree assessment to help them understand "where they are currently" in their style and their application of leadership on a day-to-day basis. The NEC Group believes that 360-degree assessment can provide an important means of encouraging debate about each manager's development needs. However, it says that managers were initially wary of taking part in the assessments and had to be "brave" to receive what might have been unfavourable feedback on their own performance.

It began by using a manual system to administer the 360-degree process, but found this was labour intensive, and has since investigated the use of an online system available from a secure part of its intranet.

Employees who apply for internal posts participate in development centres where they undertake activities based on key competencies. They receive feedback on their strengths and weaknesses from assessors drawn from HR consultants and line managers who have already received behavioural-assessor training. To give a range of feedback, provisions are made for different assessors to make observations of different candidates carrying out different activities. This type of multi-assessor/multi-activity arrangement is favoured as it ensures high levels of objectivity and greater fairness for candidates.

Volunteering

An estimated 22 million adults contribute 90 million hours of voluntary work every week in the UK, providing a vital resource to charities and other not-for-profit organisations. Of course, many of these adults are also in paid employment, with the result that their employers have a willing army of volunteers at their disposal should they wish to use it.

Many employers engage in some form of charitable work, donating goods and services, hosting visits from schoolchildren, sponsoring charities' work, and so on. And encouraging voluntary work by their employees often seems a natural part of this involvement in the community. This may involve no more than providing publicity and moral encouragement to employees to undertake voluntary work in their own time at weekends or after hours. But, in some cases, employers also contribute in a tangible way by giving volunteers paid time off and providing the facilities they need for their voluntary work (lending office equipment, donating materials, and so on).

Longer-term involvement can act as a form of secondment (see above), where particular employees provide their skills and expertise to a particular charity, school or other not-for-profit organisation. In exchange, they will face fresh challenges and unfamiliar situations that can potentially provide a form of self-development or action learning through work experience.

Shorter-term volunteering also offers benefits to those involved. Where groups of employees have to work together on a project – renovating a classroom or organising a fund-raising event, for example – their teamworking skills can be enhanced, as can skills associated with problem-solving and decision-making. Self-confidence and enthusiasm can be developed, too.

These and other skills can be valuable to the employer, should they be transferred to the workplace. But, where volunteering represents a conscious form of learning and development, the experience needs managing and the participants benefit from support.

Volunteering may be discussed as part of the individual's plans to address their training needs, and the manager and participant may actively seek out opportunities most likely to provide an effective learning experience. There may be health and safety factors to consider, and whether or not the charity and the activities that the volunteer will undertake are likely to reflect badly on the employer. Practical issues of providing cover for the employee while they are away from work need addressing and, as with other forms of learning, some post-learning debriefing and evaluation needs to be planned and carried out.

There are several organisations providing information on volunteering, including Business in the Community (tel: 0870 600 2482; www.bitc.org.uk) and Time Banks UK (tel: 0870 702 7428; www.time-banks.co.uk).

Case study K. UnumProvident

An insurer providing income-protection insurance, UnumProvident has been taking part in a Business in the Community venture called MAD 4 IT – a national scheme where employers provide IT skills and expertise to voluntary bodies. Among a range of organisations benefiting from UnumProvident's voluntary work is Brambles, a respite hostel for people with multiple sclerosis. Two of the company's process management staff spent more than 13 days on a project designed to improve the efficiency of its administrative functions. Generally, as well as the involvement of IT staff, human resources specialists have volunteered to help train charities' staff in using software packages.

The company's head of social responsibility pointed out that not only are community organisations benefiting from its involvement, "but our own staff benefit by way of self-development, teamwork and pride in giving something back to the community".

e-learning

Electronic, computer-based media represent a natural development of distance learning packages as a means of providing training opportunities. See chapter 3 (Using electronic media effectively) for more information on e-learning and our checklist on using it (checklist 3 in that chapter).

10. Legal checklist

● Protected groups should be given equal access to training and development opportunities – Sex Discrimination Act 1975; Race Relations Act 1976; Disability Discrimination Act 1995; Part-Time Workers (Prevention of Less-Favourable Treatment) Regulations 2000; Fixed-Term Employees (Prevention of Less-Favourable Treatment) Regulations 2002; Trade Union and Labour Relations (Consolidation) Act 1992; and Codes of Practice associated with these Acts.

● Induction and training practices in the public sector must support equality of opportunity on the grounds of ethnicity – Race Relations (Amendment) Act 2000; guidance from the Commission for Racial Equality recommends that public sector employers should conduct regular reviews of their personnel policies and monitor their use to ensure there is no unfair discrimination on the grounds of ethnicity.

● Reasonable adjustments should be made to the arrangements for induction, training and development to accommodate people with disabilities – Disability Discrimination Act 1995.

● Employers must assess the risks to the health and safety of employees and identify groups of workers who might be particularly at risk. If there are such groups, then induction will have to be tailored to them and the special risk factors they might face – Management of Health and Safety at Work Regulations 1992; Health and Safety (Young Persons) Regulations 1997.

● Employers covered by some regulated occupations must ensure that employees are competent and that their competence is maintained; this has implications for induction, training-needs analyses and the provision of training.

● Some contracts of employment contain training provisions that may confer legal obligations on employers, such as apprenticeship agreements – common law of contract.

● Under-qualified young people have a legal right to claim paid time off to attend training or education (see this chapter for more information) – Right to Time Off for Study or Training Regulations 1999.

● Union learning representatives in organisations that recognise trade unions have legal rights to reasonable paid time off for training and conducting their duties; trade union members have a right to reasonable unpaid time off to consult their representatives (see this chapter for more information) – Trade Union and Labour Relations (Consolidation) Act 1992 as amended by the Employment Act 2002.

● Where a trade union is granted statutory recognition rights, and it and the employer fail to agree the content of the recognition agreement, the CAC will impose a procedure that includes compulsory consultation and information rights in respect of training (see this chapter for more information) – Trade Union and Labour Relations (Consolidation) Act 1992, as amended by the Employment Relations Act 1999.

6. Pay and benefits and other terms and conditions

See also: 1. Filling your vacancies; 7. Retaining the best staff; and 9. Equal opportunities and diversity.

This chapter covers:
- Overview: an introduction to pay and benefits;
- Grading systems;
- Job evaluation;
- Market rates and market premia;
- Performance-related pay;
- Skills-based pay;
- Long-term pay awards;
- Profit sharing;
- Benefits packages: an overview;
- Holidays;
- Sick pay: see chapter 12 Attendance and absence;
- Private medical insurance;
- Company cars;
- Pensions;
- Parental and compassionate leave: see chapter 9 Equal opportunities and diversity;
- Shiftworking;
- Overtime; and
- Flexible benefits schemes.

Checklists in this chapter:
1. The pros and cons of job evaluation
2. Salary surveys: their advantages and disadvantages
3. Performance-related pay: the advantages and disadvantages
4. Introducing performance-related pay
5. Legal checklist

Case studies in this chapter:
A. Examples of location payments
B. AXA Sun Life
C. Scottish and Newcastle Retail
D. Examples of long-term pay awards
E. Examples of profit sharing

F. Six Continents
G. Examples of private medical insurance
H. Examples of company car schemes
I. Examples of shiftworking
J. Examples of flexible benefits schemes

Overview

Pay, benefits and allowances provide three of the cornerstones of effective performance management. The impact of reward on taking performance a stage higher remains controversial, yet it is undoubtedly a crucial factor in helping to maintain current standards. Where pay levels fall significantly out of line with the market then reward practices will also contribute to the loss of high-performing staff to competitors.

Personnel, HR and remuneration specialists responsible for reward systems face a double challenge. They must ensure their systems maintain employees' motivation and performance, largely through balancing the financial constraints on the organisation with the need to follow market trends and practices, while keeping their reward practices fresh and up to date.

"Familiarity breeds contempt" provides a good rule of thumb for the impact of most reward practices – especially those that aim to provide a directly motivational effect, such as bonus schemes. This means that reward practices, as well as the actual value of pay and benefits, have to be kept under more or less continuous review.

With that in mind, what is the current position regarding organisations' reward practices? To find out, IRS conducts an annual research project, gaining feedback from several hundred personnel, HR and pay specialists about their practices and plans. The latest position about the use of various reward practices is as follows, shown in descending order of prevalence:
● individual performance-related pay has been introduced by two-thirds (63.9%) of employers;
● a direct link has been created between pay levels and salary scales and those found in the marketplace by half (52.7%) of employers;
● targeted incentive payments, most often in the form of cash bonuses, are now provided by one-third (31.5%) of employers;
● all-employee share schemes are run by one-fifth (22.4%) of employers;
● some form of profit sharing is provided by one-fifth (22.0%) of employers;

- short salary scales have been merged into broad bands by one-sixth (18.3%) of employers;
- some part of individual reward is related to competency assessment among one-sixth (17.4%) of employers; and
- some form of skills-based reward scheme is in place in one-tenth (10.8%) of employers.

Looking ahead, employers are most interested in investigating the introduction of the following practices:
- one-fifth (19.0%) are interested in the concept of linking reward to competency assessment;
- one-seventh (14.1%) are interested in introducing individual performance-related pay;
- one-seventh (13.3%) are interested in replacing their salary scales with broad bands;
- one-tenth (10.4%) are interested in skills-based reward; and
- one in 13 (7.9%) are interested in incorporating a direct link between their pay levels and salary scales and those found in the marketplace.

However, this series of annual studies of ours shows that expressions of interest do not always translate into action. Take competency-related reward, for example. This is a concept that attracts many employers on an intellectual level. It offers the potential to link individuals' reward to a more rounded assessment of their performance, taking in the ways in which they achieve their objectives and carry out their jobs alongside the attainment of personal targets.

Many employers find, though, that their investigations reveal that there are difficulties in introducing this form of reward and take no further action.

Grading systems

Pay is a complex issue, and almost all employers bring some logic and order to this challenge by creating a formal grading system. It creates a structure of pay scales, enabling employees to be assigned to a particular level according to their job, responsibilities, skills, seniority or other factors.

The clarity and predictability that grading systems offer employers also provides benefits for the employees concerned. They can see their place in the pay hierarchy, understand the potential financial rewards of working for promotion and, hopefully, accept the fairness of their employer's practices.

Most employers' pay structures consist of a series of grades, each of which has a minimum and maximum salary. In conventional grading systems, there are several pay scales, each of which may have a relatively narrow gap between the minimum and maximum amounts. Broadbanded schemes, in contrast, have fewer scales, and each of them has a relatively broad span between the top and bottom of the range.

In the public sector, in particular, there may be basically just one grade: a vertical range, into which particular jobs are slotted. These pay spines have a series of pay ranges, each of which applies to a particular type of jobs.

Pay for groups of related jobs, particularly in the private sector, can also be addressed via job families, where similar types of occupations are grouped together and given their own pay structure.

Most simply, the grading system may consist of a series of spot rates, often linked to external relativities or market rates, each of which is allocated to an individual or a group performing similar roles. Pay increases are provided through uplifts in the spot rate, by awarding cash bonuses or promoting an individual to a different rate, rather than by means of progression through a pay scale.

Each of these and other approaches has its own advantages and disadvantages; pay specialist e-reward provides a useful summary of their pros and cons ("Pay structures" in its *Reward Guides* series; www.e-reward.co.uk).

Job evaluation

Most grading systems, of whatever kind, continue to be based on a job evaluation exercise. As its name implies, this is a process of analysing the demands of the jobs in an organisation. The information is then often used to help design the grading system as well as allocating job-holders to particular grades in the structure. Checklist 1 highlights some considerations about whether or not to use job evaluation.

1. The pros and cons of job evaluation

Pros: Formal job evaluation processes offer several advantages to employers:

● Objectivity: they are often more objective than alternative methods of deciding on individuals' basic salaries;

● Perceived fairness: properly carried out, job evaluation exercises are often more likely than alternatives to be accepted by employees as a fair method of deciding individuals' position in the pay hierarchy. They are most likely to be accepted where employees (and any employee representatives) are involved in conducting the evaluations and have been briefed on the approach being used;

● Benchmarking: some proprietary systems are widely used, and salary surveys linked to a particular job evaluation scheme enable employers to benchmark their pay rates against competitors in a reasonably accurate way; and

● Unfair discrimination: a job evaluation scheme that has been carefully constructed and applied, and is then checked to ensure it is not discriminating unfairly, provides a good defence against tribunal complaints under the Equal Pay Act 1970.

Cons: However, there are also disadvantages, including:

● Bureaucracy: job evaluation exercises can be time-consuming, require considerable amounts of management time, and become an end in themselves;

● Inflexibility 1: job evaluation methods must be carefully developed and audited to ensure they are objective and do not discriminate unfairly; it is often difficult to revise the basic methodology as needs arise;

● Inflexibility 2: in addition, where jobs change, they will have to be re-analysed by the job evaluation process to assess whether or not they merit a higher pay range;

● Counterproductive: a badly-designed or poorly-applied job evaluation scheme could well make matters worse than not using one at all. It may place too much value on aspects of jobs that are not important to the employer or unfairly favour one sex or race. It may be inconsistently applied, leading to unfair decisions, or be influenced by the assessors' subjective judgments or favouritism.

● Complaints: individuals will not always accept the verdict of a job evaluation exercise, and will lodge appeals against the treatment of their jobs. These appeals will take time and resources to handle; in large job evaluation exercises, there are often a considerable number of appeals occurring at the same time; and

● Equal opportunities: formal job evaluation systems may give a false sense of security to employers about their compliance with equal pay legislation. Few organisations have audited their pay practices, despite being strongly urged to do so by the Equal Opportunities Commission and the introduction of a new equal pay questionnaire that complainants can send to employers. For more information on equal pay, see chapter 9 Equal opportunities and diversity.

Job evaluation used to consist of both analytical and non-analytical methods, such as schemes that simply ranked jobs in a non-analytical way. However, non-analytical methods cannot, by their nature, be validated to show that they do not discriminate unfairly. This means that they are unlikely to be acceptable to trade unions or other representative bodies within organisations, or provide a defence against equal pay claims.

Analytical schemes consist of a series of predetermined categories ("factors"), such as skills, responsibility and working conditions, and a scoring system. When jobs are analysed according to this classification, each factor is given a score and a total is calculated to produce the job's overall value.

Usually, the factors are given weightings to reflect their relative importance to the employer. This is a particularly crucial area in terms of the impact of job evaluation on equal opportunities. In the past, some schemes have been found by researchers to contain weightings that indirectly discriminated against women, because they tended to give higher weightings to aspect of jobs that were found most often in roles performed by men, while downvaluing the skills that women required. For example, caring skills tended to be given a lower weighting than physical effort or experience. Further information is available in a free guide produced by the Equal Opportunities Commission (*Job evaluation schemes free of sex bias;* www.eoc.org.uk).

The process of job evaluation involves an analysis of jobs within the organisation. The analysis can include observation of individuals performing their role, interviews, focus groups, questionnaires and an examination of relevant documentation, such as job descriptions. For more information on job analysis, see chapter 1. Filling your vacancies. However, many employers do not develop their own job evaluation schemes, but use proprietary ones from consultants, employers' organisations and other bodies. These schemes will usually involve the use of a particular method of evaluation, in which those involved will have to be trained.

Acas recommends that employers involve employee representatives (and their trade unions, if relevant) in job evaluation exercises: "Job evaluation is most effective as a participative exercise and this, in itself, can improve employment relations." A joint approach is more likely to lead to better and more accurate results and, says Acas, is "more likely to commit both parties to the outcome of the exercise".[1]

According to research undertaken by e-reward[2], around one in three employers in the private sector have conducted a job evaluation exercise, rising to two in three employers in the public and not-for-profit sectors.

The research also found that organisations that use job evaluation typically employ a single scheme, and most (67%) apply the scheme to their whole workforce. And a large majority of the schemes in use are analytical (79%).

Certainly, current users of job evaluation do not find that the drawbacks outweigh the advantages. Fewer than a quarter (24%) told e-reward that their job evaluation processes inhibit flexibility, and even fewer (19%) said that the process is too bureaucratic or too time-consuming (14%). However, an appreciable minority – one in three (34%) – admitted that their scheme has decayed over time or has been misused.

Market rates

When asked in public, most employers insist that their salary levels and pay rises are determined by their organisations' profitability and their ability to afford the costs involved. However, in private, they are more likely to confirm that the "going rate" – of pay rates and salary increases – is hugely influential in determining their practices.

But benchmarking their organisation against competitors is not always straightforward. Where companies compete against each other on price, and where wage costs represent a significant proportion of their costs, then they will often go to great lengths to conceal information on their pay practices.

They will remove pay and benefits details from their recruitment advertising and require employees to keep this information confidential. In these cases, jobseekers are often a source of information. When employees leave the organisation to work for a competitor, an exit interview or separation questionnaire *(see chapter 7 Retaining the best staff for information on these techniques)* could ask them for details of their new salary. Similarly, job applicants or new recruits could be asked for details of their current salaries.

There may be pay clubs or other networks to which personnel, HR and pay managers could belong. These forums share information between members, according to confidentiality guidelines and within certain limits.

Competitors may also take part in salary surveys, where their pay practices are aggregated anonymously with others to present an overall picture of pay trends and issues.

And where there is less sensitivity, there may be some information-sharing and networking between personnel, HR and pay specialists working in the same industry. Recruitment advertisements may contain pay details, and publications – such as those issued by IRS – may include information about employers' salary rises, and pay and benefits practices.

As we saw at the beginning of this chapter, more than half of employers already benchmark their pay practices against competitors, and a growing number intends to do so.

In some cases, employers maintain a watching eye on competitors to ensure they do not "steal a march" on them by restructuring and uplifting salaries or introducing or improving key employee benefits. In other instances, particularly among large organisations, there is a formal policy to benchmark salaries at a certain market level – at the upper quartile or at the upper decile, for example (meaning that they keep in line with the top 25% or top 10% of competitors' practices, respectively).

Formal linkages such as these are often based on an analysis of formal salary survey data. Salary surveys, however, have their drawbacks as well as their advantages, as checklist 2 points out.

2. Salary surveys: their advantages and disadvantages

Advantages:

● Informal methods of identifying market rates can be hit and miss, and may overlook some important data that a properly conducted salary survey may bring to light;

● Salary surveys provide a measure of certainty to the difficult process of determining pay rates; the organisation may be familiar with particular surveys' use and be less resistant to meeting the additional costs required to maintain pay parity;

● Some survey publishers offer additional services that can help users get the most from them, such as user clubs, training sessions, newsletters and advice lines. They may also be part of a consultancy's portfolio, and users could bolt-on extra services as needs arise.

Disadvantages:

● Gaps in coverage: There is not a salary survey for every job or industry in the UK;

● Comparing like with like: It is usually difficult to compare the employer's own situation with others; in particular, job titles are an unreliable guide to the content and level of a job outside the organisation, and sample job descriptions are often too brief to be fully reliable;

● Self-defeating averages: Caution should be exercised in using findings that are based on averages. These will usually be influenced by extreme examples (eg, very high or very low salaries) and, by their nature, represent a "moving target" – any improvement in pay implemented by users will feed through into higher averages, leading to a vicious circle. Instead, medians (midpoints) and cut-off points that avoid the extremes (quartiles and deciles) may be preferable alternatives;

● Numbers of participants: The larger the number of employers taking part, the more reliable the salary data is likely to be. In particular, where salaries are analysed in detail (region; type of industry; size; etc), then the number of examples may be so small as to be unsatisfactory. Good salary surveys should disclose the sample sizes of their findings;

● Topicality: It takes time and effort to compile a salary survey; employers may be tardy in supplying information and the data then has to be analysed, and the report printed and published; some surveys contain adjustment indexes so that their pay rates can be adjusted for any time lag;

● Price: The cost of salary surveys ranges from nothing (some may be free, particularly where the employer has taken part in the survey or it is conducted by an association to which the organisation belongs) up to many thousands of pounds. Given that few salary surveys cover a wide range of jobs and industries, an organisation may have to purchase several titles each year at considerable cost;

● Specific needs: Many employers have a limited number of direct competitors and it may be more effective for them to focus their efforts on these organisations, rather than trying to match the market as a whole.

Market premia

Most employers concentrate on adjusting basic salaries to ensure they keep in line with market rates. But there are other options. Market premia, or supplements, are used by some organisations as a means of ensuring employees' take-home pay matches the amount they could earn elsewhere.

Market premia are usually introduced or uprated when a particular occupation is affected by recruitment or retention difficulties, such as computer specialists, accountants or actuaries. They may also be paid to key members of staff, often at executive level, whose motivation and retention are crucial to the efficiency of the organisation.

Premia are top-up amounts, rather than market-related increases in basic pay and, as such, offer greater flexibility to employers. They do not automatically have a knock-on effect on the grading structure in the way that an increase in pay rates would. They may not be counted for overtime or holiday pay or as pensionable earnings, thus reducing their overall cost compared with basic salary increases. And, the amounts can be frozen if market conditions improve, regardless of movements in basic salary. In theory, at least, the supplements could also be withdrawn, although this is likely to cause problems with the staff affected.

A broader approach to paying market-related supplements is represented by London weighting and other location allowances. These are more prevalent than market premia, and focus on areas of the country affected by recruitment and/or retention difficulties. In the areas concerned, most employers pay the allowance to all staff who are based there, although some employers may weight the actual amounts by salary or other criteria.

Some multi-site employers, particularly in retailing and hospitality, provide two or more regional grading systems, where, in effect, their location allowances have been consolidated into hourly or weekly wages. Often, the different sets of pay scales are not given regional labels, such as London or Bristol, but use a less specific designation. This provides greater flexibility for the employer, enabling it to move a particular site from one zone to another, according to local labour market conditions.

After several years when labour market conditions were relatively favourable, there has been a flurry of activity recently in introducing, uprating and amending location allowances and regional pay zones. The case studies in box A provide some examples of the different approaches available to employers.

For more information on market premia and location payments, see chapter 1 Filling your vacancies.

A. Examples of location payments

The **Audit Commission** has merged its inner and outer London zones into a Greater London allowance worth £4,654, and has increased its location payment for the South East by 25% to £2,932 (effective from 1 November 2002).

Animals charity the **Blue Cross** provides two levels of payment for London-based staff: a London weighting payment (that was uprated by 1.7% from 1 January 2003) and an additional London regional allowance for staff earning less than £20,000. In the provinces, staff earning less than £15,000 in any of five specified locations are also eligible for the allowance.

Tesco increased its band 5 location payment (which covers City of London and London's West End stores) by 3p an hour from 30 June 2002 to £1.01 an hour.

Asda operates a regional pay structure for its supermarket staff. From 1 April 2003, salaries rose by 4.5% to £5.7625 an hour for a checkout operator in its London stores and £5.0682 in provincial stores.

Safeway supermarkets maintains five regional pay bands, broadly covering inner London together with any South East "hot spots" (band 1); outer London (2); other areas of the South East (3); the South East, South West and Wales (4); and Scotland and the Midlands (5). From 30 March 2003, the hourly starting rate for a retail sales assistant ranged from £4.50 in band 5 to £4.60 in band 3 and £5.04 in band 1.

BBC Resources increased its London allowance from 1 April 2003 so as to favour lower-paid staff. Instead of a payment of £2,904 for all staff, those earning less than £22,200 a year now receive £3,335 while those earning above this limit receive a payment of £2,988.

Moto, an operator of motorway service stations, has three regional pay structures. From 1 October 2002, motorway catering and retail staff on adult hourly rates for new starters received £4.28 in the "provincial" zone, £4.86 in its "South East and London market" and £5.15 in "Outer London".

Performance-related pay

The widespread adoption of individual performance-related pay represents probably the most important development in employers' reward practices in the past 20 years.

Formal schemes that linked an employee's annual pay rise or cash bonus to the outcome of their yearly performance review had tended to be at the margins until the 1980s. Then, employers began to realise that changing the way in which employees were rewarded could be used to create a significant cultural shift in their organisations.

This coincided with changes in such sectors as financial services, where business objectives meant that services, and the employees that provided them, needed to become more customer- and profit-focused. In the public sector, privatisation led to major parts of the economy – such as the utilities and public transport – changing to a commercial basis. Again, these businesses wanted to change their cultures to ones that had a greater emphasis on customer service and profit generation.

Around two-thirds of employers now maintain performance-related pay schemes for all or part of their workforces.

The logic of such schemes seems obvious. Employers want to encourage their staff to maintain and improve their performance, and set up systems to manage it. Line managers are trained in motivational and supervisory techniques, appraisal processes are developed and introduced, and personal development plans based on these performance assessments are then used to remedy any shortcomings. If performance is so important to employers, then how can they justify failing to reward it?

Moreover, what motivation is there for an individual to perform beyond the call of duty when their colleagues who coast along receive the same salary and the same pay rise each year? Even if the financial reward were not important to that person, the perceived lack of fairness in treating them the same would be a demotivator.

Certainly, eminent occupational psychologist Professor Adrian Furnham believes that appraisal schemes could benefit from a link to pay. He argues that performance reviews are a waste of time without "some tangible follow through". This could mean promotion, the provision of training or performance-related pay[3].

However, the logic behind performance-related pay also has some flaws, as checklist 3 highlights.

3. Performance-related pay: the advantages and disadvantages

Advantages:
● Provides a direct incentive;
● Is a tangible means of recognising an individual's achievements;
● Helps to create a performance culture;
● Creates greater flexibility in reward practices, enabling employers to focus on pressure spots, such as retention difficulties.

Disadvantages:
● "Contaminates" many aspects of performance management systems, such as employees' honest discussion of their shortcomings and training needs;
● Can demotivate if personal objectives are unrealistically high;
● Can also demotivate if the size of the pay award is too low; this is a particular problem in times of low inflation where budgets for pay awards are also small;
● Sends out the wrong message, encouraging a "lone ranger" attitude that undermines teamwork, and focuses on short-term results at the potential risk of damaging longer-term factors, such as customer relationships;
● Relies on the quality of line managers, in terms of fair, objective assessments;
● May lead to unfair discrimination.

The mechanics of assessing employees' performance are covered in chapter 10 Managing performance 1. But there are additional considerations when the result is linked to reward.

Importantly, the link needs to be as transparent, understandable and predictable as possible – and accepted as a fair result that does not reflect any favouritism or prejudice. This means that the performance management system must be carefully developed, accompanied by guidelines for its users (the line managers conducting the assessments and the employees being appraised) and supported by training for the assessors.

Most organisations also introduce some form of supervision, usually via the line managers' own managers operating a "grandparenting" scheme where they check assessors' comments, performance ratings and pay decisions. In the public sector, larger organisations are now required to monitor appraisal and performance-related pay schemes to ensure no unfair discrimination is taking place (under the Race Relations (Amendment) Act 2000). But given the potential for subjectivity in managers' performance-related pay decisions, it is desirable that all employers monitor their schemes, as guidance from the Equal Opportunities Commission recommends.

The Commission sets out a 10-point action plan for employers using performance-related pay. As well as touching on the issues we mentioned above, it also recommends that the performance criteria used for the purposes of rewarding employees should be measurable – in other words, being as objective and transparent as possible. And, interestingly, that "there is a balance between quantitative and qualitative measures"[4].

This call for assessments to take account of qualitative factors, alongside personal objectives, reflects a growing trend among employers. Feedback obtained by IRS from personnel, HR and pay specialists shows that their organisations are increasingly expanding their performance management systems to include the way in which employees achieve their goals as well as what they achieve.

In customer-facing roles, for example, assessing individuals' achievement of sales targets is undoubtedly important. But, so, too, is the employee's attitude to customers, their flexibility, interpersonal skills and other factors that are likely to encourage repeat business and a growing reputation of the organisation.

Teamworking has become an increasing part of business operations. But where performance-related pay relies exclusively on quantitative measures, individuals' willingness to cooperate with others, and contribute to teams and projects, will be overlooked. This means that individuals who go out of their way to work with others will not be financially reward and, more generally, the culture of the organisation is likely to be individualistic. In general, what is rewarded is what is valued – and what employers choose not to financially acknowledge gets much less priority.

Acas's 27-page guide to performance-related pay (*Appraisal-related pay*, free from www.acas.org.uk) offers a checklist of 28 issues that employers should consider when introducing such a scheme. It is reproduced in checklist 4.

---

4. Introducing performance-related pay

Acas recommends that employers consider the following issues when contemplating the introduction of performance-related pay. Its checklist is reproduced below, with permission (Acas uses the abbreviation "ARP" – "appraisal-related pay"):

- What are the objectives of the ARP scheme?
- Will ARP be appropriate to the organisation and its culture?
- Will ARP be linked to other changes in working practices?
- Is there an effective and systematic performance appraisal scheme in place?
- How will it be linked to ARP?
- Are there other ways in which the organisation recognises good performance?
- How will ARP fit with those?
- Will ARP be the only form of wage increase?
- What resources will be made available?
- What programme of negotiation and consultation with employee representatives is anticipated?
- How will employees be told about the proposals?
- What reaction is expected?
- What training will be provided?
- Which ARP scheme will be used?
- Will ARP be introduced gradually?
- Who will eventually receive ARP?
- How achievable will eligibility for ARP be?
- What percentage of employees can expect to receive ARP?
- What aspects of the scheme will be negotiable with employee representatives?
- How open will the scheme be?
- Who will monitor consistency and objectivity?
- How will ARP be paid?
- Will ARP be consolidated into pay?
- Will ARP awards be considered as pensionable pay?
- When will it be paid?
- What appeals procedure will there be?
- How will the operation of the scheme be monitored?
- When will the scheme be evaluated, and by whom?

Source: *Appraisal-related pay*, Acas, 2002, www.acas.org.uk.

B. AXA Sun Life

In 2001, life and pensions company AXA Sun Life replaced its team-based pay scheme with individual performance-related pay. Its compensation and benefits manager told IRS in 2002 that "the time was right for a new structure that would further motivate employees by linking their reward more effectively to performance".

Alongside replacing team-based pay, the company wanted to tackle the confusion of having 15 grading structures. Although the main clerical pay band covered most staff, 14 others had been developed for a range of typical finance-sector jobs. This hindered mobility within the company, as well as creating administrative complexity. In their place, the company introduced a broadbanded pay scheme, consisting of seven bands linked to the Hay job evaluation scheme. Movement within the bands is based entirely on performance, while moving to a different band is tied to promotion.

The individual performance-related pay scheme for "frontline" staff is based on two formal performance assessments each year, in January and July, at which up to three performance points can be awarded. The scheme, as at early 2002, involved awarding a pay rise in January and/or July based on moving along their pay band worth 5% of salary for every three points awarded. At the beginning of a new year, an individual's points are cleared and the system is reset. The company ensures that its salary scales are kept in line with market movements by undertaking an annual review. The size of this market uplift is negotiated with its recognised trade union. In addition to performance-related progression through a broad band, frontline staff are also eligible for a performance bonus, which ranged from 0% to 10% of basic salary in early 2002.

Current practice

Feedback from personnel, HR and pay specialists shows that these are the ways in which employers are implementing performance-related pay schemes:

● coverage: two-thirds (64%) do not cover their whole workforce, management-only schemes being the most common;

● basis: there is a fairly even split between basing reward solely on individual performance (45%) and employers where it is based on a combination of performance and inflation adjustment (55%);

● however, there are significant differences between sectors – performance-related pay is rarer in the public sector and, where it does occur, is based on performance plus inflation (78% of schemes in that sector); in the private sector, performance-related pay is much more common and is more likely to be based solely on performance (61%);

● ratings: most employers' schemes are based on individual appraisal results and lead to an overall performance rating; most appraisal systems (more than 90%) have between three and six possible ratings – the most common number is five;

● size of payments: two-thirds (65%) of employers give line managers discretion over individual awards, while one-third (35%) predetermines the percentage increase or cash sum for each performance rating;

● communication: almost all (98%) employers provide some information to employees about their performance-related pay scheme; mostly (54%), this concerns the employee's own performance and the consequent pay award, while three in 10 (31%) communicate details of the full range of awards possible under the scheme;

● controls: seven in 10 (68%) employers audit line managers' decisions in order to control overall costs;

● costs: few (16%) employers told us that their schemes are proving more costly than their previous pay arrangements; and

● changes: the three most common changes made by employers to their performance-related pay schemes are (1) revising the guidelines given to line managers or providing managers with training in appraisals; (2) changing the number of ratings; and (3) expanding their schemes to take account of softer skills and behaviours.

Three free guides provide more information on performance-related pay:

"Performance-related pay", *Reward Guides*, e-reward; free from www.e-reward.co.uk;

Performance pay trends in the UK, Institute of Personnel and Development, 1999; free from www.cipd.co.uk; and

Appraisal-related pay, Acas, 2002; free from www.acas.org.uk.

Skills-based pay

At one time, it seemed as though skills-based pay – rewarding employees for participating in training and acquiring new skills – would become an important aspect of reward practice in the UK. However, as we saw at the beginning of this chapter, it has not been adopted by more than one in 10 employers.

Even then, these organisations tend to be concentrated in certain sectors or among particular work groups. Skills-based pay is most likely, according to our research, to be found among manual and semi-skilled workers and, industrially, among the manufacturing, retailing and hospitality sectors. (There is also a long-standing practice – particularly, in the financial services sector – of awarding cash bonuses, or pay increases, to employees who pass relevant professional examinations.)

The UK's difficulties with its skills supply are well known, and skills-based pay offers a financial inducement for lower-skilled workers to take part in training. As well as helping to overcome any reluctance to participate in training, skills-based pay has been used by employers to encourage greater flexibility. Where trades learn each others' skills, they are able to work more flexibly, provide cover for absences and help resolve problems without undue delay.

The introduction of National Vocational Qualifications and Scottish Vocational Qualifications has provided a convenient means of defining the skills that are eligible for reward, and some employers have restructured their grading systems so that they are aligned with the various levels of these qualifications.

There are several difficulties with skills-based pay schemes, however:
● rewarding employees for skills acquisition creates a direct motivational link, but does not take account of employers' need to obtain some payback from the actual utilisation of these new skills. If employees are required to wait until opportunities are available to put these new skills to use – a situation over which they have little control – then the motivational link between skills and reward can be broken or weakened;
● linked to the above, there is a danger of pay drift, where paybill costs rise in tandem with the skills that employees acquire – without there necessarily being an improvement in profitability or efficiency to fund these increased costs;
● what happens when employees have obtained all possible skills relevant to their jobs? It is likely that skills-based pay schemes have a natural, and limited, lifespan; and
● organisations' requirements for particular skills change all the time: once an employee has been given a pay rise for a particular skill, it is difficult to withdraw it once that skill becomes obsolete. This can lead to pay drift. Where cash bonuses are used to avoid this danger, then overall paybill costs may rise because the employer may be conferring two separate pay awards each year: a rise in basic pay related to one set of factors (eg inflation) and a bonus linked to skills acquisition.

Given these considerations, many employers that might have explored skills-based pay are opting, instead, for individual performance-related pay schemes that are partly based on employees' competencies (see above). While many such schemes focus on softer types of competencies, the flex-

378

ibility of the competency approach means that hard, technical types of job-related skills could equally be assessed and rewarded.

C. Scottish and Newcastle Retail

Bar and kitchen staff working for pubs and restaurants owned by Scottish and Newcastle Retail received a higher pay award in their 1 October 2002 pay review if they held a level 2 National Vocational Qualification. Their basic minimum hourly rate rose to £4.55 for employees aged 18 and over, compared with £4.20 for staff without this qualification.

Long-term pay awards

Long-term pay awards create a formula that predetermines the cost of the annual pay increase for 18 months or more into the future. They offer two advantages to employers: a means of planning ahead, particularly where long-term contracts are being negotiated or costed; and as a deal-maker when involved in negotiations with trade unions. The unions' members may prefer an agreement that guarantees them a minimum pay rise for the next two or three years, particularly where it is based on an inflation-plus formula (as is usually the case).

Most sectors of the economy provide examples of employers using long-term pay awards, although they are most regularly used where financial controls and long-term planning are particularly important – such as manufacturing and parts of the public sector.

Usually, but not invariably, long-term pay awards are used where each employee in an organisation receives the same pay rise each year, although there are examples of individual performance-related pay schemes where the total "pot" of money available is determined through a long-term formula.

Almost always, long-term pay awards are based on an inflation-plus formula (see the case studies in box D). The measurement of inflation is usually prescribed – based on movements in the Retail Prices Index for a particular month or months. And there may be overall controls on the result of this calculation in the shape of minimum and maximum pay rises.

In the past, when inflation was more volatile and ran at higher levels, it was also customary to include a reopener provision. Once inflation reached a certain level, the pay formula would be reexamined to see whether or not it needed amending to take account of unforeseen circumstances.

D. Examples of long-term pay awards

Barclays Bank has concluded a three-year long-term pay agreement with its recognised trade union Unifi. Each year, the amount of money available for individual performance-related pay rises has been based on the rate of inflation plus 0.85%. In year two, effective 1 April 2003, this produced a "pot" worth 3.45% of the paybill. Individual employees in clerical staff grades received between 0% and 16%, rising to 20% for managers.

In the **brick manufacturing** industry, the multi-employer agreement of 7 November 2002 involves a 28-month formula. Basic rates rose by 3.5% initially, to be followed by inflation plus 0.25% from 1 March 2004, within limits of 3% (minimum) and 4% (maximum). Inflation will be measured by averaging the annual change in the Retail Prices Index for December 2003, January 2004 and February 2004.

Lafarge Cement, formerly known as Blue Circle Cement, agreed a three-year long-term pay award effective from 1 January 2002. Each year, salaries increase by a formula of inflation plus 0.75%, subject to an overall minimum rise of 2% and a maximum of 5%. Inflation is measured by averaging the increases in September, October and November in the year preceding the increase in question.

Virgin Trains introduced a two-year pay award from 1 April 2002 for catering staff, train managers, clerical staff and station staff. The formula for year two involved inflation plus 2%, within an overall minimum increase of 3.5% and a maximum of 4.5%. Inflation is based on the February Retail Prices Index increase.

Profit sharing

Profit sharing schemes are widely used by British companies. Primarily, they attract employers because they have the potential to increase employees' involvement in the organisation – another name for profit sharing being "financial participation". Greater involvement can, potentially, lead to improvements in individual performance, reduced absence and increased retention of staff.

Profit sharing that is based on shares takes a longer-term view that can reduce the likelihood of resignations, because employees will wish to avoid resigning in the period prior to the maturity of a scheme when they can buy shares or sell those they already hold.

Cash-based profit sharing schemes suffer in motivational terms from lacking a clear "line of sight" between an employee's efforts and the fortunes of the company employing them. There are many factors outside even the company's own control that can depress profits and affect an employee's bonus (the same is true of movements in share prices). For that reason, some employers treat the payment as a cause of celebration, and time it to coincide with the annual pay rise in order to gain the maximum impact from this annual event.

Acas says that: "Profit share works best in companies that emphasise communications with all their workers, and which perform consistently in generating profits. Workers need to know on an on-going basis how the organisation is doing, and what decisions are being made that might affect their pay."[5]

Share schemes, though, are tied to the fortunes of the stock exchange. The static or declining value of many companies' shares in recent years has had a significant impact on share-based profit sharing. The number of new Inland Revenue-approved save-as-you-earn plans in 2000/01 was the lowest since 1992/93.

In addition, there is a proposal from the International Accounting Standards Board that the cost of providing employee share options should appear as an expense in company accounts (the "ED2" proposal). A decision on introducing this measure in 2004 was awaited as this edition of our handbook went to press.

The potential significance of this move could be considerable. For example, one study estimated that in 2001 prior to its merger with the **Halifax**, the **Bank of Scotland** could expect to see £40 million charged to its accounts because of the cost of providing share options. This represented 7% of its profits each year that the scheme ran. In the first half of 2002, international financial services company HSBC said that share options to 70,000 employees cost it $127 million.

Set against this concern, though, is the experience of companies in the USA where a voluntary disclosure standard is in operation. There, the share price of organisations disclosing share-option costs has not under-performed the S&P 500. The prevalence of share option schemes in the UK may echo this, on the basis that there might be "safety in numbers".

Most non-executive share schemes in the UK follow Inland Revenue guidelines, because of the tax advantages that this confers. The main save-as-you-earn share option plan involves employees saving money for three or five years. They can then use the proceeds to purchase shares in their company or draw out their money together with a tax-free bonus. Other schemes include the share incentive plan, the company share option plan and enterprise management incentives.

Certainly, the save-as-you-earn share option plan includes two features that recession-proof this form of profit sharing and financial involvement – to a limited extent.

First, the money that employees save is guaranteed, as is the tax-free bonus they receive on maturity. This inflation-proofs their savings to a certain extent, although the equivalent interest rate does not tend to be over-generous.

Second, the scheme's offer of shares is based on the share price at the time when the employee enters the scheme (the employer can discount this price by up to 20%). So, the value of the shares will only be unattractive to employee purchasers if it has fallen back to such an extent that it is lower than it was three or five years previously. Of course, the examples of dramatic falls in some companies' share values in recent years make this a real possibility in some cases.

E. Examples of profit sharing

Recent examples of profit-sharing payments include:

● 9.18% of basic salary paid in May 2003 to **Co-operative Bank** staff;

● 10% as cash, shares or a combination to staff at the **Royal Bank of Scotland Group** in 2003;

● the May 2002 agreement at chemicals manufacturer **Kemira Agro UK** set down a profit-sharing formula for potential payments in February 2003, based on a sliding scale: from 0.5% of salary if the company's operating income were to reach £7 million, rising to a maximum of 3% of salary if income reached £9.5 million;

● in 2002, staff at **Scottish Widows** received profit-sharing payments under the scheme of its parent company Lloyds TSB; these were worth 9% of basic salary, based on 2001 group profits. Payments could be taken in March 2002 as cash or shares;

● **Welsh Water/Dwr Cymru** operates a company performance-related bonus scheme that pays a £500 bonus if its financial targets are met and a further £2,000 if its position in the industry regulator's league table improves;

● **BorgWarner** operates a scheme that combines individual and corporate productivity payments. Its objective is to reduce the time taken to produce each
unit of the company's output, which involves components for the automotive
industry. For each of its product lines, the company sets a target and employees receive payments ranging, in 2003, from £25.63 to £37.13 a week on average, depending on the proportion of the target that is achieved. Employees
also receive an annual payment for a full year's above-target performance. In
2003, this was worth £135 for 5% above target, £250 for 10% above target and
£450 for 15% above target.

Benefits packages

Employee benefits have generally long ceased to be seen by employees as
the "icing on the cake". Increasingly, too, the state is requiring employers to
provide certain minimum benefits as a legal minimum – paid holidays and
paternity leave, for example.

According to feedback from 507 employers obtained by the Chartered Institute
of Personnel and Development[6], only four types of benefit are provided by
more than 50% of all employers (the survey did not ask about pensions):
● paid holidays of 21 days and over;
● occupational sick pay;
● death–in–service cover; and
● free on–site car parking.

In addition, more than half of all employers provide the following benefits
to their managers:
● private medical insurance;
● company car (senior managers only); and
● a car allowance (senior managers only).

In more than one-third of employers, non-manual staff below managerial
level also receive private medical insurance.

And managers below senior management level in more than one-third of
employers also receive: a company car; or car allowance; relocation assistance; and permanent health insurance.

Holidays

Holiday arrangements are among the most frequently reviewed parts of
employees' benefits and allowances packages. Basic holiday entitlements tend,

across the economy, to improve very gradually. More frequently, employers introduce additional days of holiday to reward longer service. The amount of service-related holiday may be increased or, equally frequently, the periods of service required may be reduced.

In addition, the trend towards reducing the demarcations between different types of employee (manager, white-collar and manual, for example) mean that holiday entitlements may be harmonised upwards, with consequent gains for some of those affected. An improvement in holiday entitlements might, too, be linked to gaining union agreement to an overall pay settlement.

All in all, holiday entitlements were the third most commonly revised benefit in 2002, after pensions and company cars. For 2003, more than one in 10 employers expected to review their holiday provisions.

Management at the **Pioneer** factory in Castleford, which manufactures hi-fi systems and TV set-top boxes, agreed a half-day improvement in basic holiday entitlements as part of its 1 April 2002 agreement with Amicus. This rose to 26 days, with service-related holidays of 27 days after three years and 28 days after six years.

Supermarket group **William Morrison** agreed improvements in service-related holidays as part of its 7 April 2003 agreement with Usdaw. Employees will now receive an additional five days' holiday after six years' service as of 2 August 2004, instead of after seven years as at present.

Employees covered by the multi-employer agreement for the **paper and boardmaking** industry received improvements in holiday pay from 1 May 2003 as part of the 2003 pay settlement between employers and recognised trade unions. Previously, holiday pay was based on earnings, calculated by taking the previous tax year's total earnings (as shown on the individual's P60 statement). Now, a supplement will also be paid, linked to grade. These range, for example, from £6.23 to £8.30 a week for continuous-shift workers.

Basic holiday entitlements

IRS finds that there remains a slight status divide among British employees' holiday entitlements. Non-manual employees receive an average of 23.9 days' basic holiday a year, compared with manual employees' 22.2 days. Overall, the average British employee receives 23.5 days' basic holiday.

These averages span a wide range of different entitlements. For example, and excluding education authorities, some employers provide 15 days' paid holiday (paid public holidays will boost this to the minimum legal entitlement of four weeks) while others offer 35 days.

As well as basic holiday entitlements, many employees are also eligible for one or more of three additional types of paid leave:
● service-related leave (see below);
● public holidays; and/or
● "company days".

Company days are holidays where the organisation closes down and gives its employees paid leave. In some cases – some local authorities, for example – these are "extra statutory days" tagged on to public holidays, such as Easter and Christmas. In other instances, they are extended periods where the site or department closes down for several days to a fortnight. Traditionally, manufacturers have observed "factory weeks" during the summer, when the whole workforce took its main holiday at the same time to avoid disruption to production at other times. Latterly, service sector firms are following this trend, by filling in the gaps between Christmas and New Year. This provides savings on heating and lighting, as well as accepting the fact that many employees wish to take time off during this period. Finally, some company days are historic practices, where employees have always received a paid holiday at a certain time of year, such as a day's holiday for the Queen's birthday in parts of the Civil Service.

Service-related holiday entitlements

Most employers, around 70%, provide additional holiday entitlements to their employees, linked to length of service. However, many more non-manual employees are covered by service-related provisions than manual workers. This may reflect the greater prevalence of this practice in parts of the economy where there are few manual workers, such as the service sector. Or it may be the result of organisations that employ both white-collar and manual groups of workers restricting these entitlements to just their non-manual staff.

Rules and procedures

Most employers have developed policies that set down rules about taking holidays. And where their operations depend on continuous staff cover, their policies will also often include restrictions on when holidays can be taken.

Carry over: However, IRS's regular programme of research into employers' holiday procedures shows that many employers are trying to make their rules as flexible as possible. In particular, increasing numbers of employers allow unused holidays to be carried over to the next holiday year.

There are health issues, though, to bear in mind – there is a growing awareness that employees who fail to take their holiday entitlements may be storing up health problems for themselves as well as reducing their efficiency. And amassing large amounts of leave can mean that employees could well take extended periods of absence in one particular year, leaving the employer with problems in finding cover while they are away.

So, most employers that allow the carrying-over of holiday tell us that they set down rules to control this practice. They may set a limit on the number of days that can be carried over in any one year. And they may restrict the ways in which these additional days may be taken – for example, outside peak holiday periods, or employees normally being expected to take no more than a certain total number of weeks in a single block.

Some employers permit carried-over holidays as a right, within any restrictions on timing and duration, while others leave it to line managers' discretion. In such cases, they often provide guidelines to ensure employees are being treated fairly and consistently, and to avoid claims of unfair discrimination. For example, some organisations tell us that carried-over holiday would be allowed where the employee had been heavily involved in unusual work commitments, or whose illness had prevented them taking a planned break. In addition, and increasingly, employers are allowing carryover so that individuals can amass enough leave for a special holiday the following year – such as visiting relatives overseas, attending a religions festival or going on honeymoon.

Roughly half of all employers now permit some leave to be carried over, while others apply a "use it or lose it" policy. The latter has the advantages of administrative convenience, greater control over attendance and an acknowledgement of the health benefits of rest periods.

But one potential disadvantage lies in a stampede of staff trying to ensure they take their unused entitlement before the end of the holiday year. Where the year is also the calendar year (rather than 1 April to 31 March, for example), then this pre-deadline rush will coincide with the final weeks of December, where other employees will be pressing for holiday to do Christmas shopping, go away for a Christmas break, or simply spend time with the families over the festive season. Again, employers have found that provisions are required in their holiday procedures to control this potential problem.

Duration: It is very rare for employers to specify a minimum period of holiday that must be taken at any one time (such as one or two weeks), despite the fact that individuals who make a habit of taking odd days can add to administrative workloads and make it more difficult to arrange cover for their work.

Timing: Many employers' holiday procedures place restrictions on the timing of holidays, in order to avoid their busiest periods or to ensure that sufficient staff are available to maintain operations or services. Conversely, some employers – mainly in manufacturing and production industries – close down completely for one or two weeks, and require their employees to use some of their holiday entitlements for this period. Increasingly, organisations are closing down over the Christmas–New Year period, both manufacturers and some firms in the service sector where this would otherwise be a quiet time of year.

As well as hard-and-fast rules, some organisations tell us that they give their line managers discretion over organising holiday requests so that they do not have a major impact on business operations. Managers might take account of the time of year, expected workloads, the availability of cover and the number of other staff also requesting leave around that time.

Holiday pay

Increasingly, the feedback that IRS obtains from personnel, HR and pay specialists shows that the calculation of holiday pay is benefiting from the trends towards consolidating many allowances and plus-payments into basic salary, and of harmonising manual and non-manual employees' terms and conditions in a single-status approach. However, calculation methods remain particularly important, and controversial, for manual workers whose earnings are boosted significantly by overtime and shift payments.

Non-manual staff: Most employers tell us that the holiday pay of their non-manual staff is calculated on the basis of basic annual salary. A day's leave is usually calculated in the private sector by dividing annual salary by 260 (52 weeks x 5 working days) – or 261 in some employers. The public sector, in contrast, tends to use a formula of 365.

In a minority of employers, non-manual staff's holiday pay is based on earnings. In such cases, holiday procedures need to specify which additional payments are included (such as shift pay, overtime premia, location allowances and attendance bonuses) and, in the case of variable payments, the period that will be used to calculate them. For example, some employers stipulate that earnings over the previous 12 or 13 weeks will be averaged and used for the calculation.

Manual workers: The calculation of holiday pay for manual workers varies considerably, often reflecting the payment system used in an organisation and historical factors. Many employers, particularly where additional payments are not a significant proportion of basic pay or are not enjoyed on a regular basis, use the same formula for manual workers as other workforce groups, taking basic annual salary as the basis.

In other cases, some or all of the components of manual workers' total earnings are used as the basis for holiday pay. Shift premia, overtime pay, productivity pay, attendance allowances and location allowances are typical sources of earnings that may or may not be counted. Because some of these payments are variable, a calculation period may be set down in the holiday procedure, such as averaging the individual's earnings over the previous 12, 13 or 26 weeks.

Public holidays

According to feedback from more than 100 employers, most employees are covered by a formal arrangement that they will be paid if they are asked to work over a public holiday.

The most common compensation arrangement provides both double-time for the hours worked on a public holiday plus a day's paid holiday to be taken on another occasion (time off in lieu, TOIL). This formula is more prevalent in the public sector and in the private sector's manufacturing and production industries. It is comparatively less common among services firms.

The second most common arrangement – and the most frequent one used by services firms in the private sector – provides double-time, but omits TOIL. In some other employers that also do not offer TOIL, the premium is time-and-a-half.

The third most commonly found approach involves providing TOIL but no pay premium. This approach tends to involve managers or other senior staff who are not covered by their employers' overtime arrangements.

Fourth, and finally, some employers provide no compensation, either in pay or TOIL. In these instances, public holiday working is either not expected of their staff, or those involved – again, mainly managerial staff – are considered to be sufficiently rewarded through their normal terms and conditions.

Sick pay

As a minimum, most employees are covered by the state's basic sick payments scheme, Statutory Sick Pay, which provides a minimum level of benefit after three "waiting days". Payments are made via the individual's employer. However, many organisations have introduced occupational sick pay schemes that give employees greater financial security in the event that they are unable to work because of illness.

Some employers offer attendance allowances as a means of managing absence. Where individual or collective attendance rates reach a predetermined level, the employees involved receive a bonus payment.

Information on sick pay and attendance allowances can be found in Chapter 12 Attendance and absence.

Private medical insurance

Employers' provision of private medical insurance (PMI) has experienced considerable change in recent years, being assailed by significant rises in insurance premiums and pressure from insurers to reduce the incidence of claims, on the one hand. And, on the other hand, the continuing problems with the National Health Service mean that employers face employee resistance to cuts in PMI benefits.

Insurers are offering new or amended schemes to existing employer customers as a means of keeping price rises under some control. These may not necessarily have an overt impact on employees' level of cover, reducing the potential for resistance and damaged employee relations.

For example, some insurers are creating tiers of private hospitals, according to location and facilities, linked to differences in premiums charged. Some are tightening up their management of claims, requiring employees to make a telephone call to a contact centre prior to any use of private medical facilities being made. The calls are handled by trained nurses who check such factors as pre-existing medical conditions, the use of institutions and medical practitioners on the insurer's preferred list of suppliers and so on.

Cash plans, too, have made some inroads into existing PMI provision. But, perhaps more broadly, they are offering a route by which employers without any medical benefits can provide some form of provision to their staff. Case study F provides an example of the benefits available under cash plans.

F. Six Continents

Cash plans are lower-cost schemes, providing fixed levels of payment to employees. For example, the Hospital Saturday Fund is used by the Six Continents hotel chain, which includes Crowne Plaza, Holiday Inn and Posthouse, to provide medical benefits to its employees. They are entitled to claim half the cost of dental or optical treatment, including the cost of new spectacles or contact lenses, up to £50 a year. In addition, they can claim up to £100 a year towards the cost of a consultation or treatment by a physiotherapist, osteopath, chiropractor and chiropodist. They also receive contributions towards the cost of specialist investigations, in- and out-patient hospital treatment, recuperation and other medical fees. Membership also includes a medical information helpline, a stress-counselling helpline and a legal helpline.

According to research conducted by the Chartered Institute of Personnel and Development among 507 employers, PMI and related schemes (such as cash plans) represent a targeted, but widely available benefit[7]. This seems to be firmly linked to status, with three-quarters (72%) of senior managers receiving PMI and just over half (57%) of first-line and middle managers doing so. In contrast, only one in three (37%) non-manuals and three in 10 (29%) manuals enjoy access to employer-funded or subsidised health insurance.

Where several different staff groups all have access to PMI, the benefits may still be differentiated by status. In particular, some employers will provide cover for their employees only, below a certain level, but will also offer to include more senior members of staff's partners and family. In a further twist, some or all of those covered by PMI may be given the option of purchasing additional cover, either for themselves or in order to include partners or family.

Despite its widespread availability, PMI continues to be controversial in the context of the universal ethos of the NHS. For this and other reasons, it is rarely offered by public sector employers.

G. Examples of private medical insurance

Advertising agency **Bluestone** provides cover for monthly-paid staff only, together with an option to purchase further cover for partners or family members.

Outsourced marketing provider **Broadsystem** offers PMI cover on a family basis for management-level employees upwards, and personal cover for all non-management staff.

Capita Insurance Services in Cheadle provides cover for all staff and family cover at senior management level and above; there is a six months' service eligibility requirement in all cases.

Telephone banking company **First Direct** includes PMI in its flexible benefits package; there is a six months' service requirement.

Stroud & Swindon Building Society makes a married PMI allowance of £900 and a family allowance of £1,125 to senior-level staff. A single allowance of £450 is available to management and senior professional and technical staff and any other employees with more than five years' service.

Details current as at May 2003.

Company cars

Employers' provision of a company car as an employee benefit and, to a lesser extent, as a "tool of the trade" for sales reps and other mobile staff has come under increasing political pressure. Successive changes in the tax regime, coupled with increases in tax liability for many recipients, have led to a major reappraisal of the car's value as an incentive.

However, the culture of receiving a company car is deeply ingrained in the UK for certain types of occupation, industry and status levels. Many employers face a strong adverse reaction from staff when trying to withdraw this benefit. Instead, the provision of cash alternatives to an actual car or the inclusion of company car options in a flexible benefits package (see below) are being explored by some employers.

From our own and others' research, it seems that the use of cash alternatives is spreading rapidly. Some employers are introducing cash benefits alongside the option of a company car – eligible managers can choose either. But others are phasing out their company cars and replacing them with cash-based benefits.

Despite the advent of "green taxes" and a different means of calculating the fuel scale charge (the tax on employer-provided fuel) in 2002, the introduction of congestion charges in some cities and the stricter enforcement of speed limits, company cars are still widely available. The Chartered Institute of Personnel and Development's large-scale survey of employers shows, for example, that six in 10 (60%) employers continue to provide a car for members of their senior management. And almost four in 10 (38%) do so for managers down to first-line level.

But, increasingly, cash alternatives in the form of car allowances are being offered. For example, almost identical proportions of employers (39% versus 38%) now offer a car allowance as provide a company car itself to their managers at first-line and middle management levels. Lower down the hierarchy, season-ticket loans (often, interest-free) are much more common than either a car or car allowance. Three in 10 (28%) employers offer season-ticket loans to their non-manual staff below managerial level – more than double the proportion (12%) that offers a car allowance, and four times as many as provide a car itself (7%).

IRS's own research finds that, second only to changes in pension schemes, company car policies were reviewed and revised by larger proportions of employers than any other benefit in 2002.

Employers' car policies tend to take one of two main approaches. A car is purchased and provided to the manager, together with provision for the cost of servicing, insurance, road tax and breakdown cover. Or a lease/contract-hire car is provided. In addition, employers must decide whether to cover the total cost of car ownership, or expect the manager to meet some of the costs involved in their private use of the vehicle, such as fuel consumption and sharing the servicing costs.

Replacement cycles – the timespan between renewing the vehicle – and the issue of managers wishing to opt back into the car scheme are also factors requiring determination. The complex changes to the tax regime in 2002 and their impact on different types of car mean that some managers may find that they could be better off switching back from a cash alternative to driving a company car once more. For example, they could choose a low-emission vehicle and keep their annual business mileage at a relatively low level. They may also be prepared to trade off a slightly higher tax bill for the convenience of having their employer manage such issues as breakdown cover and maintenance.

The availability of cars is, as we saw above, usually linked to status. Beyond that, many employers tailor their provision, so that more valuable models or higher-specification options are available, linked to the grade, salary or status of the manager.

As well as procedures covering the provision of status-related cars, most employers seek to define any entitlement to cars required by essential users. In some cases, the individual's job is self-defining (such as a sales representative responsible for a large district) or a regional manager required to pay frequent visits to a number of branches. In other organisations, eligibility is defined according to a minimum number of business miles travelled a year – a threshold of 8,000 or 10,000, for example.

H. Examples of company car schemes

Company cars:

Insurance broker **Amlin** provides job-related vehicles for staff who travel at least 8,000 business miles a year.

High-tech manufacturer **e2v Technologies** provides lease cars for essential users and as a benefit for managers and key skill employees. This is a tiered benefit, worth £650, £450, £350 or £335 a month.

Guarding and security services company **Group 4 Total Security** automatically provides a fully-expensed vehicle for senior managers and, depending on business need, for other employees. The grade of car is defined by pay band and business need.

Hammicks Bookshop offers a car-leasing scheme to account managers, regional managers and directors, paying up to £360 a month towards the lease costs.

Cash alternatives:

Mail-order company **J D Williams** offers between £4,300 and £6,100 a year, depending on grade.

IT systems and solutions company **Logica CMG** in London offers a cash alternative to employees earning £31,000 a year and above, worth between £2,508 and £10,800 according to salary level.

Engineering company **Southco Europe** in Cheltenham offers between £600 and £750 a month as an option for senior managers.

Details current as at May 2003.

Pensions

Occupational pension provision has become a major issue for employers with the sluggish performance of the stock market and the recent FRS 17 accountancy standard regarding the treatment in company annual reports of changes in the market value of pension fund assets.

Personnel, HR and pay professionals may find themselves torn in two ways. They know the importance of pensions provision to their employees – in providing income security in old age and as a recruitment and retention tool.

This is confirmed by a recent MORI poll among a representative sample of adults. This found that pensions, particularly final-salary schemes, constitute the second most important benefit when potential recruits are considering working for a particular employer[8]. Furthermore, the loss of an existing final-salary pension scheme could damage the morale and motivation of existing members of staff[9].

But personnel, HR and pay professionals also know that the costs involved in pensions provision could have a major impact on their organisations' finances.

The impact of the crisis in pensions has made headline news, with some large employers reporting deficits of many billions of pounds in their schemes, while some workforces have taken strike action to resist pension-scheme closures.

An analysis by the Chartered Institute of Personnel and Development finds, however, that the recent bout of scheme closures is, in fact, part of a longer-term trend caused by such factors as longer life expectancy, falling retirement ages and the growing burden of complying with pensions rules and regulations[10].

The institute argues that personnel, HR and pay specialists can help their organisations respond to the pressures on pensions schemes in a strategic way, such as by:
● reviewing their pensions arrangements, and asking employees what they want;
● introducing flexible-benefits schemes, where employees can improve their employer's basic pensions provision by trading off other benefits against it;
● making retirement ages more flexible to take account of some employees' preferences for working after normal retirement; and
● offering two or more different arrangements to cater for the needs of different groups of staff (ibid).

Among employers with final-salary schemes, these main responses are emerging to the growing costs involved:
● topping up the payments made by employers to reduce scheme deficits;
● increasing the contributions paid by both employer and employee (including ending contributions holidays and introducing employee contributions);
● closure of the scheme to new members (who are usually offered a defined-contribution scheme instead);
● winding up the scheme;
● undertaking a review of investment strategies to improve investment returns; and

● outsourcing the administration of the pension scheme.

As a result of these changes, final-salary schemes are now offered by a minority (46%) of employers, according to the National Association of Pension Funds.

In addition, while survey evidence is patchy, it does seem that only a minority of employers in the private sector offers a pension scheme of any description. This knowledge led the government to introduce Stakeholder Pensions, a money-purchase (defined contribution) scheme that relevant employers are legally required to offer to their employees. The main exceptions involve small firms with fewer than five employees, organisations where all employees earn below the lower earnings limit for national insurance purposes, or where a qualifying personal or occupational pension scheme is already offered.

Employers make widely differing payments to their employees' pension schemes, according to such factors as the type of scheme, the size of the employer, the age profile of the workforce and so on. But, on average, the National Association of Pension Funds[11] finds that private sector employers pay 8.3% of employees' salaries, rising to 9% in schemes where employees do not make any contributions. This falls to 6.4% in the case of money-purchase schemes. A separate survey by Watson Wyatt[12] finds an even lower payment of 5.3% to money-purchase schemes.

Employees, for their part, pay an average of 3.5% to pension schemes run by their employers, according to Watson Wyatt. This represents a rise from the 3% level found just two years previously.

Parental and compassionate leave

Recent legal changes have heightened the importance of employers' provisions for maternity, paternity and adoption leave and pay, and of their provisions for compassionate leave. These issues are covered in chapter 9 Equal opportunities and diversity.

Shiftworking

Shiftworking remains a widespread requirement of British employers. Long-term structural changes in the economy mean, though, that the service sector has overtaken manufacturing industry as having the largest proportion of its workers involved in shift patterns.

In all, according the government's *Labour Force Survey*, one in six (16%) employees is a shiftworker. The survey shows that their most common working patterns are, in descending order:
● two-shift system: early/late-double day;
● three-shift system;
● sometimes nights, sometimes days;
● night shifts;
● evening or twilight shifts;
● continental shift patterns;
● split shifts;
● morning shifts;
● weekend shifts; and
● various other shift patterns.

Employers often reward shiftworkers with higher basic wages or shift premia. Based on feedback obtained by IRS, typical payments are as follows:
● permanent day shifts: often, these do not attract a payment, although day shifts that involve early-morning start times may enjoy payments of 10% to 13%;
● double-day shifts: 20% to 25%;
● three-shift, non-continuous systems: payments are often averaged out over the cycle, at around 24%; and
● permanent night shifts: 33% to 40%.

In addition, some organisations requiring shiftworking have moved to an annualised hours system. In such systems, an employee's normal hours of work are expressed as an annual total, rather than a weekly one, and there is some inbuilt flexibility for the working week to lengthen or shorten over the year according to the needs of the organisation. Overtime is usually formally abolished with all hours being paid at basic rates.

Where shiftworking is used, annualised hours schemes often involve splitting contractual hours of work into those allocated to certain shifts and unallocated shifts. The latter are held in reserve and employees may be asked to work these shifts when cover is required for absent workers or when greater numbers of staff are required to cope with additional demands.

The introduction of annualised hours may encounter resistance from the workforce – primarily, because of concerns about potential loss of earnings and of changes to individuals' work–life balance. Many employers respond by offering an additional pay increase, the upwards harmonisation of terms and conditions with non-manual staff, and guaranteed limits on the extent to which hours can alter from period to period.

I. Examples of shiftworking

Pharmaceuticals manufacturer **Alpharma** operates a range of shift systems, including permanent days (8.30 to 16.30), permanent nights, permanent twilight shift (18.00 to 20.45) and double-day (6.00 to 14.00; 14.00 to 20.00). The double-day shift premium is £53.22 a week, and the permanent nights premium is £106.44 a week.

Supermarket chain **Asda** operates a wide range of shift patterns, including permanent mornings/afternoons/days/twilight/nights; alternating early/daywork; alternating daywork/nights; and weekend working. The nightwork premium (23.00 to 6.00) is £1.61 an hour.

Printer-cartridge manufacturer **Lexmark International** operates permanent days (7.00 to 19.00), permanent nights (19.00 to 7.00), a two-week cycle with a 2-3-2 shift pattern (two days on; three days off; two days on; two days off; three days on; two days off). The daywork premium is 20% and the permanent nights premium is 30%.

Some support staff working for insurer **More Th>n** work two-shift or three-shift patterns (two-shift involves 7.00 to 14.30; 1400 to 21.30, on a six-week rotation); (three-shift involves 7.00 to 14.30; 1400 to 21.30; 22.00 to 6.00, on a six-week rotation). The daywork premium is 10% and the three-shift system premium is 25%.

Details current as at August 2002.

Overtime

British employees may have one of the longest working weeks in Europe, with much of this being attributed to working large amounts of often unpaid overtime. Paid overtime, though, is falling from favour with employers. It has been criticised because the regular availability of paid overtime creates an expectation among those involved.

Where extra hours are required, employees are likely to expect payment, usually at the higher rates provided for additional hours, rather than being willing to take compensatory time off at a later date or simply forget about the time owed. And some critics argue that it can be self-fulfilling in that the amount of work is managed by a work group to ensure that it is seldom completed without overtime working being required. All in all, institutionalised overtime can increase overheads and reduce flexibility.

Some of the feedback obtained by IRS reflects this adverse experience. A contact working for an electricity company told us, for example, that:

"Overtime is sometimes done when, probably, it could have been postponed to the next day." A contact in a pharmaceutical manufacturer said that the company suffers an "additional-hours culture, combined with a lack of monitoring in some areas".

According to the government's *New Earnings Survey*, the proportion of full-time employees receiving paid overtime has fallen from a third to a quarter in a decade. Paid overtime is very common among manual workers, where around one-half of men and three in 10 women receive it. It is uncommon among non-manual workers, though, where only one in 5.5 men and one in 6.7 women receive it. In addition, the survey finds that the amount of paid overtime that is worked is, on average, longer for manuals than non-manuals.

Based on feedback from personnel, HR and pay managers working in 150 organisations, we find that employers continue to be interested in controlling and reducing overtime, particularly paid overtime. However, the way in which overtime pay is calculated has not altered significantly.

Generally, it is calculated by applying a multiplier to the employee's basic pay:
● weekday overtime: most employers use time-and-a-half, with only small proportions paying at time-and-a-third or time-and-a-quarter; however, around one in five employers pay weekday overtime at basic rates only;
● Saturdays: most employers use time-and-a-half, although one in five pay double-time;
● Sundays: most employers pay double-time; and
● bank holidays: again, most employers pay double time.

However, overtime pay is also affected by additional factors. In particular, it is rarely given to staff in more senior positions (such as supervisors and managers). Most employers exempt certain grades from eligibility, while a minority defines entitlement to overtime pay according to a salary ceiling – often, around the £21,000 mark.

In some organisations, it may be paid to manual workers but not to non-manual workers. In a sizeable minority of organisations (around one in five employers), overtime pay may also be affected by the time of day when the extra hours are worked, and/or whether or not the individual has already worked a certain period of overtime.

Authority to sanction paid overtime working is given to line managers (75% of the employers we contacted) and/or to middle and senior managers

(50%). However, team leaders and supervisors are much less likely to be able to authorise it without higher-level approval.

The ways in which employers are reducing paid overtime are as follows, shown in descending order of prevalence:
● imposing tighter managerial controls (80% of employers);
● introducing more efficient technology and other working practices (54%);
● developing new shift patterns (33%); and
● using temporary employees (25%).

There are indications, though, that some of the impact of these changes has been to drive overtime "underground". In a significant minority of employers, reductions in paid overtime have led to an increase in unpaid overtime working.

One change that has had little impact on either paid or unpaid overtime working is the UK's implementation of the Working Time Directive and its 48-hour maximum average working week. Most of the employers we contacted told us that, even with overtime, average total hours still fall below the 48-hour limit. And others that are potentially affected said that employees are willing to opt-out of the limit and work beyond it.

Flexible benefits schemes

Interest is growing in a relatively recent approach to managing employee benefits called flexible benefits schemes (initially, these were known as "cafeteria benefits"). Such schemes provide eligible members of staff with a package of current and potential benefits, and allow them a measure of discretion over the precise nature of the benefits they receive. Usually, the flexibility operates within an overall cash limit that is often based on the actual cost to the employer of their current benefits and allowances.

The benefits are often given a cash value, and employees can increase the value of a particular benefit (such as private medical insurance or holidays) by reducing the value of one or more others or, in some cases, by contributing directly to it. This often involves a salary sacrifice, which shifts the money they receive through basic pay towards paying for a new or enhanced benefit.

The main advantage of flexible benefits lies in their potential impact on employee motivation. Bringing their benefits together, and highlighting the cost to the employer of providing them, shows employees the true worth of their overall reward package. In addition, enabling employees to create customised benefits packages that better suit their own needs, interests and family circumstances can also contribute to improved motivation. The outcome of this motivational effect could be better performance and flexibility, or improved retention rates. It might also act as a recruitment incentive.

In addition, many flexible benefits schemes are almost cost-neutral, in that the employer need not increase its overall contribution to an employee's benefits package, but merely allocate it differently according to his or her wishes. But there will be additional administration costs in launching and managing schemes, particularly at the points in time where employees are able to alter their preferences, as well as providing annual statements of the cost of benefits for employees' income tax purposes.

Decisions are also required about which staff will be eligible, which benefits can be altered, and the extent to which particular benefits can be enhanced, reduced or sacrificed. Some employers, for example, exclude their final-salary pension scheme and most or all of the basic holiday entitlement from their flexible benefits schemes.

So far, according to the Chartered Institute of Personnel and Development, one in eight (12%) employers offer flexible benefits schemes, and it is difficult to know whether this will increase significantly. A great many employers (44%) told the institute that they were intending to introduce a scheme in 2003. But, looking back at the results of its previous research, it found that "intention has not been translated into practice"[13].

J. Examples of flexible benefits schemes

Telephone banking company **First Direct** gives employees a fund (the value of which is dependent on their grade) to spend on a number of non-core benefits. These include car-breakdown cover, cinema tickets, critical-illness cover, health-club membership, nursery place funding and retail vouchers. (June 2003.)

At **Unipart DCM**, which is a provider of outsourced logistics, the benefits of dental care, health screening, an internet buying club and private medical insurance are covered by a salary-sacrifice scheme. In addition, private medical insurance, a car allowance and a company car are available at differing levels of provision depending on the individual's grade. (June 2003.)

The **Family Housing Association** is using an external provider to offer a flexible benefits package via an online system. The package includes additional holiday, private medical insurance and childcare vouchers. (May 2003; source: e-reward.co.uk.)

Details current at dates shown.

5. Legal checklist

● Pay, job evaluation, grading systems, benefits and allowances should not discriminate unfairly – Sex Discrimination Act 1975; Race Relations Act 1976; Disability Discrimination Act 1995; Part-Time Workers (Prevention of Less-Favourable Treatment) Regulations 2000; Fixed-Term Employees (Prevention of Less-Favourable Treatment) Regulations 2002; Trade Union and Labour Relations (Consolidation) Act 1992; and Codes of Practice associated with these Acts.

● Practices in the public sector must support equality of opportunity on the grounds of ethnicity; larger public sector employers should audit their practices to ensure that this is the case – Race Relations (Amendment) Act 2000.

● Retirement ages and, potentially, pensions provision will be affected once age discrimination legislation is enacted by the end of 2006.

● The minimum rates of pay of most workers aged 18 and over are covered by the provisions of the National Minimum Wage Act 1998.

● Deductions from workers' wages, including non-payments, are covered by the provisions of the Employment Rights Act 1996.

● Eligible employers must provide Stakeholder Pensions to relevant employees – Welfare Reform and Pensions Act 1999.

● Workers' hours, above an average of 48 a week, are covered by the Working Time Regulations 1998.

● Workers have a right to a minimum of four weeks' paid holiday a year – Working Time Regulations 1998.

7. Retaining the best staff

See also: 1. Filling your vacancies; 5. Induction, training and development; 6. Pay, benefits and other terms and conditions; and 12. Attendance and absence.

This chapter covers:
- Overview: an introduction to managing retention;
- Getting the information to manage retention;
- Labour turnover;
- Exit interviews;
- Separation questionnaires;
- Employee attitude surveys;
- Other sources;
- Why staff resign;
- Managing retention; and
- Aspects of retention: organisational culture; empowerment and job redesign; recruitment; induction; training; line managers' role; promotion and sideways moves; pay; benefits; childcare; working time; individuals with disabilities; retirement ages; redundancy.

Checklists in this chapter:
1. Sources of labour turnover data
2. Exit interviews: the key issues
3. Exit interviews: an interviewer's guide
4. Designing separation questionnaires
5. Managing retention: the most popular responses
6. Legal checklist

Case studies in this chapter:
A. King's College Hospital NHS Trust
B. Bupa
C. Fujitsu Services
D. Oxfam
E. Wizard Inns
F. Asda

Overview

Remember when "natural wastage" was the term used to describe the process of staff resigning and leaving the organisation? The phrase could not have better captured the sense that resignations possess an apparent inevitability and regularity beyond the control of the employer.

Certainly, the phrase is still trotted out when redundancy exercises are being planned, and staff attrition is seen as a possible means of avoiding compulsory job losses. Yet, the recent redundancy survey undertaken by the Chartered Institute of Personnel and Development[1] found that most of the 563 employers it contacted reported that upwards of 93% of their total job losses involved compulsory redundancies.

Recently, we contacted more than 430 personnel and HR specialists to gain their feedback about the relative importance of retention issues to their organisations, and any initiatives they were taking to address them.

We found that retention has become a key priority for UK employers – it is among the 10 most important challenges facing personnel and HR specialists, ranking alongside such issues as reducing absence, and complying with the wave of new Acts and Regulations covering employment. In all, almost half (48.4%) of all employers are encountering retention difficulties.

Across the economy, private sector services companies are the worst affected, with six in 10 (58.6%) experiencing problems in retaining valuable staff, while difficulties are affecting just over four in 10 (42.1%) companies in the manufacturing and production sector. In the public sector, however, only one in three (35.7%) employers are reporting retention problems.

Beyond the challenge of gaining acceptance for the argument that retention can and should be managed, the issue of retention management faces two prime difficulties. First, it is often far from easy to identify the nature of the problem – who is likely to leave? how large is our staff turnover rate? what is driving these resignations? And second, even if armed with this basic information, it is not a simple matter to develop initiatives that can control staff turnover in a cost-effective way. (For example, line managers will often argue that a universal pay rise of significant magnitude will tackle the problem of staff resignations, but this is rarely an affordable solution.)

This chapter takes these retention-management issues in turn, beginning with the challenge of identifying the scale and nature of the problem.

Getting the information to manage retention

High rates of labour turnover are bad for business; conversely, a stagnant workforce with little or no movement to and from the outside world is unlikely to provide the best conditions for dynamism and innovation. Somewhere between these extremes lies the optimum level of staff wastage.

Rates of labour turnover among comparable organisations provide a source of great interest for personnel and HR professionals. They afford a benchmark against which to test whether or not their own organisation has unusually high (or low) levels of attrition – given that there is no universal level of labour turnover that could act as a yardstick.

Labour turnover data provide but one of several sources that organisations need to use when developing a retention strategy. The data can be seen as part of a process that gradually focuses down to reach the point where the root cause of staff retention problems can be identified.

Rates of labour turnover represent the end point: they measure what has already occurred – the loss of members of staff. They do not show the reasons for staff losses (although patterns and changes over time can hint at them). Instead, the use of exit interviews (structured conversations with staff who have tendered their resignation) and separation questionnaires (survey forms distributed to leavers for their completion) provide valuable insights into such reasons. These tools are described below.

Again, however, these techniques are backward-looking; the people involved have already decided to leave (or may have actually moved on). The feedback these instruments offer can be used to infer the reasons that may prompt other members of staff to resign. There are other methods that canvass individuals who have not resigned, and may not have even considered so doing.

Attitude surveys (questionnaires that ask staff about their morale, motivation and degree of identification with the organisation) and insights from routine appraisal/performance management interviews are the most common approaches in use. They offer useful insights into the factors that might encourage individuals to resign, and provide the earliest opportunity to address them before the psychological break with the employer has been made. In other words, action can be taken before individuals have decided to look elsewhere. Left until the psychological contract has been weakened or broken, it may not be possible to encourage the individual to stay, or the action may simply delay what is now inevitable.

The active collation and use of labour turnover data should not be a fair-weather process. At times such as the present, when many organisations are under increasing economic pressures, it is all the more important to ensure that valuable staff are retained and that recruitment only takes place when it is fully justified. The greater the pressure on overheads, the less sense it makes to waste the investment that has already been made in recruiting and training valuable members of staff.

The economic impact of labour turnover

Nothing more graphically illustrates the argument for addressing labour turnover than the price of doing nothing. It can easily cost thousands of pounds to recruit a replacement for someone who has resigned, particularly when managers or professionals have to be replaced. One key individual can hold the fortunes of a department or business in their hands, while the loss of several members of staff in the same unit or team can lead to instability and fluctuations in service. Organisations with high rates of turnover can easily spend thousands of pounds a year, largely unprofitably, on replacing staff whom they did not want to lose in the first place.

The labour turnover bill to employers involves some obvious items: the expense of a recruitment advertisement (as much as several thousand pounds when advertising in a broadsheet national newspaper) or the commission paid to an employment agency, and then the staff time required to consider the applications. There is also the time involved in interviewing shortlisted candidates, and in using other selection methods, such as tests or assessment centres. Successful applicants have to be inducted and probably trained, and given a period of grace while their effectiveness gradually improves to that of experienced staff.

The people leaving will require administration time to handle their separation. And there may be cost implications of the turbulence caused by the resignation and new appointment, such as reduced customer service.

The above consequences of turnover represent the cost heads that the Chartered Institute of Personnel and Development (CIPD) uses in its annual labour turnover survey[2]. Its results show that the cost per head of labour turnover runs into four figures for each of its nine categories of vacancy. At its most extreme, the CIPD calculates that it costs more than £5,500 to replace each manager who leaves. Taken together, the average replacement cost of a leaver stands at £3,462.

Many organisations measure their levels of labour turnover, but fail to quantify its impact. The **Norwich and Peterborough Building Society**, in contrast, has calculated that it costs an average of £4,500 to replace each employee. Its new reward structure and other initiatives have reduced labour turnover from 25% to 17%, yielding considerable cash savings.

In the much larger **Nationwide Building Society**[3], the replacement of leavers costs between £5,000 and £8,000 per person. Here, labour turnover averages 10.4% a year, although it is well under half this level (around 4%) among groups of employees aged under 25 and over 55.

At Bristol-based care-home provider **BRUNELCARE**, it costs about £1,000 to replace an employee. The composition of its workforce explains much of the difference in average costs between it and the two building societies. Of its 750 employees, 650 are hourly-paid, mainly part-time care assistants. But its much higher rate of labour wastage – approximately a third of its workforce has to be replaced each year – results in a relatively high annual resourcing bill. It has taken action to address labour turnover, conducting an investigation into the typical patterns of resignations – finding that turnover peaks at 24 months from recruitment – and has introduced a new skills-based pay system. This provides greater training and development opportunities, and has already had an impact on labour turnover rates.

Labour turnover

Calculating turnover

Labour turnover is simply a term for the outflow of people from an organisation. Individuals leave their jobs for many reasons: because they are dismissed or made redundant; because they have reached their normal retirement age, or qualify under the pension rules for early retirement; because they become unable to work, or die in service; or because they voluntarily decide to leave and move to another employer.

In most cases, though, personnel and HR specialists and others involved in the management of retention are interested in just one of these categories: those who leave voluntarily. They represent by far the largest number of leavers, with the sole exception of large-scale redundancy exercises. The scale of the voluntary type of turnover inflicts significant costs on employers, as we saw above, in finding and appointing replacements – and, unmanaged, it can happen at any time in any part of the organisation's activities.

Both the costs and the apparently random nature of voluntary labour turnover make it important to manage and control it in ways that benefit the organisation. But, management first requires measurement: labour turnover statistics must be collected and analysed, and then benchmarked against appropriate comparator employers.

Crude wastage

Given that voluntary resignations represent the main focus of interest, it would be logical to ensure that the data on labour turnover rates measure this, and only this, form of turnover. Unfortunately, though, most external sources of benchmarking data measure it with far less precision, through what is known as "crude wastage".

This calculation method lumps together all and every reason for turnover. It is computed by taking the number of all types of leavers in a specified period (usually 12 months), and dividing it by the number employed during that period (often averaged) – then multiplying the result by 100 to produce a percentage.

Major surveys of labour turnover, such as the one published by the Confederation of British Industry (CBI)[4], and most of the data in the CIPD's report, provide findings based on crude wastage rates. Inevitably, this has the effect of inflating the findings.

Variances between rates computed on different bases – crude wastage versus resignations – are likely to be even more marked when the focus narrows to specific occupations or industries. Managers, for example, have far lower levels of resignations than most other groups. The April 2002 Remuneration Economics/Chartered Management Institute survey of managers and directors[5] provides a detailed analysis of labour turnover rates by five different reasons for leaving. Resignations among managers were running at only 5.0%, while the crude-wastage rate (excluding transfers) was almost two-thirds higher at 8.3%.

Frankly, although many published surveys rely on it, the crude-wastage rate is of virtually no use as the basis for managing retention. It represents a tool that is too blunt for effective use – unless the employers included in the survey are behaving in much the same way as the organisation making the comparison. That is, if the rates of redundancies and dismissals are known to be much the same generally, and to be more or less in line with the organisation's own situation – an unlikely prospect – then it may be possible to infer the underlying rate of voluntary separations buried within the overall crude-wastage figure.

To be fair, though, some survey compilers have told us that their use of crude wastage to define turnover is simply a pragmatic response to the fact that many employers do not have any more precise statistics available.

Rates of voluntary turnover

The calculation of resignations follows much the same process as for crude wastage: the number of leavers for voluntary reasons in a specified period (usually 12 months) is divided by the number employed during that period (often averaged) – then the result is multiplied by 100 to give a percentage annual rate.

(Even if an organisation's record-keeping is not sophisticated, many of the major exceptions to voluntary turnover can be established – such as redundancies, dismissals and retirements – because statistics have to be kept for legal or financial reasons. Deducting these groups from the overall number of leavers will produce a reasonable approximation to the rate of voluntary turnover.)

An organisation-wide "resignation rate" is rarely sufficient for the purposes of managing retention, because it is an average figure. Averages have the effect of glossing over significant variations in any set of numbers. An overall average rate of voluntary resignations, for example, will disguise any crucial differences in their loss of staff between departments, business units, sites and occupational groups.

For example, a respectable voluntary resignation rate of 5% might easily be based on an average of 0% for senior managers and 20% for IT staff. The overall rate indicates that no action is required; while a more detailed analysis would reveal that there are serious problems in retaining the organisation's computer specialists. Obtaining specific data, such as this, is particularly important in relation to retention management, bearing in mind the potential costs involved. Where financial adjustments are required – a market supplement, a location allowance, a bonus or even a salary increase – it is usually essential that they are focused on areas where they can have the greatest impact.

It may also be worth taking into account the typical patterns of turnover's peaks and troughs that most employers experience. According to the government's *Labour Force Survey* (a massive poll of 61,000 households conducted every three months), labour turnover is highest among three groups:
● new recruits, where turnover stabilises after two years' service;
● younger staff; and

• semi- and unskilled clerical and manual workers (as well as some short-age occupations).

Detailed turnover statistics from one of the UK's largest employers, the **Civil Service**[6], illustrate the impact of these factors on labour turnover.

Among its workforce of 482,700, voluntary turnover in the Civil Service remains at a low level of 3.7%. However, it is more than twice as high in the lowest grades as in the highest (5.0% among administrative officers and assistants, compared with just 1.0% at senior levels 6 and 7, and 2.0% in the topmost ranks of the senior civil service).

But differences are most pronounced when the age of leavers is considered. The youngest workers aged under 20 have a voluntary turnover rate almost nine times higher than that of older workers aged 40 and above (15.7% versus 1.8%). And the first two years after appointment are the peak time for the loss of Civil Service staff, with an eighth (12.9%) of the civil servants with less than a year's service handing in their resignations, and a similar proportion (11.7%) doing so during their second year of service. Turnover within the first two years is thus at least treble the organisation's overall rate.

Other indices

As well as analysing resignation rates by such factors as service, grade and age, some employers calculate a stability index, which shows the extent to which the turbulence caused by labour turnover permeates the workforce. For example, even in the hospitality industry, where high turnover rates are prevalent, some employers have found that the same posts have a succession of recruits and leavers during the course of a year, while much of the workforce is unaffected.

A stability index is calculated by dividing the number of employees having a specified length of service (one year, two years, etc) by the workforce as a whole, and multiplying the result by 100. (As with the resignation rate, this can be broken down by department, grade and so on.)

A related method of computing turnover uses a **survival rate**. This is useful in focusing on the effectiveness of the recruitment, training and management of identifiable groups of staff – it is mainly used for new graduates. Alternatively, it can be one way of gauging the impact of a change in recruitment and selection practice on retention rates, comparing survival rates before and after the modification.

The survival-rate calculation involves dividing the number of people recruited in a specified year by the number in that group who are still employed at a certain later date, and multiplying the result by a 100. This calculation is often based on a time series of individual years, so, for example, the intake of 1995 is compared with the number surviving in 1996, 1997 and so on.

Finally, resignation rates can be calculated according to the **destination of leavers**. This is a method much favoured in parts of the public sector, where turnover rates are often broken down into those moving within the same area (within state schools, or the NHS, for example) or going elsewhere.

For example, the research conducted for the Review Body covering nursing staff, midwives, health visitors and professions allied to medicine[7], analyses turnover on the basis of transfers to other NHS units, to non-NHS employment, retirement and "other". It also computes a "wastage rate" of all those who leave which excludes transfers within the NHS. For nursing staff, midwives and health visitors, the wastage rate was 8.8% in the year to 31 March 2001, compared with an overall turnover rate of 12.4%. In some other public sector surveys, however, the terms are used in the opposite way, with "wastage" being used to denote turnover for all reasons, including inter-employer transfers.

Sources of labour turnover data

Labour turnover rates provide a visible and easy means of benchmarking an aspect of the management of people in organisations. While benchmarking is often considered to be purely an external process, labour turnover in particular lends itself to internal comparisons as well – between business units, departments and work groups and, equally, over time as trends emerge and change.

Both internal and external forms of benchmarking, though, need to be based on issues that are relevant to the organisation undertaking it – in particular, the choice of the calculation method to compute labour turnover, and the selection of comparators.

Typically, the benchmarking process is one of extremes; comparisons are made against a large data-set of statistics, or against just a few, carefully chosen, comparators. The published sources of labour turnover data lend themselves to the former approach, based on relatively large sets of statistics, while informal methods – such as benchmarking clubs, employers' networks and direct approaches – are more suited to the latter method.

Clubs and networks: There are several organisations offering bench-marking services to employers, most of which use labour turnover as one of the indices measured. The operation and use of such services is being great-ly aided by the use of the internet and email. Many of these benchmarking services have a strong presence on the web, and are set up for members to provide benchmarking data online, conduct online searches of databases and contact other members via email.

Some of the services provide large sets of statistics, often customised to a limited extent by sector, occupation or size, but most provide the more in-depth, bespoke type of service. Many offer several tiers of membership, based on the amount of support provided by the benchmarking agency. At their most intensive, some will provide full consultancy services where benchmarking is simply the initial phase of a tailored solution to an organ-isation's retention and other challenges.

Published sources: Benchmarking data on labour turnover that is avail-able in a published format falls into three main groups:

● **national surveys:** these bring together data on a range of industries, locations and occupations, and provide useful headline results to map overall trends. However, they rarely have sufficiently large sample sizes to enable detailed rates for specific jobs, sectors or areas to be computed reli-ably. National sources of labour turnover data are found in several one-off or occasional publications, often based on relatively small numbers of employers. The two main regular sources that draw on larger numbers of participants are conducted by the Confederation of British Industry (CBI)[8], which is usually published each spring, and the Chartered Institute of Personnel and Development (CIPD)[9], which is usually published towards the end of each year;

● **occupational surveys:** these cover one or more related occupations – often, the information on labour turnover is gathered from participating employers as part of a salary survey covering one or more occupational groups. Provided they are carefully conducted and analysed, salary surveys often provide the best source of data on specific jobs. Coverage is patchy, however, and such sources are often expensive because the purchase price has to cover the cost of conducting the whole survey and analysing the pay data as well as the information on turnover itself; and

● **industry surveys:** these cover one or more industries or a whole busi-ness sector. They are often conducted by membership organisations for the industry concerned, such as employers' associations, professional bodies and, formerly, National Training Organisations (NTOs). These surveys do not always provide as much detail as the occupational surveys, and may not be conducted as frequently as the annual cycle of many national and occupational surveys.

Unfortunately, NTOs and the services they provide are in a state of flux, or limbo in some cases. The government announced that they were to be replaced from March 2002 with a new network of Sector Skills Councils, but progress in setting up these replacements has been very slow and most industries are not yet covered. These changes have led to delays in undertaking research work, such as gathering labour turnover data.

There are also sources that fall outside this classification, such as surveys covering a local area, or those focusing on individual employers. Some of the latter are regular annual publications (such as the Civil Service's statistics mentioned above). Or, they may appear from time to time in reports and publications (for example, where a case study of a named employer includes its annual rate of labour turnover).

1. Sources of labour turnover data

Most sources shown here are priced publications or services. Enquirers should check the latest date of compilation for labour turnover data, its calculation method (crude wastage, resignation rates, or some other basis), the number of employers covered by the research, and the extent of detailed analyses (eg by particular occupations or industries). Because of the ending of government funding, most of the titles in the People Skills Scoreboard series are unlikely to be updated.

Clubs and networks
● *The benchmark index*, Small Business Service, information from nearest Business Link, or tel: 0870 011 1143, www.benchmarkindex.com.

● *Benchmarking service for UK central government: Public sector benchmarking service (PSBS)*, Cabinet Office and HM Customs & Excise, www.benchmarking.gov.uk.

● *Analysis of personnel activities and costs* (APAC), DLA-MCG Consulting, tel: 0870 241 1690.

● *HR benchmarker*, DLA-MCG Consulting Group, tel: 0870 241 1690, www.hrbenchmarker.com.

● *The HR index system*, EP–First, tel: 01491 411949, www.ep-first.com.

● The Benchmarking Centre Ltd, tel: 01494 558062, www.benchmarking.co.uk.

● EFQM Good Practice and Benchmarking Services, EFQM (European Foundation for Quality Management), tel: (+00 32) 2 775 3511, www.efqm.org.

● Best Practice Club, tel: 01223 355905, www.bpclub.com.

National surveys
● *Labour turnover*, Chartered Institute of Personnel and Development, available free, tel: 020 8971 9000, www.cipd.co.uk.

● *Absence and labour turnover*, CBI with AXA PPP Healthcare, tel: 020 7395 8071.

Occupations and industries
● *Actuaries: Salary survey of actuaries and actuarial students*, Remuneration Economics, tel: 020 8549 8726, www.celre.co.uk.

● *Building control workers: Building control workforce survey*, Employers' Organisation for Local Government, tel: 020 7296 6765, www.lg-employers.gov.uk.

● *Call centre staff: Call centres: reward and work–life strategies*, IRS with Call Centre Association Research Institute, IRS, tel Customer Services on 020 8662 2000, email: customer.services@lexisnexis.co.uk, www.irsonline.co.uk.

● *Civil servants: Civil service statistics*, Cabinet Office, available free from www.civil-service.gov.uk/statistics/css.htm.

● Computer/IT specialists:

Computer staff salary survey, Computer Economics, tel: 020 8549 8726, www.celre.co.uk.

Salaries and staff issues in IT, National Computing Centre, tel: 0161 242 2121, www.ncc.co.uk.

● *Construction industry: People Skills Scoreboard*, Construction Industry Training Board, tel: 01485 577498, www.citb.org.uk.

● *Engineers and engineering craftspeople: Salary survey of engineers*, Remuneration Economics, tel: 020 8549 8726, www.celre.co.uk.

● *Engineering companies' workforces: People Skills Scoreboard for the engineering industry*, Engineering Employers' Federation (tel: 020 7222 7777) with the Engineering and Marine Training Authority (tel: 01923 238441).

● *Financial and accountancy specialists: Salary survey of financial staff*, Remuneration Economics, tel: 020 8549 8726, www.celre.co.uk.

● Graduates:

The IES annual graduate review, Institute for Employment Studies, www.employment-studies.co.uk.

Graduate salaries and vacancies survey, Association of Graduate Recruiters (AGR), available to AGR members only, tel: 01926 623236, www.agr.org.uk.

● Healthcare staff:

Report on nursing staff, midwives and health visitors, Review Body for Nursing Staff, Midwives, Health Visitors and Professions Allied to Medicine, the Stationery Office, free from www.doh.gov.uk.

Report on professions allied to medicine, Review Body for Nursing Staff, Midwives, Health Visitors and Professions Allied to Medicine, the Stationery Office, free from www.doh.gov.uk.

● Higher education staff: *Recruitment and retention of staff in UK higher education*, IRS Research for the Universities and Colleges Employers' Association, 2002, tel: 020 7383 2444, www.ucea.ac.uk.

● Hospitality industry: *Labour market review*, Hospitality Training Foundation, tel: 020 8579 2400, www.htf.org.uk.

● Local authorities staff: *People Skills Scoreboard*, Local Government National Training Organisation and Employers' Organisation, tel: 020 7296 6600.

● Managers and directors:

National management salary survey, Remuneration Economic with the Chartered Management Institute, tel: 020 8549 8726, www.celre.co.uk.

National management salary survey: smaller business review, Remuneration Economics with the Chartered Management Institute, tel: 020 8549 8726, www.celre.co.uk.

● Motor industry, retailing: *The retail motor industry pay guide*, Sewells Information & Research, tel: 01733 468254, www.sewells.co.uk.

● Pensions specialists: *Survey of pension managers, consultants and administrators*, Remuneration Economics, tel: 020 8549 8726, www.celre.co.uk.

● Personnel/HR specialists:

Salary survey of HR/personnel staff, Remuneration Economics, tel: 020 8549 8726, www.celre.co.uk.

Personnel rewards, Croner Reward with CIPD, tel: 01785 813566, www.reward-group.co.uk.

● Property services sector (surveying; property management; estate agency; valuation; antiques and fine art): *Property services People Skills Scoreboard*, Property Services National Training Organisation, tel: 01392 423399, www.psnto.org, free.

● Retail staff: *Retail employment trends survey*, Retail Human Resources, tel: 020 7432 8800, www.rhr.co.uk.

● Sales and marketing: *Salary survey of sales and marketing staff*, Remuneration Economics, tel: 020 8549 8726, www.celre.co.uk.

● Schools:

Survey of teacher resignations and recruitment, Employers' Organisation for Local Government, tel: 020 7296 6765, www.lg-employers.gov.uk.

Statistics of education: teachers in England, the Stationery Office, free from www.dfes.gov.uk/statistics.

● Secretarial and clerical staff in London: *London secretarial and clerical rewards*, Croner Reward , tel: 01785 813566, www.reward-group.co.uk.

● Social services and care homes: *Social services workforce survey*, free from Employers' Organisation for Local Government, tel: 020 7296 6765, www.lg-employers.gov.uk.

● Steel and metals industry:*The People Skills Scoreboard for the steel and metals industry*, Metals Industry Skills & Performance, tel: 0114 244 6833, www.sinto.co.uk.

● Trading standards: *Trading standards workforce survey*, free from Employers' Organisation for Local Government, tel: 020 7296 6765, www.lg-employers.gov.uk.

● Voluntary organisations:

Annual voluntary sector salary survey, Remuneration Economics with NCVO, tel: 020 8549 8726, www.celre.co.uk.

Charity rewards, Croner Reward with Charity and Fundraising Appointments, tel: 01785 813566, www.reward-group.co.uk.

Exit interviews

Exit interviews and separation questionnaires (see next section) provide a means of asking departing employees their reasons for leaving the organisation. Both techniques vary in their timing, from the point at which the resignation is tendered until the final day at work, or beyond that in the case of postal questionnaires sent to the ex-employee's home address.

As their name implies, exit interviews involve one-to-one meetings between the departing employee and a manager where the individual's reasons for leaving are explored. Some employers use a variant of this technique, where a group of departing employees are brought together and they discuss, compare and contrast, their reasons for resigning and their attitudes towards the organisation. These are more akin to focus groups than classic exit interviews, however.

Any interview is potentially problematic, but those involving a departing employee raise particular challenges. The employee may suspect they will need another job reference at a future date (or may still be awaiting one for the job they are moving to), and will be reluctant to be brutally honest in case this jeopardises it. Depending on the point at which the interview is held, the interviewee may be subjectively over-critical, unrealistically nostalgic about the organisation or have forgotten their true reasons for leaving.

Checklist 2 highlights the key considerations involved in using exit interviews, based on feedback from personnel and HR managers with experience of using them. And checklist 3 provides a guide to conducting these interviews.

2. Exit interviews: the key issues

Based on feedback from personnel and HR managers, these are the key issues they have found determine the success or failure of exit interviews:

● **Resources:** Exit interviewing is extremely time-consuming, particularly where the workload is not shared among line managers (see Interviewers below). It may be better to focus the use of exit interviews on key members of staff, the jobs that are most difficult to replace or of most importance to the organisation, or some other limiting factor. Where some employees are not based at the main office or work irregular hours, it may be more cost-effective to administer separation questionnaires and reserve interviews for more accessible leavers.

● **Timing:** Finding a mutually-convenient time for the interview is important, but leavers tend to be most honest and accurate when they are interviewed towards the middle of their notice period.

● **Interviewers:** Most employers ask personnel and HR specialists to conduct the interviews, with good reason. Interviewees are more likely to be open and honest where the interviewer does not have a line relationship with them. It is also more likely that specialists will have acquired the necessary interviewing and interpersonal skills, or, if not, it will be easier to train a relatively small number of personnel in them.

● **Question structure:** Most employers develop a structured interview schedule that interviewers use, and most ensure that the schedule is revised to ensure it remains up to date and accurate.

● **Questions asked 1:** The choice of questions should be governed by the organisation's own circumstances, but should aim to ensure that the interviewee's prime reasons for leaving are discovered – in particular, which reason(s) contributed most to their decision to resign. Many employers also obtain information on the individual's new salary (for pay-parity purposes), some ask about how the person heard about their new job (to check that the current employer is using the most effective recruitment methods), and ask about a range of other factors.

● **Questions asked 2:** Additional factors that could be asked during the interview include the leaver's attitude towards their induction and its perceived effectiveness, and their views on the effectiveness of internal communications systems, the state of morale within the organisation and areas for improvement within the company.

● **Analysing the feedback:** Most employers ask interviewers to record the interviewee's responses on a copy of the standard interview schedule. This ensures that the feedback from several interviewees can be readily compared and analysed. However, many personnel and HR managers tell us that they also need to find another means of capturing feedback that their interviewees find upsetting or consider highly confidential, where the use of the form would not be appropriate. Some interviewers present a supplementary report on such issues, based on brief notes made at the time, or record their impressions once the interview has been concluded.

● **Acting on the feedback:** The ways in which employers use the feedback gained from exit interviews include: using it to inform the analysis of labour turnover data; compiling reports that are presented to senior management; providing feedback to line managers; and using it to inform reviews of recruitment, retention and other personnel practices.

3. Exit interviews: an interviewer's guide

1. Develop an interview schedule, listing the topics to be covered. Ensure that most questions are open-ended: these elicit explanations, rather than closed yes–no replies. Ensure that the means of recording the answers have been considered; providing space on the schedule is one option.

2. Before the interview, the interviewer should explain to the leaver the aims of the interview and, if possible, give them a copy of the interview schedule. This will give the leaver a chance to think in advance about the topics to be covered, and could improve the quality of their feedback.

3. A room that provides a calm, undisturbed and confidential venue for the interview should be found; furniture should be arranged in an informal layout.

4. The interviewee should be given assurances that their feedback will remain confidential, unless otherwise agreed by themselves. The way in which their feedback is to be communicated to others, such as their line manager, should be explained and discussed.

5. The value of their feedback should be emphasised in order to encourage the interviewee to talk frankly and freely, such as the fact that what they say could make a difference to their colleagues and the organisation as a whole.

6. During the interview, note-taking should be limited in order to avoid inhibiting the interviewee and placing a psychological barrier between interviewer and interviewee.

7. The interviewer should remain neutral, trying not to react to or pass judgment on the information given by the interviewee, nor defend individuals or the organisation.

8. As well as discussing the shortcomings of individuals and the organisation, the interviewee should be encouraged to talk about things they enjoyed as part of working for the employer.

9. At the close of the interview, as well as thanking them for their participation, it may be appropriate to thank the interviewee for the work they have done while employed by the organisation and the contribution they have made.

Separation questionnaires

Advantages: Separation questionnaires provide another means of gathering feedback from leavers about the reasons for their departure, their attitudes towards the organisation and any of the additional factors that exit interviews can also explore.

This technique is less labour-intensive than exit interviewing; leavers are given a self-completion questionnaire that they complete at a time convenient to themselves and return to a nominated person (not always a member of staff).

Separation questionnaires, as we noted above, can also be useful where some leavers are difficult to interview because of their location, working hours or where they have already left the organisation. In such cases, the survey form can be posted to the individual's home address, enclosing a prepaid return envelope.

The ability to obtain feedback once the employee has left the organisation provides one of the main benefits of the use of separation questionnaires. There are several logistical problems in conducting exit interviews once individuals have left their jobs, although this is often the best time to obtain honest feedback on the reasons that motivated them to resign.

Individuals who are still working their notice period are still linked in several ways to the employer. They remain in the same environment, and issues concerned with the line manager, colleagues or other staff may be too sensitive for the leavers to raise while they continue working alongside them. The leavers may still be waiting for references to be provided, and could be concerned that their feedback could prejudice them. And they are in the process of working through a psychological period of separation, and this may bias their feedback in either an unrealistically positive or negative way.

Disadvantages: However, there are also serious drawbacks to the use of separation questionnaires. The design and layout of questionnaires requires considerable skill and experience, although this is not always recognised. Often, the first indication that a survey contains design flaws or suffers from a poor or unclear layout will be the difficulty that the organisation encounters in trying to analyse and interpret the forms that leavers complete. Less obviously, a very poor response rate to a questionnaire might also indicate that problems exist. (More generally, surveys often suffer from low response rates, reducing not only the quantity of data but is quality – there is often a danger that the respondents will not be a true cross-section of those surveyed.)

It is, therefore, important to pilot new questionnaires and any changes to existing forms before they are introduced. Those given the form can be asked to give feedback on it, and suggest ways in which it could be improved.

Separation questionnaires suffer from further drawbacks. They lack the interaction of interviews, so the context underlying a leaver's replies cannot always be uncovered; nor, of course, can follow-up questions be posed to clarify or elaborate an individual's answers.

More generally, survey forms are best suited to obtaining fairly structured feedback, through the use of predetermined options, such as lists of choices, straight yes–no responses and attitudinal questions, where respondents choose a number from a scale. Although questionnaires can leave space for respondents to write in their own answers, views and comments, such questions are often skipped or answered in an unsatisfactory manner. There is, too, the added time and difficulty in analysing open responses on the part of the survey administrator.

Piloting the questionnaire: A pilot exercise can provide important insights into the potential usefulness of the survey form, leading to improvements that increase the potential response rate and the quality and ease of analysis of the information supplied. The pilot should aim to address:
● the length of time it takes to complete the questionnaire;
● the wording of the questions (are questions capable of being interpreted in two, or more, different ways?) (are the questions clear or do they serve to confuse the user?);
● the clarity of the instructions provided about completing the questionnaire (such as the date by which it should be returned, the return destination, the confidentiality guarantee, and the way in which specific questions should be answered); and
● the ability of the questions to provide high-quality, easily analysed information.

It is important to use a cross-section of individuals who provide a reasonable match with the target audience of the survey. For the purposes of the pilot, an extra sheet can be attached to the questionnaire that highlights the areas where the organisation is most anxious to obtain feedback. These issues can themselves be phrased as questions, to which the extra sheet can be used to gather participants' views and comments:
● "How long did the questionnaire take you to complete?";
● "Were the instructions clear?";
● "Were any questions unclear or ambiguous"?:
● "Did you object to answering any of the questions?";
● "Was the layout of the form clear?"
● "Did you find the layout attractive?"
● "Thinking through your own experiences of working for [name of employer], has the questionnaire overlooked any important issues that you would want to be asked about if you were leaving?"
● "Do you have any other comments?"

4. Designing separation questionnaires

The points in this checklist are also relevant to the design of many other types of questionnaire, such as employee attitude surveys (see next section).

● **Keep it brief:** Ensure that all questions add real value, rather than being nice-to-know options. Long questionnaires are off-putting, reducing the response rate and encouraging respondents to skip particular questions or whole sections. They also take longer to analyse and code.

● **Confidentiality:** Where a survey is to remain confidential, this fact should be stated as often as possible: in the covering letter, at the beginning of the survey form, and at the end of the form; this guarantee, where it is trusted, will increase the response rate and the honesty and completeness of the replies.

● **Introduction:** The purpose of the questionnaire should be stated, even where it has also appeared in the covering letter. Similarly, guarantees of confidentially should be repeated. The person or body issuing the survey, and those responsible for analysing it, should also be listed.

● **Logical order:** The questions should follow a logical order, grouping related topics together and moving from general to specific in each section.

● **First questions:** The questionnaire should begin softly, asking easy and non-threatening questions. Generally, these will be descriptive-type questions ("How long did you . . ?"; "Where did you work . . ?"). Open-ended questions should be asked later on in the form.

● **Building up:** Questions that require more time to complete, or are more sensitive and probing, should be placed towards the end of the questionnaire. If a survey creates a good initial impression, by the time the respondent reaches tougher questions they should be more disposed to engage with them.

● **One issue at a time:** A classic mistake with survey design involves covering more than one issue or topic in the same question. Not only is this confusing for the respondent, the survey analysts will not be able to interpret the replies in a reliable way.

● **Simplicity:** Questions should almost invariably be straightforward, simple and short. Where a topic requires detailed investigation, a series of separate questions should be asked, each focusing on a different aspect or going successively into more and more detail.

● **Routing:** In such cases where follow-up questions are required, ensure that the respondent is given clear instructions about how they should answer the questions. In particular, where their answer to a question determines which subsequent question they should answer, routing instructions are required ("If you answered Yes to [x], now please go to question 4." "If you answered No to [x], now please go to the next question, ie question 3").

● **Variety:** Even short questionnaires benefit from providing the respondent with a variety of types of question. Alongside factual questions, attitudinal ones can be asked.

● **Design 1:** Where budgets permit, the survey should be professionally designed and printed; if not, someone with good desk-top-publishing or word-processing skills should undertake the layout of the questionnaire. If a supply of professionally-printed forms cannot be afforded, copies should each be printed out using a laser printer, rather than being photocopied.

● **Design 2:** The typeface should be chosen for legibility and appearance; there is an optimum point size for legibility, although large-print versions (and copies as computer files) should be available for people with disabilities.

● **Design 3:** Where open questions are given, there should be sufficient space for the replies, and the distance between the lines should be large enough to accommodate the size of most respondents' handwriting. Where tick boxes are provided, they should be large enough to contain a typically-sized hand-written tick or cross.

Employee attitude surveys

Exit interviews and separation questionnaires can be thought of as post-mortems – they investigate the loss of staff after the event (in this case, after the decision to leave has been taken and notice has been given). The information that these techniques provide is of use in assisting the retention of others, but rarely leads to the individual concerned being persuaded to stay.

However, if it is possible to identify the causes of discontent before they irrevocably damage the employment relationship, then this is obviously a better and more cost-effective approach.

Employee attitude surveys are one of the prime ways of investigating workforce discontent. Such surveys can show how the employer is faring in terms of its employee relations, and explore employees' attitudes to proposed changes in the organisation and to working practices. It can sound out employees on their perceptions about the fairness of reward systems, and on the abilities of those managing them.

Successful attitude surveys depend on sound research methodologies. In particular, the questionnaire used must be well designed, employees must be convinced that their replies will remain anonymous, and information about the ethical and efficient conduct, analysis and use of the survey must be effectively communicated.

Where the research is flawed, more than the usefulness of the survey itself can be impaired. The exercise can damage employee relations and morale. And even where the whole process is efficient, the mere fact of asking employees their opinions raises expectations that must be met. Surveys that lead to no perceptible action by management can cause damage internally and undermine employees' confidence in any subsequent consultation exercise.

Timing of surveys

It seems that employers conducting employee attitude surveys do so on a regular basis. Four in 10 (41%) of the personnel and HR managers we contacted whose organisations conduct surveys do so on a 12-month cycle, and the same proportion does so every 18 to 24 months.

One-off surveys can highlight particular areas of dissatisfaction that could lead to the resignation of valued members of staff (as well as reduced motivation, performance and attendance among those who do not leave). But regularly-conducted ones offer the added dimension of tracking changes over time. The effectiveness of the action taken in response to survey feedback can be tracked over successive surveys, as can the impact of the various changes that are often found in organisations. The consequences of a reorganisation, redundancy exercise, revised bonus system or a new equal opportunities policy, for example, can all be investigated and tracked.

Use of consultants

Seven in 10 (70%) organisations use consultants in some form or other to help conduct their employee attitude surveys. More than half (45%) of this group use consultants exclusively to conduct staff surveys. However, the majority of respondents (66%) uses consultants in a more limited way to analyse the results of the survey.

Using consultants in the process, especially to analyse results, should make employees feel more comfortable about being open and honest, because it provides an added guarantee of confidentiality. It should also reassure them that the organisation is committed to the process. Having an independent outsider analyse the results should also mean that findings are more balanced, less likely to be (consciously or subconsciously) biased and more objective. Consultants with experience of conducting staff surveys are also more likely to identify trends and areas for concern that may have been missed internally.

The other advantage of using outside consultants with specific expertise in the area is gaining access to their benchmarking information, gathered from conducting surveys with similar organisations.

Organisations that use consultants consider that they are value for money. More than nine in 10 (95%) told us that they felt consultants involved with employee attitude surveys add a lot or some value to the process.

Focus groups

One in five (21%) organisations indicated that they hold focus groups as part of the way they conduct employee attitude surveys. Focus groups can be conducted in the initial stages of the process, when designing the survey questionnaire. They are also useful in helping to disseminate findings and get people's reactions to the results, thus ensuring employees continue to feel involved in the process. Focus groups are also useful in developing action plans and proposals for moving forward, based on the survey's findings.

Reasons for conducting surveys

The organisations we contacted conduct employee surveys to investigate employees' perceptions of one or more of the following issues:
- the style and performance of managers (issues covered by 89% of employers' attitude surveys);
- internal communications (86%);
- morale (83%);
- job satisfaction (83%);
- the organisation's values (80%);
- opportunities for career development (79%);
- the working environment (76%);
- teamwork (73%);
- training opportunities (73%);
- senior management's performance (73%);
- relationships with work colleagues (67%);
- pay (65%); and
- benefits (59%).

Design and piloting

Attitude surveys require careful development, paying attention to the design of the questions, their wording, the completion instructions and the overall layout and appearance of the form. Piloting of the questionnaire provides a valuable means of checking that the survey has paid attention to all these criteria. Checklist 4 above highlights the main issues concerned with survey development.

Other sources

Generally, no one method of gaining insights into employees' views and motivation provides sufficient information upon which to base a retention-management strategy. There are many other sources, other than the main ones which we discussed above, that could prove useful to personnel and HR managers.

Absence rates, disciplinary cases, complaints made via the grievance procedure, tribunal applications and allegations of bullying or harassment can all suggest areas for further exploration where there may be underlying problems that could be driving high resignation levels.

Formal performance-management systems provide a forum for each employee to have a discussion with their line manager about their performance, their aspirations and the ways in which their performance could be improved. These conversations represent potentially rich sources of feedback on employees' needs (the provision of training, for example, can be a powerful retention motivator) and the frustrations and problems they face. However, performance-management systems are rarely set up to capture and communicate this information in a systematic way – ensuring confidentiality, in particular, is a major issue.

Absences from work, poor timekeeping and performance problems are often considered to be signs of demotivation, and of a psychological withdrawal from the organisation. Usually, these factors are seen as alternatives to resignation – employees "leave but stay". However, research among retail staff in the USA raises the possibility that these three "job-avoidance" factors are precursors to leaving the organisation, rather than alternatives to it.

If this is true, then data that highlights employees who have worse-than-average absence rates, timekeeping and performance could provide a useful means of targeting retention initiatives. The researchers suggest that these job-avoidance patterns have an underlying cause that could be targeted.

Often, they suggest, dissatisfaction stems from conflict between caring commitments and leisure interests, on the one hand, and inflexible working patterns on the other[10].

Why staff resign

Too much has been made in the media of the weakening of the bond between employers and workers. It is simply not true to state without qualification that "jobs for life" have ceased to exist. In some industries, long-term job tenure has never existed, but, alongside this, the average length of time that employees remain with a particular employer has hardly altered across the economy as a whole, according to the authoritative Labour Force Survey.

This means that, for many employees in many sectors of the economy, the strength of the "psychological contract" – the emotional bond between each individual and their employer – plays an important part in whether or not they decide to leave their organisation. Factors affecting their identification with, and attachment to, their employer – "push" factors – usually contribute to a large extent to someone's decision-making process about moving on.

Poor supervision (such as arbitrary, unfair or uninspiring management), lack of opportunities for training and development and, in exceptional cases, poor pay are prime contributors to the weakening of the psychological or emotional contract. Issues such as these are, to a large extent, under the control of the organisation. Through them, resignations can be influenced and controlled.

At law firm **DLA**, for example, research among lawyers (including recent graduates) who had left the organisation in the previous 18 months showed that "most people didn't leave for more money, but in search of more experience"[11]. A coordinated retention strategy, developed over a five-year period, succeeded in slashing labour turnover among DLA's recent graduate recruits from 40% to just 4%.

"Pull" factors, in contrast, tend – low-paying industries aside – to have more influence once the emotional ties between employee and employer have been weakened. Typically, research has shown that some factor or combination of factors within the organisation causes an employee to begin to look for another job. At this stage, and not before, they compare what other employers offer with their present circumstances. In particular, a jobseeker is seldom likely to move to a job that offers a lower salary, unless it offers significantly better career progression or they are so desperate to leave that a salary cut is acceptable.

This second set of factors, coming later on in the process of switching employers, naturally tends to be uppermost in the minds of those who have tendered their resignation. This is the point where many employers canvass the views of their staff about their reasons for leaving, and leads to an over-reporting of the influence of competitors' rates of pay, terms and conditions.

The *Labour Force Survey*[12], the most authoritative source of information for some aspects of employees' experience of employment, shows that about a quarter of all labour turnover is due to reasons that are under the direct control of – and are predictable by – the employer: dismissals; redundancies; temporary jobs; normal retirements. Unpredictable resignations make up a further one-half of the total, , with the final one-quarter of all departures falling into an undefined "other" category.

The survey also gathers data on the reasons that are prompting employees to consider leaving their jobs at some future point. For full-time employees, pay is cited by many of the intending leavers as a factor in their decision to look elsewhere – but almost as many also mention other issues. For part-timers, their reasons convey an impression of being driven more by personal circumstances, such as their caring commitments. For example, relatively fewer part-time employees cite pay as a factor, while a great many more mention their desire to find a job that offers longer hours of work. Unlike full-timers, many also say that their current job is just a stop-gap that they have taken while looking for a more suitable one.

An international study of retention issues by Hay Management Consultants[13] confirms the *Labour Force Survey*'s finding that pay is not the only, nor often the main, reason why employees begin to look for another job. Instead, "employees are most likely to become discontented and leave when their skills or talents or not properly developed, or when superiors fail to take an interest in an employee's career development," the study says.

Being given access to training and development opportunities represents a more important factor for some groups than others. Among new graduates, who tend to be focused on their employer's ability to cater for their longer-term career development, access to better career prospects represents the main reason why they will leave their jobs, according to a representative sample of 750 employees who had graduated in 2000[14]. The poll, conducted for the CIPD, found that four in 10 (40%) new graduates will switch employers to further their career, while only one in four (23%) will do so to gain a higher salary.

The validity of these findings was confirmed when the graduates were asked to give the reasons why they would not change jobs. Again, career factors came top (cited by 40%), with the offer of a salary increase coming a poor second (18%). Finally, to test these attitudes still further, the graduates were asked whether they would move to another employer for better career prospects but at a lower salary. Here, a third (36%) were "very" prepared to do so, and a further four in 10 (42%) were "somewhat" inclined to do so.

Acas on the impact of pay as a reason for leaving

"Pay is perhaps most frequently assumed to be the reason for workers leaving, but it is rarely the only reason. Where workers can compare their earnings unfavourably with those of others in the same industry or the same locality, then pay levels do affect labour turnover. Even so, people remain in jobs they like, although higher-paid work is available. Once a high level of labour turnover has been reached, however, low rates of pay make it much more difficult to reverse the trend."

Source: Absence and labour turnover, Acas, 2003, www.acas.gov.uk.

Changes in the psychological contract

Few surveys are able to provide accurate information about whether employees are more or less likely to want to leave their employer than in the past. However, academics Andrew Oswald and Jonathan Gardner have undertaken longitudinal research in this area.

They point out that UK employers enjoy remarkably high levels of job satisfaction among their employees, compared with their counterparts in many other advanced economies. "For example, on a standard numerical scale from 1 ('I am not satisfied at all') up to 7 ('I am completely satisfied with my job'), the single most common answer is a 6."[15]

However, comparing these and other results during the 1990s, the researchers find that there has been a "remarkably large" increase in stress among public sector workers and a smaller rise in the private sector. Job satisfaction also fell in the past decade among workers in the public sector and among women generally, while it remained much the same among men in the private sector.[16]

It does not automatically follow that these measures of dissatisfaction will lead to higher rates of labour turnover, but intuitively the loss of job satisfaction and rising levels of stress do seem likely to have an impact on retention rates.

Managing retention

We noted above that more or less any major aspect of an employee's working conditions can exert some influence over their decision to stay or go. Obviously, some issues are more important than others – their relationship with their line manager, whether or not they believe they are being fairly treated, their hours of work or pay, and gaining access to training and promotion opportunities, for example.

Checklist 5 analyses the most popular ways in which employers are currently managing retention. It serves to highlight the areas of employees' working lives where the pressure points are greatest – their lack of involvement and understanding of the business; their desire to be given access to training and development opportunities; the shortcomings of line managers' supervisory abilities; and problems with basic terms and conditions.

Several issues arise from the information given in checklist 5.

Limited action: First, many employers are taking little or no action to control their loss of staff through resignations. Of all the various actions shown in the checklist, only the top three initiatives are being taken by a majority of employers.

Narrow focus: Second, most employers are tackling retention problems in a fairly narrow way. Not only are many employers adopting just a few of the seven actions shown in the checklist, but only one in eight (12.1%) are going beyond this limited list to try out other ways of managing their labour turnover. However, there are indications that this is changing. Certainly, many of the most successful initiatives to manage retention have involved an integrated approach, where several measures are introduced at the same time.

Different emphases: Third, different types of employer are often adopting contrasting ways of managing retention. Greater proportions of public sector employers are improving communications, providing training and development, tackling line managers' skills and offering flexible working than employers in general. In contrast, service sector companies in the private sector are relatively more likely to improve pay as a retention measure than employers as a whole.

5. Managing retention: the most popular responses

The action being taken by employers to improve staff retention is focusing on the areas shown below in descending order of prevalence; the information is based on feedback we obtained from more than 430 personnel and HR specialists:

● improved communication with employees (71.0% of employers addressing their retention difficulties) – this measure is primarily intended to improve the psychological contract between employers and their employees. Better communications pave the way for a better-informed and involved workforce, that will have a greater understanding of the business and feel part of it;

● provided training and development opportunities (69.5%) – this measure can produce a direct benefit in terms of improved skills, but it can also raise employees' confidence and show them that their employer is interested in their personal development;

● improved the skills of line managers (53.2%);

● offered more flexible hours of work (46.3%) – the issue of flexible working will move higher up the agenda now that a new statutory framework giving the right to request a move to flexible working is in place (see chapter 9 Equal opportunities and diversity for more information);

● increased pay (39.5%);

● improved benefits (34.2%);

● increased opportunities to change jobs (31.0%) – fewer employees now have the assurance that they have a clear upwards career path in their organisations, following successive reorganisations and the removal of layers of management. The next best alternative for some individuals may be the offer of different work that might offer variety and fresh challenges; and

● various other measures not listed above (12.1%).

Integrated approaches

In checklist 5 above, we highlighted the seven most popular methods of managing retention, and noted that most employers are only using a few such measures.

However, personnel and HR managers are increasingly telling us that single retention initiatives prove far less effective in retaining key staff and reducing levels of labour turnover than integrated strategies where several mutually supporting measures are adopted.

For example, the NHS faces many challenges in retaining staff, and the inner-city location – high house prices, high crime rates, poor environment – makes retention a particular challenge for employers such as King's College Hospital NHS Trust. But the deployment of a range of initiatives helped it to cut voluntary staff turnover by almost a third in just one year (see case study A). And most of the other examples given later in this chapter of named employer practice involve a multi-pronged approach to managing retention.

Case study A. King's College Hospital NHS Trust

The recruitment and retention difficulties facing the NHS nationally are exacerbated by the inner-city location of King's College Hospital NHS Trust, But, as a result of a number of different initiatives aimed at improving the employment experience of its staff, King's managed to reduce its voluntary staff turnover from 17.0% in March 2002, to 12.1% a year later.

The HR department at King's has adopted a multi-pronged approach to tackling turnover. It told us that: "We can't attribute the reduction in the number of people leaving to any one initiative. There are several, equally important parts to the jigsaw that help encourage people to stay."

A key starting point in the trust's strategy is to undertake regular employee attitude surveys, and act on the results. "The survey we carried out in 2001 was used to write the 2002/03 retention strategy," we were told. "That survey threw up a number of areas for improvement that we have responded to, such as ensuring regular annual appraisals and personal development plans for all employees. Another high priority was leadership training for managers."

A crucial feature of the trust's approach to retaining staff is "Kingsflex", its flexible-working programme. The policy was introduced in 2000 and was ahead of its time in the level and range of flexible working arrangements on offer. In fact, in the year of its introduction, the trust won the Health Service Journal's "Employer of the Year" award, and other trusts have been keen to follow in its footsteps by introducing similar policies.

As well as offering a range of the more common flexible-working arrangements, such as part-time hours and jobsharing, King's does its best to be as flexible as possible to help staff balance their work and home lives. Therefore, the policy also enables employees to work staggered hours. This could mean a nine-day fortnight, for example. Staff can also buy or sell their annual leave, within certain boundaries, providing employees with the flexibility to take extra holiday to look after school-age offspring during the long summer break, for instance.

King's also continually aims to narrow the gap between the expectations of would-be recruits and the reality of the role. "New employees will be disappointed, and possibly leave, if the job does not match up to their expectations," its staff resourcing manager said. "We therefore make sure that candidates are given realistic information about the job, and we encourage people to visit the hospital so that they can view their prospective working environment."

King's College Hospital is very pleased with the impact that these initiatives have had on staff turnover. Among staff working on the hospital wards, turnover reached as high as 19.0% in some cases, but had been reduced to 6.6% by mid-2003. "Reducing the number of vacancies is a self-fulfilling prophecy, as it has resulted in a feel-good factor at ward level, which has itself had a positive effect on retention."

Aspects of retention

Organisational culture

Corporate culture is a difficult concept to describe; yet it is also difficult to deny that each organisation has its own distinct approach to "the way we do things around here".

During recruitment, many employers pay attention to ensuring a reasonable match between their culture and the interests, motivations and predispositions of potential new employees. As well as problems where there is a mismatch between corporate culture and individual employees, some organisations seem to find that their culture is causing problems on a broader scale. For some reason, the culture may provoke a reaction that encourages employees to leave and work for an organisation where the climate is more to their liking.

Many employers usually embark on cultural change initiatives for business-related reasons, such as a desire to become more customer focused, more competitive or profitable. But, in the process, some discover that the changes they introduce have broader benefits in terms of improving retention rates.

For example, the cultural change programmes at private healthcare provider Bupa (see case study B) and the Defence Aviation Repair Agency (DARA) have both had significant benefits in terms of improving these organisations' ability to retain staff.

At **DARA**, labour turnover has fallen significantly at all four of its sites. For example, staff turnover at its Almondbank plant in Scotland stood at around 20% in 1999; four years later, it stood at just 2%. However, the primary aim of its change programme was to transform the organisation from an arm of the civil service to a commercial company, rather than improve staff retention. It transformed the working climate from a hierarchical, military-style culture to one that empowers the workforce and involves them in the decision-making process.

New behavioural competency frameworks and a system of self-directed teamworking for shopfloor staff have been introduced. Leadership development training was provided for all managers to communicate the reasons for change and to equip managers with the skills to train employees. As part of this programme, managers were required to spend time working on the shopfloor in order to help build closer working relationships with employees, and widen their own perspective.

Employees at DARA have been encouraged to take a greater interest in training and improving their skills, and assuming greater responsibility for their own work. An employee development scheme has been launched that is intended to help employees gain promotion and move through the organisation.

The desired behaviours that underlie the new culture are supported by a new reward framework, which included an upfront pay rise to help embed the new culture, and harmonised terms and conditions which now apply across the business. The organisation told us that it believes that the new ways of working and enhanced job satisfaction experienced by employees account for a large part of why people are choosing to stay, rather than leave DARA.

Hillarys Blinds, a leading supplier of made-to-measure window blinds based in Nottingham and Washington-upon-Tyne, has put in place a number of initiatives aimed at increasing its profile as a quality local employer and making the company "an exceptional place to work". Part of the impetus for the change programme came from the recognition that a happier, more motivated workforce can provide better customer service, which has a direct impact on business success.

As well as introducing a new benefits package for employees, including an occupational health scheme and additional holiday entitlement, the company has enhanced its communication and recognition practices. A new intranet site, noticeboards and a relaunched staff newsletter are helping to build the employer brand, while a new charity committee and works council encourage employee involvement in the business.

Other initiatives aimed at improving the work environment include family fun days and a casual dress code. The company told us that it was very pleased with the impact of the changes on its working climate; the annual staff attitude survey has revealed that employees are happier too. Labour turnover rates have improved by 20%.

Case study B. Bupa

A five-year change programme at private healthcare provider Bupa has netted the company several top HR awards and seen its staff turnover levels drop dramatically. However, the original driver for the cultural change was much wider than staff retention. Bupa wanted to create an environment based on a new vision – "Taking care of the lives in our hands" – where employees would feel valued and respected and want to work for the company. Its HR director explained to us that: "The health and care business is very personal and that ethos should be extended to our employees."

The first stage of the cultural change initiative was to train Bupa's managers to carry through the organisation's new behaviours. This comprised a "leading-one-life" development programme that covered areas such as leadership, the role of the manager and their potential impact on people. The programme introduced new practices to reinforce the new inclusive management style, such as 360-degree assessment.

As part of Bupa's commitment to valuing employees and their contribution to the business, a new recognition scheme was introduced. The "one-life" award scheme encourages input from employees to improve customer service and, in its first year, produced more than 700 suggestions for improvements. "We generally use about one-third of the ideas that are put forward, which have a direct impact on the level of service we provide," said Bupa's HR director. "Once a year, we put on a big lunch for the top customer service employees where they can bring their partners. The event has tremendous impact, with a number of £2,000 annual prizes awarded."

"The logic of our vision for the business – that each customer is important and unique – is that employees also deserve the same treatment. Our flexible working package – 'balancing one life' – is the result of that vision. We try to accommodate employees' personal commitments by offering a wide range of possible working patterns."

Bupa has won a national award for the work–life balance approach represented by "balancing one life". Initially, it conducted a one-year pilot scheme to trial the different working arrangements it intended to offer. Each generic job was tested in every possible working pattern to determine whether the arrangement could work in practice. Now, when an employee requests flexible hours, Bupa can immediately advise on the practical options that are available for that particular role.

Before Bupa embarked on its transformation journey in 1995, its annual staff survey – termed the Service Organisation Profile (SOP) – ranked the organisation's performance around the 40th percentile, amongthe poorest ranking companies. Just a few years on, Bupa's employees have pushed this score up to the 70th percentile. The survey benchmarks other employers using the same method – based on a US index that measures factors such as leadership, adaptability to change and customer orientation.

Although improving retention was not the primary motive for its all-embracing change programme, Bupa has witnessed very tangible results in this area. In its core insurance business, staff turnover had dropped from 23% to 13% by mid-2003. Bupa's hospitals have seen the overall turnover rate drop by nearly 10 percentage points, while in its care homes the number of staff voluntarily leaving has fallen by 20%.

Empowerment and job redesign

Routine, repetitive jobs can induce boredom in many employees who then move elsewhere to find different, if not more demanding, work. Equally frustratingly – for employees and customers alike – can be the situation where the limitations of a role mean that queries and problems have to be passed up the chain to another person or department for resolution.

"Empowerment" is one term for an approach that aims to address both issues, by encouraging (or requiring) each employee to accept a certain amount of personal responsibility for making decisions and resolving problems. For employers, there is the potential for customer service to improve. Decisions can be reached without passing the customer from "pillar to post". And problems can often be resolved before they become major issues. Empowerment often means that each employee becomes their own trouble-shooter and progress-chaser.

At the same time, many employees will welcome being given greater responsibility, increased flexibility and autonomy. This can improve job satisfaction and help in the management of retention. Empowerment and job redesign are often interlinked; it is difficult to introduce empowerment without making changes to job tasks and responsibilites, as witnessed by Fujitsu Services, for example (see case study C).

Case study C. Fujitsu Services

High turnover is one of the biggest pressures facing call centres, with some parts of the industry grappling with employee turnover rates well above 100%. Not long ago, staff turnover reached as high as 42% among the front-line staff at Fujitsu Services' UK call centre.

Since implementing a major change programme that transformed the call centre operation into one based on the customer's needs, turnover has improved dramatically to around 8%. The company's head of call centre strategy and operational development told us that: "Since we have redesigned the operation of the call centre, employees are definitely more satisfied with their jobs and therefore more motivated to stay."

In order to turn around the business, Fujitsu investigated the rationale behind call centres. It knew that many sites have a simple concept. Employees in frontline jobs dealing with callers are often employed in low-level tasks, requiring considerable amounts of supervision and being measured closely. Response times, the number of calls answered per hour and other metrics are commonly used.

However, Fujitsu discovered that such a set up at the front line does not necessarily result in a low-cost operation. In its industry, many of the calls were coming from the same customers who were not satisfied with the information given to them when they first called, or who had not received a complete answer. The company realised that 50% to 70% of demand was preventable; in other words, the way in which jobs in the call centre were structured was responsible for creating its own demand.

Fujitsu therefore designed and implemented a system called "Sense and respond". The new system introduced a culture where employees are encouraged to deal with the root cause of customers' queries, and are assessed on how they address these problems.

"Front-line staff effectively now design their own jobs," the company told us. "Under the old system, if an employee couldn't answer the query, the work would get passed on to someone else. Now, frontline staff are encouraged to deal with the whole problem and, importantly, to develop the skills to do so. If extra training is needed, we provide it."

In practice, this means that responsibility for more sophisticated tasks has been transferred to the front line, with the twin effect of both upskilling those individuals and significantly reducing secondary demand from customers. This revolution in the way that work is organised at Fujitsu's call centre was supported by in-depth training programmes for all employees.

A dramatically improved retention rate is not the only successful outcome of Fujitsu's change programme. Operating costs have been cut by between 20% and 35%, and customer satisfaction ratings are up by at least 25%.

Recruitment

It is ironic that recruitment – the process at the opposite end of the staffing spectrum to retention – can have such a major impact on staff resignation rates.

The process of matching a vacancy's requirements to the skills and experience offered by a group of candidates is far from straightforward. There are clear-cut criteria, such as skills, knowledge and relevant formal qualifications. But, even here, problems can occur where recruiters raise their sights too high, or accept what is on offer even when it falls below what the job requires.

Criteria that are pitched too high can mean that the recruit is overqualified for the job, and becomes bored and leaves. Unrealistically high recruitment criteria also expose employers to potential liability for unlawful unfair discrimination.

Conversely, when an under-skilled candidate is accepted, the recruit may be overwhelmed by the job's demands, fail to do well, and is either disciplined for poor performance or becomes disillusioned and burnt out. In either scenario, an early departure is likely.

Addressing these issues involves ensuring that the recruitment criteria have been identified in a careful, objective manner (see chapter 1 Filling your vacancies), and that recruiters have been trained to conduct recruitment and selection in an effective, unbiased manner.

But there is much that organisations can do to involve candidates in the process, by ensuring that they are fully aware of the demands of the job and of what working for the organisation would be like (see chapter 1 Filling your vacancies).

At fast-food retailer **Pret a Manger**, its sophisticated recruitment and selection approach provides one of the main reasons for the company's lower-than-average attrition in a high-turnover industry. Selecting staff that are both suitable for the role and "right" for the organisation is seen as crucial by the company.

Budget hotel chain **Travel Inn** has reviewed its recruitment procedures in its bid to improve retention, generating greater awareness of the company brand in order to attract a bigger pool of potentially suitable candidates. "By increasing the number of job applicants in the first place, we can be sure that we recruit people who really want to work for us," one of its regional HR managers told us.

The **Remainders Group** employs around 1,400 staff in its four retail discount bookshops The Works, Book Depot, Banana Bookshop and Booksale. The company has put in place a number of initiatives to tackle turnover, including a review of its recruitment processes.

"We found that the majority of people were leaving within the first six months of employment," its HR manager told us. "It was therefore essential that we looked at our recruitment approach in the first instance. The company has made a big investment in training for line managers in areas such as recruitment, disability, disciplinary and objective-setting, which has had a big impact on both recruitment and initial retention rates."

As a result of the training, managers are now more confident in areas such as questioning candidates, making selection decisions and managing performance.

Jobs that fail to live up to recruits' expectations provide a source of dissatisfaction and premature resignations. **King's College Hospital NHS Trust** (see case study A) takes great care to ensure that candidates are given realistic information about their prospective role, and encourages would-be recruits to visit the hospital so that they can view their potential working environment.

Bookmaker **William Hill Organization** employs around 10,500 staff across the UK. In 2002, the company succeeded in reducing staff turnover among its frontline retail staff by more than a quarter from 52% to 38%.

As a first step, the company held workshops in order to talk to employees and collect information on the reasons why staff were leaving the organisation. Acting on the findings, it put in place a number of initiatives to reduce attrition, including providing more training and development opportunities for staff, improving the skills levels of line managers and enhancing communication with employees generally.

Two main areas that the company focused on were getting recruitment and selection right in the first place and improving the induction training for new recruits. On the selection side, William Hill has undertaken a lot of work to develop role profiles based on high-performing employees, with the aim of using these insights to identify selection criteria. The induction programme has been strengthened and a buddy system set up to help new employees settle in, where a more experienced member of staff working in a similar role offers support and guidance to the new employee during their initial stages of employment.

With the aim of encouraging buy-in from both managers and employees, William Hill identified the reduction of labour turnover as one of its "breakthrough objectives" and communicated it as a key priority for the business.

Induction

Recruitment does not end on the appointment of the successful candidate. The final stage of the process is induction training, which in itself will have a major bearing on how well new recruits settle into the organisation. A key point to bear in mind is that effective induction should not be a one-off event, but should involve an ongoing process.

Travel Inn has reviewed its induction process to aid staff retention. The main focus of its strategy is to monitor labour turnover within recruits' first 90 days with the company, because the highest levels of attrition occur during the first three months of employment.

The company has therefore established a 90-day induction programme, called "Mission Inn-possible", that is highly structured and strongly linked to its brand. New recruits plan their own induction training with their line manager, and are set important goals to achieve, such as learning about other parts of the business. Travel Inn's ability to retain employees in this early critical stage of their employment has improved by at least six percentage points.

The introduction of a new, ongoing induction programme forms a key part of the Remainders group's retention strategy. The induction training is initially a 12-week programme that contains a lot of serious material but aims to make learning fun. All new recruits are given an induction pack that is interactive, and requires the employee to undertake certain activities, such as a quiz to test product knowledge.

Training

Training and development is heavily used by employers as a means of improving their retention of staff, as our research has shown (being used by 69.5% of organisations; see checklist 5 above).

Owl Housing, a housing charity for people with learning difficulties based in London, does not experience high attrition, but still views staff retention as a priority. "Even though our turnover rate is below 10%, we are an expanding organisation and keeping staff is vital," its personnel manager told us. "We have therefore been proactive on the retention front and have introduced several initiatives that are proving successful."

As well as offering flexible hours and improving internal communications, the organisation focuses on providing training and development opportunities, career progression paths and improving line managers' skills.

Owl Housing has a structured approach to supporting employees who wish to embark on training linked to National Vocational Qualifications in the social care field and also encourages managers to pursue level 4 awards. A rolling programme of team-building events is provided for the 170-strong workforce, when groups of employees take part in training activities at a Brighton hotel. "The training and development interventions are very popular with employees, and have also had a positive impact on staff retention," we were told.

Gilesports, a chain of retail sports shops, offers training leading to the award of National Vocational Qualifications. It has found that the training acts as a powerful motivator and retention aid. Courses are tailored to the company's needs and linked to access to promotion opportunities. And the award of a nationally-recognised certificate provides a formal endorsement of the learner's skills[17].

Line managers' role

Of all the various influences on employees' decisions to leave their employer, the role of their line manager ranks among the most important. In positive ways, their power to motivate, enthuse and support their subordinates contributes greatly to the quality of employees' working lives.

The trend towards involving line managers in many aspects of personnel management also places them centre stage in helping employees gain access to training opportunities and promotion and, through their regular performance reviews, to favourable performance ratings. These assessments are often used as a selection criterion when redundancies have to be made and, where performance-related pay systems are in place, there will be a direct link to each employee's earning power.

More broadly, line managers have considerable influence over whether or not a culture of bullying and harassment is permitted, the friendliness of the workplace and the support that colleagues give each other.

Confidential research among a broad cross-section of leavers conducted by Stephen Taylor and his students at Manchester Metropolitan University shows that the most common reason for resignations lies in poor or ineffective supervision from their immediate line managers. "What also seems clear is that employers are often unaware of the extent to which their line managers are contributing directly to their [organisations' rates of] turnover," he adds.

"This often occurs because it is the line managers themselves who are responsible for recording and reporting the reasons people leave."[18]

For these and other reasons, many employers' retention strategies pay particular attention to the skills and behaviours of line managers, often introducing or improving training programmes to raise their competence.

Promotion and sideways moves

Increasing the employee development opportunities on offer, often hand in hand with opening up career paths for employees, provides a commonly used and often effective solution to improving retention. There is a huge range of different training and development interventions that can be targeted at key groups of staff or individuals.

Supermarket group **Budgens** has seen its junior-management turnover fall from a level of 30% in 2001 to around 4% at the start of 2003. This was achieved largely by providing graduates with management experience early on in their careers. The firm takes on about 30 graduates a year and allows them to manage a store within 18 months.

Safeway has also achieved a significant reduction in staff turnover through the provision of development initiatives for its managers. An executive coaching programme for 100 of its most senior staff in 2000 helped reduce turnover among the supermarket chain's staff by 15%.

Pay

Many line managers' knee-jerk reaction to the loss of valued members of staff is to argue that pay levels are uncompetitive and should be increased.

Employers that pay significantly below market rates, and have no other compensatory factors working in their favour (such as better-than-average promotion opportunities or a highly valued workplace culture), could well find that any retention difficulties they experience owe much to their low salaries.

The sums involved in matching market rates in such situations are likely to be considerable. Where the increase is incorporated into basic salary, then pension costs, overtime payments, holiday pay and other related outgoings will also increase. This means that salary-related retention initiatives should not be undertaken lightly.

Oxfam, for example, has included changes to its pay practices in a recent retention strategy – but as part of a broader programme, linked to cultural change and the improved provision of training opportunities (see case study D).

Employers have other options, apart from increasing basic salary.

Market premia can be introduced, where groups of staff are given unconsolidated payments, based on such criteria as targeting staff who would be difficult to replace because of skills shortages in the labour market or whose loss would cause serious difficulties for the organisation.

Location allowances are more generalised payments, based on areas of the country where staff are difficult to recruit and retain. Payments are made to all those based in the affected areas.

For more information on market premia and location payments, see chapter 1 Filling your vacancies.

Case study D. Oxfam

Oxfam has undertaken a major change programme to aid its strategic aims of tackling the root causes of poverty and helping to guarantee the retention of its international workforce. Its director of international HR, explained: "Staff retention is not just a housekeeping issue for us; we have employees based in around 90 countries who have built important, influential relationships with key individuals. To lose those employees, even after a couple of years, could hamper both our direct action on poverty and our campaigning work in that country. It is as a knowledge-based organisation that we have the biggest impact on poverty, and therefore knowledge is a key asset."

Oxfam has carried out a review of both its reward system and the development opportunities offered to staff as part of the organisation's change initiative. Rather than just considering the basic pay it offers staff, the charity starts from a perspective of the total reward package on offer. "We have completely reviewed the pay and benefits system," its director of international HR told us. "Although we do not concentrate exclusively on the level of salary when it comes to attracting and retaining staff, it could be the last straw for someone if they are not getting paid a fair wage. We are therefore much more focused on benchmarking pay, and ensuring that pay levels are competitive." Careful research has been carried out to determine the market salaries for its posts.

Pay progression through the pay scales is partly linked to performance, experience and competency levels. Employees also have the potential to receive additional progression increases if they achieve exceptional improvements in their competency and impact. Oxfam also now pays particular attention to the "hygiene" factors related to remuneration, to ensure that the reward system is transparent and perceived to be fair by employees. There is also increased flexibility for managers to position staff at appropriate points within the new broadband framework (Oxfam's new pay structure has merged its scales into a few, much broader pay ranges).

Career progression and development opportunities are also linked to the new ways of working at Oxfam, and a performance management system is now in place. Professional development is also taken very seriously at the charity, with one project recording best practice and turning this into learning programmes for other employees.

Another change designed to encourage retention and improve performance and learning is a reduction in the number of fixed-term contracts that, in some regions, were used to employ more than 50% of staff. Oxfam felt that individuals employed on a fixed-term contract were not as emotionally attached to the organisation.

Case study E. Wizard Inns

Wizard Inns is a fast-expanding non-branded chain of 64 pubs in the south of England. The company operates in an industry where turnover rates of 200% are the norm, particularly in London, where many of the Wizard pubs are situated. Retention is therefore an important strategic issue for the chain.

Reward and recognition both play a key role in helping to motivate staff and engender loyalty. As well as paying competitive basic salaries, there is a host of bonus schemes in place, some of which are based on meeting, or beating, financial targets.

The schemes are not restricted to those staff who are directly involved in selling the drinks or preparing the food, or managing the customer relationship. Even a cleaner working two hours a week would be eligible for a bonus if total sales targets were met or exceeded; that way, the company aims to encourage the team spirit required to run a successful pub.

Another bonus is paid to the staff of the pub that wins the annual Quality Award. The process for determining the winner takes the form of a series of visits by "mystery guests". The winning pub is selected on the basis of the highest score, and on how much it has improved. Staff at a pub that gained a recent award won a trip to Brussels. High-performing pubs and employees are also included on a "roll of honour" with categories such as Employee of the Month and Manager of the Month.

The company believes that because it is not branded and is relatively small, it has been able to foster a personable and entrepreneurial culture, or strong employer brand, to help retain staff. Its size means that it is not restricted by large corporate structures; individual managers have the freedom to gear incentives towards the interests of their own members of staff. That way, the company can discover what would motivate someone both to perform better and stay with the company.

The options here are manifold. One high-performing employee won a trip to Paris, while an individual winning the "best quality manager" accolade received a bonus of £3,000 in retail vouchers of his choice.

An informal approach to recognition is also encouraged. The operations director always has a number of bets running with his staff, as do the area managers. Called "managers' challenges" in his electronic diary, so that he can keep tabs on them, this is a list of current bets. For example, a Solihull pub manager who loves football had the opportunity to earn two Premier League football tickets worth £200 once he had beaten his profit budget, while another manager received pop concert tickets as his preferred reward.

Wizard Inns is particularly proud of its management retention rate. It told us that it had only lost one quality manager whom it did not want to lose in the past five years.

The company believes that, ultimately, the key to retaining staff is quality management. "Our aim is to build a supportive and fun culture, with open and effective relationships, as well as offering suitable incentives to staff," the company's operations director told us. "Above all, it is our managers who play the key role in boosting retention. Put simply, good managers are more effective in recruiting the right staff in the first place and fostering the loyalty to make them want to stay."

Benefits

Many personnel and HR managers tell us that their organisations are targeting their employee benefits packages as a weapon in their retention armoury. While some employers are improving some benefits, much of the activity in this area focuses on highlighting the worth of the existing benefits package or creating flexible benefits policies.

● **Cash value:** Many employers are making employees more aware of the value of the benefits they receive – employers are doing so by calculating the financial worth of the benefits package and communicating this information to the workforce; this encourages employees to include the value of benefits alongside their salary when making comparisons with other employers.

Major utility company **Yorkshire Water** does not have a particular problem with staff retention, but still recognises the importance of valuing employees and engendering high levels of staff loyalty. One weapon in the company's retention armoury is to provide employees with a total reward statement so that they can appreciate the full worth of their remuneration package. "It is very easy to take some benefits for granted, and it helps if staff can see the actual value of the whole package that they receive, not just the basic pay," the company's HR policy developer told us. The annual statement itemises how much the employee receives in benefits and pension contributions, and also lists other available benefits and the names of key contacts.

● **Flexible benefits:** Employees in a growing number of organisations are being given some measure of control over their benefits package – some benefits may be exchanged for cash (such as selling some holiday entitlement back to the employer); other benefits may be improved by the employee buying a greater entitlement through a salary reduction (such as improved private medical insurance, or an upgraded company car); some benefits may be traded off against improvements in others; or there may be a menu of options, from which a selection of benefits can be chosen.

One strand of the retention strategy of **Hertfordshire County Council** is its flexible-benefits package, which contains a number of voluntary benefits. It has set up an on-site nursery for staff, and has introduced nursery vouchers which are available as part of the council's benefits package. It also tries to provide as many voluntary benefits as possible at discounted rates to give employees an element of choice. As well as counselling and accident insurance, the scheme includes very competitive travel insurance, healthcare cover, extra holiday entitlement and the option to make additional pension contributions.

● **Recognition schemes:** Recognition, apart from financial tokens of appreciation, is very often overlooked by employers, but this non-financial aspect of reward has the potential to have a dramatic impact on employee commitment. It is also an area where employers can be creative and focus reward practices towards areas where they can be the most effective.

445

Cherwell Housing Trust, based in Oxford, has made several changes to its benefits provision to help retain staff. "Retention of staff is quite difficult in this area of the country and, like most housing associations, we do not have a lot of extra cash to direct at the problem," its HR manager told us. "However, some initiatives that can make a difference only have an indirect cost to the organisation." The housing association has therefore very recently introduced a long-service leave entitlement and career breaks for staff, as well as development days which enable employees to take time off for personal or professional development during working hours. The training is linked to development needs identified during appraisals.

Claridge's, the luxury London hotel, has implemented a highly successful recognition programme to aid retention. One scheme involves a "pot of gold", where employees can take a lucky dip if they have demonstrated one of the hotel's core values. Although the gifts do not have a direct financial value – providing, instead, such perks as an extra hour for lunch or a ride home in a limo – they do have a high perceived value for staff.

Childcare

Much of the interest in flexible working time that makes it such a potentially valuable aspect of a retention strategy lies in its appeal to employees with caring responsibilities. Many employees' commitments, although not all, relate to caring for young children, and some employers have directly addressed this issue through the provision of assistance. Options include free or subsidised vouchers that can be used to purchase childcare; the provision of advice on childcare facilities in the local area; organising out-of-school clubs and childminders; and subsidising nurseries for employees' children.

The personnel, HR and equality managers we contacted for their experience of providing childcare assistance told us that the main benefit for their organisation lies in improved retention rates. More than half (57%) highlighted retention, compared with one-third (34%) of our contacts who said that childcare assistance helps in the recruitment of staff.

Independent TV company **Mersey Television Group** has put in place a number of flexible working and supportive measures to help retain its predominantly female workforce. Famous for producing dramas such as Brookside, Grange Hill and Hollyoaks, the company employs around 365 staff at its Liverpool studios.

"This type of industry has a very mobile workforce and there is strong competition for skilled staff," the group's HR director told us. "We are unique in the television industry because we have a permanent staff base that happens to consist of a significant number of young females in skilled posts. Family-friendly initiatives are therefore vital to encourage retention and this was no more apparent than at one time when four of our production assistants were preparing to go off on maternity leave."

Flexible working patterns and childcare support were therefore considered a high priority for the company's retention strategy and, in 1994, Mersey Television opened an onsite, purpose-built crèche for staff with young children. Nursery fees are subsidised and employees also receive a couple of fee-free weeks a year for their children.

The group told us that the nursery has had a big impact on its retention levels. Its popularity is such that there is a two-year waiting list for places. "The convenient and subsidised childcare we offer is an attractive retention tool for women returnees. Nearly all our female employees with pre-school-aged children – and some dads – have used the crèche at one time, and a number of staff have cited it as a major reason for staying so long with us."

The workplace nursery is open from 7.30am to 7.30pm to help cater for the sometimes long or unsociable hours that staff work when shooting a production. A range of different work patterns is also available – such as job-sharing and working part-time hours – to boost retention and help employees balance their professional lives and personal commitments.

For more information on employers' assistance with childcare, see chapter 1 Filling your vacancies, and chapter 10 Equal opportunities and diversity.

Working time

Some types of work are innately unpopular with many employees because of their unsocial hours, where shiftworking, nightworking or weekend working are found. Often, these working patterns are required by labour-intensive industries where the high level of staffing costs imposes restrictions on offering higher levels of pay as a compensation for these working conditions.

Even where shiftworking is the norm, some employers have found that it is still possible to make modifications that improve their ability to recruit and retain staff. Introducing twilight shifts with shorter hours, for example, have helped some organisations recruit and retain workers who are able to go out to work in the evenings once their children have come home from school and their partners or grandparents have finished their jobs for the day and can look after them.

More generally, there is a growing focus of attention in managing retention on making changes to working time so that employers are able to provide greater flexibility. This can involve changing the working day, week or year, or offering special types of leave.

Changing working time can be effective simply because the majority of employees – and not only parents with young children – now expect to achieve more flexibility in their working lives in order to cater for their personal commitments.

Hertfordshire County Council has to compete for most staff in the difficult labour market of South East England, and aims to reduce employee turnover partly by its revamped flexible working package. This forms part of a broader work–life balance strategy, called LifeWISE, and has led to a reduction in voluntary staff turnover.

There is high-level commitment for the LifeWISE strategy in the council, that is promoted in many ways. For example, its *Work–life balance principles* publication includes a message from the chief executive stating that the council will be "open minded and flexible in approach and, if necessary, be prepared to do things differently in the future". The LifeWISE flexible working directory describes the different working patterns on offer for consideration by managers. These include:

- term-time working;
- voluntary reduced hours;
- jobsharing;
- compressed hours;
- career breaks; and
- location flexibility.

Any employee wishing to work more flexibly makes a formal application, which should take into account any potential impact on service delivery. "It is important that staff appreciate that any request must suit the needs of the business," a council spokesperson told us. "We have also started monitoring the take-up of the new flexible policies, with line managers providing regular feedback to central HR on the requests made."

Case study F. Asda

Staff retention in such a high-turnover industry as retailing features strongly in the HR strategy of supermarket chain Asda, and the company has put in place a range of policies and cultural initiatives to aid staff loyalty. The result is a retention rate well below the industry average.

In 2002, Asda announced that it would be increasing the percentage of older workers to 20% within one year. In a bid to "take job advertising off the page", recruitment teams and older Asda employees targeted bingo halls and tea dances to help meet recruitment targets. The company believes that the employment of older workers in its stores has a stabilising effect on the workforce that can help improve retention.

Since the number of older employees has grown, so the rates of absenteeism and labour turnover have dropped. Absenteeism levels among older employees are now one-third lower than the Asda national average, while labour turnover is 1% lower. Another associated benefit strongly in evidence, according to the company's people director, is a more motivated and flexible workforce.

Asda strives to develop and nurture a flexible and friendly culture for employees (who are referred to as "colleagues") that "engages the heart of the workforce". Each store starts the day with the "Asda cheer". Although lighthearted in its approach, the company believes that this collective action both energises staff and reminds them that they are part of a bigger team. An informal atmosphere is also encouraged, with everyone from the top down being on first name terms, and a "no jackets required" policy for managers.

The company works hard to be as supportive as possible of its colleagues' personal commitments and encourages store managers to "just say yes" when approached by staff wanting to swap shifts or take time off, and worry about the rota changes later. A whole series of work–life balance policies are in place aside from the more common types of provision, such as jobsharing and parental and maternity leave. These include:

● study leave – for students going away to college who want to return to work during the summer holiday;

● school starter scheme – allowing parents to take a half day off on their child's first day of school;

● Benidorm leave – up to three months off for the over-50s to take a longer winter break, perhaps in sunnier climes;

● religious festival leave – recognising the multi-faith backgrounds of its diverse workforce, this scheme allows up to two days' additional leave to attend religious festivals; and

● grandparents' leave – new grandparents can take up to one week's leave to help with childcare provision.

Asda's head of reward told us that flexible working is "not a pink and fluffy thing" in the company, but is a key driver of retention in its stores. The company also estimates that its family-friendly approach saves it around £4 million through reduced absence rates.

Listening to what employees have to say is a key priority for Asda. "Colleague listening groups" are held regularly in all its stores, providing a cross-section of employees with the opportunity to air their views. An annual attitude survey – "We're listening" – is also conducted to gauge employee opinion and help shape corporate strategy.

Individuals with disabilities

Each year, many individuals become disabled while working for their employers, through accidents in or outside work, age-related conditions and other causes. Research has found that early intervention is the key to ensuring that individuals on long-term sick leave are retained by their organisations, even if they develop disabilities.

Not only do employers have a vested interest in retaining valuable skills and experience, but the Disability Discrimination Act 1995 and its associated Code of Practice place a legal requirement on organisations not to discriminate unfairly against individuals with disabilities. In particular, employers should evaluate the job, working conditions, access and other factors to see if "reasonable adjustments" can be made in order to retain such individuals. Redeployment to another job is a further possibility to be considered.

More information on retaining individuals with disabilities can be found in chapter 9 Equal opportunities and diversity, and chapter 12 Attendance and absence.

Retirement ages

Retention initiatives usually focus on individuals who leave voluntarily, yet there is one group whose retention is more directly under the control of the employer: people who reach retirement age and who are obliged to resign, whether or not they wish to do so. Increasingly, however, employers are taking a more flexible approach to mandatory retirement – not least, because their occupational pension schemes are likely to be facing deficits which deferred pensions will help to alleviate.

Many of the employees who reach normal retirement age take with them valuable skills and experience gained over the course of their working lives, and employers are realising that it makes little business sense to compel all such staff to leave the organisation.

For their part, some employees may wish to continue working as a way of maintaining a familiar sense of routine and a welcome source of social interaction. Their own financial prospects may not be so bright, either, and some form of earned income may help to supplement a pension or provide a means of saving for the day when they eventually retire.

Inland Revenue rules restrict employees' options in working while drawing a pension, particularly in preventing them from moving gradually into retirement by working fewer hours for the same employer that is paying them a pension. The government is consulting about ways of making the tax regime more flexible. In addition, the forthcoming legislation on age discrimination could well require changes to retirement ages.

Barclays Bank, for example, has found that the move to increase its retirement age has enabled it to retain more than 200 employees who would, otherwise, have been forced to retire. In late 2001, it raised the retirement age by five years to 65, and is now planning to increase it by a further five years, according to *People Management*. The magazine quotes the bank's head of HR policy as saying: "We are gaining and keeping some of our most experienced people with this policy."[19]

Three case studies concerning the introduction of flexible retirement ages can be found in chapter 9 Equal opportunities and diversity (case study box J).

Redundancy

Many organisations seem to treat redundancy exercises in isolation from mainstream personnel practices. Yet the unforeseen and unwanted loss of key members of staff represents one of the most commonly found problems of redundancy programmes.

Many employers fail to manage the process of applying for voluntary redundancy, with the result that the gearing of redundancy payments and access to early retirement encourage longer-serving staff to leave. This group will usually comprise the most experienced and skilled members of staff, the ones that the organisation should be least keen to encourage to leave.

In addition, badly-handled redundancy exercises have a detrimental impact on those not selected for redundancy. What is known as the "survivor syndrome" means that those who remain with the employer – the survivors – feel resentful, become demotivated and are likely to leave at the earliest opportunity. Given that the criteria developed to select staff for compulsory redundancy are usually designed to ensure that the most valuable employees remain with the organisation, their loss at a time of reduced staffing and corporate turbulence will be particularly keenly felt.

There are, though, many ways in which redundancies can be managed effectively and the impact of survivor syndrome reduced significantly, with the result that the aim of retaining the best staff is achieved. *More information can be found in chapter 13 Redundancy and redeployment.*

6. Legal checklist

● Retention practices should not discriminate unfairly – Sex Discrimination Act 1975; Race Relations Act 1976; Disability Discrimination Act 1995; Part-Time Workers (Prevention of Less-Favourable Treatment) Regulations 2000; Fixed-Term Employees (Prevention of Less-Favourable Treatment) Regulations 2002; Trade Union and Labour Relations (Consolidation) Act 1992; and Codes of Practice associated with these Acts

● Retention practices in the public sector must support equality of opportunity on the grounds of ethnicity – Race Relations (Amendment) Act 2000.

● All aspects of retention strategies can potentially discriminate unlawfully against one or more groups, and should be reviewed for direct and indirect bias. Monitoring of resignation rates and other reasons for leaving on the basis of gender, ethnicity, disability and age can provide additional information about areas of potential concern in current strategies, as well as highlighting groups who may be affected by other discriminatory practices within the organisation.

● Separation questionnaire responses, records of exit interviews and other data gathered for retention-management purposes must follow the data protection principles in such areas as confidentiality, security of storage and disposal – Data Protection Act 1998 and its Employment Practices Data Protection Code.

8. Employee involvement and representation

This chapter covers:
- Overview: an introduction to involving employees and managing their representation;
- Informing and involving employees;
- Trade unions;
- Partnerships with staff and unions; and
- Health and safety involvement and representation.

Checklists in this chapter:
1. Employers' main participation methods
2. Staff councils
3. The coverage of collective agreements
4. Partnership arrangements: the main features
5. Main differences between traditional agreements and partnerships
6. Legal checklist

Case studies in this chapter:
A. Egg
B. EDS
C and G. Barclays Group
D. The Telegraph Group
E. Sussex Grange Furniture
F. ETOL
H. Westcountry Ambulance Services

Overview

Employees are far more likely to perform effectively, collaborate with others, contribute suggestions and cooperate flexibly when they understand as much as possible about the organisation for which they work. However, even a process as deceptively simple as information-giving rarely succeeds without some skill and creativity. Recipients will not absorb information without having an active interest – and this needs nurturing and developing. Organisations must ensure they can put questions, ask for follow-up details and contribute their own points of view. Thus, active information-giving merges almost imperceptibly with consultation and involvement.

Much of the responsibility for the day-to-day business of informing and involving employees must rest with line managers and other supervisors. This role, and the skills it requires, does not necessarily come naturally to jobholders, and personnel, HR and training specialists can contribute in a significant way to organisational effectiveness by ensuring that adequate training is available to them.

They can also contribute at a broader level; organisations need guidance to decide the extent to which they wish to involve their employees and the best means of so doing. Staff councils, newsletters, intranets and other media need developing. Beyond them, though, lies the potential to develop formal consultation and bargaining arrangements where employees are represented by organised bodies: staff associations and trade unions. Personnel and HR managers are usually centrally involved in these arrangements, and this role is becoming increasingly important since the advent of statutory recognition procedures. Finally, and ultimately, employers can adopt formal partnership agreements, as we shall see in this chapter.

Informing and involving employees

All employers provide information to their employees and involve them in running their organisations. The role of personnel and HR specialists lies in helping their organisations to determine the most productive and effective ways of doing so.

The culture, business activities, size and geographical spread of an organisation are hugely important in shaping its information and involvement practices. As a general principle, though, the more human beings understand what is required of them, and take part in decisions regarding their jobs, the more they will work willingly and enthusiastically.

Whatever the state of their official communication channels, employers can be certain that the rumour machine will always be operating at full capacity. While some authorised communications can contain an element of "spin", the employee grapevine is almost always guaranteed to create more alarm, misinformation and anger. It is far better for employers to develop channels they can control, provided they are credible and effective.

Information-sharing provides employees and managers with essential insights into their organisation's aims, products and services, as well as day-to-day operational changes and issues. It fosters good relationships, opening up and maintaining channels of communication that are so important in performance management, teamworking and other aspects of modern organisational life. Informing employees about financial data, in particular, plays a further role beyond the figures themselves. Disclosing confidential or sensitive details implies a measure of trust that helps to motivate employees and increase their commitment to the organisation.

But simply throwing information at employees in the hope that some of it will stick ignores human psychology. Individuals can only absorb limited amounts of information, particularly when they are not motivated to do so. Ensuring that individuals can play a more active role – by also acting as information-givers; by questioning the details or asking for more facts; by making recommendations, and so on – greatly increases the likelihood that the information will be retained and acted on.

The Involvement & Participation Association (IPA) has found that: "The combined effect of direct and representative participation in decisions, and, therefore, a high level of employee influence, has a positive impact on employee attitudes and behaviour. This in turn has a positive impact on labour turnover, absence, internal performance, and sales and profit."[1]

Line managers, supervisors and team leaders are, of necessity, central to much of the activity of providing information to employees, consulting them and involving them in decision-making. In many ways, these activities form an integral part of performance management (*see chapters 11 and 12*). Managers who have been convinced of the importance of managing the performance of their staff, and have been equipped with the skills and information to do so, should readily inform, consult and involve them.

In particular, formal performance-management systems (*see chapter 11*) usually involve manager and employee sitting down and discussing the employee's role in achieving the organisation's objectives. Sensible and productive discussions of this nature depend on the employee being given information about the aims and activities of the organisation, and their own role and duties. The tasks of reviewing their performance and making plans for the next performance-review period are increasingly based on equal participation between employee and manager and, often, include some input into the decision-making of performance plans by the employees themselves.

In addition, information, consultation and forms of involvement play integral parts in other systems, particularly where organisations have introduced formal teamworking structures or quality initiatives. Continuous improvement, effective teamworking and problem-solving groups cannot function without an effective communication system between those involved and with the wider organisation.

Alongside the manager–employee, employee–manager communication channel, organisations routinely use other methods to ensure that information, consultation and involvement function as effectively as possible, within the limits determined by the organisation. In all, feedback obtained by IRS from personnel and HR managers shows that six different channels of information exchange and consultation are typically used (participation methods are described below). In descending order of prevalence among employers, these are:

● noticeboards;

● email and intranets (intranets use internal networks of computers; they have the look and feel of the internet itself) (for more information, see chapter 3. Using electronic media effectively);

● team briefings;

● a magazine or newsletter for staff (although these publications are gradually being replaced by the use of emails and information published on intranets);

● opinion polls of employees (often known as "employee attitude surveys"); these are usually conducted at regular intervals (every one or two years, most often) and get feedback on working conditions, job satisfaction, business plans and other work-related issues; and, finally, two relatively less frequently used methods:

● special reports distributed to employees; and

● video presentations.

Employers also told us that email, intranets and opinion polls are relatively new methods, but have increased rapidly in popularity.

Almost all employers permit two-way communication (as opposed to one-way information-giving). Employees are able to ask questions and often make suggestions of their own. In most organisations, mechanisms are in place whereby employees can ask questions of senior managers running the organisation.

Acas defines "consultation" as follows: "Consultation is the process by which management and employees or their representatives jointly examine and discuss issues of mutual concern. It involves managers actively seeking and then taking account of the views of employees, either directly or through their representatives, before making a decision. Meaningful consultation depends on those being consulted having adequate information and time to consider it, but it is important to remember that merely providing information does not constitute consultation. It is good practice for employers when consulting employee representatives to make sure that all representations are considered and where they are not accepted that reasons are given."

Source: Representation at work, Acas guidance booklet, 2002, www.acas.org.uk.

In the **Abbey National Group**, a financial services company, the company holds a regular executive question time, where staff can attend meetings with executive directors and ask questions of them.

At the Nottingham site of **Luxfer Gas Cylinders**, the managing director conducts quarterly "state-of-the-nation" presentations to the whole workforce about the company's progress and results.

Team briefings are widely used by employers, as the checklist showed above, because they reinforce the relationship between line managers/team leaders and their staff, while gaining from economies of scale when communicating the same information to more than one person at a time. In a significant minority of employers, the managers/team leaders are given training in conducting their briefings.

Feedback from employers shows that the typical team briefing is based on all relevant employees being expected to attend, without making this expectation a formal requirement. Employees are expected to participate, by asking questions and making comments.

Some, but not all, organisations also incorporate express provision in their briefings for employees' active involvement. At engineering company **Emerson Process Management**, for example, employees are invited to talk about initiatives they are involved in. At financial services company **Liverpool Victoria Friendly Society**, responsibility for delivering the briefing rotates between different members of staff. And at **Twyford Bathrooms**, short presentations by employees are included, whenever appropriate, about particular projects they are involved in.

The content of information communicated to employees depends on the organisation's priorities and background. But, taken as a whole, employers tell us that their information-giving most frequently concerns these issues or subjects (in descending order of prevalence):

- issues concerned with the organisation's structure;
- the performance of the organisation;
- health and safety issues;
- training and development plans and opportunities;
- equal opportunities policies and action plans;
- working practices;
- pay and terms and conditions; and
- environmental issues.

Participation

Engaging employees and managers more fully in the functioning of the organisation through participation represents a move along a continuum. Limited information-giving provides the starting point, and full participation through partnership (see below) provides the upper end of the scale.

1. Employers' main participation methods

On average, based on feedback from employers, three different participation methods are used in a typical organisation. In descending order of prevalence, the main methods are:

- team meetings;

- suggestion schemes;

- quality initiatives, such as total quality management;

- customer-care initiatives;

- employee recognition programmes; and

- an intranet forum.

The content of participation channels focuses, in descending order of prevalence among employers, on:
- health and safety;
- working practices; and
- pay and terms and conditions.

A comparison with the content of information channels in the checklist earlier on in this chapter shows that the two most common information subjects – issues concerned with the organisation's structure, and the performance of the organisation – are absent from this list of topics open to participation. Training, equal opportunities and environmental issues are also absent.

What of the pay-back to employers? In one study conducted by IRS, mainly among larger organisations, three-quarters of those hoping to use participation methods to improve their employees' business awareness have found that this has been achieved. Just over half of the employers hoping to improve relationships between employees, managers and the organisation have reported success. And a similar proportion has benefited from the greater empowerment of employees they aimed to achieve (empowerment encourages employees and managers to accept greater responsibility for their actions, try to resolve problems, and improve their care of customers). However, few employers have found that participation helps to retain staff or improves their ability to recruit new employees.

Acas and the IPA are good sources of information and advice on employee involvement and participation issues. Both have websites containing much free information, as well as telephone helplines (Acas: www.acas.org.uk; its helpline number is 08457 474 747. IPA: www.partnership-at-work.com, and www.ipa-involve.com; tel: 020 7354 8040).

Company annual reports

The Companies Act 1985 requires directors in all organisations with more than 250 employees to report in their annual reports and accounts on the action they have taken during the financial year to inform and consult their staff.

Our analysis of the annual reports from FTSE-100 companies finds that most comply with the law, and that intranets, European works councils (required under EC legislation to be set up by large multinationals; see below) and trade unions are increasingly being used for information and consultation purposes. The channels used by FTSE-100 companies mirror those used by employers generally, as shown in the checklist earlier in this chapter, although there is greater emphasis on electronic methods and the use of works councils.

Collective involvement

Instead of bringing a team or a whole organisation's employees together to inform, consult or involve them more widely, some employers do so via a system of employee representatives. Each person has a constituency – a group of employees that he or she represents – and is meant to act as a conduit, passing information and views back and forth between the representative and the people they meet on the management side of the organisation.

Trade union or staff association membership is an obvious form of collective representation (practice is described below), and is the most common approach taken in the UK. However, some organisations have a staff council (also known as a "employee forum", "consultative committee" or "works council", among other names). These bodies meet on a regular basis (monthly, bi-monthly or less frequently), and are usually chaired by a senior member of management. Where trade unions are recognised, employers may reserve some seats on the council for trade union representatives, with the remainder being given to staff representatives.

Case study A. Egg

Internet bank Egg does not recognise trade unions at its data processing and customer service centre in Derby, where some 1,100 people are employed. Instead, it has set up a system of staff representatives who belong to a consultative group called the Egg Forum, where they discuss employee relations issues with management representatives. The staff representatives also act as safety representatives (see below), whose role includes conducting inspections every three months of their designated work area. In common with safety representatives generally, Egg's representatives also have a responsibility to report hazards and promote health and safety in the workplace.

The constitution of staff councils naturally varies from employer to employer, but they have the potential to encourage a considerable amount of upwards and downwards information giving, consultation (with representatives being given agendas in sufficient time to consult their constituents before the meeting) and participation in decision-making. Staff members of the council may be able to table agenda items of their own, and raise issues passed on to them by other employees. Usually, the constitution of the council sets limits on the subjects that can be discussed, particularly where other forums exist (for example, pay increases and gradings, where a trade union is recognised for pay bargaining purposes) or where management wishes to retain its prerogative.

Usefully, as Acas points out in its Representation at work guide, once an employer has set up a staff council and representatives have been elected, it "may be used to help satisfy legal requirements for consulting with and providing information to worker representatives over business transfers or redundancies"[2]. In organisations that do not recognise a trade union and lack a ready-made system of representatives, statutory information and consultation requirements will impose a delay while such representatives are appointed.

The same Acas guide contains advice on setting up a staff council. It points out that staff councils require goodwill from management, employees and any trade unions if they are to succeed. In particular, senior managers' support is essential, as one or more of them will have to attend each council meeting, provide information and approve the expenditure involved in releasing staff to attend.

2. Staff councils

Acas advises that the staff council's constitution should cover the following points:

● The title and objectives of the council;

● Its terms of reference;

● Composition;

● Training for council members;

● The procedure for electing employee representatives;

● Their period of office;

● The method of electing or nominating council officers, including chair and secretary;

● An "assurance that members will suffer no detriment because of their role";

● Meeting arrangements;

● Rules on confidentiality;

● Facilities for council members, such as travelling expenses and paid time off work;

● Recording and reporting arrangements; and

● The method of altering the constitution.

Source: "Representation at work", Acas, 2002.

The EU consultation Directive

An estimated one in three workplaces with 50 or more employees have already set up a staff council, according to Professor Keith Sisson[3], but this is set to increase significantly once the EU Information and Consultation Directive comes into force in the UK.

The Directive will require employers with workforces above a certain size (see below) to introduce mechanisms through which they can inform and consult employee representatives about significant business and employment issues. Staff councils provide an obvious basis for this mechanism.

The UK government has not yet issued the Regulations that will serve to implement the Directive. These will help answer such questions as what triggers the setting up of information and consultation mechanisms (must employees lodge a formal request? and, if so, under what procedure?), and the scope of the topics that employers must discuss (such as the nature of the confidential material that can be excluded) and the process of setting up a mechanism under the new law.

The Directive itself indicates that information and consultation will cover impending management decisions that are likely to lead to substantial changes in work organisation or employees' terms and conditions, and transfers of undertakings, together with issues concerned with the profitability/viability of the organisation[4].

Employers will be progressively covered by the Directive, according to their number of employees. It is likely that organisations with 150 or more employees will have to comply by March 2005, those with 100 or more employees by March 2007 and those with 50 or more employees by March 2008.

European works councils

European works councils constitute a particular type of staff representative body, and have a legal status under the Transnational Information and Consultation of Employees Regulations 1999, which implement an EC Directive.

The Regulations apply to large multinational "undertakings" that have at least 1,000 employees in countries of the European Economic Area (EEA), of which 150 employees must be employed in each of two separate EEA countries.

The organisation, groups of employees or their representatives can trigger the setting up of a European works council. The council can consist of representatives elected/appointed by existing employee representatives or elected by a secret ballot of all employees. Representatives must be given time off for their council duties and are protected against unfair dismissal or victimisation.

Fallback statutory arrangements apply where a council is not set up or there is a failure to agree between the parties. These arrangements lay down minimum requirements, and include the creation of a constitution for the council that sets out such factors as the frequency, venue and duration of meetings, and the resources available to help run the council. Councils must meet at least once a year, where members must be informed and consulted about the organisation's prospects, including its financial performance, employment trends and likely substantial changes in working methods.

Case study B. EDS

EDS set up its European works council in July 1996 before the implementation of the EC Directive. EDS is an international IT services and outsourcing company, with more than 140,000 employees in 60 countries, of which 44,500 staff work in 17 countries within the European Economic Area.

The council's constitution was revised in July 2001, and runs to 12 sections and some 50 sub-sections. The consultation process is now described in detail, and lays down that "appropriate written information on the subject of consultation will be provided to representatives", and at "an appropriate time". The 26 representatives are given their own forum to confer about works council issues, can conduct their own investigations and can request translations of any relevant materials from English to their own language. They have a right to training, which is provided and funded by the company, and to the reimbursement of travel, meal and accommodation expenses for council meetings, and can have paid time off "for reasonable periods" to undertake their council duties.

IRS spoke to some management and employee members of the council; they reported that the council took several years to develop a constructive relationship. Initially, meetings were adversarial, and the employee side considered that the level of communication and consultation was insufficient. Now, the level of dialogue is described as "good" and, although some meetings and issues can prove difficult, there is more confidence in the role and effectiveness of the council.

Redundancies and transfers

Where trade unions are not recognised and the employer has not set up a staff council or network of staff representatives, it may still have to organise collective consultation procedures when planning redundancies or a business transfer.

Where 20 or more redundancies are planned to take place within a 90-day period, the Trade Union and Labour Relations (Consolidation) Act 1992 stipulates that employee representatives must be informed and consulted (see below for situations where trade unions are recognised). The information must be supplied before consultations begin. Its coverage is set out in the Act, and includes the reasons for the proposed redundancies, the numbers and types of employees affected, the selection criteria to be used, and the method of calculating redundancy pay.

The consultations must be conducted in good faith ("with a view to reaching agreement"), and cover ways of avoiding the redundancies, ways in which the number of redundancies might be reduced, and ways of reducing the consequences of the redundancies. The minimum consultation periods are linked to the number of proposed redundancies and are set down in the Act.

The Act also applies where employees are to be dismissed and offered new contracts.

Under the Transfer of Undertakings (Protection of Employment) Regulations 1981, employee representatives (see below for situations where trade unions are recognised) must be informed and consulted about proposed transfers, regardless of the size of the undertaking (that is, even if only one person is affected). The Regulations require the employer to provide information to the representatives "long enough before a relevant transfer" for consultations to take place on matters set out in the Regulations.

This information includes the reasons for the transfer and its likely date, and the implications of the transfer (including its impact on contracts of employment, pay and benefits). The consultations must be conducted in good faith ("with a view to seeking agreement"). However, unlike redundancy consultation, there is no minimum consultation period set down concerning transfers of undertakings, and tribunals will consider the facts of a case before it.

The procedure for appointing employee representatives is the same in both redundancy and business transfer consultations, and is described in detail by Acas in its *Representation at work* guide[5]. In summary, representatives must be elected in a fair way, in sufficient numbers so that they are able to represent the interests of all those affected, and candidates must be "affected" employees. Everyone who is entitled must be able to stand for election and vote in the ballot. Voting must be via a secret ballot, and the votes must be counted accurately. (Where employees fail to elect representatives, the employer is then required to provide relevant information about the redundancies/business transfer to each person directly.)

Employees, those standing for election and those who are elected are protected against victimisation and dismissal for reasons connected with their participation.

Working time

Employers that do not recognise a trade union are able to conclude a "workforce agreement" with specially elected employee representatives for the purposes of varying or opting out of the Working Time Regulations 1998. The agreement can vary the limits on night working, alter the rights to rest periods and rest breaks, and extend the reference period for limits on working hours to as long as 52 weeks.

The Regulations set out in detail the conditions that a workforce agreement must meet to be valid, including the election of employee representatives. These are broadly in line with the provisions covering the elections for redundancy and business transfer consultations summarised above.

Trade unions

Pros

The trade union movement in the UK has played a significant part in the economy for well over a century, and has millions of members who are represented in their workplaces by an estimated 250,000 trade union representatives.

There are arguments for and against the recognition (or derecognition) of trade unions by employers, although the intervention of the law – following the statutory recognition rights under the Employment Relations Act 1999 (more information below) – has added a further consideration.

The media attention given to trade unions naturally focuses on points of conflict, and is not a fair guide to the normal industrial relations climate in unionised workplaces. For example, a survey of 877 trade union representatives (admittedly involving the partisan bodies of the Labour Research Department and the Trades Union Congress) has found that relationships with managers were harmonious in 88% of cases. More than half (58%) of the representatives reported that they held regular consultative discussions with managers that went far beyond the issues covered by their trade unions' recognition agreements with the employers, and concerned working practices, future business plans and staffing matters[6].

Acas in its guidance booklet *Representation at work*[7] identifies 13 possible benefits that employers might gain from consulting (and, where relevant, negotiating with) employee representatives, including representatives belonging to a recognised trade union. The essential issue, Acas says, is whether the employer (or each workplace) is sufficiently small to enable meaningful one-to-one communication and involvement between employees and managers. Where workforce numbers are too large to permit this, Acas advises employers to inform, consult and involve employees via a system of representatives.

The prime benefit of representatives, according to Acas, lies in the improved communication and involvement between the employer and individual employees. The improvements will foster greater understanding by managers of employees' concerns and, conversely, by employees of the employer's aims and objectives. Greater openness can help build relationships at work and foster greater trust, Acas says.

Employee involvement in decision-making, via their representatives, can improve the quality of decisions and increase the likelihood that employees accept and support the decisions, and help implement them. Where change initiatives are planned – an increasingly common necessity – employees' resistance to them can be greatly reduced by ensuring that their representatives understand the reasons behind the changes and what they entail.

Research conducted by Professor William Brown of the University of Cambridge confirms that trade union involvement in easing in changes at work is increasingly being seen as beneficial by employers. It seems that employers are taking a less hostile attitude towards trade unions – or consider them as less marginal to their operations – and a "convergence of interests has occurred, spurred by both legal changes and competitive pressures"[8].

Many companies' change programmes are driven by marketplace pressures. Researchers at the independent Policy Studies Institute have examined large-scale data on employers' practices to investigate the role of trade unions where companies were operating in declining or turbulent markets. It found that companies recognising trade unions reported improved financial performance compared with similarly situated counterparts where unions were not recognised. The institute attributes some of these benefits to trade unions' ability to improve communication between management and individual employees, and the positive impact good internal relationships can have on employees' productivity[9].

The legal changes noted by Professor Brown primarily involve the introduction of statutory recognition rights, where employers are required to recognise and consult trade unions, provided certain conditions are met (see below). The rights, under the Employment Relations Act 1999, apply to organisations employing more than 20 people – a workforce size that might be below the threshold for collective representation recommended for effective communication under the Acas guidance mentioned above.

Case study C. Barclays Group

Barclays Group, the financial services company that includes Barclays Bank, told us that its recognised trade union Unifi "can play a significant part in communicating and helping shape change. A good dialogue provides valuable feedback from the grass roots to senior management. Having a strong network of local representatives means that mechanisms, such as the disciplinary process, run more smoothly since employees know where to go for support and to be accompanied at hearings. And, as we devolve more responsibility to line management, the infrastructure of trained lay representatives lets consultation take place at the appropriate level."

And cons

Moving to the potential drawbacks of recognising a trade union, while many organisations have accepted that recognising and working with trade unions can be beneficial, many others have operated successfully without accepting a trade union presence, and continue to do so.

In some cases, such as several well-known household names, the company has never recognised a trade union. But, increasingly, trade union membership and influence has declined because new organisations have sprung up in parts of the economy, or geographical locations, where there was no history of belonging to a union and little or no attempt was made by unions to recruit workers.

In particular, the service sector has always been less well unionised than either manufacturing or, especially, public services. And, until recently, it is the service industries where employment growth has been strongest. Similarly, geographically, jobs have tended to expand most strongly in areas of the country with a weaker tradition of belonging to a union, such as the South East, the East, the South and parts of London.

Professors Mick Marchington and Adrian Wilkinson say that some employers offer employees a "substitute" for trade unions in the form of well-managed workplaces with a wide range of communication and involvement methods, an individualistic culture focused on rewarding performance and generally highly competitive pay and benefits packages[10]. The absence of trade unions might be seen as allowing such companies more freedom to foster their culture and manage their workforces without any external input.

Conversely, Marchington and Wilkinson point out that some employers aim to remain union-free because they offer poor working conditions and low rates of pay. They say that such employers are often highly exposed to pressures from competitors or major customers to control costs and increase flexibility. The lack of trade unions might be seen as reducing the likelihood of resistance by employees to this style of management. Small firms, particularly owner-managed companies, are also likely to reject trade unions because of the owner's (or senior manager's) distrust of them.

Industrial action and trade unionism are almost synonymous terms in some managers' minds. It is true that strikes and other forms of action are almost unknown in workplaces where trade unions are not present. Yet perceptions about the prevalence and impact of industrial action usually owe far more to media coverage of a few public sector disputes than the true position. In 2001, for example, there were only 194 disputes, of which almost half (48%) lasted no more than one day. Only a quarter (24%) lasted for more than three days. And working conditions were more often the cause of the industrial action than disputes over pay (33% and 27%, respectively, of all days lost to strikes)[11].

But, in many other organisations, the issue of trade union membership and recognition may never have arisen – particularly, among firms in the growth areas of the economy and parts of the country where unionisation has always been low. For example, averaging trade union membership across an entire industrial sector, only five in every 100 employees in hotels and restaurants are members of a union, as are only nine in every 100 employees in agriculture, forestry and fishing. Conversely, more than half of all employees have joined a union in education (53 in every 100), energy and water (also 53) and public administration (59)[12].

Unless the management of companies in poorly unionised industries and localities decides to go out of its way and encourage union membership – by distributing membership forms or allowing union officials access to new members of staff, for example – then the issue will only arise when and if a trade union targets the company for a membership drive. In such cases, the merits of recognition will have to be determined by the employer, hopefully with the advice of a personnel or HR specialist, as will its response should a trade union lodge a recognition claim that could lead to the involvement of the law.

Research conducted by the University of Cambridge's MIT Institute finds that there is roughly a 50:50 chance that an employer will attempt to resist a claim for union recognition. Opposition, according to the research findings, tends to come from senior managers, while personnel and HR specialists often support recognition. The employers use many different tactics to prevent recognition or, failing that, organise "bargaining units" (the particular groups of employees over which trade unions would have recognition and bargaining rights) to their own advantage. Only a fifth of the employers studied had taken steps to manage union recognition issues in an effective way[13].

Trade union tactics concerning recognition claims seem to be changing, following the enactment of statutory recognition rights, according to research among union officials by the Labour Research Department. In the past, prior to the new rights, unions tended to target companies where managers were less hostile to recognition. More recently, though, they are focusing on workplaces where they have "substantial" levels of membership – often, in excess of 50%. The research also found that recognition campaigns are seldom the result of a strategy. Instead, they are usually prompted by a specific event. A new recruit who is already a union member is hired by an non-unionised workplace and begins to recruit their colleagues. Or the trade union is itself approached by a group of employees who have a grievance or desire to improve their working conditions[14].

Medium-sized employers are at the forefront of successful trade union recognition campaigns, according to an analysis by IRS of 212 recognition agreements concluded between 1997 and mid-2000. The typical (midpoint) size of an organisation affected was just 100 employees in England, falling to 45 employees in Northern Ireland.

Consultation and other rights

It is important to note that the act of recognising a trade union, whether this is achieved voluntarily or through the new statutory recognition procedure, creates certain rights under the law (generally, these are restricted to unions designated by the Certification Officer as being independent; that is, of not being controlled or unduly influenced by the employer in the way that some in-house staff associations may be). In addition, it also establishes the union and its representatives as the points of contact for statutory consultation requirements concerning redundancies and business transfers. This has its advantages, however, because – in the absence of a recognised trade union, staff association or staff council – the employer would otherwise be required to delay the redundancies or transfer in order to appoint representatives for the purposes of consultation. In summary, the law affects trade union recognition in the main areas described below.

Redundancies and redeployment: Where 20 or more redundancies are planned to take place within a 90-day period, the Trade Union and Labour Relations (Consolidation) Act 1992 stipulates that trade union (or employee) representatives must be informed and consulted. The information must be supplied before consultations begin. Its coverage is set out in the Act, and includes the reasons for the proposed redundancies, the numbers and types of employees affected, the selection criteria to be used, and the method of calculating redundancy pay. Representatives must be given access to the employees they represent, to reasonable amounts of paid time off for their duties and to reasonable facilities to perform their duties.

The consultations must be conducted in good faith ("with a view to reaching agreement"), and cover ways of avoiding the redundancies, ways in which the number of redundancies might be reduced and ways of reducing the consequences of the redundancies. The consultation must begin in "good time", but must start at least 30 days prior to the redundancies where up to 100 redundancies are planned, or at least 90 days where 100 or more redundancies are planned.

The Act also applies where employees are to be dismissed and offered new contracts.

Transfers of undertakings: Under the Transfer of Undertakings (Protection of Employment) Regulations 1981, trade union (or employee) representatives must be informed and consulted about proposed transfers, regardless of the size of the undertaking (that is, even if only one person is affected). The Regulations require the employer to provide information to the representatives "long enough before a relevant transfer" for consultations to take place on matters set out in the Regulations. This information includes the reasons for the transfer and its likely date, and the implications of the transfer (including its impact on contracts of employment, pay and benefits). Representatives must be given access to the employees they represent, to reasonable amounts of paid time off for their duties, and to reasonable facilities to perform their duties.

The consultations must be conducted in good faith ("with a view to seeking agreement"). However, unlike redundancy consultation, there is no minimum consultation period set down concerning transfers of undertakings, and tribunals will consider the facts of a case before it.

Information: recognised trade unions' access to information is covered by the provisions of the Trade Union and Labour Relations (Consolidation) Act 1992, the Acas Code of Practice on Disclosure of Information to Trade Unions for Collective Bargaining Purposes and Regulations concerning disclosure of information. On request, the employer is expected to provide information to trade union representatives in respect of the issues for which the union is recognised for collective bargaining purposes; however, complaints to the Central Arbitration Committee about employers' failure to observe this right are rarely lodged by trade unions. Trade unions also have information rights in respect of health and safety consultation, concerning occupational pensions schemes (particularly under the Occupational Pensions Schemes (Disclosure of Information) Regulations 1986), and in connection with consultation concerning redundancies and business transfers (see above).

Health and safety: The Health and Safety (Consultation with Employees) Regulations 1996 and the Safety Representatives and Safety Committees Regulations 1977 require employers to consult employees or their representatives about health and safety issues. Where trade unions have appointed safety representatives, the employer is required to consult them; see below for more information.

Disciplinary and grievance hearings: Employees have the right to be accompanied by a trade union representative or full-time official (or a work colleague, if they wish) when attending certain disciplinary and grievance hearings (*see chapter 12 Managing performance 2 for more information*). Acas points out, however, that agreements with trade unions concerning recognition and bargaining "normally include rights for members to be represented by union officials at disciplinary or grievance hearings or interviews [without the restrictions contained in the statutory rights]"[15].

Industrial action: Employees undertaking official industrial action that comes under the protection of the Trade Union and Labour Relations (Consolidation) Act 1992, as amended by the Employment Relations Act 1999, and where the action has been endorsed by an approved ballot, are now protected from dismissal if the main reason relates to taking part in such action. The dismissal will only be automatically unfair where it takes place within eight weeks of the employee taking "protected industrial action", or, after that period, where the employer has "not taken such procedural steps as would have been reasonable for the purposes of resolving the dispute".

Employees' activities that are not authorised or endorsed by the union in relation to the industrial action are not protected (such as assaulting someone who refuses to take industrial action). Employers cannot usually be selective if they are to avoid dismissals being automatically unfair, but must dismiss all those involved in the industrial action.

Members and representatives: Trade union members and their representatives have a general right under the Trade Union and Labour Relations (Consolidation) Act 1992 not to be victimised or dismissed because of their membership (or non-membership) of a trade union.

Time off: The Trade Union and Labour Relations (Consolidation) Act 1992 supplemented by the Acas Code of Practice on Time Off for Trade Union Duties and Activities provides qualified rights to reasonable paid time off, on request, for trade union representatives to attend training in their duties, and for reasonable paid time off to perform these duties (as specified in the Act); the rights to paid time off only apply to times when the person would normally have been working; further information is given in the Acas Code of Practice (see below for more information on resources for representatives). Members of trade unions are entitled to unpaid time off, on request, to take part in certain union activities.

Learning representatives: The Employment Act 2002 amends the Trade Union and Labour Relations (Consolidation) Act 1992 to create a new type of trade union representative: the union learning representative. The amended 1992 Act sets out representatives' duties – which primarily involve promoting learning opportunities among trade union members. Representatives must be appointed under their union's rules (the union must already be recognised by the employer), and their details given in writing to the employer. They must receive suitable training for their role. Once the statutory conditions have been met, learning representatives will have similar rights to trade union representatives to paid time off, facilities and protection against victimisation and dismissal. Members who consult their learning representative are entitled to unpaid time off for this purpose. Provisions concerning learning representatives and members consulting them are expected to come into force during 2003. (*See chapter 6 Induction, training and development for more information.*)

Compulsory recognition: In addition, trade unions that the employer has been required to recognise under the statutory recognition procedure have a legal right to collective bargaining concerning their members' pay, hours and holidays, and to consultation concerning training (see below for more information on statutory recognition).

Agreements with trade unions

Trade union recognition is almost invariably linked to the creation of a "collective agreement" or "recognition agreement" between the employer and trade union concerned. This document sets out, usually in considerable detail, the respective rights and responsibilities of each party, the subjects about which the employer will conduct bargaining with the trade union (and, often, those second-level subjects where it will only consult or merely inform the union), the appointment and rights of union representatives, procedures in the event of a failure to agree, and so on. (Typical issues covered by a collective agreement as shown in checklist 3.)

The wave of mergers and takeovers involving trade unions, which continues to this day, has greatly simplified the confusing array of different membership organisations in the UK. It is much less common now for an employer to be faced with two, three or more unions recruiting different groups within its workforce. In instances where this remains the case, employers will have to consider whether they wish to recognise more than one union and, if so, whether they will conclude separate recognition agreements or attempt to create one unified document. In the same way, they may decide to conduct bargaining and consultation jointly, rather than negotiate and consult separately with each union.

One way in which employers have traditionally attempted to control multi-unionism lies in agreeing a "single-union agreement", which grants one union exclusive recognition and bargaining rights, and which usually involves the employer in encouraging its employees to join this union. More recently, the provisions of the statutory trade union recognition procedure (see below) function so as to encourage voluntary recognition agreements and generally prevent recognition claims from trade unions where another union is already recognised. This development may, in due course, turn out to boost the practice of single-union agreements.

Feedback from personnel and HR specialists shows that employers usually have a three- or four-stage collective disputes procedure, covering issues where management and trade union fail to agree and the union pursues a form of collective grievance.

Collective agreements usually attempt to bind the trade union (morally) to exhaust the disputes process before contemplating industrial action. To reduce this likelihood still further, employers report that they usually ensure that its final stage involves bringing in an independent third-party to deal with intractable problems.

Employers tell IRS that this usually takes the form of independent concil-iation – where the third party attempts to find common ground between the warring factions, and help them find their own solution. In some instances, however, the procedure goes further and stipulates that the inde-pendent third party will provide mediation – where both sides present evi-dence and argument, but the third party produces an independent report with recommendations. Finally, some procedures involve a third party who provides arbitration; this follows the same process as mediation but varies in that the report is binding on both parties.

Procedures containing binding arbitration are often known as "no-strike deals", because, in theory at least, the outcome of binding arbitration pro-vides its own solution and precludes any form of industrial action. It is unlikely that trade unions will be as willing to conclude such agreements now as they were in the 1980s and early 1990s, when trade union influence had reached a post-war low point. In many instances, collective agreements of all types stipulate that Acas provides the third-party intervention, whether it be conciliation, mediation or arbitration.

3. The coverage of collective agreements

Collective agreements between employers and trade unions typically cover the following issues:

● whether or not the agreement and issues covered by it are intended to have a legal status;

● the group(s) of employees for which the trade union is recognised (known as the "bargaining unit");

● the respective rights and responsibilities of each party, and their intentions towards each other;

● the employer's policy concerning employees' membership of the trade union (for example, whether employees are encouraged to join; whether the employer grants union representatives access to new recruits);

● the subjects about which the employer will conduct bargaining with the trade union;

● the subjects about which the employer will consult the trade union;

● the subjects about which the employer will merely provide information to the trade union;

● arrangements for the provision of information to the trade union concerning issues covered by the agreement;

● the role, responsibilities and typical duties of representatives; their method and duration of appointment; and their accreditation by the employer;

● the arrangements for requesting time off for representatives; the facilities and paid time off available to representatives for their duties and relevant training (see section below for more information);

● safeguards concerning disciplinary action or dismissal by the employer in respect of legitimate trade union activities by representatives and union members;

● the procedure for requesting a meeting between the employer and trade union representatives;

● provisions concerning the holding of regular meetings; arrangements for taking minutes of these meetings;

● clarification about the persons (and their status) who will represent the employer and trade union in meetings (and whether this may differ for particular types of meeting); and whether or not external officials employed by the trade union may attend meetings;

● the procedure where there is a failure to agree (a "disputes procedure");

● whether or not "status-quo" arrangements apply, and how they will operate (these are provisions preventing changes that are the subject of the dispute from being implemented until the disputes procedure has been exhausted); and

● provisions concerning the procedure for the alteration of the agreement, its termination or re-negotiation.

Resources for trade union representatives

As we saw above, trade union representatives have a right to "reasonable" amounts of paid time off to perform the duties for which they were appointed, provided that these comply with the restrictions in the Trade Union and Labour Relations (Consolidation) Act 1992 – primarily, these include duties relating to the representative's own employer and to issues covered by the recognition/collective/procedural agreement between the union and employer. The paid release does not extend to time spent outside scheduled working hours (that is, for duties undertaken in the individual's personal time).

There is also an Acas Code of Practice on Time Off for Trade Union Duties and Activities which provides guidance and whose provisions may be taken into account in a relevant tribunal or appeal case. The Code is currently being revised to incorporate the forthcoming rights of "union learning representatives" (see above).

In addition to paid time off, the Acas Code (but not the Act) suggests that representatives should be provided by the employer with some basic resources to help them perform their union duties. The Code recommends that the union–employer agreement set out representatives' entitlements, but suggests that these might include "accommodation for meetings, access to a telephone and other office equipment, the use of noticeboards and, where the volume of the official's work justifies it, the use of dedicated office space".

Personnel and HR managers tell IRS that most of their organisations' collective/recognition agreements with trade unions include details of the time off and facilities the employer will afford union representatives.

Frequently, although less commonly, agreements also cover health and safety representatives, but rarely do so in respect of pension trustees. Even prior to the recent extension of time off rights to union learning representatives, some employers had already amended their agreements to include this new role. Examples include financial services companies **Abbey National Group** and **Royal & SunAlliance**, **Great North Eastern Railway**, **Sheffield City Council**, **Cheshire Fire Service** and the **Scottish Low Pay Unit**, a five-strong body campaigning to improve low rates of pay in the Scottish economy.

Rarely are actual amounts of paid release formally specified in agreements; employers prefer to follow the statutory and flexible term of "reasonable" amounts of time off. In practice, though, employers tell us that they agree widely differing amounts. The **United Biscuits** manufacturing plant in Ashby-de-la-Zouch, for example, told us that the typical average time agreed is two to three hours over a two-week period. Social housing provider **Cherwell Housing Trust** quoted three to four hours a week, and **e2v technologies** (formerly Marconi Applied Technologies, a high-technology company) mentioned half a day each month.

Senior representatives at **Twyford Bathrooms** receive around one day a week, on average – an estimate also provided by **Great North Eastern Railway**.

Practice is not necessarily more generous in the public sector. At **Welwyn Hatfield Council** in Hertfordshire, for example, its agreement limits paid time off to between 5% and 20% of normal working hours. **Cheshire Fire Service** estimates that representatives take four days a month, on average, while the representative of lecturers at **Motherwell College** takes two to three hours a week.

Personnel and HR managers contacted by IRS emphasise, however, that practical arrangements are complex. Some agree different amounts of paid time off according to the type of representative – there may be senior representatives as well as front-line representatives; there may be "convenors" who coordinate the activities of a group of representatives; and so on. But, as an overall average, feedback from employers shows that one day a week is a typical amount of paid release actually given to trade union representatives. (Separate research by the Labour Research Department has found that one in five representatives carry out some of their duties in their own time[16].)

In terms of facilities provided to representatives, employers tell IRS that, in descending order, these are most common:
● use of the employer's email system;
● use of a telephone; and
● office space – either the provision of dedicated offices or allowing representatives' to use their work office accommodation for union purposes as well.

Statutory recognition

Since June 2000, trade unions have gained a legal right to be awarded recognition by employers – provided the employer has more than 20 employees and the recognition claim meets certain conditions (see below).

This new right introduces a major additional factor for employers to consider when determining their policy towards trade unions. Not only might the employer be compelled to grant recognition, but the law's requirements are potentially more onerous than had the organisation "jumped the gun" and concluded a voluntary agreement with a union.

This element of second-guessing trade union membership drives and recognition tactics complicates the position still further. The result, according to our analyses of trade union recognition trends, has produced a situation where recognition agreements have soared – but only a fraction of them have followed the legal route. In other words, most employers that have been faced with a request for recognition have granted it voluntarily, rather than holding out and being compelled to do so.

There are several advantages to this strategy, including:

● an agreement with one "independent" trade union effectively prevents multi-unionism, with employers having to deal with two or more unions in the same workplace or organisation (provided the statutory claim covers at least some employees who are already within the scope of the voluntary agreement);

● trade union policies and attitudes vary, and it may be advantageous to conclude a voluntary agreement with a more cooperative independent union (for example, one that favours partnership; see below for information on partnerships) and, thus, prevent less amenable ones from claiming statutory recognition rights;

● voluntary agreements with independent unions give employers much greater scope to influence the bargaining unit for which the union is recognised; while the statutory procedure allows the unit to be agreed, the union has more influence and can reject the employer's proposals (bargaining units are groups of employees for which the union has recognition rights; employers may wish them to reflect organisational divisions or limit them to exclude some classes of employee, while unions tend to press for broader definitions), and cases where the unit is determined independently need not give as much weight to the employer's concerns as the union's (see next section for more information); and

● recognition and any agreements can be cancelled (preferably with due notice); this is not usually possible for at least three years where a union gains statutory recognition.

Case study D. The Telegraph Group

At publishing company the Telegraph Group, the employer lost its bid to exclude casual and fixed-term staff from the bargaining unit when the National Union of Journalists lodged a claim under the statutory recognition process. The CAC ruled in favour of the union's proposal that the bargaining unit should include such temporary staff alongside permanent employees.

The new rights

The Trade Union and Labour Relations (Consolidation) Act 1992, as amended by the Employment Relations Act 1999, requires employers with more than 20 employees to grant recognition to a trade union under certain conditions (note that the recognition provisions are already under review by the government). In summary[17]:

● the trade union must be classed as "independent" by the Certification Officer, and must deliver a formal written recognition claim to the employer;
● the document must identify the union and the bargaining unit for which recognition is claimed (bargaining units are groups of employees over which a trade union has recognition rights; they usually constitute groups with some common bond, such as a group of related occupations, employees who share the same workplace, or who are managed separately);
● the employer must respond within 10 working days;
● where the employer agrees to negotiate, it has a further 20 working days to conclude an agreement (longer if both parties agree to an extension);
● where the employer refuses recognition or fails to respond, the trade union may take its claim to the Central Arbitration Committee (the CAC: an independent body given powers under the Act to award recognition);
● the CAC will first ensure that the claim meets various conditions; in particular, a trade union cannot lodge a statutory recognition claim where any of the employees are already covered by a voluntary or statutory recognition agreement with another independent union, nor where the present union has lodged a substantially similar claim to the CAC within a three-year period; the CAC will also check that at least 10% of the employees in the proposed bargaining unit are already members of the union lodging the claim;
● provided its checks are satisfactory, the CAC will determine the appropriate bargaining unit – various criteria are set down in the Act; in addition, recent case law involving Kwik-Fit[18], the car-servicing company, indicates that the CAC need not give as much weight to the employer's arguments as those given by the trade union. However, the union and employer will be invited to agree the bargaining unit voluntarily at this stage, and many parties do so. Otherwise, the CAC makes a ruling about the unit;
● the CAC then decides whether or not there is sufficient support among employees for recognition; if more than 50% are already members, then recognition will usually be granted immediately; if it is below this level, the CAC will usually arrange for a ballot to be held;
● when holding a ballot, the CAC will appoint an independent scrutineer, with the employer and union being required to pay equal shares of the balloting costs. The employer is required to cooperate with the balloting process, give the union "reasonable" access to the employees covered by the bargaining unit, and give the CAC the names and addresses of the employees in the unit;
● the CAC will award recognition after a ballot when at least 50% of those voting, and at least 40% of all employees in the bargaining unit, vote in favour of recognition;
● where recognition is compulsory, the employer will be required to conduct collective bargaining about pay (including some pensions issues), hours and holidays, at the very least, and to consult and inform the union at least every six months on its training policy, training provision and planned pro-

vision in respect of employees in the bargaining unit. The parties are given 30 working days to agree a method of bargaining; failure to do so involves the CAC in brokering an agreement; continued failure leads to the CAC imposing a bargaining arrangement. An imposed agreement constitutes a legally binding contract, unless both union and employer agree in writing that it will not be so;

● derecognition by the employer is not usually possible for at least three years; this applies to statutory recognition awards and those voluntary agreements concluded after the union has lodged a claim with the CAC; and

● employees are protected from victimisation or dismissal in respect of their involvement in the process concerned with a union gaining recognition or derecognition under the statutory process, unless their actions were unreasonable.

The CAC's track record

So far, as we noted above, most cases of trade union recognition concluded since the statutory rights were introduced have not involved a recourse to the law; employers have voluntarily conceded union recognition claims.

The CAC, the body responsible for the recognition process, received just 175 applications from unions for recognition in the first 18 months of having its new legal powers. Interestingly, more than half of the bids involved employers with fewer than 200 employees. At the 18-month point, Acas had granted recognition to the claims or was on the way through its procedure to doing so.

So far, there have been few legal precedents concerning the process and the CAC's powers (see above for the Kwik-Fit case). In Fullarton Computer Industries Ltd v Central Arbitration Committee[19], the company appealed against a CAC decision to award recognition to the ISTC without a ballot, although the union only just exceeded the 50% threshold (it had 51.3% of the bargaining unit in membership), and a redundancy situation made this a "moving target". The appeal failed and recognition was awarded.

Case study E. Sussex Grange Furniture

At Sussex Grange Furniture, a furniture manufacturer, the GMB lodged a recognition claim on 11 September 2002 with the Central Arbitration Committee in respect of a bargaining unit based on "all shopfloor workers" at the site in Lewes, East Sussex – five people in all. The employer and union failed to agree on the definition of the bargaining unit, mainly concerning the employer's proposal that it should include the site manager. The panel appointed by the CAC to consider the case took account of the guidelines set out in the Trade Union and Labour Relations (Consolidation) Act 1992 concerning the identification of bargaining units. In this case, it found there was a clear "two-tier structure" of manager and employees that made it "inappropriate to include that manager in the bargaining unit". Instead, quoting one of the Act's guidelines, it found it "compatible with effective management" that the unit should consist of the shopfloor workers and accepted the union's definition.

Among the decisions of the **CAC**, recognition without a ballot – showing that more than 50% of a bargaining unit's employees were already members of the relevant union – has been granted to the GPMU at **Derry Print** and **John Brown**, to URTU at **Silentnight Beds**, to BALPA at **BAC Express**, and to UCATT at **Critical Path Association**.

Partnerships with staff and unions

Organisations seldom want their working arrangements to degenerate into an "us-and-them" culture, where management and employees see themselves as opposing forces. Good lines of communication, effective management and efficient performance-management systems are most often emphasised by employers that want to improve employee relations.

Some go further, however, and adopt formal "partnership" arrangements. These may be introduced unilaterally, or be based on joint agreement – particularly, where trade unions are recognised (see next section).

There is no one accepted definition of the meaning of "partnership", but the Involvement & Participation Association (IPA), which has had a strong influence on the creation of partnerships, has said that they stand out because of a combination of features. First, there is great emphasis on informing, consulting and involving employees over matters relating to the operation of the organisation. Second, representative forums are set up for these purposes. Third, the relationship between the representatives (and employees generally) and the employer is intended to be based on a joint commitment to the success of the organisation, with reasonable levels of trust and respect. Fourth, these principles are supported in a tangible way[20].

For example, representatives will be shown respect, given guarantees that they will not suffer as a result of their role, there may be a job-security agreement, efforts to give employees greater responsibility and more interesting jobs, and forms of profit-sharing may be introduced. In return, employees will be expected to show greater cooperation and commitment, particularly in respect of change (such as being willing to be more flexible and learn new skills).

The practical implications of these principles are as follows. Based on feedback obtained by IRS, we have found that many employers' partnership arrangements involve them putting at least some of the above concepts into practice. At the same time, though, they have improved a wide range of existing mainstream personnel process to reflect best practice. In other words, partnership arrangements often go hand in hand with leading-edge personnel and HR management.

Employees are usually involved via a network of staff representatives who meet management via a partnership forum. They receive information, usually in good time, and are expected to communicate this to their constituents, discuss the issues and get their ideas and feedback. At the meeting, they are consulted about management plans and proposals, and are able to draw on the feedback they have already received in order to provide their input. Further discussion with employees may follow.

Forum meetings are held regularly, with formal agendas and minutes. Representatives are often given training to enable them to carry out their role, together with arrangements for paid time off for this and their forum duties.

In addition to the forum meetings, other joint groups are often set up. Usually, these are problem-solving groups or working parties, where representatives and managers aim to address one or more issues, find ways forward and help improve the working of the organisation.

A comparison with the nub points towards the end of the next section on partnerships with trade unions shows that there is little difference between arrangements where unions are not recognised and those where they are – except for the obvious factor of recognition creating a role for the union in the process.

Partnerships with trade unions

In terms of relations with trade unions, "partnership" agreements represent a desire by both employers and unions to improve their relationships so that they become more constructive and productive. For unions, this means helping to move the organisation forward, rather than being placed in a position where they can only criticise from the sidelines. In most instances, partnerships have been introduced where traditional collective agreements have already been tried and found wanting.

Instead of adversarial relationships, partnerships are intended to encourage employers and unions to try to work more closely together. The employer provides more information about its activities, and involves the union to a greater extent in consultations and decision-making. Trade unions told us of moving from having a "firefighting" role, where they had to react to decisions already made, towards gaining more of an opportunity to influence the employer's thinking before action was taken. The unions also had issues of their own that they saw adopting a partnership role would help advance.

Acas describes union–employer partnerships as involving collective bargaining that is conducted "on the basis of a common interest in the success of the organisation"[21]. It says partnerships that grow out of existing recognition agreements based on adversarial relations often face particular challenges. Both employer and union may be concerned about the implications of change: "For example, management may be concerned about losing the right to manage, and trade unions may worry about losing their independence and separate identity." Acas offers support to both parties (tel: 08457 474 747).

IRS's review of the experience of employers and trade unions that had entered into partnerships shows that employers are often motivated to conclude such agreements because of one or more of the following:
● to win union support for a significant change initiative;
● to increase productivity substantially in an increasingly competitive marketplace; and
● to improve communication with employees and raise their commitment to the organisation.

However, some arrangements given the "partnership" label may be less constructive, and represent attempts to incorporate the union into the organisation's structures and reduce its power and influence. The advent of statutory recognition rights is likely to encourage trade unions to refuse to enter into such situations and withdraw from existing ones.

Given that most partnerships build on existing recognition agreements, many employers told us that they require a considerable cultural change, and the development of new skills, among both managers and trade union representatives to make the new partnerships work. However, it has understandably proved difficult to achieve a complete cultural change, and there are several reports of individual managers resisting new partnership arrangements by failing to provide information, consult unions and so on.

Some employers provide training to representatives in influencing skills, negotiating skills and understanding financial figures. New agreements have to be drawn up to institute the partnership, and new structures and systems are required to foster union–management joint-working. In many cases, too, both employers and trade unions have told IRS that additional costs are incurred in sustaining their partnership arrangements.

Their experience is mainly positive, however. Trade unions have become more involved in business-related issues and decision-making generally. This involvement and the greater provision of information have contributed to reports of reductions in individual and collective grievances. Unions' fears that their closer association with the employer would undermine their influence and membership base had proved groundless among those IRS contacted. Instead, the active involvement of representatives in changes has meant that employees naturally turn to them for information and to protect their interests.

Case study F. ETOL

Utilities company ETOL is one of the most upbeat about the benefits of partnership. It signed an agreement in 2000 with MSF, AEEU and TGWU in a bid to improve its industrial relations climate and bring about cultural change. The unions have been given more information about the business and are involved in problem-solving processes. Through the unions, employees are now more involved with the company and show greater commitment to it. ETOL estimates that improved performance and cost savings that the partnership helps achieve yield around £3.8 million each year, and have helped attract additional investment. A less adversarial relationship has paved the way for the unions' acceptance of redundancies, longer working hours, greater shift flexibility and a pay freeze. Some of the savings have been used to fund private medical insurance for employees and expenditure of £500,000 on training and development[22].

Examples of partnership agreements include chemicals company **Hickson & Welch** (first signed in 1988 with the TGWU), retailer **Littlewoods** (signed in 2000 with USDAW and the GMB), **Thames Water Utilities** (signed in 2000 with Unison, GMB, AEEU and TGWU), retailer **Tesco** (signed in 1998 with USDAW) and **CSL** (signed in 1999 with PCS).

In recent years, information and material assistance to help the establishment of partnerships has become more readily available. The government has established a Partnership at Work Fund (tel: 020 7215 6252, www.dit.gov.uk/partnershipfund) to give grants to help foster partnerships between employers, their employees and trade unions. Partnerships must submit a bid for funding. Successful entrants are those that meet the scheme criteria – in particular, being seen as helping to spread "best partnership practice" more widely – and receive up to 50% of eligible costs to a maximum of £50,000 per project. In its first four years, £5 million was given to 160 projects. Several partnerships have a specific focus, such as improving safety or occupational health.

Railway infrastructure company **Amey Rail**, **Royal Mail**, **Sainsbury's**, shipping company **P&O Nedlloyd**, **Redcar and Cleveland Borough Council**, chemicals manufacturer **Tessenderlo UK**, the **Lesbian and Gay Foundation** and retailer **Ethel Austin** are examples of employers with successful joint union–management projects under the Partnership at Work Fund. However, the fund also provides assistance where no unions are involved.

The Trades Union Congress has set up the TUC Partnership Institute, offering partnership-related information on its website, together with consultancy and training services (tel: 020 8347 3748, www.tuc.org.uk/pi/).

4. Partnership arrangements: the main features

Based on feedback obtained from employers, IRS finds that partnership agreements typically include the following components.

● **Forums:** consultation and information exchange is conducted through one or more staff forums, featuring employee representatives and members of management. Representatives are given information to pass on to their constituents and are consulted about proposed changes. The structure of the forums usually aims to ensure maximum participation by employees through their representatives. In multi-site organisations, for example, there is often one forum per workplace. There may also be layers of forums, with local ones being informed and consulted by regional or national ones. Forums may supplement direct union–management negotiations, but, frequently, replace them.

● **Representation arrangements vary:** To allay unions' fears about the introduction of a partnership, some employers guarantee that representatives will be union nominees. In other employers, some seats are reserved for unions and others for staff (particularly where there are gaps in the coverage of bargaining units). Elsewhere, some employers provide for direct elections for representatives, with no restrictions or safeguards concerning union membership.

● **Joint problem-solving:** Most agreements emphasise the creation of joint problem-solving machinery. Often, ad-hoc groups are set up of employee representatives and some managers to explore a problem and identify solutions to it. Examples of ad-hoc groups found in partnership arrangements include new grading systems, changes to working practices and the introduction of multiskilling. Some problem-solving groups have an indefinite future; examples include training, and health and safety groups.

● **Training:** Employee representatives are usually given training as part of the partnership agreement. The training covers skills related to their role in the partnership structure, such as problem-solving skills, group working skills, negotiation, communication skills and understanding balance sheets.

5. The main differences between traditional agreements and partnerships

According to the experience of trade unions and employers analysed by IRS, these are the main features that distinguish a partnership from a traditional recognition agreement:

● a strong commitment from the chief executive and board to the partnership;

● a readiness by personnel and HR specialists to help introduce and foster the partnership;

● a willingness to change their attitudes and practices on the part of both managers and union representatives;

● a corporate culture that values the involvement of employees and treats them with respect;

● an ability by the union to understand business issues and the activities of the organisation;

● the provision of adequate resources by both employer and union to make the partnership function satisfactorily; and, above all

● enthusiasm and commitment from both employer and union to work together to help advance the interests of the organisation.

Health and safety involvement and representation

Health and safety issues have frequently been mentioned in this chapter in connection with employers' efforts to communicate with their staff and involve them in decision-making. The law is particularly important in this area.

In general, the law requires employers to protect the health, safety and welfare of their employees (and others on their premises) as far as is reasonably practicable. The Health and Safety at Work Act 1974 imposes this general duty, but the law's more detailed requirements are now spelled out in a long series of Regulations and Approved Codes of Practice issued to accompany the Act. Six Regulations are particularly important (known as the "six pack"), and concern undertaking risk assessments, the recording and reporting of accidents, the provision and use of equipment at work, display-screen equipment, first aid and the manual handling of loads.

Employee involvement is crucial in the prevention of accidents, in reporting potential hazards and requesting help when work becomes too stressful. The Health and Safety Commission (HSC) says that: "By consulting employees, and employer should motivate staff and make them aware of health and safety issues."[23] This argument is backed up by the imposition of legal obligations on employers to inform and consult.

Where employees are not in bargaining groups for which trade unions are recognised, the Health and Safety (Consultation with Employees) Regulations 1996 (as amended) require employers to consult them directly or via elected staff representatives.

Employees covered by a recognition agreement can be consulted via special safety representatives appointed by their union, under the Safety Representatives and Safety Committees Regulations 1977 (as amended) – note that those appointed represent all employees concerned, not merely those who are union members.

In both types of consultation (and, depending on the coverage of recognition agreements, an employer might have to observe both Regulations' requirements), individual employees and representatives are protected against victimisation or dismissal connected with their participation in the process. Representatives also have a right to paid time off to be trained in their role, and to "reasonable" paid time off and facilities to carry out their duties. The time off right also applies to those standing for election as a representative.

The legal consultation requirements involve matters concerned with employees' health and safety at work. The HSC says that this includes:
● changes that might have a substantial impact on health and safety;
● measures to reduce or remove risks and dangers;
● the planning of health and safety training; and
● the impact on health and safety of the introduction of new technology.

487

Consultation under health and safety legislation involves more than merely asking employees or their representatives for their views. The HSC explains that it includes: "Employers not only giving information to employees, but also listening to and taking account of what employees say – before they make any health and safety decisions." Timing is important, too: "If a decision involving work equipment, processes or organisation could affect the health and safety of employees, the employer must allow time to give the employees or their representatives information about what is proposed. The employer must also give the employees or their representatives the chance to express their views." And, after this: "Then, the employer must take account of these views before they reach a decision."[24]

The information that employers are expected to provide to enable effective consultation to take place is covered by a number of exemptions under the law. While, in general terms, it must be sufficient for the purposes of effective consultation, the information cannot be given if it would breach other laws or endanger national security. Nor need information be given if its disclosure would damage the organisation, with the exception of damage relating to health and safety, or if the information had been obtained in connection with legal proceedings, or if the information concerns one or more individuals and they have not given their permission for disclosure.

Safety representatives

The two sets of Regulations mentioned above concern consultation with employee representatives and safety representatives appointed by trade unions. As we saw, both types of representatives have the same rights concerning information and consultation, training and paid time off. However, their more general duties differ in scope.

Under the Health and Safety (Consultation with Employees) Regulations 1996, employee representatives (those not appointed by a trade union) have the role of:
● taking up concerns about health and safety with the employer;
● raising other matters with the employer that might affect employees' health and safety; and
● representing their constituents in consultations with official health and safety inspectors.

However, the Safety Representatives and Safety Committees Regulations 1977 gives union-appointed representatives two additional roles:
● inspecting the workplace for health and safety reasons, investigating possible dangers and hazards; and

● attending a safety committee (employers are legally obliged to set up a safety committee within three months of a request from two or more safety representatives).

There is, however, nothing to prevent an employer for expanding the role of employee representative to reflect that of the safety representative or, indeed, of widening the latter's role. In addition, changes to the consultation arrangements where no trade union is recognised have been proposed by the HSC. These have not yet been finalised, but may involve giving non-unionised employees a right to determine the way in which their employer consults them (directly or via employee representatives), and introducing a new type of representative where workplaces have a poor safety record.

Case study G. Barclays Group

Safety representatives at **Barclays Group**, the financial services company, are appointed under an agreement with Unifi, its recognised trade union. The representatives, in the words of the company's health and safety manager, "are looking at the fundamental management of health and safety. We have done the risk assessments; they carry out 'sanity checks' to see if operational processes and procedures are being followed. If not, we want them to coach and educate managers and employees to ensure that agreed procedures are working". Statutory consultation requirements about the health and safety implications of changes in working practices and new technology are addressed by involving the safety representatives in business meetings when such issues are discussed. Each part of the company has a safety manager, and representatives report their findings direct to them. For broader policy issues, the representatives have direct access to the group health and safety manager. They are members of the central health and safety committee, although local committees are planned at business level to encourage effective consultation. Once these are in place, the central committee will take on a more strategic role. Representatives are given four days' training before they take up their duties. The training programme is jointly agreed between the company, Unifi and the TUC.

Case study H. Westcountry Ambulance Services

Health and safety consultation and involvement is being improved in several multi-site employers through the introduction of roving safety representatives – trade union-appointed representatives who cover workplaces that are too small to support their own safety representative. In Westcountry Ambulance Services, the NHS trust providing ambulance services in Devon, Cornwall and Somerset, the introduction of roving representatives has been supported by the adoption of a partnership approach to health and safety. With more than

50 workplaces, it was not economic or practicable to appoint and train a safety representative for each location. The trust and unions have also found that local representatives were only exposed to a narrow range of issues, and could not retain their training nor broaden their experience. The new system is based on operational structures, where five or six ambulance stations are grouped together, although representatives also have the power to cover other sites as well.

State of play: Research from the Institute for Employment Studies[25] shows that the typical pattern of employers' consultation about health and safety is as follows:
- almost all employers have set up arrangements to consult representatives about health and safety;
- this applies to 84% of employers with 50 to 199 employees and 94% of those with 200-plus employees;
- however, in only a minority of employers are trade union-appointed representatives the only type of representative consulted (in 7% of employers with 50–199 employees, rising to 20% of employers with 200 or more employees);
- instead, larger employers (200+ employees) typically consult both trade union and employee representatives, while smaller/medium-sized ones (those with 50–199 employees) most often consult employee representatives, without trade union involvement; and
- consultation is often informal, is generally seen as productive by both employer and representatives, but has most impact where it is strongly supported by senior management.

6. Legal checklist

- Directors in organisations with more than 250 employees must report in their annual reports and accounts on the action they have taken during the financial year to inform and consult their staff – Companies Act 1985.

- Employee information and consultation: Under legislation expected to be in force by March 2005 (for employers with 150 or more employees; by March 2007 for those with 100 or more employees; and by March 2008 for those with 50 or more employees), employers will be required to introduce mechanisms through which they can inform and consult employee representatives about significant business and employment issues – forthcoming UK legislation implementing the EU Information and Consultation Directive.

- European works councils: Employees, their representatives or the employer can "trigger" legal provisions requiring "undertakings" that have at least

1,000 employees in countries of the European Economic Area (EEA), of which 150 employees must be employed in each of two separate EEA countries, to set up a European works council where the employer informs and consults employee representatives – Transnational Information and Consultation of Employees Regulations 1999.

● Redundancy consultation: Employee representatives must be informed and consulted where 20 or more redundancies are planned to take place in the same establishment within a 90-day period – Trade Union and Labour Relations (Consolidation) Act 1992.

● Consultations on business transfers: Employee representatives must be informed and consulted about proposed transfers, regardless of the size of the undertaking – Transfer of Undertakings (Protection of Employment) (Amendment) Regulations 1987.

● Election of representatives: A similar procedure applies under both Regulations; representatives must be elected in a fair way, in sufficient numbers that they are able to represent the interests of all those affected, and candidates must be "affected" employees.

● Consultation with recognised trade unions: Redundancy and business transfer consultations must involve trade union representatives where an independent union is recognised by the employer – Trade Union and Labour Relations (Consolidation) Act 1992; Transfer of Undertakings (Protection of Employment) (Amendment) Regulations 1987.

● Working time: Employers that do not recognise a trade union are able to conclude a special "workforce agreement" with specially elected employee representatives for the purposes of varying or opting out of the Working Time Regulations 1998.

● Information for recognised unions 1: On request, employers are expected to provide information to trade union representatives in respect of the issues for which the union is recognised for collective bargaining purposes – Trade Union and Labour Relations (Consolidation) Act 1992; the Acas Code of Practice on Disclosure of Information to Trade Unions for Collective Bargaining Purposes and other Regulations.

● Information for recognised unions 2: There are certain information disclosure rights relating to occupational pensions schemes – Occupational Pensions Schemes (Disclosure of Information) Regulations 1986 and other Regulations.

● Right to be accompanied: Employees have the right to be accompanied to disciplinary and grievance hearings and meetings (in the case of discipline, this applies to hearings/meetings that could lead to a sanction; in the case of grievances, this applies to issues relating to the employer's contractual or statutory duties) by a trade union representative or a colleague – Employment Relations Act 1999.

● Industrial action: Employees undertaking official industrial action that comes under the protection of the Trade Union and Labour Relations (Consolidation) Act 1992, as amended by the Employment Relations Act 1999, and where the action has been endorsed by an approved ballot, are usually protected from dismissal if the main reason relates to taking part in such action.

● Victimisation: Employees, trade union members and their representatives have a general right not to be victimised or dismissed because of their membership (or non-membership) of a trade union; this right was extended to union learning representatives from April 2003 – Trade Union and Labour Relations (Consolidation) Act 1992.

● Time off: Trade union representatives have qualified rights, on request, to reasonable amounts of paid time off for relevant training and to perform their duties; trade union members have certain rights to unpaid time off to take part in certain union activities – Trade Union and Labour Relations (Consolidation) Act 1992; Acas Code of Practice on Time Off for Trade Union Duties and Activities.

● Facilities: Employers are recommended to provide facilities to help trade union representatives perform their duties, such as office equipment and access to a telephone – Acas Code of Practice on Time Off for Trade Union Duties and Activities.

● Union learning representatives: These representatives have qualified rights to paid time off to carry out their duties under provisions of Trade Union and Labour Relations (Consolidation) Act 1992, as amended by Employment Act 2002 from April 2003. Members who consult their learning representative are entitled to unpaid time off for this purpose.

● Statutory recognition: Employers with more than 20 employees may be required to grant recognition to a trade union under certain conditions (*see the "Statutory recognition" section in this chapter for more information*) – Trade Union and Labour Relations (Consolidation) Act 1992, as amended by the Employment Relations Act 1999 (the recognition provisions are under review).

● Health and safety consultation 1: Where employees are not in bargaining groups for which trade unions are recognised, employers are required to consult them directly or via elected staff representatives; representatives' duties are set out in the Regulations – Health and Safety (Consultation with Employees) Regulations 1996 (as amended).

● Health and safety consultation 2: Employees covered by a recognition agreement can be consulted via special safety representatives appointed by

their union; those appointed represent all employees concerned, not merely those who are union members; representatives' duties are set out in the Regulations – Safety Representatives and Safety Committees Regulations 1977 (as amended).

● Health and safety consultation 3: Consultation must be conducted in good time, supported by adequate information.

● Health and safety representatives: Individual employees and representatives are protected against victimisation or dismissal connected with their participation in the consultation process. Representatives also have a right to paid time off to be trained in their role, and to "reasonable" paid time off and facilities to carry out their duties. The time off right also applies to those standing for election as a representative – Health and Safety (Consultation with Employees) Regulations 1996 (as amended); Safety Representatives and Safety Committees Regulations 1977 (as amended).

9. Equal opportunities and diversity

This chapter covers:
- Overview;
- The need for a policy;
- Monitoring;
- The role of training in promoting equality;
- Diversity
- Positive action and targets;
- Sex discrimination;
- Race discrimination;
- Disability discrimination;
- Age discrimination;
- Discrimination and specific personnel practices: recruitment and selection; performance management; pay and benefits; adoption, maternity and paternity; flexible working; emergency leave; retention; training; and redundancy and dismissal; and
- Discrimination against other groups.

Checklists in this chapter:

1. Putting diversity into practice
2. Good practice in employing individuals with disabilities
3. Making reasonable adjustments
4. Good practice in employment free of age bias
5. Emergency leave case law
6. Legal checklist

Case studies in this chapter:

A. B&Q and Sainsbury's
B. Yorkshire Electricity
C. Ford of Britain
D. Co-operative Insurance Society
E. London Underground and Royal United Hospitals Bath NHS Trust
F. The Crown Prosecution Service
G. The Patent Office
H. BT
I. Hertfordshire County Council
J. National Maritime Museum; HBOS; Marks & Spencer

Overview

Unfair discrimination continues to take place in the workplace, despite the huge shifts in public opinion in the years since the first anti-discrimination Act of Parliament was passed in 1968, and the increasing likelihood that employers' commission of discriminatory practices will be challenged by either the media or through an employment tribunal application.

In some ways, personnel and HR managers find it easier to implement equal opportunities and diversity policies now that the law has been strengthened. While the initiatives will usually involve staff time, resources and other costs, the price of doing nothing may actually be greater if its consequence could be the need to mount a defence to a legal case.

However, the adverse publicity surrounding "political correctness" can make personnel and HR managers' job more difficult if it leads to accusations of "gold-plating" the law's requirements, and if it is used as an excuse to portray their concerns about dubious practices as over-reactions lacking in common sense.

The business case for equality of opportunity is often advanced as a reason for action being taken by employers, but, critics of this approach argue that it panders to the view that only actions that support corporate objectives can ever be justified. Where the business climate changes, or strategic goals are revised, it is conceivable that the business case will no longer hold true.

The business case for employers treating unfair discrimination in a serious manner focuses on five issues:

● **Customers:** The individuals making up an organisation's customer base come from diverse backgrounds, and will welcome finding a similar diversity among the employees with whom they come into contact. Employees that share the same backgrounds and experiences as their customers are also more able to understand their interests and requirements. This can help increase customer goodwill, generate new sales and encourage repeat business. Such employees' insights into the market's needs may also ensure the success of new products and services.

● **Skills and abilities:** Individuals from all backgrounds have something to offer an employer, to restrict access to their skills and abilities on the basis of irrational prejudice and subjective judgment reduces the organisation's potential performance and productivity. This factor becomes more important when employers find it difficult to recruit and retain employees.

● **Motivation:** Many potential employees have already experienced discrimination; an employer that treats them fairly and objectively is likely to gain their goodwill and, as a result, enjoy greater motivation and above-average levels of attendance and performance.

● **Spin-offs:** Measures to improve equal opportunities often provide wider benefits involving other members of staff and, perhaps, suppliers and customers. These spin-offs can raise morale and lead to improved recruitment, retention, attendance and performance. Thorough-going equality policies can raise the professionalism of management throughout the organisation.

● **Cost-benefit analysis:** The planning for most business initiatives involves a cost-benefit analysis of the potential gains that could be expected against the project's set-up and running costs. A similar process could be applied to the costs of equal opportunity initiatives and the potential benefits, and would usually show that the rewards would exceed the costs involved.

Case study A. The business case

Do-it-yourself retailer **B&Q** has won many awards for its equal opportunities initiatives. One aspect of its thinking involves the business case for implementing its equality programmes. For example, it estimates that around 8.6 million people have some form of disability or impairment, and around seven million people have caring responsibilities for them. In all, around one in four of the population either has a disability or knows someone who has one. This large target group is far more likely to choose to shop somewhere that is easily accessible to customers and employees who have disabilities. In addition, some 90% of people with disabilities live in their own homes, which means they require access to the same range of goods, facilities and services as anyone else who lives in the same locality. But, many businesses fail to recognise that people with disabilities want to use the same services as everyone else, not just specialist ones "for the disabled". B&Q estimates that it can target some five million adults of working age who receive the national average income, and who either have disabilities or care for someone with them. In business terms, its strategy aims to capture a far higher proportion of the available market.

Supermarket company **Sainsbury's** describes the business case for its initiatives towards older people as follows: "Customer service is a high priority for us at Sainsbury's, and it is helpful to us if our staff reflect the customer base we serve. For example, older workers can identify easily with the large number of retired people who shop in our stores. Their experience and natural courtesy are particularly helpful in enabling us to meet our high standards of customer care."[1]

Alongside economic arguments, the presence of unfair discrimination should be deplored because it highlights the fact that personnel practices, and the actions of managers and, probably, their employees, are flawed. The organisation is operating on the basis of subjective judgments that take little account of individuals' actual skills and abilities, but are based on prejudice, assumptions and stereotypes. Given that all aspects of the management of people should contribute to providing the skills and abilities that the organisation requires, then discriminatory practices represent a negation of that goal – practices that will cost the employer money through poor recruitment, training, promotion, reward and retention practices.

Morally, the unfair treatment of an individual is abhorrent to most people, and employers that condone it will lose the trust and goodwill of their staff.

Fundamentally, though, it is the law of the land that unfair discrimination should not be practised on the grounds of gender or ethnicity – in other words, a 100% coverage of the population – as well as against a wide range of protected minorities.

The need for a policy

Unfair discrimination in employment can manifest itself through all or any of the many ways in which individuals are managed at work, from the point before they start work for an organisation (in its recruitment and selection practices) to the stage where they leave it (through its dismissal and redundancy procedures).

It is important to ensure that each aspect of personnel management is as discrimination-proof as possible. But this does little or nothing to address underlying attitudes. A policy that integrates all these discrimination-proofing efforts is required. Properly developed and implemented, it will represent an official endorsement by senior management of the principles of equal opportunities (and, if applicable, diversity – *see the section below*). Accompanied by enforcement measures, without which it will be empty rhetoric, the policy will also act as a code of conduct for the employees and managers of the organisation and, where relevant, its suppliers and customers.

And if it ensures that the policy is known outside the organisation, then those it deals with – including potential new employees – will expect its managers and employees to behave and act in accordance with it. This encourages compliance, and can help develop the organisation's reputation as a good place to work, or to do business with.

Many organisations have already introduced a formal equal opportunities policy. Out of 180 organisations we contacted, almost all (92%) of the larger ones have such a policy, although it is likely that employers with smaller workforces are less likely to have one. There are strong indications that the policies are not introduced then forgotten. For example, more than four in 10 (44%) of those with policies had updated them in the previous four years – largely, to ensure that they kept pace with developments in legislation. Furthermore, when we contacted them, one in four (24%) were planning to change their equal opportunities policies in the near future.

The content of a particular employer's policy needs to take account of its own circumstances, once its statutory obligations have been addressed. In particular, influential factors are likely to include the number and type of employees, the resources available to the organisation and the nature of its culture (particularly, attitudes towards formalising rules and procedures).

The Equal Opportunities Commission is one of the sources of model equality policies. Its *Guidelines for equal opportunities employers* (free of charge from www.eoc.org.uk) lists the typical contents of a policy, and sets out 10 steps that employers could take in order to be able legitimately to advertise themselves as "an equal opportunities employer" in their recruitment advertising and other corporate publicity. These steps address the important issues of ensuring that, once it has been written, a policy is implemented and its effectiveness is monitored.

It recommends that the policy is supported by senior managers, and a very senior manager is given overall responsibility for it. The policy should be written down, and actively communicated to current employees, managers and recognised trade unions, as well as to job applicants and any agencies used for recruitment purposes (such as employment agencies and jobcentres). Members of staff with responsibility for the recruitment and supervision of others should be trained in the policy and in the way in which it relates to their activities.

A member of staff should be designated equality officer with responsibility for coordinating equality activities on a day-to-day basis. But the implementation and monitoring of the policy should be supervised by a senior manager, preferably one who acts as a chair of an equality committee involving representatives of employees, managers and trade unions. The committee should examine existing personnel practices and procedures to ensure that they do not lead to unfair discrimination, and follow the requirements of the new policy. Where evidence of past unfair discrimination is found, remedial action should be taken. Finally, the policy should set up monitoring systems and the data should be analysed by the committee to check that the policy is working in practice.

Case study B. Yorkshire Electricity

Utility company Yorkshire Electricity holds a Louder than Words award from the Royal National Institute for the Deaf for its support of customers and staff who have hearing difficulties. Its equal opportunities policy covers employees, contractors, temporary recruits and job applicants, and aims to ensure that they do not receive "less favourable treatment than another on the grounds of sex, race, disability, or on the grounds that they are a member or non-member of a trade union, or have taken or propose to take parental leave or maternity leave".

The first section of its seven-point document sets out the company's commitment to equality of opportunity, the consequences of unfair discrimination and the areas of personnel management where it might occur. Sections two to six define unfair discrimination in respect of sex or race, harassment, individuals with disabilities, victimisation and bullying, and provide information on the ways in which it might occur, together with individuals' rights and responsibilities. The final section covers breaches of the policy, where committing or condoning unfair discrimination will be treated "as serious or gross misconduct by the company", and the formal disciplinary procedure will be used, potentially leading to summary dismissal.

Monitoring

Where employers set up processes to collate and analyse equal opportunities information, they obtain hard evidence that proves valuable in two ways. From a legal standpoint, they have data that will help them defend tribunal complaints of discrimination. And from a good-practice point of view, they have statistics that provide the essential management information to help them ensure their practices and policies are working as intended to promote equality of opportunity.

Because unfair discrimination can occur at any point in the employment relationship, monitoring data needs to cover all its key stages: from recruitment and selection, to access to training and promotion, and eventual departure.

All the equality commissions – the Equal Opportunities Commission, the Commission for Racial Equality and the Disability Rights Commission – recommend employers to set up monitoring systems, as does the government's voluntary Code of Practice on Age Diversity in Employment[2].

And monitoring is a legal requirement of employers in the public sector. Many firms in the private sector have also introduced it. Like other data covering personnel practices, such as labour turnover rates and the results of employee attitude surveys, the information represents a starting point and has little value unless it is used as the basis for analysis and action.

In terms of current practice, personnel, HR and equality managers tell us that their organisations' monitoring processes cover the following factors, shown in descending order of prevalence:
● gender;
● ethnicity;
● disability; and to a lesser extent
● age.

Monitoring on the grounds of age is likely to increase significantly in the run up to the forthcoming legislation on age discrimination that must be in place by the end of 2006.

It is very rare, at present, for employers to monitor additional factors, such as marital status, sexual orientation and religion (however, this is a legal requirement in Northern Ireland).

There are many ways of defining or categorising individuals' ethnicity for the purposes of monitoring, and we have found that most employers have adopted the categories used in the 2001 census of population. This is the approach recommended by the Commission for Racial Equality, although it adds that employers could consider extending or subdividing the categories where the composition of their workforce or local community warrants it. There is a recommended set of ethnic categories for employers in Northern Ireland (from the Equality Commission for Northern Ireland; www.equalityni.org).

In respect of defining disabilities, the census is less helpful as it simply asks whether or not individuals consider that they have a disability. We have found that most employers instead prefer to use the categories found in the government's Labour Force Survey.

Specific personnel practices are covered by monitoring as shown below in descending order of prevalence:
● recruitment, with many organisations monitoring each stage of recruitment and selection; and to a lesser extent
● the current workforce – usually by one or more of: grade, role, department – in respect of current job and promotions; and much less commonly

● the results of formal performance reviews, access to training, basic pay, bonus awards, grievances, disciplinary actions, dismissals and redundancy selection – only a minority of employers with monitoring systems addresses any of these practices.

Very few employers monitor the composition of those managing their personnel practices; for example, while organisations monitor job applicants, they rarely monitor the composition of those responsible for recruitment and selection.

Few employers monitor their reward practices, as we saw above, despite recent government advice that they should do so. *(See the section below in this chapter on Pay and benefits for more information on pay audits and questionnaires.)*

In the public sector, the Race Relations (Amendment) Act 2000 now places a specific duty on relevant employers to monitor the ethnicity of "staff in post, and applicants for employment, training and promotion", and publish annual reports of their findings. Relevant public bodies with more than 150 full-time employees have additional duties to monitor the ethnicity of individuals who "receive training, benefit or suffer detriment as a result of its performance-assessment procedures, are involved in grievance procedures, are the subject of disciplinary procedures, or cease employment". Again, annual reports must be produced.

Case study C. Ford of Britain

Ford of Britain came fourth in Race for Opportunity's 2002 diversity benchmarking survey of the private sector, representing a major achievement for a company that had been threatened with investigation by the Commission for Racial Equality just two years previously.

The company has introduced a comprehensive monitoring process to evaluate its progress towards equality of opportunity. In terms of ethnicity, employees are monitored by grade and location, and by overall changes in workforce composition. The representation of ethnic minorities is also monitored at key stages in its internal and external recruitment procedures to ensure that fair recruitment, selection, promotion and development decisions are being made. Internal statistics are compared with the composition of the local population and, where possible, with comparable data from previous years to illustrate change. Monitoring data is collated into a company-wide annual equal opportunities report which is distributed to managers, HR specialists and trade unions.

The role of training in promoting equality

Unlawful discrimination undoubtedly continues to occur in employment, often as a result of flawed practices, unacceptable attitudes or attempts by busy managers to "cut corners". The results will not change unless these underlying practices and attitudes do so, and this requires direct intervention by employers.

Formal policies, backed up by monitoring the results of implementing them, set the tone and overall context, but line managers, their employees and others in the organisation must also be informed and trained about the need for equality of opportunity.

The role of line managers in the day-to-day management of their employees is crucial in ensuring that each person is treated without unfair discrimination. As well as managing employees in a fair manner, line managers' responsibilities are increasingly being extended by organisations to include more formal personnel issues. In particular, they are often involved in recruitment, in formal performance assessments and in reaching promotion decisions.

However, rank-and-file employees should not be overlooked. Bullying and harassment can often involve an individual's colleagues, as well as their own manager. Conversely, employees' positive attitudes can help foster a culture that encourages equality of opportunity. And involving senior managers in a communication and training exercise acknowledges their importance in shaping policies and setting the tone of the organisation.

Communication and training play several roles:
● the effort involved in launching a communication and training initiative can send out a message that the organisation intends to take a serious view of unfair discrimination;
● communication and training serve to raise awareness of the ways in which unfair discrimination can occur, and why this is unacceptable;
● they can impart the skills and foster the attitudes necessary to ensure that unfair discrimination is less likely to occur in future; and
● communication and training provide some defence against an employer's "vicarious liability" – its responsibility at law for the actions of employees and managers.

Communicating information about equal opportunities and providing training in essential skills should never be a one-off exercise. Memories become dimmed as time passes and it becomes easy to slip back into old ways, consciously or not. And the organisation's workforce is constantly changing; new members of staff are recruited from outside, and employees are promoted to positions of additional responsibility.

The Equal Opportunities Commission recommends that the training should be tailored to the responsibilities of particular groups. Individuals with supervisory responsibilities, in particular, will need greater information and training in the ways in which personnel practices can unfairly discriminate, about stereotypes and other attitudes that could lead to subjectivity, and the ways in which more objective decisions about individuals can be made. Alongside equal opportunities issues, those involved in managing particular personnel processes – such as recruitment and performance management – need to be trained in the technical skills involved. Many employers incorporate relevant equal opportunities material into their training provision for these processes, so that equality and day-to-day practice are linked closely in participants' minds – rather than discrimination being seen as an optional "add on".

The effective design and delivery of any training programme requires special expertise and skills, but training that addresses equal opportunities issues can be particularly difficult because of the sensitivities involved. Large-scale research for the Home Office by the Institute for Employment Studies[3] has highlighted some the key issues and potential pitfalls involved in training linked to race discrimination. However, it and a good-practice guide to training based on it[4], have more general relevance.

The institute found that the most effective training is:
- tailored to participants' responsibilities and needs;
- delivered by trainers who have the credibility to overcome resistance by some participants; the trainers should have a good understanding of the organisation, including its culture, and some personal experience of some of the discrimination issues being covered;
- designed to be of high quality, where the training is interesting, well-delivered and uses an appropriate pace; the training should have been piloted to ensure that these factors have been addressed;
- based on maximum attendance, where everything possible is done to encourage all participants to attend the training; in some organisational cultures, it may be acceptable to make attendance compulsory; and
- outward-looking, in that equal opportunities issues have relevance to the organisation's customers as well as its employees.

Diversity

"Diversity" is a more recent term than "equal opportunities" and is often interpreted in different ways. For some, it provides a convenient synonym for an established equal opportunities policy. For others, it means a renewed, more vigorous approach to ensuring equality of opportunity. Others interpret "diversity" as having connotations of positive action in setting targets and launching initiatives to address a history of previous unfair discrimination.

Often, though, "diversity" is understood in the UK to mean an approach that goes beyond compliance with equal opportunities legislation to one that sees each individual employee as being unique and offering their own valuable experiences, insights and skills. Employers that value diversity positively embrace the differences in their workforces and use them as the basis for higher performance and improved products and services. To gain as much benefit from diversity as possible, many organisations take action to ensure that each person is managed in such a way that their potential is given full scope.

This may involve adjusting the way that work is organised – making it more collaborative and team-based, for example, so that the one person's strong points complement another's weaknesses. The Chartered Institute of Personnel and Development (CIPD) says an diversity approach: "Acknowledges that organisational cultures may need to become more flexible and adaptable in order to realise the full potential of a diverse workforce. Changing the way in which things have always been done is a fundamental requirement."[5]

The case for adopting a diversity approach echoes the one usually advanced in respect of equal opportunities *(see above)*. Diversity helps employers observe the law of the land, is justified morally in that subjective factors over which the individual often has little or no control are not used as the basis of decision-making about them, and is also merited economically and operationally. The CIPD puts it this way: "Managing diversity is based on the concept that people should be valued as individuals for reasons related to business interests, as well as for moral and social reasons. It recognises that people from different backgrounds can bring fresh ideas and perceptions which can make the way work is done more efficient, and [make] products and services better" (same source as above).

Checklist 1 highlights the main ways in which employers can introduce and implement a diversity approach. The second half of the checklist is based on actions that employers tell us they are currently taking to improve diversity. The feedback we have obtained shows that employers in the public and private sectors often take different routes to the same end, taking advantage of their different backgrounds and strong points.

For example, the private sector tends to have less formalised recruitment and selection practices, and employers are much more likely to be flexible and creative when making appointment decisions in order to increase diversity.

But private sector employers are less creative, or less well-resourced, in respect of recruitment advertising. Far fewer of them, compared with their public sector counterparts, advertise their vacancies in non-traditional media, such as newspapers for ethnic minority groups or homosexuals. The public sector is also more likely to notify jobcentres of its vacancies – jobcentres are part of a huge network of local branches backed up by a national online database of vacancies. And the public sector is much more likely than the private sector to provide recruitment documents in different formats that could encourage individuals from diverse backgrounds to apply.

1. Putting diversity into practice

Putting diversity into practice requires many of the same strategies and procedures as traditional equal opportunities initiatives, supplemented by specific targeted actions.

Policy and procedures:

● A senior manager needs to lead the project, gain endorsement from the most senior directors in the organisation, and establish a project team.

● The project team should consult widely to develop a draft diversity policy that is discussed and revised as necessary.

● The policy should be communicated to all employees and managers, and focused training given in understanding and implementing it. The training's focus should depend on the roles and responsibilities that the participants play in the organisation, with greater depth and breadth being given to participants who have people-management responsibilities.

● The culture of the organisation should be shifted towards one that supports diversity, using effective communication, involvement and training practices, and measuring improvements through regular employee attitude surveys.

● Existing personnel practices, such as recruitment and access to training, should be checked that they comply with the policy and foster an approach that values diversity.

● Other training programmes, such as in recruitment and selection skills, should be amended to incorporate diversity-related issues and skills.

● Individuals who experience unfair discrimination should be given encouragement to raise their concerns, including the use of grievance procedures and special harassment and bullying procedures.

● The effectiveness of the policy and changes to procedures should be monitored, and the findings analysed and acted on.

Recruitment and selection:

Based on feedback we have obtained from personnel, HR and diversity managers, these are the main actions that employers are taking to encourage diverse workforces; they are shown in descending order of prevalence:

● Monitoring applications in terms of gender, ethnicity, disabilities and so on (practised by 84.5% of the employers with diversity initiatives);

● Taking account of a broader range of qualities, such as personal skills, instead of formal qualifications when conducting recruitment and selection (76.3%);

● Notifying local jobcentres of vacancies (this is one means of broadening recruitment) (59.8%);

● Advertising vacancies beyond conventional/mainstream media (this is another means of broadening recruitment) (41.2%);

● Providing recruitment literature and forms in other formats, such as large print or in electronic format (also 41.2%);

● Setting recruitment targets so that the workforce reflects the composition of the local community or customer base (also 41.2%);

● Changing the organisation of work (35.0%); and

● Appointing applicants who may not exactly match the job requirements as specified at the time (25.8%).

● Some employers are undertaking outreach programmes to encourage a broader range of applicants to come forward; this includes making contact with community groups, publicising the employer's diversity strategy, taking part in special network organisations, and offering job placements and other forms of work experience.

Training and development:

● Many employers are providing positive encouragement to individuals from under-represented groups so that they are promoted to more senior roles in their organisations. The practices include mentoring schemes, shadowing a more senior member of staff, special training and development programmes, training in interviewing skills for job applicants and setting up support networks. Positive action must comply with legal restrictions on its use.

Support:

● Enabling individuals with caring responsibilities or special needs to work for, and remain with, the organisation by providing flexible working, such as flexible hours, working from home and special leave for domestic emergencies.

Case study D. Co-operative Insurance Society

The Co-operative Insurance Society launched its diversity and dignity at work policy in July 2002. The policy says the society's aim is: "To develop a culture where the differences between people are valued, and the full capabilities of individuals are harnessed and developed to the benefit of customers, staff and the business. We shall do this by reflecting the diversity of society in all aspects of our business and, in particular, by making measurable improvements in the diversity of our workforce". Implementing the policy includes improving its existing monitoring practices, and benchmarking the society against other organisations. Personnel practices, such as recruitment, will be reviewed to ensure they support diversity, and its diversity approach is now included in the society's management training programmes and in its training in recruitment and selection skills.

"Diversity champions" have been appointed who act as both advisers to the business on issues relating to gender, ethnicity and disability, and also provide a point of contact for members of staff.

Some specific actions being taken to implement diversity include broadening its recruitment. Its advertisements now include the Positive about Disabled People logo. Individuals with disabilities are also able to take up places on a special work preparation programme. Potential applicants from ethnic minorities are being targeted by offering work experience opportunities and mentoring to students at educational establishments with large ethnic minority populations. The society's head office has multi-faith prayer rooms, and its catering facility now offers halal food.

Positive action and targets

Positive action

Positive action aims to provide focused help to individuals from groups that are currently under-represented in the workforce, so that there is a "level playing field" – particularly when they compete for recruitment and pro-motion. Positive action provides support up to the point of a decision, such as recruitment, but, unlike positive discrimination (also known as affirma-tive action; *see below*), it stops short of favouring one individual over anoth-er on the basis of the group to which they belong.

Most commonly, employers' positive action involves:
● explicitly encouraging applicants from particular groups to apply when advertising vacancies (for example, a vacancy for a manager might contain a phrase such as: "women, ethnic minorities and people with disabilities are currently under-represented at managerial levels, and [name of employer] particularly welcomes applications from under-represented groups"); and/or
● offering training courses specifically for individuals from under-repre-sented groups to build their self-confidence and motivation, develop job-search and interviewing skills and, perhaps, to develop the specific skills required in typical vacancies.

In addition, many of the actions that employers are taking to support their diversity initiatives *(see the previous section in this chapter)* constitute forms of positive action, often in the area of encouraging applications from under-represented groups.

Positive action does not constitute unlawful discrimination where it meets the requirements of the Race Relations Act 1976 and the Sex Discrimination Act 1975. Generally, this means that the action must be tar-geted towards particular racial groups or members of one sex where they have been under-represented in the organisation over the previous 12 months. Where the action involves positive encouragement, the advertise-ment (or employment agency acting on the employer's behalf) should also remind applicants that selection will always be on merit. It is likely that the legal restrictions on positive action will be relaxed once the UK implements the revised EC Equal Treatment Directive. The government must do this on or before 5 October 2005.

Unlike the sex and race statutes where positive action is permissible under certain circumstances, there is a specific duty to make special provision in respect of individuals with disabilities. In terms of employment, organisa-tions are required to make "reasonable adjustments" to their practices, such as arrangements for testing and interviewing *(for more information, see the rel-evant sections in chapter 2)*, as well as to work, equipment, facilities and build-ings. Under the Disability Discrimination Act 1995 and the Code of Practice for the Elimination of Discrimination in the Field of Employment against Disabled Persons or Persons who have had a Disability, a reasonable adjustment is required where its absence would cause a substantial disadvantage to an individual with disabilities compared with an individual without them.

In fact, the duty to promote race equality in the public sector under the Race Relations (Amendment) Act 2000 has served to draw attention to the use of positive action. The Commission for Racial Equality's Statutory Code of Practice on the Duty to Promote Race Equality says that relevant public sector employers should consider using positive action where individuals from ethnic minorities are under-represented in certain grades or in the workforce as a whole.

The Equal Opportunities Commission has produced a helpful guide called *Managing successful positive action* (free from www.eoc.org.uk).

Target-setting

The practice of monitoring employers' practices for unfair discrimination assumes that there is a reference point against which the data can be measured. Otherwise, the data would mean little or nothing. Implicitly, the reference point is being used as a goal to which the employer's practices aspire. Target-setting, on one level, merely places this practice on a formal basis.

But, of course, the use of specific targets is more controversial than this, as it can lead to a suspicion that reverse discrimination – also known as affirmative action or positive discrimination *(see next section)* – is being practised. This could give encouragement to those who are opposed to equal opportunities, and provoke a backlash against an employer's policy of preventing unfair discrimination.

Organisations that have adopted diversity initiatives may find that they are criticised for inconsistency, in that targets focus on a class or group, and aim to increase its representation in a collective way. Yet, diversity emphasises the contribution of each individual, rather than their association with a collective entity.

There are practical difficulties with target-setting, too. It is often hard to identify appropriate comparators. For example, should the target for ethnic minorities be based on the local community, the national population or those in the relevant labour market – engineers, computer specialists, pharmacists, and so on? Should the target cover ethnic minorities as a whole, or be subdivided into particular groups? Although it is usually possible to obtain the information required, without careful thought the target might prove to be unrealistically high. This could lead to demotivation if all efforts to improve equality of opportunity seem to achieve little in tangible terms of moving towards the target.

In addition, there is always the danger that the targets might become the ultimate goal, and that satisfying them encourages managers to adopt a "tick-box" mentality. This could take attention away from the fundamental purpose of the targets, which involves using them as an indicator that progress in improving equality is being achieved. It might, for example, be possible to take limited, superficial action and still ensure that the target concerning the representation of women or ethnic minorities has been satisfied. But this might simply involve an over-representation of disadvantaged groups in the lower levels of the organisation, leaving the better-paid tiers of management untouched. In contrast, equality initiatives that focus on achieving a systematic shift in attitudes and practices are more likely to ensure that equality reaches all parts of the organisation.

The government increasingly favours target-setting. In 1999, for example, the Home Secretary set targets for the representation of ethnic minorities in the various parts of the Home Office. In the **UK Passport Service**, for example, 15.3% of recruitment in 2002 came from individuals from ethnic minorities, against "milestone" targets of 8.6% for 2002 and 2009[6]. As well as recruitment, the targets cover retention and career progression.

Targets have been adopted by other parts of the public sector. In 2000, for example, the **London Borough of Camden** set a target that 19% of senior managers (grades PO4 and above) should come from ethnic minorities, against an actual level of 15.4%. By 2002, representation had improved to 18%, leading the borough to consider revising its goal upwards.

Outside the public sector, examples of targets include charity **Oxfam**, where it aims that women will represent 50% of the managers in its most senior grade by 2006, and that the representation of ethnic minorities in its workforce will reflect the make up of the population in the regions where it is based.

Affirmative action

Affirmative action, also known as positive discrimination, is generally unlawful in the UK. The main exception involves a "genuine occupational qualification", but there are strict limitations under both the sex and race discrimination Acts. Even where the GOC appears to apply because it relates to a particular type of job, both Acts expect employers to analyse each job – and review it whenever a relevant job falls vacant – to ensure that it satisfies the criteria in the appropriate Act.

Sex discrimination

After almost three decades since the Equal Pay Act 1970 came into force, the average hourly rate of pay for men in full-time work is almost a fifth higher than that of women. Moreover, the gap is widening, taking the position back to what it was in 2000.

Most of the difference in pay levels flows from the enduring differences between the jobs that men and women perform. Not only are some jobs overwhelmingly performed by one sex – builders versus hairdressers, for example – but women are concentrated in a relatively smaller number of occupations than men. In addition, far more women than men work in part-time jobs – around 43% of all women workers are in part-time jobs – and part-timers' earning power is rarely proportionately as good as full-time workers' opportunities. In some cases, part-time work is poorly paid, but there may also be difficulties in part-timers' gaining access to the overtime pay and bonuses that some full-time workers enjoy. Even when overtime is excluded, the hourly earnings of part-time workers are about one-third below those of full-timers.

According to the 2001 Census, 84% of care assistants, childminders and hairdressers are women; as are 78% of those in administrative and clerical work; and 71% of sales and customer services staff.

In contrast, men comprise 91% of mechanics, bricklayers and electricians; they make up 83% of process, plant and machine operatives; and 66% of managers and professionals.

Discrimination awards

IRS's analysis of discrimination rulings by employment tribunals shows that sex discrimination dominated their case load of discrimination complaints in 2001, with 188 cases of the total of 329 where tribunals found in favour of the applicant. The average award for sex discriminaiton stood at £9,035. However, compensation in more than one in four decisions amounted to more than £10,000, reaching more than £20,000 in one in 10 cases.

The average award of total compensation was highest for cases of:
● dismissals on grounds of pregnancy (£9,871); followed by
● harassment (£9,651);

- terms and conditions (£8,977);
- dismissals not involving pregnancy (£8,904);
- victimisation (£8,855); and
- recruitment and promotion (£3,216).

The highest single award in 2001 was £190,663.21 (plus £7,157.38 in interest). In this case, the employer was found to have unlawfully discriminated on grounds of sex in that the employee had been selected for redundancy because she was pregnant. The compensation included £10,000 for "injury to feelings" because the tribunal considered that "to dismiss a woman when she is pregnant is to dismiss her at a time in her life when she is extremely vulnerable and when her need for employment is greater".[7]

Overall, IRS's monitoring of tribunal awards reveals that employers are increasingly having to pay higher awards in sex discrimination cases.

It is worth remembering that tribunal awards in discrimination cases represent just the tip of the iceberg. Considerably more cases involve employers paying compensation as part of a settlement under the auspices of Acas or where employers withdraw their defence before the hearing is about to commence. In addition, tribunals in some cases reach decisions against the employer but leave it to the parties to reach private agreement on the amount of compensation.

Changing legislation

The Sex Discrimination Act 1975 and the Equal Pay Act 1970 are, of course, the main statutes covering sex discrimination in the UK. However, the area of equal opportunities law is changing rapidly because of developments in case law (legal precedents), British legislation and EC Directives.

Recent changes include:
- protecting part-time workers from less favourable treatment than equivalent full-time workers unless the treatment can be justified on objective grounds, under the Part-Time Workers (Prevention of Less Favourable Treatment) Regulations 2000, effective from July 2000;
- improving maternity, paternity and adoption leave and pay, effective in respect of children born on (or adopted) after 6 April 2003, under the provisions of the Employment Act 2002 *(described below)*;
- a right to request flexible working for employees with a child under the age of six or a child with disabilities under the aged of 18; introduced in April 2003 under the same 2002 Act *(described below)*;

● shifting the burden of proof onto employers once the applicant has established a basic presumption of discrimination, under the Sex Discrimination (Indirect Discrimination and Burden of Proof) Regulations 2001;

● broadening the definition of indirect discrimination from issues involving a "requirement or condition" to a "provision, criterion or practice", under the same 2001 Regulations; and

● introducing an equal pay questionnaire from 6 April 2003 for use by individuals considering making a tribunal application under the Equal Pay Act 1970 (as amended by the Employment Act 2002); employers' completion of the questionnaire is not compulsory but tribunals can make inferences about failing to reply to the questionnaire or giving evasive answers, unless the employer can provide a good reason for doing so *(further information below)*.

Forthcoming changes include:

● changing the time limit (expected in July 2003) and arrears provisions (expected in December 2003) in equal pay claims;

● extending protection to issues relating to an individual's sexual orientation by 1 December 2003;

● narrowing employers' defence in cases of sexual harassment once the UK implements the revised Equal Treatment Directive on or before 5 October 2005;

● potentially broadening the coverage of the Equal Pay Act 1970 so that applicants do not have to name an actual comparator (EC Equal Treatment Directive);

● broadening the coverage of unfair discrimination to include all actions by employers after the contract of employment has ended (EC Equal Treatment Directive); and

● undertaking a further revision of the definition of indirect discrimination under the same EC Directive.

Race discrimination

In the words of the Prime Minister: "In recent decades, Britain has become a much more ethnically diverse country. Some ethnic minority groups have done increasingly well, not only in the education system but also in the labour market. [. . .] But, despite the marked progress made by some, too many members of ethnic minority communities are still being left behind. Even those individuals who achieve academic success do not necessarily reap the rewards in the workplace that their qualifications merit."[8]

At present, individuals from ethnic minorities make up around 10% of the population in England and Wales, but have markedly different experiences in the labour market. According to the same government report that quoted the Prime Minister, individuals from Indian or Chinese backgrounds do as well as, and often do better than, whites in terms of employment. In contrast, Pakistanis, Bangladeshis and Black Caribbeans have unemployment rates and earnings levels that are significantly worse than those of whites. However, all in all, the report says that the evidence shows "that all ethnic minority groups, even those enjoying relative success [. . .] are not doing as well as they should be, given their education and other characteristics".

According to the latest Census, 9.9% of the population in England and Wales have identified themselves as being from an ethnic minority, of which 1.2% are Irish. In all, 87.5% gave their origin as white British. But there are significant differences in the distribution of ethnic minorities. In London, for example, the Census found that one in three (32.1%) of the population are ethnic minorities.

More specifically, different ethnic minority groups are present to a greater or lesser degree in particular localities. Chinese people make up more than 2% of those living in Cambridge and the London Borough of Barnet, for example. Bangladeshis form 33.4% of the population of the London Borough of Tower Hamlets, although they comprise no more than 0.5% of everyone in the UK.

As well as regional distribution, there are also differences in terms of age and education between whites and ethnic minorities, and within particular minority groups.

A study by government statisticians has taken account of these and other factors to calculate the net differences in the experiences of minorities and whites in the labour market. Using three main divisions of black, Indian and Pakistani/Bangladeshi, it has found that Pakistani/Bangladeshi men are 2.85 times more likely to be unemployed as white men. For black men, the factor is 2.51 times, while for Indian men it is 1.64 times.

When controlled for age, educational attainment and other factors, all three groups are still less likely than white males of being employed in professional occupations, and all three groups earn less then white men.[9]

Discrimination awards

IRS's analysis of discrimination rulings by employment tribunals shows that 85 of the 188 discrimination decisions made in 2001 involved findings of race discrimination. The average award stood at £9,743. However, compensation in one in three decisions amounted to £10,000 and above, reaching £20,000 or more in almost one in six cases.

The average compensation award was highest for cases of:
- dismissals (£8,851); jointly with
- recruitment and promotion (£8,851); followed by
- terms and conditions (£8,368); and
- victimisation (£4,938).

The highest single award in 2001 was £63,029, although one of £815,000 – the second highest to date – was awarded in 2002[10].

Overall, IRS's monitoring of tribunal awards reveals that employers are increasingly having to pay higher awards in race discrimination cases (the total amount has almost doubled in three years), and that the number of complaints of race discrimination is on an upward path.

Changing legislation

The Race Relations Act 1976 is the main statute covering race discrimination in the UK. However, the area of equal opportunities law is changing rapidly because of developments in case law (legal precedents), British legislation and EC Directives.

Recent changes include:
- placing a duty on public bodies to promote race equality under the Race Relations (Amendment) Act 2000, which came into force on 2 April 2001; Forthcoming changes include those shown below, which arise from the UK implementing EC Directives, and are expected to have effect from 19 July 2003 through Regulations amending the Race Relations Action 1976:
- revising the definition of indirect discrimination;
- potentially changing the definition of harassment established under case law;
- shifting the burden of proof onto employers once the applicant has established a basic presumption of discrimination; and
- broadening the coverage of unfair discrimination to include all actions by employers after the contract of employment has ended.
Other forthcoming changes include:
- additional protection concerning discrimination on the grounds of religion and new protection on grounds of belief; these measures are expected to take effect by 1 December 2003.

Disability discrimination

One in five adults have a long-term disability, many of whom are covered by the international definition of being unemployed: actively looking for work but being unsuccessful in finding it. In all, individuals with disabilities are 1.7 times more likely to be unemployed than the rest of the population that is in or actively seeking a job. Many more individuals with disabilities have given up their search for a job and are classed as economically inactive. Overall, almost half of all people with disabilities are economically inactive, compared with just 15% of people without disabilities.

A government survey of more than 2,000 people with disabilities[11] has found that one in four (24%) have experienced discrimination. In the employment context:
● one in four (25%) of this group have experienced discrimination when applying for a job, where recruiters made unfavourable assumptions about the applicant's ability to perform the job;
● one in six (16%) have experienced discrimination from colleagues at work;
● one in six (16%) have been dismissed because of a health- or disability-related problem; and
● one in eight (13%) have worked for an employer that has failed to provide equipment or support that their disability required.

Separate research commissioned by disability insurer UnumProvident[12] also indicates widespread discriminatory attitudes among employers towards individuals with disabilities. One in three organisations would appoint a candidate without disabilities in preference over someone with disabilities, even where the two candidates were equally suitable and the disability was unlikely to be relevant to performance at work.

The survey also found that one in three employers believe that individuals with disabilities have higher levels of absence than other members of staff, and two in three employers would be concerned about employing someone with disabilities because of the cost of altering premises or providing special equipment. These perceptions reflect subjective, stereotypical views. In fact, as a whole, individuals with disabilities have the same, if not better, attendance rates as employees without disabilities, and there are usually few or no costs involved in meeting the needs of individuals with disabilities[13]. The government's Access to Work programme provides £44 million a year in subsidies for employers to help workers with disabilities find employment or remain in work.

More generally, the popular view of disability focuses on mobility problems, yet only 5% of people with disabilities actually use wheelchairs.

Discrimination awards

IRS's analysis of discrimination rulings by employment tribunals shows that 56 of the 188 discrimination decisions made in 2001 involved findings of disability discrimination. Total compensation awarded in 2001 amounted to £1,355,335, considerably higher than the total for race discrimination awards of £828,187 – and not far behind the £1,698,555 awarded to cases concerned with sex discrimination, which involved more than three times as many cases.

The average award stood at £24,202. However, compensation in more than four in 10 decisions amounted to at least £10,000, reaching £20,000 or more in almost one in three cases. Compensation for future loss of earnings is often considerably higher than in cases of sex or race discrimination because tribunals tend to take the view that individuals who have been dismissed on grounds of their disability would find it difficult to gain another job.

The average award of total compensation was highest for cases of:
● dismissal and failure to make reasonable adjustment (£38,271); followed by
● failure to make reasonable adjustment without dismissal (£32,756);
● dismissal (£23,713); and
● less favourable treatment (£7,261).

The highest single award in 2001 was £280,801, where the applicant's employer was found to have failed to make reasonable adjustments, effectively cutting short her working life[14].

Overall, IRS's monitoring of tribunal awards reveals that employers are increasingly having to pay higher awards in disability discrimination cases.

Changing legislation

The Disability Discrimination Act 1995 is the main statute covering discrimination against individuals with disabilities in the UK. The relatively recent introduction of the Act means that case law is particularly important, especially in the area of defining conditions that are eligible for protection under the complex provisions of the statute. But the law is also changing because of a government review of the Act itself and because of changes required to implement EC Directives.

Forthcoming changes include those shown below, which arise from the UK implementing EC Directives, and are expected to have effect from 1 October 2004 through Regulations amending the Disability Discrimination Act 1995:

● including a definition of harassment;

● shifting the burden of proof onto employers once the applicant has established a basic presumption of discrimination;

● broadening the coverage of unfair discrimination to include all actions by employers after the contract of employment has ended;

● abolishing the exemption from the Disability Discrimination Act 1995 for employers with fewer than 15 employees, with effect from October 2004;

● extending the coverage of the 1995 Act to occupations including fire-fighting, specialised police forces and prison officers, and work on ships and airplanes; and

● removing two potential justifications for discrimination: justification for failure to make a reasonable adjustment, and justification where the reason for less favourable treatment is simply that the person has a disability.

In addition:

● replacing or amending the existing legislation – a government Bill is expected later in 2003; this is likely to broaden the protection afforded to individuals with disabilities, including extending the definition of disability to include asymptomatic cancers requiring substantial treatment and individuals diagnosed with HIV who are otherwise in good health.

Employers' disability practices

Since the period prior to the implementation of the Disability Discrimination Act 1995, IRS has been tracking employers' practices regarding the recruitment and employment of individuals with disabilities. In particular, we have been investigating emerging best practice; see checklists 2 and 3 for feedback based on the experiences of several hundred personnel, HR and equality managers.

2. Good practice in employing individuals with disabilities

Based on our long-term research into employers' practices, feedback from personnel, HR and equality managers shows that good practice in employing individuals with disabilities often includes the following factors:

● **Policy:** the development of a formal policy regarding the organisation's employment of individuals with disabilities; most organisations incorporate it into their main equality or diversity policy;

● **Rationale:** the policy plays a valuable role in fostering positive attitudes towards individuals with disabilities and towards equal opportunities more generally – in terms of employees, recruits and customers – and of ensuring compliance with the Disability Discrimination Act 1995;

● **Emerging rationale:** A growing number of organisations also introduce policies as an expression of their corporate responsibility towards society, or as a means of improving customer service;

● **Positive action:** Actively encouraging applications for jobs from individuals with disabilities;

● **Two-ticks:** Encouragement of candidates often involves publicising the organisation's award of the disability ("two-ticks") symbol; more generally, gaining the award helps reinforce the employer's commitment to employing individuals with disabilities;

● **Recruitment:** An increasing proportion of employers are undertaking a review of their recruitment and selection procedures to ensure that they do not discriminate unfairly against applicants with disabilities *(see also the sections on discrimination in specific personnel practices later in this chapter)*;

● **Reasonable adjustments:** A growing proportion of organisations is making reasonable adjustments to premises, equipment and work organisation to make it possible to recruit and retain individuals with disabilities. *See checklist 3 below for details;*

● **Monitoring:** Many employers track their success in avoiding unfair discrimination towards individuals with disabilities by introducing monitoring processes; however, difficulties are widespread and broad-ranging, including finding suitable categories of disability, gathering the information sensitively, avoiding a superficial focus on achieving targets, and avoiding the association of data-gathering with the organisation's efforts to manage attendance;

● **Flexibility:** The availability of flexible hours of work and the ability to work from home can help individuals manage their disabilities and represent reasonable adjustments on the part of the employer; so far, only a minority of organisations offer either option to individuals with disabilities; and

● **Retention:** The involvement of occupational health specialists plays a valuable role in ensuring that individuals who develop a disability are able to continue working for the employer.

3. Making reasonable adjustments

Increasing numbers of employers are making reasonable adjustments to their premises, equipment and work organisation in order to recruit and retain individuals with disabilities. Importantly, half of the adjustments involve little or no cost to the organisation. Where expenditure is involved, in around four in 10 cases of adjustments made by the employers we contacted some resources are available through the government's Access to Work programme.

The most common types of adjustment made by employers, based on feedback obtained by IRS, are shown in descending order:

- allowing absence for rehabilitation and treatment;

- making alterations to working hours;

- obtaining or adapting equipment;

- adjusting premises;

- redeploying the individual to another job;

- changing the nature of the work the person does;

- providing training;

- providing a reader or interpreter;

- providing support workers;

- modifying procedures for testing and assessment of candidates; and

- modifying instruction manuals.

Age discrimination

At present, there is no legislation specifically covering discrimination on the grounds of age, although this will be enacted within three years. As with much of the discrimination based on gender, ethnicity and disability, age discrimination is often the result of adopting subjective, stereotypical attitudes that make assumptions about the abilities and attitudes of a whole group of people.

So, it is assumed that younger people are more energetic, less committed, quicker to learn, but more prone to moving on to another employer. Older people are seen as set in their ways, more reliable, but who find it more difficult to learn new skills. Not only do these assumptions bear little relation to reality, but discrimination is then compounded because the stereotypes are then applied to each young or old person, without taking account of their own individuality.

Age discrimination is not a synonym for discrimination against older people; many young people are also affected. Research for the Chartered Institute of Personnel and Development[15] polled a cross-section of 600 workers and retired people about age discrimination. It found that more than one in six had first-hand experience of age discrimination at job interviews. Of this group, one-third of those affected were young people. The survey also found that one in five of those polled had been discouraged from applying for a job because the advertisement overly or indirectly conveyed the impression that age discrimination would be practised against applicants.

Many individuals are likely to experience discrimination twice over on grounds of age: 100% of the population at some time fall into the youth category, while, mortality permitting, 100% of the survivors will move into the older group when they reach 40, 45 or whatever specific age an industry or occupation considers is "over the hill".

One in three of the population who have reached the age of 50 but have not yet hit state retirement age are no longer working – some 2.8 million people. Many have taken early retirement, although two-thirds of this group did not do so voluntarily[16]. The apparent widespread incidence of age discrimination makes it difficult for those who wish to return to work to do so. This barrier to employment is likely to become an even greater workplace issue now that pension ages are being harmonised – usually upwards – and shrinking pension funds force people to extend their working lives.

Legislation

The government intends to implement EC provisions against age discrimination by December 2006 in the UK. At present, the likely nature of the legislation is unclear; the government has completed one round of consultations, and a further round building on the initial feedback is expected by summer 2003.

At present, age discrimination is usually only unlawful in the UK where it has the effect of having a disproportionate impact on a group covered by existing anti-discrimination legislation, such where a maximum recruitment age would disproportionately affect a member of an ethnic minority group compared with whites.

4. Good practice in employment free of age bias

This checklist is based on practices being adopted by employers to remove unfair discrimination on the grounds of age. It draws on feedback from personnel, HR and equality managers obtained by IRS, including a special survey relating to older workers that we conducted in association with the Employers' Forum on Age. We have amplified this feedback to reflect issues concerned with young workers from several other sources, in particular the government's revised Code of Practice on Age Diversity in Employment[17].

● **Policy:** Develop a formal policy about avoiding age-related discrimination; most organisations incorporate it into their main equality or diversity policy;

● **Culture:** Age discrimination is often encouraged by corporate culture; the development of a policy supported at senior level and which is fully communicated to staff can begin to shift such attitudes; training for line managers and others with responsibilities for managing people is also important;

● **Monitoring:** Set up monitoring processes to check that personnel practices do not unfairly discriminate on the grounds of age;

● **Recruitment 1:** Provide positive encouragement that the employer bases its selection decisions on merit alone; the design and wording of job advertisements should be audited to ensure they do not explicitly or implicitly discourage candidates because of a perceived minimum or maximum age limit;

● **Recruitment 2:** Ensure that candidates are drawn from as many backgrounds and ages as possible; consider broadening recruitment. For young people, this might include using the internet, jobcentres and careers services/Connexions; for older people, this might include community newsletters, the local newspaper and social groups;

● **Selection:** Remove age and date-of-birth questions from application forms; gather monitoring data on a separate form or detachable sheet; ensure selectors are trained in equal opportunities issues as well as in technical selection skills; audit selection criteria and other aspects of recruitment and selection to ensure there is no unfair age discrimination;

● **Training:** Give access to training on need, not age; in addition, some older workers may be returners to the labour market and require tailored training, while younger workers may have no real experience of work and also benefit from training tailored to their needs;

● **Other decisions:** Base promotion and other decisions on merit;

● **Work–life balance:** Help individuals with caring responsibilities to remain at work by offering childcare and eldercare arrangements, including flexible hours of work and working from home (there is a new right in respect of child-care for individuals to request a move to flexible working);

● **Job redesign:** It is often possible to alter the tasks involved in a job or rede-ploy a member of staff to another role, and this enables individuals' particular skills and abilities to be given full scope; it also helps retain workers who develop disabilities *(see checklists 2 and 3)* and take account of any diminished levels of physical strength in the limited number of jobs where this is a rele-vant factor;

● **Health and safety:** Employers are under a legal obligation to pay particular attention to the health and safety of young people, but workplace audits should also consider the impact of jobs, equipment and other issues on older workers;

● **Part-time working:** Offer older workers the opportunity to reduce their hours of work on a permanent basis or as part of a phased retirement pro-gramme;

● **Redundancy:** Ensure that the selection criteria for redundancy do not have a disproportionate impact on the basis of age; in particular, the use of length of service (last in, first out; or even first in, last out) is likely to present difficul-ties; in addition, evaluate the use of voluntary redundancy (which is most like-ly to involve those with the longest service) and of early retirement; and

● **Pensions:** Internal and external rules about occupational pensions and asso-ciated retirement ages can present barriers to the employment of older work-ers; wherever possible, they should be relaxed to permit workers to stay on until they wish to retire.

Discrimination and specific personnel practices

Recruitment and selection

Recruitment and selection procedures act as the gateway to employment, giving them a crucial influence over equal opportunities at work. The emphasis on employers' recruitment practices in the equality commissions' statutory Codes of Practice bears witness to this fact. Yet, ironically, there are relatively fewer tribunal judgments against employers in the areas of recruit-ment and selection, and relatively low average compensation awards, than relating to other aspects of employment.

Each and every aspect of recruitment and selection can potentially discrim-inate unfairly against individuals and groups, from the method of identify-ing the selection criteria (job analysis, use of job descriptions and person specifications, and so on) right up to providing and using job references and making the final appointment decision.

Monitoring the impact of recruitment and selection provides vital information about the fairness of these practices, particularly when monitoring is used to audit each of the principal stages: the composition of the initial group of applicants; the smaller group that remains after initial shortlisting; any further shortlisting (such as following the use of tests); and the individual(s) chosen for appointment. Many organisations use more than one interview stage and, given the difficulty of removing subjectivity from interviewing, it can be valuable to monitor the composition of the groups that go forward from the first interview stage to the second, and so on.

● **Recruitment:** see chapter 1 Filling your vacancies for information on identifying selection criteria and using the various recruitment methods;

● **Monitoring recruitment and selection:** see the section on monitoring earlier in this chapter;

● **Positive action:** see the section on positive action earlier in this chapter; and the section on retention below (for such factors as helping employees to cope with their caring responsibilities);

● **Selection:** see chapter 2 Cost-effective selection for information on the equal opportunities issues concerned with the various methods of selection, including the use of application forms and CVs, interviewing methods, testing and assessment centres;

● **Job references and screening:** for the equal opportunities considerations concerned with the use of reference-checking and pre-employment screening, see chapter 4 Checking candidates' backgrounds;

● **Ex-offenders:** for the equal opportunities considerations concerned with the recruitment and selection of individuals with criminal records, see chapter 4 Checking candidates' backgrounds; and

● **Immigrants and foreign workers:** for the equal opportunities considerations concerned with the recruitment and selection of workers from outside the UK, see chapter 4 Checking candidates' backgrounds.

Case study E. Recruitment initiatives

London Underground has targeted women in its recruitment of train drivers as part of a strategy to reduce the skills shortages that were leading to a growing number of train cancellations[18]. In an 18-month campaign, it increased the number of its female tube drivers from 75 to 167. It broadened its recruitment advertising by placing an advertisement in Cosmopolitan magazine, which produced 6,000 applications. The strategy also includes improved absence monitoring and attendance management, leading to a 1.5% reduction in absences.

Royal United Hospitals Bath NHS Trust had severe problems related to its under-performance nationally, according to *People Management*[19], including recruitment difficulties, low morale and high labour turnover. Its HR specialists developed a strategy which included the introduction of flexible working, such as term-time hours, job sharing and career breaks. A training programme improved management skills, and a new performance-management system was introduced. Prior to the initiatives, there were 11 vacancies in the cardiology unit, but these had all been filled a year later.

Performance management

Properly trained supervisors and line managers can play a crucial role in fostering equality of opportunity and helping to develop a supportive organisational culture. Their day-to-day interactions with their employees, backed up by their role in conducting formal reviews of performance, mean that they are often best-placed to identify areas where individuals could benefit from additional help, provide encouragement and coaching and, conversely, intervene where bullying and harassment is suspected (although victims should always be able to take their concerns in confidence to someone who does not have line responsibilities for them).

Line managers and supervisors form judgments about their employees' performance, and these managers are increasingly involved in areas where they are able to use this information about their staff – in promotion decisions, in giving access to training opportunities and, crucially, where organisations have set up performance-related pay systems, or where they use performance assessments in selection for redundancy.

Unfair treatment by their managers can demotivate those experiencing it and reduce their performance, but where there is an outcome to this treatment – such as a reduced pay award, or denial of promotion – then there is a particular danger of employers facing tribunal applications. In most circumstances, the actions of line managers are deemed to be those of the organisation for which they work; the employer is vicariously liable, in other words.

The Commission for Racial Equality's Code of Practice is explicit: "It is unlawful to discriminate on racial grounds in appraisals of employee performance." As in other areas, managers require training in both the technical skills of conducting assessment of performance, and the issues concerned with ensuring equality of opportunity. Many employers not only provide such training, but bring together both aspects in one programme. This ensures that equal opportunities issues are integrated into organisational life, and that participants in the training can readily see the relevance of equality factors to their duties.

Equality experts Binna Kandola and Johanna Fullerton point out that there are many influences on formal performance management, alongside the impact of the manager undertaking the assessment. For example, the culture of the organisation shapes employees' and managers' thinking about the nature of performance: what is valued, what is given little value and what is not valued at all.

The criteria used for the assessment should be carefully audited, they add, to ensure that they are the most relevant factors and are defined in objective ways. Most performance systems include a process of setting goals and targets, and it should also be checked that these requirements are objective and focused on the most important aspects of the individual's job.

Finally, "there needs to be an examination of the extent to which different ways of achieving those objectives are to be tolerated. Obviously, there are certain core values that an organisation will have, and it will expect people's behaviour to conform to these. Beyond that, though, being a diverse organisation [Kandola and Fullerton are focusing particularly on diversity initiatives] means being able to respect the fact that not everybody works in exactly the same way and that there needs to be some tolerance of different working styles and patterns."[20]

● **Monitoring formal performance reviews:** many employers tell us that they routinely supervise or monitor the outcomes of line managers' formal assessments of employees' performance, particularly where these are linked to pay; see the section on monitoring earlier in this chapter and the section on pay and benefits later on in this chapter;
● **Performance management:** see chapter 11 Managing performance 1;
● **Discipline and grievances:** see chapter 12 Managing performance 2;
● **Harassment and bullying:** see chapter 12 Managing performance 2;
● **Protecting whistleblowers:** see chapter 12 Managing performance 2;
● **Reasonable adjustments:** line managers are well-placed as a point of contact where individuals with disabilities require reasonable adjustments to their work, equipment or facilities; see the section earlier in this chapter on disability discrimination, including checklists 2 and 3; and
● **Managing absences:** see chapter 13 Attendance and absence.

Case study F. The Crown Prosecution Service

The Crown Prosecution Service (CPS) has suffered from considerable unfavourable publicity linked to two critical reports, culminating in a statement by the head of the CPS that it was institutionally racist. Its head of equality and diversity told IRS that an organisation with weak management is one that will have problems with discrimination. This meant that changing the organisation's culture and raising the standard of management were high priorities. A modular management training programme was introduced, which incorporated issues concerned with equality and diversity as part of each module. Specific training is included in the race equality scheme required of large public bodies, such as the CPS. In addition, all employees are receiving training in equality and diversity, and a diversity competency has been introduced as part of the service's framework of core competencies. All staff will be given a diversity objective as part of the formal performance-management system, and will be measured against it in their annual performance assessment. The grievance procedure is also being improved.

Pay and benefits

The law on equal pay is changing rapidly. An equal pay questionnaire was introduced on 6 April 2003 for use by individuals considering making a tribunal application under the Equal Pay Act 1970 (as amended by the Employment Act 2002). Employers' completion of the questionnaire is not compulsory but tribunals can make inferences about failing to reply to the questionnaire or giving evasive answers, unless the employer can provide a good reason for doing so. (This section focuses on equal pay between men and women, although, of course, the equality legislation relating to ethnic minorities and individuals with disabilities also contains provisions on equal pay.)

In addition, there will be changes to the time limits on equal pay claims and awards; these are expected to be in force from July 2003. Changes to the provisions about compensation for arrears of pay are expected to be effective from December 2003.

Looking further ahead, the provisions of the revised EC Equal Treatment Directive, which the UK must implement by 5 October 2005, could mean that applicants do not have to name an actual comparator when making a claim of equal pay.

Employment law specialist Russell Brimelow points out that "equal pay claims are among the most disruptive that can be brought against your organisation." He advises employers to avoid litigation wherever possible by "equal-pay proofing" their practices through a three-stage process:

1. Ensure that the organisation's policies and practices implement fully the Equal Opportunity Commission's Code of Practice on Equal Pay – this includes developing an equal pay policy;

2. Communicate the organisation's equal pay policy, and provide training to managers in implementing it; and

3. Check that the organisation's pay practices are based on transparent and objective criteria, so that "it is clear what is being paid to whom and why".[21]

The Code of Practice on Equal Pay recommends that employers conduct an audit, or review, of their pay related practices. The Equal Opportunities Commission has issued an *Equal pay review kit* to help organisations undertake this process (available from the EOC, tel: 0845 601 5901, or downloaded from www.eoc.org.uk).

For smaller firms, it has recently published advice tailored to their needs (*Equal pay, fair pay: a small-business guide to effective pay practices*, available free from www.eoc.org.uk; the guidance is also available in printed format and as a CD-ROM, containing an Excel spreadsheet for collecting and comparing pay information, from 0845 601 5901).

Also available from the Equal Opportunities Commission is a 15-page checklist of *Practical tips on equal pay*. This guide examines starting pay, grading, bonus payments, progression, equal pay for like work, overtime and shift pay, and performance-related pay. The commission has also produced a short introduction to the use of software in auditing equal pay (*Equal pay reviews and human resource/payroll software*). Both guides are available free from www.eoc.org.uk.

The recently introduced questionnaire for potential complaints under the Equal Pay Act 1970 is available from the Department of Trade and Industry (www.womenandequalityunit.gov.uk; tel: 0870 1502 500 quoting ref. URN 03/806), as is the department's *Guide to the Equal Pay Act 1970*. Further advice on equal pay is available from Equality Direct (www.equalitydirect.org.uk; tel: 0845 600 3444).

A specialist information service on pay issues, e-reward, has produced a five-step guide to conducting equal pay audits (free from www.e-reward.co.uk; it has also published a fuller 58-page guide "How to conduct equal pay reviews" as issue 8 in its *E-research* series, available price £50 plus VAT from its website).

So far, few employers have undertaken an equal pay audit. According to research by the Institute for Employment Studies, only one-quarter (26%) of organisations with between 100 and 200 employees has done so, or intend to do so in 2003, rising to four in 10 (39%) organisations with between 200 and 500 employees[22]. Overall, one in four of the employers that had already conducted an audit did not cover the whole workforce.

On the plus side, though, seven in 10 employers with experience of auditing for equal pay did not find it difficult to do so. Where problems occurred, most of them involved limitations in the HR or payroll databases used by the organisations. In three out of five cases where the audit had been finished, the institute's research found that employers had not uncovered a pay gap based on gender.

Case study G. The Patent Office

The Patent Office completed its first pay audit in May 2001, which was led by its personnel and pay specialists. The audit investigated six aspects of equal pay in the organisation, including analysing individual salaries by gender, pay span and on the basis of those doing like work; it also investigated overall pay patterns by gender (highest, lowest and average salaries); it analysed bonus and overtime pay, starting salaries and promotion salaries by gender and pay span; and tracked performance assessments by gender. It found the audit was fairly straightforward. The findings added impetus to the introduction of a new pay and grading scheme, although the overall gender pay gap was less than 5% of average salaries.

Equal pay questionnaire

The recent introduction of the equal pay questionnaire means that there is little experience to share between employers. A particular potential cause for concern, though, is the fact that the questionnaire is based on comparing the individual with one or more *named* comparators ("Please give the name(s), or, if not known, the job title(s) of the person or persons with whom equal pay is being claimed," the questionnaire says). This can raise issues of privacy under the Data Protection Act 1998 and employers' common-law duty of trust and confidence, as well as potentially straining relationships within the organisation if the chosen comparators object to information about them being disclosed.

An employer does not have to reply to the questionnaire, but failure to do so, or the use of ambiguous or evasive replies, can be taken into account by a tribunal – "and the employer's position may be adversely affected should the complainant bring proceedings". However, tribunals cannot draw such inferences if "the employer has a reasonable excuse for failing to respond". There is space on the questionnaire for an employer to provide its reasons in such cases.

The advice accompanying the questionnaire says that objections by comparators could represent a legitimate excuse for a failure to answer some of the questions. However, it would help an employer's case if it were to explain on the questionnaire its reasons for refusing to supply certain details. Alternatively, an employer could take the view that it is entitled to disclose confidential information, given that the Data Protection Act permits the disclosure of some information where legal proceedings are involved. However, this could damage relationships at work and the affected individuals' trust in the employer, and employers might consider it preferable to request the consent of the individuals concerned. Tribunals always have the option of ordering the disclosure of relevant information.

Performance-related pay

The use of individual performance-related pay has become widespread in the past two decades, and is often criticised because of its potential to discriminate unfairly.

However, apparently straightforward payment systems, such as bonus and overtime pay, can also disproportionately favour men over women for more fundamental reasons. For example, men and women are often concentrated in different jobs and grades, and bonus arrangements are often restricted to those where men are predominant. Overtime pay may be triggered when an individual works beyond a normal full-time week, with the result that the relatively larger numbers of women in part-time jobs do not receive it. Overtime is also frequently restricted to certain grades, and this can also operate in a way that gives men greater access to it. Even where there are transparent, relatively rigid pay bands and across-the-board pay rises for everyone, men and women can fare differently through the common practice of taking account of a recruit's starting salary when identifying their starting rate in the new job. This means that recruits do not suffer a pay cut, but it can also serve to perpetuate patterns of lower pay among women.

Performance-related pay differs in that the potential unfairness is more individualised, through the process of assessing each person's performance over the year and identifying a pay increase, bonus or progression through a pay scale that is deemed to be a suitable reward. The bases for these judgments may be unclear, or line managers may lack the detailed guidelines and training to operate a potentially objective performance-related pay scheme in a fair way.

Most employers that operate performance-related pay schemes supervise them in some way. According to our feedback from personnel, HR and reward managers, most commonly their organisations check individual decisions for cost-control purposes and to ensure that grade boundaries are observed. But around three in 10 also monitor decisions on the basis of gender – and around two in 10 on the basis of ethnicity – as one means of tackling unfair discrimination.

A list of ways in which unfair discrimination can occur in performance-related pay, and the steps that employers can take to address them, is available in the Equal Opportunities Commission's short *Good practice guide: sex bias and performance-related pay* (free from www.eoc.org.uk).

● For more information on pay, including performance-related pay schemes, see chapter 7 Pay, benefits and other terms and conditions; and

● Job evaluation: for information on job evaluation and grading schemes, see chapter 7 Pay, benefits and other terms and conditions. In addition, the Equal Opportunities Commission has issued a free 18-page booklet: *Good practice guide: job evaluation schemes free of sex bias* (free from www.eoc.org.uk).

Adoption, maternity and paternity

There have been major changes to employees' rights to leave and pay for adoption, maternity and paternity, which were introduced on 6 April 2003.

Adoption

One of the parents of a child placed with them by a UK adoption agency for adoption is now entitled to take up to 26 weeks' paid adoption leave, followed by up to 26 weeks' unpaid leave. Previously (since 1999), employees had a right to up to 13 weeks' unpaid leave only.

The new rights are dependent on the person being an employee and having 26 weeks' service by the date he or she was notified of being matched with a child for adoption. There are no rights to paid or unpaid leave if the employee does not meet this service qualification. Nor is adoption leave available where the formal placement procedure is not used, for example where a step-parent adopts a child without going through the procedure. Office holders, such as police officers and some company directors, are not classed as employees and generally do not qualify for adoption leave, although they may qualify for adoption pay.

If the adoption arrangement unfortunately subsequently falls through, the employee will be able to stay on leave for up to eight weeks (of the remaining period of leave) after the adoption ends.

If a couple are involved in a joint adoption, only one of them can take the leave; it cannot be divided between them. However, the other half of the couple can instead take advantage of the new right to two weeks' paid paternity leave *(see below)*, as can an unmarried partner of someone who is adopting in their own right. The same individual cannot take both adoption and paternity leave in connection with the same adoption.

The adoption leave can start from either the date when the child's placement actually begins, or from a fixed date of up to 14 days before the expected placement date – but no later than the date of the placement.

Adoption pay is available to employees whose earnings reach the lower earnings limit for national insurance contributions. Payments, based on the level of statutory adoption pay which is uprated each year, are made by the employer.

Employees must give the required notice – together with evidence from the adoption agency – to claim their rights to adoption leave and pay. They must notify their employer no more than seven days after the day they are notified of having been matched with a child for adoption, or, if this is not possible, as soon as is reasonably practicable.

There are rights to return after the end of adoption leave, which, in summary, are intended to reflect the employer's likely difficulty in keeping their old job open. So, where only the shorter period of adoption leave – the 26 weeks' paid leave – has been taken, the employee usually has a right to the *same* job on the same terms and conditions (together with any improvements during their absence).

But where they have also taken some or all of the additional unpaid adoption leave, there is provision for employers to offer a suitable alternative where it is not reasonably practicable for the employee to return to their old job. The alternative job must offer no less favourable terms and conditions. (There are also complex provisions of rights to return where the employee has taken a combination of adoption and another form of statutory parental leave.)

The new rights are complex and only the main points have been summarised here; for more information, the government has issued a free 44-page booklet PL518 *Adoptive parents – rights to leave and pay when a child is placed for adoption within the UK: a guide for employers and employees* (available free from local jobcentres, the DTI Publications Orderline tel: 0870 1502 500, or from www.dti.gov.uk).

Maternity

The April 2003 changes to maternity provision included increasing the basic rate of statutory maternity pay to £100 a week, extending the period of paid maternity leave from 18 to 26 weeks and reducing the length of service required for additional maternity leave. Employees no longer have to confirm their intention to return, nor give advance warning of doing so (unless they return before the agreed date).

The provisions relating to maternity leave and pay are even more complex than those applying to adoption. Below is a summary; further information is available from the government booklet PL 958 (Rev 8) *Maternity rights: a guide for employers and employees* (available free from local jobcentres, the DTI Publications Orderline tel: 0870 1502 500, or from www.dti.gov.uk).

Employees are entitled to up to 26 weeks' ordinary maternity leave, without any service qualification. This can usually begin at any time of the employee's choice from the beginning of the 11th week before the expected week of confinement (EWC) onwards. However, if the baby is born before this date, then the leave can start from this time. The latest date for starting maternity leave is the actual date of birth. Any pregnancy-related absence in the four weeks (formerly, this was six weeks) prior to EWC serves to trigger the start of maternity leave.

Employees with 26 weeks' service by the start of the 14th week before their EWC are also entitled to up to 26 weeks' additional maternity leave. This begins once ordinary maternity leave is exhausted, and means that qualifying employees receive up to 52 weeks' leave.

In addition, statutory maternity pay is payable where employees have 26 weeks' service by the start of their 14th week before EWC, and must have average earnings that are equivalent to at least the lower earnings limit for national insurance contributions. It lasts for 26 weeks, of which the first six weeks are paid at 90% of average earnings, and the remainder at the lesser of £100 a week (this will be revised in April 2004) or 90% of average earnings.

Employees must give notice to their employer in the 15th week before their EWC, or as soon afterwards as is reasonably practicable if this is not possible. The start of their leave can be changed if they give 28 days' advance notice (or as much notice as is reasonably practicable if this is not possible). The notice applies to all eligible purposes: ordinary and additional maternity leave, and statutory maternity pay.

Once the employer receives notice, it is now legally required to write within 28 days to the employee stating her expected date of return if she were to take her full maternity leave entitlement (ordinary or additional, as relevant).

The previous right for an employer to request confirmation of the employee's intention to return has been repealed. Nor does the employee have to give advance notice of her actual date of return, unless this will occur before the date set out in the letter from her employer (which quoted the latest possible date of return). In this case, she must give 28 days' notice of her early return.

There are rights to return after the end of maternity leave, which, in summary, are intended to reflect the employer's likely difficulty in keeping the woman's old job open. So, where only ordinary maternity leave – the first 26 weeks – has been taken, the employee usually has a right to the *same* job on the same terms and conditions (together with any improvements during their absence).

But where they have also taken some or all of the additional maternity leave, there is provision for employers to offer a suitable alternative where it is not reasonably practicable for the employee to return to their old job. The alternative job must offer no less favourable terms and conditions. (There are also complex provisions of rights to return where the employee has taken a combination of maternity and another form of statutory parental leave.)

Paternity

A new right to paid paternity leave was introduced from April 2003.

Employees must have some responsibility for the upbringing of the child, and be the biological or adoptive father, or the husband or partner of the child's biological or adoptive parent. Partners including lesbian and gay partners.

To be eligible, the individual must be an employee and must have 26 weeks' service by the start of the 14th week before the mother's expected week of confinement (EWC) to be eligible, or, in the case of adoption, 26 weeks' service ending with the week in which the child's adopter is notified of being matched with the child. In addition, they must be earning at least the equivalent of the lower earnings limit for national insurance contributions.

The leave must be used to care for the baby and/or support the mother or adopter. And the leave must be taken as one or two consecutive weeks; it cannot be taken as two separate weeks or as individual days.

The employee must give notice to the employer in the 15th week before the EWC. For paternity leave in the case of adoption, the notice period is at least seven days after the adopter was notified that they had been matched for adoption. In both cases, the start of the paternity leave can be changed on 28 days' notice. Employees must give evidence of their entitlement if requested to do so by their employer.

Paternity leave can start from the date of the child's birth or adoption, or on a fixed date that must be after the EWC or adoption date. Leave must normally be taken within 56 days of the actual birth or adoption.

The entitlement is two weeks' leave and to the payment of statutory paternity pay of £100 a week (the amount will be reviewed in April 2004 and annually after that), or 90% of their average weekly earnings if this is less than £100.

There is a right to return to the same job and on the same terms and conditions. (There are also complex provisions of rights to return where the employee has taken a combination of paternity and another form of statutory parental leave.)

Unpaid parental leave: There is an existing entitlement to 13 weeks' unpaid leave to care for – or to be able to spend more time with – a child, including an adopted child (18 weeks in the case of parents of a child with disabilities). The entitlement can be taken at a time up to the child's fifth birthday, or an adopted child's fifth anniversary of being placed for adoption (until the child's 18th birthday in the case of a child with disabilities).

The individual must be an employee and have at least one year's service. A notice period of 21 days is required. The right applies to both men and women. There is a qualified right to return to the same job after the period of parental leave. This applies to leave that lasts up to four weeks. For longer periods, the right to return to the same job can be amended if the employer does not find this reasonably practicable. In this case, a similar job with the same or better status, terms and conditions should be offered. (There are also complex provisions of rights to return where the employee has taken a combination of unpaid parental leave and another form of statutory parental leave.)

Rights to unpaid parental leave were first introduced in December 1999, but when we contacted a cross-section of employers two-and-a-half years later, we found that very few of their employees had taken advantage of this entitlement. The fact that the leave is unpaid seems to be the main reason for employees' lack of interest, according to the consensus of the personnel and HR managers we contacted. In addition, although many employers have introduced contractual maternity leave and pay schemes that improve on the statutory minimum, few have done so in the area covered by this parental leave right.

The provisions relating to paternity and parental leave and pay are complex, and only a summary has been given here. Further information is available from the government booklets PL 517 *Working fathers – rights to paternity leave and pay: a guide for employers and employees*, and PL 509 *Parental leave: a guide for employers and employees* (both are available free from local jobcentres, the DTI Publications Orderline tel: 0870 1502 500, or from www.dti.gov.uk).

Other statutory provisions for caring responsibilities

Flexible working: A new right was introduced in April 2003 for employees of either sex to lodge a formal request to move to flexible working under certain circumstances:
● the worker must have a child under the age of six or a child with disabilities under the age of 18;
● they can make no more than one request a year to adopt flexible working and, if granted, the change becomes permanent and serves to amend their contract of employment;
● the employer must arrange a meeting with the employee within 28 days of receiving the request;
● following the meeting, the employer must write to the employee within 14 days to agree to the new pattern of work and give a date for its commencement, or refuse the request and support this with detailed business reasons for so doing; and
● the employee must lodge any appeal against the decision within 14 days.

The request, and the options open to both parties, can include home-based working, term-time working, shorter hours or amended hours of attendance. The statutory procedure, whose timescales are shown above, must be followed as the process used to handle the request.

There are eight possible reasons under the legislation that an employer can use to justify denying the employee's request. Employees may pursue their application to an employment tribunal, but its role is limited to checking that the employer has complied with the statutory procedure. The tribunal cannot attempt to "second-guess" the legitimacy or otherwise of the reasons given by the employer, provided they fall within those laid down. However, in some circumstances, an employer's refusal to grant a move to flexible working might be considered to constitute unlawful discrimination under the sex, race or disability discrimination Acts.

Further information is available from the detailed government booklet PL 520 *Flexible working – the right to request and the duty to consider: a guide for employers and employees* (available free from local jobcentres, the DTI Publications Orderline tel: 0870 1502 500, or from www.dti.gov.uk).

Increasing numbers of employers are offering flexible working options to their employees that improve on the statutory scheme. They find that it can help employees with caring responsibilities "juggle" work and home duties which, otherwise, might cause them to take unauthorised absence or give up work entirely.

We asked several hundred personnel and HR managers about the likely impact of the new right to request flexible working a few weeks before the law came into force. Most of them told us that they expect to receive more requests to change working arrangements and that they would be more likely to agree them. But, as the legislation provides, most of the managers we contacted would aim to balance individuals' requirements with the needs of the business.

Making such decisions, and organising work more flexibly, will place additional responsibilities on line managers, our contacts told us. In turn, this will require new skills that their organisations will have to ensure are covered in their supervisory and managerial training programmes. "Managers will need a whole range of new skills to manage properly, with so many working patterns around," as an HR director at a firm of property consultants told us.

Six in 10 of those we contacted expect that their organisations will broaden the new statutory rights to cover all employees, not simply parents of young children. If this intention is put into practice, this approach will play a major role in fostering a culture of equality of opportunity. Part-time work and other forms of non-standard working will move closer to the mainstream of organisational life.

At present, personnel and HR managers find that even those organisations that proactively offer flexible working often receive few applications. Employees are concerned that such a move will marginalise them, reducing their promotion prospects and possibly stigmatising them as lacking in commitment and motivation. Adopting a policy that enables any employee and manager to request a move to flexible working will place even greater pressures on line managers to organise workloads and ensure that cover is available at all relevant times.

On balance, the personnel and HR managers were open-minded about the new right, identifying some benefits to their organisation alongside the headaches that it would bring. In particular, they told us that an ability to move to a more flexible working pattern would improve staff retention – three-quarters of our contacts agreed with this view. And almost as many – six in 10 – considered that it would help reduce their recruitment difficulties.

These are themes that we will follow up once organisations have sufficient experience of implementing the new rights

Emergency leave: Employees have a right to unpaid leave when faced with an emergency involving a dependant of theirs (a husband, wife, child or parent of the employee, together with someone living in the same household, such as a partner or aunt, provided they are not tenants, boarders or live-in employees). There is no minimum period of service required before employees are eligible for this right.

The amount of leave is not specified, nor the number of occasions on which the same employee can exercise it. However, it should represent "a reasonable amount of time off in the circumstances". This means that the period should reflect the nature and severity of the emergency.

Government advice *(details below)* stresses that the right does not extend to leave for caring responsibilities, but is intended to help cope with unexpected emergencies. When a child falls ill, for example, the government says that the right could include immediate tasks such as the initial care, a visit to the doctor and making arrangements for a carer, but would not involve being absent from work for the whole period of illness.

5. Emergency leave case law

At the time of writing, one tribunal case about employees' rights to emergency leave had reached the appeal stage (where rulings provide precedents for subsequent cases).

In Qua v John Ford Morrison Solicitors[23], the case related to a single mother's use of emergency leave under the provision in the Employment Rights Act 1996 "to provide assistance on an occasion when a dependant falls ill". Her son suffered from several medical problems, and the employee took a considerable amount of time off to look after him. Eventually, her employer took the view that her absence made it difficult to run the office and dismissed her.

The court ruled that the right does not extend to the individual personally providing care for a dependant, beyond a reasonable amount necessary to enable them to deal with the immediate crisis linked to a particular illness. The time required should depend on the circumstances, but the court suggested that no more than a few hours would usually be reasonable – at most, one to two days.

However, the business or operational needs of the employer are not relevant for the purpose of making the assessment of the reasonable amount of leave. And the employee concerned does not need to report to their employer on a daily basis when their absence continues for more than one day.

Emergencies include where the employee's dependant suddenly falls ill, is injured, has been assaulted, is having a baby, or dies. Also covered are situations where an employee needs to take time off to make longer-term arrangements to care for a dependant who is ill or has been injured – for example, finding and employing a temporary carer or taking a sick child to stay with relatives – or where established care arrangements unexpectedly break down. The right also includes parents who need time off when their child is involved in a serious incident at school, such as being injured or suspended, or is distressed.

The right applies to both men and women, and there may be situations where both require emergency leave to deal with a problem. Government guidance says that a "commonsense approach" is required, and that the absence of both parents would depend on the severity of the circumstances. Disagreements should be addressed through the employer's normal grievance or disciplinary procedures, as appropriate, although an employee can make a complaint to an employment tribunal where an application is refused, or if they are victimised as a result of asserting their right.

Further information on the right to emergency leave is available from the government booklet URN 99/1186 *Time off for dependants: a guide for employers and employees* (available free from local jobcentres, the DTI Publications Orderline tel: 0870 1502 500, or from www.dti.gov.uk).

Employers frequently improve on the statutory right to unpaid leave in certain circumstances, by paying the employee's normal salary. Paid time off is most commonly granted in respect of the death of a close relative or partner. Most employers codify this provision in a policy and specify the number of days' leave available. This is usually a period of up to five days. Some employers are more generous where the deceased is a partner or close family member, giving a day for other individuals.

In addition, many employers are now prepared to give paid time off to employees in respect of the sudden sickness of a dependant. Practice divides into those organisations that set down a limit on the number of days a year that an employee can take for this purpose (typically, three to five days per annum), and those where the decision is left to the discretion of line managers, personnel/HR specialists, or both.

Finally, some employers grant paid leave for employees to cope with a crisis in their caring responsibilities, such as a breakdown in childcare arrangements. Where the period is set down, the typical amount of leave is between three and five days. However, four in 10 organisations that set down the amount of such leave would be prepared to increase it if circumstances warrant.

Retention

The difficulties experienced by many individuals, particularly women, in balancing the demands of a job with their caring responsibilities prompted the government's recent introduction of a range of new or improved rights for parents *(see previous sections in this chapter)*.

Where individuals are already in jobs, inflexible working hours may mean it is difficult to manage routine caring duties, such as taking a child for a regular hospital appointment, without taking sick leave – unauthorised absence, in other words. Some employees may find that the difficulties of juggling work and caring become too great and they are forced to leave their jobs.

A government survey of more than 1,200 workplaces has found that six in 10 employers that have some form of provision for employees' caring responsibilities reported that resignation rates have fallen. Other benefits include improved attendance rates and greater levels of commitment[24].

Alongside the statutory provisions described earlier in this chapter, some employers are making it easier for their staff to combine careers with caring by offering direct forms of childcare assistance, such as childcare vouchers or nursery places, or by improving the statutory minima – such as by offering full pay, instead of the statutory rates of maternity and paternity pay, or by providing longer periods of maternity (and, perhaps, paternity and adoption) leave.

Case study H. BT

At telecoms company BT, an investment of £1 million in introducing flexibility policies has yielded savings of £180 million a year, its director of employment policy told delegates to the 2002 annual conference of the Chartered Institute of Personnel and Development. Among the larger savings, she highlighted:

● £36 million from the company's real-estate budget produced by employees moving from office-based to home-based work;

● £3.5 million from the sickness budget, because employees who work from home take an average of three days' sick leave a year against 12 for office-based staff;

● £10 million from BT's expenditure on diesel fuel because homeworkers tend to have less far to travel; and

● £3 million from the training budget because the return-to-work rate after maternity leave has risen to 95%, saving the cost of recruiting and inducting 500 replacement staff each year.

Of course, BT is a huge employer with a similarly vast expenditure on staffing-related factors. But its experience illustrates the ways in which smaller organisations could expect to obtain benefits from helping employees balance work and caring – and, more generally, enabling individuals to achieve a better work–life balance.

IRS asked personnel, HR and equality managers in 120 organisations to gain their feedback on current practice in offering more flexible forms of working and helping with caring responsibilities. In order of prevalence, these are the main options being offered by employers:
● part-time working;
● jobsharing;

- flexitime;
- homeworking on an occasional basis;
- term-time working;
- annualised hours (where hours of work increase and decrease over the course of the year, often on a seasonal basis, although the total hours worked usually balance out);
- regular, but limited homeworking (eg once a week);
- a compressed working week;
- providing advice on childcare or eldercare;
- full-time homeworking;
- childcare vouchers or cash payments; and
- a crèche or playscheme.

Employers take account of a range of factors when deciding whether or not an individual will be eligible for one or more of the above options. Most commonly, and in descending order of prevalence, organisations weigh up the following considerations when a move to a different work pattern is involved:
- individual need;
- the suitability of the individual's job;
- the impact of the change on the person's colleagues;
- ability to absorb work;
- impact on productivity;
- ability to manage and monitor;
- cost implications; and
- the attitude of the individual's line manager.

One particularly important finding from our research involves the lack of information available to most personnel and HR managers to demonstrate the benefits of their measures to assist caring responsibilities and improve work–life balance. Most of those we contacted simply do not attempt to measure the impact; indeed, some do not even collate statistics on those who take up the various options on offer.

Operationally, this is a major weakness. Without measuring the impact of their practices on such metrics as absence levels, labour turnover and the findings of employee attitude surveys, employers have no means of knowing whether they are focusing their efforts in the most cost-effective way. And what is not measured is often not valued – these provisions are unlikely to be seen as more than add-ons if they are not integrated into routine operational practices.

Case study I. Hertfordshire County Council

Hertfordshire County Council is implementing a range of flexibility options under its Lifewise scheme in order to reduce labour turnover to 10% a year[25]. By the end of 2002, the scheme had already helped to cut the rate by two per-centage points to 14%. Lifewise involves four areas: flexible working, care support, health services and flexible benefits. Flexible working options include homeworking, compressed hours, flexitime and annualised hours. Other fea-tures of Lifewise include a nursery, childcare vouchers, health screening and counselling. Within the first year, the council exceeded its target of a take-up rate of 2% of the workforce.

Older employees: Traditionally, employees' caring commitments were seen solely in connection with parents who had childcare responsibilities. The pace and expense of modern life means, however, that grandparents are increasingly sharing some of the load of looking after their own off-springs' children while they are at work. This means that the childcare and flexible-working measures that employers offer could well be of as much value to older individuals on their staff, as to those of prime childrearing age.

Beyond caring for children, many employees have responsibility for look-ing after elderly or infirm parents or other relatives. They, too, would appreciate flexibility in organising their working hours when their rela-tive needs accompanying to hospital or the doctor's surgery, for example. When the caring load is heavy, the availability of reduced hours of work – part-time hours or jobsharing, for example – could well enable a valued employee to continue working for the employer instead of being forced to resign[26].

So far, only unpaid leave for emergencies covers situations other than employees' responsibilities as parents of children in terms of the statutory provisions available to carers. There have been proposals, though, that the recently introduced right to request flexible working should be extended from parents of young children to others with caring responsibilities.

Employees who reach retirement age are usually obliged to resign, whether or not they wish to do so. Increasingly, employers are taking a more flexi-ble approach to mandatory retirement – not least, because their occupa-tional pension schemes are likely to be facing deficits which deferred pen-sions will help to alleviate.

For their part, some employees may wish to continue working as a way of maintaining a familiar sense of routine and a welcome source of social interaction. Their own financial prospects may not be so bright, either, and some form of earned income may help to supplement a pension or provide a means of saving for the day when they eventually retire.

Inland Revenue rules restrict employees' options in working while drawing a pension, particularly in preventing them from moving gradually into retirement by working fewer hours for the same employer that is paying them a pension. The government is consulting about ways of making the tax regime more flexible. In addition, the forthcoming legislation on age discrimination could well require changes to retirement ages.

Individuals with disabilities: Many people with disabilities develop them during the course of their working life; some are age-related disabilities; others may have actually been caused or exacerbated by their jobs and their working conditions. The Disability Discrimination Act 1995 and its associated Code of Practice apply equally to existing employees as to job applicants. They require employers to undertake reasonable adjustments to ensure that staff with disabilities are able to continue in employment.

● **Individuals with disabilities:** see checklist 3 and the section on disability discrimination in this chapter for more information on retaining individuals with disabilities;

● **Retention generally:** see chapter 8 Retaining your best staff for more information on managing retention.

Case study J. Flexible retirement

The **National Maritime Museum** now allows its employees to retire at any age between 50 and 75 and begin drawing their pension. The museum wanted to accommodate individual preferences in choosing a retirement age, and enable it to continue to have access to the skills and expertise of its staff. Its director told IRS that: "An important step has been taken towards optimising the skills of our people, while ensuring that in our recruitment and selection processes we have access to the widest possible spectrum of the nation's resources."

At the Bank of Scotland and the Halifax, the retirement ages had been 60 and 62, respectively. Following their merger as **HBOS**, a new policy was introduced whereby employees can request to work up to the age of 70. Its diversity manager told *Personnel Today* that "about half our customer base is over the age of 50, so there are positive business benefits for us in being age positive". In addition, the raising of the retirement ceiling is helping to encourage line managers to manage performance on a consistent basis, regardless of the individual's age. Previously, there had been the temptation for managers to ignore shortcomings where the employee was due to retire in the near future[27].

At **Marks & Spencer**, mandatory retirement at 65 was abolished in 2001, with the result that the number of staff aged 65-plus rose 600 per cent in two years. Once an individual reaches age 65, they are given a health assessment, and factors such as manual handling are given close attention[28].

Training

Decisions about giving particular employees access to training opportunities have far-reaching implications. Training that focuses on the immediate job should help participants perform to higher standards. This gives those concerned an advantage over employees denied training when performance achievements are used to make decisions about pay progression, annual pay awards, promotion and selection for redundancy.

Longer-term training that helps participants gain access to higher levels of the organisation provides an important means of reinforcing or breaking the "glass ceiling", depending on who is chosen for such opportunities.

For these and other reasons, the equality legislation and its accompanying Codes of Practice give particular attention to ensuring employers do not discriminate unfairly when they decide who will participate in the training opportunities they provide. As well as more obvious sources of discrimination between men and women, and whites and ethnic minorities, denial of training to employees who are pregnant, work part time or who are on fixed-term contracts may also constitute unfair discrimination.

The ability of employees to participate in the training can also represent a source of unfair discrimination. For example, an employee with caring responsibilities may find it difficult to attend a residential course. And an individual with disabilities may find it difficult to participate in experiential learning (activity courses, such as those involving outdoor tasks), and the employer and training provider should ensure that reasonable adjustments are made.

Barriers to training may be psychological. Individuals who have experienced discrimination may be less willing to take up training opportunities; for example, they may have lost confidence in their ability to learn, or may not want to draw attention to themselves.

Research for the government into the experience of older employees found both factors lay behind their disinclination to undertake training. The research found that employers need to encourage diffident employees, and "to try to ensure that all members of staff who undertake training are fully supported by trainers and colleagues, and that they are able to 'go at their own speed'." In several of the employers studied by the researchers, the good-practice approach of tailoring training provision to each participant involved "adopting a patient approach, or allowing more time for older workers to complete particular tasks".[29]

Conversely, as we saw in the section above on Positive action and targets, training can be specifically focused towards under-represented groups to help create a level playing field in the workplace, provided certain statutory conditions are met.

● For further information on induction and training, see chapter 6 Induction, training and development.

Redundancy and dismissal

The process of selecting individuals for redundancy or dismissal is increasingly coming under the legal spotlight, as we show in chapters 14 and 15. There are now around a dozen protected groups where dismissal is likely to be unfair if the selection is based on an individual's affiliation with the group in question. Protection mainly involves individuals from groups who are covered by the anti-discrimination statutes, and individuals who might be viewed as "troublemakers" because they have asserted a statutory right – such as having claimed time off to care for a dependant.

Not only the selection criteria for redundancy are covered by the discrimination Acts. Access to voluntary redundancy, the payments made for voluntary and compulsory redundancies, the offer of alternative work, and other aspects of the redundancy process should treat all employees fairly without disproportionately affecting individuals on the basis of their gender, their pregnancy (or pregnancy-related illness), ethnicity or disability.

Where alternative employment is being considered, women returning from maternity leave and individuals with disabilities should be given priority.

The redundancy or dismissal of part-time workers may be covered by the Sex Discrimination Act 1975 where the gender balance is significantly different to that found among full-time workers. Additionally, same-sex comparisons are possible under the Part-Time Workers (Prevention of Less

Favourable Treatment) Regulations 2000. So, for example, a male part-timer selected for redundancy could base their case on a male full-time employee who was not made redundant.

● For more information on redundancies, see chapter 15 Redundancy and redeployment.

Discrimination against other groups

Members of many different groups have now been given some protection against victimisation and dismissal that relates to their membership of the group concerned. The EC's Equal Treatment Directive will bring about further changes to the UK's legislation, as we described earlier in this chapter. In particular, we noted that protection is being extended to issues relating to an individual's sexual orientation, personal beliefs and religion from 1 December 2003. And by December 2006, the UK will have to introduce protection against discrimination on the grounds of age.

● Ex-offenders: see chapter 4 Checking candidates' backgrounds;

● Immigrants and foreign workers: see chapter 4 Checking candidates' backgrounds;

● Agency workers: see chapter 1 Filling your vacancies; and

● Trade union members and representatives: see chapter 9 Employee involvement and representation.

● Fixed-term workers have been given specific protection since 1 October 2002 under the Fixed-Term Employees (Prevention of Less Favourable Treatment) Regulations 2002. As their name implies, the Regulations give protection to employees who are employed on a temporary contract against being treated less favourably than a full-time worker doing comparable work, unless the employer can show that the difference in treatment was based on objective reasons.

The Regulations cover both fixed-term contracts and those that expire once a task or project has been completed. They abolish the previous legislative provisions that enabled fixed-term employees to waive their right to redundancy payments, provided the contract was signed or revised on or after 1 October 2002.

6. Legal checklist

The law plays a much greater role in shaping employers' equal opportunity and diversity practices than is the case in most of the other chapters in this handbook. Instead of using this checklist for details of the relevant legislation, readers should refer to relevant sections of this chapter.

● Personnel practices should not discriminate unfairly, although there are limited exceptions where the employer can show an objective reason for so doing – Sex Discrimination Act 1975; Race Relations Act 1976; Disability Discrimination Act 1995; Part-Time Workers (Prevention of Less-Favourable Treatment) Regulations 2000; Fixed-Term Employees (Prevention of Less-Favourable Treatment) Regulations 2002; Trade Union and Labour Relations (Consolidation) Act 1992; and Codes of Practice associated with these Acts *(see the text of this chapter for more information on the legislation's impact on personnel practices).*

● Personnel practices in the public sector must support equality of opportunity on the grounds of ethnicity – Race Relations (Amendment) Act 2000 *(see the text of this chapter for more information).*

● Sex, race, disability and age discrimination: recent and forthcoming changes to the legislation are summarised in this chapter.

10. Managing performance 1

See also: 11. Managing performance 2 (for discipline; grievances; harassment and bullying and 12. Attendance and absence

---

This chapter covers:
- Overview: an introduction to performance management;
- Day-to-day performance management; and
- Formal performance-management systems.

Checklists in this chapter:
1. Effective performance management: the key issues
2. Tackling time-wasting
3. Formal performance-management systems
4. 360-degree assessment
5. Legal checklist

Case studies in this chapter:
A. The Royal Mail
B. Fujitsu Services
C. Mid Kent Holdings
D. Greenpeace
E. Norwich Union Life
F. Lincoln Financial Group
G. Amey Construction
H. T-Mobile
I. HSBC Bank
J. British Waterways
K. The Natural History Museum
L. HM Customs and Excise
M. Whitbread Hotel Company

Overview

No other area offers greater potential for personnel and HR specialists to contribute to their organisation's success than the improvement of performance management. The rewards are considerable, in terms of the reputation of personnel and HR specialists, greater efficiency and enhanced organisational effectiveness. But the challenges are equally formidable.

It is a rare individual who appreciates a close scrutiny of their performance at work and having their failings highlighted, and the person given the task of providing this often unwelcome feedback is usually no more likely to relish it. Instead, the management of performance is often skimped, or mishandled. In some instances, employee and manager collude to evade their responsibilities.

It is equally challenging to set targets and identify assessment criteria for use in performance-management systems. It is increasingly difficult to produce meaningful targets for many jobs, particularly in the expanding service sector of the economy. Even where objectives can be spelled out, they are likely to change with alarming frequency in today's fast-moving climate, with the result that performance management may always lag behind the reality of organisational life.

Line managers are too busy, and lack the knowledge, to try to tackle these difficulties; that is where the opportunities for personnel and HR specialists lie in offering expert advice. And it is no longer an option, if it ever was, to fail to manage performance effectively. In today's slimmed-down organisations, each person's contribution must count. After all, their sole reason for being recruited was to perform a job. How could organisations possibly justify a failure to assess and improve their workforces' performance?

Today, well over half of all employers have set up formal performance-management systems (also known as "appraisals" or "personal reviews"), and probably the majority of them are, at any one time, engaged in making changes to improve and extend them.

1. Effective performance management: the key issues

Feedback from employers' own experience shows that the following represent the key issues in effective performance management:

● **Not a bolt-on:** The management of performance must be part of mainstream activities – performance management will fail if it is seen as an add-on.

● **Line managers:** Line managers must be central to performance management. They must be equipped to do the task. Involving them in the design of the formal performance-management system and communicating its workings will greatly help to win their buy-in. Their role in managing performance must be clarified through their job descriptions, and their actual performance of day-to-day performance management and conducting formal reviews must be assessed as part of their personal objectives. Training must be given in relevant skills, including persuasiveness, assertiveness, communication, empathy, judgment, work organisation, concern for equal opportunities, administering grievance and discipline systems, and absence management.

● **Employees:** Gaining the buy-in of employees is also important. They should be involved to some extent in the design of the system, and given adequate information about its workings. Buy-in will also improve through giving employees shared responsibility for the formal review of their own perform-ance; and providing some benefit (psychological or tangible) as a result of their involvement. Rigid command-and-control attitudes will not gain employees' commitment to performance management or to any resultant training and development.

● **Support:** Set up support systems to help line managers manage perform-ance: provide training and development resources to improve individuals' per-formance; and develop proper procedures to help them manage discipline, capability (inability to perform adequately) and absence.

● **Focus:** Identify the goals of the formal performance-management system. In modern organisations, they should be to develop employees and raise per-formance. Keep it focused: systems that try to cover too many issues (training; career aspirations; poor performance; identifying high-fliers, etc) will fail to achieve any of them adequately[1].

● **Performance measures 1:** The factors assessed during formal performance-management reviews should be clear, objective and restricted to factors that make a real difference to performance and contribution (as defined by organ-isational priorities and/or factors that make a real difference to customers/clients).

● **Performance measures 2:** Whatever is assessed should be seen as realistic, achievable and legitimate (on the part of both line managers and employees).

● **Performance measures 3:** It is important to include consideration of how performance is achieved, as well as what; effective outcomes are more impor-tant than simple outputs.

● **Assessments:** Formal reviews must be fair, objective and consistent. There should be an appeals procedure. Line managers' assessments should be checked by their superiors. Where there are positive or negative consequences resulting from performance assessments, it is important to check for unlawful discrimination (such as by setting up a monitoring system).

● **Benefits 1:** Do not expect too much. The most likely benefits from performance-management systems are better communication between line manager and employee and, second, improved performance at the level of the individual. Less likely, but possible in the best systems, are improved collective performance (team, departmental, organisation) and, hardest to obtain of all, increased profitability.

> ● **Benefits 2:** Performance-management systems can help rebuild communication and commitment from the grassroots upwards after restructuring or redundancy exercises. They can also support cultural change.

Day-to-day performance management

In the course of time, performance management has been approached from many different angles. The "Taylorist" system of closely-controlled and supervised workers, each given a readily-monitored task or group of tasks, has largely fallen from favour in the 21st century. Partly, change has occurred because the decline of manufacturing has made it less easy to manage people, and divide up tasks, in this way. And, partly, employers have shifted towards a more creative approach to performance management because it often produces better results.

Today, employees are generally required to be flexible, willing to cooperate and remain motivated despite the pressures of work and the constant change underway within their organisations. Many employers have found that a positive, more participative approach to performance management encourages employees to respond in these ways – in terms of their flexibility, cooperation and commitment.

A three-year study by the Work and Employment Research Centre at the University of Bath[2] investigated employers undergoing major reorganisation and change, and interviewed some 700 managers and employees. It wanted to identify the factors encouraging "discretionary behaviour" – the demonstration of sustained commitment and "a willingness to go the extra mile" for their manager or employer. Discretionary behaviour is increasingly important in modern organisations, involving the way in which a job is performed: speed, attention to detail and quality, effort, concern for customers, ability to work with team colleagues, individual morale, and so on. Yet this behaviour is more difficult to monitor and assess than traditional outputs and outcomes.

The study has found that the management of performance, in particular discretionary behaviour, depends on having an integrated approach to the employment of people. It includes ensuring that the organisation has sufficient workers with the right ability (skills, experience and knowledge) through efficient recruitment and training, and that individuals' are motivated through the recognition of their efforts through efficient performance management and reward. Line managers must manage the performance of each person, and acknowledge good performance through praise or financial reward, and address poor performance as and when it occurs. By the same token, each individual's colleagues should acknowledge the person's contribution, and raise concerns where it slips below expectations. Finally, individuals must have the opportunity to practise discretionary behaviour – they cannot do this if their jobs are too narrow or inflexible, or if they cannot contribute to developing the work of the team or wider organisation.

Ability, motivation and opportunity make up an AMO model that the study found lies at the heart of optimum performance. All efforts of managing people should aim to support one or more aspects of AMO, including recruitment, training, reward, performance reviews and the use of teamworking.

In particular, though, the study highlighted the importance of line managers. Employees reported that they are most likely to be committed to their organisation where line managers:
● ensure each employee has an opportunity to discuss their training needs;
● provide coaching and guidance to help employees improve their performance;
● ask employees for their views; and
● treat them with respect.

Case study A. The Royal Mail

Performance coaching its being introduced by the Royal Mail as one means of tackling the troubled relationship between its managers and workers. The ability to coach employees as a means of improving their performance has been included in the core skills required of the Royal Mail's managers (a skill defined as "supports individual performance improvement through coaching"). It has developed a coaching handbook for managers, which explains that: "Performance coaching is about raising the performer's awareness and responsibility by the coach's use of effective questioning. Its purpose is to focus attention on the actual issue being tackled, provide focus for precision and detail on the output, and confirm accountabilities for action and support."

Managers are attending coaching courses, where they are trained to use interpersonal skills to coach their workers in the ways in which they can achieve their targets. Managers learn how to build relationships with their employees, deal with difficult behaviour and practise coaching skills. There is a two-day workshop for first-line managers, extended to three days for middle and senior managers. Managers' confidence in confronting unacceptable behaviour has grown, according to pre- and post-course surveys, and the organisation is investigating ways in which employees can give feedback to their managers on how they are being managed and coached.

Case study B. Fujitsu Services

At Fujitsu Services, a call-centre operator, changes to its performance management have led to a dramatic reduction in staff resignations and improvements
in productivity, alongside savings in recruitment costs through reductions in
labour turnover. Performance of staff had been measured by volume, such as
the number and length of calls handled by operators. It introduced a new culture where employees were given greater responsibility, encouraging them to
help customers address the root cause of their problems and, thereby, reducing the number of follow-up enquiries they received. A major training programme for managers and employees developed the skills required to analyse
problems and resolve them. Labour turnover has fallen by more than two-
thirds from 40% to 12% overall and, in some areas, to just 6%[3].

Call centres provide an interesting insight into effective performance management, because they are some of the most tightly managed of modern
work environments. Sophisticated electronic monitoring systems provide
feedback on call-response times, length of calls, the number of calls waiting
and other factors. Employees' behaviour is also often closely managed in
terms of their scripted responses, their behaviour on the telephone and the
frequency and duration of work breaks.

Research among more than 500 call centre staff in the UK has found that
performance management becomes more effective where such controls are
less strict. For example, where call scripts are less prescriptive, employees are
given more discretion and their work is made more varied. In particular, the
use of constant performance monitoring has been found to be counter-productive in many instances. Employees tend to respond positively where
monitoring is used more to help develop their future performance, rather
than providing evidence to judge their past activities. Overall, levels of anxiety, depression and job satisfaction were all found to improve where performance management was more professional and supportive[4].

Time-wasting

Even where employees are fully trained and capable of effective performance,
their work may suffer because they are simply wasting time on other activities – usually, because they have become bored or demotivated. Stress may be
a factor, too, with highly pressured staff looking for an escape from their
duties. So may illness in organisations where employees are discouraged from
taking sick leave. And workers whose business culture expects long hours of
attendance, regardless of what is achieved, will find ways of filling their time.

2. Tackling time-wasting

Personnel and HR managers tell IRS that this general problem of time-wasting is being addressed in one or more of three main ways:

1. controlling ways in which time can be wasted (using the telephone, emails and the internet for personal use; taking excessively long or frequent breaks; poor timekeeping);

2. encouraging use of the normal disciplinary procedure; and

3. emphasising the role of line managers in managing performance on an ongoing basis.

The particular ways in which they implement these strategies vary from employer to employer, but overall the main actions being taken are shown in descending order below:

● providing written rules on internet use;

● providing rules on email use;

● communicating their expectations of what constitutes reasonable behaviour in terms of personal use of telephone calls, emails and the internet;

● encouraging line managers to have a "quiet word" with individuals whose behaviour causes concern;

● using their disciplinary procedure;

● providing a written policy on the use of the telephone for personal calls;

● using open-plan offices to enable monitoring of employees' behaviour;

● providing guidelines on expected levels of output or work duties; and

● enforcing the timing and duration of breaks.

Fundamentally, many employers accept that many of these aspects of unacceptable performance are caused by their corporate culture of long hours. Working into the evening is seen by many organisations as sign of commitment, regardless of what the individuals concerned have achieved during their excessively long working day. However, failure to manage performance effectively is also seen as a reason for employees wasting time. Morale also suffers, we are told by personnel and HR managers, when line managers act inconsistently, addressing some issues and ignoring others, or where some line managers are energetic in managing performance and others are not.

Employers in the 21st century are rarely able to impose a management régime where discipline is so harsh that it prevents all forms of under-performance, even should they wish to do so. Instead, they need to focus on activities that cause them most damage or those that lead to disputes between individuals.

However, personnel and HR managers tell IRS that targeting action effectively is difficult because the most common forms of time-wasting are not necessarily those that cause greatest disruption. For example, excessive gossiping with colleagues is readily noticeable, and represents one of the most frequent symptoms of time-wasting. Yet employers report that it has far less impact on their business than other issues.

In fact, the worst aspect of time-wasting and under-performance, according to employers, is represented by employees who come to work with a bad hangover. This is not only a major hindrance to productivity, but presents a risk to health and safety in many situations. Second, employees who take excessive cigarette breaks are seen as a major source of disruption – but more in terms of their impact on other employees, who feel aggrieved at their colleagues' absences, and less in terms of the time lost by the smokers themselves.

Third, abuses caused by using the telephone excessively for personal purposes leads to considerable lost productivity and large telephone bills, according to employers' experience. Fourth in terms of its impact on businesses, the practice of sending emails to work colleagues on non-work matters (such as exchanging jokes) causes difficulties because it distracts both the sender and all their co-workers, and ties up considerable amounts of time. The excessive use of emails for personal reasons outside the organisation and the practice of surfing the internet for personal purposes follow in this list of major causes of disruption at work. Finally, spending excessive amounts of time gossiping or bantering with colleagues is mentioned by employers, although it is seen as a relatively unimportant issue when compared with the other factors listed above.

Formal performance-management systems

Formal performance-management systems (also known as "appraisals" or "personal reviews") provide an extra dimension to the day-to-day routine management of performance by line managers, team leaders or other personnel. They should not be stand-alone systems, but should build on ongoing activities. Their difference to day-to-day activities lies in their formality: they ensure that employee and line manager take the time and effort to discuss performance systematically, record the results, and create an action plan that helps the person improve their effectiveness. The formal reviews summarise what has already been informally discussed, and should rarely contain entirely new information.

Professor Adrian Furnham, the Professor of Psychology at University College London, and an experienced external adviser to business and regular contributor to broadsheet national newspapers, has found that performance-management systems have few friends. Discontent with the system is usually rife, with individuals objecting to their assessments and line managers objecting to their involvement in running the system. He finds that the main root causes lie in unsupportive senior managers, uncooperative line managers and personnel and HR specialists who lack impact or initiative. But the alternatives to performance assessment are even less palatable, he says. "Perhaps the best way to deal with the complaints is to encourage the disillusioned and desolate to point out not what is wrong with the current system, but how it can be fixed. Focus should be moved to alternatives or ways of correcting problems,"[5] rather than admitting defeat.

Case study C. Mid Kent Holdings

Utility company Mid Kent Holdings describes performance management as a forward-looking, positive activity: "The main objective of the appraisal is for all parties to agree on future actions needed to achieve targets, taking into account past achievements, individual aspirations, strengths and weaknesses, identified action areas and measures needed for improved performance."

Case study D. Greenpeace

Environmental campaigner Greenpeace highlights the importance of formal performance management in endorsing and building on day-to-day activities, and stresses the need to acknowledge good performance as well as bad: "Poor work does not lead to job satisfaction, and detracts from organisational effectiveness. So, it is important for the line manager to draw any weaknesses to the attention of the employee when it occurs, or as soon after as possible. Real difficulties arise when the issue is not raised explicitly until the appraisal interview. The employee is likely to feel taken by surprise, let down and misled, and will lose confidence in the line manager."

It continued: "It is very important that an employee's good work performance is acknowledged and affirmed. Positive feedback engenders confidence, a sense of self-pride and fosters commitment to the job. Praise should not be withheld until the appraisal interview, but be given whenever it is justified."

Case study E. Norwich Union Life

Life assurance company Norwich Union Life's recent performance-management initiative intends to develop a "performance culture" in the organisation. It includes setting out a form of compact, by showing what employees can expect of their managers – such as regular one-to-one discussions, clear communication of each individual's role, the nature of their contribution to the business, and the ways in which their reward is determined. Each individual receives an "individual performance plan", which sets out the objectives and accountabilities agreed for them for the course of the year. Line managers have been given greater involvement and responsibility in managing performance and in determining individual salary increases and bonuses. To provide the "tools, knowledge and skills to be able to deal with these people issues", the company has developed a series of workshops lasting from one hour to three days. They address such issues as conducting formal performance reviews, solving performance problems and highlighting effective methods of providing feedback.

Case study F. Lincoln Financial Group

A formal performance management system has been introduced at Lincoln Financial Group, a life assurance and pensions provider, in response to the regulatory requirements of the Financial Services Authority (FSA). The FSA requires that financial services companies' staff are competent in their jobs, and remain so for the duration of their careers. Lincoln's new system aims to ensure compliance with these requirements, by monitoring staff's performance and providing training and development as necessary. The company involved its managers in designing its performance management system, including helping to identify the measures they would use to assess their employees' performance – such as behaviours, technical expertise and the possession of formal qualifications. Lincoln's system involves quarterly reviews of performance, but only two of the reviews each year are formally recorded. These are linked to the creation and revision of personal development plans and personal objectives.

Case study G. Amey Construction

Major construction firm Amey Construction, has found that the motivational aspect of providing a formal performance-management system helps to retain staff, particularly younger workers and new graduates[6]. It has introduced a "young-people review", where every employee aged under 30 years is given special attention, and most of them receive a performance review at six-monthly intervals. The company finds that showing interest in each employee, conducting regular reviews of their performance and asking them how they are getting on are all important ingredients in effective retention of the best staff. Where employees raise issues and problems, Amey says that these must be addressed, and any promises must be kept.

Case study H. T-Mobile

Honouring commitments is also emphasised by telecoms company T-Mobile. Its performance-management system has been modified so that it now includes the drawing up of a formal contract between an employee and their manager. "We physically sit down and sign a contract. So, we are in a situation where we have committed to training and providing them with what they have requested, and we are signing something in front of them. We then revisit it at three-, six-, nine- and 12-month intervals"[7].

3. Formal performance-management systems

State of play: The benchmark formal performance-management system in use today, based on an analysis by IRS of feedback from employers, contains the following features:

● it covers the whole workforce, including manual workers;

● it includes an element of self-assessment alongside downward appraisal by the line manager;

● it provides full disclosure of the performance report to the individual concerned;

● it has involved personnel and HR specialists in designing, implementing and subsequently improving it; and, in a significant minority of employers,

● the how of someone's performance is assessed as well as the what of their activities (in other words, their behaviours, or competencies, alongside their outputs or functional tasks).

Focus and measures used

Many personnel and HR specialists tell us that one of the main weaknesses in their performance-management systems lies in the difficulty of identifying the factors that will be assessed in each person's performance. At one extreme, some have relied on an assumption that the relevant factors are obvious and require no definition – with the consequence that the system becomes subjective, inconsistent and loses credibility. At the other extreme, some organisations have tried to spell out the particular set of factors applying to each individual – with the danger that the system takes up too many resources, becomes too bureaucratic and loses the flexibility to cope with changing circumstances.

Many employers have found it best to concentrate on a reasonable number of factors as the basis of their performance review, and to identify them according to their importance to the job the employee performs and/or the part they play in the employee's overall contribution to the business. One approach to this task of agreeing the performance factors involves a review of inputs, processes, outputs and outcomes:

● inputs represent the skills and knowledge of the employee that they bring to their job;

● the process concerns the ways in which the employee performs the task or overall job, and includes their behaviours and attitudes. Factors derived from inputs and processes will usually be qualitative, rather than numerical;

● outputs obviously relate to the tangible results of the employee's inputs and processes, and factors based on them are quantifiable, including sales or products achieved, quality targets, accuracy and timeliness; and

● outcomes concern the impact of the individual's contribution on the activities and results of the organisation. Factors derived from outcomes are also quantifiable, and include customer satisfaction indices and contribution to profits.

At present, most employers tell IRS that they introduce a formal performance-management system for one or two deceptively simple purposes: to improve individuals' performance and/or identify their training needs. Frequently, too, employers aim to use the system to improve communication between line manager and employee.

In fact, these aims are all bound up with each other. A system can only be effective if it encourages productive communication between manager and employee, and builds a measure of trust and respect between them. And the improvement of performance of necessity involves a consideration of reasons for under-performance, such as training needs, as part of a plan to address these shortcomings. Therefore, raising each person's performance through a systematic performance-management system is likely to represent the fundamental aim of most employers' practices in this area. (Linked to these systems, though, may be elements of reward, which may often be more backward-looking and require some formal rating scheme; *see below and chapter 7*.)

To achieve their aims, employers' feedback shows that they generally rely on objectives – specific goals that are set for each individual, and whose achievement is assessed at the next performance review, before further goals are set, and so on. Other factors are often taken into account, however. For example, a sizeable minority also takes account of the way in which the individual achieves their results.

Objectives

There are considerable difficulties and limitations inherent in using objective-setting to the exclusion of other factors, and one of the main trends taking place sees employers revising their systems to incorporate additional or alternative approaches.

Objectives represent the most common focus of performance reviews because they relate individual effort to tangible results, are readily measurable and – although true more in theory than in practice – can be the means of relating corporate goals to individual activities.

The difficulties are many, though. Objectives tend to be short-term, and can take attention away from longer-term factors, such as developing transferable skills or ensuring the routine achievement of ongoing tasks and duties. They can also act as a barrier to flexibility if there is no provision to revise them when changes take place within the organisation.

And there are often practical difficulties in identifying meaningful objectives or targets for many individuals. In many jobs, it may not be possible to create objectives for the most important aspects of performance, with the result that assessment gives too much weight to relatively minor factors and downgrades those that are actually important. The increasingly team-oriented or collaborative approach of organisations adds a further difficulty, in that the objectives may not be fully under the control of any one person. Success or failure to attain them then becomes more a matter of chance than personal performance, and can demotivate managers and employees when they perceive the unrealistic nature of the performance review.

Few personnel and HR managers tell us that their organisations are abandoning the use of objectives. Instead, many are supplementing them with other factors that are also considered during performance reviews – primarily, other aspects of the job that contribute to performance in a significant way, including the assessment of behaviours ("competencies") in terms of the way in which the person undertakes their work.

Effective practice in relation to objective-setting concentrates on objectives being SMART – Specific, Measurable, Attainable (or Achievable), Realistic and Time-limited (or Time-bound). Organisations as diverse as the **Public Record Office**, the non-stop rail link, **Heathrow Express** and **HSBC Bank** (see below) require objectives to follow SMART principles. Employers have found that the potential for performance management to lose credibility and fall into disuse is less likely where the process of setting an individual's objectives is participative between the line manager and the employee and, preferably, where the individual plays the leading role.

In addition, the effect of meeting the targets should lead to an outcome that benefits both the line manager and the employee. The majority of employers use performance-related pay, so that the end-result takes the form of a payment (bonus, movement up a pay scale or pay increase). In other cases, praise or some other form of recognition provides an incentive and psychological reward. Line managers' own targets can also be linked to those of their direct reports, serving to provide them with a financial or psychological reward from their involvement in managing others' performance. Less directly, the objectives set for a line manager could include one based on implementing performance reviews in an effective manner.

Unless a job has an obvious, primary objective that can be expressed in quantitative terms, such as sales or output, then some form of job analysis will have to be undertaken to establish the performance targets to be assessed. Job descriptions and person specifications (*see chapter 1 Filling your vacancies*) provide at least a starting point, although the pace of change in most organisations demands that the prime tasks, results areas and accountabilities should be revisited on a regular basis as part of the performance-review system. The theory that personal objectives can be cascaded down from corporate and departmental level to individuals works best at levels nearest the top of the organisation: managers and senior managers. To minimise the need to revise personal targets, cascading systems need to time the performance-review cycle so that it follows shortly after the most influential date in the business-planning year.

Case study I. HSBC Bank

HSBC Bank relaunched its performance management in 2000, partly to address the role that objectives played in the system. It found that too many objectives were being set for some individuals, "which included the more obvious aspects of a person's job on a day-to-day basis, and failed to focus on the more important aspects of the role". The focus of the system has shifted to continuous improvement ("to ensure the continued success of the bank, performance management has to be more than the setting of objectives and the review of performance against these objectives").

Its revised system included the provision of guidance on drafting and agreeing personal objectives, based on a flow chart: "Check job description/profile – set key accountabilities – define key results areas (KRAs) – state aim of KRAs –

agree objectives – set performance measures – identify suggested activities – establish parameters (where appropriate)". The resultant objectives should be SMART, it adds, and written in the form of action statements.

Performance standards

HSBC's criticism of unfocused objective-setting is well-founded, but it presents employers with a difficulty: should routine but vital parts of the job be ignored in performance management? One approach adopted by HSBC and others involves identifying two types of objective: short-term (ie within the confines of a single review cycle) and long-term. The latter may be termed "performance standards". Like objectives, these standards are linked to quantified targets and are similarly assessed, but they tend to alter far less frequently. They are also carefully defined so as to focus on a few activities that represent the most important aspects of long-term, ongoing performance – rather than putting numbers to each part of a job description.

Behaviours

Increasingly, employers are extending their systems to assess not only objectives but also qualitative aspects of the job – provided these are equally vital. Using objectives as the sole criterion to assess a retail salesperson's performance would focus on sales volume, for example, but would not directly address other crucial aspects of their role, such as the way in which customers were served. To round off performance assessments, therefore, consideration of "concern for customers", "customer care" or a similar description of this type of behaviour would need to be included alongside quantified targets.

In larger organisations, these behaviours are often called "competencies". To identify the behaviours, employers either create a single set to cover the whole workforce ("core competencies") or tailor their lists to individuals performing similar tasks. (*See chapter 1 for information on competencies in recruitment, and chapter 2 for the use of competencies in selection.*) More informally, though, the activities of most importance to a job that are not capable of being expressed as objectives/standards can be identified jointly by the line manager and individual. They should then agree how these factors can be demonstrated, and what would differentiate highly effective, effective and unacceptable performance. The aim here is to minimise subjectivity, and produce a measurement aid that the employee accepts as well as the manager.

Case study J. British Waterways

At British Waterways, customer care is seen as central to the organisation's work. Therefore, everyone is required to reflect this behaviour. The organisation's documentation to managers and employees explains the rationale for each of its core skills. For customer care, it says: "We need customer care so that BW provides what customers want, when they want it, and in ways that delight the customer". For assessment purposes, it has differentiated five different levels of performance in the skill of customer care. To help identify the specific level of performance of an individual, the organisation has researched some practical examples of the way in which each level might be observed in practice. For each level, there are three to five examples. At the most basic level, for example, these examples include "can explain who the customers are" and "knows when and to whom to pass comments and queries". At level 2, the examples include "resolves complaints and confrontation constructively".

Whichever way the behaviours are identified, employers report that the single most crucial factor in winning acceptance for their assessment lies in involving employees and line managers in developing these indicators.

Other factors

The outcome of formal performance-management systems tends to follow the principle that "what you measure is what you get". In other words, the aspects of each person's performance that are discussed and assessed tend to be given more importance than those that are not – not only in terms of the review system, but also in what each manager and employee considers important in their day-to-day work.

For this reason, it is important that an organisation's performance-management system is carefully tailored to its own particular business needs. Generally, though, most employers incorporate objectives and/or performance standards and/or behaviours as the aspects of performance that their formal reviews assess. More specifically, though, research for the Chartered Institute of Personnel and Development found the most widespread measures apart from objectives are linked to quality, customer care, team contribution, relationships with colleagues and managers, flexibility, ability to learn, and business and financial awareness[8].

Assessments

Formal performance-management systems stand or fall on the ability, and cooperation, of those involved. A key issue, highlighted by personnel and HR specialists contacted by IRS, involves the role of line managers in the system. Day-to-day performance management must involve the line managers, supervisors and team leaders who are in routine contact with their direct reports. Given that formal reviews of performance must build on this day-to-day activity – rather than being an unconnected process – then line managers are inescapably central to the functioning of performance-management systems. Indeed, employers report that line managers are entirely, or largely, responsible for conducting the formal reviews of their employees' performance.

A basic willingness to undertake the performance review is an obvious precondition, but line managers must also be given the tools to perform this exacting and vital task. Their cooperation, and that of the employees being assessed, is most likely if they have been involved in the design of the performance-management system. Employers confirm that this is an important factor in helping their systems succeed. They also provide information to managers and employees that explains the system, communicate this actively (through briefings, for example), and provide training. In some instances, employers train those being assessed (usually separately) as well as those responsible for undertaking the reviews.

But line managers require more than training in understanding the workings of the system. They will also need to understand, and be able to use, disciplinary and grievance procedures because these will, at some time or another, be used in connection with performance issues. Employers may also have developed related policies, such as those concerned with equal opportunities, harassment and bullying, use of email and internet facilities, and attendance/absence (see below for specific policies). Again, line managers will need information and training in understanding and using these procedures.

There are, too, the well-known psychological factors that managers need training in addressing, such as the "horns and haloes" effects, where one bad or good aspect of performance influences the assessor's judgment in an unbalanced way. Recent events or issues may overshadow in the assessor's mind the nature of the employee's performance over the course of the whole review period. Line managers may also tend to award non-committal assessments, towards the middle of any scale. These and other factors often operate at the subconscious level, rather than through a conscious intent, and are thus more difficult to address without effective training. The process of holding the review meeting is also an art that managers can develop, through training in holding the interview in a suitable location, the role of active listening, and the mutual decision-making and planning that should occur. Broader personal and interpersonal skills are also required to help managers handle the conflicts or emotional distress that a performance review can arouse. It is thought by some psychologists that much of the reluctance of line managers to conduct reviews flows from their inability to handle such conflicts or emotions.

Employers tell us that they are shifting the focus of their performance management towards positive outcomes, such as praising employees' efforts and fostering development and career building. Yet line managers' training should not overlook the realities of workplace life, and must prepare them to deliver critical feedback and take further action where performance continues to be unacceptable.

Employees are being involved to a greater degree in their own formal performance reviews, according to feedback from personnel and HR managers obtained by IRS, and have found that this has yielded some benefits. Organisational structures are increasingly fluid, and often dependent on forms of collaborative working and, more generally, often reflect a less hierarchical approach. Encouraging employee involvement in performance reviews supports this trend towards greater individual responsibility. Changes in organisational structures are also reducing promotion opportunities, so that finding alternative ways of conferring greater responsibility have to be found, so that morale and motivation can be maintained.

The fast pace of change also increases the need for employees to be flexible and gain new skills as their roles evolve. Encouraging employees to take an interest in learning helps them adjust and, with the increasing link between performance reviews and the provision of training, it follows that giving employees a greater role in performance reviews naturally flows into their playing a greater role in their own training and development.

Employers have increased employee involvement in performance reviews in several ways, often through a gradual shift in emphasis away from top-down appraisals undertaken by their line manager. It is now usually the case that employees are given routine access to the performance report prepared by their manager and, flowing from this, many employers allow them to comment on it. Beyond that, many organisations have amended their systems so that the manager and individual both prepare for the review by conducting a review of the individual's performance. They may be given the same checklist or form; the manager will assess the individual against it, while the individual undertakes a self-assessment. The formal review then provides the opportunity for the parties to compare their versions and discuss points of agreement and disagreement. Finally, in a few organisations, employee involvement has been extended to the degree that they are responsible for writing their own performance report, to which the manager may append their own views.

The role of line managers in performance reviews is being changed too, employers report. In many organisations, the system has been set up so that managers are required to produce evidence to support their assessments (for example, to cite a particular incident that justifies their criticism or praise). Many, too, are requiring the next level of management to check line managers' assessments for consistency, objectivity and fairness.

Monitoring

In the public sector, the Race Relations (Amendment) Act 2000 places a general requirement on employers to ensure their personnel practices support equality of opportunity on grounds of ethnicity. The Commission for Racial Equality's guidance recommends that public sector employers conduct regular reviews of their personnel policies, particularly those covering performance assessment, discipline, grievance and training, and monitor their use to ensure there is no unfair discrimination on the grounds of ethnicity.

Such monitoring is also practised by employers in the private sector, although only a minority do so at present.

Equality Direct, suggests that monitoring "can be carried out on an occasional 'snap-shot' basis rather than continuously. A review would look at performance markings and remuneration decisions to see whether particular groups do significantly better or worse than other groups". (Equality Direct provides advice on a range of personnel issues in respect of their fairness and compliance with discrimination law[9]. Its partners include the Federation of Small Businesses, the equality commissions, Acas (the Advisory, Conciliation and Arbitration Service) and the Department for Trade and Industry.)

360-degree

The top-down approach to performance assessment remains the most typical format among employers. However, as we have just seen, increasingly they incorporate at least some elements of self-assessment, where the individual is encouraged to examine their own performance and report on it.

There are some instances, though, where assessments are based on the input of others with whom the person has direct contact – such as colleagues, subordinates or internal/external customers, alongside their immediate manager and their own self-appraisal. These systems are known as "360-degree assessment". The cost and resources involved, and their focus on behaviours rather than objectives, means that their use is almost exclusively confined to managerial and senior managerial levels. In such instances, 360-degree assessment is generally used for management development and leadership development.

The assessment involves the manager concerned, some of their colleagues and some subordinates, and the manager's own manager – typically 10 people in all – who each complete a form that sets out key dimensions of the person's behaviours and, perhaps, the duties of their current role. Usually, they are asked to choose a rating for each factor, from a scale provided. The feedback from all those involved is analysed, usually via computer software, and the results are produced – often as a series of graphics.

The feedback is communicated to the manager by a suitably trained individual, often a personnel, HR or development specialist or external consultant, with the intention of increasing their understanding of themselves, their strengths and their weaknesses. Where the process is expertly and sensitively handled, the manager will find the feedback convincing and valuable, particularly if there is strong agreement among those giving their assessments, and where the outcome poses no threat to the manager's pay, credibility or security. However, while 360-degree assessments are increasingly being adopted by large organisations, their use remains controversial.

4. 360-degree assessment

A two-year research project among 50-plus employers with experience of 360-degree assessment has provided the basis of government guidelines[10] on this technique. The guidelines highlight the following factors:

● 360-degree assessment works best when linked to personal development, rather than performance assessment or performance-related pay;

● Employers should consider the best way of gathering the 360-degree feedback, how they will analyse it, and how the feedback will be communicated to the employee;

● the assessment should lead to a development plan and the commitment of resources by the employer to its achievement; otherwise, employers' experience shows that managers who are the subjects of 360-degree feedback will find it a frustrating experience; and

● piloting of schemes is essential to de-bug them and help calculate the resources required.

Ratings

Most employers continue to use ratings systems in their formal performance reviews. Generally, they expect a separate rating to be produced for each factor that is being assessed. Alternatively, or additionally, most systems produce an overall performance score; where separate ratings are also used, then the overall score will be calculated from them. The overall performance score is often used for performance-related pay, promotion and selection for redundancy.

Ratings systems are controversial, in that they can over-emphasise backward-looking assessments of past performance at the expense of future improvements. Similarly, they can give too much attention to short-term goals, and less to long-term development. But it is often difficult for employers to devise objective methods of linking performance to reward without the use of scores.

The number of levels of performance on the rating scale also raises problems. Many organisations use large numbers of levels – particularly in respect of behavioural-type performance factors. But psychological research has shown that it is very difficult to make fine distinctions between performance levels. Not only can the practical differences in performance be insignificant where there are many levels in use, but busy line managers required to assess each of several performance factors according to complex rating scales will find the task overwhelming.

As in the examples of named practice below, though, an increasing proportion of employers is adopting simpler schemes, based on three to five levels of performance. This range is favoured by many occupational psychologists: three is seen as the lower level, below which gradations become too broad to be helpful, while five is seen as the maximum, beyond which the scale becomes too complex for practical application.

Rating systems do not necessarily have to use numerical levels (1, 2, 3 etc), and many organisations use a descriptive label for each scale point ("exceeds expectations", "meets expectations", etc). In any event, line managers must be given adequate information to help them assess each performance factor – providing definitions of each scale point, and examples of performance that relate to it.

Personnel and HR managers report that their organisations are increasingly moving away from rating scales that have a negative connotation. This usually means that the scale points are given fairly neutral, non-threatening labels, with the aim of making the performance-review system as positive and motivating as possible. Employees who are given ratings that imply strong criticism could well be discouraged from attempting to do better, having gained the impression that the employer has given up on them. Often, these negative connotations develop over time, and are frequently one of the prime reasons why employers revise their formal performance-management systems.

A typical group of employees' overall performance ratings will usually show a distinct pattern – most of them will be assessed around the middle of the possible range of ratings, with only a few being given ratings at the extreme ends of the scale. This is a normal pattern, particularly given that ratings towards the upper and lower ends of a scale are usually described in exceptional terms – the individual is performing unusually better or worse than the average.

However, this normal distribution of ratings may be influenced by subjective factors that serve to undermine the workings of formal performance-management systems. In particular, studies of line managers have repeatedly found that they shy away from awarding relatively high or low ratings – even where they are merited. An abnormal proportion of their assessments falls into what these managers see as the safe, uncontroversial area in the middle of the rating scale.

Some organisations have tried to reduce this effect, which they consider implies that the intentions of the performance-management system are being thwarted. In some employers, the number of levels in the rating scale avoids odd numbers, so that there is never a safe middle ground for line managers to choose (1, 2, 3, 4 instead of 1, 2, **3**, 4, 5, for example). Alternatively, some employers impose a forced distribution on line managers, where they must assign a predetermined proportion of their employees to particular parts of the rating scale (for example, 10% of employees must be given a low score of 1 or 2 in a five-point scale). The element of compulsion can increase line managers' compliance with their duties in managing performance, but it has obvious disadvantages.

Compulsion can cause resentment among both managers and the individuals being assessed, and it can undermine the whole ethos of systems that are supposed to be based on objective, consistent performance assessment. To reduce these adverse reactions, some employers set guidelines for the pattern of line managers' ratings, rather than hard-and-fast quotas.

Case study K. The Natural History Museum

At London's Natural History Museum, the formal performance review is based on a form that concentrates on assessing past performance, using the job description, and factors agreed at the previous review in a "forward job plan". Each aspect of performance is assessed on a four-point scale, from "fully met" to "not met". The review then revisits the job plan to agree the factors for the next period. This comprises the forward-looking element, and takes into account measurable objectives, important behaviours and the job's main tasks. The separate ratings are then used to produce an overall performance score, which forms the basis of an individual pay award. The score uses a five-point scale: "(1) outstanding; (2) performance significantly above standard required for the job; (3) performance fully meets standard required for the job; (4) performance not fully up to requirements, (5) some improvements are necessary; and unacceptable".

Examples of rating scales for individual behaviours: "exceeds; meets; falls short" (**Boots Opticians**); "strong; competent; development area; improvement area" ("needs improvement" in the case of production workers) (**Cereal Partners UK**, the breakfast-cereal manufacturer); and "exceeds expectations; meets expectations; partly meets expectations; and fails to meet expectations" (**Smith and Nephew Wound Management**, a manufacturer of medical supplies).

Case study L. HM Customs and Excise

HM Customs and Excise, though, has abandoned the use of ratings for behavioural factors. It found that the rating process became a time-consuming and meaningless procedure, and diverted attention away from positive measures. Now, the organisation's performance-review system focuses on personal development. Areas of strength and weakness are intended to be discussed frankly, but without the trappings of formal ratings. Customs and Excise's revised list of behaviours includes a definition of each behaviour and two sets of examples of how the behaviour can be assessed. The first set provides a checklist of acceptable behaviour ("positive indicators"), while the second exemplifies unacceptable performance ("negative indicators"). The organisation considers that three behaviours are central to its activities, and requires all employees and managers to be assessed against them. One of these behaviours is "works positively with change". Examples of negative indicators here include: "Stands in the way of new ideas; actively resists change; and nit-picking new ways of working".

Similarly, **Freeserve**, the internet-services provider which introduced its first performance-review system in late 2000, omitted performance ratings because it wanted to emphasise "talent management" and personal development.

Reflecting a growing trend, **Huhtamaki Van Leer**, a manufacturer of plastic and moulded paper fibre packaging materials, continues to use ratings for performance factors, but has adopted value-free pairs of letters instead of numerical scores which it thought would be divisive. Its ratings for behaviours are: "CE: clearly exceeds; ME: meets and exceeds; MR: meets requirements; MM: meets minimum; FM: fails to meet; and TE: too early".

Personal development

Employers report that they are shifting the balance of their performance-management systems towards training and development, and away from the simple, backwards measurement of results against objectives. Given that effective performance management must be integrated with mainstream business activities, this is no more than a reflection of wider changes taking place in workplaces.

Employers now require employees and managers to participate willingly in change initiatives, to be flexible and readily acquire different skills. All of these depend on cooperation from those involved. Involving individuals to a greater degree in their own training and development is being practised by many organisations as a means of winning this cooperation. It encourages participation in learning and fosters a view that skills development benefits the individual as well as the employer. The greater measure of control in this area will, it is hoped, translate into broader benefits of accepting greater personal responsibility and improved self-confidence.

Routinely, now, many employers' performance reviews incorporate a consideration of training needs and, perhaps, the preparation of a plan to provide training that addresses identified areas of under-performance. It is often possible for the training needs recorded in the reports from performance reviews to be extrapolated, and cost-effective training provided for groups of employees at a time.

"Personal development plans" (or "PDPs") are being introduced by some employers. These are prepared either during, or soon after, a performance review, and set out the personal learning agenda for the individual concerned, linked to the results of their performance assessment. Personnel and HR managers inform IRS that PDPs offer benefits to their organisations, by indicating to employees that they are valued and that there is a willingness to invest in them through training and development provision. And the individualised nature of the plan helps to foster the employee's motivation to participate willingly in the learning.

Some organisations also use personal development plans as part of their shift towards greater employee involvement in managing their own performance and development, and this practice extends beyond the largest employers to more modestly resourced ones, too. The plan may be drawn up with the assistance of the person concerned (or even entirely by them), and they may be given responsibility for implementing it. This can involve actively identifying suitable learning opportunities for themselves, suggesting suitable training courses and keeping a learning log that records the progress of their development. Most of these self-development initiatives are found among employers that are undergoing significant change. To gain individuals' interest, these plans are often broader in scope than the remit of their current job, and may even incorporate personal preferences and interests.

It is not an easy task for either line manager or employee to draw up a development plan that simultaneously takes account of the employee's current training needs, those likely to arise in the future in their present role, those linked to a possible move to another job, and training needs associated with broader skills of general application.

Organisations will need to provide assistance with this activity, through training in preparing and implementing the plans, and providing access to advice on learning opportunities. The development of a simple pro-forma is often helpful. This can include basic guidance on how a PDP can be drawn up and implemented, and contain a simple checklist of issues to consider – such as considering the areas highlighted in the performance review that require attention, and the types of training and development that could help the individual concerned remedy them. However, forms that are too prescriptive and complex could well be self-defeating, in that PDPs are intended to be tailored to the needs of each individual.

One prime difficulty that employers report they encounter lies in the potential clash between the use of performance reviews to generate a rating or performance category for pay purposes and their role in discussing training needs and development planning.

There are many problems inherent in this dual-purpose use of performance reviews. In particular, pay for performance will focus on results (usually short-term ones), while development planning will often consider broader issues, such as longer-term personal development. The two purposes are not always mutually compatible. Moreover, employees will be at pains to emphasise their achievements when the outcome is linked to reward, while a frank discussion about training needs requires an honest admission of areas of weakness. (*See chapter 7 for information on performance-related pay.*)

Case study M. Whitbread Hotel Company

At the Whitbread Hotel Company, whose brands include Marriott Hotels and Travel Inns, a revised performance-management system has been introduced that separates reviews for pay purposes and those considering training needs. Pay reviews take place annually in March and April, and are based on assessing an employee's personal contribution over the course of the previous year. Contribution comprises both specific achievements, known as "key tasks", that were agreed at the previous annual review, and behaviours. Each individual is assessed against four company-wide behaviours – "drive for results; implementation; thinking; working with people" – with the addition of a fifth behaviour of "leadership" in the case of senior managers.

Career and personal development reviews take place between July and September each year, and are intended to be separate, "forward-looking" processes. Guidance issued to managers said that this should ensure their employees receive a "high-quality discussion with their boss about their career goals, with honest feedback on an agreed action plan". Each employee is asked to prepare for their review, which is held with their line manager, by thinking about their "strengths and development needs". The spring pay review is not ignored, however, as its assessment of the person's achievements and behaviours is considered in terms of the training and career-development implications it highlighted. At the end of a discussion, "agreed, realistic career goals" are identified, and the employee's potential for career progression is recorded on a special form ("your potential indicator"), and development plans are made.

Record-keeping

There are several important reasons for maintaining effective records of formal performance-management systems.

Record-keeping ensures that line managers and employees pay attention to the process and treat it seriously. They are usually expected to note down (often on a special form) the main details of the employee's performance to date, details of a new set of targets, and any consequent action points (such as training). Records provide a reference document for future use when performance is revisited at the next review. And the records enable monitoring of the effectiveness of the performance-management system across the organisation (see above).

The Employment Practices Data Protection Code issued in connection with the Data Protection Act 1998 (the Code has no separate legal status, but any enforcement action under the Act by the Information

Commissioner may take account of the employer's compliance with the Code) provides general advice on record-keeping and formulating policies about it.

Records generally provide valuable evidence when aggrieved employees take the employer to tribunal or court. Requiring managers to maintain accurate records helps to impress on them that the procedure should be taken seriously and handled professionally – if for no other reason than their actions can be investigated at a later stage. Accurate records also enable the workings of the procedures to be monitored to ensure there is no unfair discrimination against individuals or groups.

Most employers report that they have developed forms for use in their procedures, containing guidance and structured sets of questions or topics to ensure managers provide information about all relevant issues in sufficient detail. They often develop policies about the storage of the records to ensure they are kept in a secure and confidential manner.

Whatever records are kept – handwritten notes, completed forms or electronically stored files – there are legal implications for their security, confidentiality and period of storage. The Data Protection Act 1998 requires secure, confidential storage, the rights of access by employees to their records (having given due notice in the prescribed way), and that records "shall not be kept for longer than is necessary for that purpose or those purposes".

The Act offers no set limits on record-keeping, and it expects that the period should reflect a real business need and take account of other legal requirements. For example, records may be relevant to potential claims on the grounds of unfair dismissal or unlawful discrimination; in such cases, individuals usually have three months to lodge a complaint. Where a procedure may be used to select individuals for redundancy, then the normal six-month limit on claims relating to statutory redundancy pay will be a consideration. Performance reviews that are linked to reward should take account of equal pay legislation, where individuals usually have six months from the end of their contract to lodge a complaint. However, individuals have a period of six years to lodge breach of contract complaints. All of these considerations highlight the need to ensure that records are filed safely and securely, and kept for as long as is relevant under the law and the organisation's requirements.

5. Legal checklist

● Protected groups must not be put at an unfair disadvantage as a result of performance management, personal development and related systems (where the outcomes have relevance to pay, and access to training and promotion opportunities) – Sex Discrimination Act 1975; Race Relations Act 1976; Disability Discrimination Act 1995; Trade Union and Labour Relations (Consolidation) Act 1992; and Codes of Practice associated with these Acts.

● Performance-management and other systems and procedures in the public sector must be checked for unfair discrimination on the grounds of ethnicity – Race Relations (Amendment) Act 2000.

● Eligible groups have the right to request a move to flexible working – Employment Act 2002.

● The groups are workers with a child under the age of six, or a child with disabilities under the age of 18.

● Employee records must follow the data protection principles – Data Protection Act 1998 and its Employment Practices Data Protection Code.

11. Managing performance 2

See also: 10. Managing performance 1 (for performance management; absence; sick pay).

This chapter covers:
- Discipline;
- Disciplinary procedures;
- Grievances and grievance procedures;
- Harassment and bullying;
- Whistleblowing; and
- Record-keeping.

Checklists in this chapter:
1. Effective disciplinary procedures: the main issues
2. Defining gross misconduct
3. Effective grievance procedures: the main issues
4. Being prepared: common grievances
5. Legal checklist

Case studies in this chapter:
A. Parceline
B. Cummins Engineering

Discipline

Discipline is an essential aspect of managing people. Performance expectations, including individual standards of work and personal conduct, should be defined as clearly as possible, and set the tone for each person's contribution at work. These expectations define the boundaries of acceptability, and discipline's role is to police these boundaries and take action where they have been deliberately crossed. Educationalists have found that pupils excel where expectations are high. Work cultures that focus on high expectations, and reasonable measures of trust and individual responsibility, are also likely to provide the best conditions for effective performance, backed up with disciplinary processes for the isolated instances of abuse and non-conformance.

Changes in society towards a less-deferential view of authority support this switch towards the use of measures that encourage high performance and away from those that manage employees closely and come down harshly on any infringements, no matter how minor.

Ford, for example, has recently abandoned the practice of "managing out" the lowest 10% of its performers because it clashed with its culture and shifting social attitudes, producing a negative reaction from employees. In place of authoritarian styles of leadership, the coaching role of managers is being emphasised, and all personnel specialists are being trained in coaching techniques[1].

Employers are torn in two ways, though. Individuals' performance is likely to benefit from line managers' encouragement, coaching and informal discussions, as and when required, about performance problems. Yet case law places considerable emphasis on conformance with formal procedures – the forthcoming statutory disciplinary procedure that will be incorporated into each employee's contract (see below) will heighten this focus still further.

Increasingly, therefore, personnel and HR managers tell us that they are equipping line managers and other supervisors with key people-management skills to improve their role in managing performance. At the same time, a considerable number of employers have been reviewing their formal disciplinary procedures to ensure they are best able to withstand legal scrutiny. This involves such issues as:

● Incorporating changes to the law, in particular the introduction of a right to be accompanied to some formal hearings (see below), and the revision of the Acas Code of Practice (see below);

● Improving the provision of information to employees about the standards of performance and conduct expected of them;

● Linked to this, providing examples of unacceptable behaviour that constitute misconduct or gross misconduct, or improving the existing lists of such examples; and

● Changing the timescales of the stages in their procedure.

Day-to-day performance management must be the responsibility of line managers and supervisors as part of their routine contact with members of their staff. Issues warranting praise or remedial action cannot be left until the time arrives for the annual or six-monthly formal performance review. However, line managers must be given the training and perspective to appreciate the role of discipline in their performance-management activities. Otherwise, not only could the organisation face costly legal actions by disciplined employees, but inconsistent and ineffective practices could develop.

Despite the central role played by employees' immediate managers, personnel and HR specialists also provide an indispensable input into performance management and discipline. Their overarching role enables them to organise suitable training, develop and revise policies and monitor the effective operation of formal systems. They are also vital in providing a trained, professional input into stages of the formal procedure where sanctions are likely, such as demotion or dismissal. All in all, personnel specialists have told us that performance and discipline represent a significant part of their workload on a day-to-day basis.

Alongside pointers from employers' best practice, guidance on formulating and applying disciplinary policies is available from such sources as Equality Direct[2] and Acas (the Advisory, Conciliation and Arbitration Service)[3].

Disciplinary procedures

The new rights

The vast majority of employers have already developed formal disciplinary procedures, and this practice will be a legal requirement once part 2 of the Employment Act 2002 comes into force (estimated to be April 2004). The act will have the effect of making its minimum disciplinary procedure part of each employee's contract of employment. This will not affect disciplinary provisions that are in addition to the act's requirements, provided they not in conflict with them. It will be important for every employer that already has a disciplinary procedure to review it against the new statutory requirements to ensure that their own process does not conflict with the new law.

In the meantime, an employer's lack of compliance with the Acas Code of Practice on Disciplinary and Grievance Procedures[4] can be taken into account by tribunals when considering issues relevant to it (the Code will be revised to coincide with the implementation of the new legal requirements). However, failure to comply with the Code does not, itself, expose employers to legal challenge. In addition, the Code does not apply to employers with fewer than 20 employees. (The Code is also valuable in providing guidance on responding to grievances, and formulating and applying grievance procedures.)

When these provisions of the Employment Act 2002 are introduced, employment tribunals will be able to take account of the failure of employers or employees to comply with the Act's minimum disciplinary and grievance requirements when calculating compensation.

The Act will also require all employers (including those with fewer than 20 employees, which will no longer be exempt) to provide employees with details of the statutory disciplinary procedure and their right of appeal. If they also have their own disciplinary provisions, then they must also communicate them to staff (an existing requirement under the Employment Rights Act 1996). In both instances, the full text must be provided or details given of where employees can find copies. (A prime advantage of producing a supplementary procedure that specifies the options open to the employer when disciplining an employee lies in giving the employer the contractual right to impose such sanctions, as long as it is clear that the employer's procedure forms part of the contract of employment. Without a contractual right to do so, employers may not be able to impose such sanctions as suspension without pay or demotion.)

The Act sets down a minimum three-stage disciplinary procedure – which is intended to apply to most types of discipline and misconduct, and to individual redundancies – although this can be modified in cases of instant dismissal (see below). However, the statutory procedure may be varied in some cases, the government has suggested, where its use would be inappropriate. These include threats of violence and serious illnesses.

Stage one requires the employer to provide a written statement to the employee detailing the alleged conduct, characteristics or other circumstances, that led it to consider disciplining (or dismissing) them. The employer must also invite the employee to attend a meeting to discuss the matter.

Stage two requires that the meeting must take place before any action is taken by the employer, with the exception of suspension. The meeting should not be held until the employee has had a reasonable opportunity to study the statement and consider their response. For their part, the employee is expected to take reasonable steps to attend the meeting. Following the meeting, the employer is required to inform the employee of their decision, and notify them of their right of appeal.

Stage three deals with appeals. The employee must inform the employer that they intend to appeal against the decision. The employer must then invite the employee to attend a further meeting, that, again, the employee is expected to take reasonable steps to attend. This appeal does not have to be held before any disciplinary action, or dismissal, takes place. Following the appeal meeting, the employer must inform the employee of its final decision.

Where the employee has already been dismissed because of a reason the employer believed justified instant or near-instant dismissal, the following modified two-stage procedure is required:

First stage: The employer must provide a written statement with details of the reasons that led to the employee being dismissed, including the basis for thinking that the employee was guilty, based on the facts available at the time. The statement must also give details of a right of appeal.

Second stage: The employee must inform the employer that they intend to appeal. The employer must invite the employee to attend an appeal meeting, and which the employee is expected to take reasonable steps to attend. Following the appeal meeting, the employer must inform the employee of its final decision.

In both the standard and modified procedures: each step and action will have to be taken without unreasonable delay; the timing and location of meetings must be reasonable; and meetings must be conducted so that both employer and employee have been given the opportunity to explain their case. In addition, in the case of appeal meetings that are not the first meeting (ie following the standard procedure, where the employee had not already been dismissed), the employer should – as far as is reasonably practical – be represented by a more senior manager than the manager who attended the first meeting, unless the more senior manager also attended that first meeting. (The use of "reasonable/unreasonable" in this paragraph has not yet been defined; unless Regulations are issued that provide explanations to the Act's wording, future case law – in other words, precedents determined by senior courts – will have to fill in these details.)

Employers will not be able to claim that a failure to follow the statutory procedures would have made no difference to the end-result and, thus, avoid being found to have unfairly dismissed someone. In other words, there are no exemptions from following the statutory disciplinary procedures, although employers may, under the act, be able use this defence in respect of their own disciplinary processes that go over and above the legal minimum. In these cases, tribunals will consider whether the decision to dismiss falls within a band of reasonable responses by the employer to the employee's actions.

Note, however, that a further right concerning disciplinary meetings has already been enacted: the right to be accompanied. Under the Employment Relations Act 1999, employers must allow an employee to be accompanied by one person to disciplinary hearings (such as the meetings covered by the forthcoming law). The companion must be allowed to address the hearing, and confer with the individual, but cannot answer questions put to the individual. Companions can be trade union officials or representatives (from the same or a different employer), provided they have been certified in writing by their union as having experience of, or received training in, acting as a companion in disciplinary or grievance hearings. Companions can also be another of the employer's workers. Where representatives working for the same employer or individuals' co-workers are involved, they have a right to paid time off to attend the hearing. The right to be accompanied excludes informal disciplinary-type meetings where the purpose is to investigate the issue, but which will not involve a formal warning or impose a sanction.

Employers' practices

Formal disciplinary procedures are found in almost all employers, and the forthcoming change in the law will ensure that the remainder introduces them. The prime aim of the government in introducing statutory disciplinary hearings is to reduce the caseload of employment tribunals. At present, many complaints about unfair dismissal succeed because the employers concerned either had a faulty disciplinary procedure or failed to observe it fairly.

1. Effective disciplinary procedures: the main issues

The main issues concerned with effective disciplinary procedures, according to feedback obtained by IRS from personnel and HR managers, are:

● **A last resort:** Formal disciplinary action is seen as a serious matter by the employee concerned, and can escalate a problem to a level where a satisfactory outcome is difficult to achieve unless the purpose is to dismiss fairly. Line managers should be trained in effective performance-management techniques, and encouraged to treat discipline as an ongoing responsibility; formal procedures should be seen as a last resort where informal methods have failed;

● **Define its purpose:** Providing a statement of purpose will help employees and line managers understand the aims and workings of the disciplinary procedure;

● **Give guidance:** Providing guidance, either in the procedure or separately, helps line managers implement the disciplinary procedure. As well as setting out the general principles of managing discipline in a fair, objective and consistent way, the guidance should cover considerations such as where, when and how to conduct the hearing, the keeping of records, and when and how to involve more senior managers or personnel specialists. Providing examples of the types of behaviour that may lead to disciplinary action can be useful to both managers and their employees in managing their conduct and performance. In particular, many employers give examples of conduct that could be classed as gross misconduct and lead to instant dismissal;

● **Stages:** Four-stage disciplinary procedures reflect Acas guidance and are found in many employers;

● **Records:** Keeping records of the use of the disciplinary procedure is essential, but there should be time limits, after which records should be safely deleted;

● **Dismissal:** The legal implications of dismissal mean that personnel specialists should always be involved in stages of the disciplinary procedure where dismissal is one possible outcome; legal advice (such as *Best Practice in HR's* free helpline) should also be taken where the situation is complicated or unclear;

● **Flawed procedures**, or poorly applied ones, may also lead to legal liability where they involve unlawful discrimination, unjustified action against someone asserting their statutory rights, or whistleblowers protected by the law. Reviewing procedures against the forthcoming statutory disciplinary procedures will help to remedy defects, as will the involvement of personnel and HR specialists in vetting them; the provision of training and guidance to line managers will help them administer the policy in a fair, consistent and objective manner;

● **Time limits:** Fair and reasonable time limits need to be specified for each stage in the procedure, and adhered to; and

● **Being accompanied:** Under the law, an employee in entitled to be accompanied to disciplinary hearings or meetings that could result in a sanction (including a formal warning or confirmation of earlier action).

Personnel and HR managers tell IRS that disciplinary procedures are vital in minimising the risk of losing employment tribunal cases, and in setting the tone for the organisation's expectations of its employees and managers. Procedures can set the boundaries of acceptable behaviour, and act as a last resort when these boundaries are infringed. But, on a daily basis, line managers' effective and proactive management of performance should provide the focus for encouraging acceptable behaviour. Therefore, line managers should not be able to abdicate responsibility to a formal procedure, because they are too busy or unwilling to manage their employees.

We mentioned above that employers aim to use their disciplinary processes as part of the boundary-setting of acceptable behaviour. This brings in the broader issue of ensuring that employees understand their performance expectations and what is, and is not, acceptable behaviour. Disciplinary actions, including informal ones, should aim to address wilful breaches of known rules rather than mistakes caused by ignorance.

2. Defining gross misconduct

Acas, in its Code of Practice mentioned above, recommends that examples should be given of unacceptable behaviour, particularly where the consequence could include instant dismissal. It says that the definition of gross misconduct (leading to dismissal without notice) depends on each employer's own circumstances, but could well include:

- theft, fraud and deliberate falsification of records;
- physical violence;
- serious bullying or harassment;
- deliberate damage to property;
- serious insubordination;
- misuse of the employer's property or name;
- actions that bring the employer into serious disrepute;
- serious incapability at work because of alcohol or illegal drugs;
- serious negligence that causes, or might cause, unacceptable loss, damage or injury;
- a serious infringement of health and safety rules; and
- a serious breach of confidence (subject to the whistleblowing protection offered by the Public Interest (Disclosure) Act 1998).

Even where an employee is guilty of gross misconduct, employers should investigate the issue through their disciplinary procedure. The forthcoming statutory disciplinary procedure that will be incorporated into every employee's contract includes a fast-track process for cases of gross misconduct (see above).

Many employers adopt four-stage disciplinary procedures: an initial warning; a final warning in writing; disciplinary action (including dismissal); and an appeal stage. Employers stress that each stage should provide details to the employee of the reason for the use of the disciplinary procedure, the status of the complaint (for example, that it represents the initial stage of a process), and the nature of the possible further action that might be taken if the employee does not address the cause(s) of complaint. A right to be accompanied (whether limited to the legal minimum described above, or being more general in coverage) and a right of appeal should also be mentioned.

The Acas Code of Practice's four-stage procedure comprises a first warning (either a formal oral warning or, for more serious issues, a formal written warning); a final written warning; a sanction; and a right of appeal.

Employers advise that regardless of whether or not the initial warning is given verbally or in writing, a report should be kept, just as adequate records should be made of the other stages of the procedure. These records help maintain consistent and fair management of the same member of staff (for example, if the same type of issue has to be addressed at a later date), and provide evidence in case the employee lodges an application with an employment tribunal.

However, employers also stress that time limits should be set on the storage of records, and their safe deletion should be ensured after that date. Records relating to the first stage of disciplinary procedures, in cases where an initial verbal warning is given, are usually deleted after six months, based on typical employer practice. A more cautious minority tends, however, to retain them for 12 months. In contrast, records of initial warnings given in writing are typically held for 12 months, with only a minority discarding them after a shorter period than this – usually, six months.

Typically, employers also set a limit of 12 months for the storage of records relating to the second stage (the final warning), although a minority of employers takes markedly different approaches. Some, for example, retain records of final warnings for only six months, while some others may keep them for as long as five years.

The Acas Code suggests that, for the first stage, a formal oral warning should be kept but disregarded for disciplinary purposes after a period of six months (that is, the Code makes no recommendation about the destruction of records), and suggests a live period of 12 months for formal warnings made in writing. For stage two – a final written warning – Acas suggests a period of 12 months after which the record should be disregarded.

Disciplinary actions expose employers to many potential legal liabilities, from discrimination and whistleblowing provisions to constructive dismissal. Effective record-keeping provides an important means of ensuring that the workings of disciplinary procedures are fair, effective and safe from legal challenge. Procedures need to be checked by personnel and HR specialists to ensure they are well-designed and conform to the law (including the forthcoming statutory disciplinary procedure).

In the public sector, the Race Relations (Amendment) Act 2000 places a general requirement on employers to ensure their personnel practices support equality of opportunity on grounds of ethnicity. The Commission for Racial Equality's guidance recommends that public sector employers should conduct regular reviews of their personnel policies, particularly those covering performance assessment, discipline, grievance and training, and monitor their use to ensure there is no unfair discrimination on the grounds of ethnicity.

Monitoring is also practised by employers in the private sector, although only a minority does so at present. Some form of coordinated supervision of the patterns of disciplinary action across the organisation will ensure that discipline is being applied consistently, fairly and lawfully – for example, through the requirement to involve personnel and HR specialists in cases where sanctions are imposed as part of disciplinary action. Where the number of disciplinary cases is found to be high in a particular area, for example, then further investigation of an underlying cause might be warranted.

The provision of training for line managers in managing disciplinary matters provides a further, important line of defence in ensuring practices comply with the law, and that line managers are best able to manage individuals' performance. Most personnel and HR managers tell us that their organisations offer training to line managers in conducting disciplinary procedures, and in managing discipline more generally. However, practice is flawed at present: only a minority of employers make the training compulsory, and only a minority ensures that all managers and supervisors responsible for discipline receive the training.

In terms of the content of the training, it may be useful to take account of the most common offences that trainees are likely to face, based on employers' experience: absenteeism; performance issues; timekeeping; theft or fraud; failure to obey instructions; aggression or verbal abuse; infringements of health and safety rules; alcohol or drug abuse; assault; and sexual or racial harassment.

Alongside training, many employers issue written guidance to line managers to help them manage discipline and apply the disciplinary procedure. Some personnel specialists say that they have helped their organisations drawn up the guidance, while many others distribute copies of the Acas handbook, *Discipline at work*[5]. As well as setting out the general principles of managing discipline in a fair, objective and consistent way, the guidance should cover considerations such as where, when and how to conduct the hearing, the keeping of records, and when and how to involve more senior managers or personnel specialists. Providing examples of the types of behaviour that may lead to disciplinary action can be useful to both managers and their employees in managing their conduct and performance. In particular, many employers give examples of conduct that could be classed as gross misconduct and lead to instant dismissal.

Case study A. Parceline

Improved training for managers at distribution company Parceline in managing disciplinary and grievance issues has helped to cut its unfair-dismissal payments by 80%. A decision to reduce the costs of tribunal complaints led the company to use its personnel specialists to design a training and support programme for managers that would improve the consistency and professionalism of their handling of discipline and grievances. Training lasts one-and-a-half days. The formal procedures have been redesigned and expressed in clear, simple language. The initiative was introduced in 2000; in the previous year, Parceline spent £104,000 in tribunal costs, while, in 2000, this fell to £3,000[6].

Record-keeping

It is essential to ensure that line managers and other users of the formal disciplinary procedure maintain accurate records, and that these are stored securely and confidentially. Most employers provide guidance about the nature of these records – the amount of detail, the format, and so on. In some organisations, pro formas are provided to ensure consistency and completeness.

The Data Protection Act 1998 requires that disciplinary records are kept in a safe place and that access to them is restricted. Employees are given a right to gain access to records about them, provided the record identifies them and their access request conforms to the process set down in the Act.

Records should be "kept no longer than is necessary for that purpose or those purposes", based on employers' real business needs to have access to that information. As we saw above, Acas and most organisations set time limits beyond which disciplinary records are considered "spent" and may not be taken into account. This is not necessarily synonymous with the secure destruction of such records.

Disciplinary records are often used for several purposes by employers, such as selection for redundancy and the imposition of discipline-related sanctions (such as demotion or dismissal). Several legal provisions need to be taken into account when deciding on the length of time that such records should be stored. For example, individuals normally have three months in which to lodge a complaint relating to unfair dismissal or discrimination, six months in respect of statutory redundancy pay, and six months from the end of the contract for equal pay claims. However, breach of contract claims have a time limit of six years. See below for more on record-keeping.

Conduct outside work

The actions of employees outside work may be viewed with such seriousness or repugnance that there is considerable pressure to dismiss them. However, the provisions of the Acas Code of Practice and several legal precedents show that hasty action is unwise. For example, Acas says that: "Workers should not be dismissed solely because a charge against them is pending or because they are absent as a result of being remanded in custody." Where the person has been tried and found guilty, employers have to decide whether or not "the offence is one that makes workers unsuitable for their type of work".

Acas's guidance booklet *Discipline at work*[7] – which is intended to provide general advice for employers, and does not have the legal status of its Code of Practice – advises that employers first obtain as many facts as possible about the offence, and consider whether or not it is sufficiently serious to justify using the employer's formal disciplinary procedure. The facts might imply that "fair and reasonable" action could be taken even before the outcome of a criminal prosecution is known.

Where an employee is absent because they are held in custody, then the employer has to take a decision on the likely length of the absence and whether or not their job can be held open for them. If not, then the employer may decide to dismiss the employee.

Defending a tribunal or court action for unfair dismissal is not always straightforward, however. The employer has to show that it had a reasonable belief that the employee was responsible for the criminal act, and that the criminal conduct made it difficult to continue to employ them because of the impact on the organisation (to its reputation or in view of the risk involved). Finally, it must show that dismissal was a reasonable sanction under the circumstances – rather than finding them alternative work or imposing a lesser disciplinary sanction. By following Acas's advice, mentioned above, about conducting an investigation of the facts and then using the formal disciplinary procedure, the employer's defence will usually be strengthened.

There are special considerations relating to employees charged or convicted of criminal offences where the jobs or industries are regulated, such as healthcare, law, work involving children or vulnerable adults, financial services and security guarding.

Grievances

Grievance procedures have been introduced by an overwhelming majority of employers, and forthcoming legislation will make this a legal requirement for all. However, effective performance management should not rely solely on policies (*see Employers' practices below*). While they are essential in ensuring fair treatment of employees, formal procedures should represent the last resort when informal measures have failed to resolve a particularly intractable issue. As with discipline, uncovering and addressing employees' grievances represent an integral part of routine day-to-day management. Alongside pointers from employers' best practice, guidance on formulating and applying grievance policies is available from such sources as Equality Direct[8] and Acas[9].

Grievance procedures

The new rights

The vast majority of employers has already developed formal grievance procedures, and this practice will be a legal requirement once part 2 of the Employment Act 2002 comes into force (estimated to take place in April 2004). The Act will have the effect of making its minimum grievance procedure part of each employee's contract of employment; this will not affect grievance provisions that are in addition to the act's requirements, provided they do not conflict with them. It will be important for every employer that already has a grievance procedure to review it against the new statutory requirements to ensure that their own process does not conflict with the law. In the meantime, an employer's lack of compliance with the Acas Code of Practice on Disciplinary and Grievance Procedures[10] can be taken into account by tribunals in relevant cases (the Code will be revised to take account of the new legal requirements from April 2004). However, failure to comply with the Code does not, itself, expose employers to legal challenge. The current Code does not apply to employers with fewer than 20 employees.

When the provisions of the Employment Act 2002 are introduced, employment tribunals will be able to take account of the failure of employers or employees to comply with the Act's minimum grievance requirements when calculating compensation.

The Act will also require all employers (including those with fewer than 20 employees, which are exempt at present) to provide employees with details of the statutory grievance procedure and their right of appeal. If they also have their own grievance provisions, then they must also communicate them to staff. In both instances, the full text must be provided or details given of where employees can find copies.

The Act sets down a minimum three-stage grievance procedure – which is intended to apply to most types of grievance, apart from appeals against disciplinary actions or dismissal (where the appeals provisions of the Act's disciplinary procedure should be used; see above). However, the statutory procedure may be varied in some cases, the government has suggested, where its use would be inappropriate. These include threats of violence by either party, or complaints of harassment, where the statutory procedure would otherwise require the employee to make the complaint to the person implicated.

The forthcoming statutory grievance procedure's three stages are as follows.

Stage one requires the employee to provide their employer with written details of the grievance and the basis for it.

Stage two requires that the employer must invite the employee to attend a meeting to discuss the matter. The meeting should not be held until the employer has had a reasonable opportunity to study the written statement and consider their response. The employee is expected to take reasonable steps to attend the meeting. Following the meeting, the employer is required to inform the employee of their decision, and notify them of their right of appeal.

Stage three deals with appeals. The employee must inform the employer that they intend to appeal against the decision. The employer must then invite the employee to attend a further meeting, that, again, the employee is expected to take reasonable steps to attend. Following the appeal meeting, the employer must inform the employee of its final decision.

There is a modified grievance procedure under the Act for use by employees who have been dismissed. This modified procedure is not intended for cases where the grievance relates to the dismissal (the appeals provision of the Act's disciplinary procedure must be used instead). The government has suggested that the modified grievance procedure for dismissed employees should apply to such issues as a belief that they have not received the correct holiday pay or redundancy pay at or following termination.

The modified, two-stage statutory procedure for former employees is as follows.

First stage: This requires the employee to provide their former employer with written details of the grievance and the basis for it.

Second stage: The employer must then set out its response in writing and send it, or a copy, to the employee.

In both the standard and modified statutory procedures: each step and action must be taken without unreasonable delay; the timing and location of meetings must be reasonable; and meetings must be conducted so that both employer and employee are given the opportunity to explain their case. In addition, in the case of appeal meetings that are not the first meeting (ie forming part of the standard procedure, where the employee had not already been dismissed), the employer should – as far as is reasonably practical – be represented by a more senior manager than the manager who attended the first meeting, unless the more senior manager also attended that first meeting. (The use of "reasonable/unreasonable" in this paragraph has not been defined in the Act; unless Regulations are issued that provide explanations, future case law – precedents determined by senior courts – will have to fill in these details.)

Note, however, that a further right concerning grievance meetings has already been enacted: the right to be accompanied. Under the Employment Relations Act 1999, employers must allow an employee to be accompanied by one person to grievance hearings (this will also cover the meetings forming part of the forthcoming statutory procedure). The companion must be allowed to address the hearing, and confer with the individual, but cannot answer questions put to the individual. Companions can be trade union officials or representatives (from the same or a different employer), provided they have been certified in writing by their union as having experience of, or received training in, acting as a companion in disciplinary or grievance hearings. Companions can also be another of the employer's workers. Where representatives working for the same employer or individuals' co-workers are involved, they have a right to paid time off to attend the hearing. The right to be accompanied is restricted to grievances that relate to an employer's contractual or statutory duties.

Employers' practices

Formal grievance procedures are almost universally found among organisations with access to professional personnel expertise. They help to set the tone of a workplace, showing that employees are granted respect and some basic rights and, importantly, can help to avoid costly tribunal complaints.

However, employers should make it clear to line managers that they should try to uncover, and resolve, grievances as soon as possible, and in an informal way. The line manager–employee relationship forms the heart of effective performance management, and grievance handling should be seen as just one part of this bigger picture. Issues that are troubling an employee could well have a detrimental impact on their performance, weaken their commitment to the organisation, and lead to absence or resignation. Employers that recognise trade unions have an extra, collective, dimension to consider, and feedback obtained by us from personnel and HR managers shows that they usually incorporate collective grievances in a single procedure that also covers individual complaints. In addition, employers need to consider whether their grievance procedure includes all possible causes of complaints, or whether such issues as harassment and bullying should be treated separately.

3. Effective grievance procedures: the main issues

The main issues concerned with effective grievance procedures, according to feedback obtained by IRS from personnel and HR managers, are:

● **Define its purpose:** Providing a statement of purpose will help employees and line managers understand the aims and workings of the grievance procedure; this will help its smooth operation and encourage employees to use it, rather than developing a grudge or taking their complaint to a tribunal;

● **Simplicity:** The procedure must be accessible, by being written in clear, simple English, and be easy to follow in terms of the steps to be taken, the stages and time limits; make sure each employee is issued with a copy of the procedure on recruitment and knows where further copies can be found;

● **Involvement:** The involvement of employee representatives (recognised trade unions, or members of a staff bodies or works council) and line managers in drawing up the procedure can improve its clarity and operation, and foster a shared understanding of the ways in which grievances should be handled;

● **One or several procedures:** Some grievances are so sensitive, or may involve the person most likely to handle a complaint under normal circumstances, that separate provision may be desirable. These include complaints of sexual or racial harassment, or bullying. Where the grievance procedure makes it difficult for complainants to use it, they are more likely to take their complaint to a tribunal or take their grievances to the media; the definition of a procedure's purpose will help to steer users in the right direction;

● **Guidance:** Guidance should be issued to line managers on the grievance procedure; the use of forms to record formal grievance hearings ensures consistency and record-keeping;

● **Communication and training:** The procedure should be publicised, so that employees and line managers are aware of it (through bulletins, staff magazines and other publicity, and by forming part of induction processes). Training in grievance handling should be given to line managers (including its role in effective performance management, the relevant interpersonal skills involved in listening to employees, and in ways of applying the formal procedure);

● **Stages:** Three-stage grievance procedures reflect Acas guidance and provide a reasonably full and fair consideration of each complaint by line manager, more senior manager and, at appeal stage, a manager at a level higher than in the previous two stages;

● **Time limits:** Grievances will fester, and the outcome will appear less satisfactory, if the procedure takes too long; fair and reasonable time limits need to be specified for each stage in the process, and adhered to;

● **Being accompanied:** Under the law, only certain types of grievance (those relating to employers' statutory or contractual duties) entitle an employee to be accompanied to grievance hearings; it is more effective if all grievance hearings expressly incorporate this right; and

● **A last resort:** Develop fair and effective formal grievance procedures, but create a climate where informal methods are explored first and, where possible, grievances are resolved before reaching the formal process.

Defining the purpose of the grievance procedure offers several advantages, personnel and HR managers tell us:

● setting out the procedure's coverage and its aims helps encourage its use by employees and line managers (bearing in mind that the alternative is less desirable, where employees' grievances are left to build up to a point where their performance or attendance suffers, or they resign, and/or take a complaint to an employment tribunal or the media);

● linked to this, guidance can offer reassurance that employees will not be victimised as a result of their use of the procedure; and

● where separate processes exist for certain complaints, this statement of purpose can clarify their respective areas of coverage.

The **Royal National Institute for the Blind**, for example, defines a grievance in its procedure as being "another word for a complaint which arises out of the course of employment [...] An employee may have a feeling of injustice or resentment, or may feel they have been unfairly or unreasonably treated". At financial services company **Bradford & Bingley**, cross-reference is made to related procedures: "The range of issues that may be raised as a grievance is wide [. . .] However, there are specific policies/procedures to deal with grievances relating to harassment, bullying and victimisation, disciplinary issues, appraisal issues and the annual pay review." Pharmaceuticals company **Bayer** provides an example of reassurance in its statement: "Anyone wishing to use this procedure may do so freely and without prejudice to their position within the company. In addition, any grievance or complaint which an employee raises will remain confidential [. . .]"

Some grievances are so sensitive, or may involve the person most likely to handle a complaint under normal circumstances, that separate provision may be desirable. These include complaints of sexual or racial harassment, or bullying. Where the grievance mechanism makes it difficult for complainants, they are more likely to take their complaint to a tribunal or to the media; the definition of a procedure's purpose will help to steer users in the right direction. It is worth bearing in mind that harassment, bullying and discrimination feature in the top five types of complaint raised by employees, according to employers. The volume of such complaints could make it highly desirable to handle them with extra care through a dedicated procedure, given the potential consequences of unresolved grievances. (*See next section for harassment and bullying procedures.*)

4. Being prepared: common grievances

The most common grounds for grievances, according to feedback obtained by IRS from personnel and HR managers, are, in descending order:
● harassment and/or bullying;
● discipline;
● the introduction of new working practices;
● grading;
● discrimination;
● work allocation and/or staffing levels; and
● non-pay terms and conditions.

Individual complaints of discrimination, harassment and bullying might hint at an underlying cause, such as the behaviour of a particular employee or manager. However, only a small minority of employers currently undertakes systematic monitoring of grievances to uncover trends on the basis of gender, ethnicity and other factors. This is set to change in the public sector, where personnel procedures are now required to be examined for their fairness in respect of ethnicity under the Race Relations (Amendment) Act

2000. Commission for Racial Equality guidance for public sector employers recommends they conduct regular reviews of their personnel policies, particularly those covering performance assessment, discipline, grievance and training, and monitor their use to ensure there is no unfair discrimination on the grounds of ethnicity.

Personnel and HR specialists tell IRS that their formal grievance procedures are most likely to consist of three stages:

1. an initial complaint to the employee's line manager (incorporating provision for this to skip a level if the complaint relates to the line manager personally);

2. a further hearing with a manager at a more senior level than the line manager; and

3. an appeals stage where a manager at a level above the one involved in stage two handles the appeal. This practice follows closely the guidance given by Acas, cited above.

Most employers require the aggrieved employee to put their complaint in writing prior to invoking the procedure. However, the first stage of their procedures is viewed by some employers as a less formal part of the process. Usually, in most employers, the initial stage involves a meeting between the employee and their immediate line manager. Some organisations treat this as a less formal stage, and follow this through by not expecting a written statement of the problem at this stage. Only when the issue goes further, to stages two and three, do such employers insist on written details of complaints.

Most employers' grievance procedures incorporate set time limits for the operation of each stage. These can apply to both employee and employer: there may be a fixed period by which an employee has to lodge a grievance after the cause of their complaint has arisen, and there may be limits to the time that can elapse between their use of each stage of the procedure. Employers for their part may be required to respond to a grievance within a certain time, and to give their decision afterwards within another fixed period.

Often, line managers must respond to an initial approach about a grievance within 24 or 48 hours, and there must be a response by the employer within seven to 10 working days when later stages are invoked. Employers' decisions following a grievance meeting often have to be communicated to the employee within five working days. In most cases, particularly beyond the initial stage involving the line manager, these decisions must be in writing, according to grievance procedures typically reported by employers.

The Acas Code of Practice, mentioned above, recommends that the first stage, involving an informal or formal approach to the line manager should lead to the employee receiving a written decision within five working days of the manager receiving the complaint. At stage two, where an unresolved grievance is taken higher to a more senior manager, there must be a hearing in response to a written request within a suggested five working days, and the result of the hearing should be communicated within a suggested 10 working days. Finally, in stage three, an unresolved grievance can be taken still higher to director level or a similar level of seniority, and the person handling the complaint at this stage must communicate the result of the hearing within a suggested 10 working days. Curiously, Acas makes no recommendation for the time limit on convening this hearing.

The law now gives employees the right to bring someone with them when they attend a grievance hearing, provided the subject relates to their employer's statutory or contractual duties. However, personnel and HR managers tell us that it is simpler, and more effective, if this right is unqualified, and organisations' own procedures usually expressly incorporate a right to be accompanied. The process and outcomes of grievance-handling need to be seen as fair and legitimate in the eyes of employees if their performance is to be maintained or improved, and employment tribunal complaints are to be avoided. Having a companion who acts as an advocate, or simply provides moral support, can ensure that the employee feels they have put their case to its best advantage.

> The **Royal Liverpool Children's NHS Trust** at Alder Hey Hospital, for example, says that the employee can be accompanied, and defines their role as being: "To address the hearing, ask questions of the manager involved and the panel, and generally support the worker". Financial services company **Prudential Corporation** says that the person: "May address the meeting on points of procedure [. . .] They may also advise and generally represent the interests of the individual." It adds, though, that: "It is recognised that it is appropriate for the individual to answer questions specifically put to them."

Most employers provide some training for their line managers in grievance handling. As with discipline issues, though, this training is not always mandatory nor comprehensive in covering all managers and supervisors likely to require it.

Some employers include important interpersonal skills in their training programmes. At retailer **Fenwick** and electronics firm **SCI**, for example, interviewing skills, counselling skills and problem-solving skills are all addressed. **Birmingham City Council's** three-day course includes case studies and problem-solving exercises. Role-playing, to develop interpersonal skills, is widely practised in employers' training in this area; examples include **Dorset County Council** and London transport company **Computer Cab**.

The central importance of performance management in line managers' duties means that some employers provide general management training to staff in managerial and supervisory roles that includes grievance and disciplinary issues. Others find that there is considerable overlap in the issues and skills involved in grievance and discipline, and combine these areas in a single course (found in such employers as distribution company **Norbain** and social housing provider **Advance**).

Harassment and bullying

The Acas Code of Practice on Disciplinary and Grievance Procedures makes the point that some types of grievance are so sensitive that employers may find it helpful to set up separate complaints procedures to handle them. Acas mentions discrimination, bullying and harassment as examples of such complaints. Separately, it has issued *Bullying and harassment at work: a guide for managers and employers*[11], which provides help for employers in handling such issues, and gives a suggested definition of bullying and harassment. Bullying, it says, "may be characterised as offensive, intimidating, malicious or insulting behaviour, an abuse or misuse of power through means intended to undermine, humiliate, denigrate or injure the recipient". Harassment is "unwanted conduct affecting the dignity of men and women in the workplace. It may be related to age, sex, race, disability, religion, nationality or any personal characteristic of the individual, and may be persistent or an isolated incident. They key is that the actions or comments are viewed as demeaning and unacceptable to the recipient".

However, Acas adds that definitions rarely suffice. Harassment and bullying, in particular, are generally recognised in extreme cases, but "it is sometimes the 'grey' areas that cause most problems". It suggests setting out some examples of unacceptable behaviour in the relevant procedure (a special harassment and bullying procedure or, where one does not exist, the main disciplinary procedure). Because of the consensus about extreme cases, the examples should include some shades of grey – for example, "copying memos that are critical about someone to others who do not need to know".

Bullying and harassment are serious forms of unacceptable behaviour for many reasons. Morally they are wrong, and can cause mental or physical harm to the victim. They lay the employer open to unlimited compensation where discrimination is involved and the employer is seen as vicariously liable for the actions of an employee or employees. There may be liability under the Health and Safety at Work Act 1974, under common law for mental or physical damage, for unfair constructive dismissal where the employee is driven out, or under criminal law for harassment-related offences. But, more generally, harassment and bullying can extend beyond the victim and perpetrator to affect the culture of a whole work unit or even the entire organisation.

Acas recommends that a separate policy be drawn up to deal with allegations of harassment or bullying. Because of their sometimes controversial nature as offences, the policy should contain a statement from senior management that such offences they will not be tolerated and that any occurrences will be addressed, and victims given protection. The status of offences as being potential disciplinary matters should be set out, Acas advises, and definitions and examples of bullying and harassment should be given. The responsibilities of managers and employees need to be specified, and a procedure given that will be used to investigate any alleged occurrences, together with timescales for the operation of the process.

More generally, Acas urges employers to ensure the culture of the organisation is not conducive to harassment or bullying. "Strong management", for example, should not stray into bullying or intimidating behaviour, and setting clear expectations of managers and supervisors that temper any authoritarian behaviour can help to reduce complaints of bullying by employees.

Acas recommends that a completely confidential, informal mechanism should be set up that employees can use to discuss alleged incidents of bullying and harassment. One or more employees may be trained in the relevant skills and issues, or the employer could set up an employee counselling or assistance service that an external provider offers under contract to the organisation. Skilled individuals will be able to help the employee understand the nature of the incident(s) and enable the employee to make a decision about what further steps they wish to take. "Counselling" – the term Acas uses for this discussion between a trained adviser and the aggrieved employee – "can be particularly useful where investigation shows no cause for disciplinary action, or where doubt is cast on the validity of the complaint," it adds.

However, Acas suggests that individuals involved in such situations, victim or perpetrator, could be covered by the normal grievance (victims' complaints) or disciplinary (action against perpetrators) procedures, provided these contain effective provisions for confidentiality and a right to be accompanied.

Case study B. Cummins Engineering

Cummins Engineering has developed a separate policy covering harassment and bullying. This manufacturer of engines and power-generation equipment says in its "treatment of each other at work policy" that: "No-one should make verbal, written or physical statements [. . .] that are intimidating, embarrassing or humiliating, or to which the other person does not feel free to reply." The policy contains guidance for victims, their alleged harassers, and those handling claims.

It creates a twin-track route, where employees are encouraged in the first instance to inform the perpetrator (verbally or in writing) that their conduct is unacceptable and that, if it continues, they will lodge a formal complaint. Victims are also encouraged to approach someone who can act as their "confidant" – their supervisor, a member of the personnel department, a trade union representative or a colleague – who will "assist the complainant to determine the next course of action", and follow up the matter after seven days.

Where the informal approach does not resolve the matter, or the victim does not feel able to contact the aggressor, then a formal procedure can be invoked. The complaint must be registered with a senior personnel specialist, and a written statement of the matter provided by the victim. A formal investigation must be held within seven days of the complaint, and involves setting up an investigation panel. It communicates details of the complaint to the alleged aggressor, interviews all the parties to the complaint, including witnesses, and considers the evidence. Its decision is communicated. A final stage makes provision for an appeal against the panel's ruling.

Whistleblowing

Since the Public Interest (Disclosure) Act 1998, employees are protected from dismissal or victimisation for making "protected disclosures". The Act encourages whistleblowers to approach their employer first, and for employers to nominate individuals to handle these grievances and respond to them effectively.

Whistleblowers are often concerned about alleged illegal acts, ethical lapses on the part of the employer, threats to public health or safety, or other issues that could provoke unfavourable media coverage and, potentially, prosecution or official investigation. With the enactment of 1998 Act, employers also face compensation claims where they take action to prevent the whistleblower airing their concerns. For example, where the main reason for an employee's dismissal is found to be a protected disclosure, the Act stipulates that the dismissal will automatically be unfair (and, unlike normal dismissal claims, there is no minimum period of service before protection is given to the employee).

There are three categories of protected disclosure (internal, regulatory and wider disclosures), of which only the most extreme – wider disclosures – provides protection for employees to go to the media or the police. Even then, there are four conditions that must first be satisfied, including:

● having a reasonable belief that they would be victimised if they were to approach their employer first;

● that important evidence would be concealed or destroyed as a result of alerting their employer in this way; or

● that they had already raised a substantially similar issue with their employer and no action had been taken.

It is likely that an effective whistleblowing procedure will provide considerable protection to employers under the Act, as well as encouraging employees to highlight abuses that otherwise would have remained secret, such as theft by members of staff, acts of discrimination, and so on. To satisfy the Act, the procedure must ensure that issues raised by employees are treated seriously, investigated fully, and remedial action taken as necessary. Because complaints may relate to the individual's manager, or manager's manager, the procedure should ensure that the employee can approach a senior manager directly. The procedure should also be designed to afford whistleblowers confidentiality and protection from victimisation.

The operation of the procedure, as well as its provisions, must also conform to the Act's requirements. These highlight the importance of training the managers who will administer the procedure. They will have to be given the skills to investigate the complaint carefully, often against a strict time limit, and often with considerable attention to confidentiality in order to protect the whistleblower's identity and ensure that evidence that might support the complaint is not tampered with.

The Act's three-tier structure means that effective procedures are likely to tackle problems and abuses before they become so serious that the wider-disclosure provision gives the employee the right to go straight to the media or the police.

Effective procedures should offer a viable means of airing employees' concerns, with the consequence that employees who fail to use the procedure and make their concerns public could well be argued to show a lack of good faith. This principal of good faith is a key test of whether or not the employee qualifies for protection under the Act.

Record-keeping

There are several important reasons for maintaining effective records of the use of formal disciplinary, grievance and related procedures. Record-keeping provides documentary evidence if the issue is taken further under the procedure, such as a second hearing or an appeal, and provides valuable evidence to help defend actions taken when aggrieved employees take the employer to tribunal or court. Requiring managers to maintain accurate records helps impress on them that the procedure should be taken seriously and handled professionally – if for no other reason than their actions can be investigated at a later stage. More generally, accurate records enable the workings of the procedures to be monitored to ensure no unfair discrimination is taking place against individuals or groups.

Most personnel and HR managers tell us that they have developed forms for use in their procedures, containing guidance and structured sets of questions or list of topics to ensure managers provide information about all relevant issues in sufficient detail. They often develop policies about the storage of the records to ensure they are kept in a secure and confidential manner.

Whatever records are kept – handwritten notes, completed forms or electronically stored files – there are legal implications for their security, confidentiality and period of storage. The Data Protection Act 1998 requires secure, confidential storage, the rights of access by employees to their records (having given due notice in the prescribed way), and that records "shall not be kept for longer than is necessary for that purpose or those purposes". Guidance on storing records about grievance and disciplinary matters is given in the Employment Practices Data Protection Code 2002.

While neither the Act nor the Code offer set limits on record-keeping, they expect that the period concerned should reflect a real business need and take account of other legal requirements. For example, records may be relevant to potential claims on the grounds of unfair dismissal or unlawful discrimination; in such cases, individuals usually have three months to lodge a complaint. Where a procedure may be used to select individuals for redundancy, then the normal six-month limit on claims relating to statutory redundancy pay will be a consideration. However, individuals have six years for breach of contract complaints. All of these considerations highlight the need to ensure that records are filed safely and securely, and kept for as long as is relevant under the law and the organisation's requirements.

5. Legal checklist

● Protected groups must not be put at an unfair disadvantage as a result of disciplinary practices and procedures, grievance procedures, and related procedures – Sex Discrimination Act 1975; Race Relations Act 1976; Disability Discrimination Act 1995; Trade Union and Labour Relations (Consolidation) Act 1992; and Codes of Practice associated with these Acts.

● Disciplinary, grievance and other procedures in the public sector must be checked for unfair discrimination on the grounds of ethnicity – Race Relations (Amendment) Act 2000.

● Compliance with the Acas Code of Practice on Disciplinary and Grievance Procedures can be taken into account by tribunals and courts.

● All employers will be covered by the forthcoming statutory disciplinary and grievance procedures when the provisions are enacted (expected in April 2004) – Employment Act 2002.

● The existence of the statutory procedures, including rights of appeal, will have to be communicated to all employees – Employment Act 2002. Employers' own procedures must also be communicated to employees – Employment Rights Act 1996.

● The statutory disciplinary and grievance procedures will be deemed to be incorporated into each employee's contract of employment. Failures by employers or employees to comply with the procedures can be taken into account by tribunals and courts when calculating compensation, eg for unfair dismissal.

● Employees have the right to be accompanied to disciplinary and grievance hearings and meetings (in the case of discipline, this applies to hearings/meetings that could lead to a sanction; in the case of grievances, this applies to issues relating to the employer's contractual or statutory duties) – Employment Relations Act 1999.

● Whistleblowers are protected from dismissal or victimisation for making "protected disclosures" – Public Interest (Disclosure) Act 1998.

● Eligible groups have the right to request a move to flexible working – Employment Act 2002.

● The groups are workers with a child under the age of six, or a child with disabilities under the age of 18.

● Employee records must follow the data protection principles – Data Protection Act 1998 and its Employment Practices Data Protection Code.

● Medical records are covered by the Access to Medical Reports Act 1988.

12. Attendance and absence

See also: 10. Managing performance 1 (for performance management; absence; sick pay) and 11. Managing performance 2 (for discipline; grievances; harassment and bullying.

This chapter covers:
- Overview: an introduction to attendance and absence management;
- Managing attendance;
- Long-term absences;
- Attendance allowances;
- Sick pay;
- Reporting sick; and
- Record-keeping.

Checklists in this chapter:
1. Effective absence management: the key issues
2. The main causes of absence
3. Getting employees back to work after a long absence
4. Legal checklist

Case studies in this chapter:
A. More Th>n
B. Bracknell Forest Borough Council
C. South Shropshire Housing Association
D. The London Borough of Merton
E. Essex County Council

Overview

Attendance management is in a fluid state. Employers are increasingly aware of its importance – because of the statistics of the costs involved or, for the public sector, because of government policy to reduce absence rates – but are struggling to find effective ways of controlling it. The coordinating role of personnel and HR specialists has been weakened in many organisations, with the transfer of many attendance-related responsibilities to line managers. Yet their overcrowded days leave little time for the systematic management of absence and taking follow-up action.

Procedures concerned with sickness, absence and other attendance issues are often in search of a home. In some employers, sick pay continues to be bargained with recognised trade unions and is seen more as a benefit than part of mainstream personnel and HR management. Where different trade unions are recognised, or different bargaining groups are in place, then employers may have two or more separate sick-pay schemes as a result. Absence forms part of a broad disciplinary procedure in many employers; in others, a special process has been devised – often, as part of an initiative to reduce absence levels.

Managing attendance

The best-known source of absence statistics is an annual survey conducted by the Confederation of British Industry (CBI) since 1987. Its latest findings[1] show that the direct cost of absence averages £476 per employee, and that 7.1 working days per head are lost each year. As well as the impact of the absent member of staff on service and output, the costs are driven up by many employers' need to pay to cover the post through overtime or the use of temporary workers.

Significantly, the CBI's research shows that employers are best able to manage attendance when senior management takes an active interest and provides support to line managers in this activity. In 2001, for example, average absence per head was more than two days lower in organisations where senior managers were involved. Partly, though, employers are suffering because of their own inaction. The CBI found that half of the organisations conferring responsibility solely on line managers failed to train them in effective absence management, and that fewer than 10% of all organisations monitored the indirect costs of absences. And fewer than 7% have investigated the impact of employees' health on organisational performance. In the public sector, less than a third of local authorities produce "useable" data on the causes of sickness absence[2].

Without adequate information, even the best trained and committed line manager will struggle to identify trends and issues in attendance.

In-depth research by the Institute for Employment Studies[3] shows that half of the costs of absence are directly under the control of the employer. Not only do absence-management practices have a bearing on these costs, but so too do the effectiveness of the arrangements made to cover for absence. Unmanaged agency costs for temporary staff, or overtime payments to other employees, are high-cost options, the institute found. The composition of the workforce and its absence patterns (primarily, the balance between short- and long-term absences) are additional, and major, factors. Together, these considerations account for the huge variation in absence costs found by the institute, which ranged from 2% to 16% of total annual salary costs.

1. Effective absence management: the key issues

An analysis of feedback obtained by IRS from employers shows that the key issues in the effective management of absence are as follows:

● Develop an attendance-management procedure that is clear, fair and applied consistently;

● Introduce and consistently apply procedures where employees formally notify their absences;

● Develop effective, preferably computerised, absence-management records that track both attendance and the causes of non-attendance;

● Calculate the cost of absence (the effectiveness of action to reduce absence rates needs to be measured against cost savings; action to cut short-term absence, for example, may not necessarily lead to cost reductions);

● Focus attention where it will produce the most cost-effective results, and where it will minimise compensation claims;

● Provide absence data from a recording system to line managers;

● Take account of previous absence records when recruiting new staff (this should not apply to groups protected by the Disability Discrimination Act 1995);

● Undertake systematic return-to-work interviews;

● Introduce a "trigger" for the investigation of absence, based on the number of instances over a year and/or the length of absences;

● Provide access to advice from occupational health specialists;

● Maintain regular contact with employees on long-term sick leave;

● Review measures that could help an employee on long-term sick leave return to work, such as reduced hours of work, changes to working time, flexible working, adjustments to the work duties and redeployment; and

● Use disciplinary procedures where absence has not been found by medical practitioners to be caused by illness or injury.

(Source: research among employers conducted by IRS, CBI (cited above) and the Institute for Employment Studies (also cited above).)

Acas's guidance booklet *Discipline at work*[4] contains advice for employers on managing attendance. It urges employers to set up efficient systems to record attendance and absence, and says that records should be routinely checked "so that problems can be spotted and addressed at an early stage". Reasons for lateness and absence need to be established, it says, and action taken accordingly. Apart from day-to-day performance management to address minor problems as they occur, more serious attendance problems need to be addressed appropriately. The disciplinary procedure should be used only where lateness or absence is not caused by illness or injury, Acas says.

For other instances of lateness or absence, its booklet sets out a recommended procedure (note that, while this provides useful advice, this does not form part of its Code of Practice and has no legal status). It recommends prompt investigation of each instance, and the use of return-to-work interviews to ask for an explanation and discuss the matter.

Where several short periods of absence occur, self-certification procedures mean that there will not normally be medical evidence from a doctor to support the employee's explanation. In such cases, Acas recommends that the employee should be required to see a doctor to establish whether or not there is medical evidence to justify the absences.

In all instances, Acas recommends that the employee should be given clear information about the nature of the improvement in time-keeping or attendance required, and about the likely consequences of their failure to achieve these improvements.

"It is essential that persistent absence is dealt with promptly, firmly and consistently in order to show both the worker concerned and other workers that absence is regarded as a serious matter and may result in dismissal," Acas adds.

However, even where illness or injury are not found to cause the lateness or absences, Acas suggests that other factors should be taken into account. In particular, research by IRS has found that employees' caring responsibilities are frequent causes of absences. Unpaid time off is available in appropriate circumstances under the Maternity and Parental Leave (Time Off for Dependants in an Emergency) Regulations 1999. More generally, though, many employers now offer flexible-working arrangements that help employees cope with their responsibilities for children, elderly parents or other dependants. Many such employers report that they have experienced a significant reduction in absence levels as a result. *Further information on flexible working, work–life balance and the Employment Act 2002's new rights to flexible working is given below, under long-term absence.*

Acas also reminds employers that they should always take account of the Disability Discrimination Act 1995. Where lateness or absence is linked to a condition that qualifies as a disability under the Act, then employers are expected to make "reasonable adjustments" to accommodate it. This might involve, for example, alterations in hours of work, to equipment or premises, or redeployment to alternative work. (Acas's guidance concerning long-term absence is covered below.)

2. The main causes of absence

According to employers surveyed by the Chartered Institute of Personnel and Development[5], the causes of absence (primarily short-term illnesses) among manual workers, are, in descending order:

● minor illnesses (mainly colds and 'flu);

● back pain;

● musculoskeletal disorders;

● recurring medical conditions; and

● stress.

Among *non-manual* workers, the causes in descending order are:

● minor illnesses (mainly colds and 'flu);

● stress;

● recurring medical conditions;

● back pain; and

● musculoskeletal disorders.

Direct intervention by employers in preventing the causes of absence is relatively uncommon, apart from addressing hazards that might lead to work-related injuries, and which are generally prompted by employers' legal obligations concerning health and safety at work. In a few cases, employers have organised mass vaccinations against 'flu, or encouraged their employees to participate in fitness classes (such as insurance company **More Th>n**; see *case study A*). **Pret A Manger**, the chain of take-away shops, offered all its 2,200 employees free 'flu inoculations at the onset of the 2002/03 winter. It aimed to reduce absenteeism and, by showing its concern for staff welfare, improve morale and productivity[6].

Generally, the main focus of attention of employers' attendance practices lies in ensuring that absences are legitimate and that absent employees are helped to return to work as speedily as possible. In addition, employers also aim to prevent the problem recurring by using attendance records as a factor when selecting employees for redundancy, when paying or not paying an attendance or other bonus, and when recruiting new members of staff. Personnel and HR specialists tell us that one of the most common pieces of information they seek from referees involves feedback on applicants' attendance and sickness records.

Increasingly, though, one cause of absence – stress – is being addressed by larger employers in particular. Overall, it is now the main work-related cause of absence. According to official health and safety statistics, "the estimated prevalence rate of stress and related (mainly heart) conditions has increased over time and is now around double the level it was in 1990"[7]. Regulation 3 of the Management of Health and Safety at Work Regulations 1999 highlights the practice of employers conducting risk assessments for factors that might cause stress (research suggests that risk assessments currently represent the most common approach by employers wishing to manage stress, and that they offer a good basis for effective remedial action[8]). And the Health and Safety Executive is developing a set of guidelines for employers on stress management that can be expected to influence employers' thinking and action in reducing this cause of absence.

A landmark Court of Appeal ruling in appeals against four stress-compensation verdicts (*Sutherland v Hatton*, 5.2.2002 [2002] EWCA Civ 76) set out 16 ground-rules for courts' future consideration of such claims. Of these 16 issues, point 11 is the most significant for employers, as it suggests employers that provide a "confidential advice service" giving access to appropriate counselling or treatment services will normally have discharged their legal "duty of care" towards employees who subsequently suffer stress-related illnesses. In other words, most professionally run employee assistance programmes that employers offer to their employees should, on the basis of this ruling, provide protection against stress-related claims. For this reason alone, regardless of whether or not such services successfully reduce stress-related absence, the take up of employee assistance programmes is likely to increase significantly.

Astute employers will do more than provide access to a counselling service, though, given that many of the measures that can reduce stress also have broader business benefits. For example, stress is often induced by loss of control, while the three-year study by the Work and Employment Research Centre at the University of Bath, mentioned in chapter 11, found that high performance at work is linked to opportunities to practise "discretionary" behaviour – in the form of jobs that give employees some responsibility and control.

Feelings of isolation may be stressors, that effective communication systems can help reduce – as well as improving organisational effectiveness more generally. Intense work pressures, too, are often important stress factors, and being able to discuss them openly with individuals' line managers may be helpful. Here, too, effective communication channels can encourage open relationships between employees and managers. Where unrealistically demanding performance requirements are at fault, then a potential solution lies in ensuring that the performance-management system operates effectively. Again, wider benefits can flow from improvements in this area. Where bullying, intimidation or discriminatory behaviour cause stress, then the development of effective bullying and harassment procedures can help tackle such problems, as well as improving morale generally and reducing exposure to legal costs and compensation (*see chapter 12 for more on bullying and harassment procedures*).

Employers will only discover the causes of absence if they investigate each occasion and ask for reasons. Acas in its Code of Practice on Disciplinary and Grievance Procedures recommends that "all unexpected absences should be investigated promptly and the worker asked to give an explanation. If, after investigation, it appears that there were no acceptable reasons for the absence, the matter should be treated as a conduct issue and be dealt with under the disciplinary procedure. It is important that the worker is told what improvement in attendance is expected and warned of the likely consequences if this does not happen."

Acas adds that absences (or under-performance) linked to an employee's disability will probably be covered by the Disability Discrimination Act 1995 and, among other requirements, employers may have to make "reasonable adjustments" to the work, equipment, premises, and so on. But, this consideration apart, Acas divides absence into two: unacceptable absences where the use of the disciplinary procedure should be considered; and absences caused by medically-certified illnesses or injuries, where a different approach based on capability should be taken. Where capability is covered by a separate procedure, then employees will be covered by the same legal right to be accompanied to any formal hearings linked to possible sanctions, as applies to hearings under disciplinary procedures.

Case study A. More Th>n

The Sunderland call centre of insurer More Th>n faced a rising absence rate, reaching 6.9% in 2001, and which threatened to breach its corporate absence target. An analysis showed that business performance and sales results would improve once absence was reduced. A special project team was set up in July 2001 and produced an action plan with four elements: revised return-to-work procedures; a new absence-monitoring system; improved management of long-term sickness; and a stress-management initiative.

The new return-to-work procedures shifted responsibility to a dedicated team of five managers in order to improve consistency and effectiveness. The team was given the role of being more proactive in the management of both short- and long-term absence, including making greater efforts to identify the under-lying reasons for absences, and providing appropriate support and direction. For example, research for the action plan found that two-thirds of staff said they would be less likely to take sick leave because of a sore throat or voice loss if alternative work were available, such as duties away from telephone duties or job swaps. Consideration of providing alternative work now forms part of the new procedure. Team leaders have been given training in con-ducting return-to-work interviews with employees.

Absence monitoring uses a computer spreadsheet that the team managers complete when notified of absences. This shows the type and frequency of absences, against absence targets. Long-term absences are referred, with the employee's agreement, to occupational health specialists who provide recom-mendations to personnel specialists and line managers. A return-to-work plan is drawn up for each employee on long-term absence. Stress management includes the provision of training to employees and their managers, and access to confidential advice and counselling through Employee Care, an employee assistance programme. Guidelines for managers have been drawn up to help them when managing stress-related absences. In addition, the call centre has introduced exercise classes, particularly for those using workstations. The ini-tiatives have led to the call centre winning a Health@Work Award, and have contributed to reduced absence, and easier recruitment through an improved "employer brand" (its reputation as an appealing place to work) in a highly competitive local labour market.

Long-term absences

Sick-pay schemes often contain "triggers" that prompt a review of an employee's absence after a set period of time – usually, around four to six weeks of illness. Employers report that investigation, and the provision of advice and support, relatively early on in an extended period of absence are crucial in ensuring a return to work. Where individuals are absent for periods of months, without such intervention, then the chances of returning to normal employment are much less likely.

The focus of each employer's management of absence must, of necessity, take account of cost-effectiveness. In some organisations, recurrent short periods of absence represent the greatest barrier to maintaining levels of service or output. In others, the long-term absence of a relatively small number of employees imposes the greatest costs and consequences. The need to identify sickness patterns and their impact in order to decide where to initiate action reinforces the vital role that effective absence recording can play in attendance management.

Acas's guidance booklet *Discipline at work*[9] recommends that long-term absence found to be caused by medically-certificated illness or injury should be treated not as a disciplinary issue, but one of capability. "Employers need to take a more sympathetic and considerate approach" in such cases, it adds.

The issues raised by Acas in its guidance reflect those reported by employers in checklist 3, as being linked to the fair and effective management of long-term absence. Acas also notes that employers do not have the right to obtain information from the absent employee's doctor; they must gain their consent in writing (and, it recommends, inform the employee of their right of refusal to grant access, and to their right to see the doctor's report under the Access to Medical Reports Act 1988). Where the doctor's report gives "reasonable doubt about the nature of the illness or injury", the employer should ask the employee to undergo an independent medical examination.

The aim, says Acas, is to obtain sufficient information to make an informed decision about the factors that might help the employee return to work, and the likely duration of their absence. In cases where the employee refuses consent to their doctor's provision of a medical report and/or will not undergo an independent examination, "the worker should be told in writing that a decision will be taken on the basis of the information available, and that it could result in dismissal".

Where alternative work is not available and the employee's own job can no longer be kept open until their return, then Acas says the worker should be informed of the likelihood of dismissal. Normal notice periods then apply.

Across the economy, the CBI absence survey for 2002, cited above, found that long-term absences make up only 5% of total absence incidents, but that they represent 31% of the total time lost by employers. In other words, their impact is six times greater than a simple tally of absent workers would suggest.

The experience of one of the UK's largest employers – the half-million-strong civil service – reflects this pattern. In 1999, more than 40% of absences lasted no more than a single day, and absences of more than 20 working days accounted for just 4.0% of the total number of absence incidents. But these long-term absences represent almost half of the total days of absence in that year[10].

For long-term absences, personnel and HR specialists say that the most likely outcome by far is a phased return to work. This is three times more likely than the three other main outcomes combined: dismissal (or a termination because of frustration of contract); redeployment; and early retirement on ill-health grounds.

3. Getting employees back to work after a long absence

The most important elements in a policy to return long-term absentees to work, according to employers, are, in descending order:

- Ensuring early intervention, above all else;

- Maintaining contact with absent employees;

- Arranging a phased return to work (in some employers, based on full pay; in others, employees are required to use annual holiday to make up the gaps);

- Arranging independent medical examinations or a review of medical reports;

- Providing time off to attend medical appointments after the return to work;

- Ensuring early intervention to prevent acute conditions becoming chronic (such as through physiotherapy or counselling);

- Permanently modifying or changing the work, or aspects of it, that the employee performed formerly;

- Providing special equipment or aids to help them perform their work;

- Permanently altering the working pattern (hours, shifts, etc) formerly applying to the employee; and

- Providing retraining.

However, major barriers stand in the way of the effective management of long-term absence. Employers report that these are the main problems to be overcome:

● Line managers' resistance to efforts to return long-term sickness absentees to work (primarily because of the additional work involved in managing their return);

● The shortcomings of the NHS in providing services to help employees return to work, such as physiotheraphy; and

● Resistance by employees, particularly where there is a possibility of financial compensation for work-related illness or injury.

The causes of long-term absence naturally vary widely, according to the job, type of employer and other factors. Across the economy, though, employers report that the most common causes are, in descending order:
● mental illness;
● back injuries;
● musculoskeletal conditions;
● stress;
● surgery; and
● cardiovascular disorders.

Case study B. Bracknell Forest Borough Council

Bracknell Forest Borough Council, a unitary authority in Berkshire, has achieved one of the lowest absence levels among local authorities (it is 20% below the average for local government). Its success is due to many factors, it reports, including the development of an effective written procedure and the expectation that long-term absences will be actively monitored, rather than being left to "drift" by busy or uninterested line managers. Access to good advice from occupational health (OH) specialists is also seen as an important contributory factor in its success.

The council uses a private supplier, Adastral Health, for its OH service (elsewhere, the NHS provides, under contract, the OH service to some employers, such as the **London Borough of Brent**). OH staff attend council premises for two days a week, including meeting individual employees, reading case notes, contacting GPs, providing preventative measures and so on. Line managers are required to refer relevant cases of long-term absence to the OH service, whose role is to provide information and advice that the council's managers will use in their decision-making. The council emphasises that OH does not make decisions as to whether an employee remains in employment.

The council's procedure incorporates a trigger of 20 consecutive days' absence, pro rata for part-time staff, for referral of the case by the individual's line manager to the OH service. However, Bracknell Forest's proactive stance means that early intervention is also possible. So, where a line manager anticipates that an absent employee is likely to be away for 20 days or more, then early referral is expected. Indeed, line managers are able to refer employees' cases to the OH service even where they are not absent, but where the manager believes a medical reason underlies the person's current difficulties in performing their work.

Short-term absences are not overlooked and, here, the trigger for an OH referral is set at three separate periods of absence within any three-month period. Alternatively, where a pattern emerges of absence often occurring on the same day each week, then a referral is possible. The procedure therefore aims to set down minimum requirements, but to accompany them with the flexibility to initiate other actions as preventive measures.

Generally, line managers are required by the sickness-absence procedure to manage absence, although processes that might lead to dismissals are referred upwards beyond a certain stage to more senior levels. Line managers also have initial responsibility for managing the two related procedures of capability and discipline. The capability procedure is used, for example, where employees' attendance is sporadic or they are performing below acceptable levels.

Under the sickness-absence procedure, line managers are expected to maintain contact on a monthly basis with employees on long-term sick leave by telephone calls, making home visits or holding meetings in the workplace. However, home visits must be pre-arranged (rather than being used for spot-checks) and after advice from personnel specialists. Referrals to the OH service under the procedure lead to advice being given by the specialist about the likely cause of the absence and its possible duration. The line manager is then expected to review the case with a personnel specialist, and discuss the employee's likely return date and the impact their absence is having on the council's operations. Consultations between OH, the line manager and a personnel specialist are expected to continue throughout the period of absence.

However, "at an appropriate time", the line manager is expected to arrange a formal review meeting with the employee in order to discuss the available options, having first taken advice from OH and a personnel specialist. These options include agreeing a date by which the employee will be fit to return to work; redeployment; the provision of assistance (such as adaptations to the work or workplace) so that the employee can return to their normal duties; retirement on ill-health grounds; or use of the capability or dismissal procedures where the employee is unfit for work and none of the other options apply. The latter may lead to dismissal. The sickness-absence procedure also incorporates a right of appeal by the employee against such decisions.

An increasing number of employers are finding that the introduction of flexible-working options contributes significantly to higher attendance rates. Employees with caring responsibilities who would previously have rung in sick when a child was ill or an aged parent needed help now find it possible to "juggle" their home and work responsibilities. Many of these initiatives are in their infancy, and it is not clear whether their initially favourable impact on attendance will be maintained in the long term.

However, legislation introduced in April 2003 (under the Employment Act 2002) now gives workers the right to request a move to flexible working under certain circumstances:

● the worker must have a child under the age of six or a child with disabilities under the aged of 18;

● they can make no more than one request a year to adopt flexible working and, if granted, the change becomes permanent and serves to amend their contract of employment;

● the employer must arrange a meeting with the employee within 28 days of receiving the request;

● following the meeting, the employer must write to the employee within 14 days to agree to the new pattern of work and give a date for its commencement, or refuse the request and support this with detailed business reasons for so doing; and

● the employee must lodge any appeal against the decision within 14 days.

The request, and the options open to both parties, can include home-based working, shorter hours or amended hours of attendance. The statutory procedure, whose timescales are shown above, must be followed to handle the request. There are eight possible reasons under the legislation that an employer can use to justify denying the employee's request. Employees may pursue their application to an employment tribunal, but its role is limited to checking that the employer has complied with the statutory procedure. The tribunal cannot attempt to "second-guess" the legitimacy or otherwise of the reasons given by the employer, provided they fall within those laid down. However, in some circumstances, an employer's refusal to grant a move to flexible working might be considered to be unlawful discrimination under the sex, race and disability discrimination Acts.

Case study C. South Shropshire Housing Association

South Shropshire Housing Association is piloting a work–life balance initiative, offering a range of options that includes childcare assistance, flexible working (flexitime), compressed working hours and encouraging women to return to work. It has found that the proportion of staff taking time off sick to look after dependants has fallen by three-quarters, from around 12% to 3%. And the proportion taking holiday to look after dependants has reduced from around one in three to one in five.

Case study D. The London Borough of Merton

The London Borough of Merton has halved its absence rate among employees covered by a pilot work–life balance initiative. Different working options are available, including a compressed working week, working from home, job sharing, career breaks and special leave for emergencies. Productivity has increased significantly, too. However, the initiative has required a cultural change, and the provision of training to managers in a new management style and in managing staff on the basis of their output rather than their attendance[11].

Attendance allowances

In a carrot-and-stick approach, some employers provide a positive incentive to employees who have good attendance records – alongside the use of rules and sanctions for those that do not. The majority of such attendance-allowance schemes are focused on groups with typically high absence rates – generally, manual workers and lower-level non-manual workers.

Examples include homecare staff employed by **Dorset County Council** (one week's pay where there has been less than four working days' absence in an eight-month period), and grounds-maintenance workers at **Tameside Metropolitan Borough Council**. Here, the payment amounts to 20% of pay, typically worth £39.50 a week, paid every four weeks. This payment is the norm, and absences serve to reduce the amount. One day's absence "costs" 12.5%, with two days losing the full 20% payment. Industrial injuries do not affect the payment, however. At **TRW Automotive**, a car-components manufacturer, the scheme is open to the whole workforce. Payments are made twice a year, each of £150. The allowance is lost where there has been any absence during the previous six months.

Sick pay

A sizeable minority of employers, just over four in 10 in the case of larger organisations, has introduced two or more sick-pay schemes, each concerned with a particular group in its workforce. While collective bargaining practices play a part in this dual or multi-level provision, so do tradition and the fact that lower-level groups often have higher absence rates (and poorer timekeeping) than others. So, such schemes often contain less generous sick-pay arrangements for manual workers, or for non-managerial versus managerial staff. There may be a minimum period of service to qualify for paid sick leave (reflecting the additional factor that non-managerial staff usually have higher resignation rates and shorter periods of service than managers) and/or the payments may be less generous or operate for a shorter period of time.

In the majority of public sector employers, sick pay is now payable from the first day of any absence, while this is the case in only a small minority of private-sector organisations. No minimum period of service is required before public sector workers are eligible for sick pay, while this is not generally true in private sector firms.

In both public and private sectors, though, sick pay usually becomes more generous (in that it lasts for longer periods) for longer-serving members of the workforce.

Most employers use a calendar year to define sick-pay arrangements, so that an entitlement to three months' pay, for example, is renewed in the following year. In some employers, though, the period is calculated from whenever sick pay is claimed. For example, food manufacturer **Northern Foods** provides 26 weeks' full pay (for monthly-paid staff) in any 12-month period. Banana producer **Geest** also uses a rolling year. During the first year of service, payment is discretionary, but limited to six weeks' full and six weeks' half pay during this time. Thereafter, there is a maximum of 26 weeks' full pay, then half pay, for sickness in any rolling 12 months. Payments remain at management discretion, though.

Payment periods among employers vary significantly, even within the initial year of service. In the majority of cases, the payment excludes statutory sick pay or incapacity benefit payable by the state. If and when the employee secures these state payments, their total income will reach the level of their normal pay.

Calculating sick pay

Treatment of additional allowances and payments – London weighting, overtime pay, shift allowance, and so on – varies significantly under sick-pay arrangements. Some employers divide such payments into those that are regular (or contractual) and those that are not, and base their sick pay on the former but exclude the latter. Most commonly, employers include London and other location payments, premia for regular shift patterns, regular weekend (or other contractual) overtime and car allowances for essential users. At restaurant chain **Pizza Hut**, for example, the company includes location allowances in its sick-pay calculations, but excludes any bonus that some of its managers receive based on performance and sales targets.

Sick-pay schemes can simply use the statutory sick pay manual from the Inland Revenue[12], but most employers prefer to set up their own procedures. However, employers must still operate statutory sick pay according to official rules, such as absence notification, the guarantee that the minimum statutory sick pay must be paid for all days when employees are entitled to it, and that a claims form for incapacity benefit must be issued to employees on long-term sick leave after 28 weeks.

Organisations will also need to formulate policy for periods of sickness that extend beyond the period of paid absence. Practice is fairly evenly divided. Some organisations tell IRS that they may continue payments, at managerial discretion, while others cease payment but maintain the contract of employment. In such cases, the employee is expected to rely on statutory sick pay or incapacity benefit.

Some employers lay down guidelines to help the exercise of discretion when making payments. At pharmaceutical manufacturer **AstraZeneca**, sick pay may be extended in exceptional circumstances where the employee is terminally ill, where the company awaits the latest medical information on the individual's condition, or where a date of return has been specified and is imminent.

Conversely, most employers' sick-pay procedures enable the withholding or clawing-back of sick pay in some circumstances. Instances of failure to report illness (*see next section*) are very common stipulations, while many employers include instances where the employee also gains payment via compensation from a third party for their illness or injury, and injuries that are seen as self-inflicted (sports injuries, primarily). Where it is suspected that the employee is harming their own recovery, some sick-pay procedures give the employer discretion to suspend or withdraw sick pay. Examples include **Essex County Council** and the **East Riding of Yorkshire Council**.

Unless an employee breaches one of the sickness or sick-pay rules, or commits a disciplinary offence, employers are generally bound by the contract of employment between them and the employee. Courts have ruled that contractual rights to sick pay, or to permanent health insurance, must be observed and employers cannot dismiss an employee on sickness grounds alone where the dismissal would deprive them of their right to the payment[13]. (Dismissal for reasons of redundancy would usually not be covered by this ruling, even though employers often take absence and attendance records into account when selecting employees for redundancy.)

"Frustration of contract" may apply to long-term sickness where sick pay has been exhausted and the contract of employment can no longer be performed. Tribunals take each case on its own facts and merits, where an employee complains of unfair dismissal or breach of contract. Frustration provides a possible defence against unfair dismissal, but its uncertain nature means that it is safer for employers to rely on developing effective procedures to handle long-term absence and applying them fairly[14].

Reporting sick

Most employers require absent employees to contact them before a set time on their first day of absence – in many instances, this is before the start of their normal time of work. The point of contact varies, although the individual's line manager is most commonly cited. It is important, though, that the act of making contact leads to absence records being kept or updated, particularly where a deputy or colleague is standing in for the usual contact person.

Case study E. Essex County Council

At Essex County Council, for example: "Employees should notify their manager by telephone by their normal time of arrival at work, or earlier where the service requires it. Failure to follow the correct procedure could result in pay being stopped and/or disciplinary action, although not on the first occasion." In addition, it requires repeat notification on the fourth day of absence, or at intervals agreed with the individual's line manager; subsequent notification during extended absences is by arrangement with the manager.

This issue of backing up reporting arrangements with penalties is practised by around three-quarters of employers, most commonly by retaining managerial discretion to do so, with only a minority applying automatic sanctions for non-compliance.

The frequency of notifications by the sick employee varies with employers, although many link this to the statutory sick pay arrangements about self-certification. Therefore, it is customary to require a further notification, accompanied by a medical certificate, on the seventh or eighth day of absence, with, perhaps, an interim informal notification after the first day of absence.

In the majority of employers, sickness during a holiday qualifies for sick pay, provided the normal notification procedures are met. Issues arising here include situations where notification is not possible (for example, where an employee is abroad and cannot contact the office), and whether or not the lost holiday entitlement is reinstated (most employers do so).

Pharmaceuticals company **Pfizer**, for example, reinstates holiday entitlement lost because of illness, provided a medical certificate is provided afterwards. This is also the practice at **Kingston upon Hull City Council** and **Cambridgeshire County Council**.

In addition to the requirement to provide medical certificates (usually from the GP), many employers include provisions in their sick-pay rules for access to a second opinion about the person's condition. Large organisations often have in-house occupational health staff who can provide an assessment, or employers can organise a report from an external medical practitioner. As we saw above, access to the advice of occupational health staff is reported by employers as an important means of managing absence.

At **W H Smith**, for example, its procedure requires that reference is normally made to the group's occupational health service within six weeks of a single period of absence. For extended absences beyond the scope of its sick-pay scheme, W H Smith provides permanent health insurance to employees who are members of its pension scheme.

This long-term insured benefit is widely available, particularly for employees of large organisations, and usually involves the insurance company concerned paying a proportion of salary for an extended period. There are, however, review provisions in schemes where employees may be required to show that they are incapable of finding alternative work. The test of acceptable employment is usually exacting, in that it will not necessarily be restricted to the same type of work as the individual most recently performed.

Record-keeping

There are several important reasons for maintaining effective records of attendance and other absence procedures. Records provide a reference document for future use when attendance and absence issues recur, and where employees' attendance is summarised in employment references or is used as part of the selection criteria for redundancy.

Absence records are given particular attention in the Employment Practices Data Protection Code issued in connection with the Data Protection Act

1998 (the Code has no separate legal status, but any enforcement action under the Act by the Information Commissioner may take account of the employer's compliance with the Code). Records that contain details of the reasons for an employee's absence, such as sickness or an accident, are classed as sensitive data requiring additional data-protection measures, such as confidentiality. The Code requires that such records, where details of the causes of absence are shown, must be kept separate from records that simply show details of dates of absence and the simple cause of it ("sickness", "accident", without giving details). The Code also provides general advice on record-keeping and formulating policies about it.

Records generally provide valuable evidence when aggrieved employees take the employer to tribunal or court. Requiring managers to maintain accurate records helps to impress on them that the procedure should be taken seriously and handled professionally – if for no other reason than their actions can be investigated at a later stage. Accurate records also enable the workings of the procedures to be monitored to ensure there is no unfair discrimination against individuals or groups.

Most employers report that they have developed forms for use in their procedures, containing guidance and structured sets of questions or topics to ensure managers provide information about all relevant issues in sufficient detail. They often develop policies about the storage of the records to ensure they are kept in a secure and confidential manner.

Whatever records are kept – handwritten notes, completed forms or electronically stored files – there are legal implications for their security, confidentiality and period of storage. The Data Protection Act 1998 requires secure, confidential storage, the rights of access by employees to their records (having given due notice in the prescribed way), and that records "shall not be kept for longer than is necessary for that purpose or those purposes".

The Act offers no set limits on record-keeping, and it expects that the period should reflect a real business need and take account of other legal requirements. For example, records may be relevant to potential claims on the grounds of unfair dismissal or unlawful discrimination; in such cases, individuals usually have three months to lodge a complaint. Where a procedure may be used to select individuals for redundancy, then the normal six-month limit on claims relating to statutory redundancy pay will be a consideration.

However, records with relevance to statutory sick pay must be kept for three years, as must records that could contain information about certain injuries, diseases and dangerous occurrences under health and safety law. Individuals have a period of six years to lodge breach of contract complaints. Even longer, records that have relevance to the monitoring of employees' exposure to certain hazardous substances must be kept for 40 years, where the employee is known personally to have been exposed, or for five years in other cases.

All of these considerations highlight the need to ensure that records are filed safely and securely, and kept for as long as is relevant under the law and the organisation's requirements.

4. Legal checklist

● Protected groups must not be put at an unfair disadvantage as a result of attendance management and related systems – Sex Discrimination Act 1975; Race Relations Act 1976; Disability Discrimination Act 1995; Trade Union and Labour Relations (Consolidation) Act 1992; and Codes of Practice associated with these Acts.

● Systems and procedures in the public sector must be checked for unfair discrimination on the grounds of ethnicity – Race Relations (Amendment) Act 2000.

● Absence management must take account of individuals covered by the Disability Discrimination Act 1995, particularly in respect of reasonable adjustments.

● The requirements of the Acas Code of Practice on Disciplinary and Grievance Procedures are relevant to absence management; compliance with the Code can be taken into account by tribunals and courts.

● Eligible groups have the right to request a move to flexible working – Employment Act 2002.

● The groups are workers with a child under the age of six, or a child with disabilities under the age of 18.

● Sick pay arrangements must take account of statutory sick pay rules – Statutory Sick Pay (General) Regulations 1982; Social Security Contributions and Benefits Act 1992.

● Employee records must follow the data protection principles – Data Protection Act 1998 and its Employment Practices Data Protection Code.

● Medical records are covered by the Access to Medical Reports Act 1988.

13. Redundancies and transfers

See also: 7. Retaining the best staff.

This chapter covers:
- Overview: an introduction to reducing employee numbers;
- Survivor syndrome;
- The management of redundancies;
- Legal definitions of redundancy;
- Information and consultation about redundancies;
- Selection for redundancy;
- Alternatives to redundancies;
- Notifying those chosen;
- Redundancy payments;
- Outplacement support;
- Business transfers; and
- Information and consultation under TUPE.

Checklists in this chapter:
1. Reducing survivor syndrome
2. The effective management of redundancies
3. Effective ways of avoiding compulsory redundancies
4. Redundancy pay
5. Legal checklist

Case studies in this chapter:
A. The Body Shop
B. Bradford & Bingley
C. Hertfordshire County Council
D. Leeds Co-operative Society
E. BP
F. The New Millennium Experience Company
G. United Utilities

Overview

Organisations seem to be in constant upheaval, embarking on reorganisations, takeovers or disposals, contracting out some of their functions or, themselves, being taken over by other companies. There are human casualties of these changes. Some employees will lose their jobs; others who escape redundancy may become demoralised, feeling they have been "left to pick up the pieces".

Personnel and HR specialists are often actors, rather than directors, in these dramas. But their role is central to ensuring that their organisations stay within the law, handle redundancies and business transfers humanely, and provide the best conditions for continued high performance among the remaining employees. The case for actively involving personnel and HR specialists in change programmes such as these is irrefutable. Too often, mergers and acquisitions fail because the cultural and people issues they know about are ignored. Redundancies are badly handled, leading to a haemorrhage of skilled and experienced staff, plummeting morale and a diminished reputation of the organisation as a good place to work. The quantity of tribunal complaints bears witness to many employers' failure to observe the statutory requirements concerning redundancy and transfers of undertakings.

Redundancy

It is well known that an individual is never "redundant"; their job may be surplus to requirements, but this casts no reflection on the person doing it. The perception among those losing their jobs is usually otherwise, and this could leave a legacy of bitterness towards the organisation that undermines its efforts to attract the best applicants when it embarks on recruitment exercises. Even employees who are not chosen for redundancy will turn against their employer if it has not managed redundancies effectively. They will continue to feel vulnerable, experience a form of grief at the upheavals taking place in their organisation and may feel guilty that their colleagues have lost their jobs while they have not. The most sought-after staff will move on at the first opportunity.

Survivor syndrome

Organisations continue to play too little attention to the impact of redundancies on those who are not among those losing their jobs. Yet there is an increasing awareness of the so-called "survivor syndrome" of reduced morale and performance, coupled with the loss through resignations of key staff to competitors.

Research conducted by the Institute for Employment Studies (IES)[1] shows that the survivor syndrome is a complex phenomenon to understand and, equally importantly, can damage the organisation in many different ways.

Employees may experience it because they consider that the organisation has behaved unjustly or unfairly in respect of the redundancy exercise that led to colleagues and/or their managers losing their jobs. They will feel less secure themselves. And they may lose the belief that efforts on their part – such as striving for high performance, generating ideas and being cooperative – will be acknowledged and influence the way in which they are treated.

This mix of emotions will affect employees' behaviour in various ways. Most frequently, morale and motivation will suffer, leading to a reduction in performance and, perhaps, to increased absence rates. In a large-scale survey of more than 550 employers, the Chartered Institute of Personnel and Development (CIPD) found that a "decline in the morale of remaining employees" was the most widely-reported manifestation of survivor syndrome. More than half of the employers cited it. And almost one in three mentioned that survivors had lost trust in their organisation[2]. The CIPD concludes that its research shows: "Redundancies generally involve some costs beyond those directly associated with making people redundant."

In addition, the IES research found that: "Survivors . . . can become unduly risk-averse and narrowly focused and, therefore, less creative and open to change." In other words, survivors adopt a "bunker mentality". They may also be less willing to assume responsibility for self-development, being less inclined to learn new skills, and be less committed to helping customers – with the result that service quality decreases and business may be lost. In addition, survivors' reduced attachment to the organisation may lead them to look elsewhere for work. One likely scenario sees those whom the organisation has carefully not selected for redundancy – because of their performance, skills and experience – will be the ones most likely to leave. And their marketability is likely to see such employees being eagerly recruited by the organisation's direct competitors.

A further consequence of redundancy exercises concerns workloads. Reports from employers increasingly suggest that the scale of an organisation's redundancies tends to be larger than the reduction in workload warrants. In other words, some of the redundant employees' workload remains and is shared out among the survivors – particularly, managers[3].

Increased workloads may lead to stress, particularly where the individuals concerned resent these additional burdens and have little control over them. For example, research by outplacement consultancy Chiumento has found that 95% of the personnel and HR directors and managers contacted reported that stress levels in their organisations had increased as a result of job losses[4].

We noted above that reducing the extent of survivor syndrome requires a strategic approach, bringing together several interlocking initiatives. Robin Tait's experience of advising organisations during redundancy exercises shows that three broad issues are of particular importance:

● the extent, detail and openness of the communication exercise during the redundancy process;

● the perceived fairness and implementation of the selection criteria used to identify those who will be made redundant; and

● the treatment of employees who are being made redundant[5].

More specific actions linked to these issues are summarised in checklist 1.

1. Reducing survivor syndrome

The extent of survivor syndrome is most likely to be reduced where all of the following are carefully planned and expertly implemented:

● making the case that the redundancies are unavoidable;

● integrating the above in a communications strategy that provides regular, clear briefings on the progress of the redundancy exercise and gives as much reassurance as possible to potential survivors;

● selecting employees for redundancy on the basis of criteria that are transparent, objective, fair, consistently applied and acceptable to the workforce;

● being seen to care for employees who are losing their jobs;

● once those to be made redundant have been selected, ensuring that the survivors are given as much clear, detailed information as possible about their own place and future in the organisation, and are involved in shaping the organisation's vision for its future;

● providing support for survivors, including visible day-to-day management, career counselling, stress counselling, performance coaching, training and development, sideways moves and other alternatives where promotion opportunities have been reduced;

● ensuring existing personnel systems, such as performance management and reward, take account of the changes linked to redundancies and are accepted as fair by survivors;

● giving survivors the opportunity to express their concerns and emotions, and raise issues they want clarified;

● ensuring line managers and supervisors understand their role in both managing redundancies and supporting survivors, and are given the skills required; and

● taking the long view: research has found that organisations and human beings operate on different timescales in terms of their ability to accept change.

More generally, organisations that implement good-practice redundancy exercises are likely to reduce the impact of survivor syndrome. However, as the research conducted by IES found, organisations should not be complacent. Further redundancies are often likely to be necessary at some point in the future, and the effectiveness of an employer's attempts to reduce survivor syndrome should be investigated.

The IES research found that some leading employers are already measuring the impact on survivors of their management of redundancies through:
● hard indicators, including changes in resignation rates ("labour turnover"), changes in absence rates and performance indicators (such as ratings from formal performance-management systems and customer-related metrics); and
● softer indicators, including employee opinion polls ("employee attitude surveys"), particularly where a series of polls is conducted to give comparisons over time, and feedback from line managers, team leaders and other supervisors that they have, in turn, gathered from their subordinates.

Case study A. The Body Shop

Ethical cosmetics company the Body Shop faced a difficult challenge when marketplace pressures caused it to implement a head-office reorganisation, which led to 200 redundancies, and outsource its manufacturing, involving a business transfer of 500 people. According to a case study in *People Management*6, a comprehensive redundancy-management initiative took account of the needs of survivors. They were invited to attend a special four-day course to reduce survivor syndrome. The training aimed to "re-energise" survivors, and covered such issues as the emotions generated by the upheaval at head office and feelings of guilt at not having lost one's job, as well as correcting some of the rumours and misunderstandings that were circulating in head office. In addition, the company undertook an opinion poll that covered survivors, those who were redeployed, those who took voluntary redundancy and those who were selected for compulsory redundancy. The results were not entirely favourable, but 60% of the survivors agreed that the company had "listened to their individual needs" and more than two-thirds of the groups of leavers said they would consider working for the Body Shop again.

The management of redundancies

The effective management of redundancies involves formulating a coordinated strategy that brings together such important, but interlinked, processes as providing suitable training to line managers, consultation, redundancy selection, notifying and providing assistance to redundant employees, and communicating with the survivors (see checklist 2). The objective is to achieve the required job losses, while ensuring that as few as possible of the organisation's pool of skilled, experienced and high-performing employees are lost – either through redundancy or voluntary resignation. At the same time, the organisation needs to ensure that the exercise is not counter-productive – that its gains through a reduced paybill are not clawed back by a slump in productivity, customer service and general motivation. And, of course, it should ensure that it complies with the law.

During redundancy exercises, organisations seem to become schizoid. They forget the time and expense they devote to ensuring they are best placed to attract the best recruits, particularly in building their "employer brand" – their reputation as being a fair employer that offers interesting jobs and good terms and conditions. Yet a redundancy exercise often attracts more negative publicity for an employer than the smaller, incremental gains it has achieved over the years in striving to become an organisation where the best performers want to apply for jobs and do not leave prematurely to work for a competitor. It is the often unwelcome duty of personnel and HR managers to point out these dangers, and do the best they can to ensure that redundancies are managed effectively.

2. The effective management of redundancies

A redundancy-management strategy should take account of the following factors:

● where a formal redundancy procedure already exists, review it for continued relevance, involving employees and any employee representatives in this review;

● identify the jobs, functions and locations most at risk as a result of the potential redundancy situation that has arisen; ensure that potential job losses are covered by either/both of the statutory definitions of redundancy;

● set up a small taskforce to manage the redundancy exercise, giving each member as much training in relevant skills as time permits;

● communicate the reasons for the potential redundancies to the workforce and any recognised trade unions and/or staff forum or works council – wherever possible, those at risk should attend one-to-one confidential meetings with one of the taskforce;

● where there is no staff forum, works council or employee representatives, inform (and, later, consult) specially-elected employee representatives in accordance with the law and do so individually with each directly affected person;

● identify any methods of reducing or avoiding compulsory redundancies, and inform and consult employee representatives about them; where voluntary redundancies and/or early retirement are to be offered, develop selection criteria to reduce the impact on the organisation's pool of high-performing, skilled and experienced staff, and agree the terms that are to be offered; ensure the criteria and terms comply with the law; where redeployment is to be offered, ensure compliance with the law;

● identify selection criteria for compulsory redundancies, based on ensuring the organisation maintains as far as possible its pool of high-performing, skilled and experienced staff, and that the criteria are transparent, objective and fair, are accepted as fair and are consistently applied; ensure the criteria and their application comply with the law;

● begin statutory communication and consultation within required timescales and in accordance with statutory requirements;

● draw up a communication plan to provide regular updates (even when there is nothing new to say), based on a commitment to be as open and detailed as possible;

● draw up appeals procedures;

● agree redundancy payments, ensuring statutory compliance (minimum amounts plus limits on maximum payments in some parts of the public sector), and determine other forms of assistance (such as outplacement support); determine whether redundant employees will be expected to work out their notice or, if not, how they can clear their desks and leave with dignity;

● following consultation and any appeals, confirm details of individuals being made redundant and those taking up any alternative voluntary options; this announcement should involve collective methods and one-to-one meetings;

● ensure those involved on the employer's side have received effective training for the task of announcing the redundancies, so that they handle it compassionately, treat each person as an individual and are fully briefed about the details of redundancy payment and other resources being provided to the employee; ensure prepared letters have been drawn up, checked and are handed out to each person at their meeting; notice periods should comply with the contract or statute, whichever is longer;

● ensure statutory paid time off is provided for job search;

● provide training and support to line managers, and then expect them to be available to meet affected employees;

● throughout the exercise, implement measures to reduce survivor syndrome (see checklist 1); and

● consider developing a formal redundancy procedure for future use; Acas recommends "full and effective consultation" in its drafting. Its guidance booklet *Redundancy handling* offers advice on its contents.

The legal definitions

The Employment Rights Act 1996 provides several situations where a redundancy could arise:
● the closure of a workplace or department;
● the need to make reductions in "work of a particular kind", or discontinue performing it entirely, within the organisation generally or in a particular workplace; and
● creating a redeployment opportunity for an employee affected by redundancy by making another employee redundant ("bumping"). (However, recent case law has cast doubt on whether bumping is considered to be redundancy. Instead, an employer may be able to argue that bumping was caused by a business reorganisation.)

Employers defending a tribunal application for unfair dismissal must satisfy one of the above criteria, and also all of the following[7]:
● inform and consult affected employees (and their representatives, where appropriate);
● adopt a fair basis for selecting individuals for redundancy; and
● make reasonable efforts, where practicable, to find suitable alternative employment for those affected by redundancies.

However, tribunals tend to attach most weight to the second of these additional criteria: the process of selecting employees for redundancy.

In addition, there is a separate, broader legal definition of redundancy under the Trade Union and Labour Relations (Consolidation) Act 1992 for the purposes of informing and consulting employees. This applies where dismissals of at least 20 employees in one establishment are expected within a 90-day period, and where the dismissals are for "any reason not related to the individual employee concerned".

Information and consultation

Informing and consulting employees as early and fully as possible about a potential redundancy situation provides an important means of reducing survivor syndrome (*see earlier section in this chapter*). It is good practice, too, in that it treats those likely to lose their jobs with care and respect. It involves employees in finding ways to minimise what must be a traumatic experience, and ensures their ideas and suggestions are passed on to management. Those who are directly involved in the jobs and duties at risk will often have the best proposals for avoiding redundancies and, failing that, for ensuring the organisation continues to function as effectively as possible afterwards.

Feedback from personnel and HR specialists highlights the role that communication can play in effective redundancy management. The process is invariably stressful and often prolonged. Communication that is accepted as being honest and as frank as possible will reduce employees' anxieties. Regular bulletins are more important than isolated "windfalls" of information that may be difficult to absorb and are preceded and followed by long silences. The role of line managers is important in acting as a point of continuity and contact throughout the redundancy process. They should be encouraged to provide as much information as possible, listen to their employees' concerns, and provide whatever advice and assistance they can – including involving personnel and HR specialists and whatever other facilities and support have been arranged by the organisation for those affected by the redundancies.

There are statutory information and consultation requirements, too, where at least 20 employees are likely to be made redundant (although there is a narrowly-defined exception to this duty). In the legislative pipeline are wider-reaching requirements under the EU Information and Consultation Directive. This will require employers above a certain size to set up on request a permanent staff council. Potential redundancies will be one of the issues about which employers will be obliged to consult their council. So far, the UK government has not yet issued the Regulations that will serve to implement the Directive. Employers will be progressively covered by the Directive, according to their number of employees. It is likely that organisations with 150 or more employees will have to comply by March 2005, those with 100 or more employees by March 2007 and those with 50 or more employees by March 2008.

The current legislation, under the Trade Union and Labour Relations (Consolidation) Act 1992 (as amended), stipulates that employee representatives must be informed and consulted where 20 or more redundancies are planned to take place in an establishment within a 90-day period (the Act's definition of redundancy also includes other situations; see above). The definition of an "establishment" depends on the facts of each case, and could take account of the EC's Collective Redundancies Directive that underpins UK law. Often, it relates to a workplace or business unit.

Where trade unions are not recognised and the employer has not set up a staff council or network of staff representatives, the employer will have to organise special collective consultation procedures.

This procedure for appointing employee representatives for the purposes of redundancy consultation is described in detail by Acas in its *Representation at work guide*[8]. In summary, representatives must be elected in a fair way, in sufficient numbers that they are able to represent the interests of all those affected, and candidates must be "affected" employees. Everyone who is entitled must be able to stand for election and vote in the ballot. Voting must be via a secret ballot, and the votes must be counted accurately. (Where employees fail to elect representatives, the employer is then required to provide relevant information about the redundancies/business transfer to each person directly.) Employees, those standing for election and those who are elected are protected against victimisation and dismissal for reasons connected with their participation. Representatives must be given access to the employees they represent, to reasonable amounts of paid time off for their duties and to reasonable facilities to perform their duties.

Where the employer recognises an independent trade union, the Act requires that the union's appointed representatives are informed and consulted about the proposed redundancies. Representatives must be given access to the employees they represent, to reasonable amounts of paid time off for their duties and to reasonable facilities to perform their duties.

However, as Acas points out, legal precedents indicate that collective methods of informing and consulting the workforce are not sufficient. Individual employees who are most likely to be made redundant should also be informed and consulted individually by their employer.

Information

Employers must supply certain information before commencing consultation. The coverage of this information is set out in the Act, and includes:
- the reasons for the proposed redundancies;
- the numbers and types of employees affected;

● the selection criteria to be used;
● the way in which the redundancies will take place, including the timescale; and
● the method of calculating any extra-statutory redundancy pay.

These requirements mean that employers should have undertaken a considerable amount of preparation (or have an existing redundancy procedure) so that they are in a position of being able to communicate this information. For example, they must have already determined the selection criteria and the payments to be made – factors that would not necessarily be involved in the initial decision that a redundancy situation was likely. However, the related consultation requirements also imply that many factors relating to the proposed redundancies should not have been fully determined. Otherwise, the consultation process will be no more than a sham if it is not capable of influencing such fundamental issues as the need for redundancies and finding alternatives to them.

Consultation

The ensuing consultations must be conducted in good faith ("with a view to reaching agreement"), and cover ways of:
● avoiding the redundancies;
● reducing the number of redundancies; and
● minimising the consequences of the redundancies.

The consultation must begin in "good time", but must start at least 30 days prior to the redundancies where between 20 and 99 redundancies are planned to take place in one establishment within a 90-day period, or at least 90 days where 100 or more redundancies are planned. Usually, the consultation process should allow representatives adequate time for them to develop proposals and counter-arguments to the employer's intentions.

Case study B. Bradford & Bingley

When financial services company Bradford & Bingley decided to close its Leamington Spa office, 275 jobs were threatened. The company had already been holding informal discussions with its independent trade union concerning its investigation of selling off the relevant functions under a business transfer. When this failed, it formally notified the union of the proposed redundancies and, one day later, the chief executive met all affected employees at a special meeting off site. The announcement to employees was made as quickly as possible to avoid affected staff first hearing about the plans from the media. The meeting was difficult and emotional, with reactions ranging from anger, betrayal and apprehension, to relief in some cases. Afterwards, though, the close-knit nature of the office meant that grief was a strong reaction. Adverse press comment was countered by providing employees with as much information as possible about the reasons for the closure decision, and with practical and emotional support – including counselling and outplacement support, and training for line managers in giving bad news. As a result, no letters from staff criticising the company appeared in the press.

Selection for redundancy

The process of selecting employees for redundancy is fraught with dangers, and will benefit greatly from the involvement of personnel and HR specialists. Organisations frequently fail to undertake selection fairly and effectively. As a result, they face additional costs by incurring legal fees to defend tribunal complaints (as well as compensation if they lose), and experience reduced effectiveness when the wrong people are chosen for redundancy. Processes that are not seen as fair by the workforce will lose the organisation valuable goodwill among both those losing their jobs and the survivors.

To comply with statutory requirements, employers need to develop a clear set of criteria that they intend to use for redundancy selection and communicate these details as part of the information and consultation process required by law. Even where redundancies are exempt from the collective requirements, developments in case law indicate that providing each individual with this information is now expected. More generally, employees cannot be expected to accept the fairness of the selection process if they are not made aware of its workings.

Acas advises that "as far as possible, objective criteria, precisely defined and capable of being applied in an independent way, should be used"9. Subjective criteria could breach one or more of the discrimination laws. Even objective criteria could contravene the statutory protection afforded to a wide range of groups – for example, on grounds of trade union membership, maternity-related grounds, or because individuals have asserted a statutory employment right. In all, there are upwards of a dozen potentially unfair reasons for selecting someone for redundancy (mainly under the Employment Rights Act 1996) – primarily, with the aim of ensuring that redundancies are not used as an excuse to dismiss "troublemakers" or an opportunity to indulge in discrimination.

However, the use of "as far as possible" by Acas indicates that there is some recognition in law that even objective criteria can involve some elements of judgment when assessing individuals against such criteria as ability and performance.

State of play: According to the CIPD's large-scale survey of personnel and HR specialists about their employers' redundancy procedures, the three most important selection criteria in current use are the individual's particular role in the organisation (used by two-thirds); the person's performance or efficiency (used by six in 10); and their ability and/or flexibility (used by just over half). Length of service – the factor formerly most commonly used – is now used by no more than a quarter of employers, with a similar proportion taking account of absence and/or disciplinary records. An employee's age is very rarely taken into account.

There are, though, some differences in practice between different types of employer. Manufacturers are more likely to take account of length of service and absence/disciplinary record than either the public sector or employers in the service industries in the private sector. The public sector is much less likely to take account of performance/efficiency; ability/flexibility; length of service; or absence/disciplinary record than employers in the private sector.

We have found similar patterns in our own research, and also evidence for the increasingly important role that formal performance-management systems play in providing assessments for use in redundancy selection. Such systems are the most important source of information when employers apply selection criteria based on individuals' performance and their levels of skill. They also contribute data in terms of assessing individuals' potential to perform other roles, where redeployment is used as an alternative to redundancy.

Acas's guide *Redundancy handling*, mentioned above, provides a useful commentary on the various methods available to employers in redundancy selection:

● **Length of service:** This used to be the most common means of identifying individuals for redundancy, usually through LIFO (last in, first out). It has fallen from favour, as we saw above. Acas notes that it has the advantages of being objective, easy to apply and was often easy to agree with trade unions. However, it can be counter-productive, in that will unbalance the workforce, removing most of the "fresh blood", discriminating (lawfully, at present) against younger workers and deterring individuals from transferring to other departments unless total service is considered.

● **Skills or qualifications:** These factors provide a good means of ensuring that the workforce selected for redundancy does not include those whom the organisation can least afford to lose. However, methods must be found to identify, in an objective way, the skills and qualifications that are most needed, and of then assessing individuals against them. Acas warns that reliance on formal qualifications may not always be advisable, as other employees may have as much or more to offer although they lack paper certificates.

● **Performance:** Both performance in the job and flexibility/adaptability can be important criteria for selecting individuals for redundancy. As with skills, however, Acas points out that employers should develop objective methods to define and assess these factors – for example, through the performance-management system. (The Sex Discrimination (Indirect Discrimination and Burden of Proof) Regulations 2001 have altered the definition of indirect discrimination, however, with the result that employers should be more cautious about using flexibility as a factor in redundancy selection.)

● **Attendance and/or discipline:** As we saw above, employers seldom take account of these factors – a surprising finding, given the importance they attach to them at the point of entry to the organisation (*see the section on using employment references in chapter 4 Checking candidates' backgrounds*) and, increasingly, in day-to-day performance management (*see chapter 13 Attendance and absence*). Acas advises that attendance and discipline should only be used as criteria in redundancy selection where accurate records exist on which to base judgments. In addition, it recommends that "before selecting on the basis of attendance, it is important to know the reasons for and extent of any absences" – although employers seldom seek out such reasons at present.

Making the selection

Redundancy selection involves both developing a set of fair, objective criteria, and then ensuring they are applied in an equally fair and objective manner. However, Acas recommends that criteria requiring some judgment in applying them – such as a factor relating to the individual's performance – should include a "comparative analysis", so that each individual in the redundancy pool is compared with the others. This comparison should be documented, to provide evidence if the employer has to defend a tribunal complaint.

Where employers have introduced an effective performance-management system, and trained the managers involved in conducting assessments, they have a good foundation to use for the purposes of making assessments for the purpose of redundancy selection. Even so, full information should be given to the assessors about the individuals in the redundancy pool, the selection criteria and the way in which they should be applied.

The methods of assessment are particularly important, in view of the fact that many organisations have moved away from a simplistic assessment based on LIFO (length of service using last in first out), towards adopting a matrix, where two or more factors are used in tandem. The managers who will have to select individuals for redundancy must be able to understand how the factors interact – often, employers devise a weighting system and a scoring scale – and apply them in a consistent way across all affected employees.

It may not always be possible to provide every manager with suitable training. In such cases, another manager (such as a personnel or HR specialist) should either undertake the task or do so in concert with the line manager.

The selection process should be documented by those involved, because employers will need this evidence should they have to defend any relevant tribunal applications.

It is good practice to consult employees about the results of applying the selection criteria so that they understand them, and can provide counterarguments where they consider that the criteria could be interpreted more favourably in their case. This is particularly important given the fact that we have found many employers using absence as a selection factor make little allowance for the reasons underlying the periods of absence. There should also be provision for a formal appeals procedure.

However, one of the consequences of moving away from "safe" criteria, such as last in first out, towards more personalised approaches is that the judgments that are made are potentially much more intrusive and threatening[10]. Performance, a key factor in many organisations' selection criteria, represents a prime example. While jobs are made redundant, not employees, the choice of those asked to leave can reflect adversely on them as individuals. This increases the importance of ensuring that the selection criteria are as fair and objective as possible, that they have been applied in a similarly robust manner, and that the persons providing feedback to employees have been trained in relevant interpersonal skills. And, as far as selection criteria based on performance, discipline and attendance are concerned, effective performance-management systems should have already ensured that there are "no surprises" – the organisation's concerns about these issues should already have been discussed with the employee and the position made clear.

Alternatives to redundancies

Employers have a statutory duty to consider ways of avoiding redundancies or reducing their number. They will have identified those affected at the initial stage of the redundancy-management process – it will either concern an entire group, where a site is being closed down for example, or those selected for redundancy among a larger pool of affected employees.

Measures to avoid redundancies are covered by the statutory information and consultation procedures where 20 or more employees are likely to be made redundant (see above). However, Acas points out that it is good practice to inform and consult whether or not the statutory requirements apply.

Overall, though, efforts to avoid compulsory redundancies seem surprisingly ineffectual – despite widely-reported uses of voluntary redundancy and recruitment freezes to reduce their number. The recent redundancy survey undertaken by the CIPD[11] found that most of the 563 employers contacted reported that upwards of 93% of their total job losses involved compulsory redundancies.

3. Effective ways of avoiding compulsory redundancies

The research conducted by the CIPD has found that employers highlight the following measures as being most effective in avoiding compulsory redundancies (shown in descending order of effectiveness):

- redeployment – offering alternative employment within the organisation;

- recruitment freezes;

- natural wastage – this takes advantage of the resignations and retirements that naturally occur in the organisation to help reduce overall employee numbers when job losses are required; natural wastage is only effective where it is accompanied by some form of recruitment freeze;

- reducing or eliminating the use of contract staff;

- retraining existing employees; and

- offering early retirement.

Voluntary redundancy is not shown in the above list because the CIPD survey did not consider it to be relevant in this context. Other more creative measures, such as offering paid or unpaid sabbaticals, career breaks, study leave, or reduced hours of work, are comparatively little used.

Source: Redundancy survey report, Chartered Institute of Personnel and Development, 2002, www.cipd.co.uk.

Voluntary redundancies

While the CIPD research did not ask employers about their use of voluntary redundancy, our feedback from employers shows that it is widely offered when organisations are reducing their workforces. This route reduces the impact of survivor syndrome, because fewer of survivors' colleagues will be seen to be leaving against their will, and can ensure that many leavers continue to have a good opinion of their employer.

However, there are several potential pitfalls to avoid. In particular, many organisations continue to fail to manage the process of offering voluntary redundancy in an effective manner. Many do not develop proper selection criteria, with the result that valuable skills and experience are lost – service-related redundancy payments tend to be more attractive to longer-serving employees who often have had sufficient length of service to develop their skills and knowledge to a considerable degree. In addition, without effective management, too many volunteers may be accepted for redundancy, leaving the organisation even more depleted of valuable expertise.

Where invitations to apply for voluntary redundancy are over-subscribed or attract those whom the employer wishes to retain, the organisation will face a challenge in retaining the morale and performance of those who, having mentally decided to leave, are then denied the opportunity. The way in which the offer is communicated – as a possibility to be explored by both employees and employer, but with no commitment on either side – is important, as is continued communication about the progress of the bids for voluntary redundancy and the sensitivity with which the final outcome is announced.

Finally, voluntary redundancy may turn out to be more expensive in terms of severance payments than the use of compulsory redundancy, given the likelihood that volunteers will be disproportionately made up of longer-serving employees attracted by the cash amounts on offer.

Redeployment

The option of offering redeployment ensures that valuable employees are not lost to the organisation if the only alternative were to make them redundant, and provides evidence that the employer followed a fair redundancy procedure. However, the use of redeployment obviously depends on the availability and suitability of vacancies elsewhere. Employees should be given written details of the alternative job, showing where it differs from their current one and where similarities exist.

Those who accept redeployment have a statutory right to a trial period of four weeks where the new post involves differences in contractual terms and conditions. At the end of this period (which can be extended by mutual agreement), either the employer or employee may decide that the new job is unsuitable, giving the individual the right to their redundancy payment.

However, where the new job offers similar earnings and status, involves work that lies within the employee's potential and does not inflict on them an unreasonable amount of additional inconvenience (such as distance or commuting time), then employees who turn down redeployment may not be able to claim a redundancy payment.

Case study C. Hertfordshire County Council

Hertfordshire County Council has been actively redeploying employees made redundant as part of a long-term process of restructuing council departments. Its personnel specialists identified that best practice in managing redundancies involved adopting a strategic approach of "recycling the workforce". A new recruitment centre set up for external recruitment maintains a register of existing staff who are facing redundancy. Most staff are offered redeployment in other departments, where they receive preference for vacancies that arise through natural wastage. Where such vacancies do not occur, the council has the option of creating temporary jobs where redundant staff can be temporarily redeployed, given retraining and, hopefully, returned to a permanent position. The restructuring process included the outsourcing of recruitment to Manpower and the loss of 10 personnel posts. Here, the lengthy negotiations with providers enabled the council to avoid compulsory redundancies through natural wastage and appointing new recruits on temporary contracts that expired once Manpower took over.

Freezes and natural wastage

Organisations generally experience a fairly regular loss of staff through voluntary resignations and retirements, and such "natural wastage" can represent a "safety valve" when compulsory redundancies are being considered. Wastage rates vary hugely, however, according to the organisation's location, industry, type of workforce, employees' age profile and other factors.

While it is easy to predict the timing of employees reaching normal retirement age, the numbers involved and the type of work they are doing, voluntary resignations are by their nature much less easy to forecast. This can make the use of natural wastage a problematic alternative to compulsory redundancies. Many employers tell us that they incorporate natural wastage in their management of redundancies – it indicates to employees and their representatives that they are serious in their intention to avoid compulsory job losses wherever possible. However, natural wastage is often a "wait-and-see" contingency.

Employers will wait for a period of some weeks to see whether any employees have handed in their resignations, the numbers involved and the types of jobs they are likely to free up. The resignations may come from within the pool of employees affected by the planned job losses and, thus, directly contribute to achieving the necessary economies. Or the departing employees may create vacancies into which affected individuals could be redeployed. Once that waiting period has passed, though, employers tend to continue with their planned job losses, rather than delay the process indefinitely.

Natural wastage almost invariably goes hand in hand with the use of recruitment freezes. Without halting the replacement of departing employees, there will obviously not be any redeployment opportunities or reductions in headcount among those affected by the redundancy plans.

Recruitment freezes may be carefully targeted at posts within the redundancy pool and those closely associated with it. But these controls may be difficult to define where redeployment is also being used to reduce the need for compulsory job losses. The alternative – a universal recruitment freeze – may prove highly disruptive to the organisation, even when its duration is strictly limited.

In some cases, the scale of voluntary labour turnover can play a considerable part in helping employers avoid compulsory redundancies. At **Liverpool City Council**, all 2,700 job losses – 10% of the workforce – were achieved through natural wastage and without provoking industrial action from the workforce's trade unions[12].

Other options

Contract staff: One of the most effective means of avoiding or reducing compulsory redundancies involves reducing or ceasing the use of flexible forms of labour – external contractors and temps supplied by agencies.

Retraining: Developing the skills of employees affected by redundancies enables them to be redeployed more easily. More strategically, though, a programme of training will enable an organisation's workforce to have the skills required to respond more readily and flexibly to changing circumstances. This might reduce the need for future redundancies.

Early retirement: Employees aged 50 years and above are able to draw enhanced pensions under Inland Revenue rules, and many organisations have traditionally offered early retirement when seeking to achieve job losses. Often, the terms offered as part of a voluntary redundancy package include early retirement as one element within it. Early retirement is particularly heavily used in the public sector. However, the rising costs associated with funding occupational pensions schemes may mean that this option is more restricted in future. In addition, early retirement shares the same drawback as voluntary redundancy in that longer-serving employees are often most affected. They will also frequently be the group of employees with the greatest levels of skills, experience and knowledge.

Lay-offs: Employers can achieve temporary economies in their paybill by using lay-offs where employees are asked not to come to work and are not paid for this time. However, this can only be used as an option where it has already been incorporated into contracts of employment. Unpaid lay-offs could also be introduced, with consent, as part of the consultation concerning alternatives to a particular round of redundancies. There are situations where employees affected by unpaid lay-offs may be entitled to guarantee payments or jobseeker's allowance. Generally, employers' ability to use unpaid lay-offs as an alternative to redundancies is limited to four consecutive weeks (or six weeks in any 13 week-period). After that time, affected employees with at least two years' service can give written notice of a claim for redundancy pay.

Alternatively, employers are generally able to use lay-offs with pay, but this only reduces excess production without saving paybill costs.

Short-time working: Like lay-offs, short-time working attempts to achieve temporary reductions in output and, where permitted by contracts of employment, related savings in wages and other paybill costs. The contractual right to invoke short-time working may have already been incorporated into contracts, or the employer might introduce it, with consent, as part of the consultation concerning alternatives to a particular round of redundancies. Short-time working involves reducing employees' hours of attendance, either by curtailing the hours worked each day or cutting the working week by one or more complete days. There are situations where employees affected by unpaid short-time working may be entitled to jobseeker's allowance.

Generally, employers' ability to use unpaid short-time working – where employees with at least two years' service receive less than half a week's pay – as an alternative to redundancies is limited to four consecutive weeks (or six weeks in any 13 week-period). After that time, affected employees can give written notice of a claim for redundancy pay.

Case study D. Leeds Co-operative Society

The 200 travel-agency staff employed by Leeds Co-operative Society agreed to vary their working week during a downturn in business after the 11 September terrorist attacks[13]. In the quiet period over Christmas, staff worked four days a week for six weeks, while drawing their normal pay. However, in the new year, the working week temporarily increased for a similar period from five to six days, while employees were paid for five days. The society aimed to change working patterns to reflect what it hoped was a temporary reduction in business, while paying staff the same amount overall. In addition, recruitment was frozen, some staff were offered temporary redeployment and overhead costs were reduced.

Notifying those chosen

The **Bradford & Bingley** announcement of the closure of its Leamington Spa office was met with a wide range of often intense emotions (*see tcase study B*). Many staff experienced – and expressed – anger, betrayal and apprehension, although a few were relieved. But, subsequently, the overriding emotion was one of grief. The office had a long history, drew many of its employees from the local area, and they had formed many friendships and acquaintanceships at work.

Personnel and HR specialists contacted by the CIPD for its research into redundancies[14] confirmed that intense, perhaps violent, emotions are commonly experienced when individuals are informed they are to be made redundant. Shock and anger were reported by many of those contacted,

alongside resignation, relief and apathy. In more than a fifth of the organisations the overriding emotion was shock.

Those giving the bad news also experienced stress. The personnel and HR
specialists contacted by the CIPD said that they and the line managers
involved found the process "traumatic", and nine out of 10 of them agreed
that it is "always" stressful for managers to tell employees they are to lose
their jobs.

The likelihood of intense emotions being experienced by both parties – the
redundant employees and the managers informing them of this fact –
increases the likelihood that the process will be mishandled and that one or
both parties will suffer as a result. Few people relish the task of giving bad
news, particularly when the reaction may be intense and for which they are
unprepared. There are many anecdotal reports[15] of employees being
extremely badly treated at this crucial point. Not only is this inhuman, it can
negate all the effort that the organisation has expended on conducting the
remainder of the redundancy process in a fair and professional manner.

It is therefore good practice that those who will communicate the redundancy decision are given sufficient training and information to perform the
task properly. The CIPD recommends[16] that this aspect of the process should
focus on notifying employees of the final decision that they are to lose their
job. Previously, in a separate meeting, the manager should have consulted
the individuals about the proposed job losses and alternatives to them, and
discussed the payments and other support that would be provided were
compulsory redundancies to become unavoidable.

According to Jane Rothwell, whose 20 years' experience of personnel management includes taking part in redundancy exercises and training line
managers in the process: "The objective is to minimise the stress on employees who are departing, while promoting an image of care, and minimising
the impact of the redundancies on the morale of those remaining."[17]

At **Bradford & Bingley**, the training provided for the line managers who
would meet employees threatened with redundancy lasted two days. The
training was conducted off site by a specialist consultancy, and coached
managers in the skills of informing individuals of bad news and in dealing
with their reactions to it. Line managers subsequently met their employees
three times. The first meeting, after the collective announcement of the site's
closure, involved managers discussing employees' aspirations and personal
circumstances. The second meeting covered the formal announcement that
the closure meant that the individuals' jobs were at risk. The final meeting

involved formal notification that the individuals would lose their jobs, giving them a letter with this information and the likely date of their redundancy. But, as with the other meetings, managers encouraged employees to take part and ask questions, which the managers were expected to answer to the best of their abilities.

Redundancy payments

The size of redundancy payments is a crucial issue in winning employees' acceptance of a redundancy exercise. The statutory minima under the Employment Rights Act 1996 are hardly generous, however, and many employers take the view that it is desirable to top them up.

They may have been convinced by humanitarian arguments that employees losing their jobs should be provided with a more generous financial "cushion" against hardship than the bare statutory minimum until they find a new job. Some employers may be more convinced by the argument that it makes economic sense to do so. Former members of staff have valuable skills and experience and, if good relations are maintained with them, could return in future to provide useful expertise to the organisation – either as a self-employed consultant or employee. Equally importantly, being seen to treat departing employees fairly will help to reduce the impact of survivor syndrome. Finally, there may be a contractual obligation to do so, for example, arising from the terms of a collective agreement with a trade union or because this has been the employer's practice hitherto and has become established as an implied term.

The statutory formula is based on age, length of service and weekly pay – but there are several exclusions and maximum amounts. Below is a summary.

Working back through the calculation and talking in general terms (see the Act for full details or the government's ready reckoner at www.dti.gov.uk/er/redundancy/ready.htm), the payment is based on multipliers of actual weekly pay, but up to a limit that is uprated in February each year (it is a maximum of £260 a week for 2003/04). Pay is gross, but excludes non-contractual payments, such as overtime and bonuses (unless the contract guarantees their payment).

Length of service is based on actual service, but up to a maximum of 20 years in all (producing a maximum payment of £7,800 for 2003/04), and is dependent on the employee have a minimum of two years' service by the "relevant date" (broadly speaking, equivalent to the date that the redundancy takes effect). In addition, only complete years of service need be counted.

Length of service is divided into three age-related bands. However, only ages between 18 years of age and the normal retirement date (or the state retirement age of 65 if earlier) are taken into account. (The upper age limit may be contrary to EC law, according to two recent tribunal rulings[18].)

Half a week's pay is payable for each year of employment in which the employee was aged between 18 and 21 years. This rises to one week's pay for each year in which the employee was aged between 22 and 40 years. And rises again to one-and-a-half weeks' pay for each year in which the employee was aged between 41 and normal retirement (as above). In addition to the statutory payment, employers are obliged to provide a period of paid notice or pay in lieu.

4. Redundancy pay

In practice, many employers offer more generous terms. Based on feedback obtained by IRS, employers' practice generally involves the following:

● covering all redundant employees, without the minimum two years' service required under the minimum statutory scheme;

● basing payments on actual weekly pay unrestricted by the statutory ceiling amount; and

● multiplying each week's pay by total service, without the maximum number of years or age limits set down in the statutory fallback scheme.

However, on the other hand:

● few employers make pro-rata payments to take account of incomplete years of service; and

● few go much beyond the legal definition of a week's pay, which excludes non-contractual payments such as overtime and bonuses that are not guaranteed under the contract of employment.

In terms of the prevalence of enhanced redundancy pay, research by the CIPD[19] has found that three-quarters (73%) of the employers in its survey follow this practice.

Private healthcare provider **BUPA Hospitals** provides 2.5 weeks' pay for each year of service and, unusually, makes pro-rata payments for incomplete years. Bookclub company **BCA** offers three weeks' pay for each year of service when employees are under 41 years of age, rising to four weeks for each year they are over 41 years old. The total payment is limited to 80 weeks' pay. Car manufacturer **Vauxhall Motors** offered 25 months' pay, or 19 months plus a car, to employees aged under 50 years as part of its plans for the closure of its Luton car plant. Older employees were offered a lump sum[20].

Some organisations simply offer one or more top-up payments. For example, manufacturing company **Senior Flexonics** provides £100 per year of service in addition to the statutory payments and notice pay.

However, local authorities' redundancy payments are limited by law (the Local Government (Early Termination of Employment) (Discretionary Compensation) (England and Wales) Regulations 2000), as amended.

Outplacement support

The arguments that convince many employers to provide enhanced redundancy payments are equally relevant to the provision of other assistance to staff losing their jobs.

● Employees who lose their jobs often suffer a blow to their self-esteem at a time when they need it most – high levels of motivation and self-confidence are required to actively search for new jobs. Trained outplacement advisers can provide the support, training and practical assistance that can help restore morale. Even the knowledge that the support is being funded by the employer can show the individual that there is a continuing commitment to them.

● In addition, many redundant employees have lost (or never acquired) the skills involved in conducting effective job searches – using networks of contacts, preparing convincing CVs and application forms, approaching potential employers, being impressive at interview, and so on. Outplacement support offers training and assistance in these areas, as well as giving employees access to resources, such as directories of employers and lists of vacancies.

● More broadly, employees who lose their jobs often wish to "take stock" of their careers and interests, and outplacement advisers can provide career counselling, information on self-employment and on managing personal finances.

Such assistance often requires expert knowledge and skills, and does not come cheap. Employers therefore usually assemble a package of support based on selecting some of the above elements, rather than all of them, or, instead, may involve the jobcentre network which provides some basic forms of support at no cost.

Overall, around half of all employers making employees redundant offer some form of outplacement support, according to the CIPD research mentioned earlier. Specifically, half (49.7%) offer some form of one-to-one counselling, and just over four in 10 (44.1%) retain a specialist outplacement company to provide some services.

Our own research among employers indicates, though, that the expense involved means that outplacement support is most often found among larger organisations, where around three-quarters provide it. Moreover, among employers generally providing outplacement support, some of them offer a two-tier service, with more personalised, in-depth and lengthier (and therefore more expensive) support being given to higher-paid staff, such as managers, with others being given access to a resource centre and more basic one-to-one provision.

Even where the cost of outplacement proves prohibitive, personnel and HR managers can do much to ease the trauma of redundancy. As well as ensuring that the process is handled professionally and sensitively (see above), they can make themselves available to individuals for confidential discussions. Acas recommends[21] that local employers should be contacted "with a view to canvassing for any vacancies which may be offered to the redundant employees". Information can be obtained from experts, internal and external, about the implications of redundancy for income tax, pensions and state benefits, and passed on to employees. Independent financial advisers could be brought in to offer advice on investing redundancy payments and other financial matters. And personnel and HR specialists can offer their own expertise in such areas as completing application forms, compiling CVs and tracking down vacancies.

Case study E. BP

At the Grangemouth site of BP, which is involved in refining, petrochemicals and oil and gas processing, a restructuring was announced that involved the loss of around a quarter of the site's workforce. The company offered the same redundancy payments to those taking voluntary redundancy and those being made compulsory redundant: one month's pay for each year of continuous service to a maximum of 24 months. This limit was increased to 27 months where the individual had no immediate pension. Employees aged 50 and above could draw an immediate pension. Its outplacement support involved using an off-site resource centre run by a specialist outplacement company.

Employees were given paid time off to use the centre, where they could look for new jobs, be given training in interview techniques and receive assistance in drafting a CV or completing application forms. Local employers were invited to hold recruitment fairs at the Grangemouth site. Survivors were offered a range of support, and were also informed of the outcome of their former colleagues' efforts to find new jobs. After the first six to eight months, around 80% had been successful.

Case study F. The New Millennium Experience Company

The London Dome, run by New Millennium Experience Company, faced closure after all efforts to find a new owner had failed. The company organised a package of outplacement support called "New Horizons" for employees that was run while the Dome was still in operation. The support was provided in two overlapping tracks. Employees were offered training in relevant job-search skills: two-hour sessions called "power hours" that covered such areas as marketing oneself and compiling an effective CV. In addition, employers with vacancies to fill were encouraged to visit the Dome and meet employees. Employers that had sponsored the Dome were given particular attention, and were invited to attend special "sponsor days" at the Dome. Seven sponsors, including Marks & Spencer, Tesco, Boots and McDonalds, visited the site and more than 400 employees attended each of the days. In addition, a careers fair was subsequently organised on site which many major employers attended. Local employers were asked to arrange open days, where Dome employees could visit their premises. A resource centre at the Dome site provided ongoing support to employees in finding new jobs, and included a full-time careers adviser provided by the local economic-development partnership, as well as staff from the jobcentre network. Advisers at the centre offered individual advice to employees on job opportunities and social security benefits.

Business transfers

The pace of change in organisational life means that many personnel and HR specialists will be involved during their careers in one or more acquisitions, takeovers, mergers or business transfers. These are some of the most difficult and complex situations that a personnel or HR manager will face. In addition to the legal complications involved, these changes in business control are usually accompanied by internal reorganisations, redeployments and redundancies that produce their own particular challenges.

Research by the CIPD among personnel and HR specialists who have been involved in a merger or acquisition shows that their role is crucial in contributing to the success of the transaction. Communication and training issues are often vital to the successful integration of groups of employees involved in mergers and acquisitions. Yet a significant minority of managers lacks a good understanding of these and other personnel management issues, while almost half of companies' external advisers are considered to have little or no such knowledge[22].

Feedback from personnel and HR specialists involved in the CIPD research highlights three related issues that they have found will lead to a failed merger or acquisition:
- failure to continue to focus on personnel issues after the merger or acquisition has taken place, leading to a lack of integration between the groups of employees;
- insufficient attention being paid to personnel management issues, including cultural clashes; and
- failures on the part of senior managers, which are attributed to lack of experience among those leading the transaction or basic lack of competence.

Outsourcing, where an organisation brings in an external supplier to provide one or more of the functions it formerly operated itself, has been investigated in depth by researchers at the Cranfield School of Management[23]. Based on feedback from almost 750 employers, they found that the most likely outcome for employees affected by an outsourcing exercise is a transfer to the supplier. Redeployment internally was almost as likely, although one in five of the employers reported that at least some of the affected employees had been made redundant.

Outsourcing and other business transactions raise many of the same people management issues that occur during redundancy exercises. In particular, there is the same danger of survivor syndrome, where the transaction leads to demoralisation among those not directly affected and the resignation of many valuable members of staff. Combating survivor syndrome and ensuring that the transaction is a success require the input of personnel and HR specialists. Effective communication and involvement processes should be developed with personnel and HR specialists' advice, and line managers need information, guidance and training to ensure their employees are kept informed, motivated and committed. In particular, employees are as likely to experience, and demonstrate, strong emotions as on the occasions when they are affected by redundancies, and line managers need the skills to manage emotions effectively and help employees deal with them.

Employees affected by a business transfer are given special treatment under the extremely complex, provisions of the Transfer of Undertakings

(Protection of Employment) Regulations 1981 – usually known as TUPE. Currently, the government is consulting about proposed changes to TUPE that will increase the protection afforded to affected employees. It has already introduced a code of conduct that reduces the freedom of manoeuvre of private sector firms taking over public sector services to alter terms and conditions of both existing staff and new recruits, and will embody the code in forthcoming legislation.

In addition, a recent European Court of Justice judgment has raised the possibility that TUPE transfers may now involve the transfer of certain employees' pension rights where these are not strictly-speaking classed as "old-age benefits"[24]. The government's forthcoming changes to TUPE are expected to clarify this issue.

The government's changes to TUPE are expected to be implemented in spring 2004, and are likely to:
● extend the coverage of the Regulations – possibly where a business service changes hands without it being an identifiable business entity;
● clarify (and possibly reduce) employers' ability to dismiss employees as a result of a transfer or change their terms and conditions;
● require the existing employer to inform the new employer about the nature of the employment liabilities they will be incurring; and
● include greater flexibility for transfers relating to insolvent businesses.

Case study G. United Utilities

United Utilities was the successful bidder for an outsourcing contract with Western Power Distribution for the operations and maintenance functions of Welsh Water, but would need to achieve cost savings to make the contract profitable. The company involved its personnel specialists in the bidding work, who identified that it could not reduce wage levels because the transfer would be covered by TUPE. They also recommended that it should try to avoid compulsory redundancies, because the company wanted to maintain a partnership approach with its trade unions. Instead, they decided to investigate the most cost-effective conditions for achieving some 200 job losses through a voluntary redundancy package. The payments had to be sufficiently large to attract sufficient volunteers, but also had to be capable of being recouped before the contract expired four years later. Personnel specialists created models of the likely cost of the package, using various scenarios of volunteers' lengths of service.

Once it had won the contract, the company arranged roadshows to meet the transferred employees. These aimed to reduce the apprehension that had built up during the 18-month run up to the transfer, and convey three key messages:

● the new employer was aiming for a long-term contract, and would not try to change all aspects of their employment within the first four years;
● employees' pensions were safe; and
● there would be no compulsory redundancies.

In addition, though, it did not hide the fact that tough decisions were required, including job losses and changes to terms and conditions.

Two days after it won the contract, United Utilities met trade union representatives to discuss its restructuring plans in more detail. The representatives provided a further communication channel between the company and the transferred employees – mainly through branch meetings and newsletters – but, as well as roadshows, the company also sent out its own newsletters.

After two months of close involvement between the new company's managers and the transferred employees and line managers, United Utilities was able to identify areas were savings could be made. Creating a single procurement system would realise a 20% saving through greater economies of scale, but 198 job losses were also identified. Its personnel specialists recommended that the redundancy package of employees' former employer, Hyder, should be offered. This provided up to 12 months' pay, depending on age and length of service. In addition, employees affected by job losses were also offered redeployment.

Personnel specialists at United Utilities believe its experience of winning and successfully managing the outsourcing contract highlights three key issues:
● the importance of developing a sound financial model, particularly in respect of staffing costs and redundancy-related payments;
● an appreciation of cultural and national differences; and
● an awareness of the political dimension to many transfers.

Information and consultation under TUPE

Many types of business transfers are covered by TUPE, both as defined in the Regulations and subsequently developed by a significant number of tribunal and court rulings. Broadly, TUPE covers the sale or purchase of all or part of a business (except those that are achieved solely through a share transfer), and often covers outsourcing (contracting out) of one or more functions by an organisation – provided the function(s) meet the criteria of being an "economic entity". Where employees are covered by TUPE, they and their contracts of employment are deemed to be transferred along with the business or function.

Where a trade union is not recognised: Employers that do not recognise an independent trade union must inform and consult other employee representatives. The representatives must be informed and consulted about proposed transfers, regardless of the size of the undertaking (that is, even if only one person is affected). The employer can choose between existing staff representatives (such as those appointed to participate in a staff council) or organise an election of representatives specifically for the purposes of consultations about the transfer.

The procedure for appointing employee representatives is the same in both redundancy and business transfer consultations, and is described in detail by Acas in its *Representation at work* guide[25]. In summary, representatives must be elected in a fair way and in sufficient numbers that they are able to represent the interests of all those affected, and candidates must be "affected" employees. Everyone who is entitled must be able to stand for election and vote in the ballot. Voting must be via a secret ballot, and the votes must be counted accurately. (Where employees fail to elect representatives, the employer is then required to provide relevant information about the redundancies/business transfer to each person directly.)

With union representatives: Where an employer recognises an independent trade union, TUPE requires that union representatives must be informed and consulted about proposed transfers, regardless of the size of the undertaking being transferred (that is, even if only one person is affected).

In both types of consultation, employees, those standing for election and those who are elected are protected against victimisation and dismissal for reasons connected with their participation. Representatives must be given access to the employees they represent, to reasonable amounts of paid time off for their duties and to reasonable facilities to perform their duties.

Information and consultation: TUPE requires the employer (some information and consultation requirements apply to the transferring employer and some to the new employer) to provide information to the representatives "long enough before a relevant transfer" for consultations to take place on matters set out in the Regulations. This information includes the reasons for the transfer and its likely date, and the implications of the transfer (including its impact on contracts of employment, pay and benefits).

The consultations must be conducted in good faith ("with a view to seeking agreement"), and the employer is expected to consider and respond to any arguments and proposals put forward by the representatives. Unlike redundancy consultation, there is no minimum consultation period set down concerning transfers of undertakings, and tribunals will consider the facts of a case before it. In addition, consultations are only required concerning issues relating to the impact of the transfer on the affected employees.

5. Legal checklist

● Redundancy situations are covered by the legal provisions of two statutes – Employment Rights Act 1996 and the Trade Union and Labour Relations (Consolidation) Act 1992.

● Employers are required to inform and consult employee representatives where 20 or more redundancies are planned to take place in an establishment within a 90-day period – Trade Union and Labour Relations (Consolidation) Act 1992 (as amended).

● Individual consultation is also required with employees likely to be made redundant, according to case law.

● Redundancy consultation is likely to be affected by the UK's future implementation of the EU Information and Consultation Directive, which may involve employers setting up permanent consultation machinery via employee representatives. It is likely that organisations with 150 or more employees will have to comply by March 2005, those with 100 or more employees by March 2007 and those with 50 or more employees by March 2008.

● Employers are also generally expected to make reasonable efforts, where practicable, to find suitable alternative employment for those affected by redundancies and, in particular, to adopt a fair basis for selecting individuals for redundancy, according to case law.

● Selection for redundancy should take account of the statutory protection afforded to a wide range of groups, including trade union membership, maternity-related grounds, or because individuals have asserted a statutory employment right. In addition, selection should not unfairly discriminate against protected groups, such as ethnic minorities and people with disabilities or for reasons of gender.

● The calculations for minimum redundancy payments are set out in the Employment Rights Act 1996; the amounts are uprated annually. Employers can generally provide more generous payments, although some parts of the public sector are limited in this regard – for example, under the Local Government (Early Termination of Employment) (Discretionary Compensation) (England and Wales) Regulations 2000), as amended.

● Business transfers, acquisitions, mergers and takeovers that have consequences for employees are covered by various laws and statutes, including the common law relating to contracts of employment, and the dismissal and redundancy provisions of the Employment Rights Act 1996.

● Employees affected by a business transfer are given special treatment under the Transfer of Undertakings (Protection of Employment) Regulations 1981.

● TUPE includes provisions for informing and consulting employee representatives over a proposed transfer (*see this chapter for more information*).

● The Transfer of Undertakings (Protection of Employment) Regulations 1981
are expected to be extended and revised by spring 2004.

14. Appendix

The methods that IRS uses to obtain its findings about best practice

This handbook is based on IRS's unique programme of research among employers in the UK. For more than 30 years, our teams of researchers have maintained contact with specialists in personnel, HR, recruitment, pay, equality, health, pensions and legal functions, and analysed their experience of effective practice across the whole area of the management of people in organisations.

We fund and manage this research programme ourselves, and are independent of government, consultancies and associations set up to further the interests of employers and trade unions.

The feedback from our contacts is obtained in many different ways, including postal questionnaires, telephone interviews, site visits, face-to-face interviews, the examination of original documentation, secondary sources and convening focus groups.

Almost all the information we obtain about effective practice is published in a wide range of IRS publications. This handbook brings this invaluable feedback together in one place, and reinterprets and updates it as necessary for today's increasingly busy personnel and HR professional – particularly those who do not have the support of large departments of staff and extensive resources.

Each research project conducted by IRS is led by staff working on the relevant IRS journal, all of whom are subject experts skilled in research methodologies. The timeframe for the information used in this handbook has been shaped carefully to ensure that it covers current practice. In most subjects, the information is no more than two years old; in some selected areas where practice is less fluid, the feedback may be up to three years old. This timespan draws on research led by, and often involving, the staff of these IRS journals:

● **Employee Development Bulletin:** Neil Rankin, Noelle Murphy, together with contributions from Sue Milsome, Debbie Sanders, Rachel Suff and Louis Wustemann;

● **IRS Employment Trends:** Mark Crail, Philip Pearson, David Shepherd, Charles Cotton, Sheila Davie, Martin Edwards, Janet Egan, Kate Godwin, Ben Louvre, Peter McGeer, Rachael McIlroy;

● **Pay and Benefits Bulletin:** David Carr, Jeremy Baugh, Phil Barnett, Louise Butcher, Charles Cotton, Sheila Davie, Adam Geldman, Kate Godwin, Bridget Henderson, Ben Louvre, Rachael McIlroy, Fiona O'Brien-Smith, Philip Pearson, Rachel Suff.

● **Industrial Relations Law Bulletin:** Akosua Buckman, Penny Christie, David Fox, Roger Walden, Elsa Booth-West, Ruth Godden, Mike Haran, Christina James, Douglas Leach, Karen Mepham, Vanessa Nicholls.

● **Equal Opportunities Review:** Sue Johnstone, Kate Godwin, Michael Rubinstein, Carol Foster, Sarah Podro, Charlotte Wolff.

● **Employee Health Bulletin/Health, Safety and Wellbeing/ Attendance and Absence:** Sarah Silcox; Philip Pearson.

● **Competency & Emotional Intelligence:** Neil Rankin, Katherine Adams, together with contributions from John Warner.

● **Occupational Pensions:** Colin Sherwood, Janice McNair, Charlotte Wolff.

For details of these and the other journals, handbooks and services published by IRS, please contact Customer Services, tel: 020 8662 2000; email: customer.services@lexisnexis.co.uk; or visit our website: www.irsonline.co.uk.

Non-IRS sources, chapter by chapter

1. Filling your vacancies

1. "Employers unlikely to value greatly a gap in experience", *Financial Times*, 7–8 April 2001.

2. *The graduate recruitment manual*, Rajvinder Kandola et al, Gower, 2001.

3. *Recruitment and retention*, Chartered Institute of Personnel and Development, 2002, www.cipd.co.uk.

4. *Recruitment and induction*, Acas, 2003, www.acas.org.uk.

5. *Recruitment and retention*, Chartered Institute of Personnel and Development, 2002, www.cipd.co.uk.

6. *Management competency frameworks*, Adrian Furnham, Careers Research Forum, 2000; and "Issues and pitfalls in using managerial competencies", Adrian Furnham in *The IRS handbook on competencies: law and practice*, edited by Neil Rankin, IRS, 2001.

7. *Recruitment and retention*, Chartered Institute of Personnel and Development, 2002, www.cipd.co.uk.

8. *Central London jobs and skills: a bi-annual review*, Focus Central London Training and Enterprise Council, 2000.

9. *BRAD: the monthly guide to advertising media*, May 2001.

10. "Recruiting and advertising", Karel De Witte, chapter 2.4 in *Assessment and selection in organizations*, edited by Peter Herriot, John Wiley, 1989.

11. "Employers stung as staff surf for jobs at work", Rupert Jones, the *Guardian*, 27 January 2001.

12. *Employee resourcing*, Stephen Taylor, Institute of Personnel and Development, 1998.

13. *Successful recruitment and selection*, Margaret Dale, Kogan Page, 1995.

14. "Psychological dimensions in recruitment-advertising design", Jonathan Hill, *Selection & Development Review*, October 1994, pp.4–6.

15. *Skill needs and recruitment practices in central London: literature review*, Spilsbury Research for Focus Central London Training and Enterprise Council, 2000.

16. Letter in *Marketing Week*, 5 October 2000, p.42.

17. "Pulling power", *Employee Benefits*, 9 February 2001, p.33.

18. *Employee resourcing*, Stephen Taylor, Institute of Personnel and Development, 1998.

19. *Skill needs and recruitment practices in central London*, Mark Spilsbury and Karen Lane, Focus Central London Training and Enterprise Council, 2000.

20. Wickland Westcott Bulletin, Autumn 1998.

21. Top jobs recruitment advertising survey, PricewaterhouseCoopers, 1999.

22. "Recruiting and advertising", Karel De Witte, chapter 2.4 in *Assessment and selection in organizations*, edited by Peter Herriot, John Wiley, 1989.

23. "Recruitment", Quick Facts series, Chartered Institute of Personnel and Development, 2000, www.cipd.co.uk

24. "Creative thinking pays dividends", *Personnel Today*, 9 January 2001.

25. *The IPD guide on recruitment*, Institute of Personnel and Development, 1996.

26. *Sex equality and advertising*, Equal Opportunities Commission, 2000.

27. *Job advertisements and the Race Relations Act*, Commission for Racial Equality, 1994.

28. Removing Sex Bias from Recruitment and Selection: a Code of Practice, Equal Opportunities Commission for Northern Ireland, 1995, www.equalityni.org.

29. Code of Practice on Age Diversity in Employment, revised edition, Department for Work and Pensions, undated, tel: 0845 7330 360, www.agepositive.gov.uk.

30. *Employing disabled people: a good-practice guide for managers and employers*, Disability Rights Commission, undated, tel: 0845 7622 633, www.drc-gb.org.

31. "Dilemmas in the management of temporary work agency staff", Kevin Ward et al, *Human Resource Management Journal*, vol. 11 no.4, 2001.

32. Proposal for a Directive of the European Parliament and of the Council on working conditions for temporary agency workers: regulatory impact assessment, Department of Trade and Industry, July 2002, www.dti.gov.uk.

33. *Recruitment agencies in the UK*, Ulrike Hotopp, Department of Trade and Industry, 2001, www.dti.gov.uk.

34. *Employee resourcing*, Stephen Taylor, Institute of Personnel and Development, 1998.

35. *Brief encounters: getting the best from temporary nursing staff*, Audit Commission, 2001, www.audit-commission.gov.uk.

36. Snapshot survey, Russam GMS, 2003, www.russam.co.uk.

37. Revision of the Regulations covering the private recruitment industry: regulatory impact assessment, Department of Trade and Industry, 2001, www.dti.gov.uk. The Revision of Regulations for the private recruitment industry: regulatory impact assessment of July 2002 draws on the same research as used in 2001; this is also available at www.dti.gov.uk.

38. "Make agencies work for you", *Personnel Today*, 20 February 2001, www.personnel today.com.

39. "Partnerships and the private recruitment industry", Ian Druker and Celia Stanworth, *Human Resource Management Journal*, vol. 11 no.2, 2001.

40. Available from www.cre.gov.uk.

41. *Being positive about age diversity at work: a practical guide for business*, Department for Work and Pensions, 2002

42. *Recruitment and retention*, Chartered Institute of Personnel and Development, 2002, www.cipd.co.uk.

43. *Core personnel and development*, Mick Marchington and Adrian Wilkinson, Institute of Personnel and Development, 1996.

44. *Recruitment and retention*, Chartered Institute of Personnel and Development, 2002, www.cipd.co.uk.

45. "Referral bonus scheme nets high-calibre staff", Ben Willmott, *Personnel Today*, 25 June 2002.

46. "Face value", Roisin Woolnough, *Personnel Today*, 15 April 2003.

47. *Skill shortages, vacancies and local unemployment: a synthesis of the exploring local areas, skills and unemployment analyses*, Terence Hogarth et al, Institute for Employment Research, 2003, www.dfes.gov.uk/research/.

48. "Centrica calls on long-term unemployed to fill skills gap", Quentin Reade, *Personnel Today*, 21 January 2003.

49. "Ambulance staff gain traffic-charge grants", Ben Willmott, *Personnel Today*, 11 February 2003.

50. "Getting a foot on the housing ladder", *Personnel Today*, 30 April 2002.

51. "Getting a foot on the housing ladder", *Personnel Today*, 30 April 2002.

52. *Policy guidelines: market supplements*, e-reward, 2003, www.e-reward.co.uk.

53. Statistics quoted in *Employer-supported childcare: EOC response to the Inland Revenue consultation*, May 2002, Equal Opportunities Commission, 2003.

54. *Skill shortages, vacancies and local unemployment: a synthesis of the exploring local areas, skills and unemployment analyses*, Terence Hogarth et al, Institute for Employment Research, 2003, www.dfes.gov.uk/research/.

2. Cost-effective selection

1. *Recruitment and retention*, Chartered Institute of Personnel and Development, 2002, www.cipd.co.uk.

2. Sources: *Recruitment and selection: a competency approach*, Gareth Roberts, Institute of Personnel and Development, 1997; *Employee resourcing*, Stephen Taylor, Institute of Personnel and Development, 1998; "Validity and fairness of some alternative employee selection procedures", Richard R Reilly and Georgia T Chao, *Personnel Psychology*, vol. 35, 1982, pp.1–62. The values given in a 1989 booklet from the British Psychological Society, *Psychological testing: guidance for the user*, tend to be lower than those shown in chapter 2.

3. *Recruitment and retention*, Chartered Institute of Personnel and Development, 2002, www.cipd.co.uk.

4. *The mirror image*, Society of Personnel Officers in Local Government, www.socpo.org.uk.

5. Free from www.eoc.org.uk.

6. *Recruitment and induction*, Acas, 2003, www.acas.gov.uk.

7. "Can interviewers learn from past mistakes?", Clive Fletcher, *People Management*, 9 January 1997.

8. "Recruitment", Quick Facts series, Chartered Institute of Personnel and Development, 2002, www.cipd.co.uk.

9. Code of Practice for the Elimination of Racial Discrimination and the Promotion of Equality of Opportunity in Employment, Commission for Racial Equality, www.cre.gov.uk.

10. *Model guidance: notes to interviewers*, Equal Opportunities Commission, www.eoc. org.uk.

11. *Recruitment and retention*, Chartered Institute of Personnel and Development, 2002, www.cipd.co.uk.

12. *Recruitment and retention*, Chartered Institute of Personnel and Development, 2002, www.cipd.co.uk.

13. *Psychological testing: a user's guide*, British Psychological Society, undated, www.psychtesting. org.uk.

14. Available from the Equal Opportunities Commission, tel: 0845 601 5901, www.eoc.org.uk.

15. Available from the Commission for Racial Equality, tel: 0870 240 3697, www.cre.gov.uk.

16. Available from the Disability Rights Commission, tel: 0845 762 2633, www.drc-gb.org.

17. *Testing people with disabilities: guidelines for test users*, ASE, 1998, available free from: www.ase-solutions.co.uk.

18. *Recruitment and retention*, Chartered Institute of Personnel and Development, 2002, www.cipd.co.uk.

19. *Development and assessment centres: identifying and assessing competence*, Charles Woodruffe, Chartered Institute of Personnel and Development, 3rd ed, 2000, www.cipd.co.uk.

20. "Centres of excellence?", Paul Iles, British Journal of Management, vol. 3, 1992, pp.79–90.

21. *Recruitment survey report*, 2001, Chartered Institute of Personnel and Development, www.cipd.co.uk.

22. "It pays to be aware of the subtle inequalities", Clive Fletcher, *People Management*, 7 November 1996.

23. *Redefining the fast stream*, Cabinet Office, 2001, www.civil-service.gov.uk.

24. "Assess your staff with a modern business plan", Widget Finn, *The Times*, 18 January 2001.

25. *Assessing management skills*, Margaret Dale and Paul Iles, Kogan Page, 1992.

26. *Recruitment and retention*, Chartered Institute of Personnel and Development, 2002, www.cipd.co.uk.

27. *Recruitment and induction*, Acas, 2003, www.acas.gov.uk.

28. *Employee resourcing*, Stephen Taylor, Institute of Personnel and Development, 1998.

29. *The validity of graphology in personnel assessment*, Psychological Testing Centre, British Psychological Society, 2002, www.psychtesting.org.uk.

30. Quoted in "The impact of personnel selection procedures on candidates", Paul Iles and Ivan Robertson, in *Assessment and selection in organizations*, edited by Peter Herriot, Wiley, 1989.

31. "Retention of personnel and other related records", *Quick Facts* series, Chartered Institute of Personnel and Development, 2002, www.cipd.co.uk.

3. Using electronic media effectively

1. *Business in the information age: international benchmarking study 2002*, Department of Trade and Industry, 2002, www.dti.gov.uk.

2. *Internet and email policies*, Acas, 2002, www.acas.org.uk. The national helpline number for Acas is 08457 474 747. Its helpline receives some three-quarters of a million calls a year.

3. *Internet and email policies*, Acas, 2002, www.acas.org.uk.

4. *Recruitment and retention*, Chartered Institute of Personnel and Development, 2002, www.cipd.co.uk.

5. *Internet access: households and individuals*, Office for National Statistics, December 2002, www.ons.gov.uk.

6. *A 10-point guide to creating an online recruitment presence*, Internet Recruiters' Network and Association, www.irna-uk.com.

7. "Online candidates 'more likely to make shortlist'", *Personnel Today*, 4 June 2002.

8. "Swansea Council ops for online recruitment", *Personnel Today*, 23 July 2002.

9. "Bargain hunt", Roger Trapp, *People Management*, 26 December 2002.

10. "Surrey goes online to attract new recruits", *Personnel Today*, 3 December 2002.

11. "Health trusts take to web to fill nursing vacancies", Ben Willmott, *Personnel Today*, 20 August 2002.

12. "B&Q starts DIY web recruitment scheme", Ross Wigham, *Personnel Today*, 30 July 2002.

13. *Training and development 2002*, Chartered Institute of Personnel and Development, 2002, www.cipd.co.uk.

14. *E-learning: the learning curve*, Chartered Institute of Personnel and Development, 2003, www.cipd.co.uk.

4. Checking candidates' backgrounds

1. *Spring v Guardian Assurance plc and others* [1994] IRLR 460.

2. *Chief Constable of West Yorkshire Police v Khan* [2001] IRLR 830.

3. *Coote v Granada Hospitality (No.2)* [1999] IRLR 452.

4. *Adekeye v Post Office (No 2)* [1997] IRLR 105.

5. *Jones v 3M Healthcare Ltd and others* 11.12.2001 EAT/0714/00.

6. *Spring v Guardian Assurance plc and others* [1994] IRLR 460.

7. *Cox v Sun Alliance Life Ltd* [2001] IRLR 448.

8. *Bartholomew v London Borough of Hackney* [1999] IRLR 246.

9. *Managing dismissals*, Daniel Barnett, Tolley in association with IRS, 2002.

10. *TSB Bank plc v Harris* [2000] IRLR 157.

11. *Wishart v NACAB* [1990] IRLR 393.

12. "Job sites on the line if law gets go-ahead", Ben Willmott, *Personnel Today*, 15 October 2002.

13. *The Data Protection Act: legal guidance, 2001*, and the *Employment practices data protection Code, part one, 2002*; both published by the Office of the Information Commissioner, www.dataprotection.gov.uk.

14. Code of Practice and explanatory guide for registered persons and other recipients of disclosure information, Criminal Records Bureau, www.crb.gov.uk.

15. *Recruitment and retention,* Chartered Institute of Personnel and Development, 2002, www.cipd.co.uk.

16. "Are references worth the paper they're written on?", Nick Cowan and Rowena Cowan, *Personnel Management,* December 1989, pp.38–42.

17. "References", *Quick Facts* series, Chartered Institute of Personnel and Development, 2001, www.cipd.co.uk.

18. "References", *Quick Facts* series, Chartered Institute of Personnel and Development, 2001, www.cipd.co.uk.

19. "Validity and fairness of some alternative employee selection procedures", R R Reilly and G T Chao, *Personnel Psychology,* vol. 33, 1982, pp.1–62.

20. "Validity and utility of alternative predictors of job performance", J E Hunter and R F Hunter, *Psychological Bulletin,* vol. 96, 1984, pp.72–98.

21. "Reference reports", Paul Dobson, in *Assessment and selection in organizations,* edited by Peter Herriot, John Wiley, 1989.

22. "Are references worth the paper they're written on?", Nick Cowan and Rowena Cowan, *Personnel Management,* December 1989, pp.38–42.

23. www.riskadvisory.net.

24. *Recruiting safely,* Nacro for the Forum on the Employment of Ex-offenders in Care Settings, 2001.

25. *Deception in selection,* Liz Walley and Mike Smith, Wiley, 1998.

26. "Employing people with criminal records", *Quick Facts* series, Chartered Institute of Personnel and Development, 2002, www.cipd.co.uk.

27. "Employing people with criminal records: risk assessment", *Quick Facts* series, Chartered Institute of Personnel and Development, 2002, www.cipd.co.uk.

28. "Bus firm scours jails for drivers", *People Management,* 7 February 2002; "Unlocking potential", Rima Manocha, People Management, 26 September 2002.

29. *Recruiting and employing offenders,* Joseph Rowntree Foundation, 2001, www.jrf.org.uk.

30. *Employing people with conviction: a good-practice guide on the employment of people with criminal records,* Chartered Institute of Personnel and Development, 2001, www.cipd.co.uk.

31. "Minimum disclosure period for ex-offenders cut to two years", Paul Nelson, *Personnel Today,* 23 May 2002, based on information supplied by the manager at the Home Office who is in charge of the review of the Act.

32. Code of Practice and explanatory guide for registered persons and other recipients of disclosure information, Criminal Records Bureau, www.crb.gov.uk.

33. *Barriers to employment for offenders and ex-offenders,* research report 155, Department for Work and Pensions, 2001, www.dwp.gov.uk.

34. *Secure borders, safe haven: integration with diversity in modern Britain,* Stationery Office, 2002, www.official-documents.co.uk.

35. *Knowledge migrants: the motivations and experiences of professionals in the UK on work permits,* Home Office, 2002, www.dti.gov.uk/migrantworkers.

36. *Migrants in the UK, their characteristics and labour market outcomes and impacts,* Home Office, 2002, www.homeoffice.gov.uk.

37. *Recruitment and retention,* Chartered Institute of Personnel and Development, 2002, www.cipd.co.uk.

38. Draft Directive on conditions of entry and residence of third-country nationals for the purpose of paid employment and self-employed economic activities, European Commission, www.europa.eu.int.

39. Immigration and Asylum Act 1999 – Section 22: Code of Practice for all employers on the avoidance of race discrimination in recruitment practice while seeking to prevent illegal working, Home Office, 2001, www.ind.homeoffice.gov.uk/employers.

40. Code of Practice for the elimination of racial discrimination and the promotion of equality of opportunity in employment, Commission for Racial Equality, 1984, www.cre.gov.uk.

41. *Employing overseas workers,* Chartered Institute of Personnel and Development, 2002, www.cipd.co.uk.

5. Induction, training and development

1. *Recruitment and induction,* Acas, 2003, www.acas.gov.uk.

2. "Forestalling the induction crisis", Stephen Taylor, *IRS Employment Review,* no.771, 7 March 2003.

3. *Learning and training at work,* Department for Education and Skills, 2003, www.dfes.gov.uk.

4. *Training and development 2002,* Chartered Institute of Personnel and Development, 2002, www.cipd.co.uk.

5. *Training and development 2002,* Chartered Institute of Personnel and Development, 2002, www.cipd.co.uk.

6. *Training trends 2002,* Capita Learning and Development, 2002.

7. "Everything you need to know about training, *IRS Employment Review,* no.749, 15 April 2002.

8. *People Skills Scoreboard for local government 2002,* Employers' Organisation, 2003, www.lg-employers.gov.uk.

9. *2001–2002 People Skills Scoreboard for the engineering industry,* EMTA/EEF, 2002.

10. *People Skills Scoreboard 2001*, Construction Industry Training Board, 2001, www.citb.co.uk.

11. *People Skills Scoreboard: chemical industry*, Department of Trade and Industry, 2001.

12. *Skills for tomorrow's media*, Skillset, 2001.

13. *Property services People Skills Scoreboard 2002*, Property Services National Training Organisation, 2002, www.psnto.org.

14. *The hopeless, hapless and helpless manager: further explorations in the psychology of managerial incompetence*, Adrian Furnham, Whurr, 2000.

15. "How to get managers' support for learning", Ian Cunningham, Topics for Trainers, Chartered Institute of Personnel and Development, 2001, www.cipd.co.uk.

16. *Development and assessment centres*, Charles Woodruffe, Institute of Personnel and Development, 3rd ed, 2000.

17. Summary of findings from piloting and market testing, Investors in People UK, 2000.

18. "Investors in People", *Quick Facts series*, Chartered Institute of Personnel and Development, 2003, www.cipd.co.uk.

19. *Learning and training at work*, Department for Education and Skills, 2003, www.dfes.gov.uk.

20. *Evaluating training programs: the four levels*, Donald Kirkpatrick, 1994.

21. *Kirkpatrick and beyond*, P Tamkin, J Yarnall and M Kerrin, Institute for Employment Studies, 2002, www.employment-studies.co.uk.

22. *Cost-effective training: a manager's guide*, Tony Newby, Kogan Page, 1992, www.kogan-page.co.uk.

23. "Survey shows it's still early days for union learning reps", *Bargaining Report*, no.235, February 2003.

24. *The quiet revolution: the rise of the union learning representative*, Campaign for Learning and Trades Union Congress, 2001.

25. *Learning and training at work*, Department for Education and Skills, 2003, www.dfes.gov.uk.

26. Press release, Engineering Employers' Federation, 25 February 2003.

27. Press release, Department for Education and Skills, 12 March 2003.

28. *Evaluation of the Union Learning Fund year 4*, Neil Shaw et al, Department for Education and Skills, 2002.

29. Individual Learning Accounts, House of Commons Education and Skills Committee, third report of session 2001/02, HMSO, 2002.

30. *Who learns at work?*, Chartered Institute of Personnel and Development, 2002, www.cipd.co.uk.

31. "On-the-job training", *Quick Facts* series, Chartered Institute of Personnel and Development, 2002, www.cipd.co.uk.

32. *Training and development 2001*, Chartered Institute of Personnel and Development, 2001, www.cipd.co.uk.

33. "Good for the soul", Carol Glover, *People Management*, 11 July 2002, www.peoplemanagement.co.uk.

34. *Learning and training at work*, Department for Education and Skills, 2003, www.dfes.gov.uk.

35. *Training and development 2002*, Chartered Institute of Personnel and Development, 2002, www.cipd.co.uk.

36. *Statistics of education: vocational qualifications in the UK,* Department for Education and Skills, 2000.

37. "Sports retailer nets training result", *Personnel Today*, 4 March 2003.

38. *New directions in management development*, Wendy Hirsh and Alison Carter, Institute for Employment Studies, 2002, www.employment-studies.co.uk.

6. Pay and benefits and other terms and conditions

1. *Job evaluation: an introduction*, Acas, 2003, free from www.acas.org.uk.

2. "What is happening to job evaluation today: a large-scale survey", e-research, no.7, January 2003, www.e-reward.co.uk.

3. "Measuring performance", Adrian Furnham, *Developing People*, Autumn 2002, p.8.

4. *Sex bias and performance-related pay*, Equal Opportunities Commission, 2003, free from www.eoc.org.uk.

5. *Pay systems*, Acas, 2001, www.acas.org.uk.

6. *Reward management*, Chartered Institute of Personnel and Development, 2003, www.cipd.co.uk.

7. *Reward management*, Chartered Institute of Personnel and Development, 2003, www.cipd.co.uk.

8. *Sixth annual employee attitudes survey*, MORI for Eden Brown, 2003, www.edenbrown.com.

9. Press release, Chartered Institute of Personnel and Development, 19 February 2002.

10. "Pensions – key issues for HR", Duncan Brown, *Impact*, October 2002.

11. *Twenty-sixth annual survey of occupational pension schemes*, National Association of Pension Funds, 2001.

12. *Pension plan design*, Watson Wyatt, 2001.

13. *Reward management*, Chartered Institute of Personnel and Development, 2003, www.cipd.co.uk.

7. Retaining the best staff

1. *Redundancy survey report*, Chartered Institute of Personnel and Development, 2002,

www. cipd.co.uk.

2. *Labour turnover*, Chartered Institute of Personnel and Development, 2002, available free, tel: 020 8971 9000, www.cipd.co.uk.

3. Press release, Employers' Forum on Age, 24 January 2002.

4. *Absence and labour turnover*, CBI with AXA PPP Healthcare, 2003, price £50 (£25 CBI members), tel: 020 7395 8071.

5. *National management salary survey*, Remuneration Economics with the Chartered Management Institute, 2002, tel: 020 8549 8726, www.celre.co.uk.

6. *Civil service statistics*, 2001, Cabinet Office, 2002, free from: www.civil-service.gov.uk/ statistics/css.htm.

7. *Nineteenth report on nursing staff, midwives and health visitors*, Review Body for Nursing Staff, Midwives, Health Visitors and Professions Allied to Medicine, the Stationery Office, 2001, www.doh.gov.uk.

8. *Absence and labour turnover*, CBI with AXA PPP Healthcare, 2003, price £50 (£25 CBI members), tel: 020 7395 8071.

9. *Labour turnover*, Chartered Institute of Personnel and Development, 2002, available free, tel: 020 8971 9000, www.cipd.co.uk.

10. "Toward a greater understanding of how dissatisfaction drives employee turnover", Peter Hom and Angelo Kinicki, *Academy of Management Journal*, vol. 44 no.5, 2001.

11. "Law firm's revamped HR policies save £2m", Quentin Reade, *Personnel Today*, 15 October 2002.

12. *Labour Force Survey*, Labour Market Statistics Helpline, tel: 020 7533 6094, basic queries are free, complex ones are charged for. Database access and/or bureau services from LFS Data Services, tel: 020 7533 5614 or Nomis, tel: 0191 374 2468, prices on application. Some findings relevant to staff retention are published irregularly in Labour Market Trends magazine. Some data is available free from: www.statistics.gov.uk and www.nomisweb.co.uk.

13. *The retention dilemma*, Hay Group, 2001, www.haygroup.co.uk.

14. *Career tracking, 2001: graduate workplace attitudes*, Chartered Institute of Personnel and Development, 2001, www.cipd.co.uk.

15. *What has been happening to job satisfaction in Britain?*, Andrew Oswald and Jonathan Gardner, 2001, www.andrewoswald.com.

16. *What has been happening to the quality of workers' lives in Britain?*, Jonathan Gardner and Andrew Oswald, 2001, www.andrewoswald.com.

17. "Sports retailer nets training result", *Personnel Today*, 4 March 2003.

18. *The employee retention handbook*, Stephen Taylor, Chartered Institute of Personnel and Development, 2002.

19. "Barclays banks on older staff". Zoë Roberts, *People Management*, 29 May 2003.

8. Employee involvement and representation

1. *Sharing the challenge ahead: informing and consulting with your workforce*, Involvement & Participation Association, 2001.

2. *Representation at work*, Acas guidance booklet, 2002, www.acas.org.uk.

3. Estimate by Professor Keith Sisson based on findings from the 1998 Workplace Employee Relations Survey, given to a 2002 conference on the EU Information and Consultation Directive organised by IRS and Warwick Business School.

4. "Understanding Europe", Richard Lister and James Davies, *Impact*, October 2002.

5. *Representation at work*, Acas guidance booklet, 2002, www.acas.org.uk.

6. Research shows vital role of union reps at work, press release, Trades Union Congress, 22 November 2002.

7. *Representation at work*, Acas guidance booklet, 2002, www.acas.org.uk.

8. Findings from research conducted by Professor William Brown as part of the Economic and Social Research Council's Future of Work project, 2001.

9. *Collective bargaining and workplace performance: an investigation using the Workplace Employee Relations Survey 1998*, Alex Bryson and David Wilkinson, Department of Trade and Industry and Policy Studies Institute, 2002.

10. *People management and development: human resource management at work*, Mick Marchington and Adrian Wilkinson, Chartered Institute of Personnel and Development, 2002.

11. *Labour Market Trends*, November 2002, www.statistics.gov.uk.

12. *Labour Market Trends*, July 2002, www.statistics.gov.uk.

13. Findings reported in "Senior managers try to resist union recognition", Ross Wigham, *Personnel Today*, 25 June 2002.

14. "Boosting membership before a deal", *Labour Research*, September 2000.

15. *Representation at work*, Acas guidance booklet, 2002, www.acas.org.uk.

16. Research shows vital role of union reps at work, press release, Trades Union Congress, 22 November 2002.

17. Further information on compulsory trade union recognition is available from the Central Arbitration Committee, tel: 020 7251 9747, www.cac.gov.uk; Acas has also issued guidance, tel: 08457 474 747, www.acas.org.uk.

18. *R v Central Arbitration Committee and another ex parte Kwik-Fit (GB) Ltd* [2002] IRLR 395.

19. *Fullarton Computer Industries Ltd v Central Arbitration Committee* [2001] IRLR 752.

20. *Towards industrial partnership, Involvement & Participation Association*, 1992, www.ipa-involve. com.

21. *Representation at work*, Acas guidance booklet, 2002, www.acas.org.uk.

22. "Partnership deal pays off for ETOL", *Personnel Today*, 5 February 2002.

23. *Consulting employees on health and safety: a guide to the law*, Health and Safety Commission, 1996, www.hse.gov.uk.

24. *Consulting employees on health and safety: a guide to the law*, Health and Safety Commission, 1996, www.hse.gov.uk.

25. *Workplace consultation on health and safety*, Institute for Employment Studies, published by the Health and Safety Executive, 2000, www.hse.gov.uk.

9. Equal opportunities and diversity

1. Quoted in "Age and employment", *Quick Facts* series, Chartered Institute of Personnel and Development, 2002, www.cipd.co.uk.

2. Code of Practice on Age Diversity in Employment, www.agepositive.gov.uk.

3. *A review of training in racism awareness and valuing cultural diversity*, Institute for Employment Studies, 2002, free from www.homeoffice.gov.uk/rds.

4. *Training in racism awareness and cultural diversity (a good-practice guide)*, Home Office, 2002, free from www.homeoffice.gov.uk/rds.

5. *Managing diversity: an IPD position paper*, Institute of Personnel and Development, 1996, www.cipd.co.uk.

6. *Race equality: the Home Secretary's race employment targets*, www.homeoffice.gov.uk.

7. *Shepherd v Brentwood Bros (Manchester) Ltd* (9 February 2001; case no.2100872/00).

8. *Ethnic minorities and the labour market: final report*, Cabinet Office, 2003, www.strategy.gov.uk.

9. *Ethnic minorities and the labour market: interim analytical report*, Cabinet Office, 2002, www.strategy.gov.uk.

10. *Chaudhary v British Medical Association* (19 June 2002; case no.2401502/00).

11. *Disabled for life? Attitudes towards, and experiences of, disability in Britain*, National Centre for Social Research for the Department for Work and Pensions, 2002.

12. Press release, 31 March 2003, UnumProvident.

13. At least half of all the adjustments made by the employers we contacted involved the organisation in little or no cost. In one in three cases, the government's Access to Work fund paid for at least some of the necessary adjustments.

14. *Newsome v The Council of the City of Sunderland* (27 November 2001; case no.6403592/99).

15. *Age, pensions and retirement: attitudes and expectations*, Chartered Institute of Personnel and Development, 2003, www.cipd.co.uk.

16. Government statistics quoted in *Good practice in the recruitment and retention of older workers*, Department for Work and Pensions, 2001.

17. Code of Practice on Age Diversity in Employment, Department for Work and Pensions, 2002, available free from DWP Publications, tel: 0845 733 0360, www.agepositive.gov.uk; Good practice in the recruitment and retention of older workers, Department for Work and Pensions, 2001, tel: 0845 733 0360, www.agepositive.gov.uk; "The wonder years", Karen Higginbottom, *People Management*, 5 December 2002; "Age and employment", *Quick Facts series*, Chartered Institute of Personnel and Development, 2002, www.cipd.co.uk.

18. "Women put the tube back on track", *Personnel Today*, 11 June 2002.

19. "Morale boost for NHS trust", Carol Glover, *People Management*, 7 November 2002.

20. *Managing the mosaic: diversity in action*, Rajvinder Kandola and Johanna Fullerton, Institute of Personnel and Development, 1994.

21. "Preventing equal pay claims", Russell Brimelow, *Personnel Today*, 4 March 2003.

22. *Monitoring progress towards pay equality*, Fiona Neathey, Sally Dench and Louise Thomson, Equal Opportunities Commission, 2003, www.eoc.org.uk.

23. *Qua v John Ford Morrison Solicitors* [2003] IRLR 184.

24. Statistics quoted in Department of Trade and Industry press release, 3 April 2003.

25. "Focusing on work–life balance helps council reduce employee turnover", *Personnel Today*, 3 December 2002.

26. *The pivot generation: informal care and work after 50*, Ann Mooney and June Statham, Policy Press, 2002.

27. "Old hands make light work", Nic Paton, *Personnel Today*, 25 March 2003.

28. "Old hands make light work", Nic Paton, *Personnel Today*, 25 March 2003.

29. *Good practice in the recruitment and retention of older workers*, Department for Work and Pensions, 2001, ww.dfee.gov.uk/research.

10. Managing performance 1

1. *Performance review: balancing objectives and content*, Marie Strebler et al, Institute for Employment Studies, 2001, www.employment-studies.co.uk. This report is based on research among almost 1,000 managers.

2. *Unlocking the black box: understanding the HR–performance link*, Chartered Institute of Personnel and Development, 2003, www.cipd.co.uk.

3. "Fujitsu stems the tide of leaving staff", *Personnel Today*, 12 November 2002.

4. *Employee well-being in call centres*, David Holman, Institute of Work Psychology, University of Sheffield.

5. *The psychology of managerial incompetence*, Adrian Furnham, Whurr, 1998.

6. "Talent management", Nic Paton, *Personnel Today*, 12 November 2002.

7. "Talent management", Nic Paton, *Personnel Today*, 12 November 2002.

8. *Performance management: the new realities*, Michael Armstrong and Angela Baron, Chartered Institute of Personnel and Development, 1998.

9. Equality Direct provides an advice line, tel: 0845 600 3444, and printed information free from www.equalitydirect.org.uk.

10. *360-degree feedback: best practice guidelines*, Department of Trade and Industry, 2001, www.dti.gov.uk.

11. Managing performance 2

1. "Ford rethinks cull of its lowest performers", Noel O'Reilly, *Personnel Today*, 6 August 2002.

2. www.equalitydirect.org.uk.

3. Guidance from Acas, including model disciplinary and grievance procedures, guidance on managing discipline, and its Code of Practice on disciplinary and grievance procedures can be found at www.acas.org.uk. The national helpline number for Acas is 08457 474 747. Its helpline receives some three-quarters of a million calls a year.

4. Available free of charge at www.acas.gov.uk.

5. *Discipline at work*, Acas, free from www.acas.org.uk.

6. "Parceline slashes unfair dismissal bills", *Personnel Today*, 24 September 2002.

7. *Discipline at work*, Acas, free from www.acas.org.uk.

8. www.equalitydirect.org.uk.

9. See reference 3 above.

10. Available free of charge from www.acas.gov.uk.

11. Available free of charge from www.acas.gov.uk.

12. Attendance and absence

1. *Counting the costs: 2002 absence and labour turnover survey*, CBI, 2002, www.cbi.org.uk.

2. *Sickness absence in local government, 2000/01*, Employers' Organisation, 2002, www.lg-employers.gov.uk.

3. *Costing sickness absence in the UK*, S Bevan and S Hayday, Institute for Employment Studies, 2001, www.employment-studies.co.uk.

4. *Discipline at work*, Acas, free from www.acas.org.uk. The national helpline number for Acas is 08457 474 747.

5. *Employee absence 2002: a survey of management policy and practice*, Chartered Institute of Personnel and Development, 2002, www.cipd.co.uk.

6. "Biker nurses dispense 'flu jabs to sandwich seller", *Personnel Today*, 12 November 2002.

7. *Health and safety statistics, 2001/02*, Health and Safety Commission, 2002, www.hse.gov.uk.

8. *Intervention to control stress at work in hospital staff*, Health and Safety Executive, 2002, www.hse.gov.uk.

9. *Discipline at work*, Acas, free from www.acas.org.uk.

10. *Analysis of sickness absence in the civil service*, 1999, Biomathematics and Statistics Scotland, 2001.

11. "Flexible working cuts sickness absence", *People Management*, 10 January 2002.

12. *Statutory sick pay manual for employers*, Inland Revenue, www.inlandrevenue.gov.uk.

13. *Adin v Sedco Forex International Resources*; and *Aspden v Webbs Poultry and Meat (Group) Holldings*.

14. *Marshall v Harland & Wolff Ltd*; *Hogan v Cambridgeshire County Council*.

13. Redundancies and transfers

1. *Employee morale during downsizing*, Polly Kettley, Institute for Employment Studies, 1995, www.employment-studies.co.uk.

2. *Redundancy survey report*, Chartered Institute of Personnel and Development, 2002, www.cipd.co.uk.

3. "The new reality for UK managers: perpetual change and employment instability", Les Worrall, Cary Cooper and Fiona Campbell, *Work, Employment and Society*, vol. 14 no.4, December 2000, pp.647–668.

4. "How to support survivors of redundancy", Richard Chiumento, *People Management*, 6 February 2003.

5. *Survivor syndrome: what is it, will your organisation catch it and what's the cure?*, Robin Tait, Taylor Clarke Partnership, www.taylorclarke.co.uk.

6. "A natural preparation", Neil Merrick, *People Management*, 26 October 2000.

7. *Polkey v A E Dayton Services Ltd* ([1987] IRLR 503 HL).

8. *Representation at work*, Acas guidance booklet, 2002, www.acas.org.uk.

9. *Redundancy handling*, Acas, 2002, www.acas.org.uk.

10. "When push comes to shove", Jane Pickard, *People Management*, 22 November 2001.

11. *Redundancy survey report*, Chartered Institute of Personnel and Development, 2002, www.cipd.co.uk.

12. "A dynamic duo", Dominique Hammond, *People Management*, 21 March 2002.

13. "Co-op travel staff agree to four-day week", *Personnel Today*, 13 November 2001.

14. *Redundancy survey report*, Chartered Institute of Personnel and Development, 2002, www.cipd.co.uk.

15. For example, see "When push comes to shove", Jane Pickard, *People Management*, 22

November 2001.

16."Redundancy", *Quick Facts series*, Chartered Institute of Personnel and Development, 2002, www.cipd.co.uk.

17. "How to break the news of redundancies", Jane Rothwell, *People Management*, 23 November 2000.

18. *Rutherford v Towncircle Ltd (t/a Harvest) (in liquidation) and Secretary of State for Trade and Industry* (23.8.2002 Case No. 3203345/98); and *Bentley v Secretary of State for Trade and Industry* (23.8.2002 Case No.2200740/01). These are employment tribunal rulings; the government may either appeal against the decisions or enact legislation to reapply the upper age limit.

19. *Redundancy survey report*, Chartered Institute of Personnel and Development, 2002, www.cipd.co.uk.

20. "Vauxhall unveils redundancy package for Luton staff", Karen Higginbottom, *Personnel Today*, 19 December 2000.

21. *Redundancy handling*, Acas, 2002, www.acas.org.uk. The national helpline number for Acas is 08457 474 747.

22. *People implications of mergers and acquisitions, joint ventures and divestments*, Chartered Institute of Personnel and Development, 2000, www.cipd.co.uk.

23. *Smart sourcing: international best practice*, Andrew Kakabadse and Nada Kakabadse, Palgrave, 2002.

24. *Beckmann v Dynamco Whicheloe Macfarlane Ltd* (4.6.2002, Case C-164/00).

25. *Representation at work*, Acas guidance booklet, 2002, www.acas.org.uk.

Index

For Product Safety Concerns and Information please contact our EU
representative GPSR@taylorandfrancis.com
Taylor & Francis Verlag GmbH, Kaufingerstraße 24, 80331 München, Germany

www.ingramcontent.com/pod-product-compliance
Ingram Content Group UK Ltd.
Pitfield, Milton Keynes, MK11 3LW, UK
UKHW042200240425
457818UK00011B/322